Young Adult Literature

Young Adult Literature

Exploration, Evaluation, and Appreciation

Second Edition

Katherine Bucher

Old Dominion University

KaaVonia Hinton

Old Dominion University

Allyn & Bacon

Boston   New York   San Francisco
Mexico City   Montreal   Toronto   London   Madrid   Munich   Paris
Hong Kong   Singapore   Tokyo   Cape Town   Sydney

Executive Editor: Aurora Martínez Ramos
Series Editorial Assistant: Jacqueline Gillen
Executive Marketing Manager: Krista Clark
Production Editor: Cynthia Parsons
Editorial Production Service: NK Graphics
Composition Buyer: Linda Cox
Manufacturing Buyer: Megan Cochran
Electronic Composition: NK Graphics
Interior Design: Cia Boynton
Cover Designer: Elena Sidorova

For related titles and support materials, visit our online catalog at www.pearsonhighered.com.

Between the time website information is gathered and then published, it is not unusual for some sites to have closed. Also, the transcription of URLs can result in typographical errors. The publisher would appreciate notification where these errors occur.

Library of Congress Cataloging-in-Publication Data

Bucher, Katherine Toth, 1947–
    Young adult literature: exploration, evaluation, and appreciation/Katherine
Bucher, KaaVonia Hinton.—2nd ed.
        p.   cm.
    Includes bibliographical references and index.
    ISBN-13: 978-0-13-714532-4
    ISBN-10: 0-13-714532-2
1. Young adult literature—History and criticism.   2. Young adults—Books and reading.
3. Young adult literature—Study and teaching (Secondary).   I. Hinton, KaaVonia, 1973–   II. Title.

PN1009.A1B79 2009
809.8'9283—dc22   2008047426

Printed in the United States of America

10   9   8   7   6   5   4   3   2   1   HAM   13   12   11   10   09

**Allyn & Bacon
is an imprint of**

www.pearsonhighered.com

ISBN-10: 0137145322
ISBN-13: 9780137145324

To my husband, Glenn, for his understanding and patience, and to those teachers and librarians who share literature, in all forms, with young adults

—KB

To my son, Tony Za'id Johnson

—KH

Brief Contents

Contents

PART TWO

CONNECTING ADOLESCENTS AND
THEIR LITERATURE   54

CHAPTER **3**

Teaching, Using, and Appreciating Young Adult Literature   54

CHAPTER **4**

Protecting Intellectual Freedom   86

PART THREE

EXPLORING YOUNG ADULT LITERATURE

CHAPTER **5**

Exploring Contemporary Realistic Fiction

CHAPTER **6**

Exploring Adventure, Mystery, and Humor   152

CHAPTER **7**

Exploring Science Fiction, Fantasy, and Horror   184

CHAPTER **8**

Exploring Historical Fiction   212

CHAPTER **9**

Exploring Biography   240

CHAPTER **10**

Exploring Nonfiction/Information Books   266

CHAPTER **11**

Exploring Poetry, Drama, and Short Stories 292

Preface

Our purpose in writing this book is to open the door for readers to explore young adult literature. To do so, we have tried to establish a foundation of knowledge about young adult literature while providing pathways leading to the literature itself.

A young adult literature text must allow you, the reader, to find a balance between actual literature and the instructional text. For you to be able to guide young adult readers, you will need to read age and developmentally appropriate literature, finding your own favorites and learning firsthand how enjoyable and meaningful these books can be.

You will need more than just your own experiences with the literature. To use this literature effectively with young adults, you will need to

- Know what literature is available and be familiar with a wide range of genres
- Appreciate, understand, and evaluate the literature
- Develop ways to connect readers with the literature

This balance is important, because young adult literature is a significant aspect of middle and secondary school curricula as well as an invaluable source of enjoyment.

With the current emphasis on literature-based instruction, literature across the curriculum, reading to learn across the curriculum, and the use of literature to integrate curricular areas, the use of young adult literature will become increasingly important for all middle and high school educators. Slim enough to guarantee that you have the opportunity to read the books themselves and comprehensive enough to ensure that you understand adolescents, their literature, and how to connect the two, the second edition of *Young Adult Literature: Exploration, Evaluation, and Appreciation* will help you provide a rich educational experience for adolescents while nourishing their love of reading.

Driving Principles

For a young adult literature text to be truly valuable, it must accomplish a few things.

- It must provide readers with the knowledge of quality, age-appropriate books.
- It needs to offer information on literary exploration, emphasizing the evaluation, teaching, and appreciation of young adult literature.
- It should be sufficiently concise, allowing readers the time to read the literature itself.
- It must use technology as a means of learning more about young adult literature and about making it an integral part of the middle and secondary curriculum.
- It should include both fiction and nonfiction as well as graphic formats in order to reflect the reading interests of all students and to meet the needs of both classroom teachers and librarians.
- Finally, it must recognize and value students' diversity.

Recognition of and Commitment to Diversity

Diversity must be respected and recognized in the middle and secondary school curriculum, and a young adult literature text needs to reflect our nation's and schools' growing diversity. Rather than segregating multicultural literature in a single genre chapter, we interweave diversity and multiculturalism throughout the text. The following threads will help you address and celebrate diversity in your classroom:

- Exploring diversity—cultural, gender, ability, and sexual orientation
- Identifying multicultural literature
- Selecting and evaluating multicultural literature
- Uncovering multicultural literature for and about specific cultural groups
- Investigating award-winning books with multicultural representations
- Integrating multicultural literature throughout the curriculum
- Discovering appropriate literature that crosses curricular boundaries

Exploring, Evaluating, and Appreciating Young Adult Literature

Special features blend with chapter content to support the book's three underlying and unifying themes.

Exploration: Get to Know the Students You Teach and the Literature That Interests Them

- Chapter 2 discusses adolescence and how it affects your students.

- Chapter 8 examines fantasy, science fiction, and horror, all popular genres with adolescents, and explains how to use a reader's interest in these areas to literacy's advantage.

- Chapters 9 and 10 examine nonfiction formats that are especially appealing to male young adults and useful for promoting reading across curricular areas.

- Chapter 12 explores the popular and burgeoning areas of graphic novels, comic books, and other nontraditional literature, providing an excellent way to motivate young readers.

- Diversity and multicultural literature are major threads that run throughout the book.

- *Suggested Readings* in each chapter list journal articles and books that will benefit your teaching.

Evaluation: Learn What Makes a Young Adult Title Great

- Chapter 2, "Evaluating and Selecting Young Adult Literature," sets the stage for a text intended to help you select the finest examples of young adult literature.

- The *Considerations for Selecting Young Adult Literature* feature in every genre chapter provides clarity on how to determine the value of specific titles.

- The *Young Adult Books* feature in each chapter helps you choose the best titles for your students.

Appreciation: Help Young Adults Learn from and Love Young Adult Literature

- Chapter 3, "Teaching, Using, and Appreciating Young Adult Literature," helps you see how best to use young adult literature in your classroom, including ways of integrating curricular areas.

- Chapter 4, "Protecting Intellectual Freedom," along with the discussions in various genre chapters, will help you learn how to address censorship.

- The *Expanding Your Knowledge with the Internet* feature enriches your teaching with technology.

- The *Connecting Adolescents and Their Literature* feature includes activities for teaching, exploring, and helping young adults appreciate young adult literature.

- The *From Page to Screen* feature in each genre chapter explores the best film adaptations of young adult literature, providing opportunities to engage readers and compare films to books.

- The *Collaborating with Other Professionals* feature provides preservice and in-service teachers and library media specialists with ideas for collaboration on topics being addressed in the text.

- The *Using Multiple Readings* feature offers sample discussion questions influenced by various literary theories for selected books.

New to This Edition

In addition to the updated popular features from the first edition such as *Considerations for Selecting Young Adult Literature, Expanding Your Knowledge with the Internet, Connecting Adolescents and Their Literature, From Page to Screen,* and *Collaborating with Other Professionals* (formerly titled *Suggestions for Collaborative Efforts*), this second edition includes a number of new features.

- The new arrangement of the chapters makes the book more user-friendly and places all of the genre chapters at the end of the book. Chapters 1 through 4 now provide information on young adults and their literature, selection and evaluation guidelines, teaching ideas, and intellectual freedom and censorship.

- Throughout the chapters, the discussions and lists of young adult literature have been updated to include literature published since the first edition of this book.

- The "Using Multiple Readings" feature is found in selected genre chapters and is designed for teachers and library media specialists. It explains the use of multiple critical viewpoints such as historical-biographic, archetypal, feminism, Black feminism, deconstruction, Marxist, and new historical criticism. Included are sample questions that demonstrate various critical viewpoints with selected young adult literature.

- Chapter 12 on graphic novels, comics and magazines has been completely revised to reflect the changes in these genres. The emphasis is on helping teachers and library media specialists understand and value the varied interests and literature formats of today's young readers.

- A new section on using picture books with young adults is included in Chapter 12. There are suggestions for picture books that teachers can use throughout the secondary school curriculum and ones to add to the school library media center.

- The completely new "Suggested Readings" section in each chapter features recent journal articles that help teachers and library media specialists continue learning about young adult literature beyond the information included in this book.

- The updated Page to Screen features movies to motivate readers and class discussions about books now available as movies.

Acknowledgments

Authors always have a number of people to whom they are grateful—people who motivated them, inspired them, challenged them, and provided actual assistance with the writing and preparation of the book. We thankfully acknowledge the assistance of Linda Bishop at Merrill Education for her encouragement and patience. In addition, we thank Kasey Garrison, a graduate assistant at Old Dominion University for her assistance. Finally, we are particularly grateful to the following individuals who served as reviewers for this book and offered numerous constructive suggestions: M. Linda Broughton, Kennesaw State University; Pauline W. U. Chinn, University of Hawaii, Manoa; Jacquelyn M. Culpepper, Mercer University; Debbie East, Indiana University; Angela Ferree, Western Illinoise University; Patricia Gantt, Utah State University; Cyndi Giorgis, University of Nevada, Las Vegas; Jackie Glasgow, Ohio University; Joan F. Kaywell, University of South Florida; Rodney D. Keller, Brigham Young University; Patricia P. Kelly, Virginia Tech; Leanna Manna, Villa Maria College; Barbara Stein Martin, University of North Texas; Marcy Merrill, California State University; Dr. Kay Moore, California State University, Sacramento; Harold Nelson, Minot State Univeristy; Andrea Neptune, Sierra College; Holly G. Willett, Rowan University; and Terrell Young, Washington State University.

KB
KH
Old Dominion University

Young Adult Literature

Chapter

1

Understanding Young Adult Literature

"Like an awkward kid who's finally shed the braces and baby fat, young adult literature is coming into its own" (Crocker, 2003) and has become an "electrifying genre for getting today's young adolescents reading and exploring who they are" (Stallworth, 2006, p. 59). Attracting the attention of middle and high school readers, as well as their teachers and library media specialists, well-written young adult literature provides adolescents with considerable reading enjoyment; assists in the development of their sense of self; allows them to explore life experiences and realities; and helps them understand the many joys, trials, successes, and problems of life. With excellent authors writing high-quality literature especially for adolescents, young adult literature has earned a respected place between children's and adult literature. Young adult literature can be used throughout the school curriculum—with an integrating theme across subjects, as part of an interdisciplinary unit, or in specific content areas to expand the information found in textbooks.

Describing Adolescents

Today's young adults differ significantly from the individuals found in the 12- to 20-year-old age group 30 or 40 years ago. Contemporary adolescents develop faster.

- Physically, they mature earlier
- Cognitively, they know more (although their cognitive experiences might not be the types that are valued in school)
- Socially, many have a preoccupation with friends and peers (Manning & Bucher, 2009)

They also face issues—such as eating disorders, including crash diets; alcohol, drugs, and tobacco; AIDS and STDs (sexually transmitted diseases); peer pressure; and physical and psychological safety concerns—that previous generations might not have confronted as young adults. Knowing adolescents' developmental characteristics will help teachers and library media specialists select appropriate literature as well as plan learning experiences around young adult literature. Table 1–1 lists some adolescent developmental characteristics in more detail. It is important to remember that these developmental characteristics are complex and interrelated. For example, physical development affects self-esteem, socialization tendencies, and abilities to handle social tasks.

Although developmental characteristics can be listed with considerable certainty, educators must remember the importance of individuality and diversity. A wide range of physical developmental characteristics can readily be seen. For example, some 14-year-olds look like 18-year-olds while others resemble 10-year-olds. Other characteristics are more subtle. Psychosocially, some adolescents place priority on friendships and socialize at every opportunity; others might continue to be somewhat shy and may avoid social opportunities. Cognitive development is even less evident, with some younger adolescents performing formal and higher-level thinking, while others continue to think in concrete terms. Every adolescent is maturing, but each is taking a different road and going at a different speed on his or her journey from childhood to adulthood (Manning & Bucher, 2009). Thus, it is important to know adolescents on an individual basis and to use this knowledge to select appropriate young adult literature.

In addition to the internal changes happening to adolescents, the environment or "communities" in which a young adult lives also mold the individual. These communities, including the family and its socioeconomic group, the neighborhood (including the school), the ethnic/racial/religious community, and young adolescent peers, impact the development of adolescents. Often these communities exert conflicting influences. Expectations from an ethnic community may be different from those of peers or the neighborhood, while family expectations may conflict with the neighborhood or peer norms.

All of these developmental and community factors have an affect on young adults and an impact on their reading. However, the outcomes are as diverse as young adults themselves. Some adolescents may read to escape the confines of their homes and communities while others may choose not to read because of peer pressure or the lack of importance placed on reading by their families. Although some young adults prefer literature that realistically addresses the problems of growing up, depicts their culture, or delves into the conflicting emotions they are experiencing, others prefer literature that will allow them to forget day-to-day life and vicariously experience adventures, travel to a fantasy world, or just have a good laugh.

TABLE 1-1   Developmental Characteristics During Adolescence

PHYSICAL

- Physical changes (e.g., growth spurt and skeletal and structural changes) are rapid and visually apparent
- Considerable diversity in physical developmental rates occur due to genetics, environmental factors, and health issues
- Distinct gender differences are evident in size, strength, and age of growth spurt (e.g., girls around age 12 and boys around age 14)
- Health risks increase due to behavioral issues such as eating disorders, sexual experimentation, and drug use

PSYCHOSOCIAL

- Friendships form and social interactions increase, potentially boosting self-esteem and reducing anxiety
- Distinct gender differences occur in socialization patterns (e.g., females tend to have smaller numbers of close friends and males tend to have larger "social networks")
- Allegiance and affiliation shifts from parents and teachers to friends and peers
- Social tasks and situations are handled without adult supervision and advice
- Self-esteem changes due to adolescents' home and school lives
- Preoccupations with the self lead to critical self-examination and, subsequently, to the formation of self-perceptions
- Argumentative and aggressive behaviors become evident and often disturb parents and teachers

COGNITIVE

- Higher levels of cognitive functioning (e.g., reasoning and higher-level thought processes) develop
- Moral and ethical choices are now possible and often guide behavior
- Developmental diversity leads to varying abilities to think and reason
- Cognitive ability is often affected by overall socialization
- Perspectives about past, present, and future develop that allow enhanced perspectives of time
- Language and overall verbalization skills increase, allowing improved communication in both school and home situations

Source: Developed from Manning, M. L., & Bucher, K. T. (2009). *Teaching in the middle school.* Boston: Allyn & Bacon.

Defining Young Adult Literature

The term *young adult literature* can be difficult to define. Is it the literature that young adults select, on their own, to read? If so, some mainstream adult novels by Danielle Steele or John Grisham might be classified as young adult literature. Or is young adult literature any book that is written specifically for a young adult audience? In that case, consider that highly recognized young adult authors such as Bruce Brooks and Robert Cormier actually became young adult authors because of their publishers. Their books, which were written as adult novels, were sent to the juvenile editors because their subjects "captured the tone and mood of a teenage character" (Aronson, 2001, p. 35). Publishers sometimes go into the final sales conference not knowing whether to market a book as a young adult or adult title (Maughan, 2000).

In fact, there really is no consensus among publishers, librarians, teachers, reviewers, and booksellers about exactly what young adult literature is (Aronson, 2002). There is not even agreement about who is a young adult. When Joan F. Kaywell (2001) surveyed members of the Conference on English Education Commission on the Study and Teaching of Young Adult Literature, she found the following definitions of young adults:

"An age group roughly between 11 and 16"

"Kids between 10–21, grades 4–college"

"Adolescents who are 12 to 18 in grades 6–12"

"Between the ages of 12 and 22" (Kaywell, 2001, p. 325)

Even professional associations and award committees do not agree on an age span. A 2-year overlap exists between the ages noted for children's literature's Newbery Award (up to age 14) and young adult literature's Michael L. Printz Award (ages 12–18). While the members of the National Council of Teachers of English (NCTE) Conference on English Education Commission on the Study and Teaching of Young Adult Literature could not reach a consensus on an age range (Kaywell, 2001), most committee members did put the range somewhere between age 11 and 18 with a grade range between 6th and 12th grades.

Adding to the difficulty of defining young adult literature is a lack of agreement on the exact term that should be used to refer to it. Poe, Samuels, and Carter (1995) noted that finding research on young adult literature can be difficult because it may be indexed as children's literature, juvenile literature, or sometimes adult literature. Barnes and Noble, a major bookseller, has changed its signage so that the term *Young Adult* has been replaced by the terms *Teen Fiction* and *Teen Series* (Maughan, 2000).

Even award committees have struggled to define young adult literature. The Young Adult Library Services Association, part of the American Library Association (ALA) gives several awards for young adult literature, including the Michael L. Printz Award and the Margaret A. Edwards Award. The Printz Award is given to the best young adult book (fiction, nonfiction, poetry, or anthology) published in the previous year, while the Edwards Award is given to an author whose "book or books have provided young adults with a window through which they can view their world and which will help them to grow and to understand themselves and their role in society" (YALSA, 1996). Although both awards are given for young adult literature, the criteria defining young adult literature are very different for each award.

In selecting the Edwards Award, the committee considers a number of questions, including:

1. Does the book(s) help adolescents to become aware of themselves and to answer their questions about their role and importance in relationships, in society, and in the world?

2. Is the book(s) of acceptable literary quality?

3. Does the book(s) satisfy the curiosity of young adults and yet help them thoughtfully to build a philosophy of life?

4. Is the book(s) currently popular with a wide range of young adults in many different parts of the country?

5. Does the book or book(s) serve as a "window to the world" for young adults? (YALSA, 1996)

In contrast, the Printz Award is given to a book that has "been designated by its publisher as being either a young adult book or one published for the age range that YALSA defines as 'young adult,' i.e., 12 through 18" (YALSA, 2004). The award is given for "quality" or "literary excellence" not "popularity" or the "message" that the book presents (YALSA, 2004). Additional criteria vary by the individual book and include story, setting, theme, voice, accuracy, style, illustration, characters, and design.

Contemporary young adult literature is more than fiction. As Chelton (2006) points out, many adolescents read nonfiction, including biographies, and turn to magazines for pleasure reading and not just for research. Graphic novels are also an important "literature" for young adults, as are comics and picture books. Sometimes the literature is not even in print format, as adolescents turn to audiobooks and downloads to MP3 players and podcasts.

A Brief History of Young Adult Literature

Perhaps a definition of young adult literature lies in its history. Poe, Samuels, and Carter (1995) contend that in the 1960s, young adult literature separated from both children's literature and adult literature with the publication of S. E. Hinton's *The Outsiders* (1967) and Paul Zindel's *The Pigman* (1968). Other critics add Robert Lipsyte's *The Contender* (1967) (Cart, 2001) and Ann Head's *Mr. and Mrs. Bo Jo Jones* (1967) (Campbell, 2003a) to this list of groundbreaking books. These early young adult books were mainly novels that addressed the problems of growing up (Aronson, 2001) with "hard-edged realism" (Cart, 2001, p. 96) and "issues of relevance to the real lives of teen readers" (p. 96). *Go Ask Alice* (Sparks, 1971), published with "anonymous" listed as the author, became a best seller, showing publishers the value of young adult literature in paperback format (Campbell, 2003a). Then, in 1974, Robert Cormier's *The Chocolate War* (1974) shook young adult literature, opening the door for "honest, fresh, stylistically daring, startling, terrifying, and wonderful fiction" (Campbell, 2003a, p. 183). The following year, Judy Blume pushed the boundaries of sexual content for adolescents in her novel *Forever* (1975). In libraries, the new young adult literature was promoted to high school or college students, while students in sixth and seventh grades were still being directed to the children's collection (Campbell, 2003a).

At the same time, scholars began to recognize the growing importance of young adult literature. In the 1960s, G. Robert Carlsen began writing his *Books for the Teenage Reader: A Guide for Teacher, Librarians, and Parents* (1967, 1971, 1980) calling for the incorporation of young adult literature into schools. In 1973, Ted Hipple became the first executive secretary of the Assembly on Literature for Adolescents (ALAN), an independent assembly of the NCTE, for individuals interested in young adult literature.

Between the 1970s and the 1990s, "the media that surrounded adolescence expanded and changed both its form and its substance" (Aronson, 2001, p. 34). Talk shows, cable television, and the Internet began to address teenagers' problems and concerns. The decline in young adult readership in the 1980s resulted in changes by publishers. There was a growth of series books such as *Fear Street* and *Sweet Valley High* (Campbell, 2003a; Cart, 2001) and an increased interest on the part of young adult readers in fantasy and science fiction, multicultural novels, and poetry (Aronson, 2002). By the late 1980s, publishers "youthen[ed]" (Cart, 2001, p. 95) their main characters in an attempt to target middle school students.

Young adult literature continued to evolve throughout the 1990s. Theme-based short story collections became popular, as did novels in verse such as those by Mel Glenn and Karen Hesse. Visual elements worked their way into young adult literature and changed the way books looked (Cart, 2001). "Graphic novels—the comic book come of age . . . [show] how words and pictures are working together in fresh, original, and exciting ways" (p. 97). These new graphic formats asked readers to examine both the words and pictures when "reading" a story (Dresang, 1999). While the *Harry Potter* phenomenon rekindled an interest in fantasy and science fiction books, there were changes in the traditional linear plot style of realistic fiction. Books began to reflect the interactivity and connectivity of the digital world with shifting perspectives, diverse voices, and even multiple genres within a single book, such as Avi's *Nothing but the Truth* (1991) and Virginia Walter and Katrina Roeckelein's *Making Up Megaboy* (1998) (Dresang, 1999). In *Seedfolks* (1997), Paul Fleischman simultaneously used several storylines, and in *Holes* (1998), Louis Sachar created a multilayered story. When the first Michael L. Printz Award for Excellence in Young Adult literature was given in 1999, it changed "the way young adult literature is regarded and published" (Michael Cart quoted in Crocker, 2003, p. 77). Now, young adult literature had its own national award equal in status to the Newbery Medal, which is given for excellence in writing in children's literature. No longer were young adult books forced to compete

COLLABORATING WITH OTHER PROFESSIONALS

If your school provides summer reading lists for students, it is important to form a team of school library media specialists, teachers, and public librarians to assist in their development. They can take nonbinding recommendations from adolescents as well. The team should know what the goal for summer reading is (e.g., to create lifelong readers) and should develop a reading list that actually promotes that goal. The team needs to remember that adolescents, like adults, do not all like the same types of books. Therefore, plenty of choices need to be on the list. Williams (2003)

indicated that one-third of Connecticut school summer reading programs in 2003 gave "students complete freedom to choose their own reading" (p. 369). However, most "offered suggested lists" (p. 369) but made it clear that "it was not necessary to read from the list" (p. 369).

SUMMER READING RESOURCES
*www.ct.webjunction.org/do/
DisplayContent?id=6087*

SUMMER READING COLLABORATIVE
www.cslpreads.org/

for recognition with books for younger readers. Aronson (2001) noted that "the constraint, the box into which we used to try to fit YA books," had vanished (p. 10).

By 2000, both young adult literature and its readers had changed significantly from its founding in the 1970s. Campbell (2003a) maintains that today, most young adult readers are in sixth to ninth grade; and Cart (2001) notes that "one of the fastest-growing segments of publishing is the book market designated for readers 10–14 years old" (p. 95). Publishers have taken advantage of the fact that the teen population has had a yearly disposable income in excess of $100 billion (Kiesling, 2002). According to Michael Wood of the marketing firm Teenage Research Unlimited, for the next two decades, teenagers will be the majority of the adult population ("The marketing battle for generation Y," 2004).

Publishers are capitalizing on this new, large, more sophisticated audience. As Campbell (2004) points out, more books are speaking "directly to teens themselves, not teachers or librarians" (p. 63). To take advantage of the changes in literature, librarians and teachers need to continually update their collections and booklists. Collaborating with Other Professionals 1–1 provides some information on the importance of keeping things like summer reading lists current.

Looking back at the first years of young adult literature, the editors at *Booklist* asked authors to identify personal favorites and/or watershed books that "pushed YA literature in new directions, challenging our ideas of what a book for youth could be" (Engberg, 2007, p. 60). A few of the recommendations and the recommending authors are listed in Table 1–2.

Young Adult Literature Today

As young adult literature has matured, authors have begun to "tackle more serious subjects and to introduce more complex characters and considerations of ambiguity" (Cart, 2001, p. 96). The boundaries of young adult literature have expanded as

TABLE 1-2   Selected Watershed Books and Personal Favorites of Young Adult Authors

Book	Recommended by
After the First Death (1979) by Robert Cormier	Robert Lipsyte
Celine (1989) by Brock Cole	Ellen Wittlinger
Harry Potter and the Sorcerer's Stone (1998) by J. K. Rowling	Tamora Pierce
I'll Get There, It Better Be Worth the Trip (1969) by John Donovan	Nancy Garden
Speak (1999) by Laurie Halse Anderson	John Green
The Chocolate War (1974) by Robert Cormier	Christopher Lynch
Weetzie Bat (1989) by Francesca Lia Block	Laurie Halse Anderson and Michael Cart
A Wrinkle in Time (1962) by Madeleine L'Engle	Meg Rosoff
Sweet Whispers, Brother Rush (1982) by Virginia Hamilton	Angela Johnson

Source: Selected from Engberg, G. (2007). 50 years of YA favorites. *Booklist, 103*(19–20), 60–61.

authors explore topics of cruelty and crime, personal abuse, and racial violence (Dresang, 1999), accompanied by a change in the perspectives represented in literature. The previously unheard voices of gays, lesbians, the homeless, and people with disabling conditions now join the voices of adolescents who are speaking out in books through their journals, diaries, and letters. Young adult literature is "as varied as the multimedia mix of teenagers' lives, as complex as their stormy emotional landscapes, as profound as their soul-shaping searches for identity, as vital as their nation-forming future" (Aronson, 2001, p. 11).

Technology is also changing young adult literature. As we mentioned, adolescents are turning to audiobooks in MP3 format and podcasts. Author websites, common for a number of years, now feature multimedia experiences (Beaman, 2006) and blogs to keep in touch with readers. Beaman (2006) reports that authors such as Sarah Dessen and Stephenie Meyer have even created iTunes playlists to accompany some of their young adult novels. A few authors have created pages on MySpace. The social networking site even has a group for Teen Lit, which provides a forum for members. In Expanding Your Knowledge with the Internet, you will find the URLs for this and a few general young adult literature websites.

What, then, is contemporary young adult literature? Aronson (2002) calls it a blend of enduring adolescence and constant change.

> An agglomeration of instabilities . . . [i]t requires us simultaneously, to define three inherently unstable terms: what are young adults, what is literature, and what is the literature that has some special link to those readers. (Aronson, 2001, pp. 31–32)

For our purposes, young adult literature will be defined as literature in prose or verse that has excellence of form or expression in its genre (*Merriam-Webster's Encyclopedia of Literature*, 1995), provides a unique adolescent point of view (Herz & Gallo, 1996), and reflects the concerns, interests, and challenges of contemporary young adults

---

EXPANDING YOUR KNOWLEDGE WITH THE INTERNET

The following websites are excellent starting points for links to information about young adult literature.

Young Adult Library Services Association (American Library Association)
www.ala.org/ala/yalsa/yalsa.cfm

The ALAN Review (Assembly on Literature for Adolescents of NCTE)
www.alan-ya.org/

Vandergrift's Young Adult Literature Page
www.scils.rutgers.edu/~kvander/YoungAdult/

Young Adult Literature from the Internet School Library Media Center
falcon.jmu.edu/~ramseyil/yalit.htm

TeenReads.com
www.teenreads.com/index.asp

High School Teachers—website at Random House
www.randomhouse.com/highschool/

MySpace—Teen Lit
groups.myspace.com/teenlit

(Brown & Stephens, 1995). In sum, it provides a roadmap for readers 12 to 20 years of age (Bean & Moni, 2003).

Criticism, Praise, and the Future

There are some who believe young adult literature only attracts the poorer readers who do not have the reading and analytical skills to enjoy the classics of literature (e.g., the plays of William Shakespeare, *The Odyssey*, or the works of Charles Dickens) that are part of the traditional literary canon. Christenbury (1997) related comments she had heard about young adult literature such as "It's just for younger kids;" "It's for weaker readers;" "We are a high school, and the parents would complain if we gave their children this watered-down stuff;" and "Our students would be bored by these books" (p. 11). Aronson (1997) maintained that some adolescents, often those praised as the best readers, purposely avoid young adult books and gravitate to adult science fiction and fantasy in an effort to avoid the conciseness of much young adult literature.

Other critics downplay the role of young adult literature, especially in the high school curriculum. Jago (2000) rationalized that because young adults do not need guidance to understand a young adult novel, young adult literature should be used for independent, pleasure reading, not studied in the curriculum. She found that the characters were frequently one-dimensional and the books lacked the rich language and complex themes found in the classics (Jago, 2000). Other critics have advocated the use of young adult literature primarily for developmental English classes, in middle schools, or for unmotivated students who would find the traditional literary canon of the high school English curriculum too challenging (Knickerbocker & Rycik, 2002).

Perhaps because of the criticism surrounding it, or because of other factors such as the widening gap between young adult literature and the media-saturated world of modern adolescents, as "recently as the mid-'90s, teen-oriented literature seemed *this close* to extinction" (Crocker, 2003, p. 76). Thankfully, this changed in 1999 (Maughan, 2000) as authors found ways to "present information—both visually and stylistically—to a generation reared on MTV, the Internet, and video games" (Crocker, 2003, p. 78). As Michael Cart, former president of the Young Adult Library Services Association, said, "Young adult literature may have had a near-death experience, but it's very very alive now . . . It's sort of like how the cosmos must have looked after the Big Bang, just expanding exponentially" (Crocker, 2003, p. 76).

Some literary critics (Hipple, 2000; Moore, 1997) note the excellence in some contemporary young adult literature. As Patty Campbell, young adult critic for *The Horn Book Magazine*, noted, there are "risk-taking, exciting books being published" (Crocker, 2003, p. 76) with the current young adult literature being some of "the finest literature you can find today . . . It is finely crafted literature that's readable and accessible . . . [with stories that are] taut and intense and utterly focused" (pp. 76–77).

While young adult literature helps younger adolescents find themselves in books and begin to think critically about literature, older adolescents use young adult literature to help them explore social issues and examine their role in society (Knickerbocker & Rycik, 2002). When adolescents perceive books, especially those in the traditional literary canon, as less relevant, they become disconnected and lose interest in reading. In contrast, many young adult novels "possess themes that merit and reward examination and commentary" (Hipple, 2000, p. 2) and appeal to adolescents. According to Knickerbocker and Rycik (2002):

> Experiences that provide opportunities for adolescents to read young adult literature, make connections between literary works, orally interpret literature and respond to literature will help create more satisfying literary experiences for adolescents, contributing to the likelihood that they will become lifelong readers. (p. 208)

Qualities of Young Adult Literature

Although some children's and adult's books appeal to young adults, literature written primarily for young adults should reflect several criteria:

- It should reflect young adults' age and development by addressing their reading abilities, thinking levels, and interest levels.
- It should deal with contemporary issues, problems, and experiences with characters to whom adolescents can relate. This includes topics such as dealing with parents and other adults in authority; facing illness and death; dealing with peer pressure, specifically relating to drugs, alcohol, and sexual experimentation; and facing the realities of addiction and pregnancy.
- It should consider contemporary world perspectives, including cultural, social, and gender diversity; environmental issues; global politics; and international interdependence.

There is no doubt among scholars that "today's young adult literature is sophisticated, complex, and powerful . . . [and that] it deserves to be part of the literary tradition in middle and high schools" (Stallworth, 2006, p. 59). In addition to helping students develop reading, writing, speaking, and listening skills, it can serve as a "bridge to alienated students" (p. 62), mirror the lives of young adults, improve literacy skills, and provide a forum for adolescents to "talk about common experiences and serious life problems, gain confidence as reflective problem solvers, and build empathy and values" (p. 63).

Characteristics. Young adult literature reflects the changes adolescents experience. As they make their first excursions into adult territory, adolescents are learning to take responsibility for their own actions. Young adult literature reflects their experiences with conflicts, focuses on themes that interest young people, includes young protagonists and mostly young characters, and has language common to young adults (Campbell, 2003b; Vogels, 1996). Rather than being watered down in content or style, it is often sophisticated, artistic, and compelling (Christenbury, 1997). Campbell (2003b) believes that young adult literature must contain "no extended introspective passages from an adult or a child's point of view" (p. 503). In addition, she says that the "point of view must have the limitations of an adolescent perspective" (p. 503).

Although young adult fiction no longer shies away from plots that center on topics once considered only for adults, authors of young adult literature use less graphic details while still conveying the reality of the situation (Campbell, 2003b; Vogels, 1996). However, the literature is not boring in subject matter or in its appeal to young people. Rather, it contains exciting and intriguing plots and characters (Christenbury, 1997) with a "minimum of description" (Campbell, 2003b, p. 503). And young adult fiction usually has a concise plot with a time span of 2 months or less, as well as a focus on the present and future in the life of one central character (Vogels, 1996).

Purposes.   Young adult literature serves a number of purposes. It

- Teaches adolescents about diverse peoples and the world beyond their community
- Provides pleasure reading
- Demonstrates the range of human emotions and allows adolescents to experience them as a result of reading quality literature
- Reveals the realities of life
- Provides vicarious experiences
- Focuses on "essentials" that make order out of chaos
- Depicts the functions of institutions of society
- Allows readers to escape into the realms of fantasy
- Introduces readers to excellent writers and writing
- Increases literacy and the ability to analyze literature

Of course, young adult literature cannot provide these benefits unless adolescents actually read the books. In Connecting Adolescents and Their Literature 1–1, Patrick Jones (2003) offers ideas on purchasing young adult literature.

1-1 • • • • .   **CONNECTING ADOLESCENTS AND THEIR LITERATURE** . . . .

One key to getting adolescents to read is providing access to the types of materials they want to read. Patrick Jones (2003) suggests an interesting approach to purchasing literature for school libraries or classroom collections. In addition to selecting books from the best booklists, look at the books that are lost, long overdue, or missing (stolen) from the local school and public library. If the library's circulation system provides the necessary information, also look at the books with the most circulation and the items that have the highest turnover rate or the most circulations per copy. Use these lists to order additional books. Keep in mind that, as Jones notes, "an old book is new to teens if they've never read it before" (Jones, 2003, p. 49). If you have not read these books, read them so that you can talk to adolescents about the books they are reading.

Young Adult Literature as Transitional Literature

Young adult literature should be appreciated and enjoyed "in and of itself," and young adults should have access to books written especially for them. Young adult literature should not be considered merely a stepping stone to "better" literature or a "holding ground" until readers are ready for adult literature. It is imperative that teachers and library media specialists provide young adults with excellent, well-written books that deal with important adolescent issues and that reflect their interests and concerns. Throughout this book, especially in Chapter 2, you will read about ways to identify outstanding young adult literature.

Nonetheless, there is no question that reading excellent young adult literature can help adolescents make the transition from children's books to adult books. Young adult novels provide the perfect bridge to help adolescents cross from literature for children into the traditional literary canon that is studied in high school and college. Generally shorter than adult novels, sometimes less complex in structure, but often well-written and tightly constructed, young adult novels can lead students to a better understanding of the novel form and the elements of fiction. By studying these novels, young adults can understand the craft of fiction so that they are better able to read and to comprehend the messages and literary conventions of the classics.

According to Gillet and Temple (2000), students move through stages of reading development. Independent reading begins in the Building Fluency State (usually second or third grade) and continues into Reading for Pleasure/Reading to Learn, and finally into Mature Reading, which includes critical reading and analysis. When teachers understand both the developmental and reading appreciation levels of their students, they are best able to help adolescents find appropriate materials that will simultaneously challenge and entertain them (Bushman & Haas, 2001). In Connecting Adolescents and Their Literature 1–2, Knickerbocker and Rycik (2002) suggest four broad categories of literature experiences that all young adults should have as they move toward becoming mature readers.

1-2 • • •.   CONNECTING ADOLESCENTS AND THEIR LITERATURE

Knickerbocker and Rycik (2002) believe that "it is inappropriate to make sharp divisions in the instructional practices for middle and high school students" (p. 200). Instead, they suggest four types of literary experiences that all adolescents should have:

1. Reading young adult literature
2. Developing bridges between young adult literature and more complex texts and revisiting texts to apply "new understandings or methods of analysis" (p. 201)
3. Interpreting literature by listening to dramatic oral readings by skilled individuals such as teachers and library media specialists
4. Responding to literature in ways including discussion groups, journals, and group conversations

In addition to using young adult novels to teach literary conventions, educators can pair young adult novels with the more sophisticated books in the literary canon. Through pairing, teachers can introduce adolescents to a theme, situation, or setting the students find appealing and manageable. After a positive reading experience in which the adolescents become familiar with the concepts presented in the young adult novel, the teacher can introduce the students to the more complex format and ideas of the adult book. Teachers can use the pairing system to match books or authors (Samuels, 1992). A variation of this is to select one adult novel as the core book and then to identify a number of young adult novels that relate to it. The teacher can divide the class into groups and have each group read a different young adult novel. Following discussions within the individual groups, the teacher can host a whole class discussion on the various young adult novels before moving to a study of the core book.

Joan F. Kaywell (1993–2000) has edited a series of books that provide detailed instructional guides for linking young adult literature with the classics. A few of the combinations include linking Arthur Miller's *Death of a Salesman* with Cynthia Voight's *The Runner* (1985); Ibsen's *A Doll House* with Sue Ellen Bridgers's *Permanent Connections* (1987); or *The Tragedy of Julius Caesar* with several novels, including Lois Duncan's *Killing Mr. Griffin* (1978), Will Hobbs's *Downriver* (1991), and Bruce Brooks's *No Kidding* (1989).

Genres and Authors

Young adult literature consists of a number of different genres or categories that serve unique purposes and satisfy individual reading choices. Many books overlap genres, making the distinction between types difficult to see. For our purposes, we will use the following categories: fantasy, science fiction, horror fiction, contemporary realistic fiction, adventure, mystery, humor, historical fiction, biography, nonfiction/information, poetry, drama, short stories, comic books, graphic novels, and magazines. The following sections provide only a brief overview of the genres. You will find detailed information in the individual chapters of this book.

Contemporary Realistic Fiction. The topic of Chapter 5, contemporary realistic fiction, sometimes called the problem novel, appeals to many adolescents and uses plots, themes, settings, and characters to reflect the world as we know it and the problems and challenges many young people face daily. By reading about characters in situations similar to their own, some adolescents can see that their personal problems though difficult are not unique. For other adolescents, realistic fiction provides a vicarious experience through which they learn to overcome their fears and accept responsibilities, and to deal with problems related to adoption, divorce, disabilities, disease, sexual relationships, changes within their families, relationships, sexual orientation, alienation, alcohol and drug abuse, and suicide.

Adventure, Mystery, and Humor. In looking for excitement, many adolescents are attracted to books about adventure and survival or mystery and suspense. Adolescents enjoy the usually fast-paced plots found in adventure stories and the challenges to find out "who-done-it" in mystery novels. Some young adults read humorous novels to have a good laugh and to escape the problems of everyday life. Chapter 6 provides information on these genres.

Science Fiction, Fantasy, and Horror. There is no doubt that science fiction, fantasy, and horror, the categories discussed in Chapter 7, appeal to many young adults. Books from these genres regularly appear in top 10 reading lists selected by young adults ("Fantasy books top the list for teens," 2004). In fantasies, readers can go to magical places while, in science fiction, they can explore the possibilities of science and technology both on Earth and on other worlds. Horror books allow readers to confront the terrors that populate their worst nightmares.

Historical Fiction. Helping adolescents experience the past, explore misfortunes and triumphs, and examine the background of current events, historical fiction can be both interesting and informative. Young adults can read and learn new perspectives of cultural diversity; perceive challenges associated with disabling conditions; examine societal ills such as poverty, drug addiction, crime, and racism; and explore almost any historical period. As discussed in Chapter 8, historical fiction includes stories based in actual events as well as stories set in the past with little or no reference to recorded history or actual people. Recurring topics include wars and clashes of people, quests for freedom and equality, and overcoming disabling conditions.

Biography. Through biographies, young adults explore the frustrations, obstacles, and achievements in the lives of all kinds of people, from the historically famous to contemporary leaders and names in the news, as well as those who have persevered through challenging circumstances. These life stories can add new perspectives to young adults' learning and reading pleasure. Chapter 9 discusses this genre of young adult literature.

Nonfiction/information. While many adolescents read fiction, others enjoy well-written informational books ("Reading remains popular among youth, according to

TABLE 1-3   Important Authors of Books for Young Adults

Louisa May Alcott	Avi	Judy Blume
Ray Bradbury	Betsy Byars	Lewis Carroll
Beverly Cleary	Anne Frank	Robert Frost
S. E. Hinton	Langston Hughes	Washington Irving
Madeleine L'Engle	C. S. Lewis	Jack London
Lois Lowry	Scott O'Dell	Gary Paulsen
Richard Peck	Christopher Pike	Shel Silverstein
R. L. Stine	E. B. White	Laura Ingalls Wilder

Source: Adapted from McElmeel, S., & Buswell, L. (1998). Readers' choices: The most important authors of books for young adults. *The Book Report, 16*(4), 23–24.

poll," 2001). Authors and publishers try to meet young adults' needs and expectations by providing books on timely topics that are written on appropriate reading and interest levels. In fact, some nonfiction authors write with reluctant readers in mind and provide lots of photographs and other illustrations. Chapter 10 discusses nonfiction in more detail.

Poetry, Drama, and Short Stories. Poetry, drama, and short stories are important categories for many young adults, especially for readers who prefer shorter pieces to longer books. Rather than relying on the classics, many adolescents look for works that deal with their contemporary concerns and daily interests and that speak directly to them with words they can understand and situations they can relate to. Information on these categories is provided in Chapter 11.

Comic Books, Graphic Novels, and Magazines. Growing up in a visual and digital society, contemporary adolescents are comfortable with the visual styles found in comic books, graphic novels, and magazines. Although they differ dramatically from the genres that educators have traditionally encouraged adolescents to read, these formats have the visual impact and clipped, pared-down writing style that adolescents have grown accustomed to. Chapter 10 discusses these categories in more detail.

Authors of Books for Young Adults. There are a number of excellent writers of young adult literature. During the spring of 1998, McElmeel and Buswell (1998) published the results of a survey of teachers, librarians, and adolescents to determine the most important authors of books for young adults. Although they based their survey on one conducted by Donald Gallo in 1988, McElmeel and Buswell (1998) changed the survey and sampled a wider population. Table 1–3 shows the individual authors who received votes from at least 40% of the respondents.

Then, in June 2001, the magazine *Voice of Youth Advocates (VOYA)* published its list of books receiving its highest ratings for quality and popularity from 1996 to 2000 and compared them to the ALA's Best Books for Young Adults list (Jones, 2001). The authors who appeared on both lists are shown on Table 1–4.

TABLE 1-4   Outstanding Authors, 1996 to 2000

The following authors appeared on both the *VOYA* Perfect Ten List 1996–2000 and the American Library Association's Best Books for Young Adults list for the same years.

Caroline Cooney	Anita Lobel	Gary Paulsen
Robert Cormier	Albert Marrin	Philip Pullman
Sarah Dessen	Carol Matas	J. K. Rowling
Jackie French Koller	Walter Dean Myers	Cynthia Voight

Source: Developed from Jones, P. (2001). The perfect tens: The top forty books reviewed in Voice of Youth Advocates 1996–2000. *Voice of Youth Advocates, 24*(2), 94–99.

TABLE 1-5   Outstanding Authors, 2001-2006

Libba Bray	Gail Giles	J. K. Rowling
Orson Scott Card	Nikki Grimes	Caroline Stevermer
Christopher Paul Curtis	Pete Hautman	Jonathan Stroud
Sarah Dessen	Julius Lester	Gloria Wehlan
Mariah Fredericks	Graham McNamee	Nancy Werlin
Helen Frost	Richard Peck	Patricia Wrede

Source: Developed from The *Perfect Tens*, 2003, 2004, 2005, 2006, 2007, and lists prepared by the Young Adult Library Services Association.

Since that time, *VOYA* has continued to issue an annual "perfect ten" list based on its own ratings and has compared its picks to the YALSA Best Books for Young Adults, the Quick Picks for Reluctant Young Adult Readers, and/or the Teens' Top Ten Books. Table 1–5 shows the authors identified in these lists (The *Perfect Tens*, 2003, 2004, 2005, 2006, 2007).

New, exciting, and skillful authors continue to enter the field of young adult literature each year. Educators often strive to help adolescents make connections with outstanding authors. Expanding Your Knowledge with the Internet features URLs of some Internet sites where you can find information about authors of young adult literature. Collaborating with Other Professionals 1–2 contains ideas for planning an author visit to your school or community.

 EXPANDING YOUR KNOWLEDGE WITH THE INTERNET

Many authors have individual websites with interesting features. Here are some links for a few of the authors listed in Tables 1–4 and 1–5.

Libba Bray
www.libbabray.com/

Sarah Dessen
www.sarahdessen.com/

Mariah Fredericks
www.mariahfredericks.com/

Helen Frost
www.helenfrost.net/

Gail Giles
www.gailgiles.com/Welcome.html

Pete Hautman
www.petehautman.com/

Jackie French Koller
www.geocities.com/~jackiekoller/

Albert Marrin
www.albertmarrin.com/

Jonathan Stroud
www.jonathanstroud.com/

Nancy Werlin
www.nancywerlin.com/

COLLABORATING WITH OTHER PROFESSIONALS

Meeting an author can generate enthusiasm for reading not only that author's books but also books that are similar.

To make an author visit more affordable, several organizations can combine resources to sponsor one in the local community. Partners can include both public and private schools; public libraries; and local reading, literacy, and friends of the library organizations. Another way to control costs is to combine the visit with an author's presentation at a nearby state convention or to see if a local bookstore will help with financial support. In addition, many humanities organizations and councils for arts and cultural affairs have grants that can be used to support authors. Some libraries have used book sales with the proceeds devoted to funding author visits. Another possibility is to schedule a paid ticket presentation or "dinner with the author" for the general public in addition to school and library visits.

Costs for the visit will vary. In addition to the author's fee, there will be travel and accommodations charges, as well as costs for promoting the event.

Preplanning is very important. As part of your plan, determine where the author will make her or his presentation(s) (i.e., in several schools, in one large auditorium, etc.); whether the presentations will be open to all students in the community, as well as parents, or if invitations will be issued; who will receive invitations

(i.e., members of school book clubs, students in particular English classes, students who work in the school or public library, etc.); and whether there will be any charge for attending the presentation(s).

Asking young adults to nominate a favorite author can be one way to involve them in the process. However, it may be better to start with a suggested list from which they can make their recommendations. Once the author has been chosen, teachers and librarians should promote the author's books either through library book discussion groups or in classroom discussions. Be sure that students have read at least some of the books written by the author.

Contact a local bookstore or paperback distributor as soon as you know the name of the author and be sure that copies of the author's books are available for sale before, during, and after the visit. Decide whether you will have a special autograph session with the author during the visit (some authors prefer to send autographed bookplates) and if you will need to limit the number of books any one individual can have autographed at one time.

For additional information on planning a visit, check online at:

www.reading.org/publications/reading_today/
samples/RTY-0504-optimizing.html
www.michigan.gov/authorvisits

Young Adult Literature and the School Curriculum

The importance of having quality young adult literature available in schools is reflected in the International Reading Association's Adolescent Literacy Commission's position statement, which notes that "adolescents deserve access to a wide variety of reading material that they can and want to read" (Moore, Bean, Birdyshaw, & Rycik, 1999, p. 4). One way to encourage young adults to read is to use "both high-powered young adult literature [that is] linked to content-area concepts and interpretive activities and discussions that engage students" (Bean, 2002, p. 37). Thus, there is an increasing trend to incorporate young adult books and other forms of literature across the middle and high school curriculum. In fact, Chapter 3 focuses entirely on this topic.

All educators agree that reading is an important skill. However, when voluntary reading declines, the problems of struggling readers are only aggravated (Worthy, Patterson, Salas, Prater, & Turner, 2002). By allowing adolescents to read good young adult literature, educators are able to encourage the independent reading that will, in turn, help adolescents develop the skills necessary to succeed. "If educators are serious about developing students' lifelong love of reading they need to incorporate in the curriculum literature that is captivating and issue-based" (Bean, 2002, p. 37).

Richardson and Miller (2001) cite four reasons for using literature in the curriculum. Although they target the social studies curriculum, their reasons are valid for other subjects as well. They found that literature can:

1. Help students become emotionally involved with events and people
2. Aid students in understanding reality
3. Provide stories with satisfactory endings
4. Provide a common, shared experience for the teacher and all students

You have already read about the use of young adult literature as a transition to the classics and the pairing of young adult and adult literature. In addition, newer trends such as using literature across the curriculum and creating a literature plan have provided more productive ways to use young adult literature not just in the English classroom but also in science, social studies, art, and physical education. By working collaboratively, teachers and library media specialists can implement a literature program that reflects the abilities and interests of young adults, that encourages adolescents to read for enjoyment, and that develops an awareness of authors and literary works. This literature program should also teach adolescents to interpret literature and develop literary awareness. When the entire school environment reflects literature and a respect for reading, young adults learn the importance the school places on literature and reading.

However, as Chapter 3 explains, the effort to use young adult literature across the curriculum does not have to be an "all or nothing" approach. Teachers may elect to implement literature-based approaches of varying degrees at various times during the year. What is essential is that teachers and library media specialists recognize the need to use a variety of materials, ranging from books, magazines, and graphic novels to short stories and poetry, and provide time for adolescents to read. By varying their approaches to literature in the content areas, teachers can assure that fiction is read from an aesthetic stance and nonfiction from an efferent stance to ensure learning for all adolescents (Galda & Liang, 2003).

Rather than working in isolation, many educators now make collaborative decisions on curricular themes and use young adult literature that crosses subject areas and helps students see new and different perspectives about issues and subject content. In addition, Bean (2002) suggests that educators provide a variety of ways for adolescents to interpret literature through the use of book clubs, journals, graphic organizers, readers' theater, or even a "dinner party" (p. 36) at which students who are playing a character from a novel are interviewed by a moderator. Today's adolescents will also welcome the opportunity to produce multigenre papers that, like some recent young adult novels, depart from the traditional linear report format and employ a variety of styles (i.e., graphic novel, essay, poetry, drama, or magazine article) as well as a number of voices and perspectives to provide "multilayered, nonlinear stories and information" (Glasgow, 2002, p. 49).

Concluding Thoughts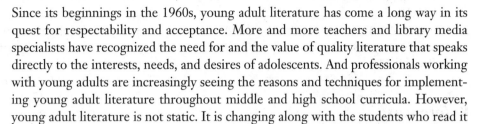

Since its beginnings in the 1960s, young adult literature has come a long way in its quest for respectability and acceptance. More and more teachers and library media specialists have recognized the need for and the value of quality literature that speaks directly to the interests, needs, and desires of adolescents. And professionals working with young adults are increasingly seeing the reasons and techniques for implementing young adult literature throughout middle and high school curricula. However, young adult literature is not static. It is changing along with the students who read it and the society in which it is written. Boundaries are pushed as new forms of graphics and multigenre or nonlinear plots become part of the accepted body of work that is young adult literature. For teachers and library media specialists, the challenge remains to identify the most appropriate strategies to provide young adult readers with well-written literature that they can appreciate and enjoy.

Young Adult Books

This section includes young adult titles mentioned in this chapter.

Anderson, L. H. (1999). *Speak*. New York: Farrar Straus Giroux.

Avi. (1991). *Nothing but the truth*. New York: Orchard.

Block, F. L. (1989). *Weetzie Bat*. New York: Harper & Row.

Blume, J. (1975). *Forever*. Scarsdale, NY: Bradbury.

Bridgers, S. E. (1987). *Permanent connections*. New York: Harper & Row.

Brooks, B. (1989). *No kidding*. New York: Harper & Row.

Cole, B. (1989). *Celine*. New York: Farrar Straus Giroux.

Cormier, R. (1974). *The chocolate war*. New York: Pantheon.

Cormier, R. (1979). *After the first death*. New York: Pantheon.

Donovan, J. (1969). *I'll get there, it better be worth the trip*. New York: Harper & Row.

Duncan, L. (1978). *Killing Mr. Griffin*. Boston: Little, Brown.

Fleischman, P. (1997). *Seedfolks*. New York: Harper-Collins.

Hamilton, V. (1982). *Sweet whispers, Brother Rush*. New York: Philomel.

Head, A. (1967). *Mr. & Mrs. Bo Jo Jones*. New York: Putnam.

Hinton, S. E. (1967). *The outsiders*. New York: Viking.

Hobbs, W. (1991). *Downriver*. New York: Bantam.

L'Engle, M. (1962). *A wrinkle in time*. New York: Farrar, Straus and Giroux.

Lipsyte, R. (1967). *The contender*. New York: Harper & Row.

Rowling, J. K. (1998). *Harry Potter and the sorcerer's stone*. New York: A. A. Levine.

Sachar, L. (1998). *Holes*. New York: Farrar, Straus and Giroux.

Sparks, B. (1971). *Go ask Alice*. Upper Saddle River, NJ: Prentice Hall.

Voight, C. (1985). *The runner*. New York: Ballantine.

Walter, V., and Roeckelein, K. (1998). *Making up megaboy*. New York: DK Publishing.

Zindel, P. (1968). *The pigman*. New York: Harper & Row.

Suggested Readings

Bradford, A. (2008). Adolescent literature in a class by itself? *Voice of Youth Advocates, 30*(6), 508–510.

Crawford, P. C. (2008). Why Gossip Girl matters. *The Horn Book, 84*(1), 45–48.

Creel, S. L. (2007). Early adolescents' reading habits. *Young Adult Literature Services, 5*(4), 46–49.

Rosoff, M. (2007). Identity crisis? Not really. *Publishers Weekly, 254*(42), 60.

Rozema, R. (2007). The book report, version 2.0: Podcasting on young adult novels. *English Journal*, *97*(1), 31–36.

Sutton, R. (2007). Problems, paperbacks, and the Printz: Forty years of YA books. *The Horn Book*, *83*(3), 231–243.

References

All works of young adult literature referenced in this chapter are included in the Young Adult Books list and are not repeated in this list.

Aronson, M. (1997). The challenge and glory of young adult literature. *Booklist*, *93*(16), 1418–1419.

Aronson, M. (2001). *Exploring the myth: The truth about teenagers and reading*. Lanham, MD: Scarecrow Press.

Aronson, M. (2002). Coming of age. *Publishers Weekly*, *249*(6), 82–86.

Beaman, A. (2006). YA lit 2.0: How technology is enhancing the pleasure reading experience for teens. *Knowledge Quest*, *35*(1), 30–33.

Bean, T. W. (2002). Making reading relevant for adolescents. *Educational Leadership*, *60*(3), 34–37.

Bean, T. W., and Moni, K. (2003). Developing students' critical literacy: Exploring identity construction in young adult fiction. *Journal of Adolescent & Adult Literacy*, *46*(8), 638–648.

Brown, J., and Stephens, E. (1995). *Teaching young adult literature*. Belmont, CA: Wadsworth.

Bushman, J., and Haas, K. P. (2001). *Using young adult literature in the English classroom*. Upper Saddle River, NJ: Merrill/Prentice Hall.

Campbell, P. (2003a). The outsiders, Fat Freddy, and me. *The Horn Book*, *79*(2), 177–183.

Campbell, P. (2003b). The sand in the oyster: Prizes and paradoxes. *The Horn Book*, *79*(4), 501–505.

Campbell, P. (2004). The sand in the oyster: YA bibliobullish trends. *The Horn Book*, *80*(1), 61–65.

Carlsen, G. R. (1967). *Books for the teen-age reader: A guide for teachers, librarians, and parents*. New York: Harper & Row.

Carlsen, G. R. (1971). *Books for the teen-age reader: A guide for teachers, librarians, and parents*. New York: Harper & Row.

Carlsen, G. R. (1980). *Books for the teen-age reader: A guide for teachers, librarians, and parents*. New York: Bantam.

Cart, M. (2001). The evolution of young adult literature. *Voices from the Middle*, *9*(2), 95–97.

Chelton, M. K. (2006). Perspectives on practice: Young adult collections are more than just young adult literature. *Young Adult Library Services*, *4*(2), 10–11.

Christenbury, L. (1997). From the editor. *English Journal*, *86*(3), 11–12.

Crocker, K. C. (2003, November/December). Teen books: The new generation. *Pages*, *11*(11/12), 76–78.

Dresang, E. (1999). *Radical change: Books for youth in a digital age*. New York: H. W. Wilson.

Engberg, G. (2007). 50 years of YA favorites. *Booklist*. *103*(19–20), 60–61.

Fantasy books top the list for teens: Young adults choose their favorite books as part of YALSA Teen Read Week. (2004). *School Library Journal*, *50*(1), 23.

Galda, L., and Liang, L. A. (2003). Literature as experience or looking for facts: Stance in the classroom. *Reading Research Quarterly*, *38*(2), 268–277.

Gillet, J. W., and Temple, C. (2000). *Understanding reading problems*. New York: Longman.

Glasgow, J. N. (2002). Radical change in young adult literature informs the multigenre paper. *English Journal*, *92*(2), 41–51.

Herz, S. K., and Gallo, D. R. (1996). *From Hinton to Hamlet: Building bridges between young adult literature and the classics*. Westport, CT: Greenwood Press.

Hipple, T. (2000). With themes for all: The universality of the young adult novel. In V. R. Monseau and G. M. Salvner (Eds.), *Reading their world: The young adult novel in the classroom* (pp. 1–14). Portsmouth, NH: Heinemann.

Jago, C. (2000). *With rigor for all: Teaching classics to contemporary students*. Portland, ME: Calendar Islands.

Jones, P. (2001). The perfect tens: The top forty books reviewed in Voice of Youth Advocates 1996–2000. *Voice of Youth Advocates*, *24*(2), 94–99.

Jones, P. (2003). To the teen core: A librarian advocates building collections that serve YA readers. *School Library Journal*, *49*(3), 48–49.

Kaywell, J. F. (Ed.). (1993–2000). *Adolescent literature as a complement to the classics*. Norwood, MA: Christopher Gordon.

Kaywell, J. F. (2001). Preparing teachers to teach young adult literature. *English Education, 33*(4), 323–327.

Kiesling, A. (2002). Tuning in to the teen soul. *Publishers Weekly, 249*(10), 30–32.

Knickerbocker, J. L., and Rycik, J. (2002). Growing into literature: Adolescents' literary interpretation and appreciation. *Journal of Adolescent & Adult Literacy, 46*(3), 196–208.

Manning, M. L., and Bucher, K. T. (2009). *Teaching in the middle school.* Boston: Allyn & Bacon.

The marketing battle for Generation Y. (2004. February). *Life Insurance International, 15.* Accessed February 11, 2005, from: http://proquest.umi.com.

Maughan, S. (2000). Teenage growing pains. *Publishers Weekly, 247*(3), 28–32.

McElmeel, S., and Buswell, L. (1998). Readers' choices: The most important authors of books for young adults. *The Book Report, 16*(4), 23–24.

Merriam-Webster's encyclopedia of literature. (1995). Springfield, MA: Merriam-Webster.

Moore, D. W., Bean, T. W., Birdyshaw, D., and Rycik, J. A. (1999). *Adolescent literacy: A position statement.* Newark, DE: International Reading Association.

Moore, J. N. (1997). *Interpreting young adult literature: Literary theory in the secondary classroom.* Portsmouth, NH: Heinemann.

The *Perfect Tens*: The top twenty books reviewed in *Voice of Youth* Advocates 2001–2002. (2003). *Voice of Youth Advocates, 26*(2), 98–99.

The *Perfect Tens*: The top ten books reviewed in *Voice of Youth* Advocates 2003. (2004). *Voice of Youth Advocates, 27*(2), 96–97.

The *Perfect Tens*: The top eleven books reviewed in *Voice of Youth* Advocates 2004. (2005). *Voice of Youth Advocates, 28*(2), 97.

The *Perfect Tens*: The top ten books reviewed in *Voice of Youth* Advocates in 2005. (2006). *Voice of Youth Advocates, 29*(2), 104.

The *Perfect Tens*: The top ten books reviewed in *Voice of Youth* Advocates 2006. (2007). *Voice of Youth Advocates, 30*(2), 112.

Poe, E., Samuels, B. G., and Carter, B. (1995). Past perspectives and future directions: An interim analysis of twenty-five years of research on young adult literature. *The ALAN Review, 22*(2), 46–50.

Reading remains popular among youth, according to poll (National Education Association survey). (2001, June). *Reading today.* Accessed January 5, 2004, from: www.findarticles.com/cf_dls/m0HQZ/6_18/76332780/print.jhtm1.

Richardson, M. V., and Miller, M. B. (2001). Motivating students to read: Using authors and literature from their home state. *Reading Improvement, 38*(3), 119–124.

Samuels, B. G. (1992). The young adult novel as transitional literature. In V. R. Monseau and G. M. Salvner (Eds.), *Reading their world: The young adult novel in the classroom* (pp. 28–47). Portsmouth, NH: Boynton/Cook.

Stallworth, B. J. (2006). The relevance of young adult literature. *Educational Leadership, 63*(7), 59–63.

Vogels, M. (1996). Young adult literature/Adult literature: What's the difference? Paper presented at meeting of National Council of Teachers of English, Chicago, November 23.

Williams, L. (2003). Summer belongs in the hands of the students: Celebrating choice in school reading lists. *Voice of Youth Advocates, 26*(5), 368–371.

Worthy, J., Patterson, E., Salas, P., Prater, S., and Turner, M. (2002). More than just reading: The human factor in reading resistant readers. *Reading Research and Instruction, 41,* 177–202.

YALSA (1996). Margaret A. Edwards Award: Policies and procedures. Accessed May 29, 2008, from: www.ala.org/ala/yalsa/booklistsawards/margaretaedwards/maepolicy/policiesprocedures.cfm.

YALSA (2004). Michael L. Printz Award Criteria. Accessed May 29, 2008, from: www.ala.org/ala/yalsa/booklistsawards/printzaward/aboutprintz/michaellprintz.cfm.

Chapter 2

Evaluating and Selecting Young Adult Literature

FOCUSING POINTS

In this chapter, you will read about:

✳ The purpose for selecting young adult literature

✳ The use of selected awards, book lists, review journals, and bibliographies in the book selection process

✳ The elements of literature that library media specialists and teachers can consider when evaluating and selecting young adult literature

✳ Our increasingly multicultural nation and the need to select young adult literature that reflects our schools' diversity

✳ The need to consider gender differences and preferences when selecting young adult literature for both females and males

"It doesn't matter what students read as long as they are reading something."

We have heard a comment like this many times and, while we agree that it is important to "hook" students on reading by offering a variety of materials, we also believe that teachers and library media specialists have the professional responsibility to lead young adults to literature that represents the best of its genre or format. In order to do this, educators must know how to evaluate and select appropriate literature, purchase it for classrooms and libraries, and then incorporate it into lesson and unit plans. By consulting recognized selection aids, checking the winners of book awards and prizes, and actually examining books for literary elements such as plot, character, theme, setting, style, and point of view, teachers and library media specialists can identify high-quality young adult literature.

When selecting literature, educators must also consider the religious, ethnic, social, racial, physical, sexual, and other diversities found in contemporary society and examine the way all groups are represented in young adult literature. Although there has been a concerted effort in the last decade to depict all groups with respect and understanding in young adult books, the challenge remains to identify appropriate literature and take the steps necessary to acquaint young adults with it. When selecting and recommending literature for adolescents, educators must also recognize gender differences and reading preferences and take them into consideration. Good books, even in the genres of science fiction or fantasy, should contain

interesting, realistic characters who play out important themes against an accurately depicted

and realistically detailed backdrop. . . . If we demand good literature,
we will get . . . the lasting pleasure that comes when we finish reading
a memorable piece of writing. (Jordan, 1996b, pp. 20–21)

The Purpose of Selecting Young Adult Literature

Thousands of new young adult books are published each year. When these are added
to the books already in print, teachers and library media specialists often face a difficult task in selecting appropriate, quality literature that meets the developmental,
intellectual, and social needs of adolescents as well as the school's curricular standards. Perhaps the ideal way to accomplish this is for educators to read young adult
literature and make their own judgments about its quality and appropriateness.
Unfortunately, given the large number of young adult books published each year, it is
not possible for any educator to read more than a sample of the new young adult literature that reaches the market. For example, 900 newly published books were nom-
inated for the annual Best Books for Young Adults list for 2004 ("Best Books for
Young Adults honors 84 books," 2004). Given that these were just a portion of the
total number of books published, teachers and library media specialists have developed other strategies for selecting quality literature.

Relying on Others When Selecting Young Adult Literature

Many teachers and all library media specialists have learned to rely on the recommendations of others when selecting materials. However, it is important not to rely
on just anyone for these recommendations. Publishers include glowing blurbs in the
catalogs and advertisements that they publish, but these publicity reviews are not recognized review sources. As one school library media specialist said, "I never met a
book that its publisher didn't love."

Thankfully, a number of resources or selection aids such as book awards, book
lists, book-length bibliographies, and review journals exist to help teachers and
library media specialists select appropriate young adult literature. We will only be able
to list a few of them in this chapter; we refer you to *The Children's and Young Adult
Literature Handbook* (Gillespie, 2005) for a detailed listing of over 1,000 bibliographies,
awards, and other resources. Expanding Your Knowledge with the Internet provides
links where you will find more information, including detailed selection criteria for the
resources we mention. Later chapters mention additional selection aids that target specific genres of young adult literature.

Book Awards

While any group can give an award, it is important to identify awards that are given
by recognized groups and associations with established committees that read and
evaluate a wide range of books. The review committee members must consider not

EXPANDING YOUR KNOWLEDGE WITH THE INTERNET

Information on book awards, including complete information on selection criteria and eligibility, is available on the Internet.

AWARDS

Alex Award
www.ala.org/ala/yalsa/booklistsawards/alexawards/alexawards.htm

Américas Award
www.uwm.edu/Dept/CLACS/outreach/americas.html

Boston Globe–Horn Book
www.hbook.com/bghb/default.asp

Carnegie Medal
www.carnegiegreenaway.org.uk/carnegie/carn.html

Carter G. Woodson Award
www.socialstudies.org/awards/woodson/

Coretta Scott King Awards
www.ala.org/ala/emiert/corettascottkingbookaward/corettascott.cfm

Garden State Teen Book Award
www.njla.org/honorsawards/book/index.html

Jane Addams Children's Book Award
home.igc.org/~japa/jacba/index_jacba.html

Los Angeles Times **Book Prize—Young Adult Fiction**
www.latimes.com/extras/bookprizes/index.html

Margaret A. Edwards Award
www.ala.org/ala/yalsa/booklistsawards/margaretaedwards/margaretedwards.htm

Michael L. Printz Award
www.ala.org/yalsa/printz

Mildred L. Batchelder Award
www.ala.org/ala/alsc/awardsscholarships/literaryawds/batchelderaward/batchelderaward.htm

National Book Award
www.nationalbook.org/nba.html

Newbery Award
www.ala.org/ala/alsc/awardsscholarships/literaryawds/newberymedal/newberymedal.htm

Orbis Pictus
www.ncte.org/elem/awards/orbispictus/106877.htm

Pura Bel Pre Award
www.ala.org/ala/alsc/awardsscholarships/literaryawds/belpremedal/belprmedal.htm

Sydney Taylor Book Award
www.jewishlibraries.org/ajlweb/awards/st_books.htm

Virginia Reader's Choice
www.vsra.org/Vyrpindex.html

BEST BOOKS LISTS

Best Books for Young Adults (YALSA)
www.ala.org/yalsa/booklists/bbya

Books for the Teen Age (New York Public Library)
teenlink.nypl.org/bta1.cfm

Outstanding Books for the College Bound (YALSA)
www.ala.org/yalsa/booklists/obcb

Popular Paperbacks for Young Adults (YALSA)
www.ala.org/yalsa/booklists/poppaper

Quick Picks for Reluctant Young Adult Readers (YALSA)
www.ala.org/yalsa/booklists/quickpicks

Fabulous Films for Young Adults (YALSA)
www.ala.org/ala/yalsa/booklistsawards/selecteddvds/fabfilms.cfm

Amazing Audiobooks for Young Adults (YALSA)
www.ala.org/ala/yalsa/booklistsawards/selectedaudio/audiobooks.cfm

Teachers' Choices list includes a category for grades 6–8
www.reading.org/resources/tools/choices_teachers.html

Young Adults' Choices
www.reading.org/resources/tools/choices_young_adults.html

Teens' Top Ten Books at YALSA
www.ala.org/ala/yalsa/teenreading/teenstopten/teenstopten.htm

REVIEW JOURNALS

Book Links
www.ala.org/ala/productsandpublications/
periodicals/booklinks/booklinks.htm

Booklist (ALA)
www.ala.org/ala/booklist/booklist.htm

Bulletin of the Center for Children's Books
lis.uiuc.edu/puboff/bccb/

English Journal (NCTE)
www.ncte.org/pubs/journals/ej

Horn Book Magazine
www.hbook.com/

Journal of Youth Services in Libraries (ALA)
www.ala.org/ala/yalsa/yalsapubs/yals/
youngadultlibrary.cfm

Journal of Adolescent & Adult Literacy
www.reading.org/publications/journals/jaal/
index.html

Kirkus Reviews
www.kirkusreviews.com/kirkusreviews/index.jsp

Language Arts (NCTE)
www.ncte.org/pubs/journals/la

Multicultural Review
www.mcreview.com/

Library Media Connection
www.linworth.com/lmc/

School Library Journal
www.schoollibraryjournal.com/

The ALAN Review (NCTE)
www.alan-ya.org/

Voice of Youth Advocates
www.voya.com/

Voices from the Middle (NCTE)
www.ncte.org/pubs/journals/vm

---

only the impact of the book on the reader but also the quality of the book and its appeal to teenagers (Gentle, 2001). Some younger adolescents enjoy reading books that have won the Newbery Medal, presented annually by the ALA for excellence in literature for children; the *Boston Globe–Horn Book* Award, given by the *Boston Globe* and *The Horn Book Magazine;* or the Carnegie Medal, presented by the British Library Association. Other young adults, however, are ready for books that are intended specifically for an older adolescent audience.

General Awards. In addition to the specialized awards that are discussed later in this book (those given to books in specific genres or to specific categories of authors), a number of general awards are also given to young adult literature. While these awards honor specific authors and books, they also promote quality young adult literature in general by heightening "public awareness of excellent literature and increas[ing] the readership of good books" (Gentle, 2001, p. 27). For example, the **Margaret A. Edwards Award** is given to an author for her or his lifetime contribution to writing for young adults. Winners have included Anne McCaffrey, Paul Zindel, and Nancy Garden.

Established in 1999 by the Young Adult Library Services Association (YALSA; a division of the ALA), and *Booklist* magazine, the **Michael L. Printz Award** recognizes, honors, and promotes excellence in young adult literature for ages 12 to 18. The award is not limited to any specific genre. Each year, a committee selects one award-winner and up to four "honor" books. For example, in 2008, the winner was Geraldine McCaughrean's *The White Darkness* (2007), while the honor books were

DreamQuake (Knox, 2007), *One Whole and Perfect Day* (Clarke, 2006), *Repossesed*, (Jenkins, 2007), and *Your Own, Sylvia: A Verse Portrait of Sylvia Plath* (Hemphill, 2007).

Given yearly since 1998 by the Adult Books for Young Adults Task Force of YALSA, the **Alex Award** identifies up to 10 adult books, such as *The Night Birds* (Maltman, 2007), *A Long Way Gone: Memoirs of a Boy Soldier* (Beah, 2007), and *Genghis: Birth of an Empire* (Iggulden, 2007) that will appeal to young adult readers. The award is named after Margaret Alexander Edwards, a public librarian who believed that adult books can help adolescents "broaden their experiences and . . . enrich their understanding of themselves and their world" ("YALSA announces 2002 Alex Awards," 2002, p. 58).

A number of other awards have young adult literature categories. For example, the **National Book Award** has a Young People's Literature category. Newspapers often give awards that have categories for young adult fiction such as the *Los Angeles Times* **Book Prize.** Several state library associations have young adult literature awards, including the **Garden State Teen Book Award** (New Jersey), the **Utah Beehive Award for Young Adult Fiction**, and the **Virginia Reader's Choice Award.** Collaborating with Other Professionals 2–1 has suggestions for participating in an award process.

Awards with Multicultural Perspectives.   Several awards have multicultural perspectives. Given by the National Council for the Social Studies, the **Carter G. Woodson Award** includes middle- and secondary-level books and recognizes works like *Freedom Walkers: The Story of the Montgomery Bus Boycott* (Freedman, 2006) and *Dear Miss Breed: True Stories of the Japanese-American Incarceration During World War II and a Librarian Who Made a Difference* (Oppenheim, 2006), which authentically depict ethnicity in the United States and examine race relations sensitively and accurately. **The Sydney Taylor Book Award** for outstanding Jewish content in children's books, given by the Association of Jewish Libraries, has a category for older readers. Given since 1953 by the Women's International League for Peace and Freedom and the Jane Addams Peace Association, the **Jane Addams Children's Book Award** honors children's books that promote peace, social justice, and world community, and has a category for older children through age 14.

Although not specifically given for young adult literature, a few awards honor multicultural literature and may include young adult literature among the award

COLLABORATING WITH OTHER PROFESSIONALS

Adolescents may not be able to select the Academy Award winners, but they can vote for the best books in their state or in the nation. For example, the national Teens' Top Ten Books list is sponsored by YALSA, (www.ala.org/ala/yalsa/teenreading/teenstopten/teenstopten.cfm).

Check your state library association(s) and your state reading association for information on existing state awards. If there is no existing award for adolescent literature in your state, lobby for one, or start your own local or regional award.

or honor winners. These include the **Coretta Scott King Award** for African Ameri-can authors and illustrators of outstanding literature for children and young adults. Winners and honor books have included Mildred Taylor's *The Land* (2001) and Julius Lester's *Day of Tears: A Novel in Dialogue* (2005). The **Pura Belpré Award,** given for books that portray the Latino cultural experience for children and youth, has hon-ored books like Julia Alvarez's *Before We Were Free* (2002) and Margarita Engle's *The Poet Slave of Cuba: A Biography of Juan Francisco Manzano* (2006). Providing an inter-national viewpoint, the **Mildred L. Batchelder Award** is given to a book originally published in a foreign language and translated into English. It has honored books like Uri Orlev's *Run, Boy, Run* (2003) and Jean-Claude Mourlevat's *The Pull of the Ocean* (2006). Other multicultural awards are mentioned later in this chapter.

Best Books Lists

In addition to awards, a number of organizations and associations develop lists of outstanding books for young adults. The New York Public Library issues an annual **Books for the Teen Age**; YALSA produces a number of these lists, including **Best Books for Young Adults, Outstanding Books for the College Bound, Popular Paperbacks for Young Adults, Quick Picks for Reluctant Young Adult Readers, Amazing Audiobooks for Young Adults,** and **Fabulous Films for Young Adults.** Some of the lists are general in nature; others are more specific. For example, each year the YALSA popular paperbacks committee identifies several themes (not neces-sarily in specific genres) and selects materials related to those themes. The 2009 themes were Dead, Dying & the Undead; Fame & Fortune; Journey & Destination; and Spies & Intrigue.

Some lists are based on suggestions by young readers themselves. The **Young Adults' Choices** is a yearly list created by adolescents in grades 7 to 12 at participating schools throughout the United States. Students make their selections from books nom-inated by publishers; in order to be nominated, each book must have received at least two positive reviews from recognized review sources. The Literature for Young Adults Committee of the International Reading Association supervises the voting. A compan-ion **Teacher's Choices** list includes a category for grades 6 to 8. The ALA sponsors an annual **Teens Top Ten** list; adolescents vote online for their favorite books.

Each year, the Children's Literature and Reading Special Interest Group of the International Reading Association lists its **Notable Books for a Global Society, K–12.** The books, including past notables such as *The Book Thief* (Zusak, 2006), *The Beast* (Myers, 2003), *Crossing the Wire* (Hobbs, 2006), and *Tangled Threads: A Hmong Girl's Story* (Shea, 2003), are culturally authentic and enhance the understanding of world cultures while showing the common bonds that exist (2000 Notable Books for a Global Society, 2001).

Review Journals

A number of reputable journals have reviews of young adult literature, including:

- *Booklist* (published by ALA)
- *Bulletin of the Center for Children's Books*

- *The Horn Book Magazine*
- *Kirkus Reviews*
- *Library Media Connection* (combination of *Library Talk* and *Book Report*)
- *School Library Journal*
- *Voice of Youth Advocates*

These journals devote a significant number of pages in each issue to reviews or, in the case of *Booklist* and *Kirkus Reviews*, contain only reviews. In addition to the regular reviews in each issue, a number of these journals, including *School Library Journal*, *Booklist*, and *Voice of Youth Advocates (VOYA)*, publish yearly best books lists. While most of these evaluate young adult literature on the basis of quality and literary merit, *VOYA* includes both a quality and a popularity rating with each review.

Other journals may include reviews or bibliographies of suggested young adult literature in addition to articles. These include *The ALAN Review* (affiliated with the NCTE), *Journal of Adolescent and Adult Literacy*, *Journal of Youth Services in Libraries* (affiliated with ALA), *Language Arts* (affiliated with NCTE), *English Journal* (affiliated with NCTE), *Multicultural Review*, *Voices from the Middle* (affiliated with NCTE), and *Children's Literature in Education*. Taking a thematic approach, *Book Links* publishes curriculum-related bibliographies and essays on linking books with topics of interest to children and young adults.

Book-Length Bibliographies

In addition to the awards and review journals, a number of books contain bibliographies of recommended books for young adults. Table 2–1 is a list of some recent titles. A number of books also examine the literary elements of young adult fiction. These include the series *Adolescent Literature as a Complement to the Classics* (Kaywell, 1993–), *Authors and Artists for Young Adults* (1989–) and the multivolume *Beacham's Guide to Literature for Young Adults* (Beetz & Niemeyer, 1989–), the latest volumes of which were issued in 2003. Each volume in the *Twayne Young Adult Author Series*, edited by Patricia Campbell, focuses on a specific young adult author and includes information about his or her works.

Evaluating Review Sources

While Internet sites such as Amazon.com and Barnesandnoble.com are not review sources, they do include reviews from reputable selection journals as part of their descriptions of many of the books found on their sites. By knowing the legitimate, quality selection aids, you can identify appropriate reviews on the websites of these and other Internet superstores. However, beware of reviews from sources that you do not know or that are from "readers." Some sources are nothing more than publishers' or distributors' catalogs. In addition, in 2004, Internet users discovered that a number of so-called reviews from readers at Internet bookstores were actually written by the book's author or by his or her friends using a variety of fictitious names in order to promote specific books. The best approach is to use only reviews from reputable sources that you know and trust.

TABLE 2-1   Recent Bibliographies of Young Adult Literature

Title	Author	Date
Best Books for Young Adults	Koelling & Carter	2007
Thematic Guide to Young Adult Literature	Trupe	2006
Popular Series Fiction for Middle School and Teen Readers	Barr	2005
Serving Teens Through Readers' Advisory	Booth	2007
Making the Match	Lesesne	2003
Middle and Junior High School Library Catalog	Price	2005
Senior High School Core Collection	Barber & Bartell	2007
Book Crush	Pearl	2007
500 Great Books for Teens	Silvey	2006
Connecting with Reluctant Teen Readers	Jones, Hartman, & Taylor	2006
Gentle Reads	McDaniel	2008
Big Book of Teen Reading Lists	Keane	2006
Best books for High School Readers	Gillespie & Barr	2006
A Core Collection for Young Adults	Jones, Taylor, & Edwards	2003

Relying on Your Own Judgment to Evaluate Young Adult Literature

While, in many cases, you can rely on selection aids to identify appropriate young adult literature, there are cases where you must rely on your own judgment. For example, there may be conflicting reviews of a book, or you may not be able to locate reviews from recognized sources. In other instances, only a publisher's advertisement that catches a school library media specialist's attention, a mention of a new book in an article, or a display at a conference or bookstore may be available. Certainly, all teachers will want to read and review the young adult books that they assign in their classes or put on their reading lists. When your own evaluation is needed, you must have a set of guidelines to use.

Elements of Literature

Throughout this book, you will read about criteria for evaluating each of the genres of literature. Behind these specific criteria are the literary elements such as character, plot, theme, setting, style, point of view, and tone. Although these elements are found in all good literature, they can vary according to the genre or type of literature as well as the age of the intended audience. While we can provide guidelines that you can use when examining these elements in books, it is important that you remain flexible when using them to select appropriate materials for a specific group of adolescents. Connecting Young Adults and Their Literature 2–1 presents one educator's view of the study of literary elements by adolescents themselves. Expanding Your Knowledge with the Internet provides links that discuss some of these elements in more detail than we can present in this chapter.

2-1 •••   CONNECTING ADOLESCENTS AND THEIR LITERATURE

While agreeing that it is important for adolescents to understand and evaluate the elements of literature, Arthea J. S. Reed (1994) suggested that educators should not lecture young adults about the literary elements of young adult novels. Rather, she believed that educators must allow young adults to discover, experience, and respond to the elements of a literary work by examining the work as a whole rather than dissecting the elements. When students are asked to dwell on the elements, they may lose sight of the work as a whole. This does not mean that readers cannot be encouraged to understand how these literary elements work. However, the elements should not be emphasized to a point where adolescents no longer enjoy reading.

Plot.   The plot is the "plan or the main story of a literary work . . . also known as the narrative structure" (*Merriam-Webster's Encyclopedia of Literature*, 1995, p. 890). Acting as a thread to hold the book together, the plot shows the characters in action and makes the reader want to continue reading (Lukens, 2007).

In young adult literature, the plot's importance cannot be overemphasized. For many reluctant readers, it is the action and movement of the plot rather than the detailed descriptions of the setting or the characters that draw them into the story. Young adults seem to prefer books with interesting plots to which they can relate. In books with well-written plots, events seem logical and natural, not contrived or artificial, and reflect the interests of adolescents. Successful authors such as Walter Dean Myers and Karen Hesse know when to allow readers to predict actions and when to surprise them.

EXPANDING YOUR KNOWLEDGE WITH THE INTERNET

Information on the elements of literature can be found at the following websites.

Lynch Glossary of Literary and Rhetorical Terms (Rutgers University)
andromeda.rutgers.edu/~jlynch/Terms/

Elements of Fiction—slide overview
www.readwritethink.org/materials/lit-elements/overview/

High School Literature—Literary Elements (Kenton County Schools)
www.kenton.k12.ky.us/TR/hslit.html

Literary Elements (Orange Unified School Division)
www.orangeusd.k12.ca.us/yorba/literary_elements.htm

Elements of Fiction—Interactive Fiction Tutorial
bcs.bedfordstmartins.com/virtualit/fiction/elements.asp

Lesson Plan on the Elements of Fiction
www.yale.edu/ynhti/curriculum/units/1983/3/83.03.07.x.html

PAL: Perspectives in American Literature—A Research and Reference Guide
www.csustan.edu/english/reuben/pal/append/AXG.HTML

Conflict is the "opposition of persons or forces upon which the dramatic action depends" (*Merriam-Webster's Encyclopedia of Literature*, 1995, p. 265) and is at the core of the plot. Conflict usually takes one or more of the following forms:

- *Person against person.* Conflict arises between the main character (protagonist) and one or more opposing characters, as in the struggle between Harry Potter and Voldemort or Draco Malfoy in *Harry Potter and the Sorcerer's Stone* (Rowling, 1998).

- *Person against society (culture).* The protagonist struggles against the rules or expectations of society, as in the struggle of Jonas against a utopia/distopia in *The Giver* (Lowry, 1993).

- *Person against nature (environment).* The protagonist struggles to survive; often found in adventure stories such as those by Gary Paulsen and Will Hobbs.

- *Person against self.* An internal emotional or intellectual conflict pulls the protagonist in different directions.

Some critics add another form of conflict, person against fate (spirit or deity). In any book, several types of conflict may be present.

Writers of young adult literature can employ a number of plot features. A plot may be linear/chronological (moving forward in a chronological pattern) or may contain flashbacks that move the action between the past and present. At times, an author may use two or more parallel plots, such as those in Robert Cormier's *I Am the Cheese* (1978), or an episodic plot that consists of a series of loosely connected stories or scenes (*Merriam-Webster's Encyclopedia of Literature*, 1995). *Holes* (Sachar, 1998) is an example of a circular or cyclical plot, in which the end of the novel returns to the beginning. Considerations for Evaluating Young Adult Literature: *Plot* provides several guidelines for evaluating plot.

Characters.   In literature, character refers to the individuals (human and nonhuman persons, animated objects, or personified animals) about whom the book is written. While the plot or action drives some books, in others, effective characterization

---

CONSIDERATIONS FOR
EVALUATING YOUNG ADULT LITERATURE PLOT

_____   Is the plot enjoyable and interesting?

_____   Is the plot logical or contrived? Natural or artificial?

_____   Is the plot credible and believable?

_____   Is there the right amount of predictability for the intended audience and genre of the book?

_____   Are the themes/topics of the book represented appropriately by the actions within the plot?

_____   Is the plot carefully constructed?

_____   Does the plot lead to a well-defined, logical, and identifiable climax?

maintains the reader's interest. When adolescents identify closely with the characters, they become involved with the experiences in the book. Authors reveal information about individual characters in a number of ways: what a character says, thinks, and does; what others say or think about the character or how they relate to the character; and the narrator's description of the character.

Several terms are used to describe the characters within a book. The *protagonist* or principal/main character (*Merriam-Webster's Encyclopedia of Literature*, 1995) is usually confronted with the *antagonist* or the "principal opponent or foil of the main character" (p. 56). While *round or dynamic characters* are "complex and undergo development throughout the story," *flat or static characters*, although essential, are "two-dimensional . . . uncomplicated, and do not change" (p. 420). Stereotypes or stock characters are usually flat and static. The static or dynamic nature of characters help the reader understand the ideas behind the action in the plot (Lukens, 2007).

All of these types of characters are found in the popular *Harry Potter and the Sorcerer's Stone* (Rowling, 1998). With Harry Potter as the protagonist, Voldemort emerges as the principal antagonist throughout the series, and although Professor Quirrel is his servant, he also serves as an antagonist as does the stereotyped or stock character of Draco Malfoy. Many dynamic characters grow in the book, including Ron Weasley and Hermione Granger, and Neville Longbottom dramatically changes from a bumbling comic to a student who stands up for his beliefs. This is in contrast to the static Dursley family, which remains cruel throughout the book. Considerations for Evaluating Young Adult Literature: *Character* details several guidelines for examining this literary element in more detail.

Setting. Basically, the setting is the time and place in which the action takes place (*Merriam-Webster's Encyclopedia of Literature*, 1995). However, the setting can be much more than a physical description, with "the makeup and behavior of fictional characters often depend[ing] on their environment quite as much as on their personal characteristics" (p. 1015). Sounds, smells, the kinds of buildings, the quality of

CONSIDERATIONS FOR EVALUATING YOUNG ADULT LITERATURE CHARACTER

_____ Are the characters' emotions, actions, thoughts, and words believable, credible, and consistent?

_____ Are the characters realistic rather than contrived?

_____ Do the characters complement each other?

_____ Do the characters contribute to the action and believability of the plot?

_____ Do the characters avoid being stereotypes?

_____ What will the readers learn from the characters?

_____ Will adolescents relate to or understand the characters?

_____ In series books, will the characters make adolescents want to continue with the series?

light, and climate may combine to create the mood and atmosphere for the characters and the conflict (Lukens, 2007). Anne Devereaux Jordan (1996c) suggested that the setting can assume the role of a character, especially in situations where nature or the environment helps or hinders characters.

By alluding to past literary and philosophical traditions, the use of setting as character adds depth to a story. For example, when nature is brought to life within a story, readers may be reminded of past mythological tales and of the pastoral and Romantic traditions (Jordan, 1996c).

While some works such as historical fiction may depend heavily on a specific realistic setting, other books may have a setting that expands rather than limits the universality of the story (Lukens, 2007). Perhaps the setting is totally imaginary—or it may be loosely defined to provide additional interpretations to the book. A setting may create a mood, create conflict, provide historical background, or add to the symbolism in the plot. Considerations for Evaluating Young Adult Literature: *Setting* provides several suggestions for examining this literary element.

Theme.   A theme is sometimes described as the "dominant idea of a book" (*Merriam-Webster's Encyclopedia of Literature*, 1995, p. 1005), or the underlying or unstated idea that provides organization. "When we ask, 'What does it all mean?' we begin to discover theme" (Lukens, 2007, p. 131). "If the plot tells us what happens in a story, the theme tells us why it happens" (Russell, 2009, p. 48). It is a statement about "society, human nature, or the human condition" (Lukens, 2007, p. 131). You may forget the exact events in a novel, but the theme will often remain with you because it goes beyond the action of the plot to reach a level of deeper meaning. This does not mean that all themes are serious; however, they should be substantial, not trivial.

A theme is more than a single word or phrase such as "love" or "growing up." As Reyes (n.d.) notes, the difference between a theme and a message is that a "message does not allow us to experience its truth—we either accept it or we don't." In contrast, a theme such as "growing up asks us to make difficult choices and decisions about who we love" is much more complex and requires more thought and analysis on the part of the reader.

Although some authors openly state an explicit theme, in most cases, the theme is implicit or implied and is revealed through the characters, the conflict, and the setting of the book. Sometimes, a book has several themes, often with one more important than the others. Common themes in young adult books usually present the

CONSIDERATIONS FOR EVALUATING YOUNG ADULT LITERATURE SETTING

_____   Even if imaginary, is the setting appropriate and consistent?

_____   Does the setting complement the other literary elements?

_____   Does the setting contribute to an understanding of the time and place?

_____   Is the setting authentic and credible?

_____   Does the author use the setting effectively?

CONSIDERATIONS FOR
EVALUATING YOUNG ADULT LITERATURE THEME

_____   What is the theme?

_____   Is the theme appropriate/worthwhile for adolescents?

_____   Will adolescents be able to understand the theme?

_____   What will adolescents learn from the theme?

_____   Is the theme too "preachy" or blatant or is it natural and objective?

_____   Does the theme complement the other literary elements?

_____   Does the theme provide cohesion to the work?

_____   How is the theme revealed to the reader?

author's perspective on concepts such as growing into adulthood or "coming of age"; accepting responsibility; confronting problems in life such as death and dying, illness, or poverty; and learning to deal with parents, other adults, and friends. Considerations for Evaluating Young Adult Literature: *Theme* provides several guidelines for examining this literary element.

Point of View. The author's perspective in telling the story is called the point of view; the three main points of view are first person, third person singular, and third person omniscient (*Merriam-Webster's Encyclopedia of Literature*, 1995). For readers, the point of view determines what the readers know, how involved they are in the story, and how the story develops.

In the first person point of view, "the story is told by 'I,' one of the characters involved in the story" (*Merriam-Webster's Encyclopedia of Literature*, 1995, p. 894), and the reader sees everything through the eyes of that character, who may or may not be the protagonist. Sometimes authors present the first person point of view through a diary or journal written by the character. When an author writes in the third person singular, he or she "writes from the point of view of a single character, describing or noticing only what that character has the opportunity to see and hear and know, but not in the voice of that character" (p. 894). Sometimes this is referred to as looking over the shoulder of one of the characters. Finally, using the third person omniscient point of view, an author is all-knowing about the details of the plot as well as the conscious or unconscious feelings of all of the characters (Lukens, 2007). Sometimes, authors use multiple points of view, perhaps by having different chapters told by different characters, switching between two major characters for alternating chapters, or interspersing short first person reflections in an otherwise third person omniscient narrative. Considerations for Evaluating Young Adult Literature: *Point of View* provides several guidelines for evaluating this literary element.

Style of Writing. In writing, the word *style* refers to the author's "distinctive manner of expression" (*Merriam-Webster's Encyclopedia of Literature*, 1995, p. 1077) or how the writer chooses and arranges words (Lukens, 2007). Using the most appropriate words and phrases, the author adds details and meanings to plots, shows characters' thoughts

CONSIDERATIONS FOR
EVALUATING YOUNG ADULT LITERATURE POINT OF VIEW

_____ Is the point of view appropriate for the plot and characters?

_____ Is the point of view appropriate for the developmental level of the intended reader?

_____ Is the point of view consistent and does it add to the understanding and appreciation of the story?

_____ Does the point of view complement the other literary elements?

_____ Is the point of view clear to the reader, and is the reader able to determine how objective or subjective it is?

_____ Does the point of view contribute to the reader's understanding of the book?

_____ Is the point of view credible and maintained throughout the book?

and reasons for actions, and provides more intricate descriptions of settings. With unique exposition, dialogue, vocabulary, imagery, figurative language, or sentence structure, the author's style conveys information, feelings, and perspectives. By putting them together, the author creates the book's mood or overall atmosphere.

The author's style also sets the *tone* of the book or the author's attitude toward both the book and the intended readers. According to Lukens (2007), the author's choice of words is a means of showing attitude toward the subject. Condescending, moralizing, didactic, sensational, cynical, or sentimental tones are usually not appropriate (Russell, 2009). In contrast, serious, humorous, passionate, sensitive, zealous, poignant, and warm tones are common in young adult literature. Considerations for Evaluating Young Adult Literature: *Style and Tone* provides several guidelines for evaluating these elements.

CONSIDERATIONS FOR
EVALUATING YOUNG ADULT LITERATURE STYLE AND TONE

_____ What literary devices comprise the author's style?

_____ Is the author's style appropriate for the plot and the theme?

_____ Is the author's style appropriate for adolescents?

_____ What mood does the style create?

_____ Does the author's style complement the other literary elements?

_____ Does the style contribute to the understanding of the book?

_____ Does the author maintain the same style throughout the book? If not, why, and is the change effective?

_____ Does the tone of the book help young adults to understand the author's perspectives and biases?

_____ Will the tone appeal to adolescents?

_____ Is the tone consistent throughout the book?

Selecting Multicultural Literature for Young Adults

The U.S. population is becoming more diverse. The U.S. Census reports show that in 1900, 85% of immigrants came from Europe. In contrast, in 1990, only 22% came from Europe (U.S. Bureau of the Census, 2003). By the 2000 census, 2.4% of the population claimed a multiracial heritage (Yakota & Frost, 2003). As the anticipated growth in selected minority groups (Table 2–2) continues, there will be an increase in the school-age population from these groups.

There are many ways of talking about diversity. In addition to nationality based on a person's specific country of birth or naturalization, there is cultural and ethnic diversity. Within a specific country, there may be different ethnic groups whose members identify with others of the same group because of common "racial, national, tribal, religious, linguistic, or cultural origin or background" *(Merriam-Webster's Online Dictionary)*. *Culture* is defined as the "customary beliefs, social forms, and material traits of a racial, religious, or social group" *(Merriam-Webster's Online Dictionary)*. Thus, people in a specific ethnic group may share cultural beliefs, values, social practices, and conventions.

Responding to Diversity: Values of Multicultural Literature

What is a common pleasure for mainstream students—connecting with a character who has a similar name and a familiar experience—truly delights children who don't typically see themselves reflected in the books they use. (Carger, 2003, p. 34)

As the U.S. population becomes more diverse, educators are attempting to reflect this diversity in both the literature that is available to adolescents and in the school's curriculum. James Baldwin maintained that literature is "vital to how people perceive reality and the world in which they live" (cited in Boyd, 2002, p. 59). Multicultural literature, described as a "vehicle for socialization and change" (Harris, 1997, p. 51), allows readers to connect to people from other cultures in a way the Western male writers in the traditional literary canon are unable to do (Chew, 1997).

TABLE 2-2   Major Cultural Groups in the United States

Cultural group	2006	Percent change 2000 to 2006
Hispanic American	44.321 million	25.5%
African American	38.343 million	7.4%
Asian American	13.159 million	24.3%
Native Hawaiian and Pacific Islanders	0.529 million	14.3%
Native American	2.903 million	9%
White Americans	239.746 million	5.1%

Source: U.S. Bureau of the Census. (2008). *Statistical abstract of the United States: 2008*. Washington, DC: Government Printing Office.

Through multicultural literature, young adults can:

- Learn about their own and others' cultural backgrounds
- Realize the many similarities that all people share and experience
- Begin to understand the injustices of the past
- Develop self-esteem and cultural identity
- Understand the problems faced by refugees and immigrant groups
- Develop a respect for a variety of cultural and individual characteristics
- "Build a positive self-image by . . . [observing] characters like themselves and their families who are able to work out problems and succeed in various ways" (McGlinn, 2002, p. 50)

In addition, "good stories from other cultures and languages help connect . . . [readers] to people around the world" (Lo, 2001, p. 87). By using universal themes such as justice, friendship, survival, or conflict resolution, authors of multicultural literature are able to make connections across cultures (Gonzalez, Huerta-Macias, & Tinajero, 1998). Authors are also able to "raise the consciousness and awareness of differences between and among people across contexts, countries, and cultures" (Boyd, 2002, p. 89). For example, in a study by Athanases (1998), a diverse group of 10th-grade students eliminated stereotypes as they read multicultural literature and learned about diversity in race, religion, ethnicity, gender, and sexual orientation.

As all adolescents begin to shape their identity, minority students begin to develop their ethnic identity (Gonzalez, Huerta-Macias, & Tinajero, 1998). In addition to learning about other cultures, multicultural literature helps adolescents "of diverse backgrounds shape cultural identity" (De León, 2002, p. 51) and their personal identity (Klein, 1992). Multicultural literature "frees the many voices in the reader" and encourages the reader to "explore all of her selves: the master and the slave, the male and the female, the black and the white" (Aronson, 2001, p. 17).

Morales, writing about "Chicano/a" (2001, p. 16) students, mentions considerations that hold true for other adolescents as well. Adolescents must learn about their cultural identity and "how it fits into their complex identity" (p. 20). When teachers promote a "shared experience" through multicultural literature while also "fostering an exuberance for one's own identity" (p. 18), the result will be a multicultural classroom that will empower all students.

A Brief History of Multicultural Literature

For many decades, children's and young adult literature focused primarily on middle-class Anglo American populations and, of course, dealt with situations, problems, and challenges representative of this cultural group. Other groups, if represented at all, were usually shown as minor characters or in menial and subservient positions. For example, American Indians were often stereotyped as savages, and African Americans were portrayed only as servants. These representations had the potential to distort the readers' views toward an entire culture of people. Table 2–3 outlines some of the historical events in the development of multicultural literature.

Recent years have brought about improvements in this representation, as authors and publishers have attempted to produce books that show more balanced perspectives

TABLE 2-3   Historical Events in the History of Multicultural Literature

Date	Event
1885	Mark Twain's *Huckleberry Finn* depicted attitudes of that time toward culturally diverse individuals.
1900–1930s	Books included stereotypical perspectives.
1940s–1950s	Books included other cultures only on a superficial level.
1960s–1970s	African American authors such as Virginia Hamilton, Alice Childress, Rosa Guy, and Walter Dean Myers began to be published.
1965	*The Saturday Review* published Nancy Larrick's article entitled "The All-White World of Children's Books."
1968/1969	The ALA established the Mildred L. Batchelder Award for translated books; the Coretta Scott King Award for African American authors was first given.
1970s	Books for children and young adults began to reflect a multicultural viewpoint as authors such as Nicholasa Mohr (Puerto Rican experience), Jamake Highwater (American Indian experience), and Laurence Yep (Asian American experience) were published.
1976	Mildred D. Taylor wrote *Roll of Thunder, Hear My Cry*, which challenged stereotypes of African American life in the South.
1980s	Retrenchment occurred. Some established minority writers had difficulty getting their books published, and many award-winning books went out of print. Small, independent presses such as Arte Publico began to publish multicultural literature.
Late 1980s–1990s	Rebirth of multicultural publishing among the major publishers.
Late 1990s–2000s	Establishment of multicultural book awards such as the Pura Belpré Award.

Source: Developed in part from Miller-Lachman, L. (1992). *Our family, our friends, our world: An annotated guide to significant multicultural books for children and teenagers.* New Providence, NJ: Bowker, pp. 5–10.

of cultural differences. However, according to a study of the publishing industry by Hill (1998), three "gatekeepers" limit the amount of multicultural literature that is published and made available. First, she found, many publishers focus on the profitability of a book and do not seek out minority authors and illustrators. Second, review journals, knowing that they do not have enough space to review all books, focus on literature that they believe will have a wide appeal to schools and libraries. Third, bookstore buyers and librarians rely in turn on the publishers and the review journals to identify the books they will carry on their shelves or purchase for their collections.

The Cooperative Children's Book Center of the School of Education at the University of Wisconsin–Madison has kept records on the multicultural books published for children and teens. Although there is no specific breakdown for just adolescent literature, Table 2–4 illustrates their statistics.

As Table 2–4 illustrates, although improvements are still needed, considerable progress has been made, and the number of books focusing on multicultural persons, themes, and issues is growing in quantity and quality. According to Dresang (1999), "the subjugated, unheard voices that are emerging in contemporary literature are not related to ethnicity alone, but speak out on previously unrecognized aspects of gender, sexual orientation, occupation, socio-economic level, and ability/disability" (p. 26). Discussing literature for Hispanic Americans, Isabel Schon (2004, p. 44) pointed out

TABLE 2-4   Statistics in Multicultural Publishing for Children and Young Adults

Year	Total number of books (est.)	Africans/ African Americans		Asian Pacifics/ and Asian Pacific Americans	American Indian	Latinos
		By	**About**	**By & About**	**By & About**	**By & About**
1985	2,500	18	NA	NA	NA	NA
1990	5,000	51	NA	NA	NA	NA
1995	4,500	100	167	91	83	70
2002	5,000	69	166	91	64	94
2007	5,000	77	150	124	50	101

NA = not available

Source: Developed from Cooperative Children's Book Center. (n.d.). *Children's books by and about people of color published in the United States.* Accessed May 9, 2008, from: www.education.wisc.edu/ ccbc/books/pcstats.htm.

that "from the joys and disappointments of Mexican migrant workers and Cuban exiles in the United States, to Gary Soto's . . . depictions of Mexican American family dynamics, to well-known legends and serious political accounts" today's literature addresses the "dreams, feelings, and celebrations" of different cultures.

Evaluating Multicultural Literature

According to De León (2002), "a multicultural approach to literature . . . is essential because it can foster a self-worth and motivation in students of diverse cultural backgrounds that was not present before" (p. 49). In addition, it can show "that there is a great deal to be learned from people who have had different cultural experiences" (Wartski, 2005). This will require a change in secondary English curricula and the ways literature is taught (Burroughs, 1999). Chew (1997) supports the study of multicultural literature with the traditional canon by pointing out that an understanding of classical literature can actually assist in the reading of multicultural works. However, the sole responsibility should not reside with the English department (Morales, 2001). Collaborating with Other Professionals 2–2 suggests developing a book selection team that includes educators from throughout the school.

While teachers and library media specialists should evaluate and select all young adult books with care, selecting appropriate multicultural literature may be even more important. As Rochman (1993) noted, a good book can help to "break down [barriers] . . . [and] can make a difference in dispelling prejudice and building community . . . with good stories that make us imagine the lives of others" (p. 19). "Fact and details should emerge naturally in description, action, and dialogue and not detract or derail the storyline or exposition. . . . Themes dealt with in the books should be of significance both to the cultural group portrayed and to the reader" (Jordan, 1996a, p. 23).

Currently, peoples from all cultures are shown from more objective perspectives, more multicultural populations are being written about, and more multicultural authors

2-2 COLLABORATING WITH OTHER PROFESSIONALS

Build a book selection team in your school. Too often school librarians and teachers forget that "if . . . collections are to be relevant to the folks we serve, we must strive to respect, and collect, materials that serve tastes not our own" (Benedetti, 2003, p. 29).

- Involve others in the selection process
- Overcome your personal biases

- Identify books that are related to the curriculum
- Determine what young adults are reading in classes and for pleasure
- Read magazines to see what books are being advertised directly to adolescents
- Check *Entertainment Weekly* to identify the new films based on novels (Benedetti, 2003)

are being published. However, too many inaccuracies, extreme dialectical differences, and stereotypical perspectives and illustrations still populate current young adult literature. As a result, teachers and library media specialists need to select and use multicultural literature that is free from bias, distortion, stereotypes, racism, and sexism. As Miller-Lachman (1992) pointed out, stereotyping may occur in characterizations (stock physical, social, and behavioral qualities are depicted), the plot (characters play set roles

EXPANDING YOUR KNOWLEDGE WITH THE INTERNET

The following are URLs of multicultural and diversity information in general and to information on multicultural literature.

GENERAL MULTICULTURAL/ DIVERSITY INFORMATION

Center for Research on Education, Diversity, and Excellence
www.crede.ucsc.edu/

Global Teach Net
www.rpcv.org/pages/globalteachnet.cfm

Multicultural Pavilion
www.edchange.org/multicultural/

National Association for Multicultural Education
www.nameorg.org/

Teaching Tolerance
www.tolerance.org/teach/

MULTICULTURAL LITERATURE

Africa Access (Montgomery County, Maryland, Public Schools)
filemaker3.mcps.k12.md.us/aad/

Bonnie O. Ericson, At Home with Multicultural Adolescent Literature (*The ALAN Review*)
scholar.lib.vt.edu/ejournals/ALAN/fall95/Ericson.html

Barahona Center for the Study of the Study of Books in Spanish for Children and Adolescents, California State University, San Marcos
www.csusm.edu/csb/

How to Choose the Best Multicultural Books (Scholastic)
teacher.scholastic.com/products/instructor/multicultural.htm

Multicultural Book Database (Montgomery County, Maryland)
www.mcps.k12.md.us/curriculum/socialstd/MBD/Books_Begin.html

Multicultural Children's Literature (Michigan State University)
www.lib.msu.edu/corby/education/multicultural.htm

"10 quick ways to analyze children's books for racism and sexism" (original)
www.birchlane.davis.ca.us/library/10quick.htm

or are unable to solve their own problems), theme (problems are faced by all members of a cultural group, and are specific to only those individuals), setting (all members of a group live in one type of house; i.e., all American Indians live in teepees), language (all members of a group have the same dialect), and illustration (all members of a group look alike). Although writing primarily about books for younger students, Reese (1999, 2007) stresses the need to select books that are both authentic and sensitive to other cultures.

In spite of the fact that "Ten quick ways to analyze children's books for racism and sexism" (1974) is 30 years old, its suggestions have served as a reliable and respected evaluation tool. We have combined this information with ideas from Miller-Lachman (1992) and other sources to provide, in Considerations for Evaluating Young Adult Literature: *Multicultural Books*, a set of questions you can ask when examining multicultural literature. Throughout this book, you will find examples of multicultural literature that have the characteristics not only of outstanding books in their genres but also of quality multicultural literature. Expanding Your Knowledge with the Internet provides URLs where you will find additional information.

CONSIDERATIONS FOR EVALUATING YOUNG ADULT LITERATURE
MULTICULTURAL BOOKS

Ask the following questions when evaluating multicultural books for young adults:

LITERARY QUALITIES

_____   Does the book meet the qualifications for good literature?

_____   Does the book exhibit the qualities expected in its genre?

ACCURACY AND CURRENCY OF FACTS AND INTERPRETATION

_____   Are thoughts and emotions portrayed authentically?

_____   In historical fiction, is the content realistic for the time period?

_____   Does the content intensify the reader's sensitivity to the feelings of others?

_____   Does the author present a balanced view of the issues in the book, especially nonfiction?

STEREOTYPES IN LIFESTYLES

_____   Are culturally diverse characters and their settings contrasted unfavorably with an unstated norm of Anglo American, middle-class suburbia?

_____   Does the story go beyond oversimplifications of reality and offer genuine insights into another lifestyle or culture?

PLOT

_____   Do European Americans in the story have all the power and make the decisions?

_____   Do people from diverse backgrounds function in essentially subservient roles?

_____   Does a character from a diverse background have to exhibit superior qualities (excel in sports, get As) to succeed?

_____   How are problems presented, conceived, and resolved in the story?

_____   Are people from diverse backgrounds considered to be "the problem"?

(Continued)

(Continued)

_____ Do solutions ultimately depend on the benevolence of a European American?

_____ Are the achievements of girls and women due to their own initiative and intelligence or their good looks or their relationships with boys?

_____ Are sex roles incidental or paramount to characterization and plot?

_____ Could the same story be told if the sex roles were reversed?

THEME

_____ Would the book limit or promote an adolescent's self-image and self-esteem?

_____ Would the book limit or promote an adolescent's aspirations?

_____ Can a reader from any culture become so involved with the book that he or she can identify with the characters and vicariously experience their feelings?

LANGUAGE

_____ Is terminology current or appropriate for the time period?

_____ Does the language refrain from including pejorative terms unless germane to the story?

_____ Do any dialects reflect the varieties found in contemporary life?

_____ Does the dialect reflect negatively on an entire culture?

AUTHOR'S PERSPECTIVE

_____ What qualifications does the author (or illustrator) have to write about a multicultural topic?

_____ Is the author (or illustrator) able to think as a member of another cultural group and to intellectually and emotionally become a member of that group?

_____ If the author (or illustrator) is not a member of the culturally diverse group being written about, is there anything in the author's (or illustrator's) background that would specifically recommend her or him for this book?

_____ If a book has to do with the feelings and insights of women, does a male author (or illustrator) present these appropriately?

ILLUSTRATIONS

_____ Are there stereotypes, oversimplifications, and generalizations in the illustrations?

_____ Do pictures demean or ridicule characters?

_____ Is there tokenism or presentation of European Americans with tinted or colored faces?

_____ Is sufficient individuality and diversity depicted within cultural groups?

Sources: Questions developed, in part, from: Jordan, A. D. (1996a). Books of other cultures. *Teaching and Learning Literature, 5*(4), 23–25; Jordan, A. D. (1996b). Welcome to my world: Books of other cultures. *Teaching and Learning Literature, 5*(4), 15–22; Miller-Lachman, L. (1992). *Our family, our friends, our world: An annotated guide to significant multicultural books for children and teenagers.* New Providence, NJ: Bowker; Ten quick ways to analyze children's books for racism and sexism. (November 3, 1974). *Interracial Books for Children, 5*(3), 6–7.

Awards and Bibliographies of Literature for a Diverse Society

Gillespie, Powell, Clements, and Swearingen (1994) conducted a study of the Newbery Medal books between 1922 and 1994 to determine the ethnicity of their characters. The results showed 90% of the books had white, Anglo-Saxon characters, as opposed to 26% with African Americans, 5% with Native Americans, 10% with Asian/Pacific Islanders, and 10% with Hispanics. This imbalance shows how important it is that teachers and library media specialists know and use reputable selection tools to assist in identifying quality multicultural literature for young adults.

Thankfully, educators and librarians can turn to a number of awards and bibliographies (Table 2–5). Several of them, such as the Coretta Scott King Award, the Pura Belpré Award, and the Mildred L. Batchelder Award, were mentioned earlier in this chapter. In addition, the **Américas Award** from the Consortium of Latin American Studies is given to works that portray Latin America, the Caribbean, or Latinos in the United States and includes some titles suitable for adolescents. The **Asian Pacific American Award for Literature,** cosponsored by the Asian Pacific American Librarians Association and the Chinese American Librarians Association, includes young adult literature. The American Indian Library Association sponsors the **American Indian Youth Literature Awards.** Finally, the **Tomás Rivera Mexican American Children's Book Award,** presented by Southwest Texas State University, has been given to some books that would appeal to younger adolescents.

TABLE 2-5 Bibliographies of Multicultural Literature

Title	Author	Date
The Best of Latino Heritage, 1996–2002	Schon	2003
Coretta Scott King Award Books 1970–2004	Smith	2004
Hearing All the Voices	Darby & Pryne	2002
Latina and Latino Voices in Literature	Day	2003
The Pura Belpré Award	Treviño	2006
The Heart Has Its Reasons: Young Adult Literature with Gay/Lesbian/Queer Content, 1969–2004	Cart & Jenkins	2006
Many Peoples, One Land	Helbig & Perkins	2001
Integrating Multicultural Literature in Libraries and Classrooms in Secondary Schools	Hinton & Dickinson	2007
Black Authors and Illustrators of Books for Children and Young Adults	Murphy & Murphy	2007
Understanding Diversity Through Novels and Picture Books	Smith & Knowles	2007
Booktalking Multicultural Literature	York	2008
Recommended Books in Spanish for Children and Young Adults, 2000 through 2004	Schon	2004

Gender Perspectives in Young Adult Literature

The two gender issues that are most important to understand when selecting literature for adolescents are (1) the representation of gender in the books, and (2) the differences in the reading habits of male and female young adults.

Gender and Reading Preferences

Worldwide literacy scores indicate that boys do not perform as well as girls. For example, in England, girls score higher than boys in English when tested at ages 7, 11, 14, and 16 (Haupt, 2003); in Australia, a 1996 survey found literacy scores for boys declining over a 10-year period (Bantick, 1996). Von Drasek (2002), reporting on the National Center for Educational Statistics National Assessment for Educational Progress of 1992–2000 reading assessments in the United States, said that between 1998 and 2000, "the gap between boys' and girls' scores increased." Although the percentage of girls at or above the proficient level in 2000 was higher than in 1992, for "boys, the percentage in 2000 was not significantly different than in 1992" (p. 72).

In *Reading Don't Fix No Chevys*, Smith and Wilhelm (2002) identified a number of general research findings about boys, girls, and reading:

- Girls comprehend fiction better than boys.
- Boys seem to prefer nonfiction, magazines, and newspapers.
- Boys tend to prefer short texts or texts with short sections.
- Girls enjoy leisure reading more than boys.
- Many boys enjoy reading about sports and hobbies.
- Some boys enjoy fantasy and science fiction.
- Graphic novels and comic books are more popular with boys than girls.
- Boys prefer visual texts.
- Boys really do judge a book by its cover.

However, Wilhelm and Smith (2001) went on to caution educators that boys can be "more different than alike" and that depending on statistics alone can cause educators to "lose sight of individual differences." Citing Millard (1997) and Telford (1999), Wilhelm and Smith (2001) noted that "teachers tend to use conventional wisdom to reinforce traditional notions of gender and gender preferences, thereby denying boys wider choices and chances to expand their tastes" (p. 60).

Gurian (2001) pointed out that most of the "reading-traumatized and reading-deficient high school students" (p. 297) are boys. In a national survey conducted during the 2001 Teen Read Week, adolescents responded to the question "If you don't read much or don't like reading, why?" Boys reported the following as obstacles to reading: boring/not fun (39.3%); no time/too busy (29.8); like other activities better (11.1%); and can't get into the stories (7.7%). Other responses constituted less than 5% (Jones & Fiorelli, 2003).

In a survey of Arizona high school students that was repeated in 1982, 1990, and 1997, Hale and Crowe (2001) found that contemporary boys' favorite books are about adventure, sports, science fiction, and mystery, while contemporary girls rank mystery and romance/love stories as their favorites. The lowest-rated categories of books for both boys and girls were historical, western, and biography/autobiography. Although humor books were favorites in 1982, they dropped significantly in popularity by 1997. It should be noted there was no category for realistic fiction on the survey and that the top pleasure reading titles in 1997 were from the genres of fantasy/science fiction/horror, mystery, contemporary realistic fiction, and historical fiction.

While these findings cannot be applied across the board to all adolescents, they must be kept in mind when selecting young adult literature. Reading takes practice. A coach would never say to a basketball player, "You know how to shoot a basket so you don't need to practice anymore." Instead, both the coach and the player know that practice improves performance. The same holds true with reading. Von Drasek (2002) notes that "skilled readers read an average of 11 pages a day" (p. 72). However, if teachers and library media specialists are not providing the kinds of materials that boys and girls enjoy reading, there is a lower probability that adolescents will spend time practicing their reading skills and thus developing reading proficiency.

To encourage boys to read, Allison Haupt (2003), coordinator of Children's and Young Adults' Services at the North Vancouver District Public Library, declared: "I've decided to be overtly and blatantly sexist in everything from the way I approach storytelling to the books I promote. It's not that I don't think that boys and girls . . . can't read and enjoy the same books. . . . But [I am convinced] . . . that our ability to promote reading can be greatly enhanced by recognizing biological and developmental differences between the guys and the gals" (p. 20). Both boys and girls need to see that reading is important and that it can blend with their academic or professional goals. For boys, if "reading is identified as being 'soft' or feminine, then reading would diminish rather than develop . . . [a boy's] fragile sense of self and growing masculinity" (p. 21). Connecting Adolescents and Their Literature 2–2 has some suggestions for encouraging boys to read.

Traditional Perspectives Toward Gender

"Everything we read . . . constructs us, makes us who we are, by presenting our image of ourselves as girls and women, as boys and men" (Fox, 1993, p. 152). A number of writers (Brown & Gilligan, 1992; Orenstein, 1994; Pipher, 1994; Sadker & Sadker, 1994; Thorne, 1993; Walker & Foote, 1999/2000) have focused on the issue of gender in education and the need for gender equity. Along with other researchers, they have documented gender inequities in educational experiences, as well as differences in socialization and ways educational experiences reflect gender.

Traditionally, in schools, educators have provided educational experiences that are based on gender-specific mindsets. For example, males, both at the top and the bottom of the class, attract a great deal of the teacher's attention (Sadker & Sadker, 1994) while textbooks and other curricular materials cater to males and their learning styles (Textbook sexism, 1994). Clark (1994) found that educators often use teaching strategies that reflect primarily male learning styles, while Levine and Orenstein (1994) found that educators often perpetuate gender-specific attitudes and beliefs about appropriate motivation and learning behaviors of males and females.

2-2 ••• CONNECTING ADOLESCENTS AND THEIR LITERATURE

A number of strategies exist that teachers and library media specialists can use to encourage adolescent boys to read.

- Identify role models and "catch" them reading. The ALA has a series of Read posters that reinforce this, but local personalities, male mentors, coaches, and community leaders can work just as well.
- Find things boys like to read and make them available.
- Include comics and graphic novels in the library and classroom.
- Make sure that both boys' and girls' reading interests are included on reading lists.
- Introduce an "all boys book club" (Haupt, 2003).
- Make magazines and newspapers available.
- Identify books that feature Brozo's 10 positive male archetypes that are relevant to male development: King, Patriarch, Warrior, Magician, Pilgrim, Wildman, Healer, Trickster, Prophet, and Lover (Brozo, 2002).
- Visit author Jon Scieszka's website for ideas: www.guysread.com.
- Display books where boys will notice them.

Beginning in the 1960s and gaining momentum from the women's movement of the 1970s, feminist criticism began as some women resisted the exclusion of women and the female consciousness in the accepted literary canon that was taught in schools. By identifying with women writers and their works and by focusing attention on the repression, trivialization, and misinterpretation of female texts, these critics called for studies of the images of women in literary works and, consequently, a feminist revision of the literary canon itself. Female critics pointed out that women bring to a work of literature different experience from that of men. Feminists also claimed that male critics not only suppressed female works but also tried to convince women that their interests reflected immature tastes. To reinterpret the literary world and change readers' consciousness, feminist criticism focused on rediscovering female authors and on establishing an alternative historical criticism that would relate literary events to both female and male social concerns (Vandergrift, 1993).

Contemporary Gender Issues

Thankfully, there have been changes over the years in the ways genders are represented in adolescent literature. Fouts (1999) reported a move away from traditional role perspectives for female characters in Spanish children's literature; and Houdyshell and Kirkland (1998) found strong, independent heroines with a sense of self in the most recent Newbery Medal books. In 2002, the Feminist Task Force of the ALA's Social Responsibilities Round Table instituted the **Amelia Bloomer List of Recommended Feminist Books for Youth** to recognize risk-taking and life-changing books about women.

Young adult literature has also begun to include gay and lesbian perspectives. Building on John Donovan's *I'll Get There, It Better Be Worth the Trip* (1969) and Nancy Garden's *Annie on My Mind* (1982), young adult realistic novels often address gay and lesbian themes while nonfiction books "provide role models of successful and creative gays and lesbians (Aronson, 2001, p. 60). "Instead of merely telling stories whose punch line is that a character is different and that is okay, we are now getting books in which a character is ambiguous, sorting out a mixed identity, and that is okay too" (p. 88). Today, books that include gay-related themes have received awards; a National Book Award went to Virginia Euwer Wolff's *True Believer* (2001), and a Printz Honor Award went to Garrett Weyr's *My Heartbeat* (2002). In 2003, Nancy Garden won a Margaret A. Edwards Award for lifetime contributions to young adult literature.

Rockefeller (2007) noted that transgender characters are beginning to make "a stumbling debut" (p. 526) in young adult fiction, although he finds many of the first books are didactic, with "an unbalanced attention to issues" (p. 519). Among those with "multidimensional characters who embody or face transgender themes in a plausible way" (p. 521), he lists *Luna* (Peters, 2004) *Choir Boy* (Anders, 2005), and *Parrotfish* (Wittlinger, 2007).

Selecting Literature for Diverse Gender Perspectives

Teachers and library media specialists need to be aware of gender perspectives when selecting and using young adult literature. This is important because the ways genders are depicted in books has an impact on attitudes and the perception of gender-appropriate behavior (Singh, 1998). Both genders deserve fair and equitable treatment. Thus, educators must identify literature that reflects respect for both females and males, shows both genders in nonstereotypical ways, and represents both female and male perspectives. When gender stereotypes are present in young adult literature, both girls and boys are deprived of a range of strong alternative role models.

Everything adolescents read, from advertisements and magazines to sports stories and romance novels, helps develop perceptions and mindsets (Fox, 1993). Too often, young adult literature portrays individuals in stereotypical ways—girls who are overly concerned with their clothes, hair, makeup, and figures or are victims in need of a male's help; men who are unable to express emotions or evidence fear. Just as educators should avoid generalizing about a particular culture, they should also avoid selecting literature that perpetuates stereotypes, false perceptions, and half-truths about both males and females.

As with multicultural literature, some critics make the argument that a book with a main character of one gender cannot be written by a writer of another gender. While having "lived" a particular gender perspective might be an advantage, requiring writers to write only about experiences they have encountered limits their imagination and creativity. Would the same critics suggest that an author must have personally been an alcoholic, drug user, or abused child to write about these real problems? In an interview with female young adult author M. E. Kerr, B. Allison Gray (1991) asked Kerr why she often wrote from a teenage male's perspective. Kerr responded that many males do not like to read stories about females. Thus, in an effort to encourage boys to read, she decided to write from a male perspective.

Contemporary young adult literature reflects the "complex identities of today's teens" (Pavo, 2003, p. 23), and "readers of all ages are proving that they are ready to move into more complex territory" (p. 25). As authors and publishers continue to diversify the representation of gender in the books that they write and publish, educators must select appropriate titles that support the social, physical, and intellectual needs of adolescents. Considerations for Evaluating Young Adult Literature: *Gender Representations* includes some guidelines for examining all gender representations in contemporary young adult literature. In Expanding Your Knowledge with the Internet, you will find additional information on gender in education and in young adult literature.

CONSIDERATIONS FOR EVALUATING YOUNG ADULT LITERATURE
GENDER REPRESENTATIONS

When examining young adult literature for gender and sexuality, ask the following:

_____   Are the characters developed as individuals, no matter what their gender or sexuality?

_____   Do the descriptions, words, and actions of the characters expand gender roles or reflect traditional stereotypes?

_____   Are occupations, aspirations, and achievements gender neutral?

_____   Do both males and females evidence emotional as well as logical characteristics?

_____   Do both males and females ask questions, confront others, interrupt, and initiate conversations?

_____   Are females "trapped in passive and whiny roles" (Singh, 1998)?

_____   Are females competitive with a desire to meet high expectations?

_____   Do the illustrations depict gender stereotypes?

_____   Does the book include any reversals of traditional gender roles (Rose, 2000)?

_____   Are various family structures shown?

_____   How do males and females gain status (sports, competitions, nurturing, or goodness)?

_____   How does the author want readers to view members of the genders?

_____   What effect does the author's gender have on the book?

_____   Is the book truthful and does it respect its readers (Aronson, 2001)?

_____   Does the book help readers overcome their personal discomfort with sexual roles (Pavo, 2003)?

Sources: Additional sources used to develop this list include: Mitchell, D. (1996). Approaching race and gender issues in the context of the language arts classroom. *English Journal, 85*(8), 77–81; Roberts, P., Cecil, N. L., and Alexander, S. (1993). *Gender positive! A teachers' and librarians' guide to nonstereotyped children's literature, K–8.* Jefferson, NC: McFarland; Rudman, M. (1995). *Children's literature: An issues approach.* White Plains, NY: Longman.

EXPANDING YOUR KNOWLEDGE WITH THE INTERNET

A number of resources that focus on gender representation and literature are available on the Internet.

Amelia Bloomer List of Recommended Feminist Books for Youth
http://libr.org/FTF/bloomer.html

Sallie Bingham Center for Women's History and Culture
http://library.duke.edu/specialcollections/bingham/

Ideas for Integrating Women of NASA into Your Curriculum
quest.arc.nasa.gov/women/teachingtips.html

Vandergrift's Feminist Page
www.scils.rutgers.edu/~kvander/Feminist/index.html

Chicago Public Library: Books for Guys
www.chipublib.org/007bibliographies/booksforguys.html

Public Library of Cincinnati—Books for Guys
teenspace.cincinnatilibrary.org/books/booklist.asp?id=teenguys

Guys Read
www.guysread.com

Male Coming-of-Age Stories
www.scils.rutgers.edu/ ~kvander/YoungAdult/male.html

GLBTQ—Young Adult Literature
www.glbtq.com/literature/young_adult_lit.html

National Coalition for Gay, Lesbian, Bisexual and Transgender Youth
www.outproud.org/

Concluding Thoughts

In spite of the number of awards, best books lists, and book-length bibliographies, evaluating and selecting young adult books will never be an easy task for teachers and library media specialists. With more books published, the realities of school budgets, and an increasing demand to select books and other forms of literature that can be integrated or at least used across the middle and secondary curricula, educators feel the pressure to select the best and most appropriate young adult literature that will, hopefully, also appeal to young adult readers. Added to the selection dilemma will be the increased diversity within school-age populations that will call for more multicultural literature in the school. Then, too, educators will likely see more accurate and realistic reflections of gender in young adult literature, with increasing numbers of powerful female protagonists, books written by exceptional female writers, and female critics, along with a more balanced view of all gender perspectives.

In response, educators will need to make the commitment to read and thoughtfully consider young adult literature and to seek out reviews in journals and resources that review it. If they are successful, the lives of all young adults and their respective needs and perspectives will be represented accurately and fairly in the literature in their schools.

Young Adult Books

This section includes young adult titles mentioned in this chapter.

Alvarez, J. (2002). *Before we were free*. New York: Knopf.

Anders, C. (2005). *Choir boy*. Brooklyn: Soft Skull Press.

Beah, I. (2007). *A long way gone: Memoirs of a boy soldier*. Waterville, ME: Thorndike Press.

Clarke, J. (2006). *One whole and perfect day*. Asheville, NC: Front Street.

Cormier, R. (1978). *I am the cheese*. New York: Dell.

Donovan, J. (1969). *I'll get there: It better be worth the trip*. New York: Harper & Row.

Engle, M. (2006). *The poet slave of Cuba: A biography of Jean Francisco Manzano*. New York: Holt.

Freedman, R. (2006). *Freedom walkers: The story of the Montgomery bus boycott*. New York: Holiday House.

Garden, N. (1982). *Annie on my mind*. New York: Farrar, Straus and Giroux.

Hemphill, S. (2007). *Your own, Sylvia: A verse portrait of Sylvia Plath*. New York: Knopf.

Hobbs, W. (2006). *Crossing the wire*. New York: HarperCollins.

Iggulden, C. (2007). *Genghis: Birth of an empire*. New York: Delacorte.

Jenkins, A. M. (2007). *Repossessed*. New York: HarperTeen.

Knox, E. (2007). *Dreamquake: Book 2 of the dreamhunter duet*. New York: Farrar, Straus and Giroux.

Lester, J. (2005). *Day of tears: A novel in dialogue*. New York: Hyperion Books.

Lowry, L. (1993). *The giver*. Boston: Houghton Mifflin.

Maltman, T. (2007). *The night birds*. New York: Soho Press.

McCaughrean, G. (2007). *The white darkness*. New York: HarperTempest.

Mourlevat, J. C. (2006). *The pull of the ocean*. New York: Delacorte.

Myers, W. D. (2003). *The beast*. New York: Scholastic.

Oppenheim, J. (2006). *Dear Miss Breed: True stories of the Japanese American incarceration during World War II and a librarian who made a difference*. New York: Scholastic.

Orlev, U. (2003). *Run, boy, run*. Boston: Houghton Mifflin.

Peters, J. A. (2004). *Luna: A novel*. New York: Little Brown.

Rowling, J. K. (1998). *Harry Potter and the sorcerer's stone*. New York: Scholastic.

Sachar, L. (1998). *Holes*. New York: Farrar, Straus and Giroux.

Shea, P. D. (2003). *Tangled threads: A Hmong girl's story*. New York: Clarion Books.

Taylor, M. (1976). *Roll of thunder, hear my cry*. New York: Dial.

Taylor, M. (2001). *The land*. New York: Fogelman.

Weyr, G. (2002). *My heartbeat*. New York: Speak.

Wittlinger, E. (2007). *Parrotfish*. New York: Simon & Schuster.

Wolff, V. E. (2001). *True believer*. New York: Atheneum.

Zusak, M. (2006). *The book thief*. New York: Knopf.

Suggested Readings

Agosto, D. E. (2007). Building a multicultural school library: Issues and challenges. *Teacher Librarian, 34*(3), 27–31.

Boston, G. H., and Baxley, T. (2007). Living the literature: Race, gender construction, and black female adolescents. *Urban Education, 42*(6), 560–581.

Bruce, H. E., Brown, S., McCracken, N. M., and Bell-Nolan, M. (2008). Feminist pedagogy is for everybody: Troubling gender in reading and writing. *English Journal, 97*(3), 82–89.

Harper, H. (2007). Studying masculinity(ies) in books about girls. *Canadian Journal of Education, 30*(2), 508–530.

Landt, S. M. (2007). Weaving multicultural literature into middle school curricula. *Middle School Journal, 39*(2), 19–24.

Walach, S. (2008). *So far from the Bamboo Grove:* Multiculturalism, historical context, and close reading. *English Journal, 97*(3), 17–20.

Whittingham, J., and Rickman, W. (2007). Controversial books in the middle school: Can they make a difference? *Middle School Journal, 38*(5), 41–45.

References

All young adult literature referenced in this chapter is included in the Young Adult Books list and is not repeated in this list.

2000 notable books for a global society: A K–12 list. (2001). *The Reading Teacher, 54*(5), 464–470.

Aronson, M. (2001). *Exploding the myths: The truth about teenagers and reading.* Lanham, MD: Scarecrow.

Athanases, S. Z. (1998). Diverse learners, diverse texts: Exploring identity and difference through literary encounters. *Journal of Literacy Research, 30,* 273–296.

Authors and Artists for Young Adults. (1989–). Detroit: Gale Research.

Bantick, C. (1996). Literacy survey. *Youth Studies, 15*(4), 5–6.

Barber, R. W., and Bartell, P. (2007). *Senior high core collection: A selection guide.* New York: H. W. Wilson.

Barr, C. (2005). *Popular series fiction for middle school and teen readers: A reading and selection guide.* Westport, CT: Libraries Unlimited.

Beetz, K. H., and Niemeyer, S. (1989–). *Beacham's guide to literature for young adults.* Washington, DC: Beacham.

Benedetti, A. (2003). Falling off my pedestal: A slippery defense of popular taste. *Alki: The Washington Library Association Journal, 19*(3), 28–29.

Best Books for Young Adults honors 84 books. (2004). Accessed January 28, 2004, from: www.ala.org/ala/pr2004/prjan2004/2004bestbooksforya.htm.

Booth, H. (2007). *Serving teens through readers' advisory.* Chicago: American Library Association.

Boyd, F. B. (2002). Conditions, concessions and the many tender mercies of learning through multicultural literature. *Reading Research and Instruction, 42*(1), 58–92.

Brown, L. M., and Gilligan, C. (1992). *Meeting at the crossroads: Women's psychology and girls' development.* Cambridge, MA: Harvard University Press.

Brozo, W. (2002). *To be a boy, to be a reader: Engaging teen and preteen boys in active literacy.* Newark, DE: International Reading Association.

Burroughs, R. (1999). From the margins to the center: Integrating multicultural literature into the secondary English curriculum. *Journal of Curriculum and Supervision, 14*(2), 136–155.

Carger, C. L. (2003). A pool of reflections: The Américas Award. *Book Links, 12*(3), 34–39.

Cart, M., & Jenkins, D. (2006). *The heart has its reasons: Young adult literature with gay/lesbian/queer content, 1969–2004.* Lanham, MD: Scarecrow Press.

Chew, K. (1997). What does e pluribus unum mean? Reading the classics and multicultural literature together. *The Classical Journal, 93*(1), 55–78.

Clark, C. S. (1994). Education and gender: The issues. *Congressional Quarterly Researcher, 4*(21), 483–487, 490–491.

Cooperative Children's Book Center. (n.d.). *Children's books by and about people of color published in the United States.* Accessed May 9, 2008, from: www.education.wisc.edu/ccbc/books/pcstats.htm.

Darby, M. A., and Pryne, M. (2002). *Hearing all the voices: Multicultural books for adolescents.* Lanham, MD: Scarecrow Press.

Day, F. A. (2003). *Latina and Latino voices in literature: Lives and works.* Westport, CT: Greenwood.

De León, L. (2002). Multicultural literature: Reading to develop self-worth. *Multicultural Education, 10*(2), 49–51.

Dresang, E. T. (1999). *Radical change: Books for youth in a digital age.* New York: H. W. Wilson.

Fouts, E. (1999). Gender and generation in contemporary Spanish children's literature. *Journal of Youth Services in Libraries, 12*(2), 31–36.

Fox, M. (1993). *Radical reflections: Passionate opinions on teaching, learning, and living.* San Diego: Harcourt Brace.

Gentle, M. (2001). The Printz Award for young adult literature. *Book Report, 20*(1), 27.

Gillespie, C. S., Powell, J. L., Clements, N. E., and Swearingen, R. A. (1994). A look at the Newbery Medal books from a multicultural perspective. *The Reading Teacher, 48*(1), 40–50.

Gillespie, J. T. (2005). *The children's and young adult literature handbook: A research and reference guide.* Westport, CT: Libraries Unlimited.

Gillespie, J. T. , and Barr, C. (2006). *Best books for high school readers: Grades 9-12: Supplement to the first edition.* Westport, CT: Libraries Unlimited.

Gonzalez, M. L., Huerta-Macias, A., and Tinajero, J. V. (Eds.). (1998). *Educating Latino students: A guide to successful practice.* Lancaster, PA: Technomic.

Gray, B. A. (1991). Her, her, her: An interview with M. E. Kerr. *Voices of Youth Advocates, 13*(6), 337–342.

Gurian, M. (2001). *Boys and girls learn differently: A guide for teachers and parents.* San Francisco: Jossey-Bass.

Hale, L. A., and Crowe, C. (2001). "I hate reading if I don't have to": Results from a longitudinal study of high school students' reading interests. *The ALAN Review, 28*(3), 49–57.

Harris, V. (Ed.). (1997). *Using multiethnic literature in the K–8 classroom.* Norwood, MA: Christopher-Gordon.

Haupt, A. (2003). Where the boys are . . . *Teacher Librarian, 30*(2), 18–24.

Helbig, A. K., and Perkins, A. R. (2001). *Many peoples, one land: A guide to new multicultural literature for children and young adults.* Westport, NH: Greenwood.

Hill, T. (1998). Multicultural children's books: An American fairy tale. *Publishing Research Quarterly, 14*(1), 36–45.

Hinton, K., and Dickinson, G. K. (2007). *Integrating multicultural literature in libraries and classrooms in secondary schools.* Columbus, OH: Linworth.

Houdyshell, M. L., and Kirkland, J. (1998). Heroines in Newbery Medal award winners: Seventy-five years of change. *Journal of Youth Services in Libraries, 11*(3), 252–262.

Jones, P., and Fiorelli, D. C. (2003). Overcoming the obstacle course: Teenage boys and reading. *Teacher Librarian, 30*(3), 9–13.

Jones, P., Taylor, P., and Edwards, K. (2003). *A core collection for young adults.* New York: Neal-Schuman.

Jones, P., Hartman, M. L., and Taylor, P. (2006). *Connecting with reluctant teen readers: Tips, titles and tools.* New York: Neal-Schuman.

Jordan, A. D. (1996a). Books of other cultures. *Teaching and Learning Literature, 5*(4), 23–25.

Jordan, A. D. (1996b). Welcome to my world: Books of other cultures. *Teaching and Learning Literature, 5*(4), 15–22.

Kaywell, J. F. (1993–). *Adolescent literature as a complement to the classics.* Norwood, MA: Christopher-Gordon.

Keane, N. J. (2006). *The big book of teen reading lists: 100 great, ready-to-use book lists for educators, librarians, parents, and teens.* Westport, CT: Libraries Unlimited.

Klein, D. (1992). Coming of age in novels by Rudolfo Anaya and Sandra Cisneros. *English Journal, 81*(5), 21–26.

Koelling, H., and Carter, B. (2007). *Best books for young adults.* Chicago: American Library Association.

Levine, E. Z., and Orenstein, F. M. (1994). *Sugar and spice and puppy dog tails: Gender equity among middle school children.* (ERIC Document Reproduction Service No. ED 389 457)

Lesesne, T. (2003). *Making the match.* Portland, ME: Stenhouse.

Lo, D. E. (2001). Borrowed voices: Using literature to teach global perspectives to middle school students. *The Clearing House, 75*(2), 84–87.

Lukens, R. (2007). *Critical handbook of children's literature.* 8th ed. Boston: Pearson.

McDaniel, D. (2008). *Gentle reads: Great books to warm hearts and lift spirits, grades 5–9.* Westport, CT: Libraries Unlimited.

McGlinn, J. (2002). Seeing themselves in what they read. *Book Links, 11*(3), 50–54.

Merriam-Webster's encyclopedia of literature. (1995). Springfield, MA: Merriam-Webster.

Merriam-Webster's online dictionary. Accessed May 10, 2008 from: www.merriam-webster.com.

Millard, E. (1997). *Differently literate.* London: Falmer.

Miller-Lachman, L. (1992). *Our family, our friends, our world: An annotated guide to significant multicultural books for children and teenagers.* New Providence, NJ: Bowker.

Mitchell, D. (1996). Approaching race and gender issues in the context of the language arts classroom. *English Journal, 85*(8), 77–81.

Morales, C. A. (2001). "Our own voice": The necessity of Chicano literature in mainstream curriculum. *Multicultural Education, 9*(2), 16–20.

Murphy, B. T., and Murphy, D. (2007). *Black authors and illustrators of books for children and young adults.* New York: Routledge.

Orenstein, P. (1994). *Schoolgirls: Young women, self-esteem, and confidence.* New York: Doubleday and American Association of University Women.

Pavo, K. (2003). Out of the closet. *Publisher's Weekly, 250*(24), 23–25.

Pearl, N. (2007). *Book crush: For kids and teens: Recommended reading for every mood, moment, and interest.* Seattle: Sasquatch Books.

Pipher, M. (1994). *Reviving Ophelia: Saving the lives of adolescent girls.* New York: Grosset/Putnam.

Price, A. (2005). *Middle and junior high school library catalog.* 9th ed. New York: H. W. Wilson.

Reed, A. J. S. (1994). *Reaching adolescents: The young adult book and the school.* Columbus, OH: Merrill.

Reese, D. (1999). Authenticity and sensitivity. *School Library Journal, 45*(11), 36–37.

Reese, D. (2007). Proceed with caution: Using Native American folktales in the classroom. *Language Arts, 84*(3), 245–256.

Reyes, N. (n.d.). Theme—Element of fiction. Accessed May 2, 2008, from: http://litera1no4.tripod.com/theme_frame.html.

Roberts, P., Cecil, N. L., and Alexander, S. (1993). *Gender positive: A teachers' and librarians' guide to nonstereotyped children's literature, K–8.* Jefferson, NC: McFarland.

Rochman, H. (1993). *Against borders: Promoting books for a multicultural world.* Chicago: American Library Association.

Rockefeller, E. (2007). The genre of gender: The emerging canon of transgender-inclusive YA literature. *The Horn Book, 83*(5), 519–526.

Rose, R. (2000). Collection development and the search for positive female characters in children's literature. *Current Studies in Librarianship, 24*(1–2), 107–115.

Rudman, M. (1995). *Children's literature: An issues approach.* White Plains, NY: Longman.

Russell, D. L. (2009). *Literature for children: A short introduction.* 6th ed. New York: Pearson.

Sadker, M., and Sadker, D. (1994). *Failing at fairness: How America's schools cheat girls.* New York: Scribner.

Schon, I. (2003). *The best of Latino heritage 1996–2002: A guide to the best juvenile books about Latino people and cultures.* Lanham, MD: Scarecrow.

Schon, I. (2004). Latinos, Hispanics, and Latin Americans. *Book Links, 13*(3), 44–48.

Schon, I. (2004). *Recommended books in Spanish for children and young adults, 2000 though 2004.* Lanham, MD: Scarecrow.

Silvey, A. (2006). *500 great books for teens.* Boston: Houghton Mifflin.

Singh, M. (1998). *Gender issues in children's literature: ERIC digest.* (ERIC Document Reproduction Service No. ED 424 591)

Smith, H. M. (2004). *The Coretta Scott King Awards, 1970-2004.* Chicago: American Library Association.

Smith, M., and Knowles, L. (2007). *Understanding diversity through novels and picture books.* Westport, CT: Libraries Unlimited.

Smith, M. W., and Wilhelm, J. D. (2002). *"Reading don't fix no Chevys": Literacy in the lives of young men.* Portsmouth, NH: Boynton/Cook.

Telford, L. (1999). A study of boys' reading. *Early Childhood Development and Care, 149*, 87–124.

Ten quick ways to analyze children's books for racism and sexism. (1974, November 3). *Interracial Books for Children, 5*(3), 6–7.

Textbook sexism. (1994). *Congressional Quarterly Researcher, 4*(21), 496.

Thorne, B. (1993). *Gender play: Girls and boys in school.* New Brunswick, NJ: Rutgers.

Treviño, R. Z. (2006) *The Pura Belpré Awards: Celebrating Latino authors and illustrators.* Chicago: American Library Association.

Trupe, A. (2006). *Thematic guide to young adult literature.* Westport, CT: Greenwood.

U.S. Bureau of the Census. (2003). *Statistical abstracts of the United States: 2003.* Washington, DC: Government Printing Office.

U.S. Bureau of the Census. (2008). *Statistical abstracts of the United States: 2008.* Washington, DC: Government Printing Office. Accessed May 9, 2008, from: www.census.gov/compendia/statab/cats/population.html.

Vandergrift, J. E. (1993). A feminist research agenda in youth literature. *Wilson Library Bulletin, 68*(2), 22–27.

Von Drasek, L. (2002, October). Boy, oh, boy—books! *Teaching K–8, 33*(2), 72–75.

Walker, C., and Foote, M. M. (1999/2000). Emergent inquiry: Using children's literature to ask hard questions about gender bias. *Childhood Education, 76*(2), 88–91.

Wartski, M. C. (2005). The importance of multicultural themes in writing and teaching. *English Journal, 94*(3), 49–51.

Wilhelm, J. (2001). It's a guy thing. *Voices from the Middle, 9*(2), 60–63.

Yaakov, J. (2002). *Senior high school library catalog.* 16th ed. New York: H. W. Wilson.

Yakota, J., and Frost, S. (2003). Multiracial characters in children's literature. *Book Links, 12*(3), 51–57.

YALSA announces 2002 Alex Awards. (2002). *Journal of Youth Services in Libraries, 15*(3), 58.

York, S. (2008). *Booktalking multicultural literature: Fiction, history, and memoirs for teens.* Columbus, OH: Linworth.

Teaching, Using, and Appreciating Young Adult Literature

In a school library, two high school students look at the shelves and mutter while they consult a list, look at a book on the shelf, and then return to the list. If we listen very closely we may hear one of them say: "Aren't there any short books on this list? If I have to read a book, why can't I read what I like instead of these lame books?"

Educators encourage and even require adolescents to read books. However, rather than appealing to student interests, many English teachers have tried to identify books, often classics, that they believe are worthy of students' time and attention. History or science teachers often assign "informational book reports" or other activities requiring students to read and digest content material. Although these approaches undoubtedly prove effective for some students, many students read as little as they can to "get by." These lists and assignments have not motivated the students or encouraged a love of reading. Fortunately, newer trends such as using literature across the curriculum and literature-based instruction have grown in popularity, suggesting more productive ways to use young adult literature. Rather than working in isolation, many educators now make collaborative decisions on curricular themes and use young adult literature that crosses subject areas and helps students see new and different perspectives on issues and subject content. This chapter explains how young adult literature can be used in single subject areas, shows how appropriate books can cross curricular boundaries, and offers a strong recommendation for incorporating young adult literature across the curriculum.

Essential Considerations

Whether you are using a single poem with a lesson, reading a book with a unit, or including multiple texts in a thematic approach, there are several things you should remember when teaching young adult literature. Although other considerations (perhaps some of equal importance) undoubtedly exist, we selected these three because if you remember to include them in your teaching, you will be a more competent and enthusiastic teacher or school library media specialist.

View Literature as Entertaining as Well as Challenging

Think back to your own days as a young adult. Can you recall reading books and poems that you considered "dry as dust"—books on reading lists that someone labeled as "must" reading for all students at some point in their education? How did reading those materials make you feel? Now, ask yourself how a teacher can help adolescents develop love for reading and the desire to become lifelong readers if the assignments actually seem designed to convince teenagers that books are difficult, boring, or totally uninteresting?

This is not to say that teachers should not challenge students or use good literature. However, there must be a balance between quality and interest; the terms are not mutually exclusive. When this balance is neglected, adolescents may become alliterate—able to read but unwilling to do so. Many adolescents do have the desire to read well-written materials that encourage them to think about what they are reading. They will even read "long" books. (Just look at the length of some of the fantasy novels they avidly read.) When teachers select quality young adult literature that is interesting, appropriate, and challenging, students enjoy both the reading process and the literature itself.

Become Familiar with a Wide Range of Literature

There are several advantages to knowing a wide range of young adult literature. In addition to planning better teaching units, especially literature-based units (discussed later in the chapter), you will be able to suggest young adult books for students' special interests or bibliotherapeutic needs, and books that compare and contrast issues and perspectives in a variety of subjects. You will also be able to discuss the books that your students are reading, comparing your reactions to theirs, suggesting similar books, and learning new titles from your students. When you know a wide range of titles and authors of young adult literature, you should feel comfortable and competent in your teaching role and should be able to make more connections to the young adults in your classes.

Share Literature with Adolescents

We believe that all teachers need to be teachers of literature. No, that does not mean that science teachers need to worry about teaching the elements of fiction. What it does mean is that all teachers need to have the skills to share literature with their students. They need to be eager and able to read to their adolescent students and to share literature that will interest, intrigue, amuse, and excite them. The effective teacher must be able to give oral performances (i.e., poetry and drama need to be read aloud). While an English teacher may read a poem and then help students explicate it, a social studies teacher may read a poem written by a Holocaust survivor as an introduction to the study of World War II. Although these teachers have different motives for reading poetry, and one teacher may focus on the form of a poem more than the other, both need to be proficient with reading literature and must be comfortable reading aloud to students (Trelease, 2006). In addition, English teachers need to be able to teach students how to use the techniques of dramatic and oral interpretation in their own reading and presentations.

Generally, teachers who have the skills and confidence for dramatic and oral interpretation are more interesting and enthusiastic. By modeling enthusiasm and appreciation of literature, you can be a powerful role model for students. What if you do not feel comfortable reading aloud? In addition to taking a course (perhaps a speech, drama, or storytelling course or workshop) in which you can learn oral reading techniques, you can seek help from a more proficient teacher or the library media specialist. Once you know skills and techniques, you can practice alone, perhaps in front of a mirror. To hone your skills even more, you can participate in a community storytelling league and take storytelling and creative dramatics classes offered by a local public library. Connecting Adolescents and Their Literature 3–1 provides some ideas for using recordings and audiobooks to present literature orally to adolescents.

3-1 ●●●● CONNECTING ADOLESCENTS AND THEIR LITERATURE

As Marjorie M. Kaiser (1999) says, when we listen to a story we no longer have the tendency to rush through it, can appreciate the words more, and can "relish the choice image or phrase" (p. 18). Providing a way for educators to bring a skilled reader into every classroom, audiobooks allow all adolescents to listen to quality literature. Rather than being viewed as a substitute for books, audiobooks are a "natural complement to print books" (Austin & Harris, 1999) and an "authentic literary experience" (p. 242). Kaiser (1999) explains that for some readers/listeners, the narrator can help shape the understanding of characters, define the setting more clearly, and bring the story to life. According to Whitten (1998), high school teachers have reported that after listening to audiobooks, their students had an appreciation for and love of literature. Teachers can:

- Encourage school and public librarians to develop collections of quality audiobooks.
- Use all or part of a book on tape or CD with an entire class.
- Use earphones to allow individuals or small groups to listen to selections.
- Set aside a short portion of a class on a regular basis during which students listen to audiobooks.

Deborah Locke (2001) lists a number of Internet resources to help teachers integrate audiobooks into the classroom and provides a list of "starter titles" (p. 28) for an audiobook collection.

Developing a Young Adult Literature Program

In encouraging adolescents to read for enjoyment, interpret events in books, and develop an awareness of authors and titles, teachers and library media specialists are most effective when they work collaboratively to implement a literature plan or program. Such a plan can be very informal, with the goal of increasing reading in the school or encouraging every teacher to use at least one piece of young adult literature during each grading period. Or a program can be very formal, with specific assignments or programs, such as Sustained Silent Reading (SSR) or Accelerated Reader (AR). To develop a literature plan or program, teachers and library media specialists need to know the young adults in their school, and know a wealth of appropriate books. Only then can they make the right matches between readers and books, suggest the right books for literature-based thematic units, or recommend appropriate books for readers who are struggling with problems or special challenges.

Purposes

Remember that young adults read books and teachers assign books for a number of reasons. While one student might read *The Land* (Taylor, 2001) because she or he enjoys reading about American history, another student might read the book only because a social studies teacher assigned it. However, regardless of whether students read by personal choice or by teacher assignment, reading is usually done for three broad purposes: enjoyment; learning and interpretation; and/or development of literary awareness.

A major purpose of any literature program is to provide young adults with an opportunity to enjoy books and other forms of literature. While some adolescents will read only assigned materials, all students should be encouraged to read and have an opportunity to enjoy reading. One of the best ways to teach young adults to appreciate novels and other literature is to provide an interesting, diverse, and well-written selection of literature that includes all the genres discussed in this book. Rather than dictating tastes or telling readers what they will like, teachers and library media specialists should encourage students to browse through books and make their own selections. Teaching young adults to enjoy literature and the reading process should be a major priority in any literature program.

The literature program should also teach adolescents to interpret literature. Literature can have many meanings, some clear and others abstract. To understand these levels of meaning, adolescents need to learn that a passage with deeper meanings may have to be read several times, digested, and then thoughtfully considered. It takes time, thought, and skills to examine and interpret events, settings, themes, characters, the author's style, and, if applicable, the illustrations to determine the author's meanings. Adolescents need help to gain confidence in expressing their beliefs, their interpretative decisions, and their conclusions. Later in this chapter, we will provide some examples of strategies teachers can use.

Finally, the young adult literature program must help adolescents develop literary awareness. This means that teachers and LMS need to convey a sense of appreciation for novels and other genres of literature. To do this, educators must teach about authors and their books, and how or why they write as they do. An author's name should bring to mind other books by the same author or by other authors who write in the same style or on the same topics. For example, educators should use and teach adolescents how to make concept maps or book webs showing relationships among books. As with appreciation for literature, awareness skills will likely increase over time and will differ among individuals.

Teachers' and Library Media Specialists' Roles and Environments

Teachers and library media specialists must set the tone for any literature program. If they are committed and enthusiastic, they will serve as models for other adults who are involved in the program and for the adolescents in the school. Educators might sometimes underestimate their powerful role and influence. If a teacher assigns a book with an attitude of drudgery that says "I had to suffer through it—you should have to suffer too," he or she will not motivate young adults to read the book or to become lifelong readers. However, by modeling respect, enthusiasm, and appreciation for novels and other genres of literature, an educator can have more far-reaching effects than by merely assigning books and being sure they have been read.

The teachers and library media specialists must be committed to the literature program and to an educational environment that reflects literature and a respect for reading. This commitment can take many forms such as providing a sufficient quantity and quality of books written for young adults, providing students with time to read in class, helping students locate appropriate books for reading enjoyment and special school projects, creating a welcoming atmosphere in the school library media center, or inviting the LMS and/or public librarian to give booktalks to students in classrooms and to teachers in faculty or departmental meetings. Connecting Adolescents and Their Literature 3–2 provides more information about the use of booktalks.

3-2 •••• CONNECTING ADOLESCENTS AND THEIR LITERATURE

Doing a booktalk is like dangling bait in front of a fish. The idea is to talk about a book in a way that tantalizes your listeners and entices them to read it. According to Terrence E. Young (2003), you need to be enthusiastic and passionate about the books you are recommending. The "talk" on each book is usually short and tells just enough to "hook" the reader without giving away too much of the story.

Teachers and librarians have many occasions to do booktalks:

- A formal presentation of several books on a related theme or topic to a whole class
- A brief talk to fellow teachers at a faculty meeting to recommend new titles
- A talk to individual students who are looking for something good to read

Young has some excellent suggestions, as well as a list of Web resources to help you booktalk. There are also several excellent books about booktalks:

- *Booktalking the Award Winners* (Bodard, 1994–1998)
- *Tantalizing Tidbits for Teens: Quick Booktalks for the Busy High School Media Library Specialist* (Cox, 2002)

- *Tantalizing Tidbits for Teens 2: More Quick Booktalks for the Busy High School Library Media Specialist* (Clark, 2007)
- *Tantalizing Tidbits for Middle Schoolers: Quick Booktalks for the Busy Middle School and Junior High Library Media Specialist* (Clark, 2005)
- *Booktalks Plus: Motivating Teens to Read* (Schall, 2001)
- *Booktalks and More: Motivating Teens to Read* (Schall, 2003)
- *Teenplots: A Booktalk Guide to Use with Readers Ages 12–18* (Gillespie and Naden, 2003)
- *The Booktalker's Bible: How to Talk about the Books You Love to Any Audience* (Langemack, 2003)
- *Still Talking That Book! Booktalks to Promote Reading Grades, 3–12* (Thomas and Littlejohn, 2003)
- *Teen Genre Connections: From Booktalking to Booklearning* (Schall, 2005)
- *Booktalks and Beyond: Promoting Great Genre Reads to Teens* (Schall, 2007)

From our experiences as a school library media specialist, public librarian, and classroom teacher, we have seen the importance of making a variety of good books available for young adults. In one school that provided a library media center (LMC) full of high-quality interesting books and classrooms with additional shelves of age- and interest-appropriate books; specific times in all classes to read; teachers and library media specialists who read and talk about books; activities such as student book clubs; and opportunities before, during, and after the school day to visit the LMC and to check-out books from both the library's and the classroom collections, adolescents saw the value of reading and responded positively. Judging from the circulation statistics in the LMC, the "wear and tear" on the books, and the discussion of young adult literature in classes throughout the curriculum, it was evident that the students in this school were reading. To us, messy shelves and a few tattered books are well worth it if students are reading and enjoying books. Connecting Adolescents and Their Literature 3–3 has some suggestions you can use to develop classroom collections to encourage reading.

3-3 ●●●. CONNECTING ADOLESCENTS AND THEIR LITERATURE

You can find quality books to develop classroom collections in schools in a number of ways. However, no matter which method you use, you should remember that you must select the materials carefully, applying the selection criteria we have provided. The idea is not just to "fill the shelves" but to provide young adults with a chance to read quality literature.

- Ask for donations from parents and former students. Check with the LMS to see if your school has a policy for donated materials and be sure everyone understands that materials you cannot use in your classroom will be donated to another agency, such as the public library—for their annual book sale. Do not forget to check out those library book sales for books to add to your classroom collection.

(Continued)

- Haunt the thrift shops and secondhand stores. Often they have quality paperbacks at rock bottom prices.
- Visit the used book stores in your area. If you let the owners know what you are trying to do, they may be on the lookout for inexpensive books for you.
- Go to yard/garage sales. We have found wonderful books being sold for 10 cents each just because the teens in the home had left for college.

Library Media Centers

Today's library media center provides services and materials that support the curriculum of the school and the reading interests of the school's students and teachers. With a collection containing a wealth of resources, including books, videotapes, DVDs, CD-ROMs, databases, and computers with Internet access, the LMC should be an inviting place where teachers, students, and parents can find carefully selected materials. In the library, students can access information from both print and nonprint resources, locate information on the Internet, evaluate that information before using it, work on projects, engage in other media- and book-oriented activities, and locate books for recreational reading.

The licensed professional school library media specialists on the staff must know the materials in the collection and their potential use, foster literature appreciation, and teach information literacy skills to both students and teachers. With the LMC open all day to serve both students and teachers, the LMS should encourage free access to materials at all times and support intellectual freedom. In addition, the LMS should work as an instructional partner with teachers throughout the curriculum, developing literature programs that meet both the instructional and recreational reading needs of young adults. To ensure that this happens, the LMS must:

- Engage in cooperative planning with teachers throughout the curriculum and help develop instruction (rather than only selecting books for specific assignments)
- Utilize technology to provide improved access to the collection
- Evaluate the impacts, outcomes, improved grades and test scores, and positive youth development that come from their efforts (Jones, 2002)

Public Libraries and Young Adult Services

Public libraries are no longer only repositories of books and now include many of the same types of resources found in school libraries, although the public library's charge is to meet the needs of all citizens rather than to support the curriculum of a particular school. At the same time that an increased population of teenagers is placing more demands on library services, public librarians are facing the tremendous task of integrating technology and information literacy into their programs while they maintain and expand other types of resources and programs (Jones, 2002). Adolescent patrons challenge public libraries in several ways: they want teen-friendly library spaces, materials and services that are more relevant, increased computer access and instruction, improved customer service, and a review of policies and hours (Meyers, 2001).

Generating an influx of young people can be an exciting challenge for public librarians, who are constantly trying to attract this most discerning and easily distracted age group. Although public libraries want adolescents to feel welcome in the library, be part of the community, obtain leadership skills, be culturally aware, and be advocates for the library, the trickiest challenge for most public librarians is to get adolescents to use public libraries and to see what they have to offer (Ishizuka, 2003). Part of the problem lies in the differences between the library culture and adolescent culture. While adolescence is a time of energy and conversation, many public libraries have a culture of solitude.

To help adolescents learn that libraries have unique resources to balance solitude with social experience, a modern library staff must provide an array of young adult programs and services. Machado, Lentz, Wallace, and Honig-Bear (2000) identified some best practices in public libraries that accommodate the needs of adolescents. These include (1) formal tutoring-style homework centers, (2) drop-in style homework centers, (3) career development/mentoring programs, and (4) cultural/recreation programs. Public libraries must also plan ways to cross the digital bridge that separates adolescents who have access to information and those who do not, use a wide variety of print and electronic information formats, and work with the school LMS and teachers (Jones, 2002). Collaborating with Other Professionals 3–1 provides some suggestions for educators and public librarians.

Some public libraries are making the effort to form partnerships with youth agencies such as Boys and Girls Clubs, Boy and Girl Scouts, park districts, art centers, and faith-based groups. Together they can provide adolescents with safe places, constructive opportunities, the guidance of respectful adults, and the companionship of peers during nonschool time. Public libraries are especially important because they encourage a disposition toward lifelong, self-directed learning, which is essential to

3-1   COLLABORATING WITH OTHER PROFESSIONALS

Educators can find a ready partner in most public libraries to help provide materials and services to young adults. The first step is for a teacher or school library media specialist to contact the public library (before a project or assignment is due), learn what the public library has to offer, and plan appropriate programs to utilize the resources of both the public library and the school. Diane P. Tuccillo (2003) lists a number of services of public libraries, including:

- Booktalking in the school library and classroom
- Coordination of resources with the school library for programs such as Accelerated Reader
- Teen library websites with links to resources for young adults
- Teen advisory boards for the public library with educators recommending members
- Newsletters about resources and programs
- Teen literary magazines
- Tours of the public library
- Recommendations on professional materials for educators
- Internet pages with links for educators
- Meetings with educators to explain programs and services
- Homework alert services: the school notifies the public library in advance of assignments that will require the use of library resources

EXPANDING YOUR KNOWLEDGE WITH THE INTERNET

A number of public libraries have websites just for young adults. Here are a few of them.

Berkeley Public Library Teen Services
www.berkeleypubliclibrary.org/content/

Public Library of Charlotte & Mecklenburg County Teen Pages
www.libraryloft.org/

Mansfield/Richland County Public Library Teen Zone
www.mrcpl.lib.oh.us/TeenZone/index.html

Hennepin County Library Web for Teens
www.mplib.org/wft/webforteens.asp

Skokie Public Library TeenScene
www.skokie.lib.il.us/s_teens/

Teen Advisory Group Site—ALA
www.ala.org/ala/yalsa/tags/tags.cfm

Internet Public Library Teen Space
www.ipl.org/div/teen/

New York Public Library Teen Link
teenlink.nypl.org/

Public Library of Cincinnati and Hamilton County TeenSpace
teenspace.cincinnatilibrary.org/books/

employment, health, and participation in civic life, home management, and recreation (Costello, Whalen, Spielberger, & Winje, 2001). Expanding Your Knowledge with the Internet highlights some programs that public libraries have developed to reach young adults.

Literature-Based Instruction Throughout the Curriculum

Traditionally, teachers have used young adult novels and other forms of literature only in English classes. However, the increase in quantity and quality of young adult literature (often called trade books, as distinguished from textbooks) now makes it possible for teachers to develop a literature plan to use these books across the curriculum. The result is that adolescents can now see that reading books is something that does not happen only in "literature class" and that books can play a major role in all content areas.

In many schools, especially middle schools, educators have begun to use literature-based integrated curricular plans in which students read trade books to develop reading skills, content knowledge, and an appreciation of literature. Connecting Adolescents and Their Literature 3–4 looks at one teacher's success story. Naturally, change is often slow, and some educators feel uncomfortable with literature-based approaches. While some teachers may work in teams or groups to adopt a total literature approach, others may elect more limited approaches. Figure 3–1 shows the progression of usage of young adult literature. We believe that all teachers, not just English and language arts educators, should muster the initial effort, commitment, open-mindedness, and time to incorporate young adult literature into their curriculum. Literature does not have to be used in every class or with every unit of study; a combination of both literature-based and traditional approaches may be most effective. Educators will move back and forth on the pyramid depending on the instructional content of the units they are teaching.

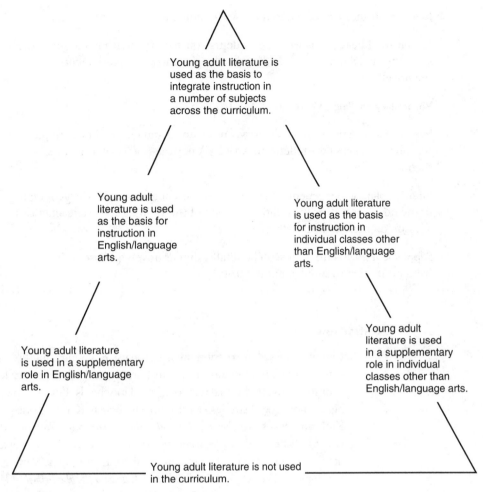

Young adult literature is
used as the basis to
integrate instruction in
a number of subjects
across the curriculum.

Young adult
literature is used
as the basis for
instruction in
English/language
arts.

Young adult literature
is used as the basis
for instruction in
individual classes other
than English/language
arts.

Young adult literature
is used in a supplementary
role in English/language
arts.

Young adult
literature is used
in a supplementary
role in individual
classes other than
English/language arts.

Young adult literature is not used
in the curriculum.

FIGURE 3-1   Integrating Literature into the Curriculum

3-4 ••• CONNECTING ADOLESCENTS AND THEIR LITERATURE

Rebecca J. Joseph (1998) writes of her success in starting each year with a "provoca-tive young adult novel" to help her students develop literature skills, make connec-tions between literature and life, and "initiate a great conversation" (p. 21). In an urban middle school, she has used Mary E. Lyons's *Letters from a Slave Girl: The Story of Harriet Jacobs* (1992) in a variety of ways:

Reading: Comprehension questions are developed that center on the skills tested on Maryland's functional reading test.

Writing: (1) City-wide prompts are used to prepare students for a high-stakes state test that are adapted to using materials from the novel. (2) Open-ended writing activities connect the novel to real life, with some small-group discussion of responses.

(Continued)

Journals: Topics are related to the novel or student reactions to the text.

Grammar: The teacher reads the students' journals and writing, identifies the skills they need to improve, and adapts the grammar text assignments to fit the novel.

Vocabulary/spelling: Words are taken from the novel.

Poetry: Connections are made between the novel and poetry. For example, Joseph introduces her students to African American poetry on the same theme as the novel.

Interdisciplinary connections: A social studies teacher focuses on the geography of the novel, as well as the political climate of the 1800s; a science teacher ties a lesson on muscles to the story.

Supplementary literature: Joseph booktalks similar novels and uses excerpts from nonfiction to supplement the story.

··

Definition

Literature-based instruction involves the use of young adult literature (e.g., trade books containing nonfiction, novels, poems, drama, and other literary forms) in place of or in addition to the traditional textbooks used in schools. For example, teachers of middle or high school social studies can use novels such as Karen Hesse's *Out of the Dust* (1997), Kathryn Lasky's *True North: A Novel of the Underground Railroad* (1996), or Carol Matas's *Greater Than Angels* (1998) to bring the Great Depression, slavery, and the Holocaust to life for readers. They can complement these fiction books with nonfiction such as Jerry Stanley's *Children of the Dust Bowl: The True Story of the School at Weedpatch Camp* (1992) (An Orbis Pictus Award–winner), Tom Feeling's narrative paintings in *The Middle Passage: White Ships, Black Cargo* (1995), and Anita Lobel's biography of her experiences in the Holocaust in *No Pretty Picture: A Child of War* (1998). By carefully matching curricular objectives and young adult trade books, teachers can make sure that students learn appropriate social studies and history concepts. The same books can then be used in the English/language arts classroom for study of literature. The ultimate goal should be to incorporate as much young adult literature as possible into the curriculum and to use young adult books to make curriculum connections across disciplines.

Rationale and Advantages

Students do not learn "subject content" only from textbooks. In fact, textbooks often break knowledge down into formal clusters of information that do not encourage reader interest, content acquisition, and meaningful retention (Smith & Johnson, 1993). In contrast, young adult trade books have the potential for making the curriculum content more understandable, comprehensible, and meaningful. For example, rather than reading in a science or health textbook about good nutrition, healthy eating, and food disorders, adolescents can read appropriate young adult literature, including both fiction and nonfiction, as shown in Figure 3–2. While the fiction books

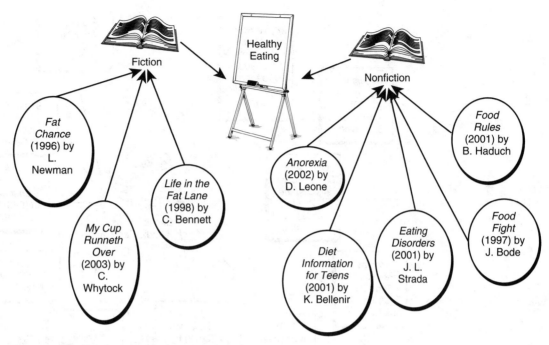

FIGURE 3-2   Books for Healthy Eating

can form the basis for class discussion, the nonfiction books can be used to provide additional health information for adolescents.

There are many benefits from using literature-based instruction. By reading and responding to young adult literature, students:

- Learn content material in all curricular areas and learn to identify meanings in what they read
- Discover knowledge and make meaning by examining age-appropriate problems, values, issues, and concerns
- Reinforce other language skills including talking, writing, and listening
- Respond, analyze, synthesize, and organize ideas in meaningful content
- Read and write often about their thoughts and ideas rather than simply concentrating on the mastery of facts and concepts in a given subject (Gerlach, 1992)

As you think about using young adult literature throughout the curriculum, you might wonder if there are enough quality books that support the curriculum. Fortunately, with the steadily increasing quantity and quality of young adult books, with the skills to select quality literature, the advice of a qualified library media specialist, and the resources of school library media centers and public libraries, all teachers who are committed to using appropriate young adult literature will be able to locate sufficient resources. It is important for teachers and library media specialists to work collaboratively and identify appropriate books for young adults to read in the various content areas. Although we cannot provide an exhaustive listing of books for each content area, we can show some representative examples. Then, you can use these examples to guide you as you develop more specific lists for your own subject content.

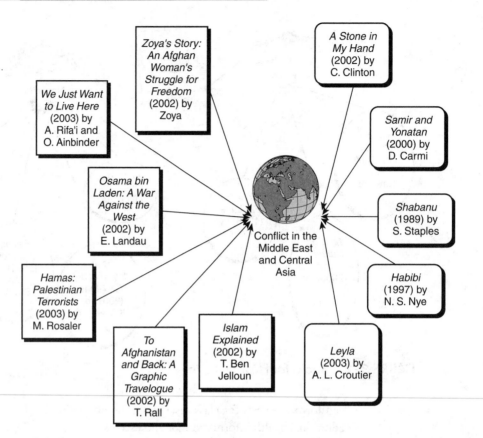

FIGURE 3-3 Literature on the Conflict in the Middle East and Central Asia

In most cases, educators can use a selection of both fiction and nonfiction books (as we did in the previous example) in all of the subject disciplines. While nonfiction will inform the reader of the facts of a particular event or issue, fiction will show how the topic, event, or issue affects people—the decisions, the happiness, the sadness, the triumphs, the failures, and the injustices. While educators must be sure that they help students understand the differences between fiction and nonfiction and keep from confusing the two, adolescents can gain considerable insights as they read fictional accounts. Figure 3–3 shows fiction and nonfiction that could be used with a curriculum unit on the conflict in the Middle East and central Asia, and Figure 3–4 shows literature that could be used with a science unit on ecology.

Feasibility

Can literature-based approaches be implemented in all curricular areas? From a realistic perspective, teachers in some curricular areas such as mathematics (particularly more advanced subjects such as algebra and trigonometry) will likely experience difficulty locating appropriate trade books. However, even with mathematics there are some young adult books that teachers can use. Pinchback (2000) reports using *A Gebra Named Al* (Isdell, 1993) with gifted middle school students. The

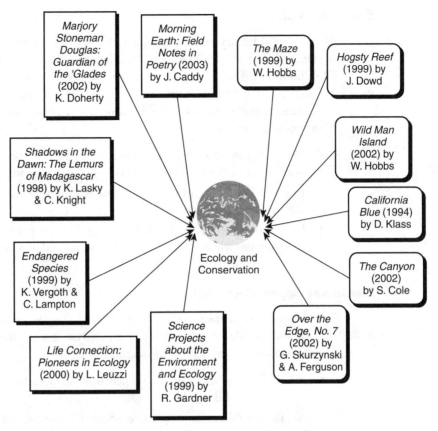

FIGURE 3-4   Literature on Ecology and Conservation

novel combines fiction with real math and science to tell the story of a frustrated algebra student. Other good choices for a mathematics class are David Blatner's *The Joy of [Pi]* (1997) and Hans Magnus Enzensberger's *The Number Devil* (1998). Whitin's and Wilde's *Read Any Good Math Lately?* (1992) and Kathryn Kaczmarksi's *Exploring Math with Books Kids Love* (1998) are excellent resources for teachers. We believe that all teachers can find at least one book per grading period or semester that relates to the topics being taught. Literature-based instruction can help readers perceive relationships between curricular areas, develop an appreciation for both young adult literature and the reading process, gain an awareness of literary characteristics, and extend their reading horizons to other areas.

While we wholeheartedly believe in the value of using literature across the curriculum and as a basis for instruction, we also believe that it is important to determine the feasibility of using literature with a particular topic before planning literature-based instruction. Some topics simply do not lend themselves to a literature-based approach. In addition, at times when educators might not feel they can use literature to teach particular learning objectives, there is no need to adopt a contrived approach. Teachers can teach without a literature-based approach or use literature (poetry, short stories, picture books) as an introduction and/or reinforcement rather than the core of the lesson.

Educators' Roles

Teachers and library media specialists have essential roles in implementing the literature-based curriculum. Together they need to develop collections of young adult literature that will support the curriculum and then identify portions of the collection that will support specific units within the curriculum. They also need to provide learning activities and educational environments that provide students with opportunities to:

- Make choices about the books they read; what projects in which to engage; whether to work individually or in cooperative learning groups
- Learn tasks relating to or building on existing schema or their previous learning and life experiences
- Learn cooperatively and collaboratively in an accepting and nonthreatening environment where they feel both physically and psychologically safe

Identifying Appropriate Books

Before deciding whether to use literature with a particular unit, educators need to identify and consider the availability of appropriate books. Teachers and LMS should work collaboratively to determine the following:

- Are novels, nonfiction, and/or other forms of literature available for use? In the LMC? Public library? As classroom sets?
- Are these books on appropriate reading and interest levels?
- Do the books meet the criteria for good literature in their genre?
- Do these books provide accurate and unbiased perspectives?
- If the topic relates to multicultural issues, are the books free of stereotypes?
- Do these books show more than one dimension or perspective (i.e., an appropriate book on war shows the various perspectives and participants of war)?
- Do these books logically lend themselves to the subject areas and the particular topics under discussion?
- Do these books show well-rounded characters in more than one-dimensional terms?
- Will these books motivate young adults to think critically about what they read and to relate the events to what they have learned previously and what they are presently learning?
- Do these books promote higher-order thinking?

When necessary, educators can use picture books and easy reading chapter books as well as young adult literature, nonprint resources, and expository texts from various sources, including newspapers, the Web, and magazines to build background knowledge on either the topic or the theme. It is important that educators select the best literature, rather than just choosing a book because it is available. In Chapter 2 and throughout the genre chapters in this book, we have noted resources that educators can use to identify appropriate young adult literature. These range from best books lists and award-winners to websites and print bibliographies.

Full-Length Young Adult Literature. Educators have always faced the dilemma of whether to use full-length books or selections from an anthology. Increasingly, educators are using full-length books for both large- and small-group instruction. Whether all students in the class read the same book or small groups of students with similar reading and overall ability levels read a particular book, this practice builds students' appreciation for literature; teaches story structures, genres, and themes; and increases reading abilities and broadens reading interests. This does not mean that educators should not use shorter pieces of literature such as short stories or poetry. Both are excellent choices for SSR as well as for introductions and reinforcement.

Young Adult Literature and the Classics. A number of teachers are reluctant to use young adult literature as a basis for instruction in middle and high schools and, for a number of reasons, prefer to focus on "the classics." While some of these teachers are successful, others succeed only in alienating adolescent readers and convincing them that reading is pure misery. Our favorite response to the question "Why shouldn't adolescents read the classics?" is to use the example of a fish and vegetables. You do not go fishing by putting a piece of broccoli on a hook and dangling it in a lake. Instead, you put a nice tasty worm or a professionally endorsed lure on your fishing rod. Quality, well-written young adult literature can be the tasty worm in your classroom that will encourage adolescents to read and maybe, eventually, to feel comfortable tackling the classics.

If you do want to include some classics in your literature instruction, we encourage you to team them with young adult literature. One way to do this is to look for books with similar themes or plots. For example, *Romiette and Julio* (Draper, 1999) has a similar plot to Shakespeare's *Romeo and Juliet*, while *Witness* (Hesse, 2001) addresses some of the issues found in *To Kill a Mockingbird. Soldier's Heart* (Paulsen, 1998) can likewise be paired with *The Red Badge of Courage.* Young adult novels can also be used to provide additional information about a period in history or about a particular setting or event in preparation for the reading of a classic. A number of resources are available to help teachers identify literature pairings, such as the series *Adolescent Literature as a Complement to the Classics,* edited by Joan F. Kaywell (1993–2000); *From Hinton to Hamlet: Building Bridges Between Young Adult Literature and the Classics* (2005), by Sarah K. Herz with Donald R. Gallo; and *Heirs to Shakespeare: Reinventing the Bard in Young Adult Literature* (2000), by Megan Lynn Isaac.

Reader Response and Young Adult Literature

Teachers who use literature as the focal point of instruction need to be familiar with the reader response theory, sometimes called a *transactional view of literature,* which holds that a reader draws meanings from and makes responses to literature based on her or his background experiences. Rosenblatt (1978, 1989) describes reading literature as a transaction between the reader and the text, whether a novel, poem, short story, or play. Whenever students read, they take a reading stance (i.e., readers read literature for enjoyment or appreciation, which Rosenblatt terms *aesthetic,* or for learning, which she calls *efferent*). While a reader's stance may remain constant during the reading of some works, it may vacillate during others. For example, a student may take an efferent stance while reading nonfiction but may switch to an aesthetic stance when viewing the illustrations (which appeal to a reader's past experiences or values) in the same book.

Drawing on past experiences, personality, and memories, readers relate to new experiences found in literature and make decisions about the theme, the characters, setting, plot, conflict, contrasts, and the author's style. On another transactional level, readers decide what the book means and make inferences about the meanings of the literature. Readers, as individuals, enter into their own transaction with the text, and each reader's transaction will be unique. In a group, each reader will respond differently, on the basis of her or his individual and personal sense of consciousness. Similarly, if a teacher or LMS reads literature aloud, the reader's tone, emphasis, and ability to read aloud may influence young people's meaning-making. While readers will make personal meanings and responses from their readings, the teacher or LMS should help readers interpret the various literary aspects and help readers identify clues that contribute to meaningful responses, provide time for experiencing personal meanings, and encourage readers to develop respect for both their and others' initial meanings.

Reading/Responding Activities to Encourage Learning. When young adults read and respond to literature, they should do more than memorize facts or summarize the plot. Instead, they should employ the full range of mental traits that comprise critical thinking (Gerlach, 1992).

According to Gerlach (1992):

> If the literature is to have meaning for readers, the readers must construct it and order it for themselves. They must respond, analyze, synthesize, organize, apply, and evaluate—all of which are tools of learning—in order to make meaning and demonstrate an understanding of literature as it applies to their own lives. Through reading and responding to young adult literature, readers come to search for and make knowledge of their worlds. (p. 120)

Thus, educators need not only to motivate students to read novels and other literature but also to teach students to respond to books, question characters' actions and motives, and ask why authors chose a particular style or point of view. Reading requires thought. When young adults simply read words without paying attention to detail, issues, and events, they are not gaining the skills necessary for learning or the dispositions to become lifelong readers. To help students develop these skills and attitudes, teachers and LMS need to talk individually with readers or establish cooperative learning groups in which adolescents can engage in reading and responding activities with their peers. In turn, these practices will help eager and enthusiastic adolescents read, enjoy, and share the books they read. Connecting Adolescents and Their Literature 3–5 explores one way to encourage reading. Later in this chapter, you will discover other strategies that allow adolescents to respond to literature.

Literary Theory and Young Adult Literature

Once students have learned to express their own responses to literature, they may be ready to use literary theories to examine young adult literature. Soter (1999) maintains

3-5 •••.   CONNECTING ADOLESCENTS AND THEIR LITERATURE

According to Dreher (2003), adolescents like oral reading—they like teachers to read aloud to them, and they like to read aloud to each other. One of the benefits of reading aloud is that it increases all students' engagement, confidence, and ability.

To take advantage of these preferences, teachers can do the following:

- Form three groups. In one group students can be read to, in another they can read aloud to each other, and in the third group they can read silently.
- 3–4 days a week, devote 25–40 minutes (of a 55-minute class) to reading. Use the remaining time to:
  - Clarify questions
  - Discuss the day's readings
  - Prepare for more formal discussions
  - Share journal reflections
- Allow the students to change groups as they move through the unit.

Dreher (2003) found that on some days students wanted to listen, on other days they wanted to read silently, and on other days they wanted to read aloud. Still, almost every student moved through all three groups.

There are several ways to expand this reading aloud activity. In addition to reading aloud in their own classroom, adolescents can read aloud to younger students in an elementary school or in a public library. They can also use their oral reading skills to read aloud in other classrooms in their school or in the school library.

that teachers often fail to encourage students to move beyond a personal response to literature to grapple with diverse interpretations and perspectives. When students apply literary theory to young adult literature, they consider the multiple ways a text might be read. Milner & Milner (2008) describe this process as peering at a literary work through a particular lens. This lens is designed to illuminate different perspectives of a text and, possibly, of the world.

Table 3–1 contains a list of several theories and their basic tenets. Some, such as feminist, black feminist, and Marxist theories, look closely at power, culture, and injustices, while others, such as new criticism approaches, look more closely at form and structure. You can use the list as a starting point for fostering multiple readings of young adult literature. Guides and dictionaries, such as *Critical Theory Today: A User-Friendly Guide* (1999), by Lois Tyson, and *The Bedford Glossary of Critical and Literary Terms* (2003), by Ross Murfin and Supryia M. Ray, provide more information on the basic ideologies of each school of criticism. Additional books about literary theory in the classroom include *Young Adult Literature and the New Literary Theories: Developing Critical Readers in Middle School* (1999), by Anna O. Soter, and *Critical Encounters in High School English: Teaching Literary Theory to Adolescents* (2000), by Deborah Appleman. Expanding Your Knowledge with the Internet provides links to some Web sites that offer guides to literary theory.

Because of the themes and issues presented, some books seem to lend themselves to a particular theoretical approach. For example, Sandra Cisneros's *House on Mango*

TABLE 3-1 Select Literary Theories

New Criticism: This type of formalist criticism requires a close reading of the text and relies solely on the text structure or form and words to determine meaning. New critics examine closely how literary elements (i.e., theme, plot, characters, irony) are interrelated and form a unified work.

Historical-Biographical Criticism: Critics following this theory look at the biographical and historical contexts of a work (including the social, cultural, and political aspects of the period).

Archetypal Criticism: With this theory, critics suggest that figures (e.g., snakes), character types (e.g., the unrequited lover), patterns (e.g., the quest), and images (e.g., gardens) that reappear in myths, folklore, and other types of literature across cultures point to the meaning of a text.

Feminism: Although it is difficult to summarize feminist criticism, at its basic level it examines women readers and writers and representations of gender in literature.

Black Feminism: This theory emphasizes the interlocking oppressions of race, class, gender, and sexuality in literature, and poses questions about subjectivity, agency, "blackness," and "whiteness."

Deconstruction: Though a close reading of the text is valued, texts do not have correct meanings. Language is imprecise, and the deconstruction theorist seeks to illustrate how the text unravels, how it is inconsistent and contradictory.

Marxist: Based on the philosophy of Karl Marx, this school of thought views the text as a product of work and focuses on class and power relationships.

New Historical: This theory focuses on a work's historical content, but differs from historical-biographical criticism in that it acknowledges that history is mediated, not objective. Dominant ideologies and omissions in texts are highlighted.

Street (1991) is ripe for a black feminist lens, which asks questions about the interlocking oppression of race, class, and gender (Hinton, 2004). However, it might not be appropriate to apply a new historical approach to the book. Theories also often overlap, allowing more than one interpretive approach to be applied to a text. Connecting Adolescents and Their Literature 3–6 provides several interpretive approaches for select young adult novels.

Literature-Based Reading Guide. There are many ways to incorporate literature into a unit and to encourage adolescents to respond to that literature. However, in a true literature-based unit, the literature will become the core. In that instance, a

EXPANDING YOUR KNOWLEDGE WITH THE INTERNET

A number of Web sites offer guides and dictionaries that summarize theories and offer additional resources such as references, key terms, and biographical information about leading theorists.

The Johns Hopkins Guide to Literary Theory and Criticism
litguide.press.jhu.edu/

Voice of the Shuttle—Links to literary theory sites
vos.ucsb.edu/browse.asp?id=2718

Bedford St. Martin's virtuaLit
bcs.bedfordstmartins.com/virtualit/poetry/critical_define/crit_marx.html

Internet Encyclopedia of Philosophy—Literary Theory
www.iep.utm.edu/l/literary.htm

3-6 ●●●● CONNECTING ADOLESCENTS AND THEIR LITERATURE

According to Moore (1997), you can use noted scholar Henry Louis Gates's theory prism to apply "multiple interpretations and multiple meanings" (p. 188) to young adult books. The following are a few examples of several theories that can be applied to a single young adult book:

- Katherine Paterson's *Jacob Have I Loved* (1980): archetypal, feminist, & new critical readings
- Virginia Hamilton's *M.C. Higgins, the Great* (1974): archetypal & new critical readings
- Gary Paulsen's *Dogsong* (1985): archetypal, feminist, & new critical readings
- Walter Dean Myers's *Fallen Angels* (1988): reader response & new critical readings

single book may be used for all students or there may be a core book that everyone reads and then four or five supplementary books that are read by small groups of students. When a single book takes the central role, teachers need to develop or identify activities that pertain to each of three reading stages: Pre-reading, during-reading, and after-reading. Table 3–2 identifies some sample strategies for each stage that teachers can modify to meet the needs, interests, and abilities of young adults in their classrooms. Then, Collaborating with Other Professionals 3–2 shows how two teachers used a single young adult book in English and music.

Thematic Literature Studies

While individual pieces of literature are often the focus of a unit, a thematic literature unit can add depth to the topic(s) being studied. Kettel and Douglas argue that the one-text-at-a-time tradition "reinforces a student's beliefs that each text is an island, that each text stands alone" (2003, p. 43). Instead, they call for multiple text–single theme teaching. By selecting books with a similar theme but various levels of difficulty, teachers can involve all students in discussions. In addition to helping young adults see connections among books, this approach helps students with diverse reading abilities. By examining

3-2 COLLABORATING WITH OTHER PROFESSIONALS

While teachers often complete a literature unit within a single classroom, many opportunities exist for collaboration. Rief and Ervin (1994) describe a unit in which the reading of Katherine Paterson's *Lyddie* (1991) served as the basis for a research project and the development of an original musical. After reading *Lyddie,* students

- Researched the Industrial Revolution
- Wrote their own story

- Turned it into a script
- Developed the poetry for the lyrics of the songs in their Language Arts class

Then, in their music class, they

- Refined the script and lyrics
- Set the lyrics to music

The final presentation occurred before parents, teachers, and other students.

TABLE 3-2   Literature-Based Reading Strategies

There are a variety of instructional strategies that educators can use to help adolescents explore literature. The following are a few basic suggestions.

PRE-READING STRATEGIES

Set the stage and provide a foundation for reading.

Identify and organize students' prior knowledge of the book or topics in it.

Establish any necessary background.

Determine where students stand on issues they will encounter.

Arouse curiosity in the book.

Motivate students to read.

SAMPLE STRATEGIES

1. *Anticipation questions:* Use questions that ask students to think critically about the issues that they will find in the book. Responses may be oral or written in a journal.

2. *New vocabulary:* Present a list of new words found in the book.

3. *Booktalk:* Booktalk the novel to spark interest. This is especially effective when several books are used in a thematic unit.

4. *Predictions/Forecasting:* Use the cover and/or the title as the basis for making predictions about possible characters, actions, and problems that may arise in the story.

5. *Agree/Disagree statement:* Provide three to five controversial or thought-provoking statements related to the topics in the books. Students either agree or disagree and explain their reasons.

6. *Shared pairs:* Use a short sentence, poem, or list of words from the book and have each student quickly list as many associations as she or he can. Then pair students to share their lists. Next, have each pair share with another pair. Finally, have the groups of four share with the entire class.

DURING-READING STRATEGIES

Facilitate comprehension.

Focus attention on characters, issues, themes, or details.

Engage students in their reading.

Relate information from the book to the students' knowledge base.

Foster literary exploration of the elements of fiction.

Encourage reflection and personal responses to the reading.

SAMPLE STRATEGIES

1. *Maps, webs, and sketches:* Provide a visual representation of the characters, the plot, the conflict, or the issues. In character maps, include the main and/or supporting characters and their characteristics. Plot maps can identify major events, conflicts, and resolutions; conflict maps can focus on the conflict, cause, participants, sources of support, and resolution; issue maps show how a particular theme or issue is explored in the book and the characters who support the theme or issue.

2. *Response journals and logs:* Write responses to teacher- or student-posed questions, make predictions, or provide reactions (written or visual) to the reading.

3. *Compare and contrast charts/activities:* Use charts to examine the similarities and differences between characters or between this book and another one.

TABLE 3-2   (Continued)

4. *Discussion:* Use both small- and large-group discussions or literature circles to provide an opportunity for students to discuss their reading. Assign roles to each member of a small group such as discussion leader (develops and asks questions), illustrator (depicts a scene from the reading), travel tracer (maps the flow of the action from place to place), literary luminary (identifies passages that illustrate the author's style of writing), vocabulary enhancer (identifies and defines new vocabulary), and connector (makes connections with real life or other books).

5. *Dramatics:* Role-play or act out interactions between characters.

6. *Poetry:* Expand the format of the poem "Book Lice" from Paul Fleischman's *Joyful Noise: Poems for Two Voices* to compare and contrast the characters in the book (Van Horn, 2000).

7. *Writing:* Create biopoems, the diary of a character, dialogue between or among characters, or an essay evaluating the use of the elements of fiction.

8. *Dialogue journals:* Use dialogue journals in which students express their thoughts about the book or respond to questions. Journals are passed between a student and the teacher or between pairs of students for responses. Dionisio (1994) finds this is an excellent way to engage adolescents in a discussion of the elements of literature.

9. *Forecasting:* Predict outcomes based on current reading.

10. *Problem solving:* Determine what a character's problem is. Then list alternative ways for the character to solve the problem.

11. *Artistic representation:* Illustrate a scene or draw a character.

AFTER-READING STRATEGIES

Continue and pull together the during-reading activities.

Provide closure to the unit.

Move beyond the book itself.

Critically analyze and evaluate the book.

Relate the book to personal experiences.

SAMPLE STRATEGIES

1. *Drama:* Provide an oral interpretation (Readers' Theater) of important scenes from the book or develop a script for a follow-up scene. Gauweiler (2003) suggests extending the Readers' Theater idea by having students make a video production of a book.

2. *Analysis of literary style:* Reread sections of a book to identify the elements of the author's style (similes, metaphor, repetition, etc.).

3. *Relationship web:* Use a graphic organizer to compare this book to others by the same author or on the same themes or issues. You can also use webs to compare the characters in the book to those in another book or to compare the elements of fiction in this book to another.

4. *Art:* Use art to create a collage or mobile with artifacts and quotes from the book, a new dust jacket/cover for the book, a diorama of a scene, a T-shirt with a message from the book, or a quilt with each square representing the book. Deringer (2003) has additional visual response ideas.

5. *Music:* Write a song based on the book.

6. *Newspaper:* Create a newspaper using the information from the book with ads, news, features, and cartoons.

7. *Research:* Research and report on a topic that comes from the story.

8. *Storyboards:* Reconstruct the story or write a sequel by creating major incident cards that represent the flow of the plot.

9. *Menu:* Develop a menu for a restaurant that one of the characters in the book might open. For help in developing the menu, read the article by Smith and Hickey (2003).

10. *Poetry:* Create "found poems" (Hobgood, 1998) by selecting a passage in the novel and turning it into a poem.

EXPANDING YOUR KNOWLEDGE WITH THE INTERNET

A number of websites have sample book units (or links to sites) and thematic units featuring young adult literature.

Scholastic Publishers—Home page with links to various resources
teacher.scholastic.com/ilp/index.asp

Teachers Resources at Bantam Doubleday Dell
www.randomhouse.com/teachers/

Literature Lesson Plans
www.eduref.org/cgi-bin/lessons.cgi/ Language_Arts/Literature

San Diego County, California—Literature CyberGuides
www.sdcoe.k12.ca.us/score/cyberguide.html

Yale–New Haven Teachers Institute—Literature Index
www.yale.edu/ynhti/curriculum/indexes/l.x.html

Doucette Index to K–12 Literature-Based teaching idea
www.educ.ucalgary.ca/litindex/

issues from a variety of perspectives, integrating information from diverse sources, and building on young adults' own interests with materials that are consistent with students' developmental levels, teachers can use literature to create units that are beneficial, meaningful, and relevant (Smith & Johnson, 1995).

Thematic units include some of the same activities already presented previously in Table 3–1; however, they require slightly different planning by the teacher and library media specialist. Table 3–3 outlines this process. To be successful, teachers may need to forsake some traditional, teacher-directed instruction to provide time for group activities that may develop as part of the overall unit. The classroom environment will undergo changes and will reflect the student-centered, participatory nature of thematic units (Smith & Johnson, 1995). Expanding Your Knowledge with the Internet provides links to a few literature units you can examine for more ideas.

Book Discussions

In both single-book and multiple-text thematic units, educators use book discussions as an instructional strategy to encourage young adults to consider what they read. Sometimes these occur as whole-class discussions, at other times teachers may use small literature circles or one-on-one literature conversations (Beers & Probst, 1998). Although discussion plans should reflect the abilities and interests of a specific group of young adults and will vary with the specific book(s) under discussion, some basic activities can be done with most literature. Table 3–4 on page 78 provides some suggestions for discussions. Collaborating with Other Professionals 3–3 profiles a student/parent/teacher book discussion group. Resources such as *Speaking Volumes: How to Get Students Discussing Books—And Much More* (Gilmore, 2006), *The Teen-Centered Book Club* (Kunzel & Hardesty, 2006), and *Discovering Their Voices: Engaging Adolescent Girls with Young Adult Literature* (Sprague & Keeling, 2007) help to promote book discussions.

TABLE 3-3 Developing a Thematic Literature Unit

IDENTIFY THE THEME

• Review the state or district curricular framework for possible topics.

• Informally survey students to determine their interests and prior knowledge.

SET GOALS AND SELECT LITERATURE

• Identify learning outcomes—Student knowledge and skills.

• Consult with the LMS to identify possible literature.

• Read possible selections and select the most appropriate.

• Use a variety of literature with different perspectives, such as biography, fiction, nonfiction, short story, and poetry.

DEVELOP THE INSTRUCTIONAL PLAN

• Plan the learning activities for the unit.

• Collaborate with the LMS and other teachers to identify specific content and interrelated concepts to be studied.

• Plan specific lessons that develop the skills as well as knowledge needed to meet the learning outcomes.

• Identify individual, small-group, and whole-group activities.

PLAN THE UNIT ASSESSMENTS

• Develop formative and summative evaluations for students, matching the assessments to the identified student outcomes.

• Prepare rubrics for those assessments.

• Develop an instructional assessment to evaluate the unit itself.

GATHER/PREPARE RESOURCES

• Collect and organize materials and resources.

• Schedule guest speakers, field trips, etc.

• Schedule any special spaces such as labs, LMC, or the auditorium.

• Inform administrators and parents of the scope and sequence of the unit.

IMPLEMENT THE PLAN

EVALUATE THE UNIT PLAN AND YOUR IMPLEMENTATION OF IT (based, in part, on Smith & Johnson, 1995)

Literature for the Reluctant Reader

Unfortunately, it is a rare educator who does not have to deal with reluctant readers. Even young adults who enjoy reading are sometimes reluctant to read a particular book and may go through a transitory stage where they do not want to read. To help reluctant readers, teachers and library media specialists need to identify the cause and utilize a number of strategies to address the problem. Too often, the stereotype of a reluctant reader is a boy who has below-grade-level reading ability and little literature and/or encouragement to read at home. This stereotype might prove dead wrong, because often good readers are reluctant to read.

COLLABORATING WITH OTHER PROFESSIONALS

Book discussions are not limited to the classroom. In fact, a number of schools and some public libraries have successfully used book discussions as a way to bring young adults and literature together. Breen and Rubin (2003) describe a program in which more than 100 middle school students, their parents, and their teachers meet four times in the evening during the school year to discuss books. The program begins with a kick-off full of booktalks, skits, videos, and contests, with refreshments to "melt the hearts of any doubting eighth-grade boys." After each parent/child team selects one of the four book choices for the month, they "locate the book, read it, discuss it at home, and come prepared for a book discussion at the following meeting" (p. 9). At the meeting (which also has door prizes and refreshments), the student/parent teams meet with others who have read the same book. While the initial discussions are led by teachers, later discussions are led by student facilitators.

TABLE 3-4   Suggestions for Book Discussions

DISCUSSION AFTER THE FIRST CHAPTER(S)

- What is your first reaction to this book?

- What characters have you met and what do you know about them? How do you feel about these characters?

- What types of conflict do you anticipate might occur in this book? What predictions can you make about the character's reactions to the conflict?

- How would you describe the author's style of writing?

- What are the setting and the point of view for the story?

DISCUSSIONS DURING THE FIRST PART OF THE BOOK

- Who are now the main characters in the book? Are they the same as in the initial chapters? How have they changed? What has caused the changes? Are there any characters that you particularly like or dislike? Why?

- What now appears to be the main conflict in the book? Has it changed since the first chapter(s)? How are the characters dealing with the conflict? Are some handling the conflict better than others? Do any have a conflict style that might lead to trouble?

- At this point in the book, knowing the conflict and the conflict styles of the characters, what predictions can you make?

- Are there any characters who need to learn something about conflict management style? What should they know or be taught? Are they capable of change?

- Whose point of view is the book told from? Does this person give us an honest story? Would other characters tell us different information?

- Are there any parallels between this book and another book that you have read or with this book and real life?

- How successful is the author in plotting the story and describing the characters?

DISCUSSIONS AT OR NEAR THE END OF THE BOOK

- Review all of the choices that led up to the climax. Discuss the character's decision. At this point does the character have a real choice?

- Have the characters learned anything or changed because of their experiences in the book?

- What is the theme of the book? (Bushman & Haas, 2001; Stanford, 1996).

Young Adult Literature and the Reluctant Reader

One way to encourage reluctant readers is for educators to use quality young adult literature that addresses reluctant readers' needs. Authors write young adult literature with adolescents' age level and interests in mind. While usually shorter and with an age-appropriate reading level, young adult literature can be well-written and more attractive than a reading book. The language and the plots of young adult literature are similar to what students are accustomed to finding in real life, on television, and in movies.

Methods of Encouraging Reluctant Readers

Educators are often concerned about why students begin to read less around the middle grades and how to motivate reluctant readers. With increased socialization, more difficult reading materials, and peer pressure that overshadows personal preferences, some adolescents read only for information and do not enjoy reading for pleasure. However, while it is helpful to understand why students read less, it is more productive to determine ways to motivate them to read.

Perhaps the best way to encourage reluctant readers is to get to know individual adolescents—their reading and interest levels and their reading preferences. Then, try some of the following strategies to encourage them:

- Provide a variety of books, both fiction and non-fiction, at appropriate reading levels.
- Stay in touch with adolescents' current interests and provide books that reflect these interests.
- Use booktalks to entice adolescents and to showcase a variety of books.
- Read books aloud and model enthusiasm for reading by carrying a book with you.
- Use audiobooks in classrooms and encourage adolescents to listen to them.
- Allow students to "self-select" their own books.
- Encourage an interest in short stories, graphic novels, and magazines and work up to full-length books.
- Use alternatives to traditional book reports.
- Give extra academic credit for books read, while trying to get learners to read for more intrinsic rewards.
- Encourage students to realize they can read and still be accepted by peers.
- Use Internet resources to find out more about favorite authors.
- Respect the reading interests of young adults and do not expect them to enjoy only the books you suggest.
- Encourage parents and families to set aside "reading times" at home.
- Relate reading to video reinforcement—read the book, see the video.
- Provide an atmosphere conducive to reading—respect for books and comfortable places for reading—and perhaps appropriate background music.
- Encourage businesses and community organizations to donate age- and interest-appropriate books.
- Encourage student booktalks, so adolescents can share the pleasures of motivating others to read.
- Encourage educators in all curricular areas to provide adolescents with reading opportunities.
- Form "reading clubs" and book discussion groups that give adolescents an opportunity to discuss their reading.
- Investigate the use of reading incentive programs such as Accelerated Reader, in which students receive points for reading and redeem the points for prizes.
- Encourage learners to bring their own books to school, ones they find interesting.
- Provide time for recreational reading, so learners realize that reading is not always schoolwork.
- Incorporate more young adult literature into the curriculum to develop interest in and a love for books.
- Provide young adults with attractive book lists, divided by subject, interest, and reading levels. Be sure there are some "thin books" on the list.
- Have a classroom collection of books that students can check out.

COLLABORATING WITH OTHER PROFESSIONALS

Working collaboratively with other teachers, the library media specialist, one or two parent volunteers, and the public librarian, decide how to most effectively address the needs of "reluctant readers." Do you recommend special books? Special rewards? How can you determine why readers are reluctant to read? Perhaps your agenda could be

(1) determining problems and needs of reluctant learners; (2) planning a literature program (e.g., books, methods, motivational techniques) that addresses those needs; and (3) planning a means of evaluation to determine program success and needed changes.

Educators can use some resources to locate books for reluctant readers and to provide more ideas for reaching this audience. These include *More Rip-Roaring Reads for Reluctant Teen Readers* (1999), by Bette D. Ammon and Gale W. Sherman, *Reaching Reluctant Young Adult Readers: A Handbook for Librarians and Teachers* (2002), by Edward T. Sullivan, and *Radical Reads: 101 YA Novels on the Edge* (2002), by Joni Richards Bodart. Jo Worthy offers suggestions for motivating reluctant readers in several articles, including "Removing Barriers to Voluntary Reading for Reluctant Readers: The Role of School and Classroom Libraries" (1996); " 'On Every Page Someone Gets Killed!' Book Conversations You Don't Hear in School" (1998); and "What Johnny Likes to Read Is Hard to Find in School" (1999). Collaborating with Other Professionals 3–4 looks at forming partnerships to reach reluctant readers.

Developing a Community of Readers

When educators incorporate literature across the curriculum, they can create a "community of readers," in which students develop the desire to become lifelong readers who read to gain information and to learn, as well as for pleasure. To create such a community, teachers and library media specialists need to promote reading by convincing students of its benefits, modeling respect for and enjoyment of books and other forms of literature, providing well-written reading materials, and using litera-

EXPANDING YOUR KNOWLEDGE WITH THE INTERNET

Find more ideas for reaching reluctant readers and for turning adolescents onto the Internet at websites such as these.

ALA Quick Picks for Reluctant Young Adult readers
www.ala.org/yalsa/booklists/quickpicks

Monroe County Public Library—Books for Reluctant readers
www.monroe.lib.in.us/childrens/reluctantbib.html

Corralling Reluctant Readers at the Ranch at Clark Middle School
litsite.alaska.edu/uaa/workbooks/ranch.html

Department. of Western Australia—Encouraging reluctant readers
www.eddept.wa.edu.au/cmis/eval/fiction/classroom/class5.htm

ture across the curriculum to show how reading relates to all aspects of one's life. By creating an atmosphere conducive to learning and appreciating literature, having well-written books and other reading materials readily available, allowing students to select books and reading materials based on their interests, and making time available for reading during classes, educators have an opportunity to foster a love of literature and promote a community of readers who will continue to read as adults. Expanding Your Knowledge with the Internet has more ideas for reaching young adults and turning them into readers.

Concluding Thoughts

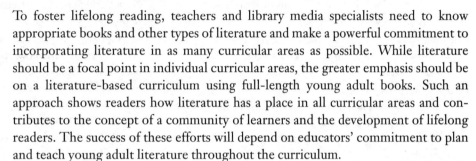

To foster lifelong reading, teachers and library media specialists need to know appropriate books and other types of literature and make a powerful commitment to incorporating literature in as many curricular areas as possible. While literature should be a focal point in individual curricular areas, the greater emphasis should be on a literature-based curriculum using full-length young adult books. Such an approach shows readers how literature has a place in all curricular areas and contributes to the concept of a community of learners and the development of lifelong readers. The success of these efforts will depend on educators' commitment to plan and teach young adult literature throughout the curriculum.

Young Adult Books

This section includes young adult titles recommended or mentioned in this chapter.

Bellenir, K. (Ed.). (2001). *Diet information for teens: Health tips about diet and nutrition.* Detroit: Omnigraphics. This book contains general sections on meal planning and specialized diets as well as information on eating disorders.

Ben Jelloun, T. (2002). *Islam explained.* New York: New Press. In addition to relating the history of Islam, the author explains Muslim beliefs.

Bennett, C. (1998). *Life in the fat lane.* New York: Delacorte. Lara cannot understand why, despite all of her attempts to diet and exercise, she keeps gaining weight.

Blatner, D. (1997). *The joy of [Pi].* New York: Walker. History, poetry, humor, and math collide in this book.

Bode, J. (1997). *Food fight: A guide to eating disorders for preteens and their parents.* New York: Simon & Schuster. Bode provides helpful information about anorexia, bulimia, and compulsive overeating.

Caddy, J. (2003). *Morning earth: Field notes in poetry.* Minneapolis, MN: Milkweed Editions. Poetry about nature and the seasons.

Carmi, D. (2000). *Samir and Yonatan.* New York: Scholastic. A Palestinian boy finds himself in an Israeli hospital with a broken leg.

Cisneros, S. (1991). *The house on Mango Street.* New York: Vintage. Vignettes describe the coming-of-age of Esperanza Cordero.

Clinton, C. (2002). *A stone in my hand.* Cambridge, MA: Candlewick. In the violence in Gaza between the Jews and Palestinians, Malaak's father and brother join the Islamic Jihad.

Cole, S. (2002). *The canyon.* New York: HarperCollins. When a land company wants to develop a canyon, Zach leads the opposition.

Croutier, A. L., and Sano, K. (2003). *Leyla: The black tulip.* Middleton, WI: Pleasant. In the 1720s, a young girl in Turkey tries to help her family and ends up on the Topkapi Palace in Istanbul.

Doherty, K. (2002). *Marjory Stoneman Douglas: Guardian of the 'Glades.* Brookfield, CT: Twenty-First Century. Douglas was a strong environmentalist who devoted her life to protecting the Everglades.

Dowd, J. (1999). *Hogsty reef.* Atlanta, GA: Peachtree. While helping their father study reef ecology, Jim and Julia become involved in a mystery. The sequel is *Rare and Endangered* (2000).

Draper, S. (1999). *Romiette and Julio*. New York: Atheneum. An African American girl and a Hispanic boy meet on the Internet and fall in love.

Enzensberger, H. M. (1998). *The number devil*. New York: Holt. When his math teacher refuses to let him use a calculator, Robert gets help from a strange person.

Feelings, T. (1995). *The middle passage: White ships, black cargo*. New York: Dial. Feelings uses 64 paintings in his depiction of the middle passage.

Fleischman, P. (1988). *Joyful noise: Poems for two voices*. New York: Harper & Row. Poems describe the activities of a variety of insects.

Gardner, R. (1999). *Science projects about the environment and ecology*. Hillside, NJ: Enslow. Projects for middle and high school students.

Haduch, B. (2001). *Food rules: The stuff you munch, its crunch, its punch, and why you sometimes lose your lunch*. New York: Dutton. This book is filled with fun food facts along with good nutrition information.

Hamilton, V. (1974). *M.C. Higgins the great*. New York: Macmillan. M.C. is stunned when it seems his family might lose the only home they have known.

Hesse, K. (1997). *Out of the dust*. New York: Scholastic. In a series of poems, Billie Jo tells about growing up in Oklahoma during the dust bowl.

Hesse, K. (2001). *Witness*. New York: Scholastic. Everyone has his or her own story to tell when the Ku Klux Klan comes to Vermont in the 1920s.

Hobbs, W. (1999). *The maze*. New York: Morrow. Can Rick and a bird biologist protect the condors in a remote canyon?

Hobbs, W. (2002). *Wild man island*. New York: HarperCollins. A storm strands Andy on remote Admiralty Island, Alaska.

Isdell, W. (1993). *A gebra named Al*. Minneapolis, MN: Free Spirit. Julie, a frustrated algebra student, takes a journey to the Land of Mathematics.

Klass, D. (1994). *California blue*. New York: Scholastic. The butterfly that John found may mean that the mill where his father works will have to close.

Landau, E. (2002). *Osama bin Laden: A war against the West*. Brookfield, CT: Twenty-First Century Books. Landau presents information about militant Islamic leader Osama bin Laden and the beliefs that fuel his terrorist actions.

Lasky, K. (1996). *True north: A novel of the underground railroad*. New York: Scholastic. Fourteen-year-old Lucy helps a fugitive slave girl.

Lasky, K., and Knight, C. (1998). *Shadows in the dawn: The lemurs of Madagascar*. San Diego: Harcourt. The authors showcase the work of a primatologist to show the relationships of people and animals in a fragile habitat.

Leone, D. (Ed.). (2002). *Anorexia*. San Diego: Greenhaven. A collection of personal essays.

Leuzzi, L. (2000). *Life connections: Pioneers in ecology*. New York: Scholastic. Leuzzi profiles eight scientists.

Lobel, A. (1998). *No pretty picture: A child of war*. New York: Greenwillow. Anita Lobel takes readers back to her experiences as a Jewish child in Poland in World War II, her capture by the Nazis, and her later life in Sweden after the war. This was a 1999 Orbis Pictus honor book.

Lyons, M. E. (1992). *Letters from a slave girl: The story of Harriet Jacobs*. New York: Aladdin. Through letters, Lyons tells a fictionalized version of the life of Harriet Jacobs in North Carolina in 1842.

Matas, C. (1998). *Greater than angels*. New York: Simon & Schuster. The people of Le Chambon-sur-Lignon in France are prepared to risk their lives to protect Jewish families.

Myers, W. D. (1988). *Fallen angels*. New York: Scholastic. Harlem native Richie Perry has to adapt to life in combat in Vietnam.

Newman, L. (1996). *Fat chance*. New York: Putnam. Judi is obsessed with being thin. But can she become too thin?

Nye, N. S. (1997). *Habibi*. New York: Simon & Schuster. Liyana's father moves the family from St. Louis, Missouri, to Jerusalem.

Paterson, K. (1980). *Jacob have I loved*. New York: Harper Trophy. Louise grows up, during the 1940s, in the shadow of her twin sister.

Paterson, K. (1991). *Lyddie*. New York: Dutton. A young girl becomes a mill girl in Lowell, Massachusetts.

Paulsen, G. (1985). *Dogsong*. New York: Puffin. Russel Susskit, an Eskimo, takes the village's last team of dogs on a life-changing journey.

Paulsen, G. (1998). *Soldier's heart: Being the story of the enlistment and due service of the boy Charley Goddard in the first Minnesota volunteers*. New York:

Delacorte. Charley leaves Minnesota full of the glory he will find in the Civil War. He returns full of the horrible images of the war.

Rall, T. (2002). *To Afghanistan and back: A graphic travelogue.* New York: NBM. Rall uses the format of a graphic novel to recount his experience in a war zone in this frank, often disturbing book.

Rifa'i, A., and Ainbinder, O., with Tempel, S. (2003). *We just want to live here: A Palestinian teenager, an Israeli teenager—An unlikely friendship.* New York: St. Martin's Press. First meeting in an exchange program in Switzerland, two teenagers exchange the letters that make up this book.

Rosaler, M. (2003). *Hamas: Palestinian terrorists.* New York: Rosen. This book presents the history and activities of this terrorist group.

Skurzynski, G., and Ferguson, A. (2002). *Over the edge, No. 7.* Washington, DC: National Geographic Society. The life of a scientist studying condors in the Grand Canyon is threatened.

Stanley, J. (1992). *Children of the Dust Bowl: The true story of the school at Weedpatch Camp.* New York: Crown. Stanley tells of the school that was built for the children of migrant workers during the Great Depression.

Staples, S. F. (1989). *Shabanu: Daughter of the wind.* New York: Knopf. In Pakistan, 11-year-old Shabanu is pledged to marry an older man.

Strada, J. L. (2001). *Eating disorders.* San Diego: Lucent. Strada looks at bulimia, anorexia, and binge eating and what they tell teens about self-perception.

Taylor, M. (2001). *The land.* New York: Phyllis Fogelman. The son of a plantation owner and a slave, Paul-Edward Logan tells his story of life during Reconstruction in the American South.

Vergoth, K., and Lampton, C. (1999). *Endangered species.* New York: Scholastic. This book provides an excellent overview of the subject.

Whytock, C. (2003). *My cup runneth over: The life of Angelica Cookson Potts.* New York: Simon & Schuster. Angel loves to cook and to eat, but she is concerned about getting too fat.

Zoya with Folian, J., and Cristofari, R. (2002). *Zoya's story: An Afghan woman's struggle for freedom.* New York: Morrow. A young woman from Afghanistan tells of her life under the rule of the Taliban and the Mujahideen.

Suggested Readings

Ariail, M., and Albright, L. K. (2006). A survey of teachers' read-aloud practices in middle schools. *Reading Research and Instruction, 45*(2), 69–89.

Follos, A. M. G. (2007). Teens take time to listen when you make time to read aloud. *VOYA, 29*(6), 499–503.

Henderson, L. (2005). The Black arts movement and African American young adult literature: An evaluation of narrative style. *Children's Literature in Education, 36*(4), 299–323.

Kilby, E. (2006). School librarian as writing mentor. *Knowledge Quest, 34*(3), 44–48.

Lesesne, T. S. (2006). Reading aloud: A worthwhile investment. *Voices from the Middle, 13*(4), 50-54.

Schneider, D. (2006). A quest for Land during reconstruction. *Book Links,* (5), 40-44.

Stallworth, B. J., Gibbons, L., and Fauber, L. (2006). It's not on the list: An exploration of teachers' perspectives on using multicultural literature. *Journal of Adolescent & Adult Literacy, 49*(6), 478-489.

Troise, M. (2007). Approaches to reading with multiple lenses of interpretation. *English Journal, 96*(5), 85–90.

References

All young adult literature referenced in this chapter are included in the Young Adult Books list and are not repeated in this list.

Ammon, B. D., and Sherman, G. W. (1999). *More rip-roaring reads for reluctant teen readers.* Englewood, CO: Libraries Unlimited.

Appleman, D. (2000). *Critical encounters in high school English: Teaching literary theory to adolescents.* New York: Teachers College Press.

Austin, P., and Harris, K. (1999). The audio argument, of sound advice about literature. *The New Advocate, 12*(3), 241–247.

Beers, K., and Probst, R. (1998). Classroom talk about literature or the social dimensions of a solitary act. *Voices from the Middle, 5*(2), 16–20.

Bodart, J. R. (1994–1998). *Booktalking the award winners* (vols. I–IV). New York: H. W. Wilson.

Bodart, J. R. (2002). *Radical reads: 101 YA novels on the edge.* Lanham, MD: Scarecrow Press.

Breen, M., and Rubin, T. (2003). Readers are survivors: A middle school student/parent/teacher book discussion group. *Voices from the Middle, 10*(4), 8–10.

Bushman, J. H., and Haas, K. P. (2001). *Using young adult literature in the English classroom.* Upper Saddle River, NJ: Merrill/Prentice Hall.

Clark, R. E. C. (2005). *Tantalizing tidbits for middle schoolers: Quick booktalks for the busy middle school and junior high library media specialist.* Worthington, OH: Linworth.

Clark, R. E. C. (2007). *Tantalizing tidbits for teens 2: More quick booktalks for the busy high school library media specialist.* Columbus: OH: Linworth.

Costello, J., Whalen, S., Spielberger, J., and Winje, C. J. (2001). Promoting public library partnerships with youth agencies. *Journal of Youth Services in Libraries, 15*(1), 8–15.

Cox, R. E. (2002). *Tantalizing tidbits for teens: Quick booktalks for the busy high school library media specialist.* Worthington, OH: Linworth.

Deringer, M. L. (2003). Visual responses to YAL that encourage higher level thinking. *Voices from the Middle, 10*(4), 11–12.

Dionisio, M. (1994). Responding to literary elements through dialogue journals and minilessons. *Voices from the Middle, 1*(1), 12–17.

Dreher, S. (2003). A novel idea: Reading aloud in a high school English classroom. *English Journal, 93*(1), 50–53.

Gauweiler, C. N. (2003). From page to stage. *Voices from the Middle, 10*(4), 29–30.

Gerlach, J. M. (1992). The young adult novel across the curriculum. In V. R. Moneau and G. M. Salver (Eds.), *Reading their world: The young adult novel in the classroom* (pp. 113–131). Portsmouth, NJ: Boynton/Cook.

Gillespie, J. T., and Naden, C. J. (2003). *Teenplots: A booktalk guide to use with readers ages 12–18.* Westport, CT: Libraries Unlimited.

Gilmore, B. (2006). *Speaking volumes: How to get students discussing books—and much more.* Portsmouth, NH: Heinemann.

Herz, S. K., with Gallo, D. R. (2005). *From Hinton to Hamlet: Building bridges between young adult literature and the classics.* Westport, CT: Greenwood.

Hinton, K. (2004). "Sturdy black bridges": Discussing, race, class, and gender. *English Journal, 94*(2), 60–64.

Hobgood, J. M. (1998). Finders keepers: Owning the reading they do. *Voices from the Middle, 5*(2), 26–33.

Isaac, M. L. (2000). *Heirs to Shakespeare: Reinventing the bard in young adult literature.* Portsmouth, NH: Boynton/Cook.

Ishizuka, K. (2003). Preparing teens for the future: A new mix of life skills and career programs has teens rushing to their local libraries. *School Library Journal, 49*(7), 46.

Jones, P. (2002). New directions for serving young adults means building more than our collections. *Journal of Youth Services in Libraries, 15*(3), 21–23.

Joseph, R. J. (1998). "Is this really English?" Using young adult literature in an urban middle school. *Voices from the Middle, 5*(2), 21–25.

Kaczmarski, K. (1998). *Exploring math with books kids love.* Golden, CO: Fulcrum.

Kaiser, M. M. (1999). Listen my children and you shall hear: Audio books for young adults. *The ALAN Review, 26*(3), 18–20.

Kaywell, J. (Ed.). (1993–2000). *Adolescent literature as a complement to the classics* (vols. I–IV). Norwood, MA: Christopher-Gordon.

Kettel, R. P., and Douglas, N. L. (2003). Comprehending multiple texts: A theme approach incorporating the best of children's literature. *Voices from the Middle, 11*(1), 43–49.

Kunzel, B., and Hardesty, C. (2006). *The teen-centered book club: Readers into leaders.* Westport, CT: Libraries Unlimited.

Langemack, C. (2003). *The booktalker's Bible: How to talk about the books you love to any audience.* Westport, CT: Libraries Unlimited.

Locke, D. (2001). Heard any good books lately? *Book Links, 11*(2), 26–29.

Machado, J., Lentz, B., Wallace, R., and Honig-Bear, S. (2000). A survey of best practices in youth services around the country: A view from one library. *Journal of Youth Services in Libraries, 15*(2), 30–35.

McCann, T. (2005). Reflective teaching, reflective learning: How to develop critically engaged readers, writers, and speakers. Portsmouth, NH: Heinemann.

Meyers, E. (2001). The road to coolness: Youth rock to the public library. *American Libraries, 32*(2), 46.

Milner, J. O., and Milner, L. F. M. (2008). *Bridging English.* 4th ed. Upper Saddle River, NJ: Pearson/Merrill Prentice Hall.

Moore, J. N. (1997). *Interpreting young adult literature: Literary theory in the secondary classroom.* Portsmouth, NJ: Boynton/Cook.

Murfin, R., and Ray, S. M. (2003). *The Bedford glossary of critical and literary terms.* New York: Bedford/St. Martin's Press.

Pinchback, C. L. (2000). Using literature in mathematics: Gifted students' comments. *Gifted Child Today, 24*(1), 36–43.

Rief, L., with Ervin, D. (1994). Threads of life: Reading, writing, and music. *Voices from the Middle, 1*(1), 18–28.

Rosenblatt, L. M. (1978). *The reader, the text, the poem: The transactional theory of the literary work.* Carbondale, IL: Southern Illinois University Press.

Rosenblatt, L. M. (1989). Writing and reading: The transactional theory. In J. M. Mason (Ed.), *Reading and writing connections* (pp. 153–176). Boston: Allyn and Bacon.

Schall, L. (2001). *Booktalks plus: Motivating teens to read.* Englewood, CO: Libraries Unlimited.

Schall, L. (2003). *Booktalks and more: Motivating teens to read.* Englewood, CO: Libraries Unlimited.

Schall, L. (2005). *Teen genre connections: From booktalking to booklearning.* Westport, CT: Libraries Unlimited.

Schall, L. (2007). *Booktalks and beyond: Promoting great genre reads to teens.* Westport, CT: Libraries Unlimited.

Smith, J. L., and Johnson, H. A. (1993). Bringing it together: Literature in an integrative curriculum. *Middle School Journal, 25*(1), 3–7.

Smith, J. L., and Johnson, H. A. (1995). Dreaming of America: Weaving literature into middle school social studies. *The Social Studies, 86*, 60–68.

Smith, S., with Hickey, B. (2003). Menu magic! *Voices from the Middle, 19*(4), 13–15.

Soter, A. O. (1999). *Young adult literature and new literary theories: Developing critical readers in middle school.* New York: Teachers College Press.

Sprague, M. M., and Keeling, K. K. (2007). *Discovering their voices: Engaging adolescent girls with young adult literature.* Newark, DE: International Reading Association.

Stanford, B. (1996). Coping with conflict in adolescent life and adolescent literature. Presentation at the annual meeting of the National Council of Teachers of English, Chicago, November 23, 1996.

Sullivan, E. T. (2002). *Reading reluctant young adult readers: A handbook for librarians and teachers.* Lanham, MD: Scarecrow Press.

Thomas, C., and Littlejohn, C. (2003). *Still talking that book! Booktalks to promote reading grades 3–12.* Worthington, OH: Linworth.

Trelease, J. (2006). *The read-aloud handbook* (6th ed.). New York: Penguin.

Tuccillo, D. P. (2003). Getting teens hooked on reading: What public librarians can do for teachers today. *The ALAN Review, 30*(2), 63–65.

Tyson, L. (1999). *Critical theory today: A user-friendly guide.* New York: Garland, 1999.

Van Horn, L. (2000). Young adult literature: An entrée into the joys of reading. *Voices from the Middle, 8*(2), 40–48.

Whitin, D., and Wilde, S. (1992). *Read any good math lately?* Portsmouth, NH: Heinemann.

Whitten, R. F. (1998). A+ for audiobooks. *Audiobook Reviews and Information, 6*(9), 17–19.

Worthy, J. (1996). Removing barriers to voluntary reading for reluctant readers: The role of school and classroom libraries. *Language Arts, 73*, 483–492.

Worthy, J. (1998). "On every page someone gets killed!" Book conversations you don't hear in school. *The Reading Teacher, 41*(7), 508–517.

Worthy, J. M., Moorman, M., and Turner, M. (1999). What Johnny likes to read is hard to find in school. *Reading Research Quarterly, 34*(1), 12–27.

Young, T. E. (2003). Working booktalks and bookchats: Tidbits that tantalize. *Knowledge Quest, 32*(1), 62–63.

Protecting
Intellectual Freedom

What do Robert Cormier's *The Chocolate War* (1974), Philip Pullman's *The Golden Compass* (1995), Mark Twain's *The Adventures of Huckleberry Finn* (1885), Maya Angelou's *I Know Why the Caged Bird Sings* (1969), and Stephen Chbosky's *The Perks of Being a Wallflower* (1999) have in common? All of these books reside among the top 10 of the ALA's Most Frequently Challenged Books of 2007 (American Library Association, 2008).

As you can see from the diversity among these books, censorship can happen to any type of literature. Thus, teachers and library media specialists need to be aware of the problems caused by censorship and must support and protect intellectual freedom. Unfortunately, authors, educators, young people, and all persons who value the freedom to read or to write whatever they wish often face the threat of censorship from people who try to impose their value systems or set restrictions on what others can read or write.

As you read this chapter, you should understand that we firmly believe in the rights of all individuals to freedom of expression and the right to read. We also believe that parents have the right and responsibility to make decisions for their own children. However, our concerns arise when a single individual or group tries to dictate what all individuals in a school may read and when materials are removed from a school without following the materials reconsideration policies of that school division.

Defining Censorship, Intellectual Freedom, and Selection

Censorship is nothing new, and its effects are constantly felt throughout society. As a result, authors may be afraid to write about certain topics and may intentionally delete or change language or characters that some readers might find offensive. Publishers may reject manuscripts that contain controversial topics, and libraries and schools may decide not to purchase materials if they believe those materials might be the target of censorship. In order to understand what is happening in each of these instances, it is important to understand the differences between censorship and intellectual freedom as well as the difference between censorship and the selection of materials.

Censorship, Intellectual Freedom, and the Relationship Between Them

The American Library Association defines *censorship* as the suppression of ideas and information that certain individuals, groups, or government officials find objectionable or dangerous (American Library Association, 2004c). In general, people act as censors when they examine books, periodicals, dramas, films, television and radio programs, and other forms of communication in order to identify and even suppress the parts they consider offensive. The rationale for their actions lies in their belief that they have the correct view of what is truthful and appropriate and that they must impose these views on others in order to protect three basic social institutions: the family, the church, or the nation (Konvitz, 2003). These people assume that if a book goes against their personal beliefs, then it must be wrong, offensive to others, and might negatively influence young minds. Table 4–1 identifies some of the most common reasons for censoring

TABLE 4-1   Reasons for Censoring Items

American Library Association (2008)	Analysis by Curry (2001)
Sexually explicit	Profanity
Offensive language	Heterosexual activity
Unsuited to age group	Homosexuality
Anti-ethnic	Sexual activity deemed immoral or illegal
Violence	Religion/witchcraft
Homosexuality	Violence/horror
Religious viewpoint	Rebellion
Racism	Racism/sexism
Sexism	Substance use/abuse
Sex education	Suicide/death
Anti-family	Crime Crude behavior Depressing/negative

Sources: Developed from information in American Library Association. (2008). Children's book on male penguins raising chick tops ALA's 2007 list of most challenged books. Accessed June 24, 2008, from www.ala.org/ala/pressreleases2008/may2008/penguin.cfm; Curry, A. (2001). Where is Judy Blume? Controversial fiction for older children and young adults. *Journal of Youth Services in Libraries, 14*(3), 28–37.

materials. Although not included on the list, event denial is a form of censorship that is evidenced in the belief that a historical even such as the Holocaust in World War II or the Armenian genocide in 1915 did not actually happen.

In their quest to mold the thinking of young adults, censors often believe that adolescents must read or see only the things that they, the adults, deem appropriate; that reflect the adults' views on living; and that espouse the positions the adults support. These individuals may fear any reading that possibly deviates from their perception of the ideal (Greenbaum, 1997). Sometimes they distrust the inclusion in books of those topics and subjects that differ from what they read when they were young. Thus, they may consider abortion, homosexuality, and incest inappropriate topics for young people to read about. While groups often lead a movement to censor certain items, censorship can be as simple as a single individual saying: "Don't let anyone read the book, or buy that magazine, or view that film, because I object to it!"

In contrast to censorship, *intellectual freedom* is the right of every individual both to seek and to receive information from all points of view without restriction (American Library Association, 2004c). A basic tenet of a democratic system, intellectual freedom protects the rights of individuals to have free access to all expressions of ideas, and to examine all sides of a question, cause, or movement before making up their own minds. Traditionally, libraries and schools have provided the ideas and information in a variety of formats, to allow people to become well-informed citizens. Intellectual freedom encompasses this freedom to hold, receive, and disseminate ideas (American Library Association, 2004c).

Censorship is tied very closely to intellectual freedom. A relationship also exists between censorship and freedom of speech, with censors exercising the freedom that they want to deny to others. Would-be censors are exercising their right to free speech, the same right that is also held by the creators and disseminators of the materials to which the censors are objecting. However, the rights of censors to voice their opinions and try to persuade others to adopt these opinions is protected only if the rights of the creators and disseminators to express those ideas are also protected. Unless the rights of both sides are protected, the rights of neither will survive (American Library Association, 2004c). In Expanding Your Knowledge with the Internet, you will find examples of websites that have basic information about intellectual freedom and censorship.

The Difference Between Censorship and Selection of Materials

Freedman and Johnson (2001) maintain that most censorship efforts have focused on the issue of who should have the authority to select the materials that are purchased for and used in schools. Undoubtedly, parents and guardians have the right to determine what their own children should read. However, the responsibility for selecting the materials that will form the basis for the curriculum and the school library collection usually falls on the shoulders of teachers and school library media specialists who identify books and other materials that have the potential to engage young adults and that are cognitively, socially, emotionally, and psychologically appropriate for them.

There is, however, a fine line between this selection of appropriate materials and censorship. In general terms, censorship is often associated with the removal of materials from a library or school—materials that educators have already selected to support the curriculum or to meet the needs of young adults for recreational reading.

EXPANDING YOUR KNOWLEDGE WITH THE INTERNET

For basic information about Intellectual Freedom and Censorship, consult some of these Internet resources. (Note: Some may present opposing viewpoints on censorship and intellectual freedom.)

American Library Association, Office of Intellectual Freedom
www.ala.org/ala/oif/Default622.htm

Banned Books Week
www.ala.org/ala/oif/bannedbooksweek/bannedbooksweek.htm

List of Intellectual Freedom Awards
www.ala.org/ala/oif/oifprograms/ifawards/intellectual.cfm

"Censored: Wielding the Red Pen." An exhibit from the University of Virginia.
www.lib.virginia.edu/speccol/exhibits/censored/index.html

Censorship and Book Banning in America: Information for secondary educators
712educators.about.com/cs/bannedbooks/a/bookbanning.htm

The Constitution, Censorship, and the Schools: *Tennessee v. John Thomas Scopes,* by Peter Neal Herndon. A teaching unit that explores intellectual freedom.
www.cis.yale.edu/ynhti/pubs/A5/herndon.html

***Catholic Encyclopedia,* History of Censorship**
www.newadvent.org/cathen/03519d.htm

"Intellectual Freedom 2002: Living the Chinese Curse": CyperCast and transcript of a lecture by Judith Krug presented on May 23, 2002
www.loc.gov/rr/program/lectures/krug.html

List of Internet resources on censorship and intellectual freedom
www.georgesuttle.com/censorship/index.shtml

"What Johnny Can't Read: Censorship in American Libraries," by Suzanne Fisher Staples. *The ALAN Review* (Winter 1996).
scholar.lib.vt.edu/ejournals/ALAN/winter96/pubCONN.html

In contrast, selection calls for evaluation and a deliberate judgment (Sipe, 1999) to identify appropriate materials for adolescents that can be included in a school or library. As author Cynthia Grant has noted: "the best collection is one that always makes you feel slightly uneasy" (1995, p. 50).

Sometimes, however, the boundaries between censorship and selection begin to blur, and what one individual calls selection may actually be censorship. According to Suhor (2003), when teachers and librarians "select" materials, they look at a wide range of items and decide what is best for the students and programs. When educators "censor," they intentionally look for undesirable language, characters, and themes. As Sutton (2007) has pointed out, excluding a book from a library because "you don't approve of one of the words it uses" (p. 228) is a violation of article 2 of the ALA's Library Bill of Rights. However, in a title analysis of the young adult book collections in a sample of Texas high school libraries, Coley (2002) found signs of self-censorship in over 80% of the schools.

Exclusion Versus Inclusion. There are instances when, as a school library media specialist or teacher deliberately and conscientiously selects books and other materials to include in a library collection or to incorporate into instruction, censorship consciously or unconsciously results. For example, a teacher might decide to exclude a book from a reading list because, even though the book is an award-winner, there may be individuals in the community who would object to the book. Or, a library media specialist might not order a particular book in spite of the fact that the book had excellent reviews; he or she might rationalize this choice by citing budget limitations when, in actuality, he or she thought there were passages in the book to which someone might object. There may also be instances where a subject or a particular author might remind the educator of a previous experience where censorship occurred or where someone made an actual complaint. In these cases, the educator does not really engage in a selection process because the book is never seriously considered. Suhor (2003) maintains that selection means that teachers develop lists of good books that are circulated as suggestions rather than prescriptions, while censorship means that teachers develop lists of "approved" books and specify ones that cannot be used.

Control Versus Advice.   As these terms imply, teachers and library media specialists may feel pressure to select or not to select a book. For example, parents, community members, or groups may try to *control* the materials that are available in a school library or taught within the curriculum. These censors, if powerful, can influence the school administration or the school board and by applying pressure or threatening legal action may succeed in preventing books from being used in the curriculum, appearing on reading lists, or being placed on library shelves. By claiming that certain topics should not be discussed or presented in schools, these censors want to control what is appropriate for all young people. For example, if an educator knows that there is a very vocal group in the community that objects to the theory of evolution, the educator may refrain from purchasing books on evolution for the school library or using books in the classroom that talk about evolution. Rather than subjecting the books to the selection criteria of the school district, the educator has allowed the threat of censorship to control his or her actions.

While not as strong as control, *advice* can have an effect on selection or become a form of censorship. An individual or group may give advice about what schools should teach in the curriculum and/or add to the library's collection. Generally, those who give advice are more open to dialogue than those who seek to control. Unlike "censorship by control," advice can be beneficial if it opens a constructive dialogue in which individuals and educators are able to consider the positions of others.

Indoctrinate Versus Educate.   Educators want to select and use books and works that offer a balanced perspective on issues and that *educate* or enlighten young adults about something that is new or unique for them. These materials should allow young adults to make their own informed decisions that are free from prejudice. In contrast, books and other reading materials that *indoctrinate* provide only one view of an issue. While it is possible to use these materials in a school, educators have to be careful to balance them with materials that present opposing points of view, and to be sure that all of these materials are equally accessible for their young adult students.

Isolation Versus the Work as a Whole.   Sometimes when selecting materials, individuals can become censors when they fail to consider an entire work and focus only on a single "dirty" word or a so-called controversial passage (e.g., a sex scene, one or two uses of profanity, or a reference to someone's sexual orientation). Educators must be careful that this form of censorship does not sneak into the selection process. For example, Jane Leslie Conly's *Crazy Lady* (1993), which was chosen as a Newbery Honor Book, an ALA Notable, and an ALA Best Books for Young Adults, contains two mild profanities that have upset some people (Reeder, 2002). When considering this book for a classroom or school library, an educator may be tempted to look only at these two words rather than to consider the entire book before making a decision on its appropriateness and whether to use it with young adults.

Relying on Review Sources and Awards: Benefits and Pitfalls

Although all teachers should read the books they plan to use in their classroom and preview all other materials, teachers may not have the time to read all the books on a booklist. Certainly, school library media specialists cannot read all of the materials they select to include in the school library's collection. Instead of relying on the name recognition of an author (for example, Shel Silverstein wrote for *Playboy* as well as for children) or publishers' recommendations (publishers promote, not review, their own products), educators must turn to review sources and awards to assist in the selection process. In general, as you read in Chapter 2, most reviews are done by experts or at least readers who are genuinely interested in young adult literature. Reviews are readily found, usually in respected journals and magazines known for their focus on young adult materials. Even on Internet sources such as Amazon.com and Barnesandnoble.com, you can locate reviews from reputable review sources.

There are pitfalls in using reviews. A review is usually just one person's opinion and might reflect only that person's taste. Although most selection journals have written selection criteria, some reviewers may have personal biases. In addition, published reviews do not always reflect local standards or values. A book or video that a reviewer finds acceptable for one community might be deemed offensive in another community. One of the authors of this book attended a panel discussion by book review editors that was held at a national conference. During the discussion, all of the panel participants noted that they did not feel it was necessary for their reviewers to note parts of the books that might be open to censorship challenges or that might be objectionable to some group.

Thus, an individual review source and/or award should be only one factor in the selection of a book or other material for use in a school. The ideal is to locate several reviews or a combination of reviews and awards, to read each review completely, and to know exactly why the award was given and by whom. When there are conflicting reviews or when the reviews raise questions, teachers and library media specialists have a responsibility to read the book or view the material themselves, discuss the appropriateness with others in the school or community, and consider community norms and expectations before making a final selection. Throughout the selection process, educators need to keep in mind the selection policies of the school division in which they work, as well as the documents that promote and defend intellectual freedom. Collaborating with Other Professionals 4–1 points out the need for teachers and library media specialists to work together when selecting materials.

COLLABORATING WITH OTHER PROFESSIONALS

4-1

Teachers and library media specialists need to collaborate when selecting materials for the curriculum and for the library collection. For example, if an individual teacher wishes to select a book to supplement a unit in the curriculum, Edward Sadler (1995) suggests that the teacher take a positive approach.

- Develop a rationale for the book:
  - Include your intentions for selecting that particular book

- Identify what students will get out of the book
- Link the book to the specific unit objectives
- Work with the library media specialist to collect reviews of the work and identify any awards or honors it might have won
- Develop informal groups within the school to provide support for members should a censorship challenge occur in the school

Parental Rights Versus Censorship

A fine line exists between parents' and guardians' supervisory rights and censorship. As we have noted, parents are ultimately responsible for raising their children. Thus, educators should try to cooperate whenever a parent or guardian makes a request about specific materials his or her child reads, hears, or sees in school. Following the rulings of the courts, most school divisions have a procedure under which a parent, guardian, or individual student may request the opportunity to read a different book from the one the entire class is reading. In addition, many teachers use a "parental permission to read" form whenever they are assigning any materials that they believe may be controversial.

Another issue concerns parental requests that a school librarian restrict what an adolescent can check out. While some library media specialists would honor such a request, Anderson (2002) cites three reasons she would not. First, depending on the size of the school, keeping track of individual student restrictions may be practically impossible. Furthermore, because most school libraries have student assistants working at the circulation desk, it would not be appropriate or ethical for these students to know about restrictions placed on their schoolmates. Second, restricting students' access to information violates the ALA Code of Ethics and the AASL (American Association of School Librarians) "Access to Resources and Services in the School Library Media Program: An Interpretation of the Library Bill of Rights." Finally, Anderson (2002) points out that, through reading, adolescents have the opportunity to explore diverse ideas and values and to experience vicariously what might prove dangerous in the real world.

The line between parental rights and censorship begins to blur when individuals or groups make a request that would limit access by all the students in a school rather than just their own children. For example, in Fairfax County, Virginia, PABBIS (Parents Against Bad Books in Schools) has lobbied to have teachers provide "written notice of any sexual depictions or graphic violence in books

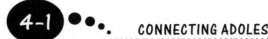

CONNECTING ADOLESCENTS AND THEIR LITERATURE

Joanne M. Marshall (2003) suggests that teachers should use open discussions to help students (and their parents) consider the use of potentially controversial books in the classroom. Her framework consists of seven steps:

1. Ask participants if they have read the book or, when appropriate, if they have seen the movie.

2. Briefly summarize the story.

3. Make a "For" and "Against" list and quickly brainstorm ideas that support or do not support using the material.

4. Introduce the concept of finding common ground and initiate a discussion by asking participants to try to see the opposing point of view.

5. Use a handout to get participants to work in small groups, to think about the events in the book, and to examine the impact of those events. Include questions about the protagonist, antagonist, violence, sex, religion, culture, moral lessons, and response to authority. For example, Marshall (2003) uses a three-column handout. In the first column, she puts questions such as *Who is the villain and who does the villain fight? What is the message behind the villain's role?* In the next column, participants record answers based on their knowledge from the book. In a third column, they indicate whether they believe the book is a positive, negative, or neutral influence.

6. Compile the responses from each small group and then lead the entire group in a discussion of the responses.

7. Ask the group to make an overall statement about the book's value or appropriateness. An alternative is to have each group member write a short persuasive essay supporting his or her position.

students might read in class." The organization also asked for a "rating system" that would alert parents to sex or violence in a book. In response to requests by PABBIS and supportive school board members, the district superintendent proposed having review panels in each school examine classroom materials for "cultural and ethnic differences, language or word choice, religion, disabilities, violence, and implied or explicit sexual situations" (Glick, 2002, p. 26). Connecting Adolescents and Their Literature 4–1 suggests one strategy that teachers and library media specialists can use when groups of students or parents consider the use of potentially controversial materials.

Since their initial action, PABBIS (Glick, 2002) has gone on to challenge several books in Fairfax County school libraries, including Morgan Llywelyn's *Druids* (1991), Lois Duncan's *Daughters of Eve* (1979), and Ken Follett's *The Pillars of the Earth* (1989). When a school district committee voted to keep the books in the schools, PABBIS appealed to the school board, which removed *Druids* and *Daughters of Eve* from middle school libraries and made *The Pillars of the Earth* available only to high school students in 10th grade and above.

Forms of Censorship

As you can see from the actions of PABBIS, once an item has been selected for inclusion in a curriculum or school library media center, a parent can ask that his or her child not be allowed to read a certain book, a community member can object to the inclusion of a specific book in the school library, or an organized group can present a list of items that they find objectionable. The result can be a restriction of what one student is allowed to read, the complete removal of an item from a school, the removal of an item from a booklist, or the deliberate exclusion of an item from a library collection. Thus, censorship in schools can take a number of different forms.

Nonselection. As you read earlier in this chapter, one form of censorship is the nonselection of materials. Suhor (2003) called nonselection an "insidious form of book banning" (p. 7). In several recent instances, school boards and school administrators have effectively censored items in advance of any challenge, not by adopting formal selection criteria or approving selection procedures but by designating one administrator to be a "gatekeeper." In the selection process, groups of teachers may have the responsibility to choose novels and supplementary materials. However, their selections must be approved by the "gatekeeper," who may base the selection decision on personal choice or by applying his or her own definition of community standards. Either way, the effect is the same—the selection process actually becomes a censoring device.

As noted, an educator can actually engage in censorship without being aware of it. For example, you have five books from which to choose one to use with a particular unit of study. In a nearby school division, there have been problems with some of the works written by the author of the first book under consideration, so you exclude it. Now you have four books to consider. You pick the fifth book because it is the safest. That means that the remaining three books were not selected and, in fact, were never even seriously considered. Nothing may be wrong with these three books, but you never subjected them to a deliberate and conscious selection process. Rather than selecting any potentially risky books, you took the safest route and made the final selection.

Orders from a Higher Authority. Sometimes intellectual freedom is curtailed when a higher authority dictates that books and other curricular materials must be removed. Administrators, either principals or individuals at the school district level, can make arbitrary decisions to remove potentially damaging books to avoid censorship threats. For example, a Virginia school principal demanded that Alice Walker's Pulitzer Prize–winning novel *The Color Purple* (1982) be removed from a high school library before any complaint was received. Considering the book potentially controversial, and acting without consulting teachers or librarians, the principal simply ordered the removal of the book. Of course, this made the book an instant bestseller at the local bookstores and actually led to more adolescents reading the novel than had read it while it was on the shelves of the school library. This unilateral act of censorship is the same as removing a book from a school in reaction to one complaint without listening to opposing points of view.

Personal Opinion of Educators. While censorship by special interest groups, minority groups, and fundamentalist religious groups is blatant and usually attracts attention, another form of censorship—by teachers and library media specialists—sometimes occurs. These educators might subscribe to the beliefs of the special interest groups, or they might be acting on their own personal beliefs and opinions. Unfortunately, this form of censorship often goes unnoticed and undetected. For example, a single teacher went to her school library's bookfair and demanded that a book of short stories be removed from the sale because it contained a story about ghosts. Her request was based solely on her personal beliefs about one story out of the entire collection.

Fortunately, most educators support the freedom of expression and the freedom to read. While they may not personally support a particular position or belief, they respect an individual's right to express that belief in writing, music, or art, and they respect the rights of other individuals to read, view, or listen to that expression. At times, however, a problem arises when the individuals doing the reading, listening, or viewing are young adults. As Small (2000) writes, especially in the Internet age, some teachers feel obligated to monitor and sometimes make difficult decisions about what students may read and observe. Again, there is the fine line between selection of what is appropriate for adolescents and censorship.

Some teachers and library media specialists may attempt to censor materials prior to any controversy erupting (O'Neal, 1990) because they fear the materials will lead to confrontations with parents, community members, or school administrators (Freedman & Johnson, 2001). They may also be afraid that they will not be supported by the administration of their own school or by the district-level administration. Thus, by providing access only to literature that does not discuss sex, politics, or violence, or that does not question the role of adults, some teachers and library media specialists may believe that they are protecting themselves. However, they are also influencing young people's minds. To help educators make wise selections and to eliminate the problems of self-censorship, school divisions need to develop sound policies for selecting materials for and removing materials from the curriculum and the school library (O'Neal, 1990). When teachers abandon their right and responsibility to select literature and other curriculum materials, they sacrifice their students to protect themselves. Self-censorship silences both teachers and students (Freedman & Johnson, 2001).

Community Pressure. Community organizations and other groups of people can pressure educators to remove materials from schools. Although most school boards and individual school libraries have planned procedures for dealing with censorship, defending a censorship challenge can still be time-consuming and emotionally draining and may sometimes lead to costly legal battles. At times, community pressure can be so powerful that educators may decide that it is easier to remove the material altogether; remove the material for a time until the controversy has quieted; restrict access to the material; or remove the item from a reading list. Unfortunately, a school or an individual educator may not have the resources (e.g., people, money, legal expertise) to engage in a possibly long, drawn-out defense. In addition, members of elected school boards may find it is politically more advantageous to remove an unpopular item than to support intellectual freedom. Finally, a school may not be willing to face the loss of community support by retaining challenged materials in the library or in the curriculum. Thus, schools often give in to community pressure.

Filters. Although it is beyond the scope of this book to discuss Internet filters in detail, we mention them because censorship challenges to print materials in schools have dropped dramatically in the past several years as some attention has shifted to materials that are available on the Internet ("Censoring school literature in the cyber age," 2001). With the Communications Decency Act—an amendment to the Tele-communications Act of 1996—the federal government attempted to prohibit the posting of "indecent" or "patently offensive" (Kravitz, 2002, p. 134) materials in public forums on the Internet, including Web pages, newsgroups, chat rooms, and online discussion lists. At a basic level, this would mean that the texts of classic fiction such as *The Catcher in the Rye* and *Ulysses*, although offensive to some, would be censored on the Internet while they would enjoy the full protection of the First Amendment if published in a newspaper, magazine, or book (Kravitz, 2002).

Internet material is unselected, and most secondary schools provide computers so that adolescents can access Internet resources both in the classroom and in the school library. Thus, in response to federal laws that require filtering software on all comput-ers purchased for schools with federal funds, and to accommodate parental and com-munity concerns, many schools have established policies regarding student Internet use and/or have installed filtering software. However, policies can be broken, and fil-ters can sometimes restrict access to inoffensive materials by mistake while allowing access to some offensive materials. Just ask the teacher who typed the name Seymour Simon (author of many nonfiction books) into a search engine and was rewarded with a listing for nude celebrity photos. As she said, that was more of Simon than she wanted the class to see. While the Internet may represent the next big censorship battleground, easy access to information will be difficult to combat ("Censoring school literature in the cyber age," 2001).

Alteration. Rather than blatantly removing books from a classroom or library, sometimes censors just make alterations by deleting words or passages that they find offensive. This alteration might be a few changed words in a new edition of Roald Dahl's classic *Charlie and the Chocolate Factory* (1964), the use of a marking pen to "raise" the bodice of a young woman on the cover of a modern romance story, the removal of a complete page that discusses wet dreams in Judy Blume's *Then Again, Maybe I Won't* (1971), or the revision of a quotation so that it no longer praises California "wine" (Kleinfield, 2002). The New York Board of Regents adopted what it called Sensitivity Review Guidelines and used them to censor literary excerpts from authors such as Chekhov, I. B. Singer, and Annie Dillard in the English Regents' Examination. The Board insisted they were only shortening the excerpts, not censoring them (National Coalition Against Censorship, 2003).

One of our college students reported that, during her practicum, the teacher she was working with received a book that had been purchased by the school division to supplement the science and literature curriculum. When the teacher reviewed the book, she found that two pages were stapled together. Curious, the teacher removed the staples and found sketches of the development of a human baby, something the school division obviously did not want the students (or the teacher) to see.

Elimination from Booklists. As we have noted, an educator may decide to exclude a book from a school list or library collection because of what the censors might say rather than worrying about responding to a censorship challenge. We know of one instance in which a high school teacher refused to add Lois Duncan's *Killing Mr. Griffin* (1978) to a booklist, in spite of student requests, because there had been an objection in a neighboring middle school. Such elimination of works is a matter of concern for many educators who think that young adults should have the opportunity to read a wide range of materials and that selection should be made on the basis of established selection criteria and curriculum content.

Relocating Controversial or Challenged Books. While public librarians might move controversial young adult books to the adult section, school librarians might remove controversial material on topics such as date rape, drugs, and witchcraft from the regular collection, place them in the librarian's office, and provide them only to adolescents who specifically ask for them. Because any mention of these materials may be removed from the library's catalog, adolescents have to know that the materials are available and that they can request them. In some cases, this means that adolescents may have to face the embarrassment of asking for information on what they see as very personal subjects. In other libraries, the materials may be placed in a restricted "Teachers' Collection" (Curry, 2001, p. 28) or on bookshelves that can be accessed only by adolescents who have permission from a guidance counselor, therapist, or parent. Although educators often justify this relocation because it may defuse a situation while still retaining some access to the material, Curry (2001) called this relocation of materials a "disturbing trend" (p. 28).

Removal from the Library or School. Perhaps the most extreme form of censorship is the complete elimination of materials. In this case, teachers, library media specialists, or administrators actually remove the book or other material from the library and/or the entire school, either in reaction to a censorship challenge or as a precautionary move to prevent censorship efforts.

   While a few educators may be able to overlook some of the other forms of censorship, to most, the actual removal of an item from a school is an assault on intellectual freedom. When an item is removed from a school, young adults do not have access to that item unless they can find it in a public library or purchase it from a local or Internet bookstore. If the decision to remove the item was based only on the beliefs of a single individual or was not made in accordance with the school division's policies, the removal has diminished intellectual freedom in the school and has constrained the rights of young adults to read, view, or listen to the item.

Censorship Through the Ages

Censorship is nothing new. In fact, it has persisted throughout the ages. Early censorship was often tied directly to government and religion. Even in ancient Greece, where the freedom to speak openly was a respected right, Socrates committed suicide rather than have his teaching censored. Later, in the fifteenth century, Pope Innocent VIII required printers to submit manuscripts to church authorities and to publish them only after church approval was given. Through the ages, many famous authors, scientists, philosophers, and historians saw their works censored, including Galileo, Jean-Jacques Rousseau, Frances Bacon, and Victor Hugo.

Censorship in the Modern Age

Although the modern period began in the eighteenth century with the Age of Enlightenment, the freedoms of expression and religion did not come easily or to all peoples. Except for a brief period in France after the Revolution of 1789, political censorship flourished in most of continental Europe until the rise of republican governments in the mid–nineteenth century. Even in the 1900s, in totalitarian countries, state censorship remained severe. One event that galvanized support for the anticensorship movement was the burning of books by the Nazis in Germany on May 10, 1933 (Cronon, 2003).

Censorship in the United States

The First Amendment to the United States Constitution forbids Congress from enacting laws that would regulate speech or the press, either before or after publication. This has not stopped attempts to censor what Americans can see and read. For example, in the years directly before the American Civil War, southern states outlawed abolitionist literature. More recently, in 1971, attempts were made to censor portions of a report on U.S. policy in Vietnam that was published as the *Pentagon Papers*.

Until the twentieth century, government policies strictly suppressed so-called obscene publications and prohibited them from being sent through the U.S. mail or from passing through customs. These prohibitions were successfully challenged in the courts in the 1930s, when *Ulysses*, by Irish author James Joyce, was found not to be obscene and was allowed into the country. Later, however, in the case of *Roth v. United States*, the U.S. Supreme Court noted that obscene materials were not protected by the Constitution and were "without redeeming social importance." This case also applied a new test of community standards for defining obscene materials, which was later defined as the standards of the national "community" rather than any local ones.

Censorship in the Schools

Censorship reaches into American education when groups and individuals attempt to control what is taught in the curriculum, what textbooks are used, and/or what other books and materials are available in classrooms and school libraries. These objections have ranged from challenges to the *Wizard of Oz* because the characters do not pray to God and to *Goldilocks* because the main character trespasses on the bears' private property (Kravitz, 2002) to the call for removal of *Annie on My Mind* (Garden, 1982) from a school because it depicts a lesbian relationship (Curry, 2001) and to the censorship of *Fallen Angels* (Myers, 1988) for offensive language, violence, and racism ("10 Most-Challenged Books of 2000," 2001). In Panama City, Florida, Robert Cormier's *I Am the Cheese* (1977) was challenged for being antigovernment.

Textbooks were challenged in Tennessee (the Basic Reading series published by Holt, Rinehart and Winston) for promoting "idolatry, demon worship, gun control, evolution and feminism" (Kravitz, 2002, p. 70) and in Kanawha County, West Virginia, because of a conflict between the religious views of groups of citizens and the multicultural content of the *Interactions* reading series. What began as a protest against a textbook spread to a call to censor *Moby Dick*, *The Good Earth*, and *Paradise Lost* and threats to firebomb the schools. When new selection guidelines were established, the National Education Association commented that "if given the interpretation obviously meant by their proponents, the guidelines would not only bar the disputed books from Kanawah County classrooms, but would proscribe the use of any language arts textbooks, including the *McGuffey's Readers*" (p. 39).

Although separation of church and state exists in the United States, some groups have charged that secular humanism, a philosophy that advocates human rather than religious values (*American Heritage Dictionary of the English Language*, 2000), is taught in public schools. Several conservative religious organizations, such as Focus on the Family and the Educational Research Analysts, have called for the elimination of courses in drug education, sex education, values clarification, and multicultural education and for a shift from an emphasis on problem solving to one of mastering the content of the disciplines (Kravitz, 2002).

Landmark Court Decisions That Affect Intellectual Freedom

Often, the struggles between individuals and groups who are attempting to censor items and those who are arguing on behalf of intellectual freedom are played out in the court system, with a few cases going all the way to the U.S. Supreme Court. A number of cases, listed in Table 4–2, have dealt with censorship topics.

Most of the court cases have centered around the following issues:

1. According to the school division's policies, who has the final authority to select materials for a school and under what circumstances?

2. Is there a procedure to follow if materials are challenged and was the procedure followed?

3. Who ultimately has the right to remove materials from a school and under what specific circumstances?

4. What are the rights of individuals who challenge materials that are in the schools and were the individuals provided these rights?

5. What is the difference between the compulsory and the optional use of materials?

6. If students are excused from using certain materials, what effect will that have on the students and on their learning?

Although there are too many cases to discuss in detail in a single chapter, several rulings are especially important.

One of the landmark cases confirming intellectual freedom in schools was *Island Trees (NY) School District v. Pico* (1982). Four high school students and one junior high school student challenged the legality of the school board's removal of nine books from the district's school libraries. A conservative group had told board members about several books in the libraries that were on a list of objectionable items. Ostensibly, the board removed the books in order to read them. However,

TABLE 4-2   Court and Other Legal Cases

Year	Case	Issue
1969	Tinker v. Des Moines Independent Community School District	Students wore black armbands to protest war.
1972	Presidents Council, District 25 v. Community School Board No. 25 (NYC)	School board removed books from the school library.
1976	Minarcini v. Strongsville (OH) City School District	School board removed books from school library.
1978	Right to Read Defense Committee v. School Committee of the City of Chelsea (MA)	Poetry anthology banned from the school library.
1980	Bicknell v. Vergennes (VT) Union High School Board	School board removed books from the school library.
1980	Loewen v. Turnipseed (MS)	School board refused to approve textbook.
1982	Pratt v. Independent School District No. 831 (MN)	School board removed a film from the curriculum.
1982	Island Trees (NY) v. Pico	School board removed eight books from the library.
1985	Grove v. Meade School District No. 354 (FL)	Parents objected to a book on the basis of secular humanism.
1986	Mozert v. Hawkins County (TN) Board of Education	Parents challenged reading textbooks.
1988	Hazelwood (MO) School District v. Kuhlmeier	Principal removed articles from student newspaper.
1989	Virgil v. School Board of Columbia County (FL)	Parents complained about literature textbook.
1994	Brown v. Woodland Jt. School District (CA)	Parents challenged reading series.
1994	Fleischfresser v. S.D. 200 (IL)	Parents challenged reading series.
2002	Counts v. Cedarville (AK) School Board	Harry Potter book placed on restricted list.
2007	Morse et al. v. Frederick	Principle confiscated banner and suspended student.

when a review committee recommended that seven of the books be returned to the library, with five to be placed on the open shelves and two in a restricted area, the board voted to remove eight of the books entirely. The case reached the U.S. Supreme Court, which found that while a school board may have "significant discretion in determining curriculum content," school officials "may not remove books from school library shelves simply because they dislike the ideas contained in those books" (Ishizuka, 2001, p. 17). The court also found that "school boards do not have unrestricted authority to select books and that the First Amendment is implicated when books are removed arbitrarily" (Reichman, 1993, p. 153). The Court suggested that books could be removed from schools when the decision to do so was based on educational suitability, when there was a recognized materials-review system with reconsideration guidelines in place, and when those guidelines were followed in the removal process.

The use of identified criteria in the selection of materials can be very important. In *Loewen v. Turnipseed* (1980), the Court found that a rating committee must follow its own stated criteria and cannot substitute personal opinion when selecting textbooks. Court decisions such as *Minarcini v. Strongsville* (1976) and *Right to Read Defense Committee v. School Committee of Chelsea* (1978) supported the rights of young people to have access to appropriately selected materials that represent diverse points of view.

Hazelwood School District v. Kuhlmeier (1988) dealt with school journalism and the school newspaper rather than young adult literature, but it has had an impact in other federal cases. In Hazelwood, Missouri, a principal objected to two stories that dealt with teenage pregnancy and divorce and banned them from the school newspaper. The student newspaper staff filed a suit. The U.S. Supreme Court finally ruled that school administrators can exercise considerable control over student expression that is not consistent with the basic educational mission of the school. Although *Hazelwood* involved only the conflict over the contents of a student newspaper, the Court's decision had implications for censorship of school plays, library holdings, and classroom instruction. In 1989, when the school board of Columbia County, Florida, locked up a state-approved literature textbook that contained selections by Aristophanes and Chaucer, some parents filed a suit. The federal judge in this case, *Virgil v. School Board of Columbia County*, based her decision on *Hazelwood* and ruled in favor of the school board (Whitson, 1993).

Censorship Today

Judging from the lists of challenged and banned books, it appears that many people believe they have the right, even the obligation, to define the literary canon. Young adult literature is well represented on the lists of challenged materials, with problem novels making a strong showing (LeMieux, 1998). While this censorship may be carried out by individuals, many times an organized group is behind the challenge. Expanding Your Knowledge with the Internet provides a list of some of these groups with URLs.

Motives for Censorship

According to Konvitz (2003), censors identify materials they believe are immoral or obscene, heretical or blasphemous, seditious or treasonable, or injurious to national security. While many factors motivate individuals to become censors, the following few reasons seem to occur most frequently.

Family Values. Most frequently, challenges to materials in schools are brought by parents, perhaps because they feel helpless sending their children into a world that seems increasingly plagued with hazards over which they have no control (Kravitz, 2002). They may also fear books and other materials that might encourage adolescents to think on their own or that contain ideas or perspectives that conflict with their own values or moral views. Often, a problem arises when parents want to influence not only what their children read, but what everyone in the school may read.

Political Views. Except for sexual issues and religion, few topics inflame people more than politics. While most people agree that young adults should learn about diverse political philosophies, there are problems with actually implementing this

EXPANDING YOUR KNOWLEDGE WITH THE INTERNET

These are a few of the organizations or pressure groups that have been associated with censorship or intellectual freedom challenges.

American Family Association
www.afa.net/

Christian Coalition
www.cc.org/

Citizens for Community Values
www.cc.org/

Citizens for Excellence in Education
www.nace-cee.org/

Citizens United for Responsible Education
www.curewashington.org/

Concerned Women for America
www.curewashington.org/

Eagle Forum
www.eagleforum.org/

Educational Research Analysts (Mel and Norma Gabler)
www.textbookreviews.org/

Family Friendly Libraries
www.textbookreviews.org/

Family Research Council
www.textbookreviews.org/

Focus on the Family
www.focusonthefamily.com/

Heritage Foundation
www.focusonthefamily.com/

John Birch Society
www.jbs.org/

Morality in Media
www.moralityinmedia.org/

National Coalition for the Protection of Children and Families
www.nationalcoalition.org/

Parents Against Bad Books in Schools
www.pabbis.com/

People of America Responding to Educational Needs of Today's Society—Save our Schools
www.soschools.org/

idea. Conservatives have charged that history and social studies textbooks often criticize America. Liberals may raise concerns about political correctness and contend that the presentation of events has been oversimplified (Reichman, 1993).

Religion. Although challenges by religious groups have always occurred, the majority of America's broad-based religious groups do not favor censoring (Kravitz, 2002). However, some individuals and organizations have questioned the portrayal of the role of women and of moral issues, religious themes, sexual issues, and witchcraft in school materials. In addition, some teachers face the dilemma of teaching evolution, creationism, or some combination of both. Whatever decision they make is virtually certain to draw the ire of some irate parent or community member, with advocates of creationism usually seeking to add materials to rather than delete them from the school curriculum (Reichman, 1993).

Minority Rights. During the 1980s and 1990s, a wide range of groups and individuals, including peoples of color, women, the elderly, homosexuals, and the disabled, challenged school materials on the basis of a concept that became known as political correctness (Kravitz, 2002). They complained about matters ranging from the words used to describe racial, ethnic, and minority groups to the manner in which members of minority groups were represented (i.e., physical characteristics, work ethic, social habits, abilities) in books and other materials. While educators must be concerned when an author stereotypes characters solely on the basis of cultural background, gender, sexual orientation, or other distinguishing characteristics, it is also realistic to assume that the whole range of individuals in society, with their flaws as well as their strengths, will be represented in literature.

The Primary Targets of Censorship

Table 4–1 (page 87) shows some of the primary reasons why individuals and groups attempt to censor materials. In the following section, we will look at a few of these reasons in more detail. Of course, some of the categories overlap, and some of the books mentioned in one category have been challenged in other categories as well.

Profanity/Curses/Offensive Language. Writers usually do not advocate the use of "bad language" (Kravitz, 2002, p. 82) when they use it in their novels. However, they do use language to portray life as it really is and to allow characters to speak as they would in their everyday lives (Kravitz, 2002). We remember the instance of a high school library media specialist who was approached by a parent demanding that she remove a book from the library that depicted the U.S. Marines landing on the beaches of a Pacific Island during World War II. Under heavy enemy fire, the Marines' language included a few instances of mild profanity, which the parent did not believe belonged in a school library media center. The LMS simply explained the benefits and "worth" of the book in regard to the curriculum, and asked the parent to consider the realism of the book and how mild the few expletives were in contrast to what the Marines might actually have been saying. As the LMS recounted to us: "I just asked him if he thought it would be realistic for the Marines to be saying 'Gee whiz, they're shooting at us.'" After considering the issue, the parent agreed that the book should remain in the school library.

A number of books have recently been challenged because of language that ranges from traditional curses (i.e., *damn, hell, bitch*) to taking the Lord's name in vain (Curry, 2001). You have already read about challenges to language in Walter Dean Myers's *Fallen Angels* (1988) and Jane Leslie Conly's *Crazy Lady* (1993). In addition, Katherine Paterson's *The Great Gilly Hopkins* (1978), Harry Mazer's *Last Mission* (1979), Robert Cormier's *The Chocolate War* (1974), Christopher Collier and James Lincoln Collier's *My Brother Sam Is Dead* (1974), Judy Blume's *Here's to You, Rachel Robinson* (1993), Chris Lynch's *Iceman* (1994) and *Shadow Boxer* (1993), and Johanna Reiss's *The Upstairs Room* (1972) have all been challenged because of profanity or foul language.

Some works contain other kinds of language that challengers find offensive. Sometimes authors use street language or dialects that differ from standard English. For example, in *A Hero Ain't Nothing but a Sandwich* (1973), Alice Childress uses street language to show the life of a young boy who is drawn into drug use.

In other instances, the challenges center on words that were once used in our culture but are no longer acceptable. These words are sometimes used in a contemporary but derogative sense and sometimes appear in historical fiction or books that were written years ago when the use of these words was accepted. The paradox is that in the historical books, the words are historically accurate; and although they are painful to some people, to change them would be to attempt to change history. A classic example is the use of racial slurs in *The Adventures of Huckleberry Finn*, which was written by Mark Twain in 1885. Some people object to the use of the word *squaw* in Sally Keehn's historical fiction book *I Am Regina* (1991), and the word *nigger* in several historical fiction titles including James Lincoln Collier and Christopher Collier's *Jump to Freedom* (1981) and *War Comes to Willy Freeman* (1983), Paula Fox's *Slave Dancer* (1973), and William H. Armstrong's *Sounder* (1969).

Heterosexually Explicit Materials.   The inclusion of sexual situations and topics in books for adolescent readers has always been a target for censors, despite the so-called sexual revolution of the 1960s and the inclusion of more graphic sexual scenes in movies and on television. Some censors either think that reading about sex in fiction or nonfiction will make young people more likely to engage in sexual experimentation or that all sexual matters and issues are inappropriate for young people.

One of the pioneers of young adult literature was Judy Blume. While her books are very popular with adolescents, they are often challenged because they explore the sexual feelings of young people and answer many adolescents' questions about the changes that are happening to their bodies and in their lives. As recently as 2004, her coming-of-age novel *Deenie* (1973) was challenged by the parent of a 7th-grade student in the Hernando County Schools in Florida. The book was retained but can be read only by students with "written parental permission" ("Deenie defeats detractors—sort of," 2004, p. 15).

A series of books that is often among the top challenged books is the Alice series by Phyllis Reynolds Naylor. In 2003, it even replaced the Harry Potter series as the most challenged ("Alice series tops most-challenged list," 2004). Complaints have ranged from "too explicit—graphic—sarcastic—mentions underwear . . . inappropriate for any age group" to "preachy—didactic—contrived" (Bucher & Manning, 2002, p. 10). Other critics called the series "full of vitality—readable—laughable . . . sensitive—true to life . . . age appropriate—cheerful, upbeat writing with a positive emphasis" (p. 10). As Naylor has said, "in my Alice series . . . I promised myself that I would write about everything that a girl would wonder about, and I am sticking to that promise. . . . I refuse to back away just because it's controversial" (West, 1997, p. 181).

In nonfiction, Robie Harris in *It's Perfectly Normal* (1994) assures adolescents that it is normal to have a wide variety of thoughts and feelings about sex and physical changes. In addition to topics such as male and female anatomy, physical changes at puberty, and fertilization, the book includes discussions of gay and lesbian relationships, masturbation, and abortion (Bayne, 2002). Harris tries to make the point that sexual subject matter is appropriate for developing readers and it is perfectly normal for them to be interested. Still, the book has been the subject of considerable criticism and censorship efforts.

A number of other well-known young adult books have been challenged because of sexually explicit material or references to sexual activity that censors deem immoral or illegal. These range from Chris Crutcher's *Chinese Handcuffs* (1989) and Alane Ferguson's *Show Me the Evidence* (1989) to Hadley Irwin's *Abby, My Love* (1985), Louise Rennison's *Knocked Out by My Nunga-Nungas* (2002), and several of Norma Klein's works, such as *Mom, the Wolfman, and Me* (1972) and *That's My Baby* (1988).

Homosexual Themes. Censors sometimes condemn books about sexual orientation as immoral and perhaps even damaging to young adult readers. However, sexual orientation is a significant issue in contemporary American life (Broz, 2002). Whether responding to external pressures or on their own initiative, many educators have promoted tolerance of gays and lesbians and opposed discrimination. Trying to recognize and accommodate the needs of all students, these educators have attempted to provide materials that include characters with diverse sexual orientations. According to Patti Capel Swartz (2003), young adult literature provides an awareness of the issues surrounding sexual orientation and can be used to counter homophobia in the schools.

However, some people have a difficult time dealing with gay and lesbian issues being discussed in young adult books or middle and high school classrooms. As a result, while there has been a growth of gay-oriented literature for adolescents, there has been a corresponding increase in the challenges to this material in some school districts (Reichman, 1993).

When *Annie on My Mind* (Garden, 1982), an ALA "Best of the Best Books for Young Adults" and one of the "most influential books of the twentieth century" (Jenkins, 2003, p. 50), was provided to 42 schools in and around Kansas City by an organization called Project 21 to promote accurate, positive materials about gays and lesbians in libraries and curricula, a number of groups and individuals raised their voices in protest. As a result, the school districts removed copies of the book. In response to that move, other individuals protested to advocate retaining the book. When the controversy ended up in court, the judge ruled that *Annie on My Mind* had been unconstitutionally removed from the shelves (Garden, 1996). Speaking about her book, author Nancy Garden noted:

> "It's . . . important to prepare teens for the world they'll meet as adults, and to help them understand it and form their own reactions to it. One can't do that by keeping the world from them. Far better for them to encounter difficult subjects when they still have adults—like their parents and teachers and librarians—to talk to than to keep them so sheltered that they know nothing of the world until they're thrust into it as independent kids in their 20s." (quoted in Jenkins, 2003, p. 50)

While other books may not have achieved the notoriety of *Annie on My Mind* (Garden, 1982), several have been challenged because of homosexual themes. *Am I Blue: Coming Out from the Silence* (1994), edited by Marion Dane Bauer, is notable as the first collection of young adult stories to address gay and lesbian themes. Censors complained that the book was inappropriate for middle school students, that it emphasized suicide, confused adolescents about sexuality, and promoted the gay and

4-2 ●●●● CONNECTING ADOLESCENTS AND THEIR LITERATURE

Discussions of sexual orientation are disconcerting to some readers. However, educators need to challenge heterosexual readers to read literature that realistically portrays lives that differ from their own and to understand the challenges faced by gay and lesbian young adults. In addition, gay and lesbian readers need books that validate the struggles they may face.

To approach this issue, you can ask adolescent students to read a book that focuses on homosexuality such as Frank Mosca's *All American Boys* (1983), Bette Greene's *The Drowning of Stephan Jones* (1991), or Nancy Garden's *Annie on My Mind* (1982). Then you can ask the students to write essays or prepare PowerPoint presentations focuses on:

- A summary of the book
- Challenges the characters face because of their sexual orientation
- Similarities and dissimilarities between gay or lesbian lifestyles and heterosexual ones
- Ways American society can change such that heterosexuals will be more tolerant of gays and lesbians (and vice versa); or how any group can become more tolerant of a group that is different from them

lesbian agenda (Broz, 2002). When Francesca Lia Block told the story of a gay man in *Baby Be-Bop* (1995), her work was censored as well. In 2002, *Achingly Alice* (Naylor, 1998) was banned from a Missouri school library for promoting homosexuality (Doyle, 2003). Other books that have undergone censorship challenges for homosexual themes include Frank Mosca's *All American Boys* (1983), Susan and Daniel Cohen's *When Someone You Know Is Gay* (1989), and Ann Heron's *Two Teenagers in Twenty* (1994). Connecting Adolescents and Their Literature 4–2 looks at a plan for creating reading and learning experiences around these books.

Witchcraft/Occult/Religion. Sometimes the depiction of witchcraft, extrasensory perception, the occult, paranormal phenomena, or even diverse religions in young adult literature prompts complaints and threats of censorship. While Roald Dahl's popular novel *The Witches* (1983) has been a perennial target (Bergson-Shilcock, 2002), more recently J. K. Rowling's Harry Potter series (e.g., 1998, 1999) has gained equal or greater notoriety for its wizardry theme. Other books that censors target for their inclusion of witchcraft include Bruce Colville's *The Dragonslayers* (1994), Mary Downing Hahn's *Wait Till Helen Comes* (1986), and Alvin Schwartz's *Scary Stories 3* (1991), which includes scary stories, songs, poems, and rhymes that appeal to a wide range of ages, interests, and tastes (Majak, 2002). Elizabeth George Speare's Newbery Medal–winning classic *The Witch of Blackbird Pond* (1958) was challenged in a Connecticut middle school in 2002 (Doyle, 2003). Complaints have also been lodged against Shakespeare's *Macbeth* because of its portrayal of witches (Morris & Ellis, 1996).

Concerned about the treatment of Christianity in young adult literature and the representation of biblical teachings and religious beliefs, some individuals and groups have questioned the inclusion of books such as Doerkson's *Jazzy* (1981) and Godard and Ribera's *The Ultimate Alchemist* (1983) in schools. Other challenges have centered on Judy Blume's *Are You There God, It's Me, Margaret* (1970) and the positive portrayal of a non-Christian religion such as Taoism in Laurence Yep's *Dragonwings* (1975).

Violence/Horror. Unfortunately, violence is a part of the American society; therefore, it has become an integral part of young adult literature. Some contend that even when violence is absent from the lives of adolescents, books and the media make it part of the adolescent experience (Isaacs, 2003). As a result, numerous censorship complaints have been filed, either to protect young adults or to prevent them from engaging in similar violent acts.

Johnston (2002) has told of Lois Duncan's *Killing Mr. Griffin* (1978), in which students plot to frighten and ridicule their English teacher. What censors fail to realize is that Duncan was attempting to show how a teacher challenges students to do their best rather than live wasted lives. Not really focusing on violence, the book deals with peer pressure, failures of communication, and inabilities to recognize potential problems among students.

Many other books have been condemned for violence. Robert Newton Peck's *A Day No Pigs Would Die* (1978), set on a 1920s Vermont farm, has been attacked because of its portrayals of violence, hatred, and animal cruelty (Curry, 2001). Caroline Cooney's *The Terrorist* (1997) has a theme of violence that censors thought was unsuitable for young adults. *Fallen Angels* (Myers, 1988) has been criticized for the violence in its portrayal of the Vietnam War; while *My Brother Sam Is Dead* (Collier & Collier, 1974), applauded for its high literary quality and strong character development, has been challenged for its depiction of the American Revolution (Short, 2002). Even *The Devil's Arithmetic* (1988), Jane Yolen's story of the Holocaust, has been challenged for being too violent (Curry, 2001).

Racism/Sexism. Many adults have concerns about the depiction of racial and ethnic minorities and about the treatment of women in young adult literature. While *The Little Engine That Could* was challenged in California because the engine was portrayed as a male (National Coalition Against Censorship, 2003), most censorship challenges have dealt with charges of racism rather than sexism (Curry, 2001). While many people realize how long-held stereotypes and prejudice have affected various cultural and racial groups, others find fault with some literature on the basis of bad language, suggestive situations, questionable literary merit, and ungrammatical English (*NCTE Guideline: The Student's Right to Read*, 2003).

As we have said, a debate rages over the use of specific words that, while no longer accepted, were used in the past. Other censorship challenges have focused not on individual words but on the depiction of minority groups in general. For example, people have objected to Mildred Taylor's *Roll of Thunder, Hear My Cry* (1976) for both antiwhite racial bias and antiblack racial bias (Curry, 2001). The textbook, *The History of the American Nation* was called biased and misleading in its presentation of minority groups, women, the civil rights movement, and the Vietnam War (Reichman, 1993). Other books that have been challenged for such reasons include Theodore Taylor's *The Cay* (1969), Laurence Yep's *Dragonwings* (1975), and Bette Greene's *Summer of My German Soldier* (1973).

Substance Use and Abuse. Censors often complain about descriptions of substance abuse in young adult literature. Perhaps they believe adolescents will be tempted or influenced to experiment with drugs. Many books, however, present a message that young people have the power to organize and be heard and can make changes in their schools, their communities, and their lives (Morgan, 2002). Challenged books in this category include Luis Rodriguez's *Always Running* (1993), Beatrice Sparks's (formerly listed as Anonymous) *Go Ask Alice* (1971), Norman Klein's *Learning How to Fall* (1989), Robert Cormier's *We All Fall Down* (1991), and Todd Strasser's *Angel Dust Blues* (1979). In books like *Road to Nowhere* (1993) and *Die Softly* (1991), Christopher Pike has upset censors because of three subjects: sex, horror, and drug use. Some censors have even attacked M. E. Kerr's *Dinky Hocker Shoots Smack* (1972) on the sole basis of the title and not the content of the book itself.

Scientific and "Historical" Theories. Scientific and historical theories have long been the focus of controversy in schools, with the teaching of evolution being a frequent target. According to a survey conducted by the National Science Foundation, a substantial majority of U.S. citizens think that evolution should be taught and that it is not incompatible with a belief in God (Crabcraft, 2004).

This has not, however, prevented challenges in a number of states. Georgia's proposed biology program is drawing fire from science educators because it omits the word *evolution* in what critics say is a nod to proponents of creationism ("GA teachers cry foul," 2004). Other topics excluded are human origins, the big bang theory, human reproduction, and much of plate tectonics ("GA teachers cry foul," 2004). In Texas, the state Board of Education rejected arguments by religious right groups and voted 11–4 to approve a series of biology textbooks with favorable treatment of evolution ("Texas ed. board rejects religious right," 2003). The Worland, Wyoming, school board hoped to adopt a new policy that critics say waters down the teaching of evolution. While the New Mexico Board of Education voted unanimously to retain science standards that emphasize evolution and do not mention creationism, North Carolina's Board of Education is reviewing state standards, and education officials in one community are lobbying to include creationism ("New Mexico rejects effort to add creationism," 2003).

Other Objections. The previous categories outline the most frequently given reasons for challenging books in schools. There are, however, other reasons. For example, people in Oregon raised objections to *Eli's Songs* (Killingsworth, 1991) because it includes instances of "logger bashing" (Reichman, 1993, p. 35) and because male characters drink (Curry, 2001). Other challenges have occurred over Phyllis Reynolds Naylor's *Outrageously Alice* (1997) (fosters rebellion), Astrid Lindgren's *The Brother's Lionheart* (1975) (too depressing), and Fran Arrick's *Tunnel Vision* (1980) (too depressing).

Lois Lowry's *The Giver* (1993), which presents a futuristic society, is a work of social criticism that speaks out against the pressures put upon young people to conform, anti-intellectualism, and the strong tendency of mass communication toward making everyone look and act alike (Avi, 2002). In this multiple award–winning book, twins are illegal and a twin baby boy is "released" from life with a fatal injection. Because of this and other subject matter, including black magic and euthanasia (Curry, 2001), Lowry's book was no. 11 on ALA's list of most challenged books of the 1990s, with challenges in at least five states since 1999 ("Lowry novel frequent censorship target," 2001).

Supporting Intellectual Freedom when Materials are Challenged

While it is important to support intellectual freedom on a daily basis, educators must also know what to do if there is a challenge to materials in a school or library. Teachers and school library media specialists must prepare themselves in advance by knowing who to turn to if a challenge arises, what documents support intellectual freedom, and what procedures to follow to deal with the challenge.

Professional Organizations That Support Intellectual Freedom

Hopkins (2003) noted that it is important for educators to seek support from outside the school when faced with a censorship challenge, because such support is a "primary factor in the retention of challenged materials" (p. 32). In spite of this, in a national survey, only 50% of the library media specialists involved in a censorship challenge sought help from others at their school, and only 22% looked outside the school for assistance. Those who received support during a challenge reported that they appreciated getting "information about the challenged materials, including reviews, awards, and distinctions" (p. 34).

A number of organizations work to address censorship issues and provide assistance in varying degrees. Expanding Your Knowledge with the Internet on page 110 provides a selected list of some of these organizations. Supplementing these national organizations, state and local groups, such as state affiliates of the ALA and AASL, can also provide help when there is a censorship challenge.

Documents That Support Intellectual Freedom

In addition to providing support, some organizations have produced well-thought-out documents that promote intellectual freedom and provide support during a censorship challenge. These resources vary from position papers and sample selection documents to resolutions and forms (e.g., book rationale forms) for protection against censors. Expanding Your Knowledge with the Internet on page 111 provides links to some of these documents.

Dealing with a Censorship Challenge

The benefits of intellectual freedom are great for both educators and students. However, the realities of promoting intellectual freedom sometimes lead to difficulties. For example, although the literature program at Mowat Middle School in Lynn Haven, Florida, was recognized as a Center of Excellence in English language arts, the superintendent wanted to ban 64 books, including Shakespeare's *Twelfth Night*. Because of their support of intellectual freedom, two teachers at the school received national awards, including the PEN/Newman's Own First Amendment Award; however, one of these teachers transferred to another school, and the other resigned (Tomasino, Zarnowski, & Backner, 2003).

Developing a Proactive Position. To cope with censorship challenges, educators must develop a positive and objective written plan before a challenge occurs. This plan should defend young adults' right to read literature of their choice, provide

EXPANDING YOUR KNOWLEDGE WITH THE INTERNET

The following organizations support intellectual freedom.

Alliance for Intellectual Freedom in Education
www.mainstream.com/nhpolitics/thinker.html

American Booksellers Foundation for Free Expression
www.abffe.org/

American Civil Liberties Union
www.aclu.org/freespeech/censorship/index.html

American Library Association, Office for Intellectual Freedom
www.ala.org/alaorg/oif/

Association of American Publishers, Freedom to Read Committee
www.publishers.org/main/FreedomToRead/freeAbout_01.htm

Authors Supporting Intellectual Freedom (AS IF!)
http://asifnews.blogspot.com/

Comic Book Legal Defense Fund
www.cbldf.org/

Directors Guild of America
www.dga.org

Electronic Frontier Foundation
www.eff.org/Censorship/

Freedom Forum
www.freedomforum.org/

Freedom to Read, Canada
www.freedomtoread.ca/default.asp

Freedom to Read Foundation
www.ala.org/ala/ourassociation/othergroups/ftrf/freedomreadfoundation.cfm

KidSPEAK: Where Kids Speak Up for Free Speech
www.kidspeakonline.org

National Coalition Against Censorship
www.ncac.org/

National Council of Teachers of English, Anti-Censorship Center
www.ncte.org/about/issues/censorship

People for the American Way
www.pfaw.org/pfaw/general/

Thomas Jefferson Center for the Protection of Free Expression
www.tjcenter.org/

guidelines for the selection of materials for classrooms and the school library media center, identify local selection criteria, include rationales for students reading young adult literature, contain procedures to educate school faculty and administration about intellectual freedom and dealing with complaints, and include guidelines for teaching controversial material. The plan should also establish a clearly defined strategy for dealing with challenges to library or classroom materials (i.e., to whom should the complainant be referred), provide a request-for-reconsideration form that the complainant can complete (all complaints should be filed in writing and signed by the individual or group making the complaint; Virginia Library Association, 1997), and outline the exact procedures to be followed if a complaint is made, including the makeup of any and all review committees that will hear the complaint. Finally, the plan should also detail any appeal process and the responsibilities of all teachers, library media specialists, staff, and administrators, and should encourage teachers to prepare written rationales for materials that might be challenged.

After the plan is approved by the central administration of the school district and the school board, all personnel should strictly adhere to the policies and fol-

EXPANDING YOUR KNOWLEDGE WITH THE INTERNET

The following organizations provide documents that support intellectual freedom.

AMERICAN LIBRARY ASSOCIATION
www.ala.org

Access to Electronic Information, Services and Networks
www.ala.org/ala/oif/statementspols/statementsif/ interpretations/accesselectronic.htm

Access to Resources and Services in the School Library Media Program
www.ala.org/ala/oif/statementspols/statementsif/ interpretations/accessresources.htm

Free Access to Libraries for Minors
www.ala.org/ala/oif/statementspols/statementsif/ interpretations/freeaccesslibraries.htm

Freedom to Read Statement
www.ala.org/ala/oif/statementspols/ftrstatement/ freedomreadstatement.htm

Freedom to View Statement
www.ala.org/ala/oif/statementspols/ftvstatement/ freedomviewstatement.cfm

Intellectual Freedom for Young People
www.ala.org/ala/oif/foryoungpeople/ youngpeople.cfm

Intellectual Freedom for Young People—Schools
www.ala.org/ala/oif/foryoungpeople/moreschool/ school.cfm

Library Bill of Rights
www.ala.org/ala/oif/statementspols/statementsif/ librarybillrights.htm

Restricted Access to Library Materials
www.ala.org/ala/oif/statementspols/statementsif/ interpretations/restrictedaccess.htm

Statement on Library Use of Filtering Software
www.ala.org/ala/oif/statementspols/ifresolutions/ statementlibrary.htm

INTERNATIONAL READING ASSOCIATION
www.reading.org

On Opposing Abridgment or Adaptation as a Form of Censorship
www.reading.org/downloads/resolutions/ resolution97_abridgment_adaptation.pdf

NATIONAL COALITION AGAINST CENSORSHIP
www.ncac.org

Censorship in Schools
www.ncac.org/education/schools/

NATIONAL COUNCIL OF TEACHERS OF ENGLISH
www.ncte.org

Students' Right to Read (with sample Reconsideration of Materials Form at the end)
www.ncte.org/about/over/positions/category/cens/ 107616.htm

Support for the Learning and Teaching of English (SLATE), Anti-Censorship Center
www.ncte.org/about/issues/censorship

Rationales for Teaching Challenged Books
www.ncte.org/about/issues/censorship/five/ 108603.htm

Guidelines for Dealing with Censorship of Nonprint and Multimedia Materials
www.ncte.org/about/over/positions/category/cens/ 107611.htm

low the procedures outlined in the plan. Collaborating with Other Professionals 4–2 provides suggestions for involving the community in these proactive efforts.

Another proactive strategy is for all educators to know about the school and the community in which it is located. Sipe (1999) suggests that educators learn the answers to questions such as the following:

COLLABORATING WITH OTHER PROFESSIONALS

Simmons and Dresang (2001) suggest creating an "open, exploratory environment" (p. 6) in the school by involving school library media specialists, teachers, parents, students, and community members in an open dialogue before there are any censorship challenges. They suggest:

- Creating a citizen's panel to discuss broad censorship issues
- Building faculty consensus in the school
- Meeting with parent and community groups for discussions of books that might be used in the curriculum
- Preparing outreach statements that explain the selection criteria, the curricular goals, and the rationales for using certain materials

In addition, Sadler (1995) suggests:

- Reading and discussing the Library Bill of Rights with students and asking them if they can think of situations in which these rights may have been violated
- Having students prepare presentations about censorship or censored books

Finally, educators can work with the local public library to:

- Celebrate Banned Books Week
- Encourage community discussions of these and other challenged materials
- Keep track of legislation pertaining to intellectual freedom and First Amendment rights (Virginia Library Association, 1997)

- How well does your school communicate with parents and community members?
- Do parents and community members feel a connection to the school and to the decision-making process?
- Do the school and district have clear, current, appropriate policies and procedures for selecting materials? What are they?
- Does the school have a policy on academic freedom and actively support it (Sipe, 1999)?

Preparing Rationales for Frequently Challenged Materials. When teachers and library media specialists are considering purchasing or using books that have been censored in other places, it may be beneficial to prepare a rationale for the book. This procedure will help the educator focus on such things as who will be the target audience for the book, how the book will be used, why the book is appropriate for the intended audience, how the book supports the lesson objectives or the curriculum of the school, and what the reviewers have said about the book. The rationale should also include an examination of the book in light of the selection criteria of the school district. While individual school districts can develop their own forms for the rationale, the NCTE has an excellent discussion of how to write a rationale on their website. In addition, Table 4–3 provides an example. McClain, Goss, and Moe (1996) suggest that a variation of the rationale can provide the basis for a permission form that teachers can use to obtain approval from a parent or guardian before students read or view controversial materials.

A number of resources to assist teachers contain rationales. Barlow (2002) recommends *Rationales for Teaching Young Adult Literature* (Reid & Neufield, 1999), which contains rationales for 22 books. Karolides's (2002) *Censored Books II: Critical Viewpoints* is a collection of essays written in support of a number of *controversial* titles, including *Killing*

TABLE 4-3   Rationale for the Purchase/Use of Materials

Title of the Material: _____

Copyright Year: _____   Type of Material: _____

Grade(s): _____   Curriculum Area: _____

Intended Audience: _____   LMS/Teacher: _____

Provide a summary of the item:

How will this item be used in the library or classroom?

_____ Placed in general circulation in the Library Media Center

_____ Placed in restricted circulation in the Library Media Center

_____ Placed in an individual classroom collection

_____ Included in a booklist of recommended readings

_____ Included in a booklist of required readings

_____ Read/viewed/heard by an entire grade level

_____ Read/viewed/heard by one/several classes

_____ Read/viewed/heard by small groups of students

_____ Read/viewed/heard by individual students on educator's recommendation

What are the reasons for selecting this material?

Have you read/seen/heard this item in its entirety? If not, why not?

What reviews (if any) has this material received? Where did the reviews appear? (Note that Publisher's catalogs are not review sources.)

What specific curricular objectives is this material designed to meet?

Does this material support the state standards of learning? If so, how?

What are the expected changes in students' skills, attitudes, and/or behaviors as the result of the use of this material?

What other materials could be used to meet the same objectives in case of parental concerns?

What objections might be raised to the purchase or use of this material? How would you counter them?

Mr. Griffin (Duncan, 1978), *Fallen Angels* (Myers, 1988), and *The Drowning of Stephan Jones* (Greene, 1991). In *Teaching Banned Books: 12 Guides for Young Readers,* Scales (2001) includes a number of books read by adolescents, including *My Brother Sam Is Dead* (Collier & Collier, 1974) and *Roll of Thunder, Hear My Cry* (Taylor, 1976).

EXPANDING YOUR KNOWLEDGE WITH THE INTERNET

A number of Internet sites provide sample intellectual freedom handbooks and resources. Here are a few of them.

INTELLECTUAL FREEDOM HANDBOOKS

Intellectual Freedom Toolkit
www.ala.org/ala/oif/iftoolkits/intellectual.htm

University of Delaware Library—Intellectual Freedom
www.lib.udel.edu/ud/freedom/

Texas Library Association Intellectual Freedom Handbook
www.txla.org/pubs/ifhbk.html

Virginia Library Association Intellectual Freedom Manual
www.vla.org/ifc/toc.htm

Northeast Iowa Library Service Area—Model Request for Reconsideration of Materials policy
www.neilsa.org/consulting/XYZ/reconsider.html

School Library.Org—Sample reconsideration-of-materials form
www.schoolibrary.org/pub/freedom/reconsideration_form.pdf

INTELLECTUAL FREEDOM AWARDS

NCTE SLATE Intellectual Freedom Awards
www.ncte.org/about/issues/slate/about/109295.htm

American Library Association—Intellectual Freedom Awards
www.ala.org/ala/oif/oifprograms/ifawards/intellectual.cfm

Responding to a Challenge. No matter how prepared you think you are, responding to an actual censorship challenge can be difficult. It is important to be calm and objective (Virginia Library Association, 1997) and to deal professionally with the complainant.

- Listen carefully and courteously to the complaint.

- Attempt to resolve the complaint informally and/or to defuse the situation without making judgments or making promises about any actions other than the written school policy (i.e., providing a copy of the request-for-reconsideration form and/or the selection guidelines).

- Be prepared to refer the complaint to the next level of authority as outlined in the plan.

- Notify the appropriate administrators of the complaint and provide a summary of the discussion with the complainant. Do this even if it appears that the complaint has been resolved.

- If a formal written complaint is filed, follow the procedures outlined in the plan. For support, contact the organizations identified earlier in this chapter.

- Keep notes on the process and maintain a file of all correspondence.

- Continue the use or circulation of the material until the entire review process is completed.

- Conduct the review openly, and inform the community through local media or other communications.

- Once the complaint has been reviewed according to procedure, communicate the results of the reconsideration process to the complainant in writing, explaining both the reevaluation procedure and justification for the final decision (National Coalition Against Censorship, 2004; Virginia Library Association, 1995, 1997).

In Expanding Your Knowledge with the Internet, you will find the URLs for some sample policies. Also included are URLs to two major awards given to supporters of intellectual freedom.

Concluding Thoughts

Censors would like to control the minds of the young. They are fearful of the educational system because students who read learn to think. Thinkers learn to see. Those who see often question (Scales, 2001, p. 2).

Intellectual freedom should be at the forefront of all teachers' and library media specialists' concerns. Undoubtedly, individuals and groups will continue to file complaints about what young adults can read, view, and hear. Educators must also remain vigilant unless they, too, fall into the role of censor rather than selector of quality materials that meet the social, cognitive, and emotional needs of young adults. To avoid being caught off guard when censorship complaints arise, it is important for educators to have a deliberate and methodical plan for dealing with censorship. The plan should be based more on careful thought than emotional reactions. Only then will educators be able to explain a rationale for the use of specific materials and be able to convince censors of young adults' right to read, view, and listen. Censorship battles will continue as long as censors believe their opinions should provide the basis for what others read. All educators need to be prepared for those challenges and to support intellectual freedom in schools and libraries.

Young Adult Books

This section includes young adult titles mentioned in this chapter.

Angelou, M. (1969). *I know why the caged bird sings.* New York: Random House.

Armstrong, W. H. (1969). *Sounder.* New York: Harper & Row.

Arrick, F. (1980). *Tunnel vision.* Scarsdale, NY: Bradbury.

Bauer, M. D. (Ed.). (1994). *Am I blue: Coming out from the silence.* New York: HarperCollins.

Block, F. L. (1995). *Baby be-bop.* New York: HarperCollins.

Blume, J. (1970). *Are you there God, it's me, Margaret.* Scarsdale, NY: Bradbury.

Blume, J. (1971). *Then again, maybe I won't.* Scarsdale, NY: Bradbury.

Blume, J. (1973). *Deenie.* Scarsdale, NY: Bradbury.

Blume, J. (1974). *Blubber.* Scarsdale, NY: Bradbury.

Blume, J. (1993). *Here's to you, Rachel Robinson.* New York: Orchard Books.

Chbosky, S. (1999). *The perks of being a wall flower.* New York: Pocket Books.

Childress. A. (1973). *A hero ain't nothing but a sandwich.* New York: Avon.

Cohen, S., and Cohen, D. (1989). *When someone you know is gay.* New York: Evans.

Collier, J. L., and Collier, C. (1974). *My brother Sam is dead.* New York: Scholastic.

Collier, J. L., and Collier, C. (1981). *Jump to freedom.* New York: Delacorte.

Collier, J. L., and Collier, C. (1983). *War comes to Willy Freeman.* New York: Delacorte.

Colville, B. (1994). *The dragonslayers.* New York: Simon and Schuster.

Conly, J. L. (1993). *Crazy lady.* New York: HarperCollins.

Cooney, C. (1997). *The terrorist.* New York: Scholastic.

Cormier, R. (1974). *The chocolate war.* New York: Pantheon.

Cormier, R. (1977). *I am the cheese.* New York: Dell.

Cormier, R. (1991). *We all fall down.* New York: Delacorte.

Crutcher, C. (1989). *Chinese handcuffs.* New York: Greenwillow.

Dahl, R. (1964). *Charlie and the chocolate factory.* New York: Knopf.

Dahl, R. (1983). *The witches.* New York: Farrar, Straus and Giroux.

Doerkson, M. (1981). *Jazzy.* New York: Beaufort Books.

Duncan, L. (1978). *Killing Mr. Griffin.* New York: Little Brown.

Duncan, L. (1979). *Daughters of Eve.* New York: Little Brown.

Ferguson, A. (1989). *Show me the evidence.* New York: Bradbury.

Follett, K. (1989). *The pillars of the earth.* New York: Morrow.

Fox, P. (1973). *Slave dancer.* Scarsdale, NY: Bradbury.

Garden, N. (1982). *Annie on my mind.* New York: Farrar, Straus and Giroux.

Godard, C., and Ribera, R. (1983). *The ultimate alchemist.* New York: Dargaud International.

Greene, B. (1973). *Summer of my German soldier.* New York: Dial.

Greene, B. (1991). *The drowning of Stephan Jones.* New York: Bantam.

Hahn, M. D. (1986). *Wait till Helen comes.* New York: Harper Trophy.

Harris, R. (1994). *It's perfectly normal.* New York: Free Spirit.

Heron, A. (1994). *Two teenagers in twenty: Writings by gay and lesbian youth.* Boston: Alyson.

Irwin, H. (1985). *Abby, my love.* New York: Atheneum.

Keehn, S. (1991). *I am Regina.* New York: Philomel.

Kerr, M. E. (1972). *Dinky Hocker shoots smack.* New York: Harper & Row.

Killingsworth, M. (1991). *Eli's songs.* New York: Margaret K. McElderry Books.

Klein, N. (1972). *Mom, the wolfman, and me.* New York: Pantheon.

Klein, N. (1985). *Family secrets.* New York: Dial.

Klein, N. (1988). *That's my baby.* New York: Viking.

Klein, N. (1989). *Learning how to fall.* New York: Delacorte.

Lindgren, A. (1975). *The brother's lionheart.* New York: Viking.

Llywelyn, M. (1991). *Druids.* New York: Morrow.

Lowry, L. (1993). *The giver.* New York: Dell.

Lynch, C. (1993). *Shadow boxer.* New York: HarperCollins.

Lynch, C. (1994). *Iceman.* New York: HarperCollins.

Mazer, H. (1979). *Last mission.* New York: Delacorte.

Mazer, N. F. (1979). *Up in Seth's room.* New York: Delacorte.

Mosca, F. (1983). *All American boys.* Boston: Alyson.

Myers, W. D. (1988). *Fallen angels.* New York: Scholastic.

Naylor, P. R. (1997). *Outrageously Alice.* New York: Atheneum.

Naylor, P. R. (1998). *Achingly Alice.* New York: Atheneum.

Paterson, K. (1978). *The great Gilly Hopkins.* New York: Crowell.

Peck, R. N. (1978). *A day no pigs would die.* New York: Knopf.

Pike, C. (1991). *Die softly.* New York: Pocket Books.

Pike, C. (1993). *Road to nowhere.* New York: Simon Pulse.

Pullman, P. (1995). *The golden compass.* New York: Knopf.

Reiss, J. (1972). *The upstairs room.* New York: Crowell.

Rennison, L. (2002). *Knocked out by my nunga-nungas.* New York: HarperCollins.

Rodriguez, L. (1993). *Always running.* East Haven, CT: Curbstone Press.

Rowling, J. K. (1998). *Harry Potter and the sorcerer's stone.* New York: A. A. Levine Books.

Rowling, J. K. (1999). *Harry Potter and the chamber of secrets.* New York: A. A. Levine Books.

Schwartz, A. (1991). *Scary stories 3.* New York: HarperCollins.

Sparks, B. (Originally published as Anonymous). (1971). *Go ask Alice.* Upper Saddle River, NJ: Merrill/Prentice Hall.

Speare, E. G. (1958). *The witch of Blackbird Pond.* Boston: Houghton.

Strasser, T. (1979). *Angel dust blues.* New York: Coward, McCann & Geoghegan.

Taylor, M. (1976). *Roll of thunder, hear my cry.* New York: Dial.

Taylor, T. (1969). *The cay.* Garden City, NY: Doubleday.

Twain, M. (1876). *The adventures of Tom Sawyer.* Hartford, CT: American.

Twain, M. (1885). *Adventures of Huckleberry Finn.* New York: Webster.

Walker, A. (1982). *The color purple.* New York: Pocket.

Yep, L. (1975). *Dragonwings.* New York: HarperCollins.

Yolen, J. (1988). *The devil's arithmetic.* New York: Viking Kestrel.

Suggested Readings

Abilock, D. (2007). Four questions to ask yourself. *Knowledge Quest, 36*(2), 7–11.

Gallo, D. (2008). Censorship, clear thinking, and bold books for teens. *English Journal 97*(3), 114–117.

Juozaitis, V. (2007). Sex and censorship in school libraries. *School Libraries in Canada, 26*(2), 43–51. www.cla.ca/casl/slic/SLICVol26Issue2.pdf.

Kauer, S. M. (2008). A battle reconsidered: Second thoughts on book censorship and conservative parents. *English Journal 97*(3), 56–60.

Kelsey, M. (2007). Are we lucky for the First Amendment? A brief history of students' right to read. *Knowledge Quest, 36*(2), 26–29.

Lent, R. C. (2008). Facing the issues: Challenges, censorship and reflection through dialogue. *English Journal 97*(3), 61–66.

Martin, A. M. (2007). Preparing for a challenge. *Knowledge Quest 36*(2), 54–56.

Martinson, D. L. (2007). Responding intelligently when would-be censors charge: "That book can make them . . . !" *The Clearing House, 80*(4), 185–189.

References

All young adult literature referenced in this chapter is included in the Young Adult Books list and are not repeated in this list.

10 most-challenged books of 2000. (2001). *Teacher Librarian, 29*(2), 56.

Alice series tops most-challenged list. (2004). *American Libraries, 35*(4), 6.

American Heritage dictionary of the English language. (2000). Boston: Houghton Mifflin.

American Library Association. (2004a). The 100 most frequently challenged books of 1990–2000. Accessed April 2, 2004, from: www.ala.org/ala/oif/bannedbooksweek/bbwlinks/100mostfrequently.htm.

American Library Association. (2004b). Challenged and banned books. Accessed March 1, 2004, from: www.ala.org/ala/oif/bannedbooksweek/challengedbanned/challengedbanned.htm.

American Library Association. (2004c). Intellectual freedom and censorship: Q & A. Accessed February 17, 2004, from: www.ala.org/ala/oif/basics/intellectual.html.

American Library Association. (2008). Children's book on male penguins raising chick tops ALA's 2007 list of most challenged books. Accessed June 24, 2008, from: www.ala.org/ala/pressreleases2008/may2008/ penguin.cfm.

Anderson, J. (2002). When parents' rights are wrong. *School Library Journal, 48*(11), 43.

Avi. (2002). Lois Lowry's *The Giver*. In N. J. Karolides (Ed.), *Censored books II: Critical viewpoints, 1985–2000* (pp. 173–175). Lanham, MD: Scarecrow.

Barlow, D. (2002). Rationales for teaching young adult literature. *The Education Digest, 68*(2), 77–78.

Bayne, N. (2002). Sexual development: Letting kids know *It's Perfectly Normal*. In N. J. Karolides (Ed.), *Censored books II: Critical viewpoints, 1985–2000* (pp. 259–263). Lanham, MD: Scarecrow.

Bergson-Shilcock, A. (2002). The subversive quality of respect: In defense of *The Witches*. In N. J. Karolides (Ed.), *Censored books II: Critical viewpoints, 1985–2000* (pp. 446–451). Lanham, MD: Scarecrow.

Broz, W. J. (2002). Defending *I Am Blue. Journal of Adolescent & Adult Literacy, 45*(5), 340–350.

Bucher, K. T., and Manning, M. L. (2002). Growing up with the *Alice* series. In N. J. Karolides (Ed.), *Censored books II: Critical viewpoints, 1985–2000* (pp. 10–19). Lanham, MD: Scarecrow.

Censoring school literature in the cyber age. (2001). *The Education Digest, 66*(9), 32–36.

Coley, K. P. (2002). *School library media research, 5.* Accessed May 4, 2004, from: http://vnweb. hwwil sonweb.com.

Crabcraft, J. (2004). The new creationism and its threat to science literary and education. *BioScience, 54*(1), 3.

Cronon, B. (2003). Burned any good books lately? *Library Journal, 128*(3), 48.

Curry, A. (2001). Where is Judy Blume? Controversial fiction for older children and young adults. *Journal of Youth Services in Libraries, 14*(3), 28–37.

Deenie defeats detractors—sort of. (2004). *American Libraries, 35*(4), 15.

Doyle, R. P. (2003). Books challenged or banned in 2002–2003. *Illinois Library Association Reporter, 21*(2), insert 1–7.

Freedman, L., and Johnson, H. (2001). Who's protecting whom? I hadn't meant to tell you this, a case in point in confronting self-censorship in the choice of young adult literature. *Journal of Adolescent & Adult Literacy, 44*(4), 356–369.

GA teachers cry foul over omission of "evolution." (2004, February 2). *Education Daily*, 1–2.

Garden, N. (1996). Annie on trial: How it feels to be the author of a challenged book. *Voices of Youth Advocates, 19*(2), 79–84.

Glick, A. (2002). Parents wage anti-porn campaign against schools. *School Library Journal, 48*(1), 26.

Grant, C. (1995). Tales from a YA author: Slightly uneasy. *School Library Journal, 41* (October), 48–50.

Greenbaum, V. (1997). Censorship and the myth of appropriateness: Reflections on teaching reading in high school. *English Journal, 86*(2), 16–20.

Hopkins, D. M. (2003). The value of support during a library media challenge. *Knowledge Quest, 31*(4), 32–36.

Isaacs, K. T. (2003). Reality check. *School Library Journal, 49*(10), 50–51.

Ishizuka, K. (2001). Librarian in censorship case honored. *School Library Journal, 47*(10), 17.

Jenkins, C. A. (2003). Annie on her mind. *School Library Journal, 49*(6) 45–50.

Johnston, S. L. (2002). In defense of *Killing Mr. Griffin.* In N. J. Karolides (Ed.), *Censored books II: Critical viewpoints, 1985–2000* (pp. 285–289). Lanham, MD: Scarecrow.

Karolides, N. J. (Ed.). (2002). *Censored books II: Critical viewpoints, 1985–2000.* Lanham, MD: Scarecrow.

Kleinfield, N. R. (2002, June 2). The elderly man and the sea? Test sanitized literary texts. *New York Times.*

Konvitz, M. R. (2003). Censorship. Accessed December 15, 2003, from: http://encarta. msn.com/text.

Kravitz, N. (2002). *Censorship and the school library media center.* Westport, CT: Libraries Unlimited.

LeMieux, A. C. (1998). The problem novel in the adult age. *The Alan Review, 25*(3). Retrieved June 17, 2003, from: http://scholar.lib.vt.edu.journals/ ALAN/spring98.

Lowry novel frequent censorship target. (2001). *Newsletter on Intellectual Freedom, 50*(5).

Majak, C. G. (2002). Conquering our fears: Alvin Schwartz's *Scary Stories* series. In N. J. Karolides (Ed.), *Censored books II: Critical viewpoints,*

1985–2000 (pp. 366–371). Lanham, MD: Scarecrow.

Marshall, J. M. (2003). Critically thinking about Harry Potter: A framework for discussing controversial works in the English classroom. *The ALAN Review, 30*(2), 16–19.

McClain, R., Goss, C., and Moe, M. S. (1996). What if I get in trouble: Self-censorship and the classroom teacher. Presentation at the annual meeting of the National Council of Teachers of English, Chicago, November 23, 1996.

Morgan, P. E. (2002). *Always Running* from the real issues: Why kids *should* read about gangs and drugs. In N. J. Karolides (Ed.), *Censored books II: Critical viewpoints, 1985–2000* (pp. 28–38). Lanham, MD: Scarecrow.

Morris, D. M., and Ellis, L. (1996). Deep trouble in the heart of Texas. *Teaching and Learning Literature, 5*(5), 2–7.

National Coalition Against Censorship. (2003). Accountability in public schools. *Censorship News Online, 90.* Accessed April 30, 2004, from: www.ncac.org/cen_news/cn90publicschools.htm.

National Coalition Against Censorship. (2004). NCAC on the issues. Accessed February 23, 2004, from: www.ncac.org/issues/ ciparuling.html.

NCTE guideline: The students' right to read. (2003). Accessed December 15, 2003, from: www.ncte. org/print.

New Mexico rejects effort to add creationism to science standards. (2003). *Church and State, 56*(9), 16.

O'Neal, S. (1990). Leadership in the language arts: Controversial books in the classroom. *Language Arts, 67*, 771–775.

Reeder, C. (2002). In defense of *Crazy Lady.* In N. J. Karolides (Ed.), *Censored books II: Critical viewpoints, 1985–2000* (pp. 120–125). Lanham, MD: Scarecrow.

Reichman, H. (1993). *Censorship and selection: Issues and answers for schools.* Chicago and Arlington, VA: American Library Association and American Association of School Administrators.

Reid, L., and Neufield, J. H. (1999). *Rationales for teaching young adult literature.* Portland, ME: Calendar Islands.

Sadler, G. E. (1995). The killing of a great book: Censorship and the classics. *Teaching and Learning Literature, 5*(5), 31–37.

Scales, P. (2001). *Teaching banned books: 12 guides for young readers.* Chicago: American Library Association.

Short, K. G. (2002). *My Brother Sam Is Dead:* Embracing the contradictions and uncertainties of war. In N. J. Karolides (Ed.), *Censored books II: Critical viewpoints, 1985–2000* (pp. 305–310). Lanham, MD: Scarecrow.

Simmons, J. S., and Dresang, E. T. (2001). *School censorship in the 21st century: A guide for teachers and school library media specialists.* Newark, DE: International Reading Association.

Sipe, R. B. (1999). Don't confront the censor, prepare for them. *The Education Digest, 64*(6), 42–46.

Small, R. C. (2000). Censorship as we enter 2000, or the millennium, or just new year: A personal look at where we are. *Journal of Youth Services in Libraries, 13*(2), 19–23.

Suhor, C. (2003). Prior censorship—Flying under false colors. *The Council Chronicle, 13*(1), 7.

Sutton, R. (2007). Here's why it's censorship. *The Horn Book, 83*(3), 228.

Swartz, P. C. (2003). Bridging multicultural education: Bringing sexual orientation into the children's and young adult literature classrooms. *Radical Teacher, 66,* 11–16.

Texas ed. board rejects religious right attempt to alter science texts. (2003). *Church and State, 56*(11), 16.

Tomasino, K., Zarnowski, M., and Backner, A. (2003). Of professional interest: Controversial books support critical literacy. *Journal of Children's Literature, 29*(1), 93–97.

Virginia Library Association. (1995). *Resource guide to intellectual freedom.* Norfolk, VA: Author.

Virginia Library Association. (1997). *Intellectual freedom manual.* Norfolk, VA: Author.

West, M. I. (1997). Speaking of censorship: An interview with Phyllis Reynolds Naylor. *Journal of Youth Services in Libraries, 10*(2), 177–182.

Whitson, J. A. (1993). After Hazelwood: The role of school officials in conflicts over the curriculum. *The ALAN Review, 20*(2), 2–7.

Chapter 5

Exploring Contemporary Realistic Fiction

Newborn baby found abandoned in local park! Drunk driver indicted in death of 16-year-old! Teenage dad charged with physical abuse of infant son! Priest accused of sexually abusing a teenager! Violence continues in Iraq and Darfur! Racially motivated attack leaves teen in critical condition! These news headlines from a single Thursday in southeastern Virginia are typical of some of the more serious events, problems, and challenges that impact many young people. Had this Thursday fallen within the school year, there might also have been reports of violence or weapons in a school.

As young adults develop and mature, they must cope with a number of issues outside of those that make the news. They must learn to overcome their fears and accept responsibilities, and to deal with problems related to adoption, divorce, disabilities, disease, sexual relationships, changes within their families, relationships, sexual orientation, alienation, alcohol and drug abuse, and suicide. Contemporary realistic fiction, sometimes called the problem novel, uses plots, themes, settings, and characters to reflect the world as we know it and the problems and challenges many young people face daily. These books often address topics in an open and frank manner. While other books, such as adventure, mystery, humorous, and other types of novels are sometimes considered realistic fiction, we have chosen to discuss these types of novels in a separate chapter and will focus here on the contemporary problem novel.

Contemporary Realistic Fiction

Some critics believe that putting the word *realistic* with the word *fiction* presents a problem. As Jordan (1995) has said:

> We may judge fiction that is labeled "realistic" by how much the various elements that compose it seem to reflect the world as we know it, how closely they mimic reality, but such literature does not nor can it capture reality as we experience it; the term itself is an oxymoron. If a realistic novel were to mirror life truly, it would consist of a plethora of random characters, actions, and events from which no overall meaning would emerge. In a novel, an author takes great pains to choose and arrange events, characters, and actions in [such] a way that, ultimately, they have meaning. Hence, we classify such literature as fiction—made-up, arranged, and graced with meaning. (p. 16)

While Jordan makes some excellent points, realistic fiction does exist as a category of literature, even though it might not capture the essence of actual events, and might not mirror peoples' lives and society exactly as the participants perceive them. What realistic fiction does attempt is to make meaning out of a number of related events in ways that present young adult readers with new ideas, add new depths to their lives, and allow them to see themselves in new ways. By creating a story that is true-to-life, realistic fiction helps young adults explore socially significant themes and events, empathize with others, and examine complex human interactions (Tyson, 1999). Today, a goal of contemporary realistic fiction may be to make adolescents think about the "challenges of life in the multichanneled, disjunctive, digital world" (Aronson, 2001, p. 82). Either because of its realism (or in some cases, sensationalism) or because young adults can often relate to the events in the story and the characters' feelings and concerns, realistic fiction is a popular genre. In 2004, Judy Blume was the first author of young adult literature to receive the Medal for Distinguished Contribution to American Letters from the National Book Foundation on the basis of her books, which provide "help in navigating the travails of growing up and . . . characters with whom [young adults] can identify" (McDuffie, 2004).

A Brief Look at Contemporary Realistic Fiction's Predecessors

Experts differ on the exact beginnings of contemporary realistic fiction. Jordan (1995) proposed that it began with moral tales, including the didactic and popular English realistic moral tale *The Renowned History of Little Goody Two Shoes*, which was attributed to Oliver Goldsmith and published by John Newbery in 1765. However, most other histories of literature suggest that realistic fiction for children appeared in the latter half of the nineteenth century with the publication of books such as Mary Mapes Dodge's *Hans Brinker, or The Silver Skates* (1865), Louisa May Alcott's *Little Women* (1868), and Mark Twain's *Adventures of Tom Sawyer* (1876) and *Adventures of Huckleberry Finn* (1884).

TABLE 5-1 Novels with Nonlinear Formats

Multiple or alternating viewpoints or formats	Nontraditional formats	Free verse novels	Nonlinear organization	Multigenre novels
Paul Fleischman, *Seedfolks* (1997)	Walter Dean Myers, *Monster* (1999) (screenplay)	Mel Glenn, *Split Image* (2000)	Robert Cormier, *I Am the Cheese* (1977)	Avi, *Nothing but the Truth* (1991)
Cynthia Voigt, *Bad Girls* (1996)	Ellen Wittlinger, *Hard Love* (1999) (magazine format)	Virginia Euwer Wolff, *Make Lemonade* (1993) and *True Believer* (2001)	Louis Sachar, *Holes* (1998)	Sharon Draper, *Tears of a Tiger* (1994)
Virginia Walter and Katrina Roeckelein, *Making up Megaboy* (1998)	Paul Fleischman, *Seek* (2001) (radio script)	Sonya Sones, *What My Mother Doesn't Know* (2001)	Paul Fleischman, *Whirligig* (1998)	Jane Yolen and Bruce Coville, *Armageddon Summer* (1999)
Walter Dean Myer, *Street Love* (2006)	Linda Sue Parks, *Project Mulberry* (2005) (character/author interview)	Juan Felipe Herrera, *Cinnamon Girl: Letters Found Inside a Cereal Box* (2005)	Sharon Creech, *Walk Two Moons* (1994)	

By the 1960s and 1970s, when young adult literature was recognized as a separate category from children's literature, realistic young adult novels began to confront contemporary problems. Books included Robert Cormier's *The Chocolate War* (1974), S. E. Hinton's *The Outsiders* (1967), and the anonymously written *Go Ask Alice* (Anonymous, 1971). Often the main character spoke to the reader, saying "I am a teenager just like you and this is my problem." The idea was that if teenagers saw the fictitious person with a problem and the ability to solve it, they would then realize that they, too, could find solutions to their own problems. While these realistic books were often labeled "problem novels," Aronson (2001) called them first-person "self-help and coping" novels (p. 55). This is not to say that they were inferior. Indeed, Judy Blume, Robert Cormier, Paul Zindel, and other writers demonstrated that such novels could be quality literature. In many instances, the familiar "happily-ever-after" ending and "phony realism" (p. 81) were replaced by uncomfortable and sometimes disturbing endings that encouraged readers to look beneath the surface to tell "truths people don't want to see" (p. 82) and to provoke thought and contemplation rather than provide neat, compact answers (Aronson, 2001).

The 1980s brought a temporary turn away from this stark realism, as paperback romance series for young adults, including a number of "Sweet Valley" titles, grew in popularity. However, in spite of predictions that the Internet and MTV would eliminate young adult fiction publishing in the 1990s, the amount of realistic young adult literature not only grew but also included more multicultural viewpoints. Jacqueline Woodson, Kyoko Mori, Walter Dean Myers, Victor Martinez, Virginia Euwer Wolff, and other writers were new voices in young adult fiction.

According to Dresang (1999), books are breaking barriers that formerly "blocked off certain topics, certain kinds of characters, [and] certain styles of language" (p. 13). Authors are also using multiple perspectives and allowing previously subjugated voices to speak in their novels. The result of these changes is books that address previously forbidden subjects, examine overlooked settings and communities, and portray characters in new and more complex ways. Even violence in realistic fiction has changed to become "more central, bold and graphic" (p. 189). Today, young adult books address a wide range of themes, including religion, sexuality and sexual orientation, ethnicity, and concern for the future.

In addition to the traditional young adult first person narrative with a typical linear, sequential plot, more books are being published that use multiple or alternating viewpoints, formats, and genres. Writers are also changing the format of realistic fiction and creating novels in verse, plots with nonlinear organization and multigenre novels (Table 5–1 gives a list of titles). Realistic graphic novels (based on the traditional comic book format and discussed in Chapter 12) are also common. Connecting Adolescents and Their Literature 5–1 suggests an inexpensive way to add realistic fiction to classroom and library collections.

5-1 ●●●● CONNECTING ADOLESCENTS AND THEIR LITERATURE

Don't be afraid of paperbacks. Because of the flimsy nature of paperbacks, some educators and librarians are reluctant to spend money on paperback novels. However, many excellent realistic fiction novels are published in paperback format and can extend a classroom or library collection. Look for bargains at garage sales, thrift stores, and half-price or used bookstores. Use your knowledge of review sources and the information from a paperback's cover to select good literature. Often quotations from reviews and lists of awards are included on the back of the book or inside the front cover. Knowing those awards and review journals will help you add quality literature to your collection at a very reasonable price.

Themes of Contemporary Realistic Fiction

What makes a young adult book feel real? Jordan (1995), Dresang (1999), Aronson (2001), and others identify characteristics found in most realistic fiction. These books

- Take their settings, characters, and plot from the real world and change the randomness of the world into meaningful patterns
- Mirror the real world and the moral and ethical dilemmas that young people face
- Are believable
- Have the literary qualities (plot, setting, character, point of view, theme, and style) of well-written fiction
- Comment on the human condition
- Confront their subjects in a direct and often intense or extreme way

Aronson (2001) maintains that, a writer of realistic fiction like a great painter, must go beneath the surface of life to explore discontinuities, examine the subconscious, and investigate unsettling truths. The results must not be sugar-coated stories of perfect lives but frank examinations of the choices young adults must make. Thus, the themes of realistic fiction are varied and range from gaining the acceptance of others, developing friendships, growing up, and understanding the role of the family to finding a place in society, coping with alienation, finding one's sexual identity, and searching for a sense of self. By using multiple voices to tell the same story, some young adult writers have attempted to show the complexities of adolescents' lives. They have also attempted to show that there are "hidden connections between things and that we can never fully know the consequences of our acts" (p. 82). In well-written young adult realistic fiction, nothing is diluted, and no condescension is permitted. Perhaps this stance is epitomized by the author Robert Cormier, who was both "unflinching and full of compassion, often brutal and always uncompromising in his depiction of the individual struggling in the face of power, corruption, victimization, betrayal and conspiracy" (Robert Cormier Remembered, 2001). Expanding Your Knowledge with the Internet identifies websites you can visit to learn more about Robert Cormier, as well as a few other authors of contemporary realistic fiction.

Rather than focusing on the subject (sports), the setting (western), or the feeling (romance) of a book, we have chosen to examine young adult contemporary realistic fiction by the theme a novel portrays. We will discuss some of the most common themes, and recommend "problem" novels for each theme. As with all such lists, we caution you that our selections are not exhaustive and that our categories are not mutually exclusive.

In deciding what novels to include, we faced the problem of how to differentiate contemporary from historical realism. For example, Walter Dean Myers's *Fallen Angels* (1988) is often included on lists of realistic fiction, as many teachers and librarians who make such lists see the Vietnam War as a contemporary event. However, 1968 is a historical time for young adolescents who were born years after the end of the war. Similarly, while Ann Head's (1967) *Mr. and Mrs. Bo Jo Jones* may address the issue of accepting responsibility for a teenage pregnancy, many modern young adults would

EXPANDING YOUR KNOWLEDGE WITH THE INTERNET

You can learn more about many authors of contemporary realistic fiction by visiting their Internet sites.

Laurie Halse Anderson
www.writerlady.com/

Joan Bauer
www.joanbauer.com/jbhome.html

Judy Blume
www.judyblume.com

Caroline Cooney
teenreads.com/authors/au-cooney-caroline.asp

Susan Cooper
www.thelostland.com

Robert Cormier
www.webenglishteacher.com/cormier.html

Chris Crutcher
aol.teenreads.com/authors/au-crutcher-chris-2.asp

Sarah Dessen
www.sarahdessen.com/

Sharon Mills Draper
sharondraper.com/

S. E. Hinton
www.sehinton.com/

Walter Dean Myers
www.harperchildrens.com/authorintro/index.asp?authorid=12522aalbc.com/authors/walter1.htm

Gary Paulsen
www.randomhouse.com/features/garypaulsen/index.html

Cynthia Voight
www.scils.rutgers.edu/ ~kvander/voigt.html

Jacqueline Woodson
www.jacquelinewoodson.com/

find the story dated and unrealistic. Thus, with the exception of a few classic novels, our discussion will focus on more recent novels.

Overcoming Fears and Accepting Responsibilities. In quality young adult literature, major or minor characters are often challenged by others (or by themselves) to meet responsibilities. For example, Tony must confront his weight and his friend's drug abuse in *Fat Kid Rules the World* (Going, 2003); Nick uses basketball to help him cope with his parent's divorce in *Night Hoops* (Deuker, 2000); Benjie fights drugs in the classic *A Hero Ain't Nothin' but a Sandwich* (Childress, 1973); Claudia must accept responsibility for her actions in *The Search* (Holland, 1991); and a young man must determine his own future in *Stetson* (Rottman, 2002). Other books with this theme are:

- *Because of Winn-Dixie* (DiCamillo, 2000)
- *Spellbound* (McDonald, 2001)
- *The Opposite of Love* (Benedict, 2007)

Connecting Adolescents and Their Literature 5–2 shows one way to create a character description web, based on the main character in a contemporary realistic novel.

5-2 •••• ⋅. CONNECTING ADOLESCENTS AND THEIR LITERATURE

Use a graphic organizer to create a character description web that is based on the main character in a contemporary realistic novel. This web is based on Joyce Park, the main character in An Na's *The Fold* (2008).

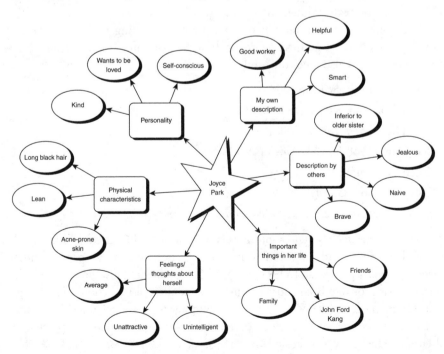

Understanding Families, Divorce, and Adoption. Relationships with parents and other family members are important to young adults. Differences of opinion about dress, curfews, and length and color of hair, as well as more serious concerns such as excessive alcohol consumption (by either the parents or the young person), physical or sexual abuse, or neglect, can exact a considerable toll on both adults and young people. While the two-parent family with a couple of children still exists today, many different types of family, including dysfunctional and disintegrating families, also occur. One-parent homes, homes with stepparents or foster children, and other family arrangements are common today and are therefore depicted in these novels.

Several authors of young adult novels deal with problems that arise in contemporary families. Tracy Mack explores divorce in *Drawing Lessons* (2000). Ian Lawrence observes a disintegrating family in *The Lightkeeper's Daughter* (2002). Trial separation is a theme in Carolyn Mackler's *Love and Other Four-Letter Words* (2000), and Gary Paulsen explores a single-parent family in *The Glass Café* (2003). Orphans and family tensions are central to the story in Patricia Reilly Giff's *Pictures of Hollis Woods* (2002), and adoption plays an important part in Julia Alvarez's *Finding Miracles* (2004). The Applewhites are a nontraditional family of writers and artists who take in a juvenile delinquent in Stephanie Tolan's *Surviving the Applewhites* (2002).

A number of young adult realistic fiction novels examine father-son or father-daughter relationships. Although they all differ in several ways, the circumstances are usually the same—differences exist between the parent and the young adult and each has to gain an understanding of both himself or herself and the other. This is the case for Brian and his father in *All That Glitters* (1996), by Jean Ferris. In Walter Dean Myers's classic *Somewhere in the Darkness* (1992), Jimmy Little is surprised when his father returns from jail. In *Seek* (Fleischman, 2001), Rob is looking for his father's voice in his life. Kate must cope with being a preacher's daughter as she tries to get into MIT in Laurie Halse Anderson's *Catalyst* (2002).

Families play a part in a number of other books, including the Alice series, by Phyllis Reynolds Naylor, and the works of Todd Strasser and Walter Dean Myers. The following novels also focus on family relationships:

- Sherri L. Smith, *Sparrow* (2006)
- Frank Portman, *King Dork* (2006)
- Mel Glenn, *Split Image* (2000)
- Jacqueline Woodson, *Miracle's Boys* (2000)
- Ellen Wittlinger, *Hard Love* (1999)
- Edward Bloor, *Tangerine* (1997)
- Rita Williams-Garcia, *Like Sisters on the Homefront* (1995)

Family relationships also enter into novels of realistic fiction as they touch on the topics of alcoholism, death of a family member, spouse abuse, a gay parent, parents embarrassing young people, and a host of others. Any problem that some real family has experienced has probably been addressed in young adult realistic fiction. For example, Michael Cadnum's *Taking It* (1995) discusses shoplifting and sexual relationships; Marion Dane Bauer's *A Question of Trust* (1994) explores the issue of trust between parents and children; and Thelma Wyss's classic *Here at the Scenic-Vu Motel* (1988) tells of the school board of Bear Flats, Idaho, deciding to stop busing seven children to the high school and instead to have them live at the Scenic-Vu Motel during the week.

Finding Friends: Relationships, Alienation, and a Sense of Belonging. Peers and friends are very important to young adults and play an influential role in many young peoples' choice of dress, mannerisms, and behaviors. Naturally, young adult fiction can portray that relationship. In *Who the Man* (Lynch, 2002), Earl uses violence to handle conflicts with peers. Ben finds he has to challenge his best friend to a wrestling match in *Wrestling Sturbridge* (Wallace, 1996). In Nikki Grimes's *Bronx Masquerade* (2001), as high school students read the poems they have written, they reveal their secret fears and their real selves to their classmates. Peer pressure is a focus in *The Battle of Jericho* (Draper, 2003), while changing friendships play an important part in *The New Rules of High School* (Nelson, 2003). Other books that present glimpses of adolescent relationships are:

- *The Kayla Chronicles* (Winston, 2008)
- *The Girls* (Koss, 2000)
- *Three Clams and an Oyster* (Powell, 2002)

In the attempt to belong, some teens are searching for their cultural identity; others are only trying to fit in with the majority culture. That is what Tara Mehtas is trying to do in *A Group of One* (Gilmore, 2001) until her grandmother arrives from India. Also from India, Dimple, in *Born Confused* (Desai Hidier, 2002), is an ABCD, American Born Confused Desi, too American for her immigrant Indian parents and too Indian for her American friends. Young Ju in An Na's *Step from Heaven* (2001) must balance her Korean heritage with her new life in America and her cruel father's demands. Contemporary American Indians searching for cultural identity appear in a number of novels, including *The Window* (Dorris, 1997), *The Heart of a Chief* (Bruchac, 1998), and *Who Will Tell My Brother?* (Carvell, 2002). Other books that include a search for cultural identity are:

- *Beacon Hill Boys* (Mochizuki, 2002)
- *Cuba 15* (Osa, 2003)
- *The Fold* (Na, 2007)
- *Off-Color* (McDonald, 2007)

Connecting Adolescents and Their Literature 5–3 looks at one technique you can use for examining the cultural conflict theme in contemporary realistic fiction.

5-3 •••• CONNECTING ADOLESCENTS AND THEIR LITERATURE

Contemporary realistic fiction provides an excellent way for teachers and library media specialists to help young adults understand their own cultural identities as well as others' cultural backgrounds. Sometimes a character in a novel feels torn between a culture's expectations and his or her own wants and desires. Students can use the information from the book to complete a graphic organizer that provides a visual representation of these feelings and the conflicts.

Accomplishing Goals in Sports. Involvement in sports can help young adults form new friendships, set goals, and discover a sense of accomplishment. There are novels that deal with nearly every sport, including extreme, or unusual, sports such as lowriders, skating, surfing, and cheerleading. Novels like Walter Dean Myers's *Slam!* (1996), Matt De la Pena's *Ball Don't Lie* (2005), and the classic *The Contender* (1967) by Robert Lipsyte feature protagonists who intend to use sports to help them accomplish their dream of transcending poverty. Some sports novels deal with social issues, such as Bruce Brooks's classic *Moves Make the Man* (1984), Chris Crutcher's *Whale Talk* (2001), and Paul Volponi's *Black and White* (2005). Other novels that feature young people who use sports to accomplish goals are:

- Kevin Waltman, *Learning the Game* (2005)
- Robert Rigby, *Goal! The Dream Begins* (2006)
- Bob Krech, *Rebound* (2006)
- Carl Deuker, *Heart of a Champion* (2007)

Developing and Maturing. As they are bombarded with messages from parents, family, peers, television, the Internet, school, and their communities, young adults must search for ways to make sense of this cacophony of voices. While attempting to discover their own identities, they ask: Who am I? What kind of person will I grow up to be? What will I be like? Developing a personal, sexual, and individual identity is a significant (although often unconscious) task for young adults. The phenomenal success of Ann Brashares's *The Sisterhood of the Traveling Pants* (2001), the first young adult debut novel to sell over 100,000 copies, shows that many young adults are turning to realistic fiction for answers.

Adolescent protagonists face the challenges and struggles of growing up in many novels. H. F. Simms seeking a sexual identity in *Finding H. F.* (Watts, 2001); Raspberry equates money with security in *Money Hungry* (Flake, 2001); wise-guy Matt emerges from his bad-boy shell in *Big Mouth and Ugly Girl* (Oates, 2002); and Myrtle tries to determine just exactly who and what she is in *Myrtle of Willendorf* (O'Connell, 2000).

While many novels, such as Virginia Euwer Wolff's stories of life in the inner city in *Make Lemonade* (1993) and *True Believer* (2001), Victor Martinez's tale of a Mexican American teenager in the California projects in *Parrot in the Oven* (1996), and Rob Thomas's novel of a gifted and troubled high school senior in *Rats Saw God* (1996), are very serious, more humorous narratives about growing up also exist, such as Louise Rennison's funny British tale of Georgia Nicholson, which begins in *Angus, Thongs, and Full-Frontal Snogging* (2000) and the diaries of Jonah Black, which begin in *Black Book Diary of a Teenage Stud: Girls, Girls, Girls* (2001). In a series of poems, Sonya Sones tells of the maturing of 15-year-old Sophie in *What My Mother Doesn't Know* (2001). Other novels that address these topics include:

- *For Now* (Friesen, 2007)
- *Alice, I Think* (Juby, 2003)
- *Goodbye, Amanda the Good* (Shreve, 2000)
- *Homeless Bird* (Whelan, 2000)

Finding Romance. The love story has always been a significant part of young adult literature. Considered one of the first young adult romance novels to be published, Maureen Daly's *Seventeenth Summer* (2002/1942) is still widely read by girls interested in escaping into a world of boy meets girl. Other classics, such as Judy Blume's *Forever* (1975) and Beverly Cleary's *Fifteen* (1996/1956) are also being read by another generation. Caroline Cooney is another veteran author who has written a number of romance series for younger teens. Since the 1980s, the Sweet Valley High series—Sweet Valley Twins, The Unicorn Club, Team Sweet Valley, Sweet Valley Saga, and Sweet Valley University have all been popular with teens, sparking the development of other series. Scholastic's First Comes Love, Avon's Teen Angels, and Harlequin's new romance line for teens are all proof that this market is lucrative and in demand.

The basic love story is told from the perspective of a young woman, involves first love, and includes trappings like the first date and the first kiss. Other stories are more complicated. Nancy Garden's classic *Annie on My Mind* (1982) is one of the first lesbian love stories, and since its publication others have followed, including Alex Sanchez's *Rainbow Boys* (2001) and Julie Ann Peter's *Keeping You a Secret* (2003). Love stories from a male's perspective include Jerry Spinelli's *Stargirl* (2000), Ellen Wittlinger's *Hard Love* (1999), Sandra Sone's *What My Girlfriend Doesn't Know* (2007), and Alex Bradley's *24 Girls in 7 Days* (2005). Some characters have to realize they have chosen someone who is not right for them, as does Isabel in Gaby Triana's *Cubanita* (2005). Other love stories include:

- *Someone Like Summer* (Kerr, 2007)
- *Prom* (Anderson, 2005)
- *The Melting Season* (Conway, 2006)
- *Getting It* (Sanchez, 2006)
- *Jason & Kyra* (Davidson, 2004)

Coping with Violence, Crime, Alcohol, and Drug Abuse. Unfortunately, violence, crime, alcohol and drug use, and various other forms of abuse are an integral part of our society and, at least in the lives of many people, take precedence over civility. Too many young adults see or experience gang-related violence and death, and feel the resulting fear, anger, and grief. No longer restricted to inner cities, violence even reaches students in rural and suburban schools in places such as Littleton, Colorado, and Red Lake, Minnesota. While shielding or protecting young people from violence and abuse is ideal, it is also impossible. However, through literature, we can help young adults explore these issues. Sometimes realistic novels offer hope; at other times they provide a forum where readers can explore options and alternatives.

Never one to shy away from violence, Robert Cormier, well known for his classic novel *The Chocolate War* (1974), often examines the topic from a new perspective. His novel *We All Fall Down* (1991) looks at violence in a small town with characters trashing a house, attacking a 14-year-old girl, and seeking revenge. Cormier's *The Rag and Bone Shop* (2001) explores the murder of a child and the attitude of authorities to do whatever is necessary to solve the crime, even if it means forcing a 12-year-old boy to confess.

These authors also examine the issue of violence in our society:

- S. E. Hinton, *The Outsiders* (1967)
- Walter Dean Myers, *Monster* (1999)
- Todd Strasser, *Give a Boy a Gun* (2000)
- Sharon Flake, *Bang!* (2005)
- K. L. Going, *Saint Iggy* (2006)

Violence happens in families, too. In *Silent to the Bone* (Konigsburg, 2000), Branwell Zamborska is accused by his family's English au pair of dropping and shaking his baby sister until she stops breathing. A physically abusive father plays a major role in Gloria Velasquez's *Rina's Family Secret* (1998). The violent "family" in Gordon Korman's *Son of the Mob* (2002) is a bit unconventional—Vince's father is a powerful Mafia boss.

Pressures from peers, television and billboard advertising, and society norms mean that most young adults are familiar with the problems associated with alcohol and drug abuse. However, the desire to experiment with the unknown too often results in disaster for young people as well as their friends and loved ones. Young adult novels that present the problems associated with substance abuse include characters who have to deal with getting addicted and working toward recovery, who experience the despair and desperation associated with substance abuse, who face problems with alcoholic or drug-dependent parents, and who confront the violence that often results from substance abuse.

Although it was published over 30 years ago, Alice Childress's *A Hero Ain't Nothin' but a Sandwich* (1973) continues to be popular. The story realistically addresses addiction problems, following Benjie's experience with drugs and his slip into desperation and despair as his family and friends try to save him. Drinking and alcoholism take center stage in Jan Cheripko's *Imitate the Tiger* (1996), as Chris Serbo plays football and drinks too much. Chris has been sent to a detox clinic and readers learn through his flashbacks about his life of despair and self-delusion.

Living with Physical and Mental Disabilities. A primary value of literature is that it provides readers with experiences which, although not always ideal, help them understand their own lives and the world around them. Contemporary realistic fiction may not always present "the best" people or places, but effective, well-written young adult realistic novels present these experiences in nonsensationalized ways.

A number of characters in contemporary realistic fiction novels must deal with disabling conditions. In the classic *Deenie* (Blume, 1973), Deenie wears a back brace. Mandy is blinded in an automobile accident in *The Window* (Ingold, 1996). Joey Pigza faces the devastating effects of learning disabilities such as attention deficit disorder in a series of books by Jack Gantos. Young adults face the challenges of cerebral palsy in Ronald Koertge's *Stoner and Spaz* (2002) and in Terry Trueman's *Stuck in Neutral* (2001). In a classic work for mature readers, a crippling automobile accident forces star athlete Willie Weaver to leave his family and friends to rebuild his shattered life in Chris Crutcher's *The Crazy Horse Electric Game* (1987). Some characters must deal not with their own disabling conditions, but with disabilities in their families. In Norma Fox Mazer's *When She Was Good* (1997), Em is finally liberated from years of being tormented by her mentally ill older sister.

Some young adults must face their own mental illness, including the serious problem of depression. Carrie, in the classic *The Language of Goldfish* (Oneal, 1980), experiences emotional and mental illness. Dani in *The Game* (Toten, 2001) must deal with a number of problems, including physical abuse, a dysfunctional family, and a psychological struggle for her own survival. In Terry Trueman's *Inside Out* (2003), readers see the torment in Zach's life as a schizophrenic when he is taken hostage during a failed robbery attempt. After being directed to see a court-appointed psychologist following her friend Aimee's suicide, Zoe learns to cope with her own depression, guilt, loneliness, and anger in Mary Beth Miller's *Aimee* (2002). Another novel that portrays characters living with disabilities is Sherri L. Smith's *Sparrow* (2006).

Coping with Death, Disease, Accidents, and Suicide. On a daily basis, many young adults see and hear about death and debilitating diseases. This takes a toll on their emotions, especially when the event is an accident or an unexpected suicide.

Both Jesse and Roxanne cope with death and loss in Martha Moore's *Under the Mermaid Angel* (1995). While Jesse grieves the death of her brother, Roxanne must deal with giving up her child at birth. Bobby in the classic *My Brother Stealing Second* (Naughton, 1989) is also grief-stricken about his brother; his brother Billy, a star athlete, while driving drunk, killed both himself and a couple celebrating their wedding anniversary. In Deborah Froese's *Out of the Fire* (2002), Dayle is seriously burned in an accident and must go through therapy and treatment for her burns.

Too often, murder and suicide find their way into the lives of young adults. In Colby Rodowsky's *Remembering Mog* (1996), the Fitzhugh family remembers Mog's violent death and tries to move toward healing. Todd, a 16-year-old African American teenager living in Denver in *Soulfire* (Hewitt, 1996), experiences grief over the death of his cousin, Tommy. Will in *Freewill* (Lynch, 2001) must deal with the suicides in his town and wonder what part, if any, he is playing.

While an accident or violence can cause a very sudden death, characters who have, or know someone who has a life-threatening disease must also struggle to cope with their feelings. Samantha and Juliana, better known as Sam and Jules, are close friends in Davida Wills Hurwin's *A Time for Dancing* (1995). Their story becomes one of death and dying when Jules learns she has cancer. In Liza Hall's *Perk!* (1997), bulimia becomes a life-threatening disease. Other novels that examine this topic are *Hope Was Here* (Bauer, 2000), the various novels by Lurlene McDaniel, and the classics *A Summer to Die* (Lowry, 1977) and *Tiger Eyes* (Blume, 1981).

During the late 1980s and 1990s, as the AIDS epidemic spread, there was an increase in the quantity and quality of young adult books that addressed the topic by looking at the loneliness of the disease, how it can change relationships with parents and friends (sometimes with outright rejection), attempts to raise awareness of AIDS, the transmission of the disease (whether from a blood transfusion or sexual contact), and HIV-positive babies. Joel keeps the memory of his uncle Michael alive in his thoughts after Michael dies of AIDS in Patricia Quinlan's *Tiger Flowers* (1994). In M. E. Kerr's classic *Night Kites* (1986), 17-year-old Jim's relationship with his family and friends changes when his older brother announces he has AIDS. A similar thing happens to Liam in *The Eagle Kite* (Fox, 1995). In *Diving for the Moon* (Bantle, 1995), Bird struggles through her mixed emotions when she discovers that her best friend,

Josh, is HIV positive. In *Earthshine* (Nelson, 1994), living with her father means that Slim will also be living with her father's longtime companion, Larry, who has AIDS. *Chanda's Secret* (Stratton, 2004) focuses on the AIDS epidemic in Africa.

Developing Sexual Relationships. As teenagers grow up, they constantly deal with problems related to their sexuality, including sexual relationships, pregnancy, incest, rape, abortions, and sexually transmitted diseases. They must not only cope with their own feelings, but also confront peer pressures and their families' expectations. In addition, they must factor in the things that they see on television and in movies. Stories of sexual relationships and pregnancy began to be published in the late 1960s and early 1970s when some of the taboos about these areas broke down. Novels that deal with these and other topics relating to sexuality are now accepted in most circles, although some novels are still challenged, especially for younger adolescents. Many of the novels we discuss in relation to other themes show young adults facing the difficulties of dating and establishing relationships.

Some teens find themselves having to cope with unwanted pregnancies. Four uncompromising views of the realities of life for some teenage girls are found in Rita Williams-Garcia's *Like Sisters on the Homefront* (1995), Connie Rose Porter's *Imani All Mine* (1999), Sharon Draper's *November Blues* (2007), and Lenora Adams' *Baby Girl* (2007). Margaret E. Bechard's *Hanging on to Max* (2002) and Angela Johnson's *The First Part Last* (2003) deal with teenage fathers who try to raise their children. In *Second Choices* (Brinkerhoff, 2000), Nikki's conversion to Christianity helps her deal with her choice to give her baby up for adoption.

In the past, rape and sexual abuse often went unreported and unaddressed in young adult realistic fiction. Although the victims' emotional scars may have lasted a lifetime, especially in the case of sexual abuse by a family member, the violence remained hidden. Therefore, books on these topics received sharp criticism from censors and other groups who wanted to limit what young people read. Those restrictions have been lifted as more novels have addressed these topics. In Hadley Irwin's classic *Abby, My Love* (1985), Chip loves Abby and questions her reluctance to be close both psychologically and physically with him; then Abby reveals that she has been sexually abused by her father. In *Out of Control* (1993), Norma Fox Mazer presents the story of Valerie Michon, who is assaulted by three respected teenage boys; and in *Speak* (Anderson, 1999), Melinda deals with the aftermath of date rape. While safe in the United States, 14-year-old Mardi tries to hide the fact that she was raped by soldiers when she was in Haiti in Jaira Placide's *Fresh Girl* (2002).

Understanding Sexual Orientation. In the past, few young adult authors wrote about sexual orientation, in part because of the nature of the topic and, perhaps, fears of censorship. However, an increasing number of writers now provide frank looks at differing sexual orientations and their surrounding challenges. One of the first books to address this topic was Nancy Garden's classic *Annie on My Mind* (1982), in which two high school girls accept their feelings for one another as their relationship develops and they fall in love. In *Deliver Us from Evie* (1994), M. E. Kerr explores the reactions of Evie Burrman's family and the small town where she lives when she reveals her sexual orientation and her affair with Patsy Duff, the daughter of the banker who holds the loan on the Burrman farm. Dirk McDonald confronts his sexual identity in Francesca Lia Block's *Baby Be-Bop* (1995); Heavenly Faith Simms discovers who she really is in Julia Watts's *Finding H. F.* (2001), and a group of gay and lesbian teenagers find support in Brent Hartinger's *Geography Club* (2003).

Some young adults face the challenge to understand the sexual orientation of friends and other family members. Mel in *From the Notebooks of Melanin Sun* (Woodson, 1995) keeps detailed notebooks telling of his anger, confusion, and denial in this story of mothers, sons, and lesbians. In *Brad's Universe* (Woodbury, 1998), Brad's father sexually harasses boys; and in *True Believer* (Wolff, 2001), LaVaughn finds out why the boy she likes is not interested in having a girlfriend.

Understanding the Difficulties Associated with Growing Old. When you are not even 20 years old, it is difficult to think about what it is like to be a senior citizen. However, many young adults do form very strong ties to older people, only to realize that, just as there are problems with growing up, there are problems with growing old. In *River Boy* (2000), Tim Bowler writes about the death of a grandfather. In *Stone Water* (1996), Barbara Snow Gilbert tells about a serious choice a teenager's grandfather asks him to make. Teenagers share unique relationships with elderly neighbors in both Paul Zindel's classic *The Pigman* (1968) and in Kazumi Yumoto's *The Friends* (1996). Alzheimer's disease and its effects on a family plays an important part in Barbara Park's *Graduation of Jake Moon* (2000).

Living in a Global Society: Prejudice, Politics, Conflicts, and War. Realistic fiction not only reflects on issues and problems that young adults find in their everyday lives in America but also asks young adults to look at issues in a global society. These multicultural themes, while often relating to some of the aforementioned issues, such as developing and maturing or family relationships, focus on other cultures or on global issues. Other novels that present pictures of teenagers in other cultures include:

- Suzanne Fisher Staples, *Shabanu* (1989)
- Naomi Shihab Nye, *Habibi* (1997)
- Gloria Whelan, *Homeless Bird* (2000)
- Nancy Farmer, *A Girl Named Disaster* (1996)
- Cathryn Clinton, *A Stone in My Hand* (2002)
- Anton Ferreira, *Zulu Dog* (2002)

Prejudice can be found almost anywhere. Kate, who is half-white, finds it in Hawaii in *Dance for the Land* (McLaren, 1999), and Zack, who has a Jewish father and a black mother, finds it with his grandfather in Mississippi in *Zack* (Bell, 1999).

Although the Cold War is over, teenagers today hear and read about conflicts, strife, and terrorism both at home and abroad. Several young adult novels look at the problems faced by teenagers throughout the world as they try to cope with conflict. In Deborah Ellis's *Parvana's Journey* (2002), a young girl tries to survive in Taliban-threatened Afghanistan. In Jan Simeon and John Nieuwenhuizen's *What About Anna?* (2002), Anna tries to learn the truth about her brother's death from a landmine in Bosnia. Because Sade's father is a muckraking journalist, she and her brother must flee Nigeria in Beverley Naidoo's *The Other Side of Truth* (2001), and in its sequel, *Web of Lies* (2006), Sade and Femi must adapt to living in asylum in London.

Understanding Religion and Its Role in Society. Many young adults are beginning their own search for spirituality and trying to determine the place religion will or will not have in their lives. Others are trying to understand the religious choices others have made and how those choices will affect their relationships with them. The inspirational Clearwater Crossing series by Laura Peyton Roberts features a diverse group of teenagers who face a series of crises that force them to increasingly rely on each other and on their faith. Lurlene McDaniel addresses the importance of religious beliefs in several of her books, including *Angel of Hope* (2000) and *Angels Watching Over Me* (1996). In Sonia Levitin's *The Singing Mountain* (1998), Mitch Green, a California teen, visits Israel and decides to join an Orthodox Jewish yeshiva there. Religion also plays a strong role in *Blind Fury* (Shands, 2001), *The Book of Fred* (Bardi, 2001), and *Conflict in California* (Stuckey, 2001).

Some young adults must deal with religious fanaticism. For example, Dorry, in *Leaving Fishers* (Haddix, 1997), finds that the group of students who befriend her are really members of a religious cult. In *The Last Safe Place on Earth* (Peck, 1995), Todd's little sister is brainwashed by his fundamentalist babysitter.

Many works of contemporary realistic fiction have been made into movies. Some of these are listed in the From Page to Screen feature.

Reasons for Using and Teaching Contemporary Realistic Fiction

Why use contemporary realistic fiction in a classroom or add it to a library collection? Perhaps because the genre developed as a didactic moral tale, many critics attempt to link it with morality by examining a realistic novel in light of the messages it delivers (Aronson, 2001). They focus on whether it "teaches" a lesson or presents a positive role model young adults can emulate. However, Aronson (2001) maintains that "realism is not concerned with morality; it is about verisimilitude" (p. 80). While morality shapes beliefs or behaviors and does provide role models, realism reflects life and focuses on the conflicts young adults face. Young adults do not want "predigested morals and fake realities" (p. 83). What they do want are works that will force them to confront their own beliefs, to identify their own messages in the story, and to grow in their own ways (Aronson, 2001). Thus, some contemporary realistic fiction novels are uncomfortable to read, while others raise more questions than they solve.

It is important for young adults to be exposed to books that reach and move them because, as Aronson notes (2001), "it can affect them as at no other age" (p. 81). Rather than looking for books that are contrived or didactic, young adults seem to look for novels that speak to them and about them in an honest and realistic way. Such books range from lighthearted, even romantic stories to more dark and disturbing examinations of the frustrations, events, and challenges of the real world in which contemporary adolescents live. Realistic characters are not always comfortable to know. As author Paul Zindel (2002) said about the protagonists he created, they are ornery, troubled, and "have an irksome itch. They always demanded a realistic story that was more than a comfortable grocery list" (p. 30).

from Page to Screen

CONTEMPORARY REALISTIC FICTION

Consider comparing these film adaptations with the original texts and discuss the ways the original was altered for the screen. Why were the changes made? Was the running time the main consideration, or were filmmakers hoping to attract a specific audience? How do the changes affect the overall quality of the piece?

THE SISTERHOOD OF THE TRAVELING PANTS
★★★ | 2005 | PG

Ken Kwapis directed this film based on the popular novel by Ann Brashares. Four friends share a magical pair of jeans during the first summer they have ever spent apart. The Sisterhood of the Traveling Pants 2, based on Forever in Blue, was released in the summer of 2008.

HOW TO DEAL
★★ | 2003 | PG-13

Neena Beber wrote the screenplay for this film that combines Sarah Dessen's Someone Like You (1998) and That Summer (1996), offering an entertaining look at romantic and familial love. The DVD includes an informative segment on the history of young adult literature, featuring young adult literature scholar Michael Cart.

HOLES
★★★★ | 2003 | PG

Louis Sachar adapted his own Newbery Award–winning novel for the screen in this delightful, funny, clever film that follows Stanley Yelnats, victim of the Yelnats bad luck, to Camp Green Lake to uncover a generations-old mystery that starts with Kissin' Kate Barlow and ends with camp inmates digging holes.

THE MIGHTY
★★★✦ | 1998 | PG-13

This adaptation of Rodman Philbrick's novel Freak the Mighty tracks an unlikely friendship between Max, the underachieving son of a convict, and Kevin, a physically handicapped genius.

TEX
★★★ | 1982 | PG

Tex is a well-crafted, beautifully acted adaptation of S. E. Hinton's authentic and layered tale of the realities and dangers of adolescence as seen by two abandoned brothers living outside Tulsa.

BECAUSE OF WINN DIXIE
★★★ | 2005 | PG-13

This lovely independent film adaptation of Kate DiCamillo's Newbury winning novel about a lonely young girl named Opal, a newcomer in town, who adopts a stray dog named for the grocery store where she found him. Together they get to know Opal's new hometown. AnnaSopia Robb stands out in her feature film debut.

Contemporary realistic fiction has many benefits. Their young adult readers can:

- Identify with characters who have similar interests and who must deal with similar problems
- Realize that while their problems and challenges are difficult, they are shared by other adolescents

COLLABORATING WITH OTHER PROFESSIONALS

Middle schools often provide time within the curriculum for advisory sessions. A realistic novel (which can also be used in the English/language arts/reading classes) can provide a basis for discussion of contemporary problems and can inspire young adults to explore their feelings freely. Teachers, school library media specialists, and counselors can work together to identify age-appropriate books and to develop group discussion guides. Discussion leaders need to beware of moralizing, oversimplifying situations, or suggesting that reading a book will solve all problems. However, these novels can provide an excellent springboard for discussion and an examination of contemporary problems. While teachers can select the first novels, young adults should be encouraged to suggest ones they would like to discuss as well.

- Extend their horizons and broaden their interests
- Better cope with grief, fear, and anger as they read about other young adults or characters who have dealt with adversity

Aronson (2001) believes that well-written realistic fiction has the potential "to touch readers deeply so that, in the struggle with it, they begin to see and to shape themselves" (p. 119). Collaborating With Other Professionals 5–1 suggests the use of contemporary realistic fiction as a basis for middle school advisory sessions.

Characteristics of Well-Written Realistic Fiction

Mirroring life as some people experience it, realistic fiction deals with many complex problems and situations, from understanding sexual orientation to dealing with family problems. At its core, a well-written realistic fiction novel is about people, their problems, and their challenges. The characters in the novel should be believable, and their language and actions should be appropriate for the setting of the story and reflective of their culture and social class. An author writing about a gang in an urban setting has a responsibility to use appropriate words, slang, phrases, and dialects.

While realism prevails, people are still considered with sensitivity; a good author is always aware of the fine line between stereotyping and realistic, objective writing. Although readers learn a lesson or a value such as being accountable for one's actions, or accepting the cultural, physical, or sexual differences of other people, well-written realistic fiction novels do not dictate specific moral and ethical beliefs. Rather, they challenge readers to learn the importance of moral and ethical behavior by drawing their own conclusions after they consider the events and facts from their personal perspectives using their own moral and ethical judgments. Some realistic fiction is expected to include violence; in fact, the genre would be failing in its mission if some novels did not mirror the violence many young people experience. However, violence should be used appropriately and to make a point—never just for sensationalism. To Aronson (2001), a well-written book "recognize[s] the depth of

CONSIDERATIONS FOR SELECTING YOUNG ADULT LITERATURE
CONTEMPORARY REALISTIC FICTION

When evaluating a contemporary realistic fiction novel, ask:

_____   Are there engaging, true-to-life, well-rounded characters, who are both wise and foolish while they are growing and changing?

_____   Is there an accurate reflection of the human condition and contemporary life, without stereotyping?

_____   Is there a sensitivity to all people regardless of sex or sexual orientation, race, religion, age, socioeconomic level, social group, or culture?

_____   Does the plot appeal to young adults? Address the challenges, hopes, and fears as well as the problems faced by contemporary adolescents? Offer hope for the future?

_____   Does the plot ask young adults to consider or reconsider their own values and beliefs, inspire without providing "handy resolutions" (Aronson, 2001, p. 119), and avoid talking down to readers or telling them what to think?

_____   Is the setting believable?

_____   Is there an appropriate treatment of violence that never glamorizes it, records it more graphically than necessary, or includes it gratuitously?

_____   Does the language accurately reflect the characters as well as their educational status, social class, culture, and the place where they live?

darkness within teenagers and yet also assume[s] that readers have the intelligence and the imagination to deal with ambiguity" (p. 120).

Due to the popularity of contemporary realistic fiction among young adults, many excellent books are published each year. Unfortunately, many others claim to be problem novels but lack the qualities that define well-written young adult literature. Considerations for Selecting Young Adult Literature: *Contemporary Realistic Fiction* lists some of the characteristics of well-written realistic fiction.

When selecting realistic fiction to use with reluctant young adult readers, you should also look for fast-paced novels that begin with a hook to get the reader's interest and that have a limited number of characters, flashbacks, or subplots. These novels should focus on high-interest topics and real-life situations that will hold the reader's interest. In the writing, look for familiar words and short sentences and paragraphs. A novel for reluctant readers will ideally have visual appeal, with an attractive cover, an easy-to-read typeface, and fewer than 200 pages in a paperback format (Jones, 1994).

Suggestions for Selecting and Teaching Realistic Fiction

Young adults are a diverse group, so selecting literature for them is never easy. Teachers and librarians need to balance the interests of individual adolescents with the reviews written by adults who work with young people. The ideal is to identify contemporary realistic fiction novels that interest young adults and have received high praise from critics and then to determine ways to use those novels in classrooms.

Awards and Best Books Lists. Fortunately, contemporary realistic novels are often found on many of the best books lists discussed in Chapter 2 such as the *School Library Journal*, the Young Adult Library Services Association best books lists, and the ALA Quick Picks for Reluctant Young Adult Readers. Others go on to win honors or awards such as the Michael L. Printz Award. Several of the multicultural book awards, such as the Pura Belpré Award, the Jane Addams Book Award, and the Americas Award, may include contemporary realistic fiction novels in their lists of winners. Many of the books that recommend young adult literature, such as the NCT English series, including *Books for You* (Beers & Lesesne, 2001), list a variety of contemporary realistic fiction novels.

Print Review Resources. In addition to the books mentioned in Chapter 2, these are some more specific print selection aids that also include realistic fiction:

- *Helping Teens Cope: A Guide to Teen Issues Using YA Fiction and Other Resources* (Jones, 2003)
- *Radical Reads: 101 YA Novels on the Edge* (Bodart, 2002)
- *Hearing All the Voices: Multicultural Books for Adolescents* (Darby & Pryne, 2002)
- *Rocked by Romance: A Guide to Young Adult Romance Genre Fiction* (Carpan, 2004)

Greenwood Press has issued the Using Literature to Help Troubled Teenagers series of books that include titles such as:

- *Using Literature to Help Troubled Teenagers Cope with Abuse Issues* (Kaywell, 2004)
- *Using Literature to Help Troubled Teenagers Cope with End-of-Life Issues* (Allen, 2002)
- *Using Literature to Help Troubled Teenagers Cope with Health Issues* (Bowman, 2000)
- *Using Literature to Help Troubled Teenagers Cope with Societal Issues* (Carroll, 1999)
- *Using Literature to Help Troubled Teenagers Cope with Identity Issues* (Kaplan, 1999)

EXPANDING YOUR KNOWLEDGE WITH THE INTERNET

Internet resources provide additional information about selecting and using contemporary realistic fiction.

The ALAN Review–Spring 1998–issue on Realistic Fiction
scholar.lib.vt.edu/ejournals/ALAN/spring98/andrews.html

YALSA's Realistic Fiction Booklist
www.ala.org/ala/yalsa/teenreading/trw/trw2005/fiction.cfm

A Quick Guide to Contemporary and Historical Realistic Fiction
www.mindspring.com/~stct42/edu/cont_his.html

Realistic Fiction Resources from Bloomington Schools
www.bloomington.k12.mn.us/indschool/HC/Genre/realfic.html

Video Booktalks for Young Adults from Scholastic
teacher.scholastic.com/products/tradebooks/booktalks.htm

Teachers' Guides from Farrar, Straus and Giroux (an example of what publishers provide)
us.macmillan.com/Content.aspx?publisher=fsgbyr&id=4627

Each book in the series includes a number of essays that review important issues and books, as well as providing suggestions for using the books in a classroom or library.

Online Resources.   Other selection aids can be found online. Expanding Your Knowledge with the Internet provides links to resources on the Internet, along with links to lesson plan ideas for teaching contemporary realistic novels.

Bibliotherapy.   Rasinski and Padak (1990) noted that

> there are few stimuli with greater potential to move people to action than literature. Because it tells the stories of human events and the human condition and not simply the facts, literature does more than change minds; it changes people's hearts. (p. 580)

In light of the impact literature can have, contemporary realistic fiction is often used for *bibliotherapy,* which, in its broadest sense, is defined as the "use of books to help people solve problems" (Aiex, 1993, p. 1). When bibliotherapy is used with individual students:

1. The reader identifies with a character in the book *(identification).*
2. The character is faced with and is able to resolve a difficult situation or problem *(catharsis).*
3. A reader reflects on the events in the story, relates them to his or her life, and internalizes them to develop personal coping strategies or problem-solving skills *(insight)* (Afolayan, 1992; Halsted, 1994).

However, bibliotherapy is more than just locating a book that discusses a problem or issue, giving the book to an adolescent, and letting him or her read it to find the answers to personal or societal problems. When bibliotherapy is used to help a young person cope with a personal problem, it is most effective if it is used as a group or individual therapeutic treatment with clearly defined roles for student(s), teacher(s), and counselor(s) (Wolpow & Askov, 2001). Furthermore, Linda Goettina (1999), a psychoanalyst working with adults and young people, cautions that it is important for individuals to have the "freedom and opportunity" (p. 13) to select the book they find helpful to meet their emotional needs rather than have an adult select the book. Sometimes books are able to "provide escape when denial is the only means of coping," to provide an "opportunity for expression of the unthinkable and undoable desires," or "to test the boundaries between what one is and what one hopes to be" (p. 14).

While some educational professionals regard bibliotherapy as a tool to be used only by skilled counselors working with individuals or with groups of students who share a similar problem, others see it as one way to help a wide range of students learn problem-solving skills. Although Forgan (2002) used bibliotherapy with students who had behavioral or learning disabilities to help them learn problem-solving strategies, he stressed that all students can benefit when they explore strategies in books as ways to solve typical personal and social problems. Bibliotherapy can also be used to provide role models for students—for example, a gifted girl who feels pressures to conform academically to a lower group standard or an African American boy who is ridiculed by his peers because he applies himself academically rather than in athletics (Ford et al., 2000). Whether used for small-group or whole-class problem solving, developmental bibliotherapy (Doll & Doll, 1997) allows young adults to focus on their developmental needs. It is important for teachers and library media specialists to select the realistic novel(s) carefully and to introduce the novel(s) so that adolescents can begin to make connections between their own experiences and those of the characters in the novel(s). Connecting Adolescents and Their Literature 5–4 outlines a process that can be used with young adults. Then, Collaborating with Other Professionals 5–2 links realistic fiction to the social studies classroom. Finally, Using Multiple Readings suggests questions influenced by various literary theories for *Cuba 15* (2003), by Nancy Osa.

CONNECTING ADOLESCENTS AND THEIR LITERATURE

To use bibliotherapy as a developmental strategy for problem solving, teachers and library media specialists can use or modify the following approach, depending on the level of the students involved and their experience in discussing literature.

Pre-reading:
1. Determine the structure of the reading. Will everyone in the class read the same book or will small groups read different books?
2. Carefully select the novel(s).
3. Introduce or booktalk the novel(s) and relate them to current or developmental issues while remaining sensitive to individuals within the group.

During Reading:
1. Depending on the group, teacher(s) and/or library media specialist may provide students with questions to guide their reading.
2. Depending on the group, students may read all or portions of the novel(s) before any discussion.
3. Encourage students to record their thoughts in their journals as they read and to write questions they may have for the discussion.

Follow-Up Discussion:
1. Conduct a discussion by using a variety of questions, moving from simple recall of facts and comprehension to more complex analytical and evaluative questions.
2. Encourage students to ask the questions they wrote as they read the novel(s).
3. Ask students to move beyond the novel(s), to explain the problem-solving strategies they found in the book, and to explain how these strategies could or could not be applied in real-life situations.

Forgan (2002) suggests using an I Solve strategy as part of the discussion with younger readers: have students identify the problem, the solutions to the problem (both those found in the book and other alternatives), and the obstacles to the solutions. Then, after examining all solutions, select one. For simple problems, it may be possible to test the solution and evaluate the outcome.

COLLABORATING WITH OTHER PROFESSIONALS

English teachers, library media specialists, and social studies teachers can work together to use contemporary realistic fiction. Many issues that are found in realistic books—such as homelessness, substance abuse, diversity in the community and nation, and individual and community responsibilities—are also studied in social studies classes. Library media specialists can booktalk various titles, social studies teachers can use the books for discussion, and English teachers can use the books as required or for supplemental reading or for book reports.

USING MULTIPLE READINGS

The following are some questions critics might ask about *Cuba 15* (2003), by Nancy Osa.

New Criticism
Why did the author choose to tell the story in first person rather than third person limited or third person omniscient narration? How do language use, character, and theme work together to form a unified work?

Historical-Biographical Criticism
Nancy Osa's father is from Cuba, and her mother's folks "came over on the Mayflower" (nancyosa.com). How might her heritage have influenced this novel?

Archetypal Criticism
How does the novel match the personal journey archetype?

Feminist Criticism
How does Violeta feel about becoming a woman at 15? What does womanhood mean to Violeta?

Black Feminist Criticism
Look closely at the Latina characters in the novel. Are there any experiences that seem unique to female characters because of their race, gender, or class?

New Historical Criticism
What conditions in Cuba could have led to Abuelo and Abuela's immigration to the United States? Why might Cubans choose to immigrate to the United States today?

Concluding Thoughts

Contemporary realistic fiction or the problem novel provides young adult readers with an excellent look at other people's lives—their problems and challenges as well as their families and relationships. Although realistic fiction, while not designated by this specific label, has been around for decades in one form or another, the literature of today is much more graphic in terms of violence, sex, and language. Unfortunately, for many young people, explicit violence and sex are everyday occurrences. The literature only mirrors the world they see. Even though censors will continue to attack many of its themes and topics, the future of realistic fiction and the problem novel looks bright. There are excellent realistic fiction writers, topics abound, and many young adults enjoy the novels.

Young Adult Books

This section includes young adult titles mentioned in this chapter.

Adams, L. (2007). *Baby girl*. New York: Simon Pulse. Pregnant, Sheree leaves home and enters Milagro House, a shelter for women and girls in Lancaster, Pennsylvania.

Alvarez, J. (2004). *Finding miracles*. New York: Knopf. Fifteen-year-old Milly Kaufman learns she was once an orphan in a Latin American country.

Anderson, L. H. (1999). *Speak*. New York: Farrar, Straus and Giroux. After she is raped at a party, Melinda does not tell anyone what happened. In fact, she does not speak at all.

Anderson, L. H. (2002). *Catalyst*. New York: Viking. Relating her life to chemistry, Kate finds that a catalyst is about to bring major changes.

Anderson, L. H. (2005). *Prom*. New York: Viking. Ashley Hannigan's involved in dating and planning the senior prom with her friends.

Anonymous. (1971). *Go ask Alice*. Upper Saddle River, NJ: Prentice Hall. A 15-year-old drug user struggles to escape the pull of the drug world.

Avi. (1991). *Nothing but the truth*. New York: Orchard. In this story told through multiple voices, Phillip Malloy is suspended for humming along with the national anthem.

Bantle, L. F. (1995). *Diving for the moon*. New York: Macmillan. Bird finds that her best friend Josh, a hemophiliac, is HIV positive.

Bardi, A. (2001). *The book of Fred*. New York: Washington Square Press. Can teenaged Mary Fred Anderson adjust to the world when she leaves her fundamentalist community and is placed in foster care? Or will she change the people that she meets?

Bauer, J. (2000). *Hope was here*. New York: Putnam. Sixteen-year-old Hope and her aunt work as the waitress and cook in the Welcome Stairways diner when the owner finds he is dying of leukemia.

Baur, M. D. (1994). *A question of trust*. New York: Scholastic. Brad and his younger brother devise a plan to get their mother to return home.

Bechard, M. E. (2002). *Hanging on to Max*. Brookfield, CT: Roaring Brook Press. Sam wants to keep his infant son even though Brittany wants to give the baby up for adoption.

Bell, W. (1999). *Zack*. New York: Simon & Schuster. Searching for his mother's roots, Zack, the son of a Jewish father and a black mother, drives to Mississippi to meet his grandfather.

Benedict, H. (2007). *The opposite of love*. New York: Viking. A young biracial girl takes responsibility for a four-year-old boy.

Black, J. (2001). *Black book diary of a teenage stud: Girls, girls, girls*. New York: Avon. In this fictional diary, Jonah is a vulnerable, humorous, likable teenage boy, but girls are a real problem for him.

Block, F. L. (1995). *Baby be-bop*. New York: HarperCollins. Dirk has to come to terms with his own sexual identity.

Bloor, E. (1997). *Tangerine*. San Diego, CA: Harcourt Brace. Paul lives in the shadow of his brother Eric, a football hero. But, what is the hidden secret about his life that Paul is trying to remember?

Blume, J. (1973). *Deenie*. Scarsdale, NY: Bradbury. Deenie's modeling career may be over when she discovers that she has scoliosis.

Blume, J. (1975). *Forever . . .* Scarsdale, NY: Bradbury. Katherine and Michael believe their love will last forever.

Blume, J. (1981). *Tiger eyes*. Scarsdale, NY: Bradbury. After the murder of her father, Davey and her family try to begin a new life in Los Alamos, New Mexico. Another classic is *Forever* (1975).

Bowler, T. (2000). *River boy*. New York: Margaret K. McElderry Books. Can grandfather finish his final painting before he dies?

Bradley, A. (2005). *24 girls in 7 days*. New York: Dutton. Jack Grammar's friends try to help him get a date for the prom.

Brashares, A. (2001). *The sisterhood of the traveling pants*. New York: Delacorte. Were they just ordinary jeans from the thrift store or was there something about them that helped everyone who wore them?

Brinkerhoff, S. (2000). *Second choices*. Minneapolis, MN: Bethany House. In this conclusion to the Nikki Sheridan Series, Nikki relies on her faith to help her live with the difficult choices that she has made in her life.

Brooks, B. (1984). *The moves make the man*. New York: Harper & Row. Basketball provides a bridge between a black boy and a troubled white boy.

Bruchac, J. (1998). *The heart of a chief*. New York: Dial. The story of Chris, a Penacook Indian, looks at some major issues in contemporary American Indian culture: gambling, alcoholism, and the racist use of American Indian names in sports.

Cadnum, M. (1995). *Taking it*. New York: Viking. Anna shoplifts as a way to vent her anger, but things seem to be getting out of control.

Carvell, M. (2002). *Who will tell my brother?* New York: Hyperion. Evan protests the use of Indian names for mascots in his high school.

Cheripko, J. (1996). *Imitate the tiger*. Honesdale, PA: Boyds Mills Press. From a detox clinic Chris Serbo reflects on his life of despair and self-delusion.

Childress, A. (1973). *A hero ain't nothin' but a sandwich*. New York: Coward-McCann. A 13-year-old Harlem boy is becoming a confirmed heroin addict. His story is told by his family and friends.

Cleary, B. (1996/1956). *Fifteen*. New York: HarperCollins. Jane Purdy is surprised when one of the popular boys at school asks her for a date.

Clinton, C. (2002). *A stone in my hand*. Cambridge, MA: Candlewick Press. Malaak, the main character, and her family live in Gaza City in the midst of the intifada of 1988 and 1989.

Conway, C. (2006). *The melting season*. New York: Delacorte. Sixteen-year-old Giselle uses her relationship with Will to help put her life into perspective.

Cormier, R. (1974). *The chocolate war*. New York: Knopf. Jerry Renault does not realize consequences of refusing to sell chocolate for his private school.

Cormier, R. (1977). *I am the cheese*. New York: Knopf. The past holds the key to survival for a young boy.

Cormier, R. (1991). *We all fall down*. New York: Delacorte. Why did four boys victimize Karen Jerome and her family and who is the Avenger?

Cormier, R. (2001). *The rag and bone shop*. New York: Delacorte. Since Alicia was Jason's friend, he could not have killed her, could he? Another novel by this author is *Tenderness* (1997).

Creech, S. (1994). *Walk two moons*. New York: HarperCollins. Sal and her grandparents retrace the route her mother took when she suddenly left home.

Creech, S. (1998). *Bloomability*. New York: HarperCollins. Dinnie has a chance to spend a year in Switzerland.

Crutcher, C. (1987). *The Crazy Horse electric game*. New York: Greenwillow. After being disabled by an accident, a high school athlete regains his mental and physical health.

Crutcher, C. (2001). *Whale talk*. New York: HarperCollins. T. J. champions the underdog Chris and forms a swimming team in this dark novel of hatred, anger, and revenge. Earlier works by Crutcher include *Running Loose, Chinese Handcuffs, Staying Fat for Sarah Byrnes*, and *Stotan!*

Daly, M. (2002/1942). *Seventeenth summer*. New York: Simon & Schuster. Angie Morrow experiences first love.

Davidson, D. (2004). *Jason & Kyra*. New York: Hyperion. Jason, a high school basketball star, and Kyra, a budding scientist, fall in love.

De la Peña, M. (2005). *Ball don't lie*. New York: Random House. Abused and abandoned, Sticky Reichard has to put the past behind him so he can focus on playing college basketball.

Desai Hidier, T. (2002). *Born confused*. New York: Scholastic. Dimple's parents are from India and Dimple seems caught between their traditional beliefs and the culture of her American friends.

Dessen, S. (1996). *That summer*. New York: Orchard. Halley is having a challenging summer because her father is remarrying and her sister is planning a wedding.

Dessen, S. (1998). *Someone like you*. New York: Viking. Halley helps her friend Scarlett deal with a pregnancy and her boyfriend's death.

Deuker, C. (2000). *Night hoops*. Boston: Houghton Mifflin. Through basketball, Nick learns that life is full of choices and, like basketball, you can make adjustments to succeed.

Deuker, C. (2007). *Heart of a champion*. Boston: Little Brown. Problems, including alcohol abuse and the loss of a love one, make it difficult for Seth Barham to focus on becoming a better baseball player.

DiCamillo, K. (2000). *Because of Winn-Dixie*. Cambridge, MA: Candlewick. When India Opal Buloni found a dog in the grocery store, she named him Winn-Dixie after the store. Her life then began to change.

Dorris, M. (1997). *The window*. New York: Hyperion. When her mother goes into alcohol rehabilitation, Rayona begins to find out about her heritage.

Draper, S. (1994). *Tears of a tiger*. New York: Atheneum. Andy's world has come crashing down around him. Is the only person he has left really his 5-year-old brother?

Draper, S. (2003). *The battle of Jericho*. New York: Atheneum. Jericho wants to join the Warriors of Distinction, an elite club. But he begins to feel uncomfortable with the initiation process.

Draper, S. (2007). *November blues*. New York: Atheneum. November and Jericho are trying to forget about Josh's death, but it is impossible, especially since November is carrying Josh's child.

Ellis, D. (2002). *Parvana's journey*. Toronto: Groundwood Books. As the Taliban takes over Afghanistan, Parvana disguises herself as a boy and tries to find her mother. *The Breadwinner* (2001) and *Mud City* (2003) complete a trilogy about Parvana.

Farmer, N. (1996). *A girl named Disaster*. New York: Orchard Books. Fleeing Mozambique and an unwanted marriage, Nhamo struggles to reach Zimbabwe.

Ferreira, A. (2002). *Zulu dog*. New York: Farrar, Straus and Giroux. In postapartheid South Africa, a young Zulu boy seeks to become the friend of a white girl.

Ferris, J. (1996). *All that glitters*. New York: Farrar, Straus and Giroux. Brian is faced with leaving Chicago and spending 6 weeks in the Florida Keys with his father, Leo, after his mother remarries.

Flake, S. G. (2001). *Money hungry*. New York: Hyperion. Money is important to 13-year-old Raspberry, but her schemes to raise some do not always work out as she planned. Another book by Flake is *The Skin I'm In* (1998).

Flake, S. G. (2005). *Bang!* New York: Jump at the Sun. After his younger brother is shot by a stray bullet, thirteen-year-old Mann's father decides to teach him to be a man by leaving him stranded in the woods with his friend, Kee-lee.

Fleischman, P. (1997). *Seedfolks*. New York: HarperCollins. Each person tells his or her story as they rehabilitate an abandoned downtown lot and turn it into a garden.

Fleischman, P. (1998). *Whirligig*. New York: Holt. Brian tries to find forgiveness by building a whirligig.

Fleischman, P. (2001). *Seek*. New York: Simon & Schuster. When Rob Radkovitz is assigned to write his autobiography, he looks back at the voices in his life, especially that of his long-absent father.

Fox, P. (1995). *The eagle kite*. New York: Orchard Books. Liam's father has AIDS and Liam has a secret that he does not want to share with his family.

Friesen, G. (2007). *For now*. Tonawanda, NY: Kids Can Press. In this sequel to *Losing Forever* (2002), Jes Miner-Cooper struggles to deal with the death of her little sister, Alberta, her mother's new marriage to Cal, and her not-so-nice stepsister, Angela.

Froese, D. (2002). *Out of the fire*. Toronto: Sumach Press. When Pete tries to light a bonfire with gasoline both he and Dayle are burned. As she recovers, Dayle thinks about revenge.

Gantos, J. (1998). *Joey Pigza swallowed the key*. New York: Farrar, Straus and Giroux. Follow-up novels include *Joey Pigza Loses Control* (2000) and *I Am Not Joey Pigza* (2007). Joey tries so hard to be good. But when his meds do not work, Joey has problems following directions and paying attention in class. In fact, Joey can get into real trouble if he is not careful.

Garden, N. (1982). *Annie on my mind*. New York: Farrar, Straus and Giroux. Liza met Annie at the Metropolitan Museum of Art. Now they must try to hide their love from people who would not understand. Garden has also written *Good Moon Rising* (1996), *Holly's Secret* (2000), and *The Year They Burned the Books* (1999).

Giff, P. R. (2002). *Pictures of Hollis Woods*. New York: Wendy Lamb Books. Although Hollis Woods is an orphan, she may have found a home with an elderly artist who needs her. But what happened at the last foster home she was in?

Gilbert, B. S. (1996). *Stone water*. Arden, NC: Front Street. When his grandfather is placed in the skilled personal care wing of the nursing home, Grant has a difficult choice to make.

Gilmore, R. (2001). *A group of one*. New York: Holt. When Tara Mehtas' grandmother arrives from India, Tara must begin to deal with her own feelings about her cultural heritage.

Glenn, M. (2000). *Split image*. New York: HarperCollins. Laura Li tries desperately to determine who she is. For some of her fellow students, she's too smart, too pretty, and too perfect. But for Laura, nothing can illuminate the gray of her days.

Going, K. L. (2003). *Fat kid rules the world*. New York: Putnam's. After Curt saves overweight Troy Billings from committing suicide when he jumps off a New York City subway platform, Troy begins to confront the problems in his life.

Going, K. L. (2006). *Saint Iggy*. New York: Harcourt. Born addicted to drugs, Iggy Corso has to find a way to graduate from high school and do something productive with his life.

Grimes, N. (2001). *Bronx masquerade*. New York: Dial. A group of high school students express their fears, concerns, joys, and values as they read the poems that they have written.

Haddix, M. P. (1997). *Leaving fishers*. New York: Simon & Schuster. Going to a new high school, Dorry is lonely until she is befriended by the members of a religious cult.

Hall, L. F. (1997). *Perk! The story of a teenager with bulimia*. Carlsbad, CA: Gurze. It takes a near disaster before anyone recognizes the serious problem that is taking over Perk's life.

Hartinger, B. (2003). *Geography club*. New York: HarperTeen. Students form a group where they can openly discuss their lives, including their sexuality.

Head, A. (1967). *Mr. and Mrs. Bo Jo Jones*. New York, Putnam. As one of the first books to address teenage pregnancy, this story is dated.

Herrera, J. F. (2005). *Cinnamon girl: Letters found inside a cereal box*. New York: HarperCollins. Yolanda and her family are wounded by the attacks on 9/11.

Hewitt, L. (1996). *Soulfire*. New York: Dutton. What will happen when Ezekiel tries to end the problem of gang violence in his Denver neighborhood?

Hinton, S. E. (1967). *The outsiders*. New York: Viking. Ponyboy feels the world is made up of two kinds of people, those with money (the socs) and those like him who live on the outside (the greasers). He has always been willing to fight the socs until the night his friend Johnny kills a soc.

Holland, I. (1991). *The search*. New York: Ballantine. Although Claudia gave her baby up for adoption, she tries to find out what happened to him.

Hurwin, D. W. (1995). *A time for dancing*. Boston: Little Brown. Life changes when 17-year-old Juliana finds that she has cancer.

Ingold, J. (1996). *The window*. San Diego: Harcourt Brace. Blind since the automobile accident that killed her mother, Mary is sent to live with relatives in Texas.

Irwin, H. (1985). *Abby my love*. New York: Atheneum. Chip cannot understand why Abby will not let him get close to her. Then he learns the horrible truth.

Johnson, A. (2003). *The first part last*. New York: Simon & Schuster. Sixteen-year-old Bobby is trying to raise his infant daughter, but sometimes the pressure gets too much to bear.

Juby, S. (2003). *Alice, I think*. New York: Harper Tempest. Home schooled since first grade, Alice is now attending a public high school. But, with her unusual background can she fit into the mainstream teen culture in a small town?

Kerr, M. E. (1986). *Night kites*. New York: Harper & Row. Life can sure get complicated when your best friend's girl makes a play for you and you find out that your brother is dying of AIDS.

Kerr, M. E. (1994). *Deliver us from Evie*. New York: HarperCollins. Things become difficult in rural Missouri for 16-year-old Parr Burrman and his family when his lesbian older sister begins a relationship with the daughter of the town's banker.

Kerr, M. E. (2007). *Someone like summer*. New York: HarperTeen. Seventeen-year-old Annabel Brown dates Esteban Santiago, an illegal immigrant.

Koertge, R. (2002). *Stoner and Spaz*. Cambridge, MA: Candlewick Press. It takes drugged-out Colleen to show Ben that his cerebral palsy does not have to keep him from living.

Konigsburg, E. L. (2000). *Silent to the bone*. New York: Atheneum. Branwell Zamborska is accused by the English au pair of dropping and shaking his baby sister. Now his sister is in a coma and Branwell has lost the ability to talk.

Korman, G. (2002). *Son of the mob*. New York: Hyperion. In this humorous tale, Vince, the son of a Mafia boss, falls in love with Kendra, the daughter of the FBI agent who is investigating his "family."

Koss, A. G. (2000). *The girls*. New York: Dial. Although she was once part of the group, Maya now finds herself on the outside.

Krech, B. (2006). *Rebound*. Tarrytown, NY: Marshall Cavendish. Discrimination and poor race relations make it difficult for Ray Wisniewski to feel comfortable on his basketball team.

Lawrence, I. (2002). *The lightkeeper's daughter*. New York: Random House. Only the McCrae family lives on Lizzie Island, but it can be a refuge from the events that threaten to tear the family apart. However, it also may be a prison that forces them to live together in captivity.

Levitin, S. (1998). *The singing mountain*. New York: Simon & Schuster. On a trip to Israel, a California teen decides to stay and join an Orthodox yeshiva, but his family is sure he has been brainwashed.

Lipsyte, R. (1967). *The contender*. New York: Harper. After he's introduced to boxing, Alfred Brooks finds strength and courage.

Lowry, L. (1977). *A summer to die*. Boston: Houghton Mifflin. Molly, who was always pretty and popular, is now dying.

Lynch, C. (2001). *Freewill*. New York: HarperCollins. Is there really a relationship between Will, the woodcarvings, and the suicides that begin to happen in town? Lynch has also written the Blue Eyed Son series that includes *Blood Relations* (1996), *Dog Eat Dog* (1996), and *Mick* (1996).

Lynch, C. (2002). *Who the man*. New York: HarperCollins. Just who is Earl Pryor? Is he the giant freak that his classmates see, a beloved son as his parents claim, or someone else?

Mack, T. (2000). *Drawing lessons*. New York: Scholastic. What is the relationship between Rory's father and the female art model?

Mackler, C. (2000). *Love and other four-letter words*. New York: Delacorte. When her parents agree to a trial separation, Samantha "Sammie" Davis learns about several four-letter words including *hate*, *gain*, and *grow*.

Martinez, V. (1996). *Parrot in the oven: Mi vida*. New York: HarperCollins. We see life in the projects of a California city through the eyes of a Mexican American teenager.

Mazer, N. F. (1993). *Out of control*. New York: Morrow. Valerie Micho is assaulted by three respected teenage boys.

Mazer, N. F. (1997). *When she was good*. New York: Scholastic. Em's life is complicated by her abusive, emotionally disturbed sister.

McDaniel, L. (1996). *Angels watching over me*. New York: Bantam. While Leah is in the hospital, she meets Rebekah, an Amish girl with strong religious beliefs.

McDaniel, L. (2000). *Angel of hope*. New York: Random House. When Heather (the central character in *Angel of Mercy*) (1999) becomes ill with hepatitis, her sister Amber decides to return to Africa in Heather's place.

McDonald, J. (2001). *Spellbound*. New York: Farrar, Straus and Giroux. When 16-year-old Raven becomes a single mother, she drops out of school and her dreams of college evaporate. Another excellent title by this author is *Swallowing Stones*.

McDonald, J. (2007). *Off-Color*. New York: Farrar, Straus and Giroux. Cameron Storm discovers that her father is African American.

McKean, T. (1997). *My evil twin*. New York: Avon. When Jellimiah tries to get his first name taken out of his school record before it is sent to a new school, he winds up with two identities instead of one.

McLaren, C. (1999). *Dance for the land*. New York: Atheneum. When her father moves the family to his home in Hawaii, Kate is ostracized because she is half-white and longs to return to California.

Miller, M. B. (2002). *Aimee*. New York: Dutton. After being acquitted of helping her best friend Aimee commit suicide, Zoe begins a journal to help her understand her life and her unhappiness.

Mochizuki, K. (2002). *Beacon hill boys*. New York: Scholastic. As a Japanese American, Dan searches for his cultural identity.

Moore, M. (1995). *Under the mermaid angel*. New York: Delacorte. Jesse grieves the death of her brother while Roxanne feels the loss of the child she gave up at birth.

Mori, K. (1993). *Shizuko's daughter*. New York: Holt. Shizuko commits suicide and her husband marries his mistress. Now Shizuko's daughter Yuki must try to make sense of her life.

Myers, W. D. (1992). *Somewhere in the darkness*. New York: Scholastic. Jimmy Little's life in New York with Mama Jean changes dramatically when Crab, his father, returns from jail and takes Jimmy away to Chicago and Arkansas.

Myers, W. D. (1996). *Slam!* New York: Scholastic. Greg Harris faces more challenges from his Harlem neighborhood than he ever did on the basketball court. Other books by this popular author include *Hoops* and *Somewhere in the Darkness*.

Myers, W. D. (1999). *Monster*. New York: HarperCollins. Sixteen-year-old Steve Harmon is being called a monster, as he's on trial for murder.

Myers, W. D. (2006). *Street love*. New York: HarperCollins. Though Damien Battle and Junice Ambers seem to be headed in different directions, they connect and fall in love.

Na, A. (2001). *Step from heaven*. Asheville, NC: Front Street. Korean immigrant Young Ju must adjust to her new life in America and the unraveling of her family as changes begin to drive her father toward violence.

Na, A. (2008). *The fold*. New York: Putnam. Joyce's Gomo offers to pay for a plastic surgery procedure Joyce believes will make her more attractive.

Naidoo, B. (2001). *The other side of truth*. New York: HarperCollins. Because their father is a muckraking journalist, two Nigerian children must flee to England. But even there, they still face problems.

Naidoo, B. (2004). *Web of lies*. New York: HarperCollins. This sequel to *The Other Side of Truth*, follows Sade and her brother Femi to London, where they hope to begin a new life.

Naughton, J. (1989). *My brother stealing second*. New York: Harper & Row. Bobby's brother might have been a star athlete, but when he was drunk, he killed himself and a couple celebrating their wedding anniversary.

Naylor, P. R. (1997). *Outrageously Alice*. New York: Atheneum. In this entry in the popular series of Alice books, Alice is suffering an identity crisis. Other recent books in the popular series include *Alice on the Outside* (1999), *The Grooming of Alice* (2000), *Alice Alone* (2001), and *Simply Alice* (2002).

Nelson, B. (2003). *The new rules of high school*. New York: Viking. One day Max has it all—good grades, editor of the school newspaper, and debate team captain with a beautiful girlfriend. The next day, his whole life starts to change dramatically.

Nelson, T. (1994). *Earthshine*. New York: Orchard. Slim watches her father die of AIDS.

Nye, N. S. (1997). *Habibi*. New York: Simon & Schuster. When her Palestinian-American family moves from St. Louis to Jerusalem, Liyana finds herself in the middle of the conflict between Arabs and Israelis.

Oates, J. C. (2002). *Big mouth and ugly girl*. New York: HarperCollins. Everyone believes Matt really threatened to blow up the school and Ursula lost the basketball game on purpose. Can two misunderstood high school juniors help each other learn who they really are?

O'Connell, R. (2000). *Myrtle of Willendorf*. Asheville, NC: Front Street. Myrtle, soon to be a college sophomore, looks back at her years in high school and tries to find out who she really is underneath the layers of fat.

Oneal, Z. (1980). *The language of goldfish*. New York: Viking. Something is happening to 13-year-old Carrie as she experiences dizzy spells and her mind begins to wander. But no one seems to realize how serious the problem is.

Osa, N. (2003). *Cuba 15*. New York: Delacorte. Violet Paz is preparing for her quincera-ero, a celebration of womanhood, but she is having problems relating her Cuban heritage with her life in suburban Chicago.

Park, B. (2000). *Graduation of Jake Moon*. New York: Atheneum. Granddad has Alzheimer's disease and is becoming increasingly irresponsible.

Parks, L. S. (2005). *Project mulberry*. New York: Houghton Mifflin. When Julia Song and her best friend Patrick decide to raise silk worms, Julia discovers an appreciation for her Korean heritage.

Paulsen, G. (2003). *The glass café*. New York: Wendy Lamb Books. The trouble began when 12-year-old Tony drew pictures of the dancers at the Kitty Kat Club where his mother works.

Peck, R. (1995). *The last safe place on earth*. New York: Delacorte. Walden Woods looks like the perfect suburban community to raise a family, safe from the violence of the city. But Todd and his family soon find out that things are not what they seem.

Peters, J. A. (2003). *Keeping you a secret*. Boston: Little, Brown. Holland Jaeger is shunned by family and friends when she begins dating Cece Goddard.

Placide, J. (2002). *Fresh girl*. New York: Wendy Lamb Books. Mardi's uncle is a political activist in Haiti, and Mardi blames him for all of her problems, even after she escapes to the United States.

Porter, C. R. (1999). *Imani all mine*. Boston: Houghton Mifflin. Fifteen-year-old Tasha loves her daughter Imani, even though Imani was conceived as the result of a rape.

Portman, F. (2006). *King dork*. New York: Random House. Using clues in an old copy of *Catcher in the Rye*, Tom Henderson discovers the truth about his father's death.

Powell, R. (2002). *Three clams and an oyster*. New York: Farrar, Straus and Giroux. When Cade, the "Oyster," misses the first four-man flag football game, Rick, Dwight, and Flint have a weekend to find a replacement or be dropped from the league.

Quinlan, P. (1994). *Tiger flowers*. New York: Dial. When his uncle Michael dies of AIDS, Joel uses his thoughts and dreams to keep Michael's memory alive.

Rennison, L. (2000). *Angus, thongs, and full-frontal snogging*. New York: HarperCollins. Fourteen-year-old Georgia Nicholson shares her crazy life in this humorous diary. Follow-ups include *On the Bright Side, I'm Now the Girlfriend of a Sex God* (2001), *Knocked Out by my Nunga-Nungas* (2002), and *Dancing in my Nuddy-Pants* (2003).

Rigby, R. (2006). *Goal! The dream begins*. New York: Harcourt. Santiago Munez leaves Los Angeles to pursue a career as a soccer player in Europe. Other books in the series include *Goal! II: Living the Dream* (2007) and *Goal! III* (2008).

Rodowsky, C. (1996). *Remembering Mog*. New York: Farrar, Straus and Giroux. Annie struggles to deal with the murder of her sister.

Rottman, S. L. (2002). *Stetson*. New York: Viking. If being abandoned by his mother and living with his alcoholic father isn't enough of a challenge, 17-year-old Stetson suddenly finds he has a 14-year-old sister and she is moving in with him.

Sachar, L. (1998). *Holes*. New York: Farrar, Straus and Giroux. Stanley Yelnats is sent to a correctional camp in the Texas desert where he finds a friend, a treasure, and himself.

Sanchez, A. (2001). *Rainbow boys*. New York: Simon & Schuster. Jason Carrillo, Kyle Meeks, and Nelson Glassman cling to each other for support as they discover their sexuality. Other companion books include *Rainbow High* and *Rainbow Road*.

Sanchez, A. (2006). *Getting it*. New York: Simon & Schuster. Desperate to attract Roxy Rodriguez, Carlos Amoroso asks Sal, a gay classmate, to make his appearance more fashionable.

Shands, L. I. (2001). *Blind fury*. Grand Rapids, MI: Fleming H. Revell. Fifteen-year-old Wakara Sheridan watches as her mother's death changes everyone in the family in a different way.

Shreve, S. (2000). *Goodbye, Amanda the good*. New York: Knopf. Purple hair, dark clothes, and a new boyfriend are all signs that Amanda is changing.

Simeon, J., and Nieuwenhuizen, J. (2002). *What about Anna?* New York: Walker. Anna is living in Belgium when she learns that her brother may not have been killed by a landmine in Bosnia.

Smith, S. L. (2006). *Sparrow*. New York: Random House. Seventeen-year-old Kendall Washington is devastated when her grandmother dies and she becomes homeless, reaching out to family members with no avail.

Sones, S. (2001). *What my mother doesn't know*. New York: Simon & Schuster. In a series of poems, Sophie must decide between her own feelings and those of her friends. The sequel, *What My Girlfriend Doesn't Know* (2007), features Sophie's boyfriend, Robin.

Spinelli, J. (2000). *Stargirl*. New York: Random House. Leo Borlock falls in love with the new and different student at school named Stargirl. A sequel, *Love, Stargirl*, was published in 2007.

Staples, S. F. (1989). *Shabanu: Daughter of the wind*. New York: Knopf. Only 11 years old, Shabanu, a Pakistani girl, wonders if she will be able to obey her father and marry an older man.

Strasser, T. (2000). *Give a boy a gun*. New York: Simon & Schuster. Strasser provides a multi-viewpoint look at a shooting at a high school dance.

Stratton, A. (2004). *Chanda's secrets*. Toronto: Annick. Chanda Kabele is distraught when AIDS destroys her family and friends.

Stuckey, K. (2001). *Conflict in California*. Grand Rapids, MI: Baker Books. The members of the Thunderfoot Ballet Company, the support crew for a racing team, are attending the drag races where they use their Christian faith to help others.

Thomas, R. (1996). *Rats saw God.* New York: Simon & Schuster. Steve was an outstanding student. Now he's on drugs. What happened?

Tolan, S. S. (2002). *Surviving the Applewhites.* New York: HarperCollins. Add Jake, the juvenile delinquent, to the unconventional Applewhite family's Creative Academy and you get a crazy, humorous story.

Toten, T. (2001). *The game.* Calgary: Red Deer Press. Will Dani ever be able to confront the truth about her own family and the reasons that she is now in a New York clinic for detox?

Triana, G. (2005). *Cubanita.* New York: HarperCollins. Mami warns seventeen-year-old Isabel that Andrew is not right for her, but she refuses to listen.

Trueman, T. (2001). *Stuck in neutral.* New York: HarperCollins. Would Shawn's father really try to kill him just because Shawn has cerebral palsy?

Trueman, T. (2003). *Inside out.* New York: HarperCollins. Can Zach's schizophrenia help him survive in a hostage crisis?

Velasquez, G. (1998). *Rina's family secret.* Houston: Arte Publico. Rina cannot understand how her mother can continue to put up with the beatings from her alcoholic husband. Check out other books in the Roosevelt High School series.

Voigt, C. (1996). *Bad girls.* New York: Scholastic. Margalo and Mikey help each other in and out of trouble. A follow-up is *Bad, Badder, Baddest* (1997).

Volponi, P. (2005). *Black and white.* New York: Penguin. Marcus Brown and Eddie Russo are high school basketball stars who decide to rob people. When the crimes are discovered, Marcus is arrested and refuses to tell authorities that Eddie was involved.

Wallace, R. (1996). *Wrestling Sturbridge.* New York: Knopf. Wrestling provides a focus for Ben's life, but it seems that things are always stacked against him.

Walter, V., and Roeckelein, K. (1998). *Making up megaboy.* New York: DK Publishing. Robbie Jones shot the old man in the liquor store, but he will not tell anyone why he did it.

Waltman, K. (2005). *Learning the game.* New York: Scholastic. Nate Gilman admits that he and other members of his basketball team were involved in a robbery.

Watts, J. (2001). *Finding H. F.* Los Angeles: Alyson. Heavenly Faith Simms left her home in Kentucky to find her mother and wound up finding herself.

Whelan, G. (2000). *Homeless bird.* New York: HarperCollins. Koly is 13 years old, a widow, and alone in modern India.

Williams-Garcia, R. (1995). *Like sisters on the homefront.* New York: Lodestar. When 14-year-old Gayle gets pregnant for the second time, she is sent to live with her relatives in the country.

Winston, S. (2008). *The Kayla chronicles.* New York: Little, Brown. Determined to prove that teen girls can be smart, pretty, and athletic, Mikayla Dean competes for a position on the Lady Lions dance team.

Wittlinger, E. (1999). *Hard love.* New York: Simon & Schuster. In this 'zine format novel, John/Gio struggles to find out who he really is in the aftermath of his parents' divorce.

Wolff, V. E. (1993). *Make lemonade.* New York: Holt. In a novel in free verse, Verna LaVaughn tries to help a teenage mother with two small children without letting go of her own dreams.

Wolff, V. E. (2001). *True believer.* New York: Atheneum. In another novel in poetic form, LaVaughn finds her life is changing as her friends join a Christian group, her mother starts dating, and she falls in love. But she learns that things are not always what they seem on the surface.

Woodbury, M. (1998). *Brad's universe.* Victoria, BC, Canada: Orca. Did Brad's father really spend a year in a mental hospital, or was there some other reason that he had to leave the family?

Woodson, J. (1995). *From the notebooks of Melanin Sun.* New York: Blue Sky Press. What do you do when you find out that your mother is in love with another woman?

Woodson, J. (2000). *Miracle's boys.* New York: Putnam. After Mamma dies, all Lafayette has left are his brothers. But, while Ty'ree works to support the family, Charlie seems changed by those years in Rahway Correctional. Will anything bring the brothers back together again? Three other books by Woodson are *I Hadn't Meant to Tell You This* (1994), *Hush* (2002), and *Locomotion* (2003).

Wyss, T. H. (1988). *Here at the Scenic-Vu Motel.* New York: Harper & Row. Living too far from town to commute to school, Jake and six other teenagers spend each week at the Scenic-Vu Motel.

Yolen, J., and Coville, B. (1999). *Armageddon summer*. New York: Harcourt. Marina and Jed help their parents and members of a cult prepare for the end of the world.

Yumoto, K. (1996). *The friends.* New York: Farrar, Straus and Giroux. The friendship between three boys and their elderly neighbor changes all of them.

Zindel, P. (1968). *The Pigman.* New York: Harper & Row. Sophomores John and Lorraine meet Mr. Pignati, the Pigman, but then something destroys the happiness that they found. A follow-up is *The Pigman's Legacy* (1981).

Suggested Readings

Belben, C. (2007). There are no booktalking police: Alternatives to stand-and-deliver presentations. *Library Media Connection, 26*(2), 28–29.

Blasingame, J. (2008). Interview with Chris Crutcher. *Journal of Adolescent & Adult Literacy, 51*(6), 519–520.

Burner, J. A. (2007). Keeping it real. *School Library Journal, 4*(2), 12–15.

Emge, D. (2006). I'm pregnant! Fear and conception in four decades of young adult literature. *Young Adult Library Services, 4*(2), 22–27.

Jackett, M. (2007). Something to speak about: Addressing sensitive issues through literature. *English Journal, 96*(4), 102–105.

Sutton, R. (2007). "Annie on My Mind." *The Horn Book, 83*(5), 543–546.

References

All works of young adult literature referenced in this chapter are included in the Young Adult Books list and are not repeated in this list.

Afolayan, J. A. (1992). Documentary perspective of bibliotherapy in education. *Reading Horizons, 33,* 137–148.

Aiex, N. K. (1993). *Bibliotherapy.* (Report No. EDO-CS-93-05). Bloomington: Indiana University, Office of Educational Research and Improvement. (ERIC Document Reproduction Service No. ED 357 333)

Alcott, L. M. (1868). *Little women, or, Meg, Jo, Beth, and Amy.* Boston: Roberts.

Allen, J. (Ed.). (2002). *Using literature to help troubled teenagers cope with end-of-life issues.* Westport, CT: Greenwood Press.

Aronson, M. (2001). *Exploring the myths: The truth about teenagers and reading.* Lanham, MD: Scarecrow.

Beers, G. K., and Lesesne, T. S. (Eds.). (2001). *Books for you: An annotated booklist for senior high.* Urbana, IL: National Council of Teachers of English.

Bodart, J. R. (2002). *Radical reads: 101 YA novels on the edge.* Lanham, MD: Scarecrow Press.

Bowman, C. A. (Ed.). (2000). *Using literature to help troubled teenagers cope with health issues.* Westport, CT: Greenwood Press.

Carpan, C. A. (2004). *Rocked by romance: A guide to young adult romance genre fiction.* Westport, CT: Libraries Unlimited.

Carroll, P. (Ed.). (1999). *Using literature to help troubled teenagers cope with societal issues.* Westport, CT: Greenwood Press.

Darby, M. A., and Pryne, M. (2002). *Hearing all the voices: Multicultural books for adolescents.* Lanham, MD: Scarecrow Press.

Dodge, M. (1865). *Hans Brinker, or the silver skates: A story of life in Holland.* New York: Scribner's.

Doll, B., and Doll, C. (1997). *Bibliotherapy with young people: Librarians and mental health professionals working together.* Englewood, CO: Libraries Unlimited.

Dresang, E. T. (1999). *Radical change: Books for youth in a digital age.* New York: H. W. Wilson.

Ford, D. Y., Tyson, C. A., Howard, T. C., and Harris, J. J. (2000). Multicultural literature and gifted Black students: Promoting self-understanding, awareness, and pride. *Roper Review, 22*(4), 235–240.

Forgan, J. W. (2002). Using bibliotherapy to teach problem solving. *Intervention in School and Clinic, 38*(2), 75–82.

Goettina, L. (1999, Spring). When books help. *Riverbank Review,* 12–14.

Halsted, J. W. (1994). *Some of my best friends are books: Guiding gifted readers from pre-school to high school.* Dayton, OH: Ohio Psychology Press.

Jones, J. B. (2003). *Helping teens cope: A guide to teen issues using YA fiction and other resources.* Worthington, OH: Linworth.

Jones, P. (1994). THIN books, BIG problems: Realism and the reluctant teen reader. *The ALAN Review, 20*(2), 18–28.

Jordan, A. D. (1995). True-to-life: Realistic fiction. *Teaching and Learning Literature, 5*(1), 16–22.

Kaplan, J. S. (1999). *Using literature to help troubled teenagers cope with identity issues.* Westport, CT: Greenwood Press.

Kaywell, J. F. (Ed.). (2004). *Using literature to help troubled teenagers cope with abuse issues.* Westport, CT: Greenwood Press.

McDuffie, C. (2004). 2004 Medal for Distinguished Contribution to American Letters. Accessed November 19, 2004, from: www.nationalbook. org/dcal_2004_pr.html.

Myers, W. D. (1988). *Fallen angels.* New York. Scholastic.

Rasinski, T. V., and Padak, N. D. (1990). Multicultural learning through children's literature. *Language Arts, 67*(6), 576–580.

Robert Cormier Remembered. (2001, January 1). *Publishers Weekly.* Accessed December, 30, 2002, from: http://publishersweekly.reviewsnews.com/index/asp?layout:articlePrint&articleID=CA16892.

Twain, M. (1876). *The adventures of Tom Sawyer.* Hartford, CT: American.

Twain, M. (1884). *Adventures of Huckleberry Finn (Tom Sawyer's comrade).* New York: Charles L. Webster.

Tyson, C. A. (1999). "Shut my mouth wide open": Realistic fiction and social action. *Theory into Practice, 38*(3), 155–159.

Wolpow, R., and Askov, E. N. (2001). Widened frameworks and practice: From bibliotherapy to the literacy of testimony and witness. *Journal of Adolescent & Adult Literacy, 44*(7), 606–609.

Zindel, P. (2002). The 2002 Margaret A. Edwards Award Acceptance Speech. *Journal of Youth Services in Libraries, 15*(4), 30–34.

Exploring Adventure, Mystery, and Humor

On a cold, fretful afternoon in early October 1872, a hansom cab drew up outside the office of Lockhart and Selby, Shipping Agents, in the financial heart of London, and a young girl got out and paid the driver. . . . Her name was Sally Lockhart; and within fifteen minutes, she was going to kill a man. (Pullman, 1987, p. 3)

Whether waiting for the murderer to strike, jumping at every little noise while reading an edge-of-the seat suspense story, figuring out how the characters can survive a plane crash in the jungles of the tropics or even LOL (laughing out loud) at improbable situations, adolescents like to escape from everyday life into worlds of mayhem, dangerous situations, techno-thrills, mysteries, and humor.

Americans in general seem to be fascinated with mystery, adventure, and humor. According to *Publishers Weekly*, mystery books make up at least half of the books on the national bestseller lists each week (Dahlin et al., 2007). True-life adventure stories such as Sebastian Junger's *The Perfect Storm* (1998) and Jon Krakauer's *Into Thin Air* (1998) and *Into the Wild* (1996), mystery/thrillers such as Dan Brown's novel *The Da Vinci Code* (2003), as well as humorous books by Bill Bryson regularly top the bestseller lists. While some adolescents read contemporary realistic fiction or speculative fiction, others follow the adult trend and turn to adventure and survival, mystery and suspense, or humorous novels for an escape from the problems of everyday life. While these books may explore values and social morality, they also examine the disruption and restoration of order in a person's life in an exciting or funny way. Some might suggest that the escape these books provide can give adolescents a break from the day-to-day routine they often perceive as troubling or boring and provide the thrill and excitement of the unknown. Whatever the reasons for the popularity of these novels, educators and library media specialists can take advantage of it.

The Genres: Adventure, Mystery, and Humor

Through vicariously experiencing adventure, using their sleuthing abilities to solve murders and other mysteries, outwitting a criminal in a suspense novel, and enjoying a laugh that results from a funny situation, young adults have demonstrated a liking for novels of adventure, mystery, and humor. In addition to applauding the fact that so many young people enjoy reading these books, teachers and library media specialists should also be glad that these books can be used to support the curriculum and to encourage reluctant readers.

Adventure

From the *Odyssey* and *Gilgamesh* to *Beowulf* and the Hindu epic of the *Mahabharata*, the ancient epics of wars and the challenges to survive, first told in the oral tradition, have evolved into today's adventure books. Faced with fighting to survive and the possibility of death, the main characters, either the protagonist alone or a group of people, struggle against people and elements that place them in dangerous situations. Adventure novelists such as Caroline Cooney, Mary Casanova, Will Hobbs, and Gary Paulsen—to name just a few—provide stories that attract the interest of many young adults.

A Brief Look at Adventure's Predecessors. With their roots in oral tradition stories and the quests of the knights in medieval tales, written adventure stories first became popular in the eighteenth century with the publication of Daniel Defoe's novel *Robinson Crusoe* (1719), about survival on a desert island. In the nineteenth century, books such as James Fenimore Cooper's *Leather-Stocking Tales* (1850–1851), Robert Louis Stevenson's *Treasure Island* (1883), and Mark Twain's *The Adventures of Tom Sawyer* (1876) and *Adventures of Huckleberry Finn* (1884) continued the adventure genre (Rigby, 1999). By the end of the nineteenth century, adventure books, or "boy's stories" (p. 14), dominated children's literature. American stories were set at home, and British stories were set in foreign countries or waters (Russell, 2009). In the twentieth century, survival stories in which the hero or heroine adapted to, rather than conquered, the environment became popular with the publication of children's books such as Scott O'Dell's *Island of the Blue Dolphins* (1960), and Jean Craighead George's *My Side of the Mountain* (1959) and *Julie of the Wolves* (1972).

Types of Adventure Novels. According to Rigby (1999), adventure stories have a basic theme of exile, physical challenge, and survival/return of the hero or the group. While he divides the adventure into two main categories, the human and the superhuman, our discussion will look only at realistic stories of human adventures. (Superhuman adventures that appear in fantasy novels are discussed in Chapter 7, and those in graphic/comic book novels are discussed in Chapter 12.)

Russell (2009) points out that modern adventure and survival stories have taken on a new meaning. With "technology and impersonal bureaucracy threaten[ing] our identity and . . . even the nature of society and civilization," adventure stories today are set not only in the wilderness but also in the urban environment. However, no matter what the setting, the protagonist(s) must locate food and shelter and provide "protection from threatening forces" (p. 243). In contemporary stories, rescue is no longer an overarching concern. Instead, the focus is on individuals "rising above adversity . . . and discovering themselves" (p. 243).

As you have seen with other genres, it is difficult to divide young adult literature into discrete categories. Thus, adventure and survival books overlap with some of the other genres we discuss in this book. For example, we discuss many excellent nonfiction adventure novels in Chapter 10, and many realistic novels are included in Chapter 5.

Person against nature. A very popular type of adventure novel is that in which an individual or group is pitted against nature. These are often tales of survival in the wilderness; good examples are the series of novels by Gary Paulsen about a boy named Brian and his life in the woods of northern Canada, beginning with *Hatchet* (1988), as well as the novels of Mary Casanova (1995, 1997, 2002). In *Wild Man Island* (Hobbs, 2002), Andy washes ashore on a wild and remote Alaskan island with bears, wolves, and a mysterious bearded man. In *Lucy the Giant* (Smith, 2002), 15-year-old Lucy runs away from her alcoholic father to work on a commercial fishing boat in Alaska where she must endure not only the seas but someone who wants to tell the truth about her age and identity. Not all adventures are set in current times. In Karen Hesse's *Stowaway* (2000), a young boy keeps a diary of his adventures with Captain James Cook on board *the Endeavor* during its round-the-world trip of 1768–1771.

Person against person and nature. Adventure novels become more complex when a person-to-person conflict is added to the challenges supplied by nature. In *Downriver* (Hobbs, 1991) and *River Thunder* (Hobbs, 1997), Jessie and her friends must survive the Colorado River rapids and each other. Likewise, in the Everest series by Gordon Korman (2003), a group of teenagers must learn to work together to conquer the world's tallest mountain. Other wilderness adventure stories include:

- Robb White, *Deathwatch* (1972)
- Jean Craighead George, *Julie's Wolf Pack* (1997)
- Harry Mazer, *The Island Keeper* (1981)
- Roland Smith, *Jaguar* (1997)
- Curtis Parkinson, *Storm-Blast* (2003)

Disasters. Disasters often feature prominently in adventure stories, as nature unleashes floods, famine, epidemics, blizzards, and wildfires, while accidents or conflicts produce plane crashes, shipwrecks, or massacres. Nory tries to save her family when the blight attacks Ireland's potato crop in *Nory Ryan's Song* (Giff,

2000); 14-year-old Emily fights to survive after the sinking of a ferry off Sumatra in *Overboard* (Fama, 2002). In *Walks Alone* (Burke, 1998), a young Apache girl and her family try to survive capture and imprisonment by the "White Eye" soldiers in 1880. In Alexandria, Egypt, in 45 B.C., Damon has just begun a quest to find his father when his ship sinks and he is attacked by sharks in *The Wadjet Eye* (Rubalcaba, 2000). Caroline Cooney has written a number of novels with adventure/survival themes, including *Diamonds in the Shadow* (2007), *Hit the Road* (2006), and *Code Orange* (2007).

Urban adventures. Not all adventure novels are set in the wilderness. Some take place in the suburbs or in the city and include a different type of conflict and survival. Focusing on the conflict of person against other person(s) or person against society, these novels are sometimes considered problem novels and may contain gangs and violence. Several were previously mentioned in Chapter 5. In Francine Prose's *After* (2003), Tom and Becca, trying to survive the aftermath of a school shooting, encounter something just as deadly as the shooting itself.

Four classic urban survival stories are Virginia Hamilton's *The Planet of Junior Brown* (1971), in which a group of homeless boys survive against the odds; Felice Holman's *Slake's Limbo* (1974), in which Aremis Slake tries to escape his problems by going underground in the New York City subways; Walter Dean Myers' *Scorpions* (1988), in which Jamal must decide whether to join his brother's gang; and Ineke Holtwijk's *Asphalt Angels* (1999), in which Alex joins a group of street children in Rio de Janeiro.

Terrorists, assassins, and kidnappers. Other person-against-person conflicts are found in stories of terrorists, assassins, kidnappers, and threats of revenge. Toswiah and her family must enter the witness protection program in Jacqueline Woodson's *Hush* (2002), and Laura becomes involved with terrorists when a package carried by her brother explodes in Carolyn Cooney's *The Terrorist* (1997). Sometimes teens assume the role of eco-saboteur, for example Mullett Fingers in *Hoot* (Hiaasen, 2002). Finally, in *The Kidnappers* (Roberts, 1998), Joey loves to tell tall tales so much that, when he witnesses a kidnapping, no one believes him.

Reasons for using and teaching adventure books. Extreme sports may not appeal to you, but many young people relish the idea of snowboarding Mt. Everest, kayaking 13 of the world's greatest rivers, climbing all 15 of California's 14,000-foot and higher peaks in fewer than four and a half days, or sailing around the world in the 29,000-mile "Around Alone" yacht race. Many adolescents, especially reluctant readers who do not usually pick up a book unless it is part of a school assignment, willingly read books about such adventure and survival experiences.

One way to encourage reluctant readers, especially boys, may be to recommend some of the excellent adventure and survival books that are currently available. At one time, this was barely possible. When Gary Paulsen, a leading author of adventure and survival fiction, was beginning to write for children and young adults, he asked why there were not more books written for boys. After being told that people do not write for boys because boys do not read, Paulsen noted the paradox in this reply. Drawing on his own experiences in the wilderness, he began to write adventure novels that, while they are read by both boys and girls, have a special attraction for many male reluctant readers. Connecting

Adolescents and Their Literature 6–1 suggests another way to encourage reluctant readers using adventure novels.

6–1 • • • •   CONNECTING ADOLESCENTS AND THEIR LITERATURE

To build good readers, you have to encourage young adults to read on a daily basis. One way to do that is to capitalize on teenagers' interests and to use a variety of literary formats, including magazines. These two periodicals regularly contain articles about adventures and survival:

> *National Geographic Adventure*
>
> (www.nationalgeographic.com/adventure)
>
> *Outside*
>
> (www.outsideonline.com)

You can use articles from these magazines or their websites to generate interest in a topic. Then suggest both fiction and nonfiction adventure and survival novels that will expand the topic while appealing to a wide range of readers.

Characteristics of Adventure Novels. Characterized by exciting, fast-moving plots, adventure and survival novels are set in realistic places, although they may be remote or exotic. For the most part, the characters are believable, and the protagonist is usually a strong individual, although those attributes may not be apparent until he or she is placed in a survival situation. However, the focus is always on the interaction between the protagonist and the forces pitted against him or her.

**CONSIDERATIONS FOR
SELECTING YOUNG ADULT LITERATURE ADVENTURE**

When examining young adult adventure literature, ask yourself the following questions:

_____   Is there an exciting, clearly defined plot that develops naturally and logically from the actions and decisions of the characters—one that grabs readers' attention at the beginning of the book?

_____   Are the basic conflicts believable and credible (i.e., conflicts may result from people, nature, or events, but readers must believe that the conflict could have happened)?

_____   Can young adults understand and relate to the protagonist?

_____   Are the characters convincingly real, multidimensional (i.e., they have good and bad traits like most people), and lifelike (with personalities and mannerisms that readers can believe)?

_____   Is there a detailed setting, whether in snow-filled mountains or the streets of an inner city, that contributes to the sense of adventure?

Considerations for Selecting Young Adult Literature: *Adventure* outlines the characteristics of good adventure novels.

Suggestions for Selecting and Using Adventure Novels. Historically, adventure stories were viewed as primarily appealing to boys, while girls read family stories. However, thanks to the increased number of female protagonists in these stories, this view has changed. Today, all young adults, including many reluctant readers, enjoy reading adventure stories, many of which are written for the middle and junior high school level. However, few readers, male or female, will struggle through an adventure book (or any other type of book) if they find it dull and not believable. By carefully selecting contemporary adventure novels with fast-paced plots and interesting characters, you should be able to encourage reluctant young adult readers. Although no specific awards exist for this type of literature, many adventure novels do win major book awards and honors and are included on some of the best books lists that are published each year, especially the lists for reluctant young adult readers. *More Rip-Roaring Reads for Reluctant Teen Readers* (Ammon & Sherman, 1999) includes adventure novels as well as mystery and humor stories. *Blood, Bedlam, Bullets and Badguys: A Reader's Guide to Adventure/Suspense Fiction* (Gannon, 2004) focuses on adventure and suspense novels. Some excellent lists of adventure and survival books are available on the Internet (see Expanding Your Knowledge with the Internet). Connecting Adolescents and Their Literature 6–2 suggests another way you can help adolescents discover good adventure novels.

EXPANDING YOUR KNOWLEDGE WITH THE INTERNET

The following lists of adventure stories and selected authors are available on the Internet.

LIBRARIES ON THE INTERNET

Logan, Utah, Public Library
library.loganutah.org/books/YA/Action.cfm
library.loganutah.org/books/YA/Survival.cfm

Menasha, Wisconsin, Public Library
www.menashalibrary.org/teens/read/booklists/adventure

Los Angeles Public Library
www.lapl.org/ya/books/adventure.php

ADVENTURE NOVELISTS ON THE INTERNET

Will Hobbs
www.willhobbsauthor.com/
www.randomhouse.com/teachers/guides/grade/grade68.html

Gary Paulsen
www.randomhouse.com/features/garypaulsen/about.html
www.randomhouse.com/teachers/guides/pdf/guts.pdf
scholar.lib.vt.edu/ejournals/ALAN/spring99/unwin.html
www.scils.rutgers.edu/~kvander/paulsen.html

Carolyn Cooney
www.teenreads.com/authors/au-cooney-caroline.asp
www.bookpage.com/9611bp/childrens/thevoiceontheradio.html

6-2 ••••• CONNECTING ADOLESCENTS AND THEIR LITERATURE

Try something as simple as a bookmark to lead adolescents to good literature. Reproducible mystery bookmarks appear in the December issue of *VOYA*, or you can make your own. Visit a few of the websites mentioned in this chapter or use the list of books we provide. Keep the list short, with 10 or fewer titles on a variety of reading levels. Be sure your school and public libraries have the titles you include.

Our sample bookmark includes some fantasy, historical, and contemporary adventure novels.

ADVENTURE AND SURVIVAL— PAST, PRESENT, AND FUTURE

FOR ADVENTURE IN THE PAST:

***Adaline Falling Star* by Mary Pope Osborne. 2000.**
Kit Carson's "half-breed" daughter runs away from her cruel relatives to find her father somewhere in the Rocky Mountains.

***The Legend of Bass Reeves: Being the True and Fictional Account of the Most Valiant Marshal in the West,* by Gary Paulsen. 2006.**
Join Bass Reeves, and African American federal marshal in the Indian Territory of the late 1800s.

***The Castaways* by Iain Lawrence. 2007.**
Escaping from a cannibal-infested island, Tom returns to London in this sea faring historical novel. This is the third in a series including *The Convicts* and *The Cannibals*.

FOR PRESENT-DAY ADVENTURE:

***Shipwreck* by Gordon Korman. 2003.**
This is the first in the Island series. Things go wrong when a big storm throws six troubled kids together in order to survive in the middle of the Pacific Ocean. Follow up with the other books in the series: *Survival* and *Escape*.

***Peak* by Roland Smith. 2007.**
Will Peak Marcello become the youngest person to scale Everest?

***The Trap* by John Smelcer. 2006.**
The arctic is an unforgiving place for people who make mistakes and Johnny Least-Weasel finds out.

FOR A FANTASY ADVENTURE:

***Firestorm* by David Klass. 2006.**
Can Jack save Earth from ecological disaster?

Mystery

> People who read mysteries hate mysteries. What they like are solutions. A mystery novel is the only kind of book a reader can pick up knowing that, after some two hundred pages of turmoil, order will be restored at the end. Questions will be answered, problems will be solved, and the disruptive force in the world of the book will be routed out to allow that world to return to its own norm. (Paul, 1999, p. 121)

A good mystery encourages reasoning and problem solving, as well as questioning and examining evidence, fact, and motives. Like a problem novel, a good mystery also explores values and social morality. Behind the plot of each mystery is the idea of "good versus evil, order versus chaos, illusion versus reality, and the necessity of thought as a tool for survival" (DeAndrea, 1994, p. ix).

Mystery books for young adults reflect a wide array of topics including murders, missing or disappearing people, missing items, lies and deceit, games ending in questionable deaths, perplexing or sinister letters and phone calls, and a host of other suspicious occurrences. While some mysteries just tell an interesting story, others have a message about improving people's lives (such as promoting civil rights or conserving natural resources). In a mystery, the "real message . . . is that even in the worst of circumstances, a [person] . . . can make things right using courage, tenacity, and brainpower" (DeAndrea, 1994, p. ix). Although some mysteries are written as novels, others are short stories. And some are written in narrative form, while others—such as Mel Glenn's *Who Killed Mr. Chippendale?* (1996)—are written in free verse. Taken as a whole, mysteries make up 28.1% of all popular fiction sales in North America (Charles, Morrison, & Clark, 2002).

A Brief Look at Mystery's Predecessors. Mysteries first became popular among adults in the early nineteenth century, thanks to Wilkie Collins (e.g., *The Woman in White* and *The Moonstone*) and Edgar Allan Poe (e.g., *The Murders in the Rue Morgue* and *The Purloined Letter*). The trend continued in the late nineteenth and early twentieth centuries, courtesy of Sir Arthur Conan Doyle and his adventures of Sherlock Holmes (e.g., *A Study in Scarlet* and *The Hound of the Baskervilles*). Mystery has long been a favorite of young readers. The 1920s and 1930s saw growth in mystery series featuring juvenile detectives, including the Hardy boys, Nancy Drew, Judy Bolton, the Dana girls, and Cherry Ames (Herbert, 1999). These books were very popular, although they rarely involved the crime of murder and had no ghosts that could not be rationally explained at the end of the story (Nixon, 1994).

These parameters changed when young adult literature broke away from children's literature in the 1960s. Authors became free to include more situations and problems in longer novels that provided more opportunities for character and plot development. Lois Duncan included murder in *Killing Mr. Griffin* (1978), Norma Fox Mazer had a kidnapping by a parent in *Taking Terry Mueller* (1983), and Joan Lowery Nixon wrote of a suspicious suicide in *Secret Silent Screams* (1988). Robert Peck introduced the psychic Blossom Culp in *The Ghost Belonged to Me* (1975) (Nixon, 1994). In addition, Rosa Guy and Virginia Hamilton brought multicultural voices to the mystery field.

Currently, a wide variety of mysteries, both stand-alone and series books, are written by a number of outstanding authors for teens of all interests and all reading levels.

In addition, many older adolescents are reading adult mystery and suspense novels by John Grisham, Sharyn McCrumb, Laurie King, Kathy Reichs, Mary Higgins Clark, and others, while more serious mystery fans read P. D. James, Charles Todd, Ruth Rendell, Ian Rankin, Ed McBain, and Tony Hillerman. A spinoff of the genre consists of the many CD-ROM interactive mysteries and role-playing games now available.

Types of Mystery Books. According to young adult mystery author Lesley Grant-Adamson, "labels are for jam; a novel is too subtle a blend for simple tagging" (Moody, 1990, p. 77). Nevertheless, many attempts have been made to categorize mysteries, with talk of classic British mysteries or locked room and coded mysteries. Novelist Carol Gorman broke the genre into two categories, maintaining that in a mystery you do not know who committed the crime or what the answer is to the mystery until the end of the story, whereas in a suspense novel there is a race against time because the protagonist knows who committed the crime but must prove it before the criminal is able to silence her or him (Crowley, 1998). Another simple way to categorize mysteries is to divide the genre into two types, cozy (with an optimistic outlook) and noir (dark and despairing with a bleak view of life) (DeAndrea, 1994). Others look at themes and distinguish culinary, legal, needlework, craft, and animal mysteries. We use the categories in the yearly mystery review in the December issue of *VOYA*, and shown in Table 6–1.

In our discussion of mysteries, we made several decisions. Like *VOYA*, because of young adults' great interest in adult mysteries, we include a few of them in the following discussion. And given the popularity of mystery series, we mention a number of them as well—usually identifying the first book in the series. Later in this chapter you will find aids for identifying all of the books in a particular series.

P.I. mysteries. Teenagers enjoy reading private investigator (P.I.) novels, even though most are written for adult audiences. Teenagers may enjoy them because they respond to the figure of the "lone seeker of truth . . . who, although disillusioned and even cynical, is never afraid to plunge into the seamy underside of society in the search for truth" (Charles & Morrison, 2000, p. 318). Today these mysteries are often social commentaries with a focus on contemporary themes such as identity theft or mistreatment of the elderly (Gulli, 2008). Although this subgenre began primarily with male protagonists in the classic mystery stories of Sir Arthur Conan Doyle, Dashiell Hammett, and Raymond Chandler, female private investigators are now very popular. Sara Paretsky's V. I. Warshawski is based in Chicago, Sue Grafton's Kinsey Millhone works in California, and Linda Barnes's Carlotta Carlyle calls Boston home.

TABLE 6-1   Types of Mystery

Private investigator (P.I.)

Amateur sleuths

Police procedural

Historical mysteries

Suspense and thriller (including gothic mysteries, also known as romantic suspense)

Mystery blends (mystery blended with fantasy or science fiction)

Amateur sleuths. While many older teens read adult mysteries about amateur sleuths such as those written by Earlene Fowler and Sujata Massey, a number of such novels are written specifically for young adults. For younger adolescents, Wendelin Van Draanen's series focuses on seventh-grade sleuth Sammy Keyes (e.g., *Sammy Keyes and the Art of Deception*, 2003), while Gloria Skurzynski and Alane Ferguson's series are set in national parks (e.g., *Escape from Fear*, 2002). John Feinstein combines sports and mysteries in *Cover Up* (2007) and *Last Shot* (2005). Carl Hiaasen's sleuths look at ecological problems in *Flush* (2005). Two teens become involved with a stolen Vermeer painting in *Chasing Vermeer* (Balliett, 2004). Popular series include Mark Delaney's Misfits, Inc. series, including *Hit and Run* (2002), and Peter Abrahams' Echo Falls mysteries, including *Behind the Curtain* (2006).

Many books for older teens include murder, even though the actual killing does not occur in the book. In *The Angel of Death: A Forensic Mystery* (Ferguson, 2006), Camryn helps her medical examiner father find the murder of a popular teacher. In Tim Wynne-Jones's *The Boy in the Burning House* (2001), Jim Hawkins tries to solve the mystery of what happened to his father by looking into the past. Although not really a series, Daniel Parker's *The Wessex Papers* (2002) is a mystery trilogy set in a ritzy boarding school. Joan Lowery Nixon has been a perennial favorite among teens with her blend of mystery and suspense, such as *Nightmare* (2003), which was published after her death. Other books with amateur sleuths include:

- *Facing the Dark* (Harrison, 2000)
- *The Night the Penningtons Vanished* (Heusler, 2002)
- *Snatched* (Hautman and Logue, 2006)
- *Drawing a Blank: Or How I Tried to Solve a Mystery, End a Feud and Land the Girl of My Dreams* (Ehrenhaft, 2006)

Some mysteries appear in graphic novel format. In *Shutterbug Follies* (Little, 2002), Bee tries to find a killer. In *The Dead Boy Detectives* (Thompson, 2005), two dead teens try to find a missing girl.

Police procedurals. While police play a role in many mysteries featuring amateur sleuths, mysteries in the police procedural subgenre take the reader directly into the professional world of law enforcement, both the criminal investigations and the routine work. Cops are the main focus in the adult novels of Deborah Crombie, Ian Rankin, P. D. James, Ridley Pearson, and Louise Penny.

Perennial favorites among adolescents are Tony Hillerman's Lieutenant Joe Leaphorn and Sergeant Jim Chee novels, set on the Navajo Reservation; and stories of Ute tribal policeman Charlie Moon in the series by James D. Doss. We have already mentioned Robert Cormier's *The Rag and Bone Shop* (2001) in our discussion of realistic fiction; however, it is also a first-class young adult mystery story with the police as main characters.

Historical mysteries. These are very popular; a number of authors write adult series that appeal to adolescents. While these books are good mysteries, they are also able, like good historical fiction, to make another time and place come alive in the reader's mind. Beginning in *The Beekeeper's Apprentice* (1994), Laurie King writes about teenager Mary Russell and her future husband, Sherlock Holmes. In

The Cater Street Hangman (1979), Anne Perry begins the story of Victorian British policeman Thomas Pitt and his upper-class wife, Charlotte. In other series, Barbara Hambly writes of antebellum New Orleans, Stephanie Barron returns to the world of Jane Austen, Tasha Alexander presents a strong Victorian heroine, Lynda S. Robinson sets her mysteries in ancient Egypt, Lindsey Davis returns to ancient Rome, Elizabeth Peters explores Egypt in Victorian times, Jacqueline Winspear examines post–World War I England, and Ellis Peters makes her hero a medieval monk.

Several excellent historical mysteries are available for adolescents. Rachel tries to find the source of mysterious fires in 1872 Boston in *Firehorse* (Wilson, 2006). Philip Pullman sets his mysteries, beginning with *Ruby in the Smoke* (1987), in 1870s England. Avi takes readers to 1849 London in *Traitors' Gate* (2007); Mary Hoffman sets *The Falconer's Knot* (2007) in fourteenth-century Italy. Middle school reluctant readers may also enjoy the Roman Mysteries series by Caroline Lawrence.

Suspense novels. Many of these novels have as their protagonist an innocent individual in a familiar everyday setting who is drawn into a threatening situation. The protagonist may have deal with "the results of the villain's conspiracies and plots" or may be "drawn into committing a crime" (Reid, 1999, p. 438). Some suspense novels have romantic themes and were formerly called gothic novels. Adult suspense novels that are favorites of young adults include those by Mary Higgins Clark and Thomas Perry.

Several authors of young adult literature write suspense. An early suspense novel for young adults was Richard Peck's *Are You in the House Alone?* (1976), one of the first novels to address the terror of date rape. More recently, Nancy Werlin has created a psychological suspense story in *Rules of Survival* (2006). In Elaine Marie Alphin's *Counterfeit Son* (2002), the abused son of a serial killer assumes the identity of one of his father's victims. Many teens who enjoy a story of intrigue and action-packed adventure will enjoy reading the suspenseful spy series of Anthony Horowitz. His books, featuring 14-year-old Alex Rider as the protagonist, include *Stormbreaker* (2001) and *Skeleton Key* (2003). Another suspense series is Jordan Cray's danger.com, which features crimes related to the Internet. In Carol Plum-Ucci's *The Body of Christopher Creed* (2000), when the class outcast disappears, some of his classmates are suspected of playing a role in his disappearance. Several other young adult novels of suspense include:

- Nancy Werlin, *Locked Inside* (2000)
- Robert Cormier, *Tenderness: A Novel* (1997)
- Shelley Sykes, *For Mike* (1998)
- Gail Giles, *Shattering Glass* (2002)

Mystery blends. Finally, there are novels that combine elements from speculative fiction with a mystery. Adult fantasy writer Katherine Kurtz's *St. Patrick's Gargoyle* (2001) follows Paddy, a gargoyle who witnesses an act of vandalism at the church. Michael Crichton's *Timeline* (1999) involves a time-travel mystery, and in Jim Butcher's *Grave Peril* (2001) (part of the Dresden File series), professional wizard Harry Dresden solves mysteries in Chicago.

Writing for adolescents, Charlie Price blends extrasensory perception and mystery in *Dead Connection* (2006), and Joyce McDonald takes a 17-year-old boy back 200 years to meet the ghost of a murderer in *Shades of Simon Gray* (2001). Jenny Carroll (who also writes under the name Meg Cabot) writes *Safe House* (2002), one of the books in the popular 1-800-WHERE-R-YOU mystery series about Jessica and her psychic visions. Steven-Elliott Altman and Michael Reaves combine graphic novel with mystery and a touch of horror in *The Irregulars: In the Service of Sherlock Holmes* (2005). Jasper Fforde combines humor and parody with mystery and fantasy in *The Big Over Easy: A Nursery Crime* (2005). Other mystery blends include:

- Lois Duncan, *Gallows Hill* (1997)
- Elizabeth Chandler, *Dark Secrets: Legacy of Lies* (2002)
- Kathryn Reiss, *PaperQuake* (1998)

Reasons for Using and Teaching Mystery Books. According to young adult novelist Laurence Yep,

> a good mystery challenges the mind. It presents a set of clues, some of which appear so contradictory they seem as tangled as the mythological Gordian knot. The detective wields reason like a knife slicing though the knot to the truth. . . . The stroke must be exact and sure because a mystery must reveal some truth about society and what we hope are the workings of our universe. The knife that cuts is also the knife that shapes us as creatures of reason, as social beings, as readers and writers. (2003, p. 1521)

Although the mystery author creates an exciting or dangerous plot, he or she cleverly plants clues to help the reader solve the mystery along with the protagonist. With the many interesting stand-alone books and series currently available on a wide range of reading levels, there is a mystery to appeal to the reading tastes of almost every young adult.

Series mysteries continue to be popular, as readers enjoy the ongoing characters and the familiar settings. Readers want not only to solve the mystery but also to know more about the characters and to watch them grow and change, something that did not happen in the early formulaic Nancy Drew and Hardy Boys series. In contemporary series, readers can connect with the characters and enjoy reading the solid, orderly format in a very disorderly time. As editor Kate Miciak states: "If a mystery is about disrupting order, then reinstating it, a series mystery is about how the characters who shape the plot not only bring order to their world, but also about how they change and grow because of what has just happened" (Dahlin, 2002). Connecting Adolescents and Their Literature 6–3 suggests one way to use mysteries across the curriculum.

Characteristics of Good Mystery Literature. Plot and characters are very important in both the young adult and adult mysteries that adolescents read. In the former, the protagonist is usually an adolescent who assumes the role of the amateur sleuth, sometimes following in the footsteps of a parent or adult friend who is a P.I. or

6-3 •••• **CONNECTING ADOLESCENTS AND THEIR LITERATURE**

Every teacher has days when the lesson ends early or the class activities are completed in record time. For a change of pace, have a collection of short mysteries close at hand. Teens will enjoy listening to and solving the puzzles without realizing that they are developing their problem-solving skills.

- Check with your library media specialist to identify some collections such as Vicki Cameron's *Clue Mysteries: 15 Whodunits to Solve in Minutes* (2003).
- Join The Two Minute Mystery "Writing" club, sponsored by the Quebec English Schools Network on the Web, at: www.qesnrecit.qc.ca/cc/2mmsolve/ index.html.
- Use short mysteries as a springboard to writing in the English classroom.

police officer. The characters should be engaging, interesting, and multidimensional; and most of them, with the exception of the protagonist, could conceivably be the murderer or perpetrator of the crime.

The plot usually begins with elements of action, intrigue, or suspense to hook the reader. By pursuing a series of clues, the protagonist eventually solves the mystery, and sometimes faces real or perceived danger. All information in the plot (clues) can be important in solving the case, yet in some cases, the author plants misleading information (a red herring) to challenge the reader and the detective. Foreshadowing is often used to heighten the suspense, and there are usually several motives for the crime, lots of plot twists, and plenty of alibis to be investigated. The solution must come from known information, not a surprise villain introduced in the last chapter of the book; yet the clues must be cleverly planted so that the mystery is not solved too easily or too soon. In a suspense novel, the setting often becomes very important, with violent storms, a deserted island, an abandoned mine, or a spooky old house playing an important role. Collaborating with Other

6-1 **COLLABORATING WITH OTHER PROFESSIONALS**

Amy Shimberg and Heidi Meehan Grant (1998) developed a mystery thematic unit combining English and science to build on their students' interest in criminology, forensics, and law. Here's what they suggest:

- Begin with a mystery genre study in the English classroom.
- Ask local attorneys to visit and answer questions about legal procedures.

- Ask police to visit the science class to demonstrate fingerprinting and other basic forensic sciences.
- Host a simulated murder investigation, with a "murder" in the school's hallway, clues planted by the teachers, and science labs for ink, poison, fabric, fingerprint, and handwriting analysis.

CONSIDERATIONS FOR
SELECTING YOUNG ADULT LITERATURE MYSTERY

When examining young adult mystery books, ask the following questions:

_____   Does the author provide clues and endings that seem realistic, not contrived and phony?

_____   Are the characters well-developed and believable?

_____   Does the setting create a mood or present information about a time or a place (e.g., period in history, type of art or music, particular location) without becoming didactic?

_____   Are there clear descriptions of the locale, the events, and the characters and other descriptive material that might lead to or suggest clues?

_____   Is there a "twist" in the plot to that challenges readers to think and to consider new clues?

_____   At the end, after the conflict is convincingly resolved, is the mystery solved, even if some uncertainty remains about the future of some characters?

_____   Does the book provide enjoyment for the reader—a chance to enjoy reading, to be challenged to think and consider all clues, and to want to read additional mysteries or books by the same author?

Professionals 6–1 shows how two teachers used good mysteries to develop an interdisciplinary unit. Considerations for Selecting Young Adult Literature: _Mystery_ summarizes some of the characteristics of a good mystery.

Suggestions for Selecting and Using Mystery Novels. In addition to reading mysteries yourself and evaluating them by looking for the characteristics of good mysteries, you can consult a number of guides.

Awards and best books lists. The Edgar Awards (short for the Edgar Allan Poe Awards), given by the Mystery Writers of America, Inc., have had categories for both children's and young adult mysteries since 1989. Before that only a single children's mystery category existed. The Agatha Award, given by Malice Domestic for traditional or "cozy" mysteries, has a combined children's/young adult category. Other awards for adult mysteries include the Anthony and the Macavity. A number of excellent specialized magazines also review mystery books, including _Mystery Scene_, _The Strand Magazine_, and _Mystery Readers Journal_. We have already mentioned that since 1997 the December issue of _VOYA_ has featured adult mysteries recommended for young adults.

Print review resources. For young adults, Jeanette Larson has written _Bringing Mysteries Alive for Children and Young Adults_ (2004). In addition, although they cover primarily adult mysteries, several excellent mystery reference books provide information on the genre. Examples include:

- *Detecting Women* (Heising, 2000) and *Detecting Men* (Heising, 1998)
- *The Mammoth Encyclopedia of Modern Crime Fiction* (Ashley, 2002)
- *The Encyclopedia of Murder and Mystery* (Murphy, 1999)
- *Killer Books* (Swanson and Dean, 1998)
- *Silk Stalkings* (Nichols and Thompson, 2000)
- *100 Favorite Mysteries of the Century* (Huang, 2000)
- *St. James Guide to Crime & Mystery Writers* (Pederson, 1996)
- *Murder in Retrospect: A Selective Guide to Historical Mystery Fiction* (Burgess and Vassilakos, 2005)
- *Critical Survey of Mystery and Detective Fiction* (Rollyson, 2008)
- *The Essential Mystery Lists: For Readers, Collectors, and Librarians* (Sobin, 2008)

In addition, the December listing of adult mysteries for young adults in *VOYA* often includes reference books.

Online resources. A number of Internet sources have information about writing mysteries and incorporating mystery writing into the English curriculum. The Two Minute Mystery Writing Club provides detailed information on the writing process and specific guidelines for creating the essential ingredients of a good mystery. Project activities and teaching ideas can be adapted for working with a wide range of adolescents; for example, Joan Lowery Nixon provides an entire mystery writing workshop on the Web. Expanding Your Knowledge with the Internet lists some of the previously mentioned sources and other Internet sites.

Muse (1999) notes that young adult mysteries often have themes of social responsibility and social realism. By centering the moral debate around a conflict between good and evil, mysteries encourage readers to question values and even to combine

EXPANDING YOUR KNOWLEDGE WITH THE INTERNET

On the Internet you can find information on mysteries—awards and prizes, periodicals, book lists, teaching guides, and selected writers at sites such as the following:

MYSTERY WRITERS OF AMERICA, INC.

Mystery Writers of America, Inc., an organization for mystery writers and other professionals in the mystery field, has a database of the Edgar Award winners and nominees
www.mysterywriters.org/

AWARDS AND PRIZES

Mystery Writers of America, Inc., an organization for mystery writers and other professionals in

the mystery field, has a database of the Edgar Award winners and nominees
www.mysterywriters.org/

The members of Mystery Readers International vote for their favorite mysteries in four categories
www.mysteryreaders.org/macavity.html

A list of recent Anthony Award–winners and other awards given at the Bouchercon World Mystery Convention
www.bouchercon.info/

Agatha Award winners
www.malicedomestic.org/agathaawards.html

PERIODICALS

Mystery Readers Journal
www.mysteryreaders.org/

Ellery Queen Mystery Magazine
www.themysteryplace.com/eqmm/

The Strand Magazine
www.strandmag.com/guidlines.htm

MYSTERY BOOK LISTS ON THE WEB

Adult Mysteries for Teens
www.ala.org/ala/yalsa/booklistsawards/
popularpaperback/1998popularpaperbacks.
cfm#adult

Page Turners—Adult Novels for Teens
www.ala.org/ala/yalsa/booklistsawards/
popularpaperback/1998popularpaperbacks.cfm#adult

Carol Hurst's Children's Literature Newsletter for January 1998 features mysteries for younger adolescents
www.carolhurst.com/newsletters/
31bnewsletters.html

A number of public libraries provide lists of mysteries for young adults: Mercer County Library System, New Jersey
www.mcl.org/ys/bibmystya.html

Hewlett-Woodmere Public Library, New York
www.nassaulibrary.org/hewlett/yamystery2.html

Menasha WI Public Library
www.menashalibrary.org/teens/read/booklists/
mystery

OTHER RESOURCES

Ideas and lesson plans for using mysteries in the classroom
mysterynet.com/learn/

A mystery timeline with links to famous mystery authors
mysterynet.com/timeline/

Millinium Mystery Madness was created by students at Ss. Peter & Paul School (K–8), Naperville, Illinois
library.thinkquest.org/J002344/

AUTHORS OF MYSTERIES

Yahoo maintains a page of links to information about mystery authors
dir.yahoo.com/Arts/Humanities/Literature/
Authors/Mystery/

Lois Duncan
loisduncan.arquettes.com/

TEACHING AIDS

The Two Minute Mystery Writing Club is designed to help students write their own "twistedly plotted whodunits"
www.learnquebec.ca/en/content/pedagogy/cil/
cc-registry/lbdoing/2mmclub/index.html

Mystery Writing with Joan Lowery Nixon is a writers' workshop with a teacher's guide available from Scholastic
teacher.scholastic.com/writewit/mystery/
index.htm

The 42eXplor project lists mystery Web sites that can be connected to classroom projects
www.42explore.com/mystery.htm

A WebQuest on writing a historical mystery involves social studies, English, and information literacy skills for high school students
dina17.tripod.com/mywebquest/index.htm

entertainment with lessons on history and culture. Thus, mystery units can go beyond the English classroom and involve a number of other subjects. Collaborating with Other Professionals 6–2 identifies some Internet WebQuests that incorporate mysteries throughout the curriculum. Connecting Adolescents and Their Literature 6–4 suggests some additional ways to share mysteries with adolescents.

COLLABORATING WITH OTHER PROFESSIONALS

Teachers can work together and with a library media specialist and/or technology facilitator to have students complete WebQuests, a number of which center around mysteries.

- In a forensic mystery WebQuest, students use logical thought processes and scientific inquiry skills to determine whether or not the science accurately explains the crime:
  projects.edtech.sandi.net/kearny/forensic/
- Was It Murder? The Death of King Tutankhamun is a social studies and science WebQuest:
  www.pekin.net/pekin108/wash/webquest/

CONNECTING ADOLESCENTS AND THEIR LITERATURE

Look for ways to capitalize on the interest of young adults in mysteries.

- Host a mystery night program in the school or public library and allow adolescents to help solve an imaginary case. For more information on a successful program, visit: www.ala.org/Content/NavigationMenu/YALSA/For_Members_Only/YAttitudes/Archives.

- *The Mystery Readers' Advisory: The Librarian's Clues to Murder and Mayhem* (Charles, Morrison, and Clark, 2002) has a number of suggestions for promoting mysteries that both teachers and librarians can use:

  - Annotated book lists, bookmarks, and bibliographies
  - Displays that focus on topics (culinary mysteries, crime around the world, teens as sleuths), types (historical mysteries), or authors
  - Book discussion groups
  - Booktalks
  - Linking films and books
  - Celebrations of events in the history of mysteries

Finally, From Page to Screen identifies some mystery and adventure novels that have been released as movies.

Humor

According to author James Howe, "humor is nature's way of saying, 'Lighten up'" (1995, p. 5). It is a form of play (Boyd, 2004; Caron, 2003), an "affirmation of the resilience of humanity and an expression of hopefulness" (Russell, 2000, p. 176). It has also been called a "mechanism for survival" (Heins, 1979, p. 637) and an "antidote to the anxieties and disasters of life" (Opie & Opie, 1992, p. 14). Thus many young adults turn to humorous books when they want a good laugh or maybe a polite chuckle. When they read about others' antics, sayings, mishaps, and puns, adolescents

from Page to Screen

ADVENTURE, MYSTERY, AND HUMOR

Good cinematography can add a visual thrill to stories of adventure and mystery, but simplified and shortened stories sometimes compromise the details that make the original texts riveting. Consider comparing the following films with the novels they were based on to see how well these filmmakers realized their cinematic potential.

HOUNDS OF THE BASKERVILLES

★★★ | 1959 | Unrated

In this atmospheric and subdued adaptation of Sir Arthur Conan Doyle's classic mystery, director Terence Fisher reimagines Doyle's world of logic as a realm of evil. His version is spooky and effective, if often far afield from the original novel. This adaptation makes for an interesting comparison to the original text when considering artistic interpretation.

JAWS

★★★★ | 1975 | PG

Peter Benchley's novel is a favorite among adolescents. Charged with the task of coscripting his own work for the screen, Benchley succeeded where most screen adaptations fail: he wrote a movie that is superior to the novel.

SOMETHING WICKED THIS WAY COMES

★★★ | 1983 | PG

Ray Bradbury adapted his own novel for the screen, focusing as much on the mystery behind "Dark's Pandemonium Carnival" as on the fantasy that made the novel famous.

THE MALTESE FALCON

★★★★ | 1941 | Unrated

Among the best cinematic mysteries ever filmed, director John Huston's noir adaptation of Dashiell Hammett's novel ranks at #23 on the American Film Institutes list of the 100 best films.

may see themselves in these humorous situations, or they may just be escaping from the ordeals they perceive themselves experiencing in their everyday lives. Either way, they enjoy the humorous works of such authors as Joan Bauer, Richard Peck, Todd Strasser, Terry Pratchett, Gordon Korman, Louise Rennison, and Carolyn Mackler.

Joan Bauer, a writer of humorous fiction, regards humor as a survival tool. She believes that seeing humor in life shows that an individual has moved from looking at life as a series of problems to gaining a greater sense of clarity and control it; she sees humor as a series of mirrors. When young adults look into these mirrors, they learn to distinguish between the laughter that shames and ridicules and the laughter that brings redemption and goodhearted feelings (Bauer, 1996).

A Brief Look at Humor's Predecessors. "Humor is seeing the Emperor without his clothes" (Howe, 1995, p. 7). Humorous stories may have begun with the droll, simpleton, or noodlehead tales and the tall tales found in the oral folk tradition, which often poked fun at human foolishness and the stupidity of some people. Miguel de Cervantes incorporated these characteristics into his classic sixteenth-century novel of Don Quixote. Adding foolishness to their own children's stories written in the late 1800s and early 1900s, Lucretia P. Hale (e.g. 1880) told stories of the Peterkin family, and P. L. Travers (e.g., 1934) recounted the adventures of Mary Poppins.

By the middle of the twentieth century, Beverly Cleary (e.g., 1955) wrote about Ramona and her family, Sid Fleischman (e.g., 1965) told stories about McBroom, Judy Blume (e.g., 1972) provided funny stories of Fudge and his family, and James Howe (e.g., 1979) invented a vampire rabbit named Bunnicula. For adolescents, Douglas Adams added humor to space travel in *The Hitchhiker's Guide to the Galaxy* (1979), Sue Townsend penned *The Secret Diary of Adrian Mole, Aged 13 3/4* (1984), Paula Danziger wrote *The Cat Ate My Gymsuit* (1988), and Jill Pinkwater introduced Brenda Tuna and her friend India Ink Tiedlebaum in *Buffalo Brenda* (1989). Today a number of writers continue this tradition by writing humorous tales for adolescent readers.

Types of Humor in Books. Humor can be found in any type of novel (historical fiction, science fiction, realistic fiction, mystery) as well as in short stories, poetry, and graphic novels. There have been many attempts to categorize humor. Hogan (2005) arranges his study of humor in "stages of adolescent development" (p. xii), starting with family and peers and leading to authority figures, romance, and adulthood. In contrast, Farber (2007), suggests a taxonomy based on the "kind of payoff that an instance of humor provides" (p. 72) including derisive, empathetic, counter-restriction, aggressive, sexual, and nonsense humor. However, as Max Eastman noted in 1936 in the introduction to *Enjoyment of Laughter*, "nothing kills the laugh quicker than to explain a joke" (Howe, 1995, p. 4). Thus, rather than try to categorize humorous books, we have decided to list, in Table 6–2, some of the types of humor found in young adult literature, along with young adult books where you can find each type. Keep in mind that any one of these books may contain other types of humor as well.

TABLE 6-2   Types of Humor Found in Young Adult Literature

Strange and/or funny characters: *Enter Three Witches* (Gilmore, 1990)

Impossible, absurd, and/or ridiculous situations: *Lawn Boy* (Paulsen, 2007)

Suspense, surprise, and/or unexpected actions and endings: *Count Karlstein* (Pullman, 1998)

Wordplay: jokes, puns, malapropisms: *Math Curse* (Scieszka, 1995)

Exaggeration, fabrication, irony, and incongruity: *Swindle* (Korman, 2008)

Slapstick comedy: *Who Put That Hair in My Toothbrush?* (Spinelli, 1984)

Satire: *The Amazing Maurice and His Educated Rodents* (Pratchett, 2001)

Hyperbole: *Year of the Griffin* (Jones, 2000)

Innuendoes and double-entendres: *Geography Club* (Hartinger, 2003)

Tricks and twists: *The Bad Beginning* (Snicket, 1999)

Sarcasm: *Rats Saw God* (Thomas, 1996)

In addition to some we mentioned in Chapter 4, many other young adult novels combine humor and realistic fiction. Carolyn Mackler has written a number of funny realistic novels, including her celebration of a plus-size girl in the Michael L. Printz honor book *The Earth, My Butt, and Other Big Round Things* (2003), and the story of a serious girl whose planned life is turned upside down in *Vegan Virgin Valentine* (2004). In *Confess-O-Rama* (Koertge, 1996), when Tony calls the self-help hotline, he does not realize who he is telling all his secrets to. Brad in *Behaving Bradley* (Nodelman, 1998) tries to gather student opinion for the school's new code of conduct. In *Absolutely, Positively Not* (LaRochelle, 2005), Steven has lots of ideas, which are usually humorously wrong, for ways to prove he is not gay.

Some diary and journal formats provide humor for adolescents. Courtney Von Dragen Smith shares her feelings as she tries to survive her senior year and breaking up with her boyfriend in *Truth or Diary* (Clark, 2000). Mary Lou documents the ups and downs of a typical 13-year-old girl interspersed with her thoughts about her summer reading assignments in *Absolutely Normal Chaos* (Creech, 1995).

Several authors have written a number of humorous novels for young adults. Gordon Korman is a perennial favorite, with *Son of the Mob* (2002), *No More Dead Dogs* (2000), *The Chicken Doesn't Skate* (1996), *Losing Joe's Place* (1993), and others. In *Squashed* (1992), Joan Bauer writes of overweight Ellie Morgan who has a fascination with growing giant pumpkins; in *Rules of the Road* (1998) Bauer sends shoe-selling sophomore Jenna Boller on a road trip with elderly Mrs. Gladstone. David Lubar provides humorous insights about life in both *Dunk* (2002) and *Flip* (2003). Louise Rennison takes readers to England in her stories of Georgia Nicolson, including *Angus, Thongs and Full-Frontal Snogging* (2000), *On the Bright Side, I'm Now the Girlfriend of a Sex God* (2001), and *Dancing in My Nuddy-Pants* (2003).

Humor crosses genres. Fantasy author Patricia Wrede has written several humorous books, including *Dealing with Dragons* (1990), in her Enchanted Forest Chronicles series and, with Caroline Stevermer, *Sorcery and Cecelia, or the Enchanted Chocolate Pot* (2003). Todd Strasser also combines speculative fiction and humor in books such as *Help! I'm Trapped in an Alien's Body* (1998) and *How I Spent My Last Night on Earth* (1998). *Zap* (2005), by Paul Fleischman, is a parody of the theatre. Novel and cartoon combine in Gary Larson's *There's a Hair in My Dirt! A Worm's Story* (1998). Root Nibot has three talking monkeys in his graphic novel *Banana Sunday* (2006). Kevin Rubio unleashes two bumblers in the graphic novel *Star Wars: Tag and Bink Were Here* (2006). Finally, Terry Pratchett has created the bizarre land of Discworld, featuring fantasy spoofs and madcap adventures that begin with *The Colour of Magic* (1983) and continue with *Thief of Time* (2001) and *Making Money* (2007).

Historical novels also incorporate humor. In Karen Cushman's *Catherine, Called Birdy* (1994), readers meet a medieval girl who is determined not to get married. In Richard Peck's *A Long Way from Chicago* (1998), a brother and sister visit their grandmother in rural Illinois during the Great Depression and find that she is constantly involved in outlandish schemes.

Reasons for Using and Teaching Humor. Attempting to provide a theoretical framework for an exploration of the role of humor in literature, Farber (2007) found that the traditional theories of humor—including the classical superiority theory, Spencer and Freud's release or relief theory, and the incongruity theory—do not adequately explain contemporary humor. Most people "bypass theory entirely and simply accept humor as a given: an unanalyzable fact of human life" (p. 67).

Humor for adolescents is "not just a weapon. It helps them deflect some of life's more perplexing problems" (Davis, 1999, p. 15), which they experience every day in their own lives and vicariously through the media. By helping them work through and with their emotions, humor can be both a barrier and a tool for overcoming that barrier. An author must find a balance between the serious and the humorous to make the humor effective. Even in the midst of pain, laughter can be a positive force when it brings hope for the future and helps characters overcome fears and adversity. Humor can also allow readers to look at social problems and cultural differences because it lowers barriers to discussion while revealing problems and issues in a new light. Comedy questions "the accepted social structures" (Russell, 2000, p. 167) as it holds up a "mirror to society" (p. 176). By asking readers to "evaluate society's artificial limitations in the form of customs, habits, mores, and manners" (p. 167), it leads to deeper understanding.

As Paul Lewis (1995) has said:

> The suggestion that we should work the study of humor into English curricula starting in middle school is based . . . on a sense that humor can be a powerful force in the expression of any value or idea. . . . We should take [students] inside jokes to expose the subtle way humor can convey information, images, and assertions. (p. 10)

A number of researchers (Gentile & McMillan, 1978; Jalonga, 1985; Klesius, Laframboise, & Gaier, 1998; Kuchner, 1991; McGhee, 1979; Monson & Sebesta, 1991) have studied the humor preferences of various developmental groups. While children enjoy books with incongruous events, riddles, and linguistic wordplay, younger adolescents usually enjoy more complex, aggressive, or "sick" humor, as well as slapstick comedy. When puberty begins, humor often becomes more aggressive and sexual, with lewd jokes and with authority figures bearing the brunt. Interest in riddles is replaced with an appreciation of the humor in real-life stories. Finally comes an understanding of more complex intellectual humor, including parody.

CONSIDERATIONS FOR
SELECTING YOUNG ADULT LITERATURE HUMOR

When evaluating humor, ask the following questions:

_____ Is the work well-written? Are wording, sentences, and paragraphs well-constructed?

_____ Is the plot interesting? Does it capture and hold the readers' attention?

_____ Are the chapters easy to read and of a length that will appeal to young adult readers?

_____ Are the characters developed to a point where readers can see both strengths and weaknesses?

_____ Is the humor developmentally appropriate (i.e., do various ages of readers understand and appreciate the humor)?

Given the popularity of humor, why are teachers reluctant to use more humorous works? To Cart (1995), "humor is the Rodney Dangerfield of literary forms: It gets no respect" (p. 1). In his Zena Sutherland lecture, Jon Scieszka (2005) wonders why tragedy or sadness is seen as a "more valid and deeper emotion than happiness" (p. 655) and tragedy "more substantial than comedy" (p. 655). Building on E. B. White's comment that humor is like a frog—it dies when we dissect it—Scieszka believes that teachers are often reluctant to use humor because they cannot analyze and discuss it without destroying it.

Characteristics of Humor. Humor comes from unusual, ludicrous, or incongruous events, characters, and settings that appeal to adolescents across a wide range of ages, developmental levels, and reading abilities. Subjects of humor can range from perfectly normal people who wind up in funny, but realistic, situations to zany, whimsical, nonsensical characters. While some humorous books are straight narratives, others, like works of contemporary realistic fiction, break from the traditional narrative pattern and include clippings, drawings, memos, newspaper ads, and other artifacts that add to the story. Whatever the format of the book, the adolescent protagonist should be placed in realistic situations where he or she can do things that readers can relate to. In addition to being well-written stories, humorous novels should make the reader laugh; since different things make different people laugh, humorous tales need to reflect the wide-ranging interests of adolescents. Considerations for Selecting Young Adult Literature: *Humor* lists some important features of well-written humor.

Suggestions for Selecting and Using Humor. According to Teri Lesesne (2000), while humorous books for children abound, humor is "in terribly short supply for middle and high school readers" (p. 60). Unfortunately, no awards are given specifically for humorous stories. A number of websites do include lists of recommended titles. Expanding Your Knowledge with the Internet contains some pertinent information.

 ## Expanding Your Knowledge with the Internet

You can find information about humor at these websites:

BOOK LISTS

The YALSA has a list of recommended humor books
www.ala.org/ala/yalsa/booklistsawards/ popularpaperback/07ppya.cfm.

The Tigard, Oregon, Public Library has a list of books of humorous fiction
www.ci.tigard.or.us/library/teens/reading_for_fun/ humor_list.asp

HUMOROUS AUTHORS ON THE INTERNET

Lemony Snicket
www.lemonysnicket.com/

Gordon Korman
www.gordonkorman.com/

Carolyn Mackler
www.carolynmackler.com

LOL @ YOUR LIBRARY—RESOURCES ON HUMOR BOOKS

wikis.ala.org/yalsa/index.php/Teen_Read_Week

Several resources provide information on humor. A recent reference book is *Humor in Young Adult Literature: A Time to Laugh* by Walter Hogan (2005). The March 1999 issue of *English Journal*, published by the NCTE for secondary school educators, and the September 1995 issue of *Voices from the Middle*, the NCTE publication for educators in the middle grades, focus on using humor in the English classroom. Barbara S. Morris (1999) discusses the use of character studies from comedy television shows. Colleen A. Ruggieri (1999) explains how she uses humor to capture her students' attention as well as to teach a lesson. Tom Tatum (1999) tells how he uses puns in his vocabulary reviews with college-bound students. Andrew Dunn (1999) describes a clever bulletin board idea: he uses paper cutouts of tee shirts and prints literature-related slogans on them such as "Ahab Was a Whale of a Guy" or "King Arthur Used a Knight Light" (p. 65). While teaching in a middle school, Michele McInnes (1995) explained how she uses humor with her advisees, and Dan Rothermel (1995) wrote about how he takes everyday events, twists and turns them, and comes up with the unexpected in his writing workshop. We encourage you to read these and other articles to discover ways to use humor and humorous literature in your classroom. Finally, Using Multiple Readings contains some questions that reflect various critical approaches to Carolyn Mackler's *The Earth, My Butt, and Other Big Round Things (2003)*.

USING MULTIPLE READINGS

The following are questions critics might ask about *The Earth, My Butt, and Other Big Round Things* (2003), by Carolyn Mackler.

New Criticism
Why did the author choose to interject email messages? How do the email messages extend the story?

Archetypal Criticism
How does Virginia's impression of Byron change throughout the novel, and how does this relate to her own transformation?

Feminist Criticism
What comments does the author seem to make about body image and its impact on self-esteem?

Marxist Criticism
What is the importance of money to Virginia? To Mr. and Mrs. Shreves?

Historical-Biographical Criticism
What characteristics, images, and/or motifs make it clear that this novel is a product of the twenty-first century?

Concluding Thoughts

Obviously, adventure and survival, mystery and suspense, and humorous novels are a very important part of young adult literature. While we have tried to include many of them in this chapter, we encourage you to consult the selection guides we have mentioned to locate additional titles. Because these books provide vicarious experiences, a sense of enjoyment, and an opportunity to get away from the trials of everyday life, they should remain popular with adolescents. Recognizing this popularity, educators and library media specialists should seek to incorporate quality and age-appropriate books into both classroom and media center book collections and to integrate these books into the middle and secondary school curriculum.

Young Adult Books

This section includes young adult titles mentioned in this chapter.

ADVENTURE AND SURVIVAL—FICTION

Burke, B. (1998). *Walks alone*. San Diego: Harcourt Brace. A young Apache girl struggles to survive after an attack on her village.

Casanova, M. (1995). *Moose tracks*. New York: Hyperion. Twelve-year-old Seth lives an exciting life in northern Minnesota.

Casanova, M. (1997). *Wolf shadows*. New York: Hyperion. Seth becomes involved in the conflict over the wolves in northern Minnesota.

Casanova, M. (2002). *When eagles fall*. New York: Hyperion. After she paddles to a remote island to band some eaglets, Alex is stranded by a storm.

Cooney, C. (1997). *The terrorist*. New York: Scholastic. Everything changes when a package carried by Laura's brother explodes.

Cooney, C. (2005). *Code orange*. New York: Laurel-Leaf. Was it really smallpox in the envelope Mitty found?

Cooney, C. (2006). *Hit the road*. New York: Delacorte. It should have been an easy drive to her grandmother's college reunion, but Brittany becomes involved in a theft and kidnapping.

Cooney, C. (2007). *Diamonds in the shadow*. New York: Delacorte. When the Finches sponsor an African refugee family, they endanger their own survival.

Fama, E. (2002). *Overboard*. Chicago: Cricket Books. When the ferry Emily is on sinks off the coast of Sumatra, she fights to save herself and a young Indonesian boy.

George, J. C. (1997). *Julie's wolf pack*. New York: HarperCollins. This continues the story begun in *Julie of the Wolves* (1972). Julie begins a third adventure with the wolf pack that saved her life.

Giff, P. R. (2000). *Nory Ryan's song*. New York: Delacorte. Can Nory and her family survive the 1845 Irish potato famine?

Hamilton, V. (1971). *The planet of Junior Brown*. New York: Macmillan. Streetwise Buddy Clark leads a group of homeless boys and befriends Junior Brown as Junior begins to slip into madness.

Hesse, K. (2000). *Stowaway*. New York: Margaret K. McElderry Books. Captain James Cook sets out on an around-the-world trip in 1768.

Hiaasen, C. (2002). *Hoot*. New York: Knopf. To save the burrowing owls, Mullett Fingers and his friends sabotage the building site for the proposed Pancake House by putting alligators in the portable toilets and releasing cottonmouth snakes to terrorize the guard dogs.

Hobbs, W. (1991). *Downriver*. New York: Atheneum. Jessie and her friends ditch their guide from "Hoods in the Woods" camp and decide to run the rapids of the Grand Canyon on their own.

Hobbs, W. (1997). *River thunder*. New York: Delacorte. In the sequel to *Downriver*, Jessie and her crew return for another adventure on the Colorado River. Can they forget their differences and work together as a team?

Hobbs, W. (2002). *Wild man island*. New York: HarperCollins. When Andy tries to visit the site of his father's death, his sea kayak is blown to a remote Alaskan island. Other adventure books by Hobbs set in Alaska include *Jason's Gold* (1999) and *Down the Yukon* (2001).

Holman, F. (1974). *Slake's limbo*. New York: Scribner. As his life seems to crumble all around him, Aremis Slake flees into the New York City subway tunnels, where he intends to spend the rest of his life.

Holtwijk, I. (1999). *Asphalt angels*. Asheville, NC: Front Street. The Asphalt Angels, a gang of street kids, provide protection and support, but there is a price to pay for security.

Korman, G. (2003). *The contest.* London: Scholastic. Four adolescent boys want to be the youngest expedition to climb Everest, but their troubles begin before they leave Base Camp. Other books in the series are *The Climb* (2003) and *The Summit* (2003).

Mazer, H. (1981). *The island keeper.* New York: Delacorte. Cleo tries to escape personal problems by fleeing to a desolate Canadian island, where her major problem becomes survival.

Myers, W. D. (1988). *Scorpions.* New York: Harper & Row. With his older brother Randy in jail, Jamal must decide whether to join the gang known as the Scorpions.

Parkinson, C. (2003). *Storm-blast.* New York: Random House. Regan does not get along with his sister Carol and cousin Matt. But when the three are swept out to sea, they will only survive if they learn to cooperate with each other.

Paulsen, G. (1988). *Hatchet.* New York: Viking Penguin. After a plane crash in northern Canada, Brian learns to survive in the wilderness with only a hatchet. Sequels include *The River* (1991), *Brian's Winter* (1996), and *Brian's Return* (1999).

Prose, F. (2003). *After.* New York: HarperCollins. The school shooting was bad enough. Now Tom and his friends find that friends who refuse to conform to the new school rules are disappearing.

Roberts, W. D. (1998). *The kidnappers.* New York: Atheneum. Joey sees the men kidnapping Willie Groves. But will anyone believe his story before it's too late?

Rubalcaba, J. (2000). *The wadjet eye.* New York: Clarion. Damon leaves Alexandria, Egypt, in 45 B.C. to find his father in the Roman army in Spain.

Smith, R. (1997). *Jaguar.* New York: Hyperion. Jacob finds adventure on the Amazon River when he accompanies his father to a jaguar preserve.

Smith, S. L. (2002). *Lucy the giant.* New York: Delacorte. Leaving her alcoholic father, 15-year-old Lucy takes a job on a commercial fishing boat in Alaska.

White, R. (1972). *Deathwatch.* Garden City, NY: Doubleday. A college boy accepts a job as a guide on a desert hunting trip and soon finds that he is the hunted, not the hunter.

Woodson, J. (2002). *Hush.* New York: Penguin. When her father testifies against two of his fellow police officers, Toswiah's family must enter the witness protection program.

MYSTERY AND SUSPENSE—FICTION

Abrahams, P. (2006). *Behind the curtain: An Echo Falls mystery.* New York: Laura Geringer Books. Investigating town secrets, eighth-grader Ingrid Levin-Hill is kidnapped. Other books in the series include *Down the Rabbit Hole* (2005) and *Into the Dark* (2008).

Alphin, E. M. (2002). *Counterfeit son.* San Diego: Harcourt. After the police shoot Hank Miller, a serial killer, his son assumes the identity of one of his father's victims.

Altman, S., and Reaves, M. (2005). *The Irregulars: In the service of Sherlock Holmes.* Illustrated by Bong Dazo. Milwaukie, OR: Dark Horse Books. When Dr. Watson is accused of murder, the Irregulars help Holmes prove Watson's innocence.

Balliett, B. (2004). *Chasing Vermeer.* New York: Scholastic. Two teens become involved with a stolen Vermeer painting.

Barnes, L. (1987). *Trouble of fools.* New York: St. Martin's. When P.I. Carlotta Carlyle takes a missing person case, she does not expect to find ties to the IRA. A more recent novel in this series is *Heart of the World* (2006).

Butcher, J. (2001). *Grave peril.* New York: Roc. Magician Harry Dresden and his friend Michael, a knight, take on vengeful ghosts loose in modern-day Chicago.

Cameron, V. (2003). *Clue mysteries: 15 whodunits to solve in minutes.* Philadelphia: Running Press. These 15 short mysteries take only minutes to solve.

Carroll, J. (2002). *Safe house.* New York: Pocket Pulse. Should Jess try to keep a low profile or use her psychic powers to find a missing girl?

Chandler, E. (2002). *Dark secrets: Legacy of lies.* New York: Pocket Books. In this first of the Dark Secrets series, Megan visits her grandmother and finds that her nightmares are coming true. The second book in the series is *Dark Secrets: Don't Tell* (2002).

Chandler, R. (1939). *The big sleep.* New York: Knopf. The first of the Philip Marlowe private investigator stories.

Cooney, C. B. (1999). *Burning up.* New York: Delacorte. Macey's school project leads her to investigate a 1959 arson case and uncover prejudice in her Connecticut town.

Cormier, R. (1997). *Tenderness: A novel.* New York: Delacorte. Eric Poole is a serial killer and Lori is the 15-year-old runaway who is drawn to him.

Cormier, R. (2001). *The rag and bone shop.* New York: Delacorte. Since Alicia was his friend, Jason could not have killed her, could he?

Cray, J. (1997). *Gemini 7.* New York: Aladdin. After meeting a girl on the Internet, Jonah's life begins to fall apart.

Crichton, M. (1999). *Timeline.* New York: Knopf. Historians travel back in time to 1357 to rescue a colleague who is stuck in the past.

Delaney, M. (2002). *Hit and run.* Atlanta, GA: Peachtree. Mattie and the other Misfits investigate a car-theft ring.

Duncan, L. (1978). *Killing Mr. Griffin.* Boston: Little, Brown. Playing a trick on a high school English teacher leads to his death.

Duncan, L. (1997). *Gallows hill.* New York: Delacorte. When Sarah runs the fortune-telling booth at the Halloween carnival, her fortunes and nightmares come true! Other suspense books by this author include *The Third Eye* (1985), *Twisted Window* (1987), and *Stranger with My Face* (1981).

Ehrenhaft, D. (2006). *Drawing a blank: Or, how I tried to solve a mystery, end a feud, and land the girl of my dreams.* New York: HarperCollins. Carlton searches for his kidnapped father.

Feinstein, J. (2005). *Last shot: A final four mystery.* New York: Knopf. Who is blackmailing a basketball player in the college championship tournament?

Feinstein, J. (2007). *Cover-up: Mystery at the Super Bowl.* New York: Knopf. Two teenage sports reporters investigate suspicious activities at football's premier event.

Ferguson, A. (2006). *The angel of death: A forensic mystery.* New York: Sleuth/Viking. Camryn helps her medical examiner father find the murder of a popular teacher and puts her own life in danger.

Fforde, J. (2005). *The big over easy: A nursery crime.* New York: Viking. Detective Inspector Jack Spratt and Detective Sergeant Mary Mary tackle the case of Humpty Dumpty.

Giles, G. (2002). *Shattering glass.* Brookfield, CT: Roaring Brook Press. Rob and his friends transformed Simon Glass from a nerd into a popular guy. Then, they killed him.

Glenn, M. (1996). *Who killed Mr. Chippendale?* New York: Lodestar. As the school day begins, a high school teacher is shot to death. Fellow teachers, students, and others describe their reactions in free verse poems.

Guy, R. (1979). *The disappearance.* New York: Delacorte. When the 7-year-old daughter of a Brooklyn family disappears, everyone suspects the young boy from Harlem who has been living with them.

Hammett, D. (1930). *The Maltese falcon.* New York: Knopf. When a beautiful redhead asks P.I. Sam Spade for help, there is trouble ahead.

Harrison, M. (2000). *Facing the dark.* New York: Holiday House. Did Simon's father kill Charley's dad? The two teens decide to find out the truth.

Hautman, P., and Logue, M. (2006) *Snatched.* New York: Sleuth/Putnam. A reporter for a high school newspaper investigates a kidnapping.

Heusler, M. (2002). *The night the Penningtons vanished.* Prides Crossing, MA: Larcom Press. Two love birds vanish and Isabella is determined to recover them even if it means hunting a murderer.

Hiaasen, C. (2005). *Flush.* New York: Knopf. Can Noah and Abbey prove that the owner of the floating casino is polluting the Florida Keys?

Hoffman, M. (2007). *The falconer's knot.* New York: Bloomsbury. Two teens set out to solve a series of murders in Renaissance Italy.

Horowitz, A. (2001). *Stormbreaker.* New York: Philomel Books. After his uncle's death, Alex is approached by the British government about following in his uncle's footsteps as a spy.

Horowitz, A. (2003). *Skeleton key.* New York: Philomel Books. Alex goes to Wimbledon and finds Chinese gangs, illegal nuclear weapons, and a possible Russian psychopath.

King, L. (1994). *The beekeeper's apprentice.* New York: St. Martin's Press. A young teenager stumbles across Sherlock Holmes on the Sussex Downs and goes on to join him in a series of adventures. A more recent novel in this series is *Justice Hall* (2001).

Kurtz, K. (2001). *St. Patrick's Gargoyle.* New York: Ace. In Dublin, Ireland, a gargoyle witnesses a crime and decides to bring the perpetrator to justice.

Little, J. (2002). *Shutterbug follies.* New York: Doubleday. When she sees a corpse in a photo she is developing, Bee tries to find a killer.

Mazer, N. F. (1983). *Taking Terry Mueller*. New York: Morrow. When Terri is 14, she learns that her mother is still alive and that her father kidnapped her after their divorce.

McDonald, J. (2001). *Shades of Simon Gray*. New York: Delacorte. What has caused the plagues of frogs and crows in a New Jersey town and does it have anything to do with Simon Gray breaking into the school computers?

Nixon, J. L. (1988). *Secret silent screams*. New York: Delacorte. Almost everyone thinks that Marti's friend Barry committed suicide, but Marti is convinced it was murder.

Nixon, J. L. (2003). *Nightmare*. New York: Delacorte. Will a stay at a camp for underachievers help Emily find the source of her nightmares?

Parker, D. (2002). *The Wessex papers: Trust falls*. New York: Avon. Although each book in this trilogy tells its own story, together they tell one long mystery. The other titles are *Fallout* (2002) and *Outsmart* (2002).

Peck, R. (1975). *The ghost belonged to me*. New York: Viking. In 1913, Blossom Culp and friends set out to exorcise a ghost.

Peck, R. (1976). *Are you in the house alone?* New York: Viking. Whenever she babysits, 16-year-old Alison gets threatening phone calls.

Perry, A. (1979). *The Cater Street hangman*. New York: St. Martin's Press. Someone is killing women on Cater Street, and it is up to Investigator Thomas Pitt to find the secrets hiding behind the walls of the Victorian mansions. A more recent novel in this series is *Seven Dials* (2003).

Perry, T. (2001). *Pursuit*. New York: Random House. What is the meaning behind the massacre of 13 diners in a local restaurant?

Plum-Ucci, C. (2000). *The body of Christopher Creed*. New York: Harcourt. Tory finds that things are not always what they appear to be when he begins a search for a boy in his class who has disappeared.

Price, C. (2006). *Dead connection*. New Milford, CT: Roaring Brook Press. Can the voice of a dead cheerleader help solve her murder?

Pullman, P. (1987). *Ruby in the smoke*. New York: Knopf. In nineteenth-century London, a young girl looks for the man who killed her father and for a valuable ruby. Other books in this series are *Shadow in the North* (1988) and *Tiger in the Well* (1990).

Reiss, K. (1998). *PaperQuake*. San Diego: Harcourt Brace. A force from the past tries to help Violet solve a mystery.

Skurzynski, G., and Ferguson, A. (2002). *Escape from fear*. Washington, DC: National Geographic Society. In St. John National Park, a young boy is searching for his birth mother who, he believes, is in danger. Other books in the series include *Over the Edge* (2002) and *Buried Alive* (2003).

Sykes, S. (1998). *For Mike*. New York: Delacorte. In a blend of mystery, suspense, and romance, Jeff begins an investigation into the disappearance of his friend Mike.

Thompson, J. (2005). *The dead boy detectives*. New York: Vertico. Two dead teens try to find a missing girl.

Van Draanen, W. (2003). *Sammy Keyes and the art of deception*. New York: Knopf. Sammy is off to investigate the strange things that are happening at an art gallery. Another book about Sammy is *Sammy Keyes and the Wild Things* (2007).

Werlin, N. (2000). *Locked inside*. New York: Delacorte. The story begins with the computer game Paliopolis and ends with Marnie locked in a windowless basement.

Werlin, N. (2006). *The rules of survival*. New York: Dial. Who can Matt and his sisters turn to for help in surviving their mother's violent moods?

Wilson, D. L. (2006). *Firehorse*. New York: Simon & Schuster. Rachel tries to find the source of mysterious fires in 1872 Boston.

Wynne-Jones, T. (2001). *The boy in the burning house*. New York: Farrar, Straus and Giroux. Jim does not know what to believe. Did his father commit suicide or did the local pastor kill him?

HUMOR—FICTION

Adams, D. (1979). *The hitchhiker's guide to the galaxy*. New York: Harmony. Arthur Dent and Ford Perfect take a very funny journey through outer space.

Bauer, J. (1992). *Squashed*. New York: Delacorte. Ellie stakes everything on winning the Rock River Pumpkin Weigh-In with her 611-pound pumpkin.

Bauer, J. (1998). *Rules of the road*. New York: Putnam. Jenna accepts a summer job driving the elderly president of a shoe company from Chicago to Texas. Other books by Bauer include *Thwonk* (1995) and *Sticks* (1996).

Clark, C. (2000). *Truth or diary*. New York: HarperTempest. Can Courtney really give up boys until she graduates?

Creech, S. (1995). *Absolutely normal chaos*. New York: HarperCollins. It's a summer of reading, romance, and growing up for 13-year-old Mary Lou.

Cushman, K. (1994). *Catherine, called Birdy*. Boston: Houghton Mifflin. Peek into the diary of a 14-year-old girl in the Middle Ages and read about her attempts to keep her father from finding her a rich husband.

Danziger, P. (1988). *The cat ate my gymsuit*. New York: Dell. Marcy hates everything, including herself. Then something changes her life.

Fleischman, P. (2005). *Zap*. Cambridge, MA: Candlewick Press. Seven plays are performed simultaneously, with characters shifting from one play to another.

Gilmore, K. (1990). *Enter three witches*. Boston: Houghton Mifflin. A family of witches attends a school production of Macbeth.

Hartinger, B. (2003). *Geography Club*. Calling the high school gay and lesbian club the "Geography Club" leads to interesting surprises.

Jones, D. W. (2000). *Year of the Griffin*. New York: Greenwillow. Surprises await Elda at the Wizards' University.

Koertge, R. (1996). *Confess-o-rama*. New York: Orchard. Tony calls the self-help hotline and gets more than he bargained for.

Korman, G. (1993). *Losing Joe's place*. New York: Scholastic. Jason and his friends have Jason's older brother's apartment for the summer, until they lose their jobs, fight over girls, and deal with a difficult landlord.

Korman, G. (1996). *The chicken doesn't skate*. New York: Scholastic. Henrietta the chicken goes from being Milo's science project to serving as the mascot of the hockey team.

Korman, G. (2000). *No more dead dogs*. New York: Hyperion. Wallace Wallace, a football player, gets to serve his detention by working on the school play. Other titles by Korman include *Something Fishy at McDonald Hall* (1995), *Semester in the Life of a Garbage Bag* (1987), and *The Twinkie Squad* (1992).

Korman, G. (2002). *Son of the mob*. New York: Hyperion. Being the son of a Mafia boss can be a problem when you want to date the daughter of an FBI agent.

Korman, G. (2008). *Swindle*. New York: Scholastic. How far will Griffin Bing go to get his baseball cards back from an unscrupulous collector?

LaRochelle, D. (2005). *Absolutely, positively not*. New York: Arthur A. Levine Books. Steven has lots of ideas, which are usually humorously wrong, forways to prove he is not gay.

Larson, G. (1998). *There's a hair in my dirt: A worm's story*. New York: HarperCollins. When a young worm finds a hair in his supper, father worm tells him how the hair got there.

Lubar, D. (2002). *Dunk*. New York: Clarion. Chad wants to be the clown on the New Jersey boardwalk, but life tries to get in the way.

Lubar, D. (2003). *Flip*. New York: Tom Doherty. Magic disks can turn twins Taylor and Ryan into famous people from the past.

Mackler, C. (2003). *The Earth, my butt, and other big round things*. Cambridge, MA: Candlewick. Virginia tries to deal with her self-image and her family.

Mackler, C. (2004). *Vegan virgin valentine*. Cambridge, MA: Candlewick. Two teenagers with opposite personalities clash.

Nibot, R. (2006). *Banana Sunday*. Portland, OR: Oni Press. Trying fitting into a new high school when you have three talking monkeys.

Nodelman, P. (1998). *Behaving Bradley*. New York: Simon & Schuster. Eleventh-grader Brad Gold learns about school politics and bureaucracy when he tries to get input for creating the new code of conduct.

Paulsen, G. (2007). *Lawn boy*. New York: Wendy Lamb Books. When a 12 year-old boy gets a lawn mower as a present, he never dreams that it will lead to his owning a prizefighter.

Peck, R. (1998). *A long way from Chicago*. New York: Dial. Grandma Dowdel has her own ways of surviving in the Great Depression, as she lies, trespasses, and outwits her neighbors in rural Illinois.

Pinkwater, J. (1989). *Buffalo Brenda*. New York: Macmillan. Things begin to happen when Brenda Tuna takes over the high school newspaper and suggests a live bison for the school mascot.

Pratchett, T. (1983). *The colour of magic*. New York: St. Martin's Press. Twoflower, the tourist, and Rincewind, his wizard guide, set off into the zany Discworld.

Pratchett, T. (2001). *The amazing Maurice and his educated rodents*. New York: HarperCollins. Intelligent rats, a talking cat, and a boy with a magical pipe try to con the wrong town.

Pratchett, T. (2001). *Thief of time: A novel of Discworld*. New York: HarperCollins. If Jeremy Clockson builds a totally accurate glass clock, will he be able to put the Grim Reaper out of business?

Pratchett, T. (2007). *Making money: A novel of Discworld*. New York: Harper. What better job for an arch swindler than to oversee the printing of a country's currency?

Pullman, P. (1998). *Count Karlstein*. New York: Knopf. What will happen when the wicked count abandons his orphaned nieces in a remote hunting lodge?

Rennison, L. (2000). *Angus, thongs and full-frontal snogging: Confessions of Georgia Nicholson*. New York: HarperCollins. Rennison provides a British look at growing up and getting a serious boyfriend. Other books about Georgia include *On the Bright Side, I'm Now the Girlfriend of a Sex God* (2001), and *Dancing in My Nuddy-Pants* (2003).

Rubio, K. (2006). *Star Wars: Tag and Bink were here*. Milwaukie, OR: Dark Horse Comics. Two bumblers create chaos wherever they go.

Scieszka, J. (1995). *Math curse*. New York: Viking. Did you know that you can think of almost anything as a math problem?

Snicket, L. (1999). *The bad beginning*. New York: HarperCollins. Can the three Baudelaire children outwit their evil guardian in this first book in the series.

Spinelli, J. (1984). *Who put that hair in my toothbrush*. Boston: Little Brown. Sibling rivalry gets out of hand after Megin ruins her brother's science project.

Strasser, T. (1998). *Help! I'm trapped in an alien's body*. New York: Scholastic. Jake switches bodies with a funny-looking alien, and now Jake wants his own body back.

Strasser, T. (1998). *How I spent my last night on Earth*. New York: Simon & Schuster. Allegra "Legs" Hanover does not know whether to believe the rumor about an asteroid headed for Earth, but, just in case, there are a few things she wants to do. A book in the Time Zone High series.

Thomas, R. (1996). *Rats saw God*. New York: Simon & Schuster. What made Steve go from promising student to troubled teen?

Townsend, S. (1984). *The secret diary of Adrian Mole, aged 13 3/4*. New York: Avon. A 13-year-old English boy keeps a diary of his funny, funny life.

Wrede, P. (1990). *Dealing with dragons*. San Diego: Jane Yolen Books. Cimorene is a very unconventional princess who volunteers to become the captive of the female king of the Dragons. Other funny books in this fantasy series are *Searching for Dragons* (1991), *Calling on Dragons* (1993), and *Talking to Dragons* (1993).

Wrede, P., and Stevermer, C. (2003). *Sorcery and Cecilia, or the enchanted chocolate pot*. Orlando, FL: Harcourt. Cecilia and Kate keep each other informed of events in London and the country through their letters about their silly families and the mysterious wizards that they meet.

Suggested Readings

Farber, J. (2007). Toward a theoretical framework for the study of humor in literature and other arts. *The Journal of Aesthetic Education, 41*(5), 67–86.

Gray, B. A. (2006). Return of the gumshoe. *School Library Journal, 53*(9), 57–61.

Lupa, R. (2007). LOL on screen. *Young Adult Library Services, 5*(4), 41–42.

Mehegan, D. (2006, February 27). An adventure in finding books for boys. *Boston Globe*. Accessed March 21, 2008, from www.boston.com/news/globe/living/articles/2007/02/27/an_adventure_in_finding_books_for_boys/

Onofrey, K. A. (2006). "It is more than just laughing": Middle school students protect characters during talk. *Journal of Research in Childhood Education, 20*(3), 207–217.

Penzler, O. (2005). Anatomy of a mystery. *Publishers Weekly, 252*(16), 30.

Robertson, G. (2007). Mystery madness: Understanding the demand for *crime fiction* in libraries. *Feliciter, 53*(4), 202–204.

References

All young adult literature referenced in this chapter is included in the Young Adult Books list and are not repeated in this list.

Ammon, B. D., and Sherman, G. W. (1999). *More rip-roaring reads for reluctant teen readers*. Englewood, CO: Libraries Unlimited.

Ashley, M. (2002). *The mammoth encyclopedia of modern crime fiction*. New York: Carroll & Graf.

Bauer, J. (1996). Humor, seriously. *The ALAN Review, 23*(2), 2–3.

Blume, J. (1972). *Tales of a fourth grade nothing*. New York: Dutton.

Boyd, B. (2004). Laughter and literature: A play theory of humor. *Philosophy and Literature, 28*(1), 1–22.

Brown, D. (2003). *The Da Vinci Code*. New York: Doubleday.

Burgess, M., and Vassilakos, J. H. (2005). *Murder in retrospect: A selective guide to historical mystery fiction*. Westport, CT: Libraries Unlimited.

Caron, J. E. (2003). From ethology to aesthetics: Evolution as a theoretical paradigm for research on laughter, humor, and other comic phenomena. *Humor: International Journal of Humor Research, 15*(3), 245–281.

Cart, M. (1995). *What's so funny? Wit and humor in American children's literature*. New York: HarperCollins.

Charles, J., and Morrison, J. (2000). Clueless? Adult mysteries with young adult appeal 2000. *Voice of Youth Advocate, 23*(5), 318–321.

Charles, J., Morrison, J., and Clark, C. (2002). *The mystery readers' advisory: The librarian's clues to murder and mayhem*. Chicago: American Library Association.

Cleary, B. (1955). *Beezus and Ramona*. New York: Morrow.

Collins, W. (1860). *The woman in white*. London: Sampson Low.

Collins, W. (1868). *The moonstone: A romance*. London: Tinsley Brothers.

Cooper, J. F. (1850–1851). *The leather-stocking tales*. New York: G. P. Putnam.

Crowley, C. (1998). Pathways, pointers and pearls: Interview with Carol Gorman. In J. Grape, D. James, and E. Nehr (Eds.), *Deadly women: The woman mystery reader's indispensable companion* (pp. 255–257). New York: Carroll & Graf.

Dahlin, R. (2002). Publishers are getting really series-ous. *Publisher's Weekly 4/22/2002*. Accessed 12/30/02 http://publishersweekly.reviewsnews.com/ index.asp?layout=articlePrint&articleID=CA21357.

Dahlin, R., Mantell, S., Dyer, L., and Danford, N. (2007). Booksellers drop clues. *Publishers Weekly, 254*(47), 18–21.

Davis, J. (1999). Speaking my mind: On humor. *English Journal, 88*(4), 14–15.

DeAndrea, W. L. (Ed.). (1994). *Encyclopedia mysteriosa: A comprehensive guide to the art of detection in print, film, radio, and television*. New York: Prentice Hall.

Defoe, D. (1719). *The farther adventures of Robinson Crusoe being the second and last part of his life, and of the strange surprising accounts of his travels round three parts of the globe*. London: W. Taylor.

Doyle, A. C. (1887). *A study in scarlet*. London: Ward Lock.

Doyle, A. C. (1900). *The hound of the Baskervilles*. Garden City, NY: Doubleday.

Dunn, A. (1999). "Lit-TEE-raries," or "Getting it off your chest." *English Journal, 88*(4), 56.

Farber, J. (2007). Toward a theoretical framework for the study of humor in literature and the other arts. *Journal of Aesthetic Education, 41*(4), 67–86.

Fleischman, S. (1965). *McBroom tells the truth*. New York: W. W. Norton.

Gannon, M. B. (2004). *Blood, bedlam, bullets, and badguys: A reader's guide to adventure/suspense fiction*. Westport, CT: Libraries Unlimited.

Gentile, L. M., and McMillan, M. M. (1978). Humor and the reading program. *Journal of Reading, 21,* 343–349.

George, J. C. (1959). *My side of the mountain*. New York: Dutton.

George, J. C. (1972). *Julie of the wolves*. New York: Harper & Row.

Gulli, A. F. (2008, February–May). Interview: Sue Grafton. *The Strand Magazine, 24,* 50–57.

Hale, L. P. (1880). *The Peterkin papers*. Boston: James R. Osgood.

Heins, E. L. (1979). A cry for laughter. *The Horn Book, 55*(6), 631.

Heising, W. L. (1998). *Detecting men: A reader's guide and checklist for mystery series written by men*. Dearborn, MI: Purple Moon Press.

Heising, W. L. (2000). *Detecting women: A reader's guide and checklist for mystery series written by women*. Dearborn, MI: Purple Moon Press.

Herbert, R. (Ed.). (1999). *Oxford companion to crime and mystery writing*. New York: Oxford University Press.

Hogan, W. (2005). *Humor in young adult literature: A time to laugh.* Lanham, MD: Scarecrow Press.

Howe, J. (1979). *Bunnicula: A rabbit tale of mystery.* New York: Atheneum.

Howe, J. (1995). Mirth & mayhem: Humor and mystery in children's books. *Voices from the Middle, 2*(3), 4–9.

Huang, J. (Ed.). (2000). *100 favorite mysteries of the century: Selected by the Independent Mystery Booksellers Association.* Carmel, IN: Crum Creek Press.

Jalonga, M. R. (1985). Children's literature: There's some sense to its humor. *Childhood Education, 62,* 109–114.

Junger, S. (1998). *The perfect storm: A true story of men against the sea.* New York: HarperPaperbacks.

Klesius, J., Laframboise, K. L., and Gaier, M. (1998). Humorous literature: Motivation for reluctant readers. *Reading Research and Instruction, 37*(4), 253–261.

Krakauer, J. (1996). *Into the wild.* New York: Villard Books.

Krakauer, J. (1998). *Into thin air: A personal account of the Mount Everest disaster.* New York: Anchor Books.

Kuchner, J. (1991). *The humor of your children.* (Report No. PS 020 516.) Paper presented at the National Association for the Education of Young Children. (ERIC Document Reproduction Service No. 348–139)

Larson, J. (2004). *Bringing mysteries alive for children and young adults.* Worthington, OH: Linworth.

Lesesne, T. (2000). A passion for humor: An interview with Joan Bauer. *Teacher Librarian, 27*(3), 60–62.

Lewis, P. (1995). Why humor. *Voices from the Middle, 2*(3), 10–16.

McGhee, P. E. (1979). *Humor: Its origin and development.* San Francisco: Freeman.

McInnes, M. (1995). Backing into the hallway, one step at a time. *Voices from the Middle, 2*(3), 17–19.

Monson, D., and Sebesta, S. (1991). Reading preferences. In J. Flood, J. M. Jensen, D. Lapp, and J. R. Squire (Eds.), *Handbook of research on teaching the English language arts* (pp. 664–673). New York: Macmillan.

Moody, S. (Ed.). (1990). *Hatchards crime companion: The top 100 crime novels selected by the Crime Writer's Association.* London: Hatchards.

Morris, B. S. (1999). Why is George so funny? Television comedy, trickster heroism, and cultural studies. *English Journal, 88*(4), 47–52.

Murphy, B. F. (1999). *The encyclopedia of murder and mystery.* New York: St. Martin's Minotaur.

Muse, D. (1999). Detectives, dubious dudes, spies, and suspense in African-American fiction for children and young adults. *Multicultural Education, 6*(3), 37–41.

Nichols, V., and Thompson, S. (2000). *Silk stalkings: More women write of murder.* Lanham, MD: Scarecrow Press.

Nixon, J. L. (1994). Juvenile mysteries. In W. L. DeAndrea (Ed.), *Encyclopedia mysteriosa: A comprehensive guide to the art of detection in print, film, radio, and television* (pp. 186–187). New York: Prentice Hall.

O'Dell, S. (1960). *Island of the blue dolphins.* Boston: Houghton Mifflin.

Opie, I., & Opie, P. (Eds.). (1992). *I saw Esau.* Cambridge, MA: Candlewick Press.

Paul, B. (1999). Putting an end to the mystery. In H. Windrath (Ed.), *They wrote the book: Thirteen women mystery writers tell all* (pp. 121–130). Duluth, MN: Spinsters Ink.

Pederson, J. P. (Ed.). (1996). *St. James guide to crime & mystery writers.* Detroit: St. James Press.

Poe, E. A. (1841). *The murders in the Rue Morgue.* Philadelphia. (No publisher is listed)

Poe, E. A. (1844). The purloined letter. *Chamber's Edinburgh Journal, 2*(48), 343–347.

Reid, R. A. (1999). Suspense novel. In R. Herbert (Ed.), *Oxford companion to crime and mystery writing* (pp. 437–438). New York: Oxford University Press.

Rigby, N. (1999). Adventure story. In R. Herbert (Ed.), *The Oxford companion to crime and mystery writing* (pp. 7–8). New York: Oxford University Press.

Rollyson, C. E. (2008). *Critical survey of mystery and detective fiction.* Pasadena, CA: Salem Press.

Rothermel, D. (1995). What's so funny in 303? *Voices from the Middle, 2*(3), 20–25.

Ruggieri, C. A. (1999). Laugh and learn: Using humor to teach tragedy. *English Journal, 88*(4), 53–58.

Russell, D. L. (2000). *Pippi Longstocking* and the subversive affirmation of comedy. *Children's Literature in Education, 31*(3), 167–177.

Russell, D. L. (2009). *Literature for children: A short introduction.* Boston: Pearson/Allyn & Bacon.

Scieszka, J. (2005). What's so funny, Mr. Scieszka? *The Horn Book, 81*(6), 653–667.

Shimberg, A., and Grant, H. M. (1998). Who-dun-it? A mystery thematic unit. *Science Activities, 35*(3), 29–35.

Sobin, R. M. (2008). *The essential mystery lists: For readers, collectors and librarians.* Scottsdale, AZ: Poisoned Pen Press.

Stevenson, R. L. (1883). *Treasure Island.* London: Casell.

Swanson, J., and Dean, J. (1998). *Killer books: A reader's guide to exploring the popular world of mystery and suspense.* New York: Berkley Prime Crime.

Tatum, T. (1999). Cruel and unusual PUNishment (LOW humor is better then NO humor). *English Journal, 88*(4), 62–64.

Travers, P. L. (1934). *Mary Poppins.* New York: Harcourt, Brace.

Twain, M. (1876). *The adventures of Tom Sawyer.* Hartford, CT: American Publishing.

Twain, M. (1884). *Adventures of Huckleberry Finn (Tom Sawyer's comrade).* New York: Charles L. Webster.

Yep, L. (2003). The knife that cuts: Writing mysteries for young readers. *Booklist, 99*(17), 1521.

Exploring Science Fiction, Fantasy, and Horror

Many young adults enjoy speculative fiction or works of fantasy, science fiction, and horror. Consider the phenomenal success of the Harry Potter and *Lord of the Rings* series of fantasy books and movies; the continued popularity of the horror novels of Stephen King, R. L. Stine, and Dean Koontz; and the sales of horror-based role-playing games. Why are these genres so popular with young adults? Perhaps they provide an escape from the difficulties of life, or they allow young adults to enjoy vicarious experiences and investigate worlds where the impossible becomes possible or where technology makes dreams come true. Whatever the reasons, it is clear that young adults greatly enjoy speculative fiction. Therefore, perceptive teachers, library media specialists, and others who work with young adults need to be aware of the wealth of books that are available and the need to share this literature with adolescents.

Speculative Fiction: Science Fiction, Fantasy, and Horror

While young adults enjoy reading about the past in historical fiction and the present in contemporary realistic fiction, they also enjoy escaping to the strange worlds of speculative fiction. Science fiction, fantasy, and horror books allow readers to enter imaginative worlds that are full of endless possibilities. Readers can vicariously face the future, explore the possibilities of science and technology, wrestle with the fantastic in a make-believe world, or confront the horrors that populate their worst nightmares.

It can sometimes be difficult to distinguish between science fiction, fantasy, and horror. Some critics place all speculative fiction in the genre of fantasy, and consider science fiction and horror to be subgenres. Others use the term *fantastic* (Clute & Grant, 1999) or *speculative fiction* (Card, 1990) as an umbrella to cover all three categories, and then discuss each category independently. In this book, we use the term *speculative fiction* to refer to all nonrealistic fiction, including fantasy, science fiction, and horror.

Orson Scott Card (1990), a writer of both science fiction and fantasy and the only author to win both the Nebula Award and the Hugo Award two years in a row for the best science fiction novel (*Ender's Game*, 1985; *Speaker for the Dead*, 1986), suggests the following way to differentiate between science fiction and fantasy: "If the story is set in a universe that follows the same rules as ours, it's science fiction. If it's set in a universe that doesn't follow our rules, it's fantasy" (p. 22). He goes on to say that while plot devices such as time travel can be found in both fantasy and science fiction, if the story contains metal, plastic, and/or heavy machinery, it is science fiction; and the reader can assume, until told otherwise, that the known laws of science apply. If the story contains talismans or magic, it is fantasy; the reader must then rely on the author to describe the natural laws that exist in this fantasy world (Card, 1990). Horror, the final type of speculative fiction, looks at phenomena young adults like to read about but would not want to experience, such as vampires, monsters, werewolves, and the supernatural.

It is important to remember that some books cross category lines. For example, some horror books can also fit into the categories of fantasy or science fiction. Some time travel or time warp books are considered science fiction; others are considered fantasy. Some ghost stories are more adventure (Chapter 6) than horror. Lois Lowry's novel *The Giver* (1993) can be classified as science fiction or as mystical fantasy. We have tried to make logical decisions based on certain guidelines that you will find throughout the chapter. In addition, although we discuss short stories in Chapter 11, we have included a few collections of speculative fiction in this chapter's list of young adult books. Furthermore, some books that are classified as nonfiction are directly tied to speculative fiction, for example *Robots: From Science Fiction to Technological Revolution* (Ichbiah, 2005), *Encyclopedia Horrifica: The Terrifying TRUTH! About Vampires, Ghosts, Monsters, and More* (Gee, 2007), and *The Tough Guide to Fantasyland* (Jones, 2006). Rather than worrying about categorizing these works, we encourage you to read them, enjoy them, and recommend them to young adults.

The Popularity of Speculative Fiction

In a survey of high school students, Diaz-Rubin (1996) found that horror and fantasy were two of the top 10 areas of interest out of a list of 49 categories. Interest in speculative fiction has been spurred by the continued success of series such as the Harry

Potter and *Lord of the Rings* fantasy books and movies, the release of the *Star Wars* film trilogy, and the *X-Men* films with accompanying books, among others. In 2007, the Harry Potter film series displaced the James Bond movies to become the highest grossing movie series in box office history, with the *Star Wars* films in third place ("Harry Potter soars above James Bond at the box office," 2007). In July, 2007, Scholastic reported selling 8.3 million copies of J. K. Rowling's *Harry Potter and the Deathly Hallows* (2007) in the first 24 hours after it was released ("Harry's in a league of his own," 2007). Philip Pullman's *The Amber Spyglass* (2000) won the British Whitbread Children's Book of the Year and went on to win the overall Whitbread Award, something never before accomplished by a children's or young adult book. In 2008, Orson Scott Card won the Margaret A. Edwards Award for lifetime achievement in writing for young adults for his science fiction novels.

Science Fiction

Science fiction stories appeal to many middle and high school students, transporting them to a world where science makes dreams—and sometimes nightmares—come true. Paperbacks, comics, and magazines combine with movies, television shows, and computer games, to give young adults an opportunity to escape from the difficulties and tedium of everyday life and enter a world that is based on current science as well as trends and technology (Ochoa & Osier, 1993). Clute and Grant (1999) define science fiction as "a text whose story is explicitly or implicitly extrapolated from scientific or historical premises" (p. 844). While science fiction was originally written for adults (though young adults read it as well), writers such as Ursula LeGuin, began to write science fiction aimed specifically at the young adult reader (Owen, 1987). Currently, adolescents read a mixture of young adult as well as mainstream adult science fiction.

Many literature critics dismiss science fiction as a literary genre and consider it unworthy of any serious reader's time. This may be in part because much original science fiction is still published in paperback rather than hardcover format. Other critics point out that the stories are plot-driven or setting-driven (rather than character-driven) almost to the exclusion of believable or likable characters (Hughes, 1992). In addition, well-written science fiction demands a high level of scientific accuracy; errors and inconsistencies found in many science fiction books ruin the credibility of the story (Ochoa & Osier, 1993). Still other readers may see the scientific information as detracting from the story. In addition, many science fiction books have lurid, pin-up style covers or contain steamy sex scenes. Finally, fearing censorship challenges, some teachers and librarians may be reluctant to use novels that present alternative worlds, challenge the supremacy of life on Earth, or present alternatives to contemporary religious beliefs.

However, there are those who maintain that science fiction can be a means of opening students' minds and imaginations. Anne Devereaux Jordan (1995) has said that "science fiction for both adults and young people has developed into a sophisticated literary form worth reading and worthy of study" (p. 17). According to author David Brin, science fiction is the "jazz," or most American, of all literary genres (Moltz, 2003). Because well-written science fiction is alive, vibrant, and exciting, its use may yield unexpected dividends (Hughes, 1992). As science fiction challenges readers to think about the past, present, and future, the reader's imagination comes into play. As readers begin to consider the future of the world presented in the novel they are reading, they also begin to consider the world they live in. Often science fiction is written for political purpose (Levy, 2007) or to critique the problems in current society. For example, Gross (2007) suggests that educators can use *Ender's Game* (Card, 1985) to examine child abuse and its "relationship to the development of creativity, hatred, and violence" (p. 115). Well-written science fiction both warns and teaches readers to build the future they want, based on logic and knowledge, and does so in a pleasing and entertaining manner (Jordan, 1995). Science fiction writing is full of magic moments "when the writer discovers more in her work than she believed she had put into it. They happen at the subconscious level, perhaps more readily in science fiction and fantasy because the setting and situations therein are removed from the mundane to the more mythical, containing elements that echo the folk tales and legends of the past" (Hughes, 1992, p. 4).

A Brief Look at Science Fiction's Predecessors. Some would argue that the first science fiction book was Mary Shelley's *Frankenstein* (1818)—a book that warned about tampering with science and the unknown. Surely the genre was helped along by books such as *From the Earth to the Moon* (Verne, 1865) and *The Time Machine* (Wells, 1895). Traditionally using either a paperback or magazine format, science fiction publishing began in earnest in the 1950s, with authors such as Robert Heinlein and Ray Bradbury (Louvisi, 1997) as well as Isaac Asimov, Frank Herbert, and Robert C. Clarke. In these "pulp" formats (so called because of the cheap pulp paper on which they were printed), the stories were often more concerned with action and scientific gadgets than with the plausibility and logic of the plot (Jordan, 1995). Frequently, the writing was poor, plots were heavily dependent on coincidence, and the themes were limited to "good versus evil" (p. 19). Fortunately, since the 1950s, science fiction has grown into a respected and popular field of literature (Jordan, 1995). Three good overviews of the history of science fiction for young adults are *The History of Science Fiction* (Miller, 2001), *The History of Science Fiction* (Roberts, 2006), and the brief *Modern Masters of Science Fiction* (Hamilton, 2007).

Types of Science Fiction. It is always difficult to categorize literature, especially with the diversity found in science fiction. Too often, readers lump all science fiction into a category known as "space opera," which takes the old "good guys versus bad guys" scenario of Western movies and places it in the realm of outer space. This may have been an accurate description of such early works as Edgar Rice Burroughs's *A Princess of Mars* (1912), in which the protagonist, after being teleported to Mars, battles his way across a planet filled with villains and ultimately wins the hand of Princess Deiah Tjoris. In contrast, contemporary science fiction is much more complex. *The Space Opera Renaissance* (Hartwell & Cramer, 2006) a collection of short stories, provides a historical overview of the genre.

In identifying the following types of science fiction, we have combined the works of Card (1990) and Jordan (1995) with our own ideas. Recall that, as we have mentioned, any attempt to categorize literature is fraught with problems, since elements from more than one category can be found in a single book. For a list of science fiction books of all types recommended for young adults, see the end of this chapter.

Earth's future. Some science fiction books focus on the future of Earth and its inhabitants including the threat of nuclear or biological war, holocaust brought about by pollution or toxic wastes, the decline of humans and the development of robots or superintelligent machines or beings, and alien invasions. In films, the alien is often portrayed as a threatening entity; in books, aliens may arrive either to help or to threaten humankind. Representative young adult novels in this category include:

- *The White Fox Chronicles* (Paulsen, 2000)
- *Ender's Shadow* (Card, 1999)
- *Parable of the Talents* (Butler, 1998)
- *The Kindling* (Armstrong and Butcher, 2002)
- *Feed* (Anderson, 2002)
- *Memory Boy* (Weaver, 2001)
- *Old Man's War* (Scalzi, 2005)

Contradiction of known laws. This type of science fiction focuses on Earth, with a contradiction of known laws of nature such as time travel. Time travel became firmly established as a convention in science fiction when H. G. Wells used it in his story *The Time Machine* (1895). Caroline Cooney (e.g., 2001), Roger Allen (e.g., 2002), and others build on this idea in contemporary young adult novels, creating alternative Earth societies that are not bound by our laws of nature. In a future world, Margaret Haddix in *Turnabout* (2000) allows people to un-age and go back to their childhoods. Other recent time travel novels that combine historical and science fiction include:

- *Johnny and the Bomb* (Pratchett, 2007)
- *London Calling* (Bloor, 2006)
- *Gideon the Cutpurse* (Buckley-Archer, 2006)

Other worlds. The next group of science fiction books are those set on other (sometimes alien) worlds. The difficulty a writer faces in constructing an alien world is that it cannot be too alien. The characters must share some of the basic fears, needs, and drives humans have—otherwise, the reader cannot identify with or understand them. Anne McCaffrey, the first science fiction author to win the Margaret A. Edwards Award for lifetime achievement in young adult literature, created a classic series of this type of science fiction with her books set on the planet of Pern. One of the early entries in this series, *Dragonsinger* (McCaffrey, 1977), tells of the struggles of a girl, Menolly, who is growing up and trying to find her place within her world. The search for self and a place in the adult world is a task all young people confront as they grow up, and one with which they can identify even if the story is set on a foreign planet. A well-written introduction to Pern is McCaffrey's *A Gift of Dragons* (2002). Alastair Reynolds presents a modern variation of the world created by Arthur C. Clarke in *Pushing Ice* (2006). Scott Westerfeld creates a futuristic society in *Uglies* (2005). Other writers who have created successful worlds include C. J. Cherryh (e.g., 2001), Ian Banks (e.g., 1997), Frank Herbert (e.g., 1965), Nancy Kress (e.g., 2003), and Kathy Tyers (e.g., 1999).

After spending a great deal of time creating other worlds, authors often set sequels and complete series in them. If the books are successful, publishers expect the authors to continue the series even when the authors wish to turn to other topics. Thus, some authors "sharecrop their universes" (Levy, 2006, p. 134) by creating detailed outlines or plot summaries and allowing others to actually write the books. In some cases, series are even continued long after the death of the author with the author's name still appearing on the book (Levy, 2006).

Utopias or dystopias. Located in another world or existing as a community in our own world, a utopia is a society that embodies, on the surface, a perfect social, economic, religious, and/or political system. In contrast, a dystopia is a repressive or totalitarian society. Some scholars also distinguish between a dystopia, which is intentionally negative, and an antiutopia, a utopia that has become twisted or flawed. Authors use these settings to "explore their hopes and fears for human society" (Benfield, 2006, p. 128) and to show the need to balance perfection with freedom, and pain and sorrow with joy and humanity. Lois Lowry has explored closed communities that seem on the surface seem to be utopian communities but turn out to be dystopian or anti-utopian, in books such as *The Giver* (1993), *Gathering Blue* (2002), and *The Messenger* (2004).

Alternative history. Finally, there are some science fiction books that focus on alternate histories of the world or of a prehistoric Earth. Sometimes using time travel, this type of science fiction may present an alternate reality that is often the result of a rewriting of history. Both Henry Turtledove, with a number of alternative history series (e.g., Turtledove & Greenberg, 2001), and Orson Scott Card (e.g., 1993), with his Alvin Maker books set in a North America where there was no American Revolution, have created series of books based on the premise of "contrahistory."

Steampunk, a type of alternative history, examines the redirection of technology (Reid, 2005). For example, mechanical electricity ceases to exist in *Dies the Fire* (Stirling, 2004), while twenty-first-century technology exists without twentieth-century industrial sprawl in *Conquistador* (Stirling, 2003).

Reasons for Using and Teaching Science Fiction. Science fiction puts an emphasis on imagination and offers an escape from the demands and practicalities of the real world that appeal to many readers, and deals with more that just "the good versus the bad." Current science fiction engages many topics such as future worlds, superintelligent mechanical and human beings, time travel and altered historical events, robots, DNA experiments, nuclear holocaust and survival, toxic wastes, and germ warfare. These works encourage readers to investigate social concerns and ecological problems (Harris, 1996). In addition, science fiction attracts some adolescents who reject other kinds of books or who are interested in scientific concepts. Adolescents can read these books and evaluate the extent to which science is accurately reflected (Harris, 1996). A strength of science fiction is its diversity and appeal to adolescents of various reading abilities and on a wide range of grade levels (Bucher & Manning, 2001). Collaborating with Other Professionals 7–1 illustrates how science fiction can be a springboard to scientific inquiry.

Characteristics of Well-Written Science Fiction. Of the wide range of science fiction published each year, some are excellent, while others fall far short of meeting even the basic requirements for any work of fiction. Considerations for Selecting Young Adult Literature: *Science Fiction* lists items to consider in evaluating science fiction.

COLLABORATING WITH OTHER PROFESSIONALS

Link literature and science. As students read a work of science fiction, encourage them to use a Possible, Plausible, or Futuristic chart to identify the elements in the book that are currently possible and scientifically accurate, those that are plausible and an extension of current science, and those that are truly futuristic. When in doubt, students can consult a science teacher or use the library media center for research. They can also visit Internet sites, such as NASA (www.nasa. gov/home/index.html), to learn more about space travel.

Suggestions for Selecting and Using Science Fiction. It can be very difficult for teachers and librarians to select, use, and recommend well-written science fiction, especially if they themselves do not enjoy reading novels in the genre. Fortunately, there are many resources that can aid in the selection of quality science fiction titles. Expanding Your Knowledge with the Internet lists many of these resources.

Awards and best books lists. There are awards and annual best books lists that feature science fiction. Two of the most prestigious awards are the Nebula Award, given by the Science Fiction Writers of America, and the Hugo Award, presented by the World Science Fiction Society. Although the Hugo Awards are given in more categories, the Nebula Awards have been called the Academy Awards of science fiction (Card, 1990). Lists of the winners can usually be found online at the *Locus* Index to Science Fiction Awards. This website also contains information on the Arthur C. Clarke Award for

CONSIDERATIONS FOR
SELECTING YOUNG ADULT LITERATURE SCIENCE FICTION

When evaluating science fiction, look for the following:

_____   Strong themes that are basic to human existence and that do not rely on time or place

_____   Nonstereotypical characters who believe in the science and who rise to meet and overcome challenges

_____   Well-developed and plausible plots

_____   Believable details

_____   Accurate and well-researched science and/or technology

_____   Rules for imaginary or invented science

_____   Details that support the science

_____   Pleasing writing style that does not talk down to the reader

_____   Escapist aspects with an interesting story

_____   Consistency in the plot, characters, and setting

_____   Reliance on science, not on coincidence

EXPANDING YOUR KNOWLEDGE WITH THE INTERNET

These Internet sources provide information about works of speculative fiction and ways to teach about them.

AWARDS AND REVIEWS

Locus Index to Science Fiction Awards
www.locusmag.com/SFAwards/index.html

Golden Duck Awards for Excellence in Children's Science Fiction Literature
www.goldenduck.org

Orson Scott Card
www.hatrack.com/osc/

Ellen Datlow
www.datlow.com/index.html

ONLINE JOURNALS

Locus: The Newspaper of the Science Fiction Field
www.locusmag.com.

Science Fiction Chronicle
www.angelfire.com/mn/scififantasynews/

Science Books & Films Online
www.sbfonline.com/index.htm

GENERAL SCIENCE FICTION RESOURCES

SF Zines WebRing
c.webring.com/hub?ring=sfzines

Fantasy and Science Fiction website (University of Michigan)
www.umich.edu/~umfandsf/

The Internet Speculative Fiction DataBase
isfdb.tamu.edu/

Reading for the Future—Literacy through speculative fiction
readingforfuture.com

SFF Net—science fiction, fantasy, horror, and young adult fiction
www.sff.net/

Science Fiction and Fantasy Writers of America
www.sfwa.org

Talk of the Nation: Science Friday—"The Science of Science Fiction"
www.sciencefriday.com/pages/1998/Nov/hour2_112098.html

science fiction published in Great Britain, as well as brief listings of a variety of other award-winners and nominees, such as the Prix Aurora Award for Canadian science fiction and fantasy. Another excellent source of information on science fiction is *Locus: The Newspaper of the Science Fiction Field* and its website. Super-Con-Duck-Tivity, a group of parents, teachers, and librarians based in Illinois, presents the Golden Duck Awards for Excellence in Children's Science Fiction Literature, including the Hal Clement Award for Young Adult Science Fiction and the Eleanor Cameron Award for Middle Grades.

Another excellent source is the annual best books list published in the April issue of *VOYA*. Featuring fantasy and horror as well as science fiction, this annotated bibliography consists of excerpts from the reviews of highly rated titles that were published in *VOYA* in the previous year (June to April). One outstanding feature of this journal is that in addition to identifying the suggested grade level for each title (middle school through senior high), the reviewers rate each title for both popularity (1P to 5P) and the quality (1Q to 5Q) of the writing. Adult-marketed titles that the reviewers recommend for young adults are included.

Print review resources. In 1999, *Science, Books and Films*, a publication of the American Association for the Advancement of Science, began to include science fiction reviews. With background in the pure and applied sciences, its reviewers are qualified to evaluate the scientific as well as the literary qualities of the novels (Gath, 1999). Subscribers can view a database of reviews online as well as in the traditional hard copy of the periodical.

Other professional resources are available to aid in book selection and to help you become familiar with the genre. These include:

- *What Fantastic Fiction Do I Read Next?* (Barron, 1999b)
- *Presenting Young Adult Science Fiction* (Reid, 1998)
- *Strictly Science Fiction: A Guide to Reading Interests* (Herald and Kunzel, 2002)
- *Anatomy of Wonder: A Critical Guide to Science Fiction* (Barron, 2004)
- *Encyclopedia of Science Fiction* (D'Ammassa, 2005)
- *Brave New Words: The Oxford Dictionary of Science Fiction* (Prucher, 2007)
- *Reference Guide to Science Fiction, Fantasy and Horror* (Burgess and Bartle, 2002)
- *The A to Z of Science Fiction Literature* (Stableford, 2005)

Online resources. Naturally, the Internet has become home to a number of excellent websites with information on science fiction. Many web-based magazines, or "Webzines," can be located through *SF Zines WebRing*. The University of Michigan maintains a web page for all who wish to study fantasy and science fiction—especially useful in high schools that offer specialized classes on speculative fiction.

Reviews and information on the major science fiction awards are also available on the Internet. Both Orson Scott Card and Ellen Datlow, former *Omni* magazine reviewer and editor of SCI FI Channel's SCIFI.COM, have large databases of reviews at their websites. In addition to information on science fiction award–winners, The Internet Speculative Fiction DataBase gives sources of reviews and has information on both published and forthcoming books.

A good starting point for information on science fiction authors is the *SFF Net* site, The website of the Science Fiction and Fantasy Writers of America, with more than 1,200 members. This site provides news, reviews, and information on writing speculative fiction. In addition, many major science fiction publishers, such as Del Rey Books, Tor/Forge, HarperCollins, Voyager, and Penguin Putnam/Ace, also provide information at their websites.

Evaluating science fiction. In addition to using the checklist for well-written science fiction, if you want to evaluate individual science fiction titles, you should apply many of the same standards used to evaluate any work of fiction. While the plot, setting, and characters might be simpler in science fiction than in other genres, simplicity need not mean poor quality. Contrived plotting, stereotypical characterization, and ineptly portrayed settings are weaknesses in any work of fiction (Harris, 1996). As Jordan (1995) maintains, well-written science fiction must be believable. Readers will be skeptical and fail to believe the setting or events if the work does not present a logical world or presents poorly researched and flawed science. A discussion of this important part of science fiction writing can be found on the Internet in "The Science of Science Fiction," an installment of the National Public Radio program *Talk of the Nation: Science Friday*.

Teaching with science fiction. When selecting a work of science fiction to use in a classroom, you need to consider your purpose in using the work and the context in which you will use it. Certainly, a novel that is taught for the sake of its literary concepts may be judged differently from one taught for the sake of other concepts, such as ecological or social awareness. You also need to determine whether the book meets the materials selection standards of the local governing bodies for the school. Many of the early works of science fiction might appear sexist by today's standards, but the introduction of strong female characters has led to the inclusion of sexual situations that might cause difficulties in many classrooms (Harris, 1996). To help teachers and librarians promote science fiction, writers Greg Bear and David Brin have developed Reading for the Future, a Web project that includes answers to questions posted by teachers.

Various books and articles suggest ways teachers can connect science and science fiction. Recent books include *No Limits, Grades 7–10: Developing Scientific Literacy Using Science Fiction* (Czerneda, 1999); *The Science in Science Fiction: 83 SF Predictions That Became Scientific Reality* (Bly, 2005); *Science Fact and Science Fiction: An Encyclopedia* (Stableford, 2006); *Teaching Science Fact with Science Fiction* (Raham, 2004); and *Teach Science with Science Fiction Films: A Guide for Teachers and Library Media Specialists* (Cavanaugh & Cavanaugh, 2004). Writing in *The American Biology Teacher*, Andrea Bixler (2007) presents ideas for using science fiction to encourage higher level thinking while confronting misconceptions about biology.

The Internet offers a number of other resources teachers can use to teach specific works of science fiction. Connecting Adolescents and Their Literature 7–1 lists a number of websites that offer ideas for teaching Lois Lowry's award-winning novel *The Giver*.

7-1 •••• CONNECTING ADOLESCENTS AND THEIR LITERATURE

The Internet offers a number of excellent resources to help you teach young adult novels, including works of speculative fiction. You can start with reviews from reputable review sources (discussed in Chapter 2) which can be found on sites such as Amazon.com or Barnesandnoble.com. If you are planning to teach a novel such as *The Giver* (Lowry, 1993), you might consult websites where you will find sample lessons and ideas you can incorporate into your own lessons. Other sites may have background information on the author. After viewing the following resources for *The Giver*, select another novel of speculative fiction and locate links that you think will be helpful in teaching that novel.

Random House teacher's guide
www.randomhouse.com/teachers/guides/give.html

Carol Hurst's Children's literature site
www.carolhurst.com/titles/giver.html

Schools of California Online Resources for Educators Project
www.sdcoe.k12.ca.us/score/Giver/givertg.htm

Teacher's Net
www.teachers.net/lessons/posts/664.html

Fantasy

One of the most recent genres to be accepted in young adult literature, fantasy has its roots in fairy tales, myths, and legends. For children and younger adolescents, fantasy stories often consist of "modern" fairy tales, stories of magical or talking animals or toys, or travels to imaginary lands. In books targeted at adolescents, the emphasis is often on high fantasy, in which the story is set in whole or in part in a created or secondary world and the focus is on the epic and heroic.

The popularity of fantasy in our modern culture cannot be denied. For confirmation, consider the sales of fantasy video/computer games, the success of the Harry Potter books and the box-office draw of *The Lord of the Rings* film trilogy. Publishers and booksellers find that fantasy readers tend to devour books (Corbett, 2006). Why are fantasy items so popular? Some educators write off fantasy as escapist and insufficiently serious for young people to read (Charmas, 1992). Others suggest that fantasy replaces the boredom of everyday life with the strange and unusual and provides an escape from the problems of modern society (Sanders, 1996). With its appeal to the senses, fantasy may provide adolescents with a feeling of overcoming the odds and being triumphant at a time when their own lives often feel like a series of "battles" that they lose or never even get to fight (Bucher & Manning, 2000).

In the past, writers of fantasy have received less respect and experienced more problems than other fiction writers (Service, 1992) although this is beginning to change (Bond, 2006). While some critics consider writing fantasy a literary copout (there are no rules except those the author creates, so the author can make up anything he or she wants), Service (1992) disagrees and suggests that writing fantasy involves considerable mental effort. Fantasy writer Terry Brooks claims that it is "harder to write good fantasy than any other form of fiction" *(The Writers' Complete Fantasy Reference*, 1998, p. 1). Even when a writer invents a completely new world, consistency is important. In addition, all fantasy must speak to the reader, reflect the human condition, and "resonate in some identifiable way with truths we have discovered about ourselves" (p. 1).

If you think back to your own school days, you can probably recall reading and enjoying favorites such as C. S. Lewis' Narnia books, Susan Cooper's books in the Dark Is Rising series, Lloyd Alexander's Prydain series, Diane Duane's Young Wizards series, Diana Wynne Jones's Chrestomanci series, or even Brian Jacques's Redwall books, Robin McKinley's Damar books, and J. R. R. Tolkein's Middle-Earth books. The fantasy genre has been enriched in recent years by authors such as J. K. Rowling (e.g., 1998, 2000, 2003, 2005, 2007), Philip Pullman (e.g., 1996, 2000, 2008) , Garth Nix (e.g., 1996, 2003), Megan Whalen Turner (e.g., 2006), Jonathan Stroud (e.g., 2003), Christopher Paolini (e.g., 2003) and Gerald Morris (e.g., 2000). In addition, writers such as Donna Jo Napoli (e.g., 1998), Patricia McKillip (e.g., 1999), Katherine Kurtz (e.g., 2000), Mercedes Lackey (e.g., 2001), L. E. Modesitt (e.g., 1997), Patricia Wrede (e.g., 1990), Tamora Pierce (e.g., 1999), Sherwood Smith (e.g., 1997), G. C. Levine (e.g., 1997, 2001) and Tanith Lee (e.g., 2000) have created strong characters and series. Many of these fantasy favorites bridge the gap between adolescent and adult fantasy.

A Brief Look at Fantasy's Predecessors. Certainly, fantasy has its roots in the myths, epic tales, and legends that existed in the oral tradition before the spread of literacy. In the mid-1800s, when Hans Christian Anderson began writing literary fairy tales and Lewis Carroll wrote *Alice's Adventures in Wonderland* (1865), fantasy became its own genre. By the early 1900s, fantasy spread to the United States, with the publication of *The Wonderful Wizard of Oz* (Baum, 1900). In the middle of the twentieth century, C. S. Lewis's and Tolkein's works of fantasy created a renewed interest in fantasy, which has been strengthened by the success of Terry Brooks's (e.g., 1997) Shannara series, J. K. Rowling's Harry Potter books (e.g., 1998, 2000, 2003, 2005, 2007), and Philip Pullman's (e.g., 1996, 2000) His Dark Materials trilogy and the popularity of other series such as Brian Jacques's Redwall books (e.g., 2001, 2002), a number of series by Tamora Pierce (e.g., 1999), and books based on computer games such as Mage Knight. By 2005, the top three bestsellers in children's hardcover publishing were all fantasy novels (Roback, 2006). In 2006, the editors of *VOYA*, faced with the explosive growth of young adult fantasy, science fiction, and horror books, had to tighten the criteria for books they would include on their annual best books list ("Best science fiction, fantasy, & horror 2005," 2006).

Types of Fantasy Books. According to Clute and Grant (1999), fantasy is a "self-coherent narrative" (p. 338) that, if set in our world, "tells a story which is impossible in the world as we perceive it" (p. 338) or, if set in another world, is possible only in terms strictly relating to that other world. Young adult fantasy has been influenced by an array of diverse factors, including traditional folk literature. It builds on the categories of children's fantasies, including animal and toy fantasy, the imaginary worlds of high fantasy (including religious allegories and heroic quests), time fantasy (including time travel and timeslips), exaggerated characters and preposterous situations, ghosts and the supernatural, and magic. Even comics and graphic novels, which we discuss in Chapter 12, often feature fantasy themes.

"High" fantasies, which are popular with older readers, are defined as fantasies that are set in other worlds and that "deal with matters affecting the destiny of those worlds" (Clute & Grant, 1999, p. 466). Often the hero or heroine in these books is engaged in a quest to save the fantasy kingdom from an all-powerful evil force or a dark menace that is threatening to take over. Consisting of a series of emotional and sometimes tragic adventures, high fantasies center on the conflict between good and evil and the ultimate triumph of the forces of right and justice.

Reasons for Using and Teaching Fantasy. Why is fantasy literature often forgotten in many secondary schools? Do educators focus on the critical things students need to know and ignore the need of many students to escape? In an effort to prepare students to respond with the "right answer" on standardized tests, do educators fail to encourage students to dream? Are teachers and librarians afraid of censorship when they exclude fantasy titles? Do educators allow their own preferences for realistic and historical fiction to overshadow this genre?

While adults often ignore fantasy literature, some young adults, especially boys, are devouring it. Research into reading habits (Fronius, 1993; Leonhardt, 1996; Moffitt & Wartella, 1992; Thomason, 1983; Traw, 1993) has shown that adolescent boys and girls have different reading preferences. Many girls have been "suspicious of anything called fantasy" (Harris, 1996). Thankfully, with the success of the Harry Potter books and the growth of strong female characters in fantasy literature by authors such as Philip Pullman (e.g., 1996), Garth Nix (e.g., 1996), Tamora Pierce (e.g., 1999), Tanith Lee (e.g., 2000), Patricia Wrede (e.g., 1990), and Robin

EXPANDING YOUR KNOWLEDGE WITH THE INTERNET

A number of authors of fantasy books have their own websites. Here are a few.

Tamora Pierce
www.tamora-pierce.com

Brian Jacques
www.redwall.org/dave/jacques.html

Garth Nix
www.garthnix.com/

Philip Pullman
www.philip-pullman.com/

J. K. Rowling
www.jkrowling.com/

Patricia Wrede
www.dendarii.co.uk/Wrede/

Ursula K. Le Guin
www.ursulakleguin.com/

Robin McKinley
www.robinmckinley.com/

McKinley (e.g., 1978, 1982), fantasy is now reaching a wider audience of readers. Expanding Your Knowledge with the Internet guides you to the Web sites of a number of authors of speculative fiction for young adolescents. Our own observations indicate that students who read fantasy books are not always those who follow directions. They are often divergent thinkers who use these books as focal points for thinking, creating, and imagining.

Fantasy books provide a way for young adults to look at codes of behavior and the human psyche. As Rockman (2001) notes, allegory and metaphor are two excellent techniques that authors use to explore the concepts of good and evil. In fantasy, readers can consider concepts that are often too scary to consider in real life. Through

7-2   COLLABORATING WITH OTHER PROFESSIONALS

Plan a movie discussion and comparison of a specific fantasy book, such as one of the Harry Potter books or another fantasy that has been adapted to film. After selecting an appropriate work, plan your discussion carefully with either adult or student discussion leaders. Read reviews of both the book and the movie to learn what the critics have said. Then develop a list of questions to help students compare the two.
   Sample questions might be:

- Were there any parts of the book that were not included in the movie?
- Why do you think they were omitted? Did this help or hurt the story?

- Were the characters in the movie true to what you expected after reading the book?
- Why do you think the changes were made? If you could change any one thing about the book or movie, what would it be?
- Do you agree or disagree with the critics' comments?
- If you were writing a review of either the book or the movie, what would you say?

   While you can hold the discussion in your classroom or in the school library media center, you can also work with a local public library. For more information on conducting a book/movie discussion, consult Vaillancourt and Gillispie (2001).

fantasies, readers can contemplate dark forces of evil. Often adolescents find that courage, friendship, their own resourcefulness, and the help of trusted elders enables the characters in the books to overcome such evil forces (Rockman, 2001). Fantasies such as Ursula K. Le Guin's *Powers* (2007) may also mirror the coming-of-age stories found in contemporary realistic fiction. Collaborating with Other Professionals 7–2 shows how to involve a number of people in a discussion of fantasy.

Characteristics of Well-Written Fantasy. Readers demand two things from fantasy, whether written for adults or young adults: it cannot contain nonsense or betray the reader (Snyder, 1986). According to successful fantasy writer Terry Brooks, fantasy must be grounded "in both truth and life experience if it is to work" (*The Writer's Complete Fantasy Reference*, 1998, p. 1). A well-written fantasy should have the following characteristics:

- The impossible must seem to be possible.
- Characters should behave in reasonable and expected ways.
- Magic must work consistently.
- Rules must be followed.
- The fantasy world must bear a relationship to our own.
- The fantasy should not be unfairly taken away at the book's end under the pretext that everything that happened was just a dream.
- Once the reader is committed to the fantasy world, the author should never trick or deceive the reader.

Considerations for Selecting Young Adult Literature: *Fantasy* lists some characteristics to look for in evaluating fantasy.

Of all fantasy's characteristics, originality may be the most important. Jon Scieszka (e.g., 1993) may not be a great writer, but the books in his Time Warp series are so original and imaginative that they have gained a wide following among younger adolescents. The characters of well-written fantasy—Alice and her friends from Wonderland, Harry Potter and his classmates at Hogwarts, Bilbo Baggins and the

CONSIDERATIONS FOR
SELECTING YOUNG ADULT LITERATURE FANTASY

When evaluating science fiction books, ask the following:

_____ Is there consistency—with rules or "laws of nature" for the fantasy world?

_____ Are the plot and setting believable—through vivid descriptions?

_____ Is the story original and imaginative?

_____ Are there restraints or limits to the fantastic or magical?

_____ Does realism root the fantasy in reality and human nature?

_____ Are there worthwhile themes such as struggles of good versus evil, heroism, or order versus anarchy?

other inhabitants of Middle-Earth, Lyra Belacqua and the armored bears, or Taran the assistant pigkeeper to the wizard Dalben—remain indelibly marked in our minds, and become the standard against which we measure all other characters. We believe in them and in the values they represent; even though they are make-believe people residing in fantasy worlds, they are rooted in human nature and are imbued with a strong sense of reality and a deep seriousness (Russell, 2009).

A good fantasy writer should provide vivid descriptions of things so that readers can actually visualize the scenes. In this way, the fantasy world comes to life, if only in the mind of the individual reader. In contrast to the sparseness of folk tales, in a fantasy, "description lends weight and substance to ideas" (*The Writer's Complete Fantasy Reference*, 1998, p. 2) so that a reader can see, taste, smell, hear, and feel the new world. A well-written fantasy must "establish a whole new set of natural laws, explain them right up front, and then faithfully abide by them throughout" (Card, 1990, p. 23). These rules prevent the story from slipping into sheer absurdity because there are consistent limits on even magical powers. For example, Princess Cimorene in Patricia Wrede's (e.g., 1990) dragon stories learns that soapy water is very powerful against even the strongest wizard.

Suggestions for Selecting and Using Fantasy. You can use many of the same resources you use to select science fiction (such as *VOYA*, *Locus*, and *Speculative Fiction Book Awards*). There are also a number of specialized resources, such as the following:

- *Encountering Enchantment: A Guide to Speculative Fiction for Teens* (Fichtelberg, 2007)
- *Read on . . . Fantasy fiction: Reading Lists for Every Taste* (Hollands, 2007)
- *The Wand in the Word: Conversations with Writers of Fantasy* (Marcus, 2006)
- *Mapping the World of Harry Potter: Science Fiction and Fantasy Writers Explore the Best Selling Fantasy Series of All Time* (Lackey, 2006)
- *Encyclopedia of Fantasy and Horror Fiction* (D'Ammassa, 2006)
- *Fantasy Literature for Children and Young Adults: A Comprehensive Guide* (Lynn, 2005)
- *Reference Guide to Science Fiction, Fantasy, and Horror* (Burgess and Bartle, 2002)
- *Alternative Worlds in Fantasy Fiction* (Hunt and Lenz, 2001)
- *Encyclopedia of Fantasy* (Clute and Grant, 1999)
- *The Greenwood Encyclopedia of Science Fiction and Fantasy: Themes, Works, and Wonders* (Westfahl, 2005)
- *Fantasy and Horror: A Critical and Historical Guide to Literature, Illustration, Film, TV, Radio, and the Internet* (Barron, 1999a)
- *Barlowe's Guide to Fantasy* (Barlowe, 1996)

Do not forget to check the lists of winners of general young adult book awards and prizes to locate outstanding fantasy books. As we mentioned, Philip Pullman's *The Amber Spyglass* (2000) won the Whitbread Award. *Skellig* (1999), the first young adult book written by David Almond, won both the British Carnegie Medal and the Whitbread Award and was an honor book for the Michael L. Printz Award. *Dreamquake* (Knox, 2007) was a Michael L. Printz 2008 honor book.

When evaluating a work of fantasy on your own, look for the characteristics of well-written fantasy books listed earlier in this chapter, and be sure to evaluate the elements of fiction (listed in Chapter 2) as well. Ask yourself, does the story reflect the characteristics of well-written fantasy? Are the plot and characters believable and original? What has the author done to make the story believable? What message does the story convey? In addition to a well-constructed plot, are there higher level meanings in the story? How do the setting (e.g., visual aspects, smells, and sounds) and the characterization (e.g., language, actions, and attitudes) contribute to the believability of the story? Connecting Adolescents and Their Literature 7–2 illustrates one way to keep track of the large number of characters that are found in many fantasies.

7-2 ••••• CONNECTING ADOLESCENTS AND THEIR LITERATURE

Fantasy books often have a complex cast of characters. Use a graphic organizer such as the computer program *Inspiration* to keep track of the characters in a book and their relationships. Here is an example of the beginning of a web for the characters in the first Harry Potter novel.

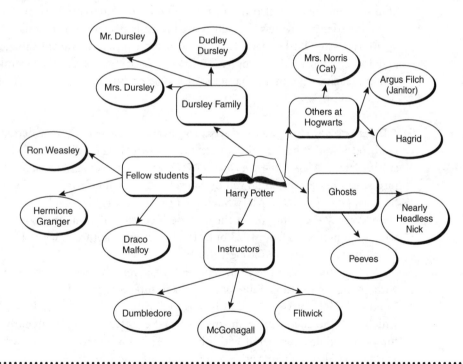

Horror

Horror is the only form of literature that is named "solely after the effect it is intended to produce" (Clute & Grant, 1999, p. 337). According to Card (1990), horror books include "believable events that are so gruesome or revolting that the audience reacts with fear or disgust" (p. 19). While some science fiction and fantasy books may have a "horror 'feel'" (Clute & Grant, 1999, p. 478), true horror fiction creates a feeling of something "obscenely, transgressively impure" (p. 478). Along with this comes the belief that there is a "threat to one's body and/or culture and/or world," as well as "a sense that there is something inherently monstrous and wrong . . . in the invasive presence" (p. 478). Although Dracula, Frankenstein, and the Headless Horseman continue to be popular with adolescents (Lodge, 1996), modern horror stories frequently include elements of romance, mystery, even comedy. Vampires and werewolves can have human dimensions; serial killers can acquire immortality and possess supernatural powers. Good still triumphs over evil, but the hero or heroine often pays with his or her life.

Perhaps the best known writers of horror fiction are R. L. Stine (e.g., 1999, 2001, 2002, 2005) and Stephen King (e.g., 1999). In his Goosebumps 2000 series for children and younger teens, the original Fear Street Series and the new Fear Street Nights for older adolescents, R. L. Stine creates both easy reading tales and spine-chilling dramas that have attracted a wide audience of readers and made him a bestselling author in the United States (Jones, 1998). His works "give kids a positive reading experience to which they can respond since the horror is fun, yet also familiar" (p. 211). In addition, it is the teenagers themselves who, through their own talents and ingenuity, overcome the evil forces. Writing for teenagers and adults, Stephen King also masterfully blends the mundane with the fiendish and fantastic. Many of King's characters are basically decent, normal folk who reside in small towns and lead uneventful lives until some powerful, inexplicable, and usually evil force (such as the vampire in *Salem's Lot*) invades their peaceful existence. Others (such as the main character in *Carrie* or *Firestarter*) have special talents or psychic abilities.

A Brief Look at Horror's Predecessors.   Some of the early horror fiction that is still read today was written in the nineteenth century. Edgar Allan Poe's works included stories such as *Mask of the Red Death* (1842), a tale of terror, and *Berenice* (1835), a vampire story. These were followed by Sheridan Le Fanu's *Carmilla* (1871–1872), Bram Stoker's *Dracula* (1897), Mary Shelley's *Frankenstein* (1818), and a "penny dreadful" about Varney the Vampire. In the twentieth century, the pulp magazine *Weird Tales*, which was published from 1923 until 1954, presented authors such as H. P. Lovecraft, Frank Belknap Long, and Robert Bloch.

In the later part of the twentieth century, several horror writers became popular with young adults. R. L. Stine produced a number of series. His popularity was indicated in a 1997 survey of 3,200 English educators (McElmell & Buswell, 1998) in which 80% included R. L. Stine on a list of the 100 most important authors of books for young adults, compared with only 17–45% for award-winning author Virginia Hamilton. Also popular with young adults are the horror novels of Stephen King (e.g., 1999) and Dean Koontz (e.g., 1998, 1999). Fueled by the popularity of the television series about Buffy, the Vampire Slayer, teens have turned to the vampire novels of Amelia Atwater-Rhodes (e.g., 2001) and Annette C. Klause (e.g., 1997), as well as those by adult author Anne Rice. Rice "paved the way for the undead to be portrayed as complex, even sympathetic, characters" (Altner, 2005). Recently, interest in novels that deal with the paranormal has increased. While not as scary as mainstream horror books or psycho-slasher novels, these books include demons, witches, and ancient gods and goddesses (Herald, 2002). Short story collections such as Neal Shusterman's *Darkness Creeping* (2007) contain a number of different types of horror story.

Types of Horror Books. It is difficult to categorize works of horror. There are "dark fantasies" or "gothic fantasies," which incorporate a feeling of horror but are set in a fantasy world (Clute & Grant, 1999), and paranormal romances, which combine romance with the occult. Books of supernatural horror, which may include vampires, ghosts, werewolves, and the occult, are set in the normal world and are often called "weird fiction" (p. 478). Included in this type are *Blood and Chocolate* (Klause, 1997) and *The Transition of H. P. Lovecraft* (Lovecraft, 1996).

Works of "pure horror" (p. 478) are shaped entirely by the sense of horror they produce. In these, both the protagonist and the reader recognize that a threat exists from a monstrous, invasive presence (Clute & Grant, 1999). Representative books are:

- *Fear Nothing* (Koontz, 1998)
- *The Girl Who Loved Tom Gordon* (King, 1999)
- *Haunting Hour: Chills in the Dead of Night* (Stine, 2001)
- *Nightmare Hour: Time for Terror* (Stine, 1999)
- *Coraline* (Gaiman, 2002)
- The Point Horror Trilogy (e.g., *The Fog*, Cooney, 1989)

Works of "romantic horror," or gothic fiction, include elements of both romance and physical or psychological horror. For example, in vampire romances, the main character may fall in love with a vampire, as in *Vampire Kisses* (Schreiber, 2003). Works of paranormal or unexplained phenomena include series such as the Circle of Three (e.g., Bird, 2001), Daughters of the Moon (e.g., Ewing, 2000), and the Young Adult Witches' Chillers (e.g., Ravenwolf, 2000). From Page to Screen lists a number of films based on speculative fiction, including some horror movies.

Reasons for Using and Teaching Horror Books. Given that mysteries, thrillers, and horror capture the adult best seller lists, it should not be surprising that horror books also capture the attention of adolescents (Dunleavey, 1995) who want to experience, albeit vicariously, frightening situations. They enjoy reading about the vampires, the walking dead, the invasions, and the assaults because they realize that everything is just make-believe. Perhaps this is an extension of the thrill that children get when they sit in the dark and tell ghost stories. In horror fiction, young adults can read about situations in everyday events (such as school, proms, malls, sports, and parties) in which they, not adults, are in control. By confronting imaginary fears, they are confronting their own anxieties in a safe place while learning to accept the responsibilities associated with becoming adults.

Many educators, however, are reluctant to use horror novels in the classroom. This may be, in part because, like science fiction, they have a history based in pulp magazines. Horror fiction is often seen as sensational rather than serious, and with a focus on popularity rather than quality. Then, too, there may be a reluctance to use horror fiction because of anticipated complaints from parents or others in the community. However, not all horror fiction can be written off so easily. Certainly, the works of Edgar Allen Poe have entered the canon of respected literature. The appeal of this type of literature among young adults provides an avenue to reach even reluctant readers. The key is to balance quality and popularity and to find books that both entertain and enrich readers.

from Page to Screen

SCIENCE FICTION, FANTASY, AND HORROR

Two books can help you select science fiction films: *Teach Science with Science Fiction Films* (Cavanaugh and Cavanaugh, 2004) and *The Rough Guide to Sci-Fi Movies* (Scalzi, 2005). An article in "School Library Media Activities Monthly" (Zingher, 2006) has recommendations of films for middle-grade students. Tales of fantasy are often made into films, but their dense and complicated stories are sometimes difficult to fit into a feature-length running time. Consider comparing these films with their novel counterparts and evaluating how well these stories make the leap to the big screen.

THE LORD OF THE RINGS TRILOGY
★★★ | 2001–2003 | PG-13

Peter Jackson's breathtakingly realized vision of J. R. R. Tolkien's classic epics of Hobbits, elves, kings, and evil is surprisingly faithful to the original text.

HARRY POTTER AND THE PRISONER OF AZKABAN
★★★ | 2003 | PG

The third and most impressive adaptation of J. K. Rowling's phenomenally successful novels of witchcraft and wizardry, this film has a cinematic quality that is lacking in the previous Potter films, with impressive visual effects and a more exciting storyline.

TUCK EVERLASTING
★★★ | 2003 | PG

Natalie Babbitt's (1975) beloved story of an ageless family and the girl who stumbles upon them takes a surprising turn in director Jay Russell's hands. Reenvisioning Winnie as an adolescent, the film adaptation turns the story of a girl who latches on to new parent figures into a story of budding romance.

FRANKENSTEIN
★★★ | 1931 | Unrated

Director James Whale's classic interpretation of the Mary Shelley novel no longer packs the scares that thrilled audiences of old, but his principled direction and fantastic eye for gothic staging, alongside Boris Karloff's heartbreakingly humane performance as the monster, create a wonderful film to watch in tandem with reading the novel.

NOSFERATU
★★★ | 1922 | Unrated

F. W. Murnau was unable to get the rights from Bram Stoker's widow to bring the novel Dracula to the screen, so he improvised, changing just enough to avoid prosecution. Murnau's groundbreaking directorial style gives this silent picture an eerie quality far ahead of its time.

Characteristics of Horror Books. Horror literature shares several characteristics with well-written science fiction and fantasy, as listed in Considerations for Selecting Young Adult Literature: *Horror*. Horror, however, has at least one special characteristic—the horror should not be just for sensationalism. It should encourage the reader to explore the reasons behind the actions rather than merely portray a terrifying or gory situation. For example, Dean Koontz's *By the Light of the Moon* "casts a mirror on social responsibility in a world that has become both increasingly dangerous and overly self-absorbed" (Halem, 2003, p. 57).

CONSIDERATIONS FOR
SELECTING YOUNG ADULT LITERATURE HORROR

When examining young adult horror literature, ask the following:

_____ Does the work have the characteristics of well-written science fiction and fantasy?

_____ Does it have strong themes, well-developed plots, nonstereotypical characters, and pleasing writing styles?

_____ Does it provide a sense of escape or sheer enjoyment?

_____ Does it encourage the reader to explore the reasons behind the actions rather than merely portraying a terrifying or gory situation?

Suggestions for Selecting and Using Horror. Select horror fiction the same way you select other literature—by looking for books that are well-written and age-appropriate. Look to see if females are singled out as victims or stereotyped as being helpless and in particular need of assistance because of their gender. The events of violence or horror in the novel should teach a lesson or have a meaning and not be used just for sensationalism. If written well, at a pace that young adults will enjoy, the book should have a believable plot, with a setting and characters that contribute to and complement it. It should be the characters and the plot, not the events of horror or the paranormal, that hold the reader's attention. Using Multiple Readings illustrates how questions influenced by select literary theories can be used to explore one horror novel, *Twilight* (2005) by Stephenie Meyer.

USING MULTIPLE READINGS

The following are some questions critics might ask about *Twilight* (2005), by Stephenie Meyer:

New Criticism
Bella repeatedly mentions her clumsiness and knack for attracting danger. How does this character trait connect to the larger meaning of the novel?

Historical-Biographical Criticism
How might Meyer's experience as a Mormon influence the novel?

Archetypal Criticism
How are archetypes such as soulmate, fatal woman, transformation, immortality, and so on reflected in the novel?

Feminist Criticism
How would you describe Bella's relationship with her mother? How do mother and daughter attempt to take care of one another?

Deconstructionist Criticism
What happens to Bella, and how does she help decide her own fate?

Fortunately, some resources are available to help you select horror fiction. The Horror Writers Association gives the Bram Stoker Award each year; between 2001 and 2004, there was a special category that included books for young people. Since 2005, the categories have included novel, first novel, short fiction, long fiction, fiction collection, poetry collection, anthology, and nonfiction, as well as a lifetime achievement award. In addition to the information mentioned earlier in this chapter, consult:

- *Hooked on Horror: A Guide to Reading Interests in Horror Fiction* (Fonseca and Pulliam, 2003)
- *What's so Scary About R. L. Stine?* (Jones, 1998)
- *Stephen King's Danse Macabre* (King, 1981)
- *Supernatural Horror in Literature* (Lovecraft, 1945)
- *The Vampire Book* (Melton, 1999)
- *Horror Literature: A Reader's Guide* (Barron, 1990)
- *The Vampire Companion* (Ramsland,1993)
- *The Complete Vampire Companion* (Guiley and Macabre, 1994)
- *Vampire Readings* (Altner and Ofcansky, 1998).

The periodical *Rue Morgue, Horror in Culture and Entertainment* (www.Rue-Morgue.com), covers horror. Connecting Adolescents and Their Literature 7–3 suggests a way to promote speculative fiction.

7-3 ••• CONNECTING ADOLESCENTS AND THEIR LITERATURE

To promote the reading of speculative fiction, put displays of science fiction, fantasy, and horror books in the classroom, near the computers in the school library media center, or on your school's website. Bookmark approved websites for speculative fiction and provide the information as links from the school, class, or library homepage.

Considering Gender and Speculative Fiction

For many years, speculative fiction was seen as primarily read by boys; female authors were considered "fantasy" writers and male authors "science fiction" writers (Charmas, 1992). Research into reading habits (Fronius, 1993; Leonhardt, 1996; Moffitt & Wartella, 1992; Thomason, 1983; Traw, 1993) has shown that adolescent girls read more romance and historical romance, while adolescent boys read more fantasy and science fiction. To confirm this research into reading preferences, all you need to do is visit a modern book superstore such as Barnes and Noble or Borders. You'll typically find women browsing through the large sections of romance books, men in the science fiction/fantasy section, and both genders in the mystery and adventure sections. However, as more female authors write quality science fiction and the number of strong female characters in these works begins to grow, this gender-related preference is beginning to change.

It is important for teachers and library media specialists to keep these reading preferences in mind when recommending books to adolescents. Unfortunately, in our college young adult literature classes, we often find that secondary teachers and school library media specialists frankly admit that they do not like fantasy, horror, or science fiction and prefer to read realistic and historical fiction. As a result, they are less likely to use speculative fiction in their classrooms or suggest it to their students. While educators need to take special care to identify, select, and use appropriate speculative fiction with all adolescents, they need to use science fiction books, in particular, to attract male adolescents to reading.

Concluding Thoughts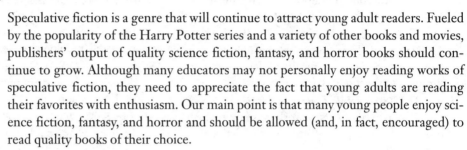

Speculative fiction is a genre that will continue to attract young adult readers. Fueled by the popularity of the Harry Potter series and a variety of other books and movies, publishers' output of quality science fiction, fantasy, and horror books should continue to grow. Although many educators may not personally enjoy reading works of speculative fiction, they need to appreciate the fact that young adults are reading their favorites with enthusiasm. Our main point is that many young people enjoy science fiction, fantasy, and horror and should be allowed (and, in fact, encouraged) to read quality books of their choice.

Young Adult Books

This section includes young adult titles mentioned in this chapter.

SCIENCE FICTION

Allen, R. M. (2002). *The depths of time*. New York: Bantam. Journey to A.D. 5211 and a galaxy where timeshaft wormholes permit time travel through outer space. However, these wormholes can also allow intruders to enter.

Anderson, M. T. (2002). *Feed*. Cambridge, MA: Candlewick. Imagine a world where a communications system that can influence your life is installed in your head at birth.

Armstrong, J., and Butcher, N. (2002). *The kindling*. New York: HarperCollins. In this first volume of the Fire-Us trilogy, a small group of children form their own community after a virus kills most of the inhabitants of Earth. Their story continues in *The Keepers of the Flame* (2002).

Banks, I. M. (1997). *Excession*. New York: Bantam. When something from another dimension appears in the galaxy, every civilization rushes to control it.

Bloor, E. (2006). *London calling*. New York: Knopf. Martin travels back in time to London during the Blitz.

Buckley-Archer, L. (2006). *Gideon the cutpurse*. New York: Simon & Schuster. Travel back with Peter and Kate to 1763.

Butler, O. (1998). *Parable of the talents*. New York: Seven Stories Press. Lauren and her daughter try to survive in a postapocalyptic world.

Card, O. S. (1985). *Ender's game*. New York: Tor. When aliens attack Earth, young Ender Wiggin and his battle skills may be the only hope for survival.

Card, O. S. (1986). *Speaker for the dead*. New York: Tor. In this award-winning sequel to *Ender's Game*, Ender confronts a new group of aliens on the planet Lusitania.

Card, O. S. (1993). *Seventh son*. New York: Tor. This series of alternative histories begins in nineteenth-century America.

Card, O. S. (1999). *Ender's shadow*. New York: Tor. Building on the story in *Ender's Game* (1985), this is the story of Bean, a classmate of "Ender" during the war with the insectile race of aliens called the Buggers. Sequels include *Shadow of the Hegemon* (2002) and *Shadow Puppets* (2002).

Cherryh, C. J. (2001). *Defender*. New York: DAW. Can the starship *Phoenix* successfully reach the damaged station in outer space before disaster strikes?

Cooney, C. B. (2001). *For all time*. New York: Delacorte. Annie, a time-traveler, tries to go back to the Egyptian pyramids in 1899 but ends up in ancient Egypt.

Haddix, M. P. (2000). *Turnabout*. New York: Simon & Schuster. The year is 2085. Melly and Anny Beth are going to unage, going back from their 16 years to the time of their births. Another futuristic book by this author is *Among the Hidden* (1998).

Hamilton, J. (2007). *Modern masters of science fiction*. Edina, MN: ABDO. This brief, easy-to-read history will appeal to reluctant readers.

Hartwell, D. G., and Cramer, K. (Eds.). (2006). *The space opera renaissance*. New York: Tor. A chronological collection stories from the subgenre.

Herbert, F. (1965). *Dune*. Philadelphia: Chilton. On the desert planet Arrakis, when Duke Paul Atreides is exiled after the overthrow of his father's government, the results are felt throughout the interstellar empire.

Ichbiah, D. (2005). *Robots: From science fiction to technological revolution*. New York: Abrams. Ichbiah provides the past, present and future of fictional and real robots.

Kress, N. (2003). *Crossfire*. New York: Tor. Selecting between two alien races will determine the future of humankind.

Lowry, L. (1993). *The giver*. Boston: Houghton Mifflin. When Jonas is chosen as the Receiver of Memories, he learns the truth about his utopian world.

Lowry, L. (2000). *Gathering blue*. Boston: Houghton Mifflin. Kira has exceptional weaving skills that save her from death. But will the Council of Guardians really protect her?

Lowry, L. (2004). *The messenger*. Boston: Houghton Mifflin. This story returns to the worlds of her earlier books *The Giver* (1993) and *Gathering Blue* (2000).

McCaffrey, A. (1977). *Dragonsinger*. New York: Atheneum. Menolly begins her studies to become a Harper of Pern and learns about firelizards and dragons.

McCaffrey, A. (2002). *A gift of dragons*. New York: Del Rey. These four short stories are a good introduction to the land of Pern.

Miller, R. (2001). *The history of science fiction*. New York: Watts. Although nonfiction, this history is sure to appeal to science fiction fans.

Paulsen, G. (2000). *The white fox chronicles*. New York: Delacorte. When dissidents overthrow the U.S. government in 2057, 14-year-old Cody Pierce is thrown into a prison camp.

Pratchett, T. (2007). *Johnny and the bomb*. New York: HarperCollins. Will traveling back to 1941 change the future?

Reynolds, A. (2006). *Pushing ice*. New York: Ace Books. One of Saturn's moons leaves its orbit and heads into interstellar space taking a starship and its crew with it.

Roberts, A. (2006). *The History of Science Fiction*. New York: Palgrave Macmillan. This is a great reference book for science fiction fans.

Scalzi, J. (2005). *Old man's war*. New York: Tor. In the style of Robert A. Heinlein, Scalzi examines the concept of being a "human" as he serves in the interstellar Colonial Defense Force.

Stirling, S. M. (2003). *Conquistador*. New York: Roc. Time travel and steampunk combine in this novel set in New Virginia.

Stirling, S. M. (2004). *Dies the Fire*. New York: Roc. Imagine what would happen to the world. if there suddenly were no mechanical electricity—just fire and flashlights.

Turtledove, H., and Greenberg, M. H. (Eds.). (2001). *Best alternative history stories of the twentieth century*. New York: Del Rey. Byzantium falls seven centuries early, Mozart becomes a cyberpunk, and Shakespeare is shipwrecked in North America in this anthology of stories.

Tyers, K. (1999). *Firebird*. Minneapolis, MN: Bethany House. Lady Firebird Angelo of the planet Netaia joins a Federate Sentinel to fight the development of genocidal bombs.

Weaver, W. (2001). *Memory boy*. New York: Harper-Collins. As the ash from volcanoes covers the world and chaos reigns, Miles Newell has a plan to get his family out of Minneapolis to a safe haven.

Westerfeld, S. (2005). *Uglies*. New York: Simon Pulse. Before Tally gets her operation that will turn her from an "ugly" into a "pretty," she comes to question the government rules.

FANTASY

Almond, D. (1999). *Skellig*. New York: Delacorte. Why is Skellig, the man-owl-angel, crumpled in the abandoned garage behind Michael's new house? Another book by Almond is *Kit's Wilderness* (2000).

Babbitt, N. (1975). *Tuck everlasting*. New York: Farrar, Straus and Giroux. The Tuck family drinks from the fountain of youth and comes to question the wisdom of eternal life.

Brooks, T. (1997). *First king of Shannara*. New York: Ballantine. Breman tries to unite the Four Lands in this book in popular Shannara cycle. *Morgawr*

(2002) is a recent title in the Voyage of the Jerle Shannara series.

Jacques, B. (2001). *Taggerung*. New York: Philomel. Deyna, a young otter, is captured by the ferret leader of a vermin clan who wants to use Deyna in his evil plans. This is part of the Redwall series.

Jacques, B. (2002). *Triss*. New York: Philomel. Join Triss, a squirrelmaid, and her friends as they elude the evil ferret king and discover Brockhall, the ancient home of the badgers.

Jones, D. W. (2006). *The tough guide to fantasyland*. New York: Firebird. Humor abounds in this dictionary/encyclopedia of the fantasy genre. Don't forget your magic pebble!

Knox, E. (2007). *Dreamquake: Book 2 of the dreamhunter duet*. New York: Frances Foster Books. Laura tries to determine the role the Regulatory Body has in the disappearances and mysterious activities.

Kurtz, K. (2000). *King Kelson's bride: A novel of the Deryni*. New York: Ace Books. In the conclusion to the King Kelson series, Kelson is pressured to find a wife and keep his ward Prince Liam safe.

Lackey, M. (2001). *Take a thief*. New York: DAW. After a mysterious fire, Skif sets out with vengeance on his mind in this prequel to the Valdemar tales.

Lee, T. (2000). *Wolf tower*. New York: Dutton. Escaping from the house where she is a maid, Claidi journeys through the Waste with a stranger, only to find a worse fate in Wolf Tower.

Le Guin, U. K. (2007). *Powers*. Orlando, FL: Harcourt. In the third book in the Annals of the Western Shore series, a young slave flees the city after the brutal death of his sister.

Levine, G. C. (1997). *Ella enchanted*. New York: HarperCollins. The gift of obedience turns into a curse.

Levine, G. C. (2001). *The two princesses of Bamarre*. New York: HarperCollins. Addie has always been the timid princess. Now only she can save her sister from the Gray Death.

McKillip, P. (1999). *Riddle master, the complete trilogy*. New York: Ace. This reissue of the Riddle-Master trilogy contains *The Riddle-Master of Hed*, *Heir of Sea and Fire*, and *Harpist in the Wind*, an epic tale.

McKinley, R. (1978). *Beauty: A retelling of the story of Beauty and the Beast*. New York: Harper & Row. McKinley tells her own version of this traditional tale.

McKinley, R. (1982). *The blue sword*. New York: Greenwillow. Corlath, the King of the Hillfolk of Damar, kidnaps Harry Crewe and trains her to fight the evil forces threatening his country.

Modesitt, L. E. (1997). *The Chaos balance*. New York: Tor. Can Nylan the Smith use the forces of Chaos to help the world survive? Try others in Modesitt's Saga of Recluse series or the Spellsong cycle.

Morris, G. (2000). *The savage damsel and the dwarf*. Boston: Houghton Mifflin. Will Lady Lynet find a champion to save her castle from the Knight of the Red Lands?

Napoli, D. J. (1998). *Sirena*. New York: Scholastic. A young siren rescues Philoctetes, a Greek soldier. But can she release him to face his destiny?

Nix, G. (1996). *Sabriel*. New York: HarperCollins. Can Sabriel save the Old Kingdom from destruction by the undead and rescue her necromancer father, who is trapped in Death? The saga continues in *Lirael* (2001) and *Abhorsen* (2003).

Nix, G. (2003). *The keys to the kingdom: Mister Monday*. New York: Scholastic. The first in a new fantasy series.

Paolini, C. (2003). *Eragon*. New York: Knopf. In this first book in the Inheritance trilogy, a 15-year-old boy finds a mysterious stone that will change his life.

Pierce, T. (1999). *Protector of the small*. New York: Random House. Ten-year-old Keladry of Mindalen begins her quest to become a knight in this first book in the Protector of the Small series. Other series by Pierce include the Trickster's books (e.g., *Trickster's Choice*, 2003, *Trickster's Queen*, 2004), Circle of Magic (e.g., *Sandry's Story*, 1997), The Circle Opens (e.g., *Cold Fire*, 2002), The Immortals (e.g., *Realm of the Gods*, 1996), and Song of the Lioness.

Pullman, P. (1996). *The golden compass*. New York: Knopf. In this first of the His Dark Materials trilogy, Lyra Belacqua begins her quest to learn about the mysterious Dust and to rescue the missing children in the far north. The second book in the trilogy is *The Subtle Knife*.

Pullman, P. (2000). *The amber spyglass*. New York: Knopf. Will sets out to rescue Lyra in the conclusion to the trilogy.

Pullman, P. (2008). *Once upon a time in the north*. New York: Knopf. Lee Scoresby and the armored bear Iorek Byrnison join forces against an evil politician.

Rowling, J. K. (1998). *Harry Potter and the sorcerer's stone*. New York: Scholastic. Harry Potter is rescued from the home of his Muggle aunt and uncle Dursley to begin school at Hogwarts School of Witchcraft and Wizardry.

Rowling, J. K. (2000). *Harry Potter and the goblet of fire*. New York: Scholastic. In his fourth year at Hogwarts Academy, Harry Potter is mysteriously entered in an unusual contest.

Rowling, J. K. (2003). *Harry Potter and the order of the phoenix*. New York: Scholastic. In this fifth book in the series, Harry Potter learns to face new challenges as he studies for his Ordinary Wizarding Levels and begins the transition into adulthood.

Rowling, J. K. (2005). *Harry Potter and the half-blood prince*. New York: Arthur A. Levine Books. This sixth book in the series is darker now that more people are aware that Voldemort has returned.

Rowling, J. K. (2007). *Harry Potter and the deathly hallows*. New York: Arthur A. Levine Books. Book seven in the series provides a conclusion to the conflict between Harry and Voldemort.

Scieszka, J. (1993). *The time warp trio, your mother was a Neanderthal*. New York: Viking. When Sam, Joe, and Fred look at the pictures of cavemen in a book, the time travel mist appears, and the three boys are transported back to prehistoric times.

Smith, S. (1997). *Crown duel*. New York: Harcourt. Will Meliara be able to keep her promise to her father and protect her country?

Springer, N. (1998). *I am Mordred: A tale of Camelot*. New York: Philomel. Mordred tells his side of the legend of King Arthur.

Stroud, Jonathan. (2003). *The amulet of Samarkand*. New York: Hyperion. In this first book in the Bartimaeus trilogy, Nathaniel instructs the djinni Bartimaeus to steal the Amulet of Samarkand.

Turner, M. W. (2006). *The King of Attolia*. New York: Greenwillow. In this third book in the series of Eugenides, the thief of Eddis proves himself to his new kingdom and his queen. The first book in the series was a Newbery Honor book.

Wrede, P. C. (1990). *Dealing with dragons*. New York: Harcourt Brace. Not content with being a bored princess, Cimorene runs away to live with a dragon. This is the first book in the series.

Yolen, J. (1982). *Dragon's blood*. New York: Delacorte. In the first of the Pit Dragons series, Jakkin steals a dragon hatchling and trains it to become a fighter.

HORROR

Atwater-Rhodes, A. (2001). *Shattered mirror*. New York: Delacorte. Sarah is a high school vampire-hunter. Other vampire books by this author include *Demon in My View* (2002), *Midnight Predator* (2002), and *In the Forests of the Night* (1999).

Bird, I. (2001). *So mote it be*. New York: Avon Books. In this first book in the Circle of Three series, Morgan uses a spell in a book and then must locate others who have checked out the book in an attempt to undo the damage she has caused.

Cooney, C. (1989). *The fog*. New York: Scholastic. In this first book of the Losing Christina series or the Point Horror Trilogy, the Shevvingtons almost destroy Christina's friend Anya. Other books in the series are *The Snow* (1990) and *The Fire* (1990).

Ewing, L. (2000). *Goddess of the night*. New York: Hyperion. Meet Vanessa, a typical teenager except for her special talents, in this first book in the Daughters of the Moon series.

Gaiman, M. (2002). *Coraline*. New York: Harper. Coraline is living the good life, until she wants to return home.

Gee, J. (2007). *Encyclopedia horrifica: The terrifying TRUTH! about vampires, ghosts, monsters and more*. New York: Scholastic.

King, S. (1999). *The girl who loved Tom Gordon*. New York: Scribner. What is the beast that is following Trisha McFarland through the Maine woods? Other horror books by King include *Salem's Lot*, *Carrie*, and *Firestarter*.

Klause, A. C. (1997). *Blood and chocolate*. New York: Delacorte. Vivian and her werewolves are blamed for unexplained deaths of humans. Another vampire tale by Klause is *Silver Kiss* (1990).

Koontz, D. (1998). *Fear nothing*. New York: Bantam. Can Chris Snow come out of the darkness and save his world? A sequel is *Seize the Night*.

Koontz, D. (1999). *False memory*. New York: Bantam. Can Martie protect herself from herself?

Koontz, D. (2002). *By the light of the moon*. New York: Bantam. Dylan and Jilly only have 24 hours to stop the people who want to kill them.

Lovecraft, H. P. (1996). *The transition of H. P. Lovecraft: The road to madness*. New York: Ballantine. Here are 29 weird tales by a master of the genre.

Meyer, S. (2005). *Twilight*. New York: Little Brown. Bella meets a handsome boy who is not completely human.

Ravenwolf, S. (2000). *Witches' night out.* St. Paul, MN: Llewellyn. The first book in the Witches' Chillers series.

Schreiber, E. (2003). *Vampire kisses.* New York: HarperCollins. Is there really a vampire living in the old mansion on Benson Hill? Raven is determined to find out.

Shusterman, N. (2007). *Creeping darkness: Twenty twisted tales.* New York: Puffin. A collection of spooky and creepy tales.

Stine, R. L. (1999). *Nightmare hour: Time for terror.* New York: HarperCollins. These 10 tales of fear and horror are for younger teens.

Stine, R. L. (2001). *Haunting hour: Chills in the dead of night.* New York: HarperCollins. A collection of 10 horror stories. Another collection by Stine is *Beware: R. L. Stine Picks His Favorite Scary Stories* (2002).

Stine, R. L. (2002). *The stepsister.* New York: Simon Pulse. Emily learns a terrifying secret from Jessie's past. This book is from the Fear Street series.

Stine, R. L. (2005). *Midnight games.* New York: Simon Pulse. Can the evil of Fear Street come back to haunt the new teens at Shadyside High?

Suggested Readings

Arnold, M., and Kunzel, B. (2007). Speculative fiction: Classroom must-reads. *English Journal,* 97(1), 118–122.

Czerneda, J. E. (2006). Science fiction and scientific literacy. *The Science Teacher* 73(2), 38–42.

Hunt, J. (2007). Epic fantasy meets sequel prejudice. *Horn Book 83*(6), 645–653.

Luedtke, A., Wentline, S., and Wurl, J. (2006). The brood of Frankenstein: Great literature? Maybe not, but teens love horror. *School Library Journal,* 52(7), 34–37.

Silvey, A. (2007). The unpredictable Lois Lowry: The Edwards Award–winner talks about *The Giver*'s controversial past and, yes, its enigmatic ending. *School Library Journal,* 53(6), 39–42.

Wallace, D. L., and Pugh, T. (2007). Playing with critical theory in J. K. Rowling's Harry Potter series. *English Journal,* 96(3), 97–98.

Zigo, D., and Moore, M. (2005). Chicken soup for the science fiction soul: Breaking the genre lock in the high school literacy experience. *Journal of Curriculum Theorizing,* 21(3), 29–45.

References

All young adult literature referenced in this chapter are included in the Young Adult Books list and are not repeated in this list.

Altner, P. (2005). Bloody good reads: Vampire tales with bite. *Library Journal,* 130(17), 96.

Altner, P., and Ofcansky, T. (1998). *Vampire readings.* Lanham, MD: Scarecrow.

Barlowe, W. D. (1996). *Barlowe's guide to fantasy.* New York: HarperPrism.

Barron, N. (1990). *Horror literature: A reader's guide.* New York: Garland.

Barron, N. (Ed.). (1999a). *Fantasy and horror: A critical and historical guide to literature, illustration, film, TV, radio, and the internet.* Lanham, MD: Scarecrow Press.

Barron, N. (1999b). *What fantastic fiction do I read next? A reader's guide to recent fantasy, horror, and science fiction.* Farmington Hills, MI: Gale.

Barron, N. (2004). *Anatomy of wonder: A critical guide to science fiction.* Westport, CT: Libraries Unlimited.

Baum, L. F. (1900). *The Wonder Wizard of Oz.* Chicago: G. M. Hill.

Benfield, S. S. (2006). The interplanetary dialectic: Freedom and equality in Ursula Le Guin's *The Dispossessed. Perspectives on Political Science,* 35(3), 128–134.

Best science fiction, fantasy, & horror, 2005. (2006). *Voice of Youth Advocates,* 29(1), 10–12.

Bixler, A. (2007). Teaching evolution with the aid of science fiction. *The American Biology Teacher,* 69(6), 337–340.

Bly, R. (2005). *The science in science fiction: 83 SF predictions that became scientific reality.* Dallas: BenBella Books.

Bond, G. (2006). Fantasy goes literary. *Publisher's Weekly,* 253(14), 29–31.

Bucher, K. T., and Manning, M. L. (2000). A boy's alternative to bodice-rippers. *English Journal,* 89(4), 135–137.

Bucher, K. T., and Manning, M. L. (2001). Taming the alien genre: Bringing science fiction into the classroom. *The ALAN Review,* 28(2), 41–45.

Burgess, M., and Bartle, L. R. (Eds.). (2002). *Reference guide to science fiction, fantasy, and horror.* Englewood, CO: Libraries Unlimited.

Burroughs, E. R. (1912). *A princess of Mars.* Garden City, NY: Nelson Doubleday.

Card, O. S. (1990). *How to write science fiction and fantasy.* Cincinnati: Writer's Digest Books.

Carroll, L. (1865). *Alice's adventures in Wonderland.* London: MacMillan.

Cavanaugh, T. W., and Cavanaugh, C. (2004). *Teach science with science fiction films: A guide for teachers and library media specialists.* Worthington, OH: Linworth.

Charmas, S. M. (1992). A case for fantasy. *The ALAN Review, 19*(3), 20–22.

Clute, J., and Grant, J. (Eds.). (1999). *Encyclopedia of fantasy.* New York: St. Martin's Griffin.

Corbett, S. (2006). Reality check for fantasy. *Publisher's Weekly, 253*(28), 57–59.

Czerneda, J. E. (1999). *No limits, grades 7–10: Developing scientific literacy using science fiction.* Toronto: Trifolium Books.

D'Ammassa, D. (2005). *Encyclopedia of science fiction.* New York: Facts on File.

D'Ammassa, D. (2006). *Encyclopedia of fantasy and horror fiction.* New York: Facts on File.

Diaz-Rubin, C. (1996). Reading interests of high school. *Reading Improvement, 33,* 169–175. Accessed December 30, 2002, from WilsonWeb: http://vnweb.hwwilsonweb.com.

Dunleavey, M. P. (1995). Children's writers plumb the depths of fear. *Publishers Weekly, 242*(13), 28–29.

Fichtelberg, S. (2007). *Encountering enchantment: A guide to speculative fiction for teens.* Westport, CT: Libraries Unlimited.

Fonseca, A., and Pulliam, J. M. (2003). *Hooked on horror: A guide to reading interests in horror fiction.* Englewood, CO: Libraries Unlimited.

Fronius, S. K. (1993). *Reading interests of young adults in Media County, Ohio.* (ERIC Document Reproduction Service No. ED 367 337)

Gath, T. (1999). Exploring new worlds: Finding science in science fiction. *Science, Books and Films, 35*(3). Accessed July 26, 2000, from: http://ehrweb.aaas.org/~sbf/313.htm.

Gross, M. (2007). Prisoners of childhood? Child abuse and the development of heroes and monsters in *Ender's Game. Children's Literature in Education, 38*(2):115–126.

Guiley, R., and Macabre, J. B. (1994). *The complete vampire companion.* New York: Macmillan.

Halem, D. (2003). Night light: Dean Koontz finds brightness in life's dark mysteries. *Pages, 11*(1/2), 56–59.

Harris, J. (1996, May 28). State of fantasy. *Discussion List* [online]. Accessed February 9, 1999, from: www.igloo-press.com/disc.fantasy. html.

Harry Potter soars above James Bond at the box office. (2007, September 11). *Press Association National Newswire.* Accessed September 24, 2007, from: Faciva database:global.factivia.com.

Harry's in a league of his own. (2007). *Publisher's Weekly, 254*(30), 4.

Herald, D. T. (2002). Dead but not gone. *Booklist, 98*(22), 1950.

Herald, D. T., and Kunzel, B. (2002). *Strictly science fiction.* Englewood, CO: Libraries Unlimited.

Hollands, N. (2007). *Read on—fantasy fiction: Reading lists for every taste.* Westport, CT: Libraries Unlimited.

Hughes, M. (1992). Science fiction as myth and metaphor. *The ALAN Review, 19*(3), 2–5.

Hunt, P., and Lenz, M. (2001). *Alternative worlds in fantasy fiction.* New York: Continuum.

Jones, P. (1998). *What's so scary about R. L. Stine?* Lanham, MD: Scarecrow.

Jordan, A. D. (1995). Future reading: Science fiction. *Teaching and Learning Literature, 4*(5), 17–23.

King, S. (1981). *Stephen King's Danse Macabre.* New York: Everest House.

Lackey, W. (Ed.). (2006). *Mapping the world of Harry Potter: Science fiction and fantasy writers explore the best selling fantasy series of all time.* Dallas: BenBella Books.

Le Fanu, S. (1871–1872). Carmilla. *The Dark Blue, 2–3:* Chapters 1–3 (December 1871); 4–6 (January 1872); 7–10 (February); 11–16 (March).

Leonhardt, M. (1996). *Keeping kids reading: How to raise avid readers in the video age.* New York: Crown.

Levy, M. (2006). Sharecropped universes. *Voice of Youth Advocates 29*(2), 134–135.

Levy, M. (2007). Politics and science fiction. *Voice of Youth Advocates 34*(4), 318–319.

Lodge, S. (1996). Life after Goosebumps. *Publishers Weekly, 243*(3), 24–27.

Louvisi, G. (1997). *Collecting science fiction and fantasy.* Brooklyn: Alliance.

Lovecraft, H. P. (1945). *Supernatural horror in literature*. New York: B. Abramson.

Lynn, R. N. (2005). *Fantasy literature for children and young adults: A comprehensive guide*. 5th ed. Westport, CT: Libraries Unlimited.

Marcus, L. S. (2006). *The wand in the word: Conversations with writers of fantasy*. Cambridge, MA: Candlewick.

McElmell, S., and Buswell, L. (1998). Readers' choices: The most important authors of books for young adults. *Book Report, 16*(4), 23–24.

Melton, J. G. (1999). *The vampire book: The encyclopedia of the undead*. Detroit: Visible Ink Press.

Moffitt, M. A. S., and Wartella, E. (1992). Youth and reading: A survey of leisure reading pursuits of female and male adolescents. *Reading Research and Instruction, 31*(2), 1–17. Accessed February 9, 1999, from: www.cyfc.umn.edu/Documents/C/B/CB1025.html.

Moltz, S. (2003). Forging futures with teens and science fiction: A conversation with Greg Bear and David Brin. *Voice of Youth Advocates, 26*(1), 15–18.

Ochoa, G., and Osier, J. (1993). *The writer's guide to creating a science fiction universe*. Cincinnati: Writer's Digest Books.

Owen, L. (1987, October 30). Children's science fiction and fantasy grows up. *Publishers Weekly, 232*, 32–37.

Poe, E. A. (1835, March). Berenice. *Southern Literary Messenger 1*, 333–336.

Poe, E. A. (1842). Mask of the red death. *Graham's Magazine, 20*(5), 257–259.

Prucher, J. (Ed.). (2007). *Brave new words: The Oxford dictionary of science fiction*. Oxford: Oxford University Press.

Raham, G. (2004). *Teaching science fact with science fiction*. Portsmouth, NH: Teacher Ideas Press.

Ramsland, K. M. (1993). *The vampire companion: The official guide to Anne Rice's "The Vampire Chronicles."* New York: Ballantine.

Reid, S. E. (1998). *Presenting young adult science fiction*. Farmington Hills, MI: Twayne.

Reid, S. (2005). What if the lights went out? Alternate stories. *Voice of Youth Advocates, 27*(6), 464–465.

Roback, D. (2006). Potter leads the pack. *Publisher's Weekly, 253*(13), 37–42.

Rockman, C. (2001). Up for discussion—Give them wings. *School Library Journal, 47*(12), 42–43.

Russell, D. L. (2009). *Literature for children: A short introduction*. 6th ed. Boston: Pearson/Allyn & Bacon.

Sanders, L. M. (1996). "Girls who do things": The protagonists of Robin McKinley's fiction. *The ALAN Review, 24*(1), 38–42.

Scalzi, J. (2005). *The rough guide to sci-fi movies*. Longon: Rough Guides.

Service, P. F. (1992). On writing scifi and fantasy for kids. *The ALAN Review, 19*(3), 16–19.

Shelley, M. W. (1818). *Frankenstein, or, the modern Prometheus*. London: Lackington, Hughes, Harding, Mayor & Jones.

Snyder, Z. (1986). Afterword. *Tom's midnight garden* (by Philippa Pearce). New York: Dell.

Stableford, B. M. (2005). *The A to Z of science fiction literature*. Lanham, MD: Scarecrow Press.

Stableford, B. M. (2006). *Science fact and science fiction: An encyclopedia*. New York: Routledge.

Stoker, B. (1897). *Dracula*. Garden City, NY: Nelson Doubleday.

Thomason, N. (1983). *Survey reveals truths about young adult readers*. (ERIC Document Reproduction Service No. ED 237 959)

Traw, R. (1993). *Nothing in the middle: What middle schoolers are reading*. (ERIC Document Reproduction Service No. ED 384 864)

Vaillancourt, R. J., and Gillispie, J. (2001). Read any good movies lately? *Voice of Youth Advocates, 24*(4), 250–253.

Verne, J. (1865). *From the Earth to the Moon*. New York: Bantam.

Wells, H. G. (1895). *The time machine: An invention*. London: Heinemann. *The writer's complete fantasy reference*. (1998). Cincinnati: Writer's Digest Books.

Westfahl, G. (2005). *The Greenwood encyclopedia of science fiction and fantasy: Themes, works and wonders*. Westport, CT: Greenwood Press.

The writer's complete fantasy reference: An indispensable compendium of myth and magic. (1998). Cincinnati: Writer's Digest Books.

Zingher, G. (2006). Gentle beings from other worlds. *School Library Media Activities Monthly, 22*(9), 47–48.

Chapter 8

Exploring Historical Fiction

"I was mesmerized by the Grandma Dowdel."

"She has a complex personality."

"She's a large character with an equally large heart who appears to be antisocial, unapproachable, and perhaps bitter."

"My students would truly enjoy her."

These comments were made by teachers engaged in an online discussion about Richard Peck's character Grandma Dowdel in his novels *A Long Way from Chicago* (1998) and *A Year Down Yonder* (2000). In addition to telling a good story, Peck's books, and historical fiction in general, provide readers with information about life, customs, and events in the past while taking readers into the lives of the characters.

> [Historical fiction] makes us feel . . . what otherwise would be dead and lost to us. It transports us into the past. And the very best historical fiction presents to us a TRUTH of the past that is NOT the truth of the history books, but a bigger truth, a more important truth—a truth of the HEART. (Lee, 2000)

Young adults often know the important dates and events in history and realize that historical events occurred many years ago but may have difficulty comprehending the magnitude of historical events and how they affected many aspects of people's lives. By going beyond the mere presentation of facts, young adult historical fiction allows adolescents to explore history through the eyes of characters their own age. They can see how the Civil War changed families and the nation; how the Salem witchcraft trials brought fear and threats; and how people have struggled to achieve personal and national freedom.

Thankfully, both adult and young adult readers can enjoy a current resurgence of interest in historical novels. Not only have a number of mainstream adult writers such as Michael Crichton, John Grisham, and Amy Tan begun to write in the genre (Nesbeitt, 2002) but also a number of historical fiction books have won major awards and prizes. In 2001, historical novels won the Pulitzer Prize for Fiction in the United States, the Booker Prize in Great Britain, and the Governor General's Literary Award in Canada. Recent bestselling adult historical fiction has included Philippa Gregory's *The Other Boleyn Girl* (2004), Charles Frazier's *Cold Mountain* (1997), Tracy Chevalier's *Girl with a Pearl Earring* (1999), and Arthur Golden's *Memoirs of a Geisha* (1997). In the children's and young adult publishing world, seven historical fiction novels won the Newbery Award from 1996 to 2008: Laura Amy Schlitz, *Good Masters! Sweet Ladies! Voices from a Medieval Village* (2007); Cynthia Kadohata, *Kira-Kira* (2004); Avi, *Crispin, The Cross of Lead* (2002); Linda Sue Park, *A Single Shard* (2001); Richard Peck, *A Year Down Yonder* (2000); Christopher Paul Curtis, *Bud, Not Buddy* (1999); and Karen Hesse, *Out of the Dust* (1997). M. T. Anderson's novel *The Astonishing Life of Octavian Nothing, Traitor to the Nation*, Volume 1, *The Pox Party* (2006), won a Michael L. Printz honor citation and the National Book Award. Laurie Halse Anderson's *Fever, 1793* (2000) showed up as an ALA Best Book for Young Adults, a New York Public Library Best Books for the Teen Age, and an IRA Teacher's Choice. Aidan Chambers's *Postcards from No Man's Land* (2002), a book that interweaves contemporary and historical fiction, won both Britain's Carnegie Medal and America's Michael Printz award. In 2002, historical fiction author Karen Hesse became the second young adult author (the first was Virginia Hamilton) to win a prestigious "Genius" fellowship from the John D. and Catherine T. MacArthur Foundation.

Historical Fiction

What exactly is historical fiction? Most writers and educators agree that it is fiction that is set in the past. The problem seems to revolve around the definition of "the past." Does a novel have to be written originally as historical fiction or can a contemporary novel become historical fiction as time marches forward and the contemporary events become history? What role do the ages of the author and the reader play in this definition?

According to *Merriam Webster's Encyclopedia of Literature* (1995), a historical novel is one that "has as its setting a period of history and that attempts to convey the spirit, manners, and social conditions of a past age with realistic detail and fidelity to historical fact" (p. 549). Some commentators set additional criteria. For example, the *Historical Novels Review* indicates that a historical novel must be set at least 50 years in the past and the author must base the book on historical research rather than personal experiences (Nesbeitt, 2002). While these criteria might be appropriate for adult historical fiction, young adult novels are written for readers to whom anything that happened 15 years ago is historical. Thus we define historical fiction as a novel that was set in the past (at least one generation approximately 15 to 20 years) when it was originally written. We also apply Nesbeitt's (2002) criterion that the historical period must be so well represented that the novel could not have been set in any other time or place in history. Collaborating with Other Professionals 8–1 explores one way to use historical fiction as a basis for examining history.

Whatever historical period they depict, good historical fiction writers achieve a sense of authenticity, such that readers believe that the cultural, social, and political events as well as the feelings, joys, disappointments, and frustrations of the characters actually could have happened. Without using artificiality or sensationalism, good historical novels genuinely relate historical perspectives to the plot, setting, and characters, so that as contemporary adolescents view the past through the eyes of characters their own age, they learn not only about the past but also how it has contributed to the world as it is today. As author Katherine Paterson says: "When we write about . . . the past, we are really writing about our present . . . shedding light on our own time. . . . History becomes a pair of spectacles to focus our vision on the chaotic present" (Johnson & Giorgis, 2001/2002, p. 400).

A Brief Look at Historical Fiction's Predecessors

Historical fiction began as a genre for adults in the 1800s, with Sir Walter Scott's *Waverley* novels (1822) and *Ivanhoe* (1820) and continued with classics such as Leo Tolstoy's *War and Peace* (1869). Along the way, many other not-so-notable novels featured historical settings only as a backdrop for improbable adventures (*Merriam Webster's Encyclopedia of Literature*, 1995).

During the late nineteenth century, historical novels such as Charlotte Yonge's *The Dove in the Eagle's Nest* (1866) and Howard Pyle's *Otto of the Silver Hand* (1888), among a number of others, were written for children. After a decline in popularity

COLLABORATING WITH OTHER PROFESSIONALS

In addition to its literary value, historical fiction, with its links to actual events and people, can be used in social studies as well as language arts classes. You can:

- Have students identify elements of the story pertaining to food, clothing, shelter, social norms, government, and education. Then, with the help of the library media specialist and social studies teacher, students can check these representations against the known historical facts.
- Pair historical fiction with nonfiction that covers the same events or periods. Have

students compare and contrast the information from both books, checking for accuracy. The *Diary of Anne Frank,* a biography, can be paired with a historical fiction book such as *The Devil's Arithmetic* (Yolen, 1988) or *Good Night, Maman* (Mazer, 1999).

- Use the American Memory website of the Library of Congress to check facts; correlate the fictional events in a historical novel with actual historical photographs, recordings, and other primary source materials; and provide information students can use to create their own historical fiction.

during the early twentieth century, children's historical fiction flourished again after the 1930s, with books such as Laura Ingalls Wilder's Little House series, Elizabeth Forbes's *Johnny Tremain* (1943), and Elizabeth George Speare's *Witch of Blackbird Pond* (1958) (Hillman, 2003).

Another decline came in the 1970s when the youth rebellion and the maxim of not trusting anyone over 30 led to a rejection of historical fiction (Russell, 2001). In the 1980s, according to Leo Garfield, historical fiction was "something of an embarrassment . . . tolerated out of a sense of duty and reluctantly supported in a condition of genteel poverty" (Brown, 1998, p. 7). The emphasis in young adult literature was on contemporary realistic fiction and nonfiction instead.

However, by the late 1990s, historical fiction was again popular with adolescents, with publishers producing both series and stand-alone novels (Brown, 1998). A number of writers of young adult literature turned to the genre, including Avi, Christopher Paul Curtis, Karen Cushman, Karen Hesse, Walter Dean Myers, Katherine Paterson, Anne Rinaldi, and Mildred Taylor. Expanding Your Knowledge with the Internet provides links to information about a few of these authors.

Types of Historical Fiction

A number of ways exist to categorize historical fiction; perhaps the most basic is to divide it into two broad types. Some novels are set in the past but not directly tied to specific historical events or actual historical characters. While the characters and

EXPANDING YOUR KNOWLEDGE WITH THE INTERNET

The Internet has information on some of the outstanding authors of young adult historical fiction.

ANN RINALDI

www2.scholastic.com/browse/contributor.jsp?id=1753
www.secondaryenglish.com/ameliaswar.html

KAREN CUSHMAN

www.karencushman.com

Reviews and other information
www.carolhurst.com/titles/midwifesapprentice.html
www.carolhurst.com/titles/catherinecalledbirdy.html

Teaching guides
www.harperchildrens.com/schoolhouse/TeachersGuides/cushmanindex.htm
www.sdcoe.k12.ca.us/score/ccb/ccbtg.html

KAREN HESSE

www2.scholastic.com/browse/contributor.jsp?id=3214
www.kidspoint.org/columns2.asp?column_id=1221&column_type=author

Lesson plans
www.eduscapes.com/newbery/98a.html
www.carolhurst.com/titles/outofthedust.html

WALTER DEAN MYERS

www.eduplace.com/kids/hmr/mtai/wdmyers.html
www.randomhouse.com/teachers/authors/myer.html

Lesson plans
urbandreams.ousd.k12.ca.us/language_arts/core/09/myers/index.html
www.sparknotes.com/lit/fallenangels/
www.mcdougallittell.com/disciplines/_lang_arts/litcons/glory/guide.cfm

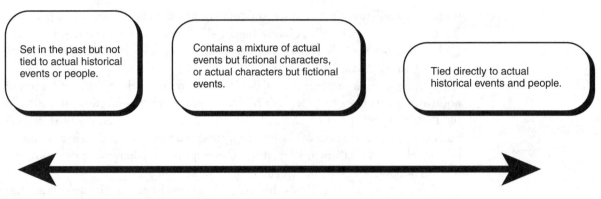

Figure 8-1 Continuum of Historical Fiction

their behaviors are appropriate for the historical setting, they are the creation of the author. In contrast, some novels relate directly to actual historical events, with factual supporting characters and perhaps a fictitious protagonist. In between these two extremes fall novels with a mixture of historical and fictional events and characters (see Figure 8–1).

For example, Ann Rinaldi's *Mine Eyes Have Seen* (1998) is based on historical events and actual characters. Through the eyes of his adolescent daughter, readers watch abolitionist John Brown plot the attack on the federal arsenal at Harpers Ferry, West Virginia. In contrast, using an actual historical event, Laurie Halse Anderson sets her novel *Fever 1793* (2000) during the yellow fever epidemic in Philadelphia but with a cast of fictional characters. While the book provides an accurate description of the life and times of the busy port city, protagonist Mattie Cook is the author's creation. Finally, although Robert Cormier sets his *Frenchtown Summer* (1999) in a post–World War I community, the novel is mainly about a young boy facing problems and trying to understand his conflicting emotions about his life and family.

Topics in Historical Fiction

Another way to categorize historical fiction is to look at some of the recurring themes that appear in the novels. As you might expect, historical novels often focus on the clash of cultures, the human cost of war, the quest for individual and group freedom, the overcoming of disease and disabling conditions, and the struggle to survive the challenges of everyday life.

Clashes of Cultures. People have long fought to preserve their cultures for a number of reasons: they considered their culture superior and thought others should embrace it; they thought others wanted to destroy their culture; and/or they considered their cultural heritages and traditions worthy of honor and protection. Understandably, young adult literature reflects these cultural clashes and their effects on peoples' lives.

Authors such as Kirkpatrick Hill in *Minuk: Ashes in the Pathway* (2002), Scott O'Dell in the classic *The King's Fifth* (1966), Caroline Cooney in *The Ransom of Mercy Carter* (2001), Joseph Bruchac in *The Arrow over the Door* (1998), and Beatrice Harrell in *Longwalker's Journey: A Novel of the Choctaw Trail of Tears* (1999) have written young adult novels about the clash of American Indian and European cultures. In Virginia Euwer Wolff's *Bat 6* (1998), cultural prejudices left over from World War II simmer in a community and come to the surface during a girl's softball game. In *Beacon Hill Boys* (Mochizuki, 2002), a young boy becomes an activist for Asian American rights in Seattle.

Other books look at cultural clashes in other countries. In *Forgotten Fire* (Bagdasarian, 2000) and *Daughter of War* (Skrypuch, 2008), the tensions between Turks and Armenians erupt in the Armenian massacres of the early twentieth century. In *Neela: Victory Song* (Divakaruni, 2002), a 12-year-old girl becomes involved in India's fight for independence. Cathryn Clinton's *A Stone in My Hand* (2002) is set in a Palestinian community during the intifada of the late 1980s and provides some background on the current fighting in the region.

Wars and Conflicts. Clashes over culture and individual or group freedoms have often led to war. Figure 8–2 shows a book web of young adult historical fiction novels related to the American Civil War, and Figure 8–3 is a book web of some novels

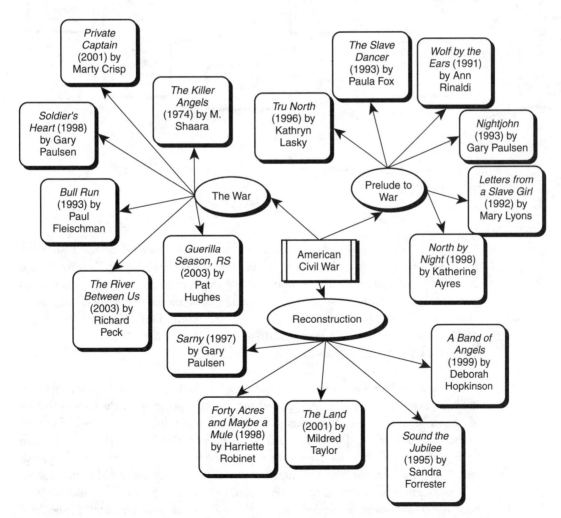

Figure 8-2 Historical Fiction About the American Civil War

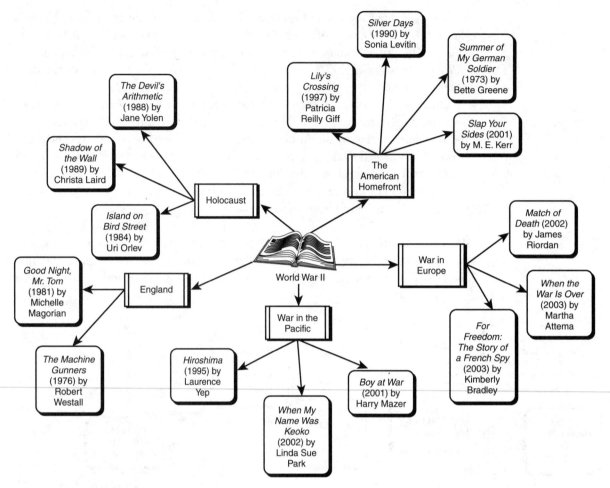

Figure 8-3   World War II Book Web

related to World War II. Other novels about war include Joseph Bruchac's *Codetalker: A Novel about the Navajo Marines of World War Two* (2005) which tells how Navajo Marines created an unbreakable code based on the Navajo language that was used to communicate secretly during the war; Theresa Breslin's *Remembrance* (2002) shows the effect of World War I on five British teenagers; Walter Dean Myers's *Fallen Angels* (1988) looks at the Vietnam War; and Brian Burks's *Soldier Boy* (1997) follows a young boy from Chicago to Custer's cavalry.

The Quest for Freedom. Throughout history, freedom has meant different things to different people. While some protagonists may be attempting to flee the bonds of actual slavery or imprisonment, other protagonists may be attempting to break free of the social or cultural rules and traditions. In the classic *I, Juan De Pareja* (de Trevino, 1965), Juan risks everything to paint, in spite of the fact that he is a slave belonging to the Spanish artist Velazquez. Lyddie tries to escape the servitude of being a mill girl in the Lowell, Massachusetts, textile mills in *Lyddie* (Paterson, 1991). Rosa's family fights against unfair working conditions in textile mills in *Bread and Roses, Too* (Paterson, 2006). The 2008

Newbery honor book and the Scott O'Dell Historical Fiction Award–winning *Elijah of Buxton* (2007), by Christopher Paul Curtis, focuses on abolition.

Many times, freedom is associated with attaining civil rights and equal treatment under the law. In Karen Hesse's *Witness* (2001), a young Jewish girl and an African American girl both learn about bigotry when the Ku Klux Klan comes to Vermont. In *The Watsons Go to Birmingham, 1963* (1995), Christopher Paul Curtis contrasts the Watsons' life with the terror of the church bombing in Birmingham, Alabama. In *A Friendship for Today* (2007), by Patricia C. McKissack, and *Fire from the Rock* (2007), by Sharon M. Draper, school integration is the primary concern. Other works of historical fiction that look at civil rights in the United States include:

- John Armistead, *The Return of Gabriel* (2002)
- Sue Monk Kidd, *The Secret Life of Bees* (2002)
- Chris Crowe, *The Mississippi Trial, 1955* (2002)

Other authors look at freedom in other parts of the world. In *Before We Were Free* (Alvarez, 2002), Anita and her family are involved in the underground movement that is trying to end dictator General Trujillo's rule in the Dominican Republic. Su Phan tells about her life growing up in North Vietnam in *Sing for Your Father, Su Phan* (Pevsner & Tang, 1997), and Ying flees an arranged marriage in China in *Child Bride* (Russell, 1999).

Overcoming Natural Disasters, Death, Disease, and Disabling Conditions. This is another recurring theme. Billie Jo in Karen Hesse's *Out of the Dust* (1997) copes with not only the Dust Bowl in Oklahoma but also the violent death of her mother. Nat Field's response to his father's suicide in Susan Cooper's novel *The King of Shadows* (1999) is to journey back in time to Elizabethan London to perform at the Globe Theater, where he meets Shakespeare. Amari holds on to hope while enduring the disease and hardship of the Middle Passage in Sharon M. Draper's *Copper Sun* (2006).

At many times in history, people have had to fight to survive pestilence and disease. In *Fever, 1793* (Anderson, 2000), Mattie flees the yellow fever epidemic. In *A Time of Angels* (Hesse, 1995), Hanna strives to help her family survive the Boston influenza epidemic of 1918. A young girl and her family struggle to survive the Irish potato famine in *Nory Ryan's Song* (Giff, 2000), and a plague almost destroys an English village in *A Parcel of Patterns* (Walsh, 1983).

Many types of disabling conditions have been depicted in historical fiction. In *The Dark Light* (Newth, 1998), a young girl in the nineteenth century is diagnosed with leprosy. In *Charlie Wilcox* (McKay, 2000), a 14-year-old boy sets out to disprove everyone's belief that his club foot makes him unfit for work in his 1915 Newfoundland community by stowing away on what he thinks is a seal-hunting ship, only to find himself on a troop ship headed for Europe. Sometimes a disabling condition comes after a trauma. In *Motorcycle Ride on the Sea of Tranquility* (Santana, 2002), a young Hispanic girl tries to help her brother deal with his emotional problems when he returns home from the Vietnam War.

Surviving the Challenges of Everyday Life. In the past, the mere attempt to survive from day to day has often been a struggle for a number of people. In *The Birchbark House* (1999), Louise Erdrich tells about the daily life of an Ojibwa family in 1847; in

The Ballad of Lucy Whipple (1996), Karen Cushman tells about life in the California gold fields; in *Search of the Moon King's Daughter* (2002), Linda Holeman describes life in Dickensian London; and in *The Borning Room* (1991), Paul Fleischman tells the history of a single family through the events that take place in one room in their home. Fifteen-year-old Getorix, in *Getorix: The Eagle and The Bull* (Geary, 2006), has to adjust to being a slave to the son of an official in Republican Rome. Sometimes survival is a life-or-death matter, as Mary Chase finds out in Kathryn Lasky's *Beyond the Burning Time* (1994), when her mother is accused of being a witch. Srulik Friedman makes the same discovery inside the Warsaw Ghetto in Uri Orlev *Run, Boy, Run* (2003), which is based on the experiences of an actual Holocaust survivor.

Humor can go a long way toward helping people through the challenges of everyday life. Richard Peck is a master, having written several humorous stories set in the past, including *Fair Weather* (2001), *A Long Way from Chicago* (1998), *A Year Down Yonder* (2000), and *The Teacher's Funeral: A Comedy in Three Parts* (2004). In *Harris and Me* (1993), Gary Paulsen tells the very funny tale of a young city boy who is sent to live with his country cousins for the summer.

By using a diary format, authors can take readers inside the daily lives of characters. In *Catherine, Called Birdy* (1994), Karen Cushman takes readers back to 1290, as a young girl tells about her attempts to keep her father from selecting a husband for her. Sometimes the diary keepers come from higher stations in life. The Royal Diaries series include, Carolyn Meyer's *Anastasia: The Last Grand Duchess, Russia, 1914* (2000), and Kathryn Lasky's *Marie Antoinette: Princess of Versailles, Austria-France, 1769* (2000). These diaries take readers into the lives of historical characters through fiction rather than biographies. Connecting Adolescents and Their Literature 8–1 suggests using literature to examine social issues.

Chronology of Young Adult Historical Fiction

A final way to categorize young adult historical fiction is to arrange books chronologically according to the time periods they depict. Many of the bibliographies listed later in this chapter use this categorization. The selected young adult historical

8-1 ••••. CONNECTING ADOLESCENTS AND THEIR LITERATURE

Developmentally, adolescents begin to explore their feelings about themselves and the world around them when they are in middle school. Toni Sills-Briegel and Deanne Camp (2001) suggest using excerpts from a variety of genres to focus on selected social issues or problems. You can also use entire works rather than just excerpts with older adolescents. Some suggested topics:

- Facing the constraints of family and society: *A Northern Light* (Donnelly, 2003)
- Rights and freedoms for all people: *Saturnalia* (Fleischman, 1990)
- Growing up in an inner city: *Jazmin's Notebook* (Grimes, 1998)
- Civil rights for all: *Kinship* (Krisher, 1997)
- Challenges for immigrants: *An Ocean Apart, a World Away* (Namioka, 2002)

novels in Figure 8–4 present a worldview of historical events. In addition, the books mentioned earlier in this chapter and in Figures 8–2 and 8–3 could be added to these.

Reasons for Using and Teaching Historical Fiction

Why should we encourage young adults to read historical fiction? Haven't most professionals at some time heard young people complain of reading about history? Don't many young adults prefer contemporary realism?

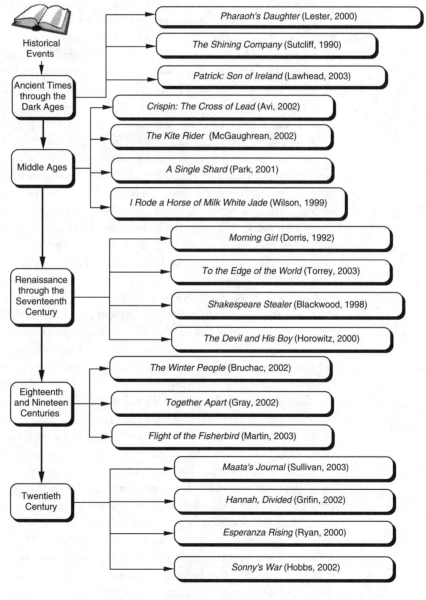

Historical Events

Ancient Times through the Dark Ages
- *Pharaoh's Daughter* (Lester, 2000)
- *The Shining Company* (Sutcliff, 1990)
- *Patrick: Son of Ireland* (Lawhead, 2003)

Middle Ages
- *Crispin: The Cross of Lead* (Avi, 2002)
- *The Kite Rider* (McGaughrean, 2002)
- *A Single Shard* (Park, 2001)
- *I Rode a Horse of Milk White Jade* (Wilson, 1999)

Renaissance through the Seventeenth Century
- *Morning Girl* (Dorris, 1992)
- *To the Edge of the World* (Torrey, 2003)
- *Shakespeare Stealer* (Blackwood, 1998)
- *The Devil and His Boy* (Horowitz, 2000)

Eighteenth and Nineteen Centuries
- *The Winter People* (Bruchac, 2002)
- *Together Apart* (Gray, 2002)
- *Flight of the Fisherbird* (Martin, 2003)

Twentieth Century
- *Maata's Journal* (Sullivan, 2003)
- *Hannah, Divided* (Grifin, 2002)
- *Esperanza Rising* (Ryan, 2000)
- *Sonny's War* (Hobbs, 2002)

Figure 8-4   Chronology of Historical Fiction

Historical fiction helps adolescents to make connections between the past and the present, to view problems and situations over a period of time, and to place events in a historical context. As adolescents vicariously experience the past with its conflicts, joys, and challenges, they can see how a single decision may have far-reaching ramifications. Young adults, like most people today, have a sense of preoccupation with daily events. These preoccupations vary with age and developmental period, and may differ from those of previous times. Through historical fiction, readers may see that there are some concerns that have remained constant throughout the ages. For example, while adolescents today do not concern themselves with traveling west in a covered wagon, many do deal with problems that have concerned people for centuries: cultivating honesty, developing friendships, overcoming loneliness, dealing with crime and criminals, finding a place in society, and dealing with family members.

Charlotte in *The True Confessions of Charlotte Doyle* (Avi, 1990) faces a personal struggle. Stone confronts discrimination in *Just Like Martin* (Davis, 1992). Ben faces family problems in *Borderlands* (Carter, 1990), and Celeste appreciates the power of friendships in *The Starplace* (Grove, 1999). By reading about these characters, their lives, and the difficult decisions they have to make, readers are drawn into their decision-making processes. Exploring the extremes of human behavior encourages readers to think about the causes and effects of events, the consequences of human actions, and the impact events can have on personal choices (Nawrot, 1996).

Young adult historical fiction also encourages readers to think beyond historical events. Adolescents can read social studies and history texts to learn "facts"—events that have shaped the nation and the world. However, much is lost when young adults learn historical events yet fail to perceive the human perspectives surrounding the events. Historical fiction helps readers develop a context for the names, dates, and events of history. While textbooks focus on the results of an action, historical fiction allows readers to look at why it occurred. History provides objective analysis; historical fiction offers synthesis. Reading a textbook, the reader is on the outside, looking in. Reading historical fiction, the reader becomes involved in the events and the lives of the people in the story (Nawrot, 1996).

For example, many history books present the events of the Civil War—the reasons for it, the states' roles, the battles, and the numbers killed. While this information is undoubtedly important, young adults also need an understanding of the human perspectives such as the suffering the war brought, its effects on family relationships, and the terror and worry. War tears friends apart in *The Best of Friends* (Rostokowski, 1989) and families apart in *My Brother Sam Is Dead* (Collier & Collier, 1974). Readers can begin to appreciate the feelings that convince an escaped slave to join the Union army in *Which Way to Freedom* (Hansen, 1986), and can wonder at the hostile attitudes of many Americans during the Vietnam War in *The Road Home* (White, 1995).

Young adult historical fiction also helps readers to identify and judge the mistakes our nation and its peoples, both collectively and individually, have made in the past— errors that young adults will want to understand and strive to avoid. Bilof suggests using historical fiction in high schools to provide a "credible insight into the motive forces and values of the era or society under study" (1996, p. 19). Because historical fiction allows readers to see historical and societal events from various perspectives, it is an excellent genre to help adolescents understand their own cultural heritage, as well as the heritage of other ethnic groups.

Finally, historical fiction is ideal for use in an integrated curriculum and with literature-based approaches across the disciplines. These novels can address the problem of history being taught from a singular dimension void of human emotion or from an approach that does not show the interrelationships among the disciplines. Readers can benefit when they learn about the "human" aspects of historical and societal events and when they see relationships among subject areas.

Characteristics of Good Historical Fiction

As we have cautioned with other genres, you should select historical fiction for young adults carefully. Perhaps more than any other genre, historical fiction calls for interweaving of both fiction and nonfiction, because historical fiction should be both good history and good fiction. Without stereotyping, historical fiction must be true to the time period and reflect the values and attitudes of the period presented in the novel. Accurate details of daily life in a given time period dictate what a character can and cannot do (Clarke, 1999). For example, a character cannot use a kerosene lamp or take photographs in the 1600s or talk about being strong as steel or escaping a mob in the 1700s. These inventions and expressions would be anachronisms, as they simply did not exist at that time. While being well written and entertaining, historical fiction must also be well researched, with characters who are true to their time period. In addition, the language must fit the period and the person while still being understandable to a modern reader.

Because some readers may accept everything in the novel as true, an author must constantly ask himself or herself two questions: (1) How historically accurate must this be? and (2) What fiction is acceptable and necessary? According to author Chris Crowe, it is difficult to blend fact and fiction because "the fictional plot and characters . . . [keep] bumping up against real history" (Blassingame, 2003, p. 24). An author must constantly recheck facts so as to stay faithful to the actual historical events.

However, historical accuracy is not everything. Caro Clarke (1999) maintains that good historical fiction demonstrates a balance between story and fact and that a good writer must know what history to include and what to omit. "The good historical novel is the wise selection of the right fact for the right effect. It doesn't surfeit . . . [readers] by too much information; it doesn't starve them with too little . . . in the end, it is the story that must rule" (Clarke, 1999).

As these authors are writing about the past, they are still influenced by their own political, economic, social, or religious biases. Even historical fiction is a reflection of the time in which it is written as well as the time it portrays (Brown, 1998). Some authors have a definite agenda to present, cause to advance, or perceived wrong to right. In addition, history is constantly being revised as contemporary society reflects on its own past (Lee, 2000). Views on topics such as colonialism and imperialism, the role of women, yesterday's heroes, the contributions of minorities, and the government's treatment of individuals and groups change over the years. Such changes are often reflected in historical fiction; they are discussed in more detail later in this chapter. Considerations for Selecting Young Adult Literature: *Historical Fiction* outlines additional criteria that you will want to keep in mind when examining historical fiction.

CONSIDERATIONS FOR SELECTING YOUNG ADULT LITERATURE HISTORICAL FICTION

When evaluating historical fiction, ask the following questions:

_____   Is the plot interesting and enjoyable?

_____   Are the historical events accurate and authentic?

_____   Do the background details reflect the historical period?

_____   Do the events, attitudes, and behaviors reflect the values and spirit of the time?

_____   Are various points of view represented?

_____   Is the dialogue realistic and conversational in tone?

_____   Are the characters and situations believable?

_____   Are the events, actions, and situations historically possible and plausible?

_____   Do the themes provide insights into contemporary problems?

Suggestions for Selecting and Teaching Historical Fiction

Unless you are a historian, it may be difficult for you to evaluate the historical accuracy of a novel. A number of awards, prizes, bibliographies, and websites that can help you select quality historical fiction. Expanding Your Knowledge with the Internet provides information on Internet resources.

Awards and Best Books Lists. The oldest award for historical fiction is the Scott O'Dell Award for Historical Fiction, established in 1982 by author Scott O'Dell. This annual award is given to a children's or young adult book set in the New World that will help readers understand the history that has helped shape their world and their country. In 1983, the Virginia Library Association established the Jefferson Cup, awarded for quality writing in historical fiction, biography, or U.S. history. The Geoffrey Bilson Award is given annually by the Canadian Children's Book Center for a work of historical fiction by a Canadian author. Works of historical fiction regularly appear on many of the young adult book lists (e.g., Best Books for Young Adults, Quick Picks for Reluctant Readers, Notable Children's Trade Books in the Social Sciences).

Print Review Sources. A number of excellent bibliographies of outstanding historical fiction, are available in print and on the Internet, provided by public and school libraries. Lynda Adamson has written a number of guides that include historical fiction, including:

- *American Historical Fiction: An Annotated Guide to Novels for Adults and Young Adults* (1999a)

- *World Historical Fiction: An Annotated Guide to Novels for Adults and Young Adults* (1999b)

- *Literature Connections to American History: Resources to Enhance and Entice, 7–12* (1997)

- *Literature Connections to World History: Resources to Enhance and Entice, 7–12* (1998)

EXPANDING YOUR KNOWLEDGE WITH THE INTERNET

You can find information on awards and prizes, bibliographies, and teaching resources on the Internet. Here are just a few sources.

AWARDS AND PRIZES

Scott O'Dell Historical Fiction Award
www.scottodell.com/odellaward.html

Virginia Library Association Jefferson Cup
www.vla.org/cyart/jefferson_cup/Jeffersoncup_index.html

Geoffrey Bilson Award
www.bookcentre.ca/awards/bilson/index.shtml

REVIEWS

Historical Fiction Review
historical-fiction-review.blogspot.com/

Copperfield Review
www.copperfieldreview.com/

Historical Novel Society
www.historicalnovelsociety.org/

Historical Fiction Network
www.histfiction.net/

BIBLIOGRAPHIES

www.suffolk.lib.ny.us/youth/bibhf19.html
www.fcps.k12.va.us/FranklinMS/research/hisfic.htm
home.pacbell.net/zindel/historical/
www.pkwy.k12.mo.us/west/lmc/Bibliographies/Historical%20Fiction%20Bibliography.htm

TEACHING IDEAS

Using Historical Fiction in the History Classroom
www.yale.edu/ynhti/curriculum/units/1981/cthistory/81.ch.10.x.html

Why and How I Teach with Historical Fiction
teacher.scholastic.com/lessonrepro/lessonplans/instructor/social1.htm

Social Studies for Kids
www.socialstudiesforkids.com/

Other print bibliographies include:

- *America as Story: Historical Fiction for Middle and Secondary Schools* (Coffey and Howard, 1997)
- *An Annotated Bibliography of Historical Fiction for the Social Studies, Grades 5–12* (Silverblank, 1992)
- *Recasting the Past: The Middle Ages in Young Adult Literature* (Barnhouse, 2000)
- *Historical Fiction: A Guide to the Genre* (Johnson, 2005)
- *Read On—Historical Fiction: Reading Lists for Every Taste* (Hooper, 2006)

Other references focus on individual authors—for example, Jeanne M. McGlinn, *Ann Rinaldi: Historian and Storyteller* (2000)—or on topics, for example, Edward T. Sullivan, *Holocaust in Literature for Youth: A Guide and Resource Book* (1999), and Rebecca L. Berg, *The Great Depression in Literature for Youth* (2004).

Online Resources. The Internet resources on historical fiction are varied. Although not limited to young adult fiction, the *Copperfield Review* is a quarterly online journal for writers and readers of historical fiction, the *Historical Fiction Review* is a blog about historical fiction that includes reviews, and the Historical Novel Society has excellent information. Another comprehensive site for historical fiction is the Historical Fiction Network. All four sites maintain links to other historical fiction sites.

Several other Internet sites provide ideas about using historical fiction in the curriculum. Although Tarry Lindquist's article "Why and How I Teach with Historical Fiction" (1995) was written for teachers of intermediate and middle school children, it provides an excellent rationale for using historical fiction in any grade. The website Social Studies for Kids provides ideas for incorporating historical fiction into social studies lessons.

Nawrot (1996) maintains that while historical fiction is not the most efficient way to teach history, it is the most effective. By reliving the past and internalizing the characters' feelings and emotions and the events, readers become able to remember more than the facts found in a textbook. Teachers can use historical fiction to help students make comparisons of life today and in the past, create timelines, write a sequel, produce a newspaper based on the novel, write letters to characters, or keep a diary. Because some writers of historical fiction attempt to revise history, challenge existing ideas, or refute previous theories about the way things were, it is always important to select young adult historical fiction carefully.

One book that discussed a mystery in history when it was written is *Wolf by the Ears* (Rinaldi, 1991). Connecting Adolescents and Their Literature 8–2 provides a unit to use with this novel. Using Multiple Readings on page 228 provides questions that indicate how various critical interpretations can be applied to a work of historical fiction.

8-2 CONNECTING ADOLESCENTS AND THEIR LITERATURE

Instructional Unit for *Wolf by the Ears*, by Ann Rinaldi

Summary

Harriet Hemings was born in 1798 at Monticello to Sally Hemings, an educated slave owned by Thomas Jefferson. Now, Harriet's twenty-first birthday is approaching, and she must make a decision. Will she stay at Monticello, will she receive her freedom and leave as a free person of color, or will she receive her freedom and leave Monticello to pass as a white woman? As Harriet watches her brother Beverly, who wants to leave to go to college but cannot do so, she realizes that if she decides to take her freedom, she will have to leave behind the security of her family and everything she loves. She finally makes her decision, fully understanding its cost.

Through the eyes of Harriet, readers see the conflict Thomas Jefferson felt about the issue of slavery, when he says, "As it is, we have the wolf (slavery) by the ears, and we can neither hold him, nor safely let him go. Justice is in one scale, and self-preservation the other."

Introducing the Book

1. Explore the setting of the book. Use the Internet to view Monticello and other southern plantations. What would you expect daily life to be like at Monticello? How would you expect life at Monticello to differ from your life today?

2. Explore the social situation of the early 1800s. What constraints does society put on the book?

3. Explore the recent DNA findings about the parentage of some of Sally Hemings's children.

4. Have you ever wondered what life would be like if your father was someone rich or famous? How would you feel if people in your neighborhood said your dad was a

member of an important or wealthy family but your mother refused to tell you if you were really that person's child? How would you feel if that man had other children who lived with him and enjoyed his lifestyle, but you were his servant?

Discussing the Book

1. What changes take place in Harriet from the time Mr. Jefferson gives her the diary until she makes her last entry almost 2 years later? Why did Jefferson give her the diary?

2. What role do each of the following people play in Harriet's life: Sally Hemings, Isobel's Davie, Mammy Ursula, Charles Bankhead, Thad, and Thomas Jefferson?

3. Why does Sally Hemings have such passionate feelings about freedom? Why does Harriet call these feelings a sickness?

4. What most influences Harriet's final decision? Would you have made the same choice? Why or why not?

5. Why did Harriet and Beverly make different choices?

6. Sally Hemings could have stayed in France as a free woman. Why didn't she? What did she lose/gain?

7. Alienation is a theme in this novel. For example, Beverly and Jefferson are alienated, as are Martha and Sally. Who else feels alienation? Why are these feelings so strong?

8. Examine the way Rinaldi portrays Jefferson. Does she put him on a pedestal or does she try to take him off one? Is she sympathetic or unsympathetic to his feelings and actions?

9. Why does Jefferson tell Beverly the Wythe story?

10. Why is Randolph confused about his feelings for his father-in-law?

11. What are Harriet's feelings toward Thruston? What role do they play in her decision?

12. When Harriet leaves Monticello, she calls Jefferson "mister" rather than "master." What does this signify?

Moving Beyond the Book

1. Thomas Jefferson, the third president of the United States and author of the Declaration of Independence, was rumored to be the father of Sally Hemings's children. What have been the findings of recent DNA investigations? Why do you believe that Jefferson refused to comment on the allegations during his lifetime?

2. Some writers put historical figures on a pedestal and show only their good side. Other writers prefer to debunk the hero and focus on the flaws in his or her character. How has Rinaldi treated Thomas Jefferson?

3. As president, what actions, if any, did Jefferson use to curtail slavery or to curb its spread?

4. Contrast life on Monticello to life on other southern plantations. Would you consider Jefferson an "enlightened" slave owner?

5. Find a map of the United States as it was in 1819. Use the book and other resources to identify the free states and the slave states. Locate your town on the map if you can. Was it part of the United States in 1819? If so, was it in a free or slave state?

6. Thomas Jefferson was known as an inventor and an amateur scientist. What things did he invent?

(Continued)

(Continued)

7. Harriet may be a slave, but she is also a well-educated woman of the early nineteenth century. Contrast her education to education for women today as well as to education for other women in her time period.

8. While little is known about Harriet after she leaves Monticello, there is information on some of her brothers. Locate that information and explain what it adds to your knowledge about Thomas Jefferson and his relationship with Sally Hemings.

Literature Activities

1. Research is very important in historical fiction. However, in researching the novel, Rinaldi found very little direct information about Harriet. Thus, much of her portrayal of Harriet is indeed fiction. Using your imagination and common sense, you could possibly create a very different young woman in the same setting. You could make her a rebel or a coward. Write a character sketch of the Harriet you would write.

2. Rinaldi tells the story from Harriet's point of view. What constraints does this put on her as an author? How does she deal with these constraints? Is her work effective?

3. Discuss the ways Rinaldi uses figurative language throughout the story, identifying similes, metaphors, oxymorons, and symbols.

4. How does Rinaldi use both dialect and formal speech to advance the story?

5. Select a scene from the story you would like to dramatize. What does this scene show about Harriet's life and/or her relationship to Thomas Jefferson?

6. Little is known about Harriet after she leaves Monticello. Use your imagination to continue her diary. Remember to anticipate that she will encounter both success and sorrow. Go back and reread Thad's words to Harriet about leaving her friends and family.

USING MULTIPLE READINGS

The following are some questions critics might ask about the novel *Kira-Kira* (2004), by Cynthia Kadohata.

New Criticism
Kira-Kira is mentioned throughout the book. How is the word linked to characterization, theme, and plot in the novel?

Feminist Criticism
What does Katie's mother's life and work teach her children?

Black Feminist Criticism
What types of race, class, and gender discrimination does Katie's family face? How do they stand up against prejudice?

Marxist Criticism
What role does class play in this novel? How does class impact the Takeshima's livelihood?

New Historical Criticism
Could the poverty and poor working conditions depicted in this novel occur in the United States today? Why or why not?

Changing Perspectives in Historical Fiction

As the world has changed, so has our view of history. At one time, young adults read only about majority-culture males with little negative said or implied about these males. Flaws and weaknesses went undiscussed, and societal ills were ignored. Over the past 25 years perspectives in historical fiction have changed somewhat: young adult historical fiction increasingly includes characters from all backgrounds; looks at all sides of individuals to present their strengths, weaknesses, and challenges; portrays realism; and examines social problems. Because every piece of history, whether fiction or nonfiction, reflects the author's interpretations of the events, complete with his or her biases (Brown, 1998), these changes have presented some challenges for both writers and readers of historical fiction.

From Page to Screen looks at the historical accuracy of some films based on historical fiction novels.

Increased Diversity. Our nation's increased diversity means that historical fiction is needed that accurately reflects the many cultures, races, and ethnic groups in our nation, as well as all gender orientations. The novels we discuss in this chapter reflect this diversity in their protagonists and supporting characters. But merely changing names or identifying the ethnicity of the characters is not enough. As contemporary writers look back on the past, it is important to reflect the past as accurately as possible. We need to remember that we cannot erase bigotry or racism from our history by writing historical fiction that portrays relations as we wish they

from Page to Screen

HISTORICAL FICTION

Consider comparing the historical authenticity of these films to that of their original text. Does the visual aspect of the film clarify the time period, or does the book feel more historically true?

DANCES WITH WOLVES
★★★ | 1990 | PG-13

Michael Blake adapted his own young adult novel for the screen in Kevin Costner's directorial debut. Dances with Wolves, a tale of 1860s hardship, humanity, and cultural identity, received an Oscar for Best Picture.

NIGHTJOHN
★★★★ | 1996 | PG-13

During slavery, Sarney tries to avoid punishment when a slave named Nightjohn secretly teaches her how to read. Some scenes are violent, as slaves caught learning to read were severely punished.

WHEN ZACHARY BEAVER CAME TO TOWN
★★★ | 2003 | PG

Director and screenwriter John Schultz brings to the screen Kimberly Holt's novel set in the 1970s in Texas. The title character is an obese boy whose guardian uses him as a sideshow to make money.

GIRL WITH A PEARL EARRING
★★★ | 2003 | PG-13

Based on Tracy Chevalier's novel that imagines a backstory for Vermeer's famous painting, the film is worth watching as much for the way cinematographer Eduardo Serra mimic's the artist's use of light as it is for the solid performances.

COLLABORATING WITH OTHER PROFESSIONALS

A library media specialist and members of an interdisciplinary team (or just two or three other teachers, if your school does not have interdisciplinary teams) can work together to plan an integrated curriculum unit and to select appropriate historical novels that accurately portray the realities of diversity.

- Take advantage of the perspectives of all the educators on the team. For example, opinions may vary on accurate portrayals of historical events, depictions of people with culturally

diverse backgrounds, and the extent the diversity contributes to or diminishes the overall worth of the book.

- Explain:
  a. How the diversity (e.g., characters, plot, setting) makes a genuine contribution to the book
  b. How the diversity makes a genuine contribution to the unit
- Use only books that have merit and that make a legitimate contribution to the unit.

had been. For example, today, shameful and hurtful words to describe certain cultural groups have, for the most part, been removed from the vocabularies of all but the most extreme racists. But these terms were used in the past. As we examine historical fiction, we must determine whether the use of what we now consider racial or ethnic slurs provides accuracy and advances the plot of the novel or whether the words are used gratuitously or for their shock value. Collaborating with Other Professionals 8–2 looks at some ways educators can work together to select multicultural historical fiction.

Connecting Adolescents and Their Literature 8–3 suggests a way to use the strong historical characters as role models for students.

8-3 •••• CONNECTING ADOLESCENTS AND THEIR LITERATURE

In an informal survey of girls in grades 6–12 by Samantha Melnick (2002), 66% of the respondents indicated that "there had been characters in books that they felt they could use as role models in their lives" (p. 44). Melnick was surprised when an "overwhelming number of girls" (p. 45) mentioned a historical person as being an inspiration to them. She concluded that "fictional characters that display good qualities and traits, such as honesty, bravery, creativity, and kindness, can teach the girls . . . to possess these same qualities in their own lives" (p. 45). Thus, teachers and library media specialists need to:

- Identify historical fiction books that contain positive role models for girls
- Use these books in displays
- Incorporate these books into instructional activities
- Include these books on book lists

More Accurate Portrayal of All Types and All Sides of Individuals. At one time in our history, authors created many stereotyped, one-dimensional characters. For example, Indians were portrayed as ignorant savages who would be rescued from their pitiful lives if they turned over their lands and submitted to the demands of the white settlers. The settlers, in contrast, were depicted as struggling people who embodied the best qualities of the American "pioneer." Now, as writers of historical fiction do more accurate research, multifaceted characters populate historical novels. Not all of the pioneers were upstanding individuals. As Kathryn Lasky has pointed out, some who went west in the wagon trains robbed, killed, and raped other settlers, and not all of the women who went west were schoolmarms (Brown, 1998). The problem for writers of historical fiction is whether to produce accurate characters or to maintain the myth of the American pioneer. Thankfully, in deciding to debunk many of the myths of history, authors have incorporated a wider variety of characters from all ethnic, religious, and cultural groups and all genders.

In the past, many people considered disabling conditions to be evil, a jinx, or an imperfection to be ignored and, certainly, not written about. While exceptions exist, contemporary perceptions of disabling conditions today are more accepting and positive, and more characters with disabling conditions are included in historical fiction. As Baskin and Harris (1984) said in the preface of their book *Notes from a Different Drummer: A Guide to Juvenile Fiction Portraying the Handicapped*:

> Like everyone else, people with impairments are still just people—
> individuals who are good and bad, wise and foolish, congenial and aloof.
> Their core human needs are the same, and their differences are in degree,
> not in kind. Undeniably, their pursuit of goals is affected by the fact and
> severity or complexity of their disabilities. (p. xv)

Increased Realism. With interest in multiculturalism and in representing all peoples fairly in historical fiction, authors have begun to sharpen their sensitivities and to reexamine historical events and viewpoints (Brown, 1998). The concern is that in doing so, these authors must still retain historical accuracy. A racist view, while not accepted today, might have been the norm in the 1700s. Likewise, acceptable behavior today might have been unthinkable in the past. Most young adult novels have adolescents as the protagonists and/or main characters. Usually these characters are able to overcome obstacles and succeed in spite of their youth and lack of power. However, "by inflating their valor and courage, an author may diminish or even sacrifice their humanity as well as challenge the reader's suspension of disbelief" (p. 7). For example, although it is true that today authors create many strong positive women and girls as role models, many critics have questioned whether a young, sheltered, upper-class girl of the early 1890s like Charlotte in *The True Confessions of Charlotte Doyle* (Avi, 1990) would have actually been able to lead a rough crew of sailors and captain a trading ship (Brown, 1998).

The inclusion of violence is also an issue. For example, although some would have us believe that in the 1700s and 1800s most slave-owners were benevolent, this was not the case in the majority of situations. Any writers who incorporate these settings in their novels must deal with the unsavory, cruel, and repugnant aspects of

COLLABORATING WITH OTHER PROFESSIONALS

Most teachers believe they have a responsibility to work toward social justice in schools and society. Many think social ills need to be addressed whenever possible. While teachers cannot address all societal ills, they can make significant contributions toward eliminating or at least reducing them.

Four or five teachers (working collaboratively with the library media specialist) can discuss societal ills (e.g., racism, sexism, and classism) to determine

how these issues are affecting students in their school. Next, they can:

- Select historical fiction that accurately portrays these ills and shows some deliberate action to lessen their effects
- Include the selected books in lessons and units (being sure to choose books that students will see as relevant to contemporary society)
- Identify Internet sites that complement or enhance the selected books

the situations. In *Nightjohn* (1993), Gary Paulsen realistically includes references to forced sex, castration, and cruel punishment.

Increased Examination of Societal Ills. Historical fiction increasingly addresses societal ills—situations such as racism, injustice, discrimination, and inhumane treatment of others—that once were not considered ills or were simply ignored. In some instances, similar situations may even exist today. For example, in the 1800s and early 1900s, the owners of coal mines were not always fair and honest individuals who were looking out for the good of their "employees." In *Breaker* (1988), Perez shows the deplorable conditions that led to the coal miners' strike of 1902. Increasingly, authors have addressed societal ills in an attempt to promote social justice; to help young adults understand prejudice, discrimination, and inhumane treatment; and to recognize the need to improve all people's living and social conditions. The problem is that in looking at these issues, novelists may ignore complexities and nuances and "forego the expansive canvas that historians use in order to create clear characterizations and forward-moving plot lines that arrive, finally, at resolutions often denied to history" (Brown, 1998, p. 8). Thus, Brown (1998) cautions teachers to look for books that blend literary art with historical information. Collaborating with Other Professionals 8–3 contains ideas for combating "isms" in schools.

Concluding Thoughts

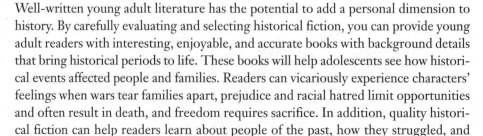

Well-written young adult literature has the potential to add a personal dimension to history. By carefully evaluating and selecting historical fiction, you can provide young adult readers with interesting, enjoyable, and accurate books with background details that bring historical periods to life. These books will help adolescents see how historical events affected people and families. Readers can vicariously experience characters' feelings when wars tear families apart, prejudice and racial hatred limit opportunities and often result in death, and freedom requires sacrifice. In addition, quality historical fiction can help readers learn about people of the past, how they struggled, and how they overcame obstacles and their own fears. Many adolescents will appreciate recent historical fiction and its changing perspectives on diverse cultures and on societal ills. You can use historical fiction to help young adults see that there is more to history than bare facts and dates and that their heritage is a rich tapestry of feelings, emotions, fears, joys, and satisfactions.

Young Adult Books

This section includes young adult titles mentioned in this chapter.

Alvarez, J. (2002). *Before we were free*. New York: Knopf. In the 1960s, Anita and her family become involved in the attempts to overthrow Trujillo's dictatorship in the Dominican Republic.

Anderson, L. H. (2000). *Fever, 1793*. New York: Simon & Schuster. It seems like any other hot August in Philadelphia until disease begins to spread and Mattie begins to wonder if she can outrun it even if she flees from the city.

Anderson, M. T. (2006). *The astonishing life of Octavian Nothing, traitor to the nation: Vol. 1: The pox party*. New York: Candlewick. Set in the 1700s; scholars study Octavian and his mother, who are Africans, to determine their humanity. The story continues in *The Astonishing Life of Octavian Nothing, Traitor to the Nation: Vol. 2: The Kingdom on the Waves* (2008).

Armistead, J. (2002). *The return of Gabriel*. Minneapolis, MN: Milkweed Editions. When the civil rights movement and the Klan both come to their Mississippi hometown in 1964, the lives of three young boys are changed forever when their families and friends start taking opposite sides.

Attema, M. (2003). *When the war is over*. Custer, WA: Orca. Sixteen-year-old Janke joins her father and brother in the Resistance in Holland in World War II.

Avi. (1990). *The true confessions of Charlotte Doyle*. New York: Orchard. As a passenger on a sailing ship in 1832, Charlotte is accused of murder.

Avi. (2002). *Crispin: The cross of lead*. New York: Hyperion. After a 13-year-old orphan is declared a "wolf's head" (meaning that he is anyone's prey), he flees across England and meets a juggler named Bear in this adventure story of the Middle Ages.

Ayres, K. (1998). *North by night*. New York: Delacorte. Through Lucy's journal, readers learn the rules of hiding slaves and the operation of a station on the underground railroad.

Bagdasarian, A. (2000). *Forgotten fire*. New York: Dorling Kindersley. When the Turkish leaders begin to massacre Armenians, young Vahan must flee for his life.

Blackwood, G. L. (1998). *The Shakespeare stealer*. New York: Dutton. When Widge is sent to copy the script of Will Shakespeare, his first job is to survive in London. The sequel is *Shakespeare's Scribe* (2000).

Bradley, K. (2003). *For freedom: The story of a French spy*. New York: Delacorte. Sixteen-year-old Suzanne becomes a spy for the French Resistance.

Breslin, T. (2002). *Remembrance*. New York: Delacorte. By watching five teenagers, we see the reality of war, the slaughter on the battlefield, and the changes that World War I made in the lives of women.

Bruchac, J. (1998). *The arrow over the door*. New York: Dial. A Quaker boy and an Abenaki Indian scout explore their beliefs in this tale of the American Revolution.

Bruchac, J. (2002). *The winter people*. New York: Dial. A young Abenaki boy tries to rescue his mother and sister from Rogers' Rangers in the French and Indian War.

Bruchac, J. (2005). *Codetalker: A novel about the Navajo Marines of World War Two*. New York: Dial. Ned Begay tells his grandchildren about his service in the United States Marine Corps during World War II.

Burks, B. (1997). *Soldier boy*. San Diego: Harcourt. After Johnny "The Kid" McBane throws a boxing match, he ends up in Custer's cavalry at the Battle of the Little Big Horn.

Cadnum, M. (2000). *The book of the lion*. New York: Viking. Edmund travels to the Holy Land as the squire of a crusader.

Carter, P. (1990). *Borderlands*. New York: Farrar, Straus and Giroux. Ben Curtis learns that there is both cruelty and adventure in the Old West.

Chambers, A. (2002). *Postcards from no man's land*. New York: Dutton. In this novel for mature readers, two stories, one contemporary and one set during World War II, come together as a young British boy goes to the Netherlands to learn about his grandfather.

Clinton, C. (2002). *A stone in my hand*. Cambridge, MA: Candlewick. Through the eyes of a young Palestinian girl, we see life in Gaza during the intifada of the 1980s.

Collier, J. L., and Collier, C. (1974). *My brother Sam is dead*. New York: Four Winds Press. Sam runs away to join the army of Benedict Arnold in the American Revolution. But no one anticipates how he dies. Another book about the Colliers set in the same time period is *Jump Ship to Freedom* (1981).

Cooney, C. B. (2001). *The ransom of Mercy Carter*. New York: Delacorte. Captured by Mohawks in 1704, Mercy Carter recounts her life and her hopes to return to her home.

Cooper, S. (1999). *The king of shadows*. New York: McElderry Books. After his father's suicide, Nat Field goes back in time to the Elizabethan England of William Shakespeare.

Cormier, R. (1999). *Frenchtown summer*. New York: Delacorte. In the aftermath of World War I, Eugene watches his tenement community and thinks about the unanswered questions in his life.

Crisp, M. (2001). *Private captain: A story of Gettysburg*. New York: Philomel. Searching for his older brother, Ben leaves home with his brother's dog and his cousin Danny and arrives at Gettysburg, where he helps bury the bodies and nurse the wounded.

Crowe, C. (2002). *The Mississippi trial, 1955*. New York: Dial. Hiram meets Emmett Till, an African American boy who is visiting his town and who is soon murdered for speaking to a white woman. Now Hiram begins to look at the people he knows who might have been involved in the killing.

Curtis, C. P. (1995). *The Watsons go to Birmingham, 1963*. New York: Delacorte. Kenny and his family lead a funny life until they travel south to visit a family in Alabama where there is a church bombing.

Curtis, C. P. (1999). *Bud, not Buddy*. New York: Delacorte. After his mother's death, Bud begins his search for his father in the depths of the Great Depression.

Curtis, C. P. (2007). *Elijah of Buxton*. New York: Scholastic. Elijah is the first free-born black growing up in Buxton, Canada.

Cushman, K. (1994). *Catherine, called Birdy*. New York: Clarion. In 1290, Birdy's diary shows the lengths to which she will go to discourage all suitors.

Cushman, K. (1996). *The ballad of Lucy Whipple*. New York: Clarion. When Lucy Whipple's mother moves the family from New England to the California gold fields, everyone is in for a major change in life. Another title by Cushman is *Rodzina* (2003).

Davis, O. (1992). *Just like Martin*. New York: Simon & Schuster. When Stone's father keeps him from attending the March on Washington in 1963, he decides to find other ways to protest.

de Trevino, E. B. (1965). *I, Juan De Pareja*. New York: Bell Books. Although he is a slave, Juan De Pareja risks his life to follow his dream of being a painter like his master Velazquez.

Divakaruni, C. B. (2002). *Neela: Victory song*. Middleton, WI: Pleasant Company. In this book in the Girls of Many Lands series, a young girl searches for her father and becomes involved in India's fight for independence from Great Britain.

Donnelly, J. (2003). *A northern light*. San Diego: Harcourt. In 1906, waitress Matie Gokey seeks to find a balance between her dreams of becoming a writer and the expectations of her family.

Dorris, M. (1992). *Morning girl*. New York: Hyperion. Life changes for Morning Girl and her brother when the white men land on their Caribbean island.

Draper, S. (2006). *Copper sun*. New York: Simon & Schuster. Amari is stolen from Africa and enslaved on a Carolina plantation in 1738.

Draper, S. (2007). *Fire from the rock*. New York: Penguin. Sylvia Patterson has to decide if she wants to be one of the Little Rock nine who integrated Central High School.

Erdrich, L. (1999). *The birchbark house*. New York: Hyperion. In this book for younger teens, we see the life of a young Ojibwa girl in 1847.

Fleischman, P. (1990). *Saturnalia*. New York: Harper & Row. At the end of the Indian War, William, a Narraganset Indian, tries to find his twin brother in a Boston that is tombstone-cracking cold.

Fleischman, P. (1991). *The borning room*. New York: HarperCollins. The Civil War, World War I, women's suffrage, and medical folklore are all reflected in the events that take place in one room.

Fleischman, P. (1993). *Bull Run.* New York: HarperCollins. Soldiers and slaves, men and women, adults and children tell the story of the first battle of the Civil War. Another novel by Fleischman is *Dateline: Troy* (1996).

Forrester, S. (1995). *Sound the jubilee.* New York: Lodestar. Maddie's family joins a colony of former slaves on Roanoke Island, North Carolina.

Fox, P. (1973). *The slave dancer.* Scarsdale, NY: Bradbury. A young boy is kidnapped so that he can provide music on a slave ship to keep the "cargo" in good shape.

Geary, J. (2006). *Getorix: The eagle and the bull: A Celtic adventure in ancient Rome.* Boone, NC: Ingalls. A spoil of war, Getorix wants to die a noble death instead of serving as a slave.

Giff, P. R. (1997). *Lily's crossing.* New York: Delacorte Press. When Lily befriends a Hungarian refugee, she begins to understand World War II.

Giff, P. R. (2000). *Nory Ryan's song.* New York: Delacorte. Nory and her family try to survive the Irish Potato Famine of 1845.

Gray, D. E. (2002). *Together apart.* Boston: Houghton Mifflin. After the Great Blizzard of 1888, two children cope with life on the Nebraska prairie and their "luck" at being survivors.

Greene, B. (1973). *Summer of my German soldier.* New York: Dial. What exactly is freedom and what is prison? That is the problem that a young Jewish girl in Arkansas must face when German prisoners-of-war come to her town.

Griffin, A. (2002). *Hannah, divided.* New York: Hyperion. Against all odds, Hannah wins a scholarship and leaves the farm to attend school in Philadelphia during the Great Depression.

Grimes, N. (1998). *Jazmin's notebook.* New York: Dial. The notebook of 14-year-old Jazmin reflects life in Harlem in the 1960s.

Grove, V. (1999). *The starplace.* New York: Putnam. Celeste, an African American girl, enrolls in a school in Oklahoma in 1961.

Hansen, J. (1986). *Which way to freedom?* New York: Walker. After escaping from slavery, Obi joins a black Union regiment.

Harrell, B. O. (1999). *Longwalker's journey: A novel of the Choctaw trail of tears.* New York: Dial. This short novel for younger adolescents recounts the walk of the Choctaw people from Mississippi to Oklahoma.

Hesse, K. (1995). *A time of angels.* New York: Hyperion. During the Boston influenza epidemic in 1918, Hanna becomes responsible for her younger sisters.

Hesse, K. (1997). *Out of the dust.* New York: Scholastic. As if the Dust Bowl did not provide enough challenges, Billie Jo must also cope with the sudden death of her mother.

Hesse, K. (2001). *Witness.* New York: Scholastic. Everyone has his or her own story to tell when the Ku Klux Klan comes to Vermont in the 1920s.

Hill, K. (2002). *Minuk: Ashes in the pathway.* Middleton, WI: Pleasant Company. A young Yup'ik girl in Alaska watches the arrival of Christian missionaries.

Hobbs, V. (2002). *Sonny's war.* New York: Farrar, Straus and Giroux. The Vietnam War and the civil rights movement become personal for Corin.

Holeman, L. (2002). *Search of the Moon King's daughter.* Toronto: Tundra Books. Emmaline goes to London to search for her brother, who has been sold as a chimney sweep in Victorian England.

Hopkinson, D. (1999). *A band of angels: A story inspired by the Jubilee Singers.* New York: Atheneum. After Ella enrolls at Fish, the school for freed slaves, she is invited to join the chorus. But will the school be able to survive the financial difficulties that threaten it?

Horowitz, A. (2000). *The devil and his boy.* New York: Philomel. In 1593, a young boy becomes involved with a group of actors who are really thieves and rebels.

Hughes, P. (2003). *Guerrilla season, RS.* New York: Farrar, Straus and Giroux. In the 1860s, when Quantrill's raiders come closer to his Missouri farm, 15-year-old Matt has to make some difficult choices about a brutal war.

Kadohata, C. (2004). *Kira-Kira.* New York: Simon & Schuster. Katie Takeshima's family is one of the few working-class Japanese American families living in Georgia in the 1950s and 1960s.

Kerr, M. E. (2001). *Slap your sides.* New York: HarperCollins. When Jubal's brother registers as a conscientious objector during World War II, his Quaker family becomes the target of hostility from residents of his small town.

Kidd, S. M. (2002). *The secret life of bees: A novel.* New York: Viking. Running from racial unrest in the 1960s, Lily and Rosaleen, her adult companion, flee to Tiburon, South Carolina, where Lily hopes to learn more about her mother, who was killed when she was four.

Krisher, T. (1997). *Kinship*. New York: Delacorte. When Pert's father shows up at her home in a small town in Georgia in 1961, she does not realize that he has brought trouble with him.

Kurtz, J. (1998). *The storyteller's beads*. San Diego: Harcourt. When famine and social unrest strike Ethiopia in the 1980s, two young girls attempt to flee to a refugee camp in Sudan.

Laird, C. (1989). *Shadow of the wall*. New York: Greenwillow. When a young boy joins a resistance group, he misses the deportations from the Warsaw ghetto to the Treblinka concentration camp. The sequel to this is *Beyond the Wall*. Another book by this author on the Holocaust is *But Can the Phoenix Sing* (1993).

Lasky, K. (1994). *Beyond the burning time*. New York: Blue Sky Press. Mary Chase tries to save her mother from being executed as a witch.

Lasky, K. (1996). *True north: A novel of the underground railroad*. New York: Scholastic. Lucy decides to help a young slave escape.

Lasky, K. (2000). *Marie Antoinette: Princess of Versailles, Austria-France, 1769*. New York: Scholastic. Marie Antoinette's diary shows her rise to queen of France and wife of Louis XVI.

Lawhead, S. R. (2003). *Patrick: Son of Ireland*. New York: Morrow. This novel fills in the gaps in the life of a young boy who is captured as a slave and who eventually returns to Ireland and becomes a legend.

Lester, J. (2000). *Pharaoh's daughter: A novel of ancient Egypt*. San Diego: Silver Whistle. A fictionalized story about the birth of Moses.

Levitin, S. (1990). *Silver days*. New York: Atheneum. Escaping from Nazi Germany, the Platts find a home in America.

Lyons, M. (1992). *Letters from a slave girl*. New York: Scribner. Before she is able to escape to the North in 1842, Harriet Jacobs hides where she is able to watch her children grow up.

Magorian, M. (1981). *Good night, Mr. Tom*. New York: Harper & Row. When the Germans begin to bomb London, Willie Beech is among the children who are sent to the country for safety.

Martin, N. (2003). *Flight of the fisherbird*. New York: Bloomsbury. When Clementine rescues an illegal Chinese immigrant on the coast of Washington in 1889, she must decide what to do with him.

Mazer, H. (2001). *Boy at war: Novel of Pearl Harbor*. New York: Simon & Schuster. Growing up as the son of a U.S. naval officer in Honolulu in 1941 is not easy for Adam. Then the Japanese planes come.

Mazer, N. F. (1999). *Good night, Maman*. San Diego: Harcourt Brace. Karin Levi, her mother, and her brother flee the Nazis who have invaded France. But Karin and her brother must leave their mother behind when they flee on an American refugee ship.

McCaughrean, G. (2002). *The kite rider*. New York: HarperCollins. To save his mother from marriage to the man who killed his father, Haoyou becomes a "wind tester."

McKay, S. E. (2000). *Charlie Wilcox*. Toronto: Stoddard Kids. When Charlie tries to stow away on a seal hunting ship, he finds himself on a troop ship headed to the war in Europe where his courage will be tested in the trenches during the battle of the Somme.

McKissack, P. (2007). *A friendship for today*. New York: Scholastic. Loosely based on the author's own life, the main character is one of the first blacks to integrate a school in Missouri.

Meyer, C. (2000). *Anastasia: The last grand duchess, Russia, 1914*. New York: Scholastic. This book in the Royal Diaries series takes readers inside the life of Russian nobility from 1914 to 1918.

Mochizuki, K. (2002). *Beacon Hill boys*. New York: Scholastic. Tensions are high in Seattle in the 1970s as a high school student decides to stand up for his rights as an Asian American.

Myers, W. D. (1988). *Fallen angels*. New York: Scholastic. A young African American boy tries to escape his neighborhood by enlisting for the Vietnam War.

Namioka, L. (2002). *An ocean apart, a world away*. New York: Delacorte. Leaving China for life in the United States in the 1920s, Yanyan finds that she has two strikes against her: she is Asian and she is a woman.

Newth, M. (1998). *The dark light*. New York: Farrar, Straus and Giroux. When Tora is diagnosed with leprosy, she learns that she still may be able to help others.

O'Dell, S. (1966). *The king's fifth*. Boston: Houghton Mifflin. The conquistadors' search for gold is not a peaceful one.

Orlev, U. (1984). *Island on Bird Street*. Boston: Houghton Mifflin. When his father disappears, a young boy tries to survive in an abandoned house in the Warsaw Ghetto.

Orlev, U. (2003). *Run, boy, run*. Boston: Walter Lorraine. A Jewish boy's experiences in Poland during World War II.

Park, L. S. (2001). *A single shard*. New York: Clarion. In twelve-century Korea, a young boy must deliver the work of a master potter.

Park, L. S. (2002). *When my name was Keoko*. New York: Clarion. Sun-hee and her brother Tae-yul lose more than their names when the Japanese invade Korea during World War II.

Paterson, K. (1991). *Lyddie*. New York: Lodestar. When tragedy strikes her family, Lyddie runs away to work in the textile mills rather than be bound out as a servant. But Lyddie finds a different kind of servitude in the mills of Lowell, Massachusetts.

Paterson, K. (2006). *Bread and roses, too*. New York: Houghton Mifflin. Rosa and her family are affected by the 1912 Textile Mill strike in Lawrence, Massachusetts.

Paulsen, G. (1993). *Harris and me*. San Diego: Harcourt. Get ready for laughs when a young city boy spends the summer with his country cousins.

Paulsen, G. (1993). *Nightjohn*. New York: Delacorte. Sarny wants to learn to read, but that is forbidden for slaves.

Paulsen, G. (1997) *Sarny: A life remembered*. New York: Delacorte. Leaving the plantation at the end of the Civil War, Sarny journeys south to find her children and begin a new life.

Paulsen, G. (1998). *Soldier's heart: Being the story of the enlistment and due service of the boy Charley Goddard in the First Minnesota Volunteers*. New York: Delacorte. Charley leaves Minnesota full of the glory he will find in the Civil War. He returns full of the horrible images of the war.

Peck, R. (1998). *A long way from Chicago*. New York: Dial. Two children are sent to rural Illinois to spend the summer with their grandmother during the Great Depression.

Peck, R. (2000). *A year down yonder*. New York: Dial. Because of the Great Depression, Mary Alice has to spend a year in rural Illinois with her grandmother.

Peck, R. (2001). *Fair weather*. New York: Dial. What's more interesting: The 1893 World's Fair or grandfather?

Peck, R. (2003). *The river between us*. New York: Dial. When Howard visits his grandparents, his grandmother tells him of the strange events of

1861 when two young ladies from New Orleans arrived in their Mississippi town.

Peck, R. (2004). *The teacher's funeral: A comedy in three parts*. New York: Dial. When the county schoolteacher dies, Russell Culver has to adjust to a new teacher: his sister.

Perez, N. A. (1988). *Breaker*. Boston: Houghton Mifflin. Pat, a Polish breaker boy in the Pennsylvania coal mines, tries to survive the brutality of the mine owners and the mistrust of the Irish miners.

Pevsner, S., and Tang, F. (1997). *Sing for your father, Su Phan*. New York: Clarion. Growing up in North Vietnam, Su Phan tells about her life after her father is sent to prison.

Rinaldi, A. (1991). *Wolf by the ears*. New York: Scholastic. Harriet Hemings, a young slave on Thomas Jefferson's plantation, must decide whether to accept her freedom or stay at Monticello. Other books by this author include *Ride the Morning: The Story of Tempe Wick* (1991), *The Secret of Sarah Revere* (1995), and *In My Father's House* (1993).

Rinaldi, A. (1998). *Mine eyes have seen*. New York: Scholastic. Annie follows John Brown, her father, to Maryland, where he will plan his raid on the U.S. arsenal at Harpers Ferry, West Virginia.

Riordan, J. (2002). *Match of death*. Oxford: Oxford University Press. The Kiev Dinamos are scheduled to play a football match against the Germans in 1942. Then a referee tells the team members that if they win the game, they will all die.

Robinet, H. (1998). *Forty acres and maybe a mule*. New York: Atheneum. At the end of the Civil War, Pascal, his brother, and their friends set out to get the 40 acres that have been promised to all of the freed slaves.

Rostkowski, M. I. (1989). *The best of friends*. New York: HarperCollins. When one of two friends becomes a peace activist and the other enlists as a soldier in the Vietnam War, can the two remain good friends?

Russell, C. Y. (1999). *Child bride*. Honesdale PA: Boyds Mills. Eleven-year-old Ying tries to flee an arranged marriage in 1940s China.

Ryan, P. M. (2000). *Esperanza rising*. New York: Scholastic. When her father is murdered by bandits, Esperanza and her mother flee from Mexico to a migrant camp in California, during the Great Depression.

Santana, P. (2002). *Motorcycle ride on the sea of tranquility*. Albuquerque, NM: University of New Mexico Press. When Chuy returns from Vietnam in 1969, his sister is frightened by the emotional changes in him.

Schlitz, L.A. (2007). *Good masters! sweet ladies! voices from a Medieval village.* Cambridge, MA: Candlewick. Set in England in 1255. Short monologues introduce 22 characters in a village.

Shaara, M. (1974). *The killer angels.* New York: Ballantine. The battle of Gettysburg comes alive in this classic novel.

Skrypuch, M. F. (2008). *Daughter of war.* Markham, Ontario: Fitzhenry & Whiteside. During World War I, the Turkish government abandoned Armenians in the Syrian Desert. Kevork, Marta, and her sister Mariam manage to survive.

Sullivan, P. (2003). *Maata's journal: A novel.* New York: Atheneum. Through a young Inuit girl's journal, we learn about survival in the Arctic in 1924.

Sutcliff, R. (1990). *The shining company.* New York: Farrar, Straus and Giroux. A young shield bearer tells the story of the Saxon invasion of Britain in the seventh century. Other books by Sutcliff on early British history include *The Shield Ring* (1957), *Dawn Wind* (1961), *Knight's Fee* (1960), *The Silver Branch* (1959), *The Lantern Bearers* (1959), and *The Eagle of the Ninth* (1961).

Taylor, M. (2001). *The land.* New York: Phyllis Fogelman. The son of a white plantation owner and a slave mother, Paul-Edward Logan, tells his tale of the Reconstruction South. The sequel to this novel is the classic *Roll of Thunder, Hear My Cry* (1976). Other books about the Logan family include *The Road to Memphis* (1990) and *Mississippi Bridge* (1990).

Torrey, M. (2003). *To the edge of the world.* New York: Knopf. A young orphan joins Ferdinand Magellan on his first successful circumnavigation of the world in 1519.

Walsh, J. P. (1983). *A parcel of patterns.* New York: Farrar, Straus and Giroux. In 1665, a plague comes to an English village.

Westall, R. (1976). *The machine gunners.* New York: Greenwillow. A group of English children find a German machine gun and decide to hide it from the adults.

White, E. E. (1995). *The road home.* New York: Scholastic. After spending a year with the soldiers in Vietnam, Becky Phillips comes home to a hostile America.

Wilson, D. L. (1999). *I rode a horse of milk white jade.* New York: HarperCollins. Disguised as a boy, Oyuna joins the army of Kublai Khan.

Wolff, V. E. (1998). *Bat 6.* New York: Scholastic. Tradition had the sixth-grade girls playing a softball game at the beginning of the new school year for 50 years. But this year's game was filled with danger.

Yep, L. (1995). *Hiroshima.* New York: Scholastic. Through Sachi, we see the effects of the atomic bomb on Hiroshima, Japan.

Yolen, J. (1988). *The devil's arithmetic.* New York: Viking. Hannah is transported back in time to 1942, when the Nazi soldiers come to her family's village in Poland.

Suggested Readings

Anderson, M. T. (2007). Printz award honor speech. *Young Adult Library Services, 6*(1), 20–21.

Brooks, W., and Hampton, G. (2005). Safe discussions rather than firsthand encounters: Adolescents examine racism through one historical fiction text. *Children's Literature in Education, 36*(1), 83–98.

Carbone, E. (2007). Making it real: Bringing historical fiction alive. *Teacher Librarian, 34*(5), 27–30.

Crawford, P. A., and Zygouris-Coe, V. (2008). Those were the days: Learning about history through literature. *Childhood Education, 84*(4), 197–203.

Walach, S. (2008). "So far from the bamboo grove": Multiculturalism, historical context, and close reading. *English Journal, 97*(3), 17–20.

Wasta, S., and Lott, C. (2006). Where are the facts? Jason's gold gives meaning to the Yukon gold rush. *The Social Studies, 97*(1), 3–7.

References

All young adult literature referenced in this chapter is included in the Young Adult Books list and are not repeated in this list.

Adamson, L. G. (1997). *Literature connections to American history: Resources to enhance and entice, 7–12.* Englewood, CO: Libraries Unlimited.

Adamson, L. G. (1998). *Literature connections to world history: Resources to enhance and entice, 7–12.* Englewood, CO: Libraries Unlimited.

Adamson, L. G. (1999a). *American historical fiction: An annotated guide to novels for adults and young adults.* Phoenix: Oryx Press.

Adamson, L. G. (1999b). *World historical fiction: An annotated guide to novels for adults and young adults.* Phoenix: Oryx Press.

Barnhouse, R. (2000). *Recasting the past: The Middle Ages in young adult literature*. Portsmouth, NH: Boynton/Cook.

Baskin, B. H., and Harris, K. H. (1984). *Notes from a different drummer: A guide to juvenile fiction portraying the handicapped*. New York: Bowker.

Berg, R. L. (2004). *The Great Depression in literature for youth: A geographical study of families and young lives: A guide and resource book*. Lanham, MD: Scarecrow Press.

Bilof, E. G. (1996). *The killer angels:* A case study of historical fiction in the social studies curriculum. *The Social Studies, 87*(1) 19–23.

Blassingame, J. (2003). "A crime that's so unjust!" Chris Crowe tells about the death of Emmett Till. *The ALAN Review, 30*(3), 22–24.

Brown, J. (1998). Historical fiction or fictionalized history? Problems for writers of historical novels for young adults. *The ALAN Review, 26*(1), 7–11.

Chevalier, T. (1999). *Girl with a pearl earring*. New York: Dutton. After becoming a model for the seventeenth-century Dutch painter Vermeer, a young maid describes life in his household.

Clarke, C. (1999). Writing advice from Caro Clarke: 19. Historical fiction: Who rules, researcher or story-teller? Accessed August 4, 2003, from: www.caroclarke.com/historicalfiction.html.

Coffey, R. K., and Howard, E. F. (1997). *America as story: Historical fiction for middle and secondary schools*. Chicago: American Library Association.

Forbes, E. (1943). *Johnny Tremain: A novel for old and young*. Boston: Houghton Mifflin.

Frazier, C. (1997). *Cold mountain*. New York: Atlantic Monthly Press.

Golden, A. (1997). *Memoirs of a geisha*. New York: Knopf.

Gregory, P. (2004). *The other Boleyn girl*. New York: Simon & Schuster.

Hillman, J. (2003). *Discovering children's literature*. Upper Saddle River, NJ: Merrill/Prentice Hall.

Hooper, B. (2006). *Read on—historical fiction: Reading lists for every taste*. Westport, CT: Libraries Unlimited.

Johnson, N. J., and Giorgis, C. (2001/2002). Stepping back, looking forward. *The Reading Teacher, 55*(4), 400–408.

Johnson, S. L. (2005). *Historical fiction: A guide to the genre*. Westport, CT: Libraries Unlimited.

Lee, R. (2000). *History is but a fable agreed upon: The problem of truth in history and fiction*. Paper presented at the annual meeting of Romantic Novelists' Association. Accessed August 4, 2003, from: www.historicalnovelsociety.com/historyis.htm.

Lindquist, T. (1995). Why and how I teach with historical fiction. Accessed November 17, 2008, from: teacher.scholastic.com/lessonrepro/instructor/social1.htm.

McGlinn, J. M. (2000). *Ann Rinaldi: Historian and storyteller*. Lanham, MD: Scarecrow Press.

Melnick, S. (2002). Fictional characters in books as positive role models for adolescent females. *Gifted Child Today, 25*(2), 44–45.

Merriam-Webster's Encyclopedia of Literature. (1995). Springfield, MA: Merriam-Webster.

Nawrot, K. (1996). Making connections with historical fiction. *The Clearing House, 69*(6), 343–345.

Nesbeitt, S. (2002, March). *What are the rules for historical fiction?* (Panel discussion.) Paper presented at the annual conference of the Associated Writing Programs. Accessed August 4, 2003, from: www.historicalnovelsociety.com/historyic.htm.

Pyle, H. (1888). *Otto of the silver hand*. New York: Scribner.

Russell, D. L. (2001). *Literature for children: A short introduction*. New York: Longman.

Scott, W. (1820). *Ivanhoe: A romance*. Edinburgh: A. Constable.

Scott, W. (1822). *The Waverly novels*. New York: Routledge.

Sills-Briegel, T., and Camp, D. (2001). Using literature to explore social issues. *The Clearing House, 74*(5), 280–284.

Silverblank, F. (1992). *An annotated bibliography of historical fiction for the social studies, grades 5–12*. Dubuque, IA: Kendall/Hunt.

Speare, E. G. (1958). *Witch of Blackbird Pond*. Boston: Houghton Mifflin.

Sullivan, E. T. (1999). *Holocaust in literature for youth: A guide and resource book*. Lanham, MD: Scarecrow.

Tolstoy, L. (1869). *War and peace*. New York: Modern Library.

Van Meter, V. (1997). *American in historical fiction: A bibliographic guide*. Englewood, CO: Libraries Unlimited.

Wilder, L. I. (1932). *Little house in the big woods*. New York: Harper.

9 Exploring Biography

Peering in at someone's life experiences in the pages of a book can be captivating and akin to eavesdropping or gossiping. Anyone who has read Ned Vizzini's autobiographical essays chronicling his tumultuous teen years in *Teen Angst Naah . . . : A Quasi-Autobiography* (2000), Gary Paulsen's *Guts* (2001), a partial autobiography about adventures that influenced the writing of his novels, or Samantha Schutz's description of life battling a psychological disorder in *I Don't Want to Be Crazy* (2006) knows exactly what we mean. In addition, biographies are an important resource young adults can use to learn more about people, themselves, history, and society in general.

"If democratic citizenship education—the ability to make informed and reasoned decisions for the public good—is the goal . . . then students must develop an understanding of the lives of those who lived before them, who are different from them, and whose struggles created the kind of world in which they live" (Akmal & Ayre-Svingen, 2002, p. 272). Biographies can provide young adults with such descriptions of individuals' lives, serve as information resources, and offer considerable reading enjoyment, by illuminating the frustrations, obstacles, and achievements of a wide spectrum of people from the past and the present. In doing so, biographies can add new perspectives to young adults' learning and reading pleasure.

Many adolescents enjoy reading biographies. According to Moss and Hendershot (2002), 50–85% of the juvenile books circulated by libraries are nonfiction, including biographies. David McCullough's books on Harry Truman and John Adams, Debby Applegate's biography of Henry Ward Beecher, Alfred Habegger's biography of Emily Dickinson, *My Wars Are Laid Away in Books* (2001), and Joan Didion's autobiography *The Year of Magical Thinking* (2005) are a few of the serious biographies that have recently appeared on adult bestseller lists and have been read by adolescents. Laura Hillenbrand's bestselling biography *Seabiscuit* (2001) was made into a successful movie. Arts and Entertainment (A&E) television features the series *Biography*, with companion website, magazine, and radio versions. For both adults and young adults, biographies continue to be a genre that is read, viewed, and listened to for both enjoyment *and* learning.

In this chapter we explore the types of biography that are available for young adult readers, provide guidelines for evaluating and selecting biographies, and identify ways teachers and librarians can use biographies in schools to help adolescents appreciate biographies.

Biography

Well-written biographies are more than a series of facts about a biographee (the person about whom a biography is written) thrown together in more or less chronological order. A biographer (the author) must sort through the truths and fictions, decide what is important and what is inconsequential, identify relevant details, eliminate superfluous trivia, and create a narrative that presents a person's life. Instead of depicting only the best about an individual, contemporary biographies for young adults portray all sides of a person and present a well-rounded, realistic character whom adolescents can relate to or begin to understand. A well-written biography encourages curiosity by challenging readers to revisit their own beliefs and prior knowledge about the subject (Carter, 2003). Without ignoring the flaws in the individual, the author must strive to be empathetic (Townsend & Hanson, 2001). A novelist creates a legend; a biographer portrays a life. "Biography's ties to fiction lie in its story narrative; its allegiance to nonfiction, in its history" (Carter, 2003, p. 166). It is important to remember that biographies can "easily pass into fiction when rational inference or conjecture pass over into imaginative reconstruction or frank invention" (*Merriam-Webster's Encyclopedia of Literature*, 1995). Thus, it is as important to identify and select quality biographies as it is to select well-written fiction.

A Brief Look at Biography's Predecessors

According to the *Merriam-Webster's Encyclopedia of Literature* (1995), the earliest biographies were probably funeral oratories that lauded and praised the deceased. In time, these speeches evolved into books that contained biographies of a number of noteworthy rulers and leaders. One early example is Plutarch's moralizing tales of prominent Romans and Greeks. The field of biography changed in the eighteenth century and was finally recognized as a distinct genre when Samuel Johnson produced his *Lives of the English Poets* and James Boswell wrote *The Life of Johnson*, in which he combined psychological insight with exhaustive records of events and conversations. As more biographies were written, Thomas Carlyle voiced the opinion that history was actually the record of great men and that the key to understanding society was through the lives of the individuals who shaped it.

With that in mind, it is surprising that early children's literature did not include more quality biographies. To be sure, there were numerous "wordy, repetitive, and didactic" (Hillman, 2003, p. 229) biographies, but even during the "golden age" of children's literature in the nineteenth and early twentieth centuries, there were only "lackluster" (p. 229) biographies. With a few exceptions, including Cornelia Meigs's Newbery Medal–winning *Invincible Louisa* (1933) and James Daugherty's *Daniel Boone* (1939), as well as the autobiography *Diary of a Young Girl* (1952), by Anne Frank, biography was, according to Mary Mehlman Burns (1995), "the stepchild among the genres of children's literature. Not that there were too few but rather that there were too few that qualified as literature, let alone good biography" (p. 60).

Thankfully, the genre has changed, and a number of individuals now write quality biographies for young adults thus giving biographies more recognition. Since the 1970s, Milton Meltzer, the recipient of the 2001 Laura Ingalls Wilder Award, has published a number of excellent biographies, including ones about Dorothea Lange, George Washington, Mark Twain, Langston Hughes, and Mary McLeod Bethune. In 1988, Russell Freedman's *Lincoln: A Photobiography* (1987) won the Newbery Medal. In 1997, Diane Stanley won the Orbis Pictus Award for Outstanding Nonfiction for *Leonardo da Vinci* (1996). Expanding Your Knowledge with the Internet provides more information on Russell Freedman, Diane Stanley and their biographies.

The focus of book awards began to change when the Orbis Pictus Award (given by NCTE) was established for nonfiction writing and the Boston Globe-Horn Book Award included a nonfiction category. In 2001, the Association for Library Service to Children created the ALSC/Robert F. Sibert Information Book Award. Although

EXPANDING YOUR KNOWLEDGE WITH THE INTERNET

Russell Freedman and Diane Stanley have won a number of awards for their biographies and other informational books. On the Internet, you can find information about them and their books, as well as teaching ideas.

RUSSELL FREEDMAN

www.eduplace.com/kids/hmr/mtai/freedman.html
www.indiana.edu/~reading/ieo/bibs/freedman.html

Units and CyberGuides
Eleanor Roosevelt: A Life of Discovery
eduscapes.com/newbery/94d.html

Lincoln: A Photobiography
www.sdcoe.k12.ca.us/score/civwnov/civilwar16.htm

Russell Freedman Webcast
www.loc.gov/today/cyberlc/feature_wdesc.php?rec=3428

DIANE STANLEY
www.dianestanley.com/
www.harperchildrens.com/hch/author/author/stanley/
biography.jrank.org/pages/1899/Stanley-Diane-1943.html
www.teachingk-8.com/archives/author_interview/following_the_path_by_becky_rodia_senior_editor.html

Literature Guide
Bard of Avon
www.maslibraries.org/infolit/samplers/bard.html

these awards did not specifically target biographies, they did serve to draw attention to well-written nonfiction in general. Several biographies suitable for young adults have won these awards.

Types of Biography

A number of ways are available to categorize biographies. You may consider the amount of historical evidence in the book, or the amount of a person's life covered. Still other ways are to consider the author, or whether the book is about one or several persons.

Authentic or Pure Biography/Fictionalized Biography/Biographical Fiction. Biographies may be divided into three basic categories—pure or authentic biography, fictionalized biography, and biographical fiction (see Figure 9–1)—based on the emphasis on factual information in the book. In this biography continuum, the emphasis on the amount of facts changes as you move from left

Authentic or Pure Biography. Pure or authentic biographies are based only on the known or verifiable facts about a person. For example, conversations are included only when they can be documented. Well-researched, well-written pure or authentic biographies are gaining in popularity, even though some are very scholarly. Tonya Bolden won the 2008 Orbis Pictus Award for her authentic biography *M.L.K.: Journey of a King* (2007). Kathleen Krull's series Giants in Science, which includes *Marie Curie* (2007), *Isaac Newton* (2006), and *Sigmund Freud* (2006), also offers authentic biographies for younger adolescents.

Fictionalized Biography. In contrast to authentic biographies, many works about historical figures are fictionalized because little or no primary source documentation of their lives exists. Even when authors can identify primary sources, they might need to add some fictionalized details such as a conversation to make a point about the person, to describe the person's thoughts, or to show the person's relationship to other historical figures. However, even in fictionalized biography, the invented dialogue is based on actual events and people. It does not matter whether these biographies are contemporary or historical. For younger adolescents, the Childhood of Famous Americans series offers fictionalized biographies such as *Harry S. Truman: Thirty-Third President of the United States* (Stanley, 2004). Walter Dean Myers has written a fictionalized biography of Sarah Forbes Bonetta, *At Her Majesty's Request: An African Princess in Victorian England* (1999).

Figure 9-1   Types of Biographies

Biographical Fiction. An easy way to remember the distinction between fictionalized biography and biographical fiction is to focus on the noun in each phrase—fictionalized *biography* is more factual than biographical *fiction*. Biographical fiction includes accurate historical events and individuals as well as invented characters and events. In *The King's Swift Rider* (1998), Mollie Hunter uses the fictional character of Martin Crawford to explore the life of the thirteenth-century Scottish hero Robert the Bruce.

Biography and Autobiography. While a biography is written by the author about the life of another individual, an autobiography is written by the biography's subject. Many autobiographies must actually be considered fictionalized autobiographies, because most people rely on their memories rather than on actual notes of conversations to re-create the stories of their lives.

An autobiography may take the form of a personal narrative or a memoir, although this format often focuses more on the interaction of the author with external events than in a traditional autobiography (*Merriam-Webster's Encyclopedia of Literature*, 1995). Some would argue that, when a person writes his or her autobiography but changes details to suit the writer's personal perspective, perhaps by including events as the writer wishes they had happened, the autobiography moves toward becoming autobiographical fiction. As you evaluate autobiographies, you need to keep this in mind.

Partial and Complete Biographies. Biographies can also be divided into partial or complete. In a partial biography, the author focuses on one period in the subject's life. It may be the period of his or her greatest accomplishment, such as a sports career or the period an individual spends in public office. It may also be the subject's childhood. In *Jack: The Early Years of John F. Kennedy* (2003), Ilene Cooper looks at the struggles that shaped the life of the future president. Peter Sis's *The Wall: Growing Up Behind the Iron Curtain* (2007) describes his childhood in postwar Czechoslovakia. Walter Dean Myers's autobiography *Bad Boy: A Memoir* (2001) concentrates on his childhood in Harlem in the 1950s. Jack Gantos's autobiography *A Hole in My life* (2002) focuses on his life before he became a writer. Esmeralda Santiago's *When I Was Puerto Rican* (1993) tells of growing up in Puerto Rico and New York. In contrast, a complete biography traces the entire life of an individual, as in Freedman's *Eleanor Roosevelt: A Life of Discovery* (1993) or Myers's *At Her Majesty's Request: An African Princess in Victorian England* (1999).

Individual and Collective Biographies. Whether authentic or fictionalized, biographies can also be divided into individual or collective. Individual biographies are written about one person; collective biographies are collections of biographies about a number of individuals. Some collective biographies include individuals from many backgrounds, such as Kathleen Krull's *Lives of Extraordinary Women: Rulers, Rebels (And What the Neighbors Thought)* (2000) and Penny Colman's *Adventurous Women: Eight True Stories About Women Who Made a Difference* (2006). Others have an organizing theme, such as politicians and world leaders, as in Jill S. Pollack's *Women on the Hill* (1996) or Milton Meltzer's *Ten Kings and the Worlds They Ruled* (2002b); scientists, as in Kim K. Zach's *Hidden from History: The Lives of Eight American Women Scientists* (2002) and Erica Stux's *Achievers: Great Women in the*

Biological Sciences (2005); successful business leaders, as in Laura S. Jeffrey's *Great American Businesswomen* (1996); or notable achievers, as in Julie Danneberg's *Women Artists of the West: Five Portraits in Creativity and Courage* (2002) and Cherie D. Abbey and Kevin Hillstrom's *Biography Today Performing Artists: Profiles of People of Interest to Young Readers* (2008). Later, when we look at the criteria for evaluating biographies, we will identify some special things to look for when examining collective biographies. Connecting Adolescents and Their Literature 9–1 suggests a way to use collective biographies across the curriculum.

9-1 ····· CONNECTING ADOLESCENTS AND THEIR LITERATURE

Taylor (2002/2003) describes link-up activities that are ideal to use with younger adolescents. Students should:

- Read the biography of a historical individual.
- Note interesting, intriguing, and unique but also actual characteristics of that individual.
- Search newspapers, magazine articles, and biographical databases to identify a contemporary individual who shares a majority of these characteristics.
- Report the results in a paper, electronic presentation, or art project.

   In addition to practicing public-speaking and listening skills, this activity helps students develop critical thinking skills.

Biography in Contrast to Historical Fiction

In our look at biographies and autobiographies, we will concentrate on pure/authentic and fictionalized biographies. Works of biographical fiction tend to place a greater emphasis on the plot rather than the character and are sometimes categorized as historical fiction. Whether to place a book in the genre of biography or historical fiction depends on the degree to which a historical figure plays a central role in the book and on the amount of accurate information in the book about that individual. Often, in historical fiction, the real individual is included only to advance the central story or to add a sense of authenticity and credibility.

Biographical Subjects

At one time in history, biographies examined the lives and perspectives of only historical people (and mostly western European or American males) such as explorers; political leaders and social activists; artists, scientists, and sports figures; and people who persevered through difficult or challenging circumstances. Now biographies focus on contemporary people or historical individuals who interest young people. Movie stars, popular artists and musicians, sports figures, characters from sitcoms, and just about anyone who is in the public spotlight has had a biography written of her or him. Some of these subjects will remain important over time.

Others are less enduring, so teachers and library media specialists who select biographies must remain current with the interests of young adults. Connecting Adolescents and Their Literature 9–2 suggests a way to develop a collection of biographies that are both interesting to young adults and well-written.

9-2 ••••   CONNECTING ADOLESCENTS AND THEIR LITERATURE

Keeping up with the latest sports and entertainment figures can be difficult for educators. To ensure that the biography collection contains information on individuals adolescents will enjoy reading about as well as those they should read about, enlist their help.

- Have a biography advisory board for the library media center that contains representatives from each grade level.
- Use recommendations from teachers and guidance counselors to be sure these students represent a wide range of abilities and interests.
- Have students make a list of the individuals they would like to see in the library collection.
- Have the students themselves, with the assistance of the library media specialist or the library staff determine
  (a) what, if any, books have been published about the people on the list.
  (b) what reviewers have said about these books.
- Give the group a budget and have them determine what biographies from their list should be added to the collection with the budgeted funds.

Remember that not all biographies are about heroes and people we would want young adults to emulate or revere. For example, James Giblin's award-winning *Life and Death of Adolf Hitler* (2002) and Susan Bartoletti's *Hitler's Youth: Growing up in Hitler's Shadow* (2005) ask readers to confront some difficult questions about power and its use or misuse. Carter (2003) suggests that well-written biographies "present individuals as people readers might *want* to know rather [than] those they *should* know" (p. 170) and helps readers "understand the historical context that sets the stage for the story" (p. 166). Collaborating with Other Professionals 9–1 suggests one way a number of educators can work together to incorporate collective biographies into the curriculum.

Categories of Biographies

Although biographies focus on individuals with achievements in many areas, we have tried to group them into categories and have identified some representative examples in each category. While other groupings can be devised, the following categories show the richness of the biographies, both individual and collective, that are currently available for young adults.

9-1   COLLABORATING WITH OTHER PROFESSIONALS

Using collective biographies, English teachers, social studies teachers, art teachers, and library media specialists can help adolescents explore the lives of important individuals and see the contributions they have made.

- Before beginning the project, the teachers and the library media specialists meet to determine the availability of appropriate collective biographies.

- The social studies teacher introduces the assignment of historical figures, and the English teacher begins a study of biography as a literary genre.

- From a list compiled by the teachers, students draw names of people, read about those individuals in the collective biographies, and create a mobile that represents the individuals.

- After the mobiles are hung in the classroom or library, teachers challenge the students in the school to guess the subject of each of them.

Although the individual biographies in the collections are short, they should provide basic information that, if necessary, can be supplemented with additional resources from the school library media center. More detailed information on this project can be found in Akmal and Ayre-Svingen (2002).

Politicians and Leaders. As you might expect, many biographies have been written about American presidents and the founders of the United States. These include Albert Marrin's portrait of George Washington in *George Washington and the Founding of a Nation* (2001) and Abraham Lincoln in *Commander in Chief: Abraham Lincoln and the Civil War* (1997); Marc Aronson's *Up Close: Robert Kennedy* (2007); Natalie S. Bober's collective biography of colonial patriots in *Countdown to Independence: A Revolution of Ideas in England and Her American Colonies: 1760–1776* (2001); and Russell Freedman's biographies of a president and his wife in *Eleanor Roosevelt: A Life of Discovery* (1993) and *Franklin Delano Roosevelt* (1990). However, young adult biographies also include other leaders as well. Leaders in other parts of the world are the focus of Jeff C. Young's *Hugo Chavez: Leader of Venezuela* (2007) and Peter Limb's *Nelson Mandela: A Biography* (2008). Russell Freedman examines the life of an American Indian leader in *Life and Death of Crazy Horse* (1996). For younger adolescents, Diane Stanley takes a look at a French leader in *Joan of Arc* (1998) and *Saladin: Noble Prince of Islam* (2002). June Estep Fiorelli writes about a political activist who ran for the Mississippi state senate in *Fannie Lou Hamer: A Voice for Freedom* (2005). James I. Robertson, Jr., depicts Civil War general Thomas J. Jackson in *Standing Like a Stone Wall* (2001). Tracy Barrett explores an eleventh century teenage princess in *Anna of Byzantium* (1999). However, not all biographees are inspiring subjects. As mentioned, James Cross Giblin has written *Life and Death of Adolf Hitler* (2002), Elaine Landau *Osama bin Laden: A War Against the West* (2002), and Mitch Young published a collective biography, *Terrorist Leaders* (2004).

Religious Leaders. While there are few young adult biographies about religious leaders, a few recent ones deserve mention, including Sandra Donovan's *Billy Graham* (2007), Russell Freedman's *Confucius: The Golden Rule* (2002), Bruce Feiler's *Abraham:*

A Journey to the Heart of Three Faiths (2002), and Stephen Mitchell's controversial *Jesus: What He Really Said and Did* (2002).

Scientists and Inventors. A number of excellent biographies highlight notable scientists and their achievements. Lorraine Jean Hopping explains forensic anthropology while sharing details about Diane France's life and work as a forensic anthropologist in *Bone Detective: The Story of Forensic Anthropologist Diane France* (2005), Ellen Levine tells of Rachel Carson's work as an environmentalist in *Rachel Carson* (2007), and Lisa Yount describes the life of the founder of biochemistry and chemistry in *Antoine Lavoisier: Founder of Modern Chemistry* (2008). M. F. Delano explores the life of Thomas Alva Edison in *Inventing the Future: A Photobiography of Thomas Alva Edison* (2002). Mary Collins examines man's first successful flight in *Airborne: A Photobiography of Wilbur and Orville Wright* (2003). John Severance looks at Albert Einstein in *Einstein: Visionary Scientist* (1999), and Frances A. Karnes describes female inventors in *Girls & Young Women Inventing* (1995). Marilyn Nelson uses poetry to reveal the life and work of scientist and inventor George Washington Carver in *Carver: A Life in Poems* (2001), while Leslie Dendy and Mel Boring provide a collective biography of scientists who experimented on themselves in *Guinea Pig: Bold Self-Experimenters in Science and Medicine* (2005). Two collective biographies of women scientists are *Twentieth-Century Women Scientists* (1996) and *Contemporary Women Scientists* (1994), both by Lisa Yount.

Explorers and Adventurers. Some people have lives full of thrills, excitement, and exploits throughout the world. In *The Adventures of Marco Polo* (2006), Russell Freedman explores the credibility of Marco Polo's legacy; in *Emperors of the Ice: A True Story of Disaster and Survival in the Antarctic, 1910–13* (2008), Richard Farr reimagines Apsley Cherry-Garrard's adventure in Antarctica; in *Far Beyond the Garden Gate: Alexandra David-Neel's Journey to Lhasa* (2002), Don Brown tells the story of an unconventional woman's travels in 1911; in *Extraordinary Explorers and Adventurers* (2001), Judy Alter appeals to younger adolescents; while in *Sir Walter Ralegh and the Quest for El Dorado* (2000), Marc Aronson provides a carefully researched book for all ages. Younger adolescents will enjoy *Onward: A Photobiography of African American Polar Explorer Matthew Henson* (2005), by Dolores Johnson.

Artists and Writers. There are several excellent biographies of artists and authors who have also led very interesting lives. Looking at photographers, Beverly Gherman has written *Ansel Adams: America's Photographer* (2002), and Elizabeth Partridge penned *Restless Spirit: The Life and Works of Dorothea Lange* (1998). Jan Greenberg and Sandra Jordan chronicle an artist's life in *Runaway Girl: The Artist Louise Bourgeois* (2003). Russell Freedman compiled *Kids at Work: Lewis Hind and the Crusade Against Child Labor* (1994). Diane Stanley has written a number of picture-book biographies for younger adolescents, including *Michelangelo* (2000) and *Leonardo da Vinci* (1996). Jan Greenberg and Sandra Jordan use letters and paintings to help tell the story in *Vincent van Gogh: Portrait of an Artist* (2001), and Barbara O'Connor has written *Leonardo da Vinci: Renaissance Genius* (2003).

A number of biographies are available on a wide range of authors. In their Authors Teens Love series, Enslow Publishers offer biographies about Jerry Spinelli, Lois Lowry, S. E. Hinton, Robert Cormier, and Richard Peck. Rowman and Littlefield offer the Scarecrow Studies in Young Adult Literature Series, edited by Patty Campbell. Recent books in the series include Mary Ann Tighe's *Sharon Creech: The Words We Choose to Say* (2006) and KaaVonia Hinton's *Angela Johnson: Poetic Prose* (2006).

Writers are also the subject of several Alex Award–winning autobiographies, including Pulitzer Prize–winning correspondent Rick Bragg's memoir *All Over but the Shoutin'* (1997) and poet June Jordan's *Soldier: A Poet's Childhood* (2001). *Something to Declare* (1998) is Hispanic American author Julia Alvarez's series of autobiographical essays about her life as a "hyphenated American." Caroline Lazo tells the story of the novelist Alice Walker in *Alice Walker: Freedom Writer* (2000). In *Shakespeare: His Work and His World* (2001), Michael Rosen combines art and quotes from plays. In his autobiography *Sometimes the Magic Works: Lessons from a Writing Life* (2003), Terry Brooks includes advice to aspiring writers.

Athletes. Sports are important to many adolescents. Thus, biographies of sports stars, past and present, focus on the achievements of athletes, including their hardships, determination, and trials of endurance. Readers might enjoy biographies of current sports figures in books such as Bill Gutman's *Lance Armstrong: A Biography* (2003) and Glen MacNow's *Sports Great Allen Iverson* (2003); as well as works like the bestselling *Brett Favre: The Tribute* (2008), by *Sports Illustrated*; and autobiographies such as *Dropping in with Andy Mac: The Life of a Pro Skateboarder* (2003), by Andy MacDonald with Theresa Foy DeGeronimo, and *A Journey: The Autobiography of Apolo Anton Ohno* (2002), by Apolo Anton Ohno with Nancy Ann Richardson. Biographies of sports greats from the past are popular as well. Some current titles include David L. Porter, *Michael Jordan: A Biography* (2007); Jane Leavy, *Sandy Koufax: A Lefty's Legacy* (2002); Jim Haskins, *Champion: The Story of Muhammad Ali* (2002); John Stravinsky, *Muhammad Ali* (1997); and Thomas Streissguth, *Jesse Owens* (1999). There are also a number of biographies about women athletes, including:

- Russell Freedman, *Babe Didrikson Zaharias: The Making of a Champion* (1999)
- Joan Anderson, *Rookie: Tamika Whitmore's First Year in the WNBA* (2000)
- Jacqueline Edmondson, *Venus and Serena Williams: A Biography* (2005)

Entertainers and Musicians. While there are a number of biographies of popular current and past performers, many are little more than carefully contrived publicity packages. Mixed with these less-than-quality titles, however, are a few biographies that examine the real lives of performers. These include:

- Rita J. Markel, *Jimi Hendrix* (2001)
- Elizabeth Partridge, *This Land Was Made for You and Me: The Life and Songs of Woody Guthrie* (2002)
- Savion Glover, Bruce Weber, and Gregory Hines, *Savion! My Life in Tap* (2000)
- Rachel Stiffler Barron, *John Coltrane: Jazz Revolutionary* (2002)
- Elizabeth Partridge, *John Lennon: All I Want Is the Truth* (2005)

Sue Macy reaches back into history in *Bull's Eye: A Photobiography of Annie Oakley* (2001), and Carole Boston Weatherford uses poetry in *Becoming Billie Holiday* (2008).

Uncommon Individuals. Young adults enjoy reading about individuals who have overcome hardships and struggles in their lives or have distinguished themselves through their valor, courage, and conviction of beliefs. For example, several biographies have been written by or about Holocaust survivors and rescuers. Anita Lobel recounts her experiences as a Polish Jew in *No Pretty Picture: A Child of War* (1998). Irene Gut Opdyke tells of her experiences in *In My Hands: Memories of a Holocaust Rescuer* (1999). Ruth Jacobsen tells of her family in *Rescued Images: Memories of a Childhood in Hiding* (2001). Howard Greenfeld examines the struggles of survivors in *After the Holocaust* (2001), and Carla Killough McClafferty's *In Defiance of Hitler: The Secret Mission of Varian Fry* (2008) introduces a man who risked his life to help artists who were enemies of the Nazi regime of the 1940s.

Several biographies tell the stories of individuals who fought for equal rights throughout American history. In *Elizabeth Cady Stanton: The Right Is Ours* (2001), Harriet Sigerman writes of an early feminist. Ruby Bridges remembers the struggle for school integration in *Through My Eyes* (1999). Dennis Brindell Fradin and Judith Bloom Fradin examine the life of an unconventional activist in *Ida B. Wells: Mother of the Civil Rights Movement* (2000). Christine M. Hill explores the life of a civil rights activist in *John Lewis: From Freedom Rider to Congressman* (2002).

Young Adults Growing Up. A number of biographies focus on adolescents' feelings and emotions. Esmeralda Santiago tells of growing up in Puerto Rico and her shock when she moves to New York to live with her grandmother in *When I Was Puerto Rican* (1993). Gary Paulsen recounts his life after running away at the age of 16 in *The Beet Fields: Memories of a Sixteenth Summer* (2000). Rebecca Walker explores her own identity as the child of a white father and black mother in the Alex Award–winning *Black, White, and Jewish: Autobiography of a Shifting Self* (2002). In *Barefoot Heart* (1999), E. T. Hart remembers her childhood as a Mexican American whose family worked as migrant laborers. Jennifer Roy's *Yellow Star* (2006) tells of her aunt's childhood in the Lodz ghetto during World War II. Two outstanding biographies examine a child's life in a communist culture. In *Red Scarf Girl: A Memoir of the Cultural Revolution* (1997), Ji-Li Jiang tells about her life in China, and in *Blessed by Thunder: Memoir of a Cuban Girlhood* (1999), Flor Fernandez Barrios recounts her family's struggle for survival in Cuba under Castro and their flight to the United States.

From Page to Screen lists some films that are based on the lives of famous individuals.

Reasons for Using and Teaching Biographies

At the most basic level, biographies satisfy an adolescent's need to know and desire to find out more about a person, event, or topic. But there is more than that. According to Hurst (2001), biographies personalize history by focusing on the motivations and driving forces behind personal actions. Through biographies, adolescents can see that while social constructs can be harmful to some individuals and helpful to others, these constructs can be challenged and changed (Taylor, 1996). When they see the choices others have made and how those choices determined the

from Page to Screen

BIOGRAPHY

Just as there are many fascinating biographies to share with adolescent readers, there are countless biopics illustrating the same lives these biographies narrate in their pages. Consider pairing a biography with one of these appropriate biopics, and discussing the commonalities and the differences in the two versions of one life. What could account for some of the differences? Which version seems more authentic? Why?

ANNE FRANK'S DIARY
★★★ | 1999 | unrated

This provocative animated version of the famous journals of the young Jew living in hiding from the Nazis during World War II explores many passages from the actual journal that were cut from the book, providing an image of a more fully realized human being than the better known upright, well-behaved adolescent.

AMADEUS
★★★★ | 1984 | PG (note: director's cut is rated R)

While the storylines are not parallel, it is interesting to compare the innocent and ornery character portrayed in F. N. Monjo's book Letters to Horseface: Young Mozart's Travels in Italy with the depiction of Mozart in director Milos Forman's brilliant Amadeus.

MUHAMMAD ALI, THE GREATEST
★★★★ | 1969 | unrated

William Klein's 1969 documentary chronicles the iconic boxer's very early career. Compare these two documentaries—When We Were Kings and Muhammad Ali, the Greatest—with the biographies by Haskins (2002) and Stravinsky (1997). How do the documentaries mirror the themes in the biographies? How is the impact on American history, as discussed in the text, highlighted in the films?

MALCOLM X
★★★ | 1992 | PG-13

Follow a reading of Arnold Adoff's Malcolm X with a screening of the Spike Lee film. Although Lee's version is based on the biography written by Alex Haley and Malcolm X's autobiography, Adoff's text is more appropriate for younger adolescent readers.

BECOMING JANE
★★★★ | 2007 | PG

Anne Hathaway and James McAvoy portray a couple—based on a romantic relationship Jane Austen had with Tom Lefroy when she was 20 years old—deeply in love, but separated by uncontrollable circumstances. Jon Spence's biography Becoming Jane Austen: A Life (2007), would be great for those intrigued by the film.

courses of individual's lives, adolescents can begin to realize that they too can make choices and that their decisions will influence their future. As Akmal and Ayre-Svingen (2002) note, if adolescents are to realize that history is more than the study of dead people, educators must use the connection between inquiry and biography to help young adults see the relationship between past events and the realities of the present. Connecting Adolescents and Their Literature 9–3 suggests one way to make individuals of the past come alive.

9-3 •••• CONNECTING ADOLESCENTS AND THEIR LITERATURE

Engage young adults with biographies by having a Dressing Up for History day. English, social studies, science, mathematics, art, and music teachers as well as the library media specialist can work together, or this project can be done by an individual teacher with the help of the library media specialist.

- After reading a biography and exploring other resources about an individual, each student plans a costume that represents the individual and prepares a brief presentation that contains information about the individual's accomplishments.

- When the student appears in class dressed as the individual and gives the presentation, classmates attempt to guess who the individual is.

- The student may even prepare a set of questions others can ask to aid in the identification.

- If this is done with several classes, the best from each class can present to other classes, other grade levels, or the entire school.

A variation on this idea is to host a "dinner party" (Buehler, 2003) and everyone attends as the historical person they have researched.

Characteristics of Well-Written Biographies

According to research cited by Carter (2003), biography reading declines between fourth and tenth grades, with the exception of books for the yearly required biography book report. However, sports and entertainment magazines that feature biographies are eagerly read by teenagers. Perhaps, then, these statistics are more a comment on the quality and subjects of many of the biographies written for adolescents than on young adults' interest in biographies. As with all young adult literature, it is important to look for the best biographies. We will explore the characteristics that distinguish excellent biographies from the adequate, mediocre, or unacceptable. Unfortunately, not all the biographies marketed for adolescents have these characteristics. After examining juvenile biographies in general, Lechner (1997) found inaccuracies resulting from carelessness and oversimplification, inadequate or incomplete data, unreliable primary sources, and social mores and taboos. On the basis of her own experiences, Carter (2003) suggests dismissing those biographies that feature a

> larger-than-life, near-perfect individual to be honored and emulated; a lack of historical context within which to place the subject; an endless tally of accomplishments that show little relationship to either character or reader; and an organizing structure that revolves around birth and death dates rather than an implied theme concerning the subject's life. (p. 165)

What, then, are the characteristics of excellent biographies? Obviously, well-written biographies should:

- Be engaging
- Be authentic and honest
- Provide an objective treatment of the subject

- Be accurate (controversial information and personal fallacies should be neither omitted nor glossed over)
- Reveal a complex individual, including human strengths as well as weaknesses
- Depict the life of the individual in ways that allow the reader to question, evaluate, and analyze the narrative to identify the pattern or meaning in the person's life

A well-written biography should avoid didacticism. Sermon should not "substitute for story," and fictionalization should not "enhance factual material" (Carter, 2003, p. 168). Included should be the feelings, beliefs, actions, and daily decisions made by the individual (Townsend & Hanson, 2001). To keep a biography from becoming a chronology of events or a collection of dates without any unifying theme, a strong narrative thread is needed. A biography must be grounded in the historical context of the time period in which an individual lived and must tell the story of his or her life in a way that captures and holds the reader's interest (Carter, 2003).

Biographies must also avoid stereotypes based on things such as gender, culture, religious background, and ethnicity. This does not mean distorting the truth or allowing inaccuracies. For example, one cannot disguise the fact that women received second-class treatment for many decades, and this treatment should be accurately portrayed. However, in writing about these times, writers should avoid placing women in stereotypical roles such as being helpless and dependent on a male. According to Lucy Townsend (Townsend & Hanson, 2001), many earlier biographies of women show them achieving success only through their relationships with others (e.g., wife, mother, daughter). While historical perspectives and events cannot be changed, women need to be shown as individuals with unique strengths as well as weaknesses (Bucher & Manning, 1998). The same can be said about the members of any minority group.

Remember that "biography is as much a product of the times in which it is written as it is of the times and lives it portrays" (Carter, 2003, p. 167). This means that, first, an author must respect the accepted beliefs and traditions of the time period he or she is writing about. Some conditions (such as segregation or the absence of most women from positions of political power) that are not acceptable today must be included for the sake of historical accuracy. As Steve Weinberg (2003) notes, "the most intellectually honest biographies capture subjects as they lived in their own times, not as an author alive centuries later thinks they ought to have comported themselves" (p. 30). However, while writing a biography, the author is also affected by the social institutions of the period he or she is depicting. A Franklin Roosevelt biography written in the 1950s with the idea of the leader as a role model is likely to present a less well-rounded portrait than one written in the 1990s that includes a discussion of the motives for his actions and his personal life.

Julia Mickenberg (2002) has pointed out that juvenile literature, especially biography, is used as a vehicle both for activism and to support the status quo. Authors use biographies to deal with issues of race, to challenge gender norms, and to present life stories of role models who lived outside the prescribed, traditional expectations of society. She maintains that by publishing a number of biographies between 1945 and 1965 of early civil rights leaders, authors were able to lay the groundwork for the involvement of young adults in the civil rights movement in the 1960s and 1970s (Mickenberg, 2002).

Finally, the treatment of the subject, the theme, and the writing style should be appropriate for adolescent readers. When reviewing biographies, Carter (2003) suggests you begin by thinking about what you know and what you do not know about the person and/or the time period in which he or she lived. Hold this information up against what the author provides. Then think about the author as a "partner in discovery" (p. 172) who will help you learn even more about the person by showing you his or her character, rather than telling you about it. Considerations for Selecting Young Adult Literature: *Biography* contains additional information for evaluating biographies.

Suggestions for Selecting and Using Biographies

As with all young adult literature, proper selection and evaluation of biographies are absolute essentials. Young adults deserve accurate biographies in which controversial information and personal fallacies have neither been omitted nor glossed over. Readers should see the biographee as a human being with both strengths and weaknesses and be

CONSIDERATIONS FOR SELECTING YOUNG ADULT LITERATURE BIOGRAPHY

When evaluating biographies, ask the following questions:

_____ What are the author's credentials, experience, background, and perspectives that indicate his or her competence to write about this individual?

_____ Is the biography authentic or fictionalized? If fictionalized, is there an explanation of the rationale for creating the fictionalized parts?

_____ Are the fictionalized parts identified?

_____ Is the content up-to-date, complete, and objective, with language or dialect that reflects the subject?

_____ Is the book accurate?

_____ Does the book avoid misrepresentations of events and facts?

_____ Is the biography free from bias and not patronizing?

_____ Does it present all sides of controversial issues?

_____ Does it neither debunk the subject nor place him or her on a pedestal?

_____ Is the biography relevant to young adults?

_____ Will the style of writing attract young adults?

_____ Are a bibliography of sources, endnotes or footnotes, and a list of recommended readings included?

_____ Are there special features such as period art work, photographs, or other illustrations; replicas of documents, letters, and other artifacts; and an index?

When evaluating collective biographies, ask these additional questions:

_____ What is the scope of the entire collection?

_____ What criteria did the author use to select (and exclude) individuals?

_____ Is the writing consistent across the selections?

_____ How is the collection organized?

_____ Is a consistent amount of information presented for each individual?

able to understand and, at least sometimes, relate to his or her feelings of frustration and happiness. Remember that not all authors write and not all companies publish accurate and well-written biographies, thus you must refer to the characteristics of well-written biographies when reviewing books for purchase for a school library or for incorporating them into the curriculum.

Awards and Best Books Lists.   While there are no specific awards for biographies, the genre is included in a number of best books lists and awards. For example, *Your Own, Sylvia: A Verse Portrait of Sylvia Plath* (Hemphill, 2007) was a 2008 Michael L. Printz Award honor book. The Orbis Pictus Award, given by NCTE, has honored several biographies. In 2002, the ALSC/Robert F. Sibert Information Book Award, created in 2001, was awarded to James Cross Giblin for *Life and Death of Adolf Hitler* (2002), with honor also going to Jack Gantos for *A Hole in My Life* (2002). The National Science Teachers Association (NSTA) has a biography category in its annual list of Outstanding Science Trade Books for Students K–12. The Notable Social Studies Trade Books for Young People, issued annually by the National Council for the Social Studies (NCSS), has a section on biographies. The YALSA list of Outstanding Books for the College Bound and Lifelong Learners features a number of excellent biographies. Educators can also use a variety of Internet resources to locate biographies and to cross-check resources when evaluating biographies. Expanding Your Knowledge with the Internet lists several of these awards and other resources.

Expanding Your Knowledge with the Internet

A number of Internet resources list quality biographies and provide biographical information. A few are listed here.

Orbis Pictus
www.ncte.org/elem/awards/orbispictus/106877.htm

Arts and Entertainment Network's Biography.com
biography.com

Internet biographical dictionary
www.s9.com/biography

Distinguished Women of Past and Present
www.distinguishedwomen.com

Women's biographies
www.gale.com/free_resources/whm/bio/index.htm

Politician and leaders
www.americanpresidents.org/22.asp
bioguide.congress.gov/biosearch/biosearch.asp

Scientists and inventors
www.mnsu.edu/emuseum/information/biography/
www.astr.ua.edu/4000WS/summary.shtml
www.asap.unimelb.edu.au/bsparcs/bsparcshome.htm
www-groups.dcs.st-and.ac.uk/~history/BiogIndex.html
www.science.ca/scientists/scientists/php

Artists
www.the-artists.org
www.getty.edu/research/tools/vocabulary/ulan/
www.ibiblio.org/wm/paint/auth

Writers
voices.cla.umn.edu/newsite/index.htm
www.blupete.com/Literature/Biographies/Literary/BiosPoets.htm

Entertainers and performers
www.pbs.org/jazz/biography
www.allmusic.com
www.rockhall.com/hof/allinductees.asp?sort=ln%2Cfn

Teaching with Biographies in the Classroom. Teachers and library media specialists can use biographies throughout the curriculum in many ways, from reading them to creating them. While expanding adolescents' knowledge about themselves and others, biography study can be an engaging, stimulating, and motivational activity for readers that addresses a number of the NCTE standards for the English language arts, including using "a variety of strategies to comprehend, interpret, evaluate, and appreciate texts" (Taylor, 2002/2003, p. 342); exploring a wide range of print materials in a variety of genres; developing an understanding of themselves and the cultures of the world; communicating with others; and using all the language arts (Taylor, 2002/2003).

We have room to mention only a few of the many excellent activities educators can use with the study of biographies. After reading biographies, students can research their own histories and write family genealogies that are more than ancestor charts. Adolescents can construct their own biographies about the subjects of biographies or other interesting people. Based on a biography they have read, a student can write a resume, eulogy, or obituary; appear as a "guest" on an imaginary talk show in the classroom; or write a journal entry about a specific event from the point of view of the biographee. Teachers can extend the study of the biography by asking adolescents to think critically about the biographies they have read, having them describe what the subject of the biography might have put in a backpack, make a class or school hero quilt with each square representing a different biography, or develop a class or school biography timeline on which they locate their biographies. Students can create biopoems or vanity license plates about the subjects of their biographies. Connecting Adolescents and Their Literature 9–4 gives a few examples of these.

9-4 •••• CONNECTING ADOLESCENTS AND THEIR LITERATURE

Encourage adolescents to read biographies by moving beyond the required book report. Two possible approaches are biopoems, or acrostic poems—poems that use the initial letter in a word or name to begin each line—and vanity license plates.

Here are a few license plates (limited to eight characters) based on biographies:

Shakespeare	IN2WRTNG
Alexandra David-Neel	TIBET-11
Allen Iverson	#1HOOPS

There are a number of possible formats for biopoems or acrostic poems. You can take the letters of the subject's name (last only or first—full or initials—and last) and write a brief description that begins with each of the letters:

L	Leader of the nation
I	Interested in maintaining the union
N	Not supported by all in the country
C	Conflicted over the wisdom of his actions
O	Overcame adversity
L	Left a country that was trying to heal
N	Now revered as a great president

Another form of the biopoem uses the following format:

Line 1   First name of the subject of the biography
Line 2   Four words that describe the individual
Line 3   "Who is a lover of" (three ideas, objects, things, etc.)
Line 4   "Who believes in" (one idea)
Line 5   "Who learns" (three things)
Line 6   "Who notices" (three things)
Line 7   "Who dreams" (three things)
Line 8   "Who says" (one quotation)
Line 9   Last name of the subject of the biography
Line 10   Who is the subject of the biography _____ (title), by _____ (author).

Working with the art teacher, students can make a collage, mobile, sculpture, or model based on the book; prepare an ad that could be used to sell the biography; create a new book jacket; design a bulletin board based on its theme; make a flip book or animated presentation of the key events in it; or illustrate scenes from the subject's life.

One interesting way to create a biography is to produce an Interactive BioCriticism of a favorite author. In this activity, outlined in Collaborating with Other Professionals 9–2, students read young adult literature and then use databases in the library and Internet resources to create a "biography" of the author. Instead of copying the information that is available on the Internet about the individual, the Interactive BioCriticism provides the links to the appropriate Internet sites. In this project adolescents learn a number of Internet skills, from using search engines to evaluating websites.

Expanding Your Knowledge with the Internet provides links to some additional Internet resources to use with biographies across the school curriculum.

9-2   COLLABORATING WITH OTHER PROFESSIONALS

An English/language arts teacher, library media specialist, and computer resource teacher could teach an Interactive BioCriticism of an author using Web resources.

Here are a few examples for the author Philip Pullman:

To find a bibliography of Philip Pullman's works, visit

my.linkbaton.com/bibliography/pullman/philip/

To find biographical information on Philip Pullman, visit

www.philip-pullman.com/

www.randomhouse.com/author/results.pperl?authorid=24658

www.teenreads.com/authors/au-pullman-philip.asp

To find Philip Pullman's Carnegie Acceptance Speech, visit

www.randomhouse.com/features/pullman/author/carnegie.html

To find interviews and commentary, visit

www.powells.com/authors/pullman.html
www.moreintelligentlife.com/node/697

EXPANDING YOUR KNOWLEDGE WITH THE INTERNET

A number of Internet resources help young adults write and use biographies. A few are listed here.

Biography Writer's Workshop, with Patricia & Fredrick McKissack
teacher.scholastic.com/writewit/biograph/index.htm

Student Biographers Lesson Plan, for grades 5–8
www.teachersdesk.com/lessons/language_arts/ Student%20Biographers.htm

Writing Biographies, with Kay Cornelius
www.longridgewritersgroup.com/rx/tr01/ kay_cornelius.shtml

Lesson Plan for writing the biography of an author
www.readwritethink.org/lessons/lesson_ view.asp?id=271

Kathleen Krull's Resources and Ideas for Using Biographies in the Classroom
home.san.rr.com/kathleenkrull/ teachers.html

Education World's ideas for integrating biographies in classroom activities
www.educationworld.com/a_curr/ curr230.shtml

Using Biographies in Science, Math, and Social Studies. As we have mentioned, there are a number of benefits of using biographies throughout the curriculum, not just in the English/language arts classroom. Biographies can serve as advanced organizers or as a summarizing activity for the study of a historical time period, can enrich a science unit, or can help build critical thinking skills through the use of concept maps or Venn diagrams. When young adults look at the past through biographies, history becomes more than a series of static events but the "intersection of numerous human actors, creative minds, and innovators" (Rudelson, 2003).

Daisey (1996a, 1996b, 1997) has noted that the use of biographies in secondary science and mathematics instruction helps promote students' construction of knowledge, the development of positive attitudes toward instruction, and positive growth. By presenting information about scientists and mathematicians in a genre other than traditional textbooks, biographies complement secondary instruction, appeal to a wider range of students, and ask both teachers and students to examine the factual, discipline-specific information they contain (Daisey, 1997).

In Collaborating with Other Professionals 9–3, Daisey and José-Kampfner (2002) discuss the use of biographies to help students develop a positive sense of self in the mathematics classroom. Another way to use biographies in a math class is to create a personal budget, graph, or pie chart illustrating how the subject of a biography probably spent his or her money (Taylor, 2002/2003).

Using Biographies in Guidance and Advising. Because biographies can paint compelling portraits of a wide range of individuals, educators have often recommended biographies for providing role models for adolescents and for use in bibliotherapy. Fortunately, there are many excellent biographies of diverse individuals who have struggled against bias or personal circumstances to achieve their goals.

Sue S. Minchew (2002) suggests using sports literature, including biographies, for character education. With more states committed to including it in their standards,

9-3 COLLABORATING WITH OTHER PROFESSIONALS

In response to a number of studies that have documented the school experiences of Latino teenagers and have highlighted their discouragement and high dropout rate, Peggy Daisey and Cristina José-Kampfner (2002) designed a biographical storytelling project in a middle school.

- Teachers selected biographies that presented Latinas with a number of positive role models.

- In storytelling sessions, the teachers and students told or reenacted the stories for others in their classes.

We have mentioned some Latino biographies in this chapter. To find additional ones, consult York (2001).

the question is not whether but how to teach character education. Although it is sometimes taught through minilessons on various traits, the trend now is to integrate it into lessons throughout the curriculum. Minchew (2002) has found that sports biographies can help young adults learn about the importance of setting goals, thinking positively, triumphing over adversity while learning from it, overcoming physical fears and demonstrating psychological courage, playing honestly and fairly, developing a sense of humor and an ability to laugh at oneself, learning tolerance and the importance of working with others, developing self-discipline and a strong work ethic, and believing in oneself. While Minchew looked at sports novels, short stories, and poems as well as biographies, it is evident that all of these important character traits are exhibited by the subjects of well-written young adult sports biographies.

Concluding Thoughts

Biographies today focus on people of all ethnic, cultural, religious, social, and gender groups and all nationalities. In doing so, they provide young adults with more than the descriptions of lives of famous individuals. By providing valuable information along with reading enjoyment, biographies let young adults share in the frustrations, obstacles, and achievements of individuals from all walks of life and in all levels of society. Biographies also add new dimensions to young adults' learning and reading pleasure. By carefully evaluating and selecting biographies and by incorporating these books into the curriculum, teachers and library media specialists can introduce adolescents to quality biographies.

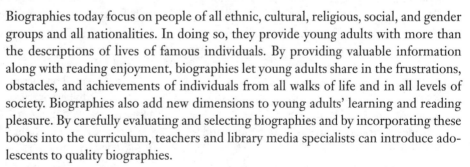

Young Adult Books

This section includes young adult titles mentioned in this chapter.

Abbey, C. D., and Hillstrom, K. (Eds.). (2008). *Biography today performing artists: Profiles of people of interest to young readers* (Biography Today Subject series). Detroit: Omnigraphics. Shares the lives of performers such as the Dixie Chicks, Usher, and Bernie Mac.

Alter, J. (2001). *Extraordinary explorers and adventurers.* New York: Children's Press. Historical figures from Sacagawea and Jim Bridger to Juan Ponce de Leon, Marco Polo, and Sir Ernest Shackleton are included in this collection.

Alvarez, J. (1998). *Something to declare.* Chapel Hill, NC: Algonquin Books. In 24 autobiographic essays, Alvarez shares the story of her youth in the Dominican Republic and America as well as her adult life as a successful author.

Anderson, J. (2000). *Rookie: Tamika Whitmore's first year in the WNBA.* New York: Dutton. Read about the life and basketball career of a player with the New York Liberty in the WNBA.

Aronson, M. (2000). *Sir Walter Ralegh and the quest for El Dorado.* New York: Clarion. This literary biography provides a fresh look at an important historical figure.

Aronson, M. (2007). *Up close: Robert Kennedy.* New York: Viking. Explores Kennedy's youth and work in politics.

Barrett, T. (1999). *Anna of Byzantium.* New York: Delacorte. In the eleventh century, princess Anna Comnena fights for the throne of the Byzantine Empire.

Barrios, F. F. (1999). *Blessed by thunder: Memoir of a Cuban girlhood.* Seattle, WA: Seal Press. From living in Cuba under Castro to moving to America as a 14-year-old, Flor Fernandez Barrios tells the story of her life.

Barron, R. S. (2002). *John Coltrane: Jazz revolutionary.* Greensboro, NC: Morgan Reynolds. Barron looks at the life of an innovative jazz saxophonist.

Bartoletti, S. (2005). *Hitler's youth: Growing up in Hitler's shadow.* New York: Scholastic. Explores how a large number of youth were manipulated by Adolf Hitler.

Bober, N. S. (2001). *Countdown to independence: A revolution of ideas in England and her American colonies: 1760–1776.* New York: Atheneum. Bober provides portraits of patriots, both familiar and less known.

Bolden, T. (2007). *M.L.K.: Journey of a king.* New York: Abrams. Photographs and text tell the story of King's life.

Bragg, R. (1997). *All over but the shoutin'.* New York: Pantheon. Growing up in poverty, Rick Bragg followed his dreams to become a writer and a Pulitzer Prize–winning correspondent.

Bridges, R. (1999). *Through my eyes.* New York: Scholastic. As a 6-year-old, Ruby Bridges walked through a hostile crowd on the first day of school integration in New Orleans. Now she looks back and tells her story. The 2000 Orbis Pictus winner.

Brooks, T. (2003). *Sometimes the magic works: Lessons from a writing life.* New York: Del Rey. Fantasy author Terry Brooks reflects on his life and the lessons that he has learned about writing.

Brown, D. (2002). *Far beyond the garden gate: Alexandra David-Neel's journey to Lhasa.* Boston: Houghton Mifflin. Leaving her family behind, a woman journeys to Tibet in 1911 and stays 14 years to study Buddhism.

Collins, M. (2003). *Airborne: A photobiography of Wilbur and Orville Wright.* Washington, DC: National Geographic. The individual personalities of these brothers come through in this book.

Colman, P. (2006). *Adventurous women: Eight true stories about women who made a difference.* New York: Holt. Shares the lives of eight women, including Mary McLeod Bethune and Louise Boyd, who had different experiences.

Cooper, I. (2003). *Jack: The early years of John F. Kennedy.* New York: Dutton. This biography for younger adolescents portrays the pressures and struggles that shaped the future president.

Danneberg, J. (2002). *Women artists of the West: Five portraits in creativity and courage.* Golden, CO: Fulcrum. Danneberg looks at five notable women who influenced the art of the western United States.

Delano, M. F. (2002). *Inventing the future: A photobiography of Thomas Alva Edison.* Washington, DC: National Geographic Society. Photographs bring to life the story of a famous scientist.

Dendy, L., and Boring, M. (2005). *Guinea pig: Bold self-experimenters in science and medicine.* New York: Holt. Focuses on scientists like Marie Curie who experimented on themselves and made noteworthy discoveries.

Donovan, S. (2007). *Billy Graham.* Minneapolis, MN: Lerner. Presents Graham's career as a minister.

Edmondson, J. (2005). *Venus and Serena Williams: A biography.* (Greenwood Biography series). Westport, CT: Greenwood. Examines the lives of two sisters who achieved success as tennis players.

Farr, R. (2008). *Emperors of the ice: A true story of disaster and survival in the Antarctic, 1910–13.* New York: Farrar, Straus and Giroux. Through the perspective of Apsley Cherry-Garrard, Farr reimagines his dangerous journey to the South Pole.

Feiler, B. (2002). *Abraham: A journey to the heart of three faiths.* New York: Morrow. This biography for advanced readers looks at the truth and the fantasy in the life of the patriarch of three religions.

Fiorelli, J. E. (2005). *Fannie Lou Hamer: A voice for freedom.* Greensboro, NC: Avisson. During the 1960s, Hamer fought for voting rights in Mississippi and ran for the Mississippi state senate.

Fradin, D. B., and Fradin, J. B. (2000). *Ida B. Wells: Mother of the civil rights movement.* New York: Clarion. Photographs help tell the story of this often forgotten civil rights leader.

Freedman, R. (1987). *Lincoln: A photobiography.* New York: Clarion. This 1988 Newbery Medal–winner focuses on Lincoln as president and his impact on the country.

Freedman, R. (1990). *Franklin Delano Roosevelt.* New York: Clarion. Although weakened by polio, Roosevelt led the United States through the Great Depression and World War II.

Freedman, R. (1993). *Eleanor Roosevelt: A life of discovery.* New York: Clarion. Although she began her public life as the wife of an American president, Eleanor remained active as a crusader for human rights, serving as a delegate to the United Nations and as chairman of the Human Right Commission.

Freedman, R. (1994). *Kids at work: Lewis Hind and the crusade against child labor.* New York: Clarion. Traveling throughout the United States in the early 1900s, Lewis Hind became an investigative photographer who documented the abuses of child labor. A 1995 Orbis Pictus honor book.

Freedman, R. (1996). *Life and death of Crazy Horse.* New York: Holiday House. Freedman tells the story of the Oglala leader and his resistance to the takeover of Indian lands.

Freedman, R. (1999). *Babe Didrikson Zaharias: The making of a champion.* New York: Clarion. Constantly testing the boundaries set for women in sports, Babe was named the best female athlete of the first half of the twentieth century.

Freedman, R. (2002). *Confucius: The golden rule.* New York: Arthur Levine Books. Freedman explores the life of a religious teacher and the links between his writings and the visions of Thomas Jefferson. Other biographies by Freedman include *Out of Darkness: The Story of Louis Braille* (1997) and *Martha Graham: A Dancer's Life* (1998).

Freedman, R. (2006). *The adventures of Marco Polo.* New York: Scholastic. Questions whether Polo made the discoveries attributed to him.

Gantos, J. (2002). *A hole in my life.* New York: Farrar, Straus and Giroux. Award-winning young adult author Jack Gantos reflects on his youth, including his arrest for drug trafficking.

Gherman, B. (2002). *Ansel Adams: America's photographer.* Boston: Little, Brown. With a timeline, bibliography, and notes, the author presents the life of a famous photographer.

Giblin, J. C. (2002). *Life and death of Adolf Hitler.* New York: Clarion. An award-winning biography.

Glover, S., Weber, B., and Hines, G. (2000). *Savion! My life in tap.* New York: Morrow. This young tap dancer choreographed the Tony Award–winning Broadway show *Bring in da Noise, Bring in da Funk.*

Greenberg, J., and Jordan, S. (2001). *Vincent van Gogh: Portrait of an artist.* New York: Delacorte. Brilliance and intensity filled the life and the paintings of this tortured artist.

Greenberg, J., and Jordan, S. (2003). *Runaway girl: The artist Louise Bourgeois.* New York: Abrams. The authors use Bourgeois's works and words to tell the story of this Franco-American sculptor.

Greenfeld, H. (2001). *After the Holocaust.* New York: Greenwillow. Howard Greenfeld examines the lives of survivors of the Holocaust after their liberation.

Gutman, B. (2003). *Lance Armstrong: A biography.* New York: Simon & Schuster. Looks beyond the world of sports to portray the entire life of this Tour de France winner.

Hart, E. T. (1999). *Barefoot heart: Stories of a migrant child.* Tempe, AZ: Bilingual Press. As the youngest of six children, Hart remembers life as part of a family of migrant workers.

Haskins, J. (2002). *Champion: The story of Muhammad Ali.* New York: Walker. Provides a view of the life of a famous athlete.

Hemphill, S. (2007). *Your own, Sylvia: A verse portrait of Sylvia Plath.* New York: Knopf. A poetic look at the life of Sylvia Plath.

Hill, C. M. (2002). *John Lewis: From freedom rider to Congressman.* Berkeley Heights, NJ: Enslow. Hill explores the civil rights movement through the eyes of one of the participants.

Hinton, K. (2006). *Angela Johnson: Poetic prose.* Lanham, MD: Rowman & Littlefield. This biography is part of the Scarecrow Studies in Young Adult Literature series of biographies of young adult authors.

Hopping, L. J. (2005). *Bone detective: The story of forensic anthropologist Diane France.* New York:

Scholastic. Describes France's work as a forensic anthropologist.

Hunter, M. (1998). *The king's swift rider: A novel on Robert the Bruce*. New York: HarperCollins. Sixteen-year-old Martin becomes a spy for Robert the Bruce of Scotland.

Jacobsen, R. (2001). *Rescued images: Memories of a childhood in hiding*. New York: Mikaya Press. Using collages and photographs, Jacobsen tells the story of her family.

Jeffrey, L. S. (1996). *Great American businesswomen*. Springfield, NJ: Enslow. Jeffrey profiles 10 twentieth-century American women who have achieved success in business. Jeffrey has also written *Betty Shabazz: Sharing the Vision of Malcolm X* (2000).

Jiang, J. (1997). *Red scarf girl: A memoir of the cultural revolution*. New York: HarperTrophy. What can a young girl do when her government wants her to turn her back on her ancestors and inform on her parents?

Johnson, D. (2005). *Onward: A photobiography of African American polar explorer Matthew Henson*. Washington, DC: National Geographic Society. Tells how Henson, took part in Robert Peary's expedition to the North Pole.

Jordan, J. (2001). *Soldier: A poet's childhood*. New York: Basic Civitas. Poet and professor of African American studies June Jordan tells her own story in this coming-of-age autobiography.

Karnes, F. A. (1995). *Girls and young women inventing*. Minneapolis, MN: Free Spirit. Describing how each inventor began and continued the process of inventing, Karnes includes inventions such as labor-saving devices, objects that improve safety, and gadgets that make life more convenient.

Kraft, B. H. (2003). *Theodore Roosevelt: Champion of the American spirit*. New York: Clarion. From the Rough Riders in the Spanish-American War to his years in the White House.

Krull, K. (2000). *Lives of extraordinary women: Rulers, rebels (And what the neighbors thought)*. San Diego: Harcourt. Krull uses lots of humor to tell the stories of important women throughout history. Another anthology by Krull is *Lives of the Writers: Comedies, Tragedies (and What the Neighbors Thought)* (1994).

Krull, K. (2007). *Marie Curie*. (Giants in Science series). New York: Penguin. Reveals the unique difficulties Curie faced because of her gender. *Sigmund Freud* (2006) and *Isaac Newton* (2006) are also featured in this series.

Landau, E. (2002). *Osama bin Laden: A war against the West*. Brookfield, CT: Twenty-First Century Books. Presents information about militant Islamic leader Osama bin Laden and the beliefs that fuel his terrorist actions.

Lazo, C. (2000). *Alice Walker: Freedom writer*. Minneapolis, MN: Lerner. Using quotations from Walker's writings, Lazo explores the life of an American author.

Leavy, J. (2002). *Sandy Koufax: A lefty's legacy*. New York: HarperCollins. Although Koufax guards his private life, Leavy has written an excellent biography of one of baseball's greatest pitchers.

Levine, E. (2007). *Rachel Carson*. New York: Penguin. Highlights Carson's contribution as a writer and environmentalist.

Limb, P. (2008). *Nelson Mandela: A biography*. (Greenwood Biography series). Westport, CT: Greenwood. Focuses on the life of the South African leader.

Lobel, A. (1998). *No pretty picture: A child of war*. New York: Greenwillow. Anita Lobel takes readers back to her experiences as a Jewish child in Poland in World War II, her capture by the Nazis, and her later life in Sweden after the war. A 1999 Orbis Pictus honor book.

MacDonald, A., with DeGeronimo, T. F. (2003). *Dropping in with Andy Mac: The life of a pro skateboarder*. New York: Simon Pulse. This autobiography takes readers into the world of skateboarding.

MacNow, G. (2003). *Sports great Allen Iverson*. Berkeley Heights, NJ: Enslow. Follow this basketball player from the projects to his career as an NBA superstar.

Macy, S. (2001). *Bull's eye: A photobiography of Annie Oakley*. Washington, DC: National Geographic Society. Macy's text, along with outstanding photographs and quotations, brings this woman of the Old West to life.

Markel, R. J. (2001). *Jimi Hendrix*. Minneapolis, MN: Lerner. Markel recounts the life of the famous rock-and-roll guitarist.

Marrin, A. (1997). *Commander in chief: Abraham Lincoln and the Civil War*. New York: Dutton. *School Library Journal* (January 1998) called this the best book on Lincoln since Russell Freedman's Newbery Medal–winning book. Another biography of a Civil War leader is *Unconditional Surrender: U. S. Grant and the Civil War* (1994).

Marrin, A. (2001). *George Washington and the founding of a nation.* New York: Dutton. Using primary resources, Marrin provides an honest portrait of one of the founding fathers. Marrin has also written *Terror of the Spanish Main: Sir Henry Morgan and His Buccaneers* (1999).

McClafferty, C. K. (2008). *In defiance of Hitler: The secret mission of Varian Fry.* New York: Farrar, Straus and Giroux. Fry helped artists who were enemies of the Nazis.

Meltzer, M. (1985). *Dorothea Lange: Life through the camera.* New York: Viking Kestrel. Lange's photographs of migrant workers and poverty in rural America became an impetus to social reform. Other biographies by Meltzer include *Langston Hughes* (1997), *Lincoln, in His Own Words* (1993), *Mary McLeod Bethune: Voice of Black Hope* (1987), *Captain James Cook: Three Times Around the World* (2002), and *Starting from Home: A Writer's Beginnings: A Memoir* (1988), his own autobiography.

Meltzer, M. (2002a). *Walt Whitman: A biography.* Brookfield, CT: Twenty-First Century Books. Meltzer explores Whitman's life and the events of the nineteenth century. Meltzer has also written *Carl Sandburg: A biography* (1999).

Meltzer, M. (2002b). *Ten kings and the worlds they ruled.* New York: Scholastic. The stories of rulers from Attila and Charlemagne to Kublai Khan, Atahualpa, and Mansa Musa.

Mitchell, S. (2002). *Jesus: What he really said and did.* New York: HarperCollins. Mitchell tries to distinguish fact from legend and to identify the authentic sayings and actions of Jesus.

Myers, W. D. (1999). *At her majesty's request: An African princess in Victorian England.* New York: Scholastic. Saved from becoming a ritual sacrifice, an Egbado princess is taken to London and presented to Queen Victoria as Sara Forbes Bonetta. Myers tells the tragic story of her life and the cultural conflicts she faced. A 2000 Orbis Pictus honor book.

Myers, W. D. (2001). *Bad boy: A memoir.* New York: HarperCollins. Award-winning author Walter Dean Myers tells of his youth in Harlem in the 1950s.

Nelson, M. (2001). *Carver: A life in poems.* Asheville, NC: Front Street Books. Poems tell the story of Carver's life from slave to scientist.

O'Connor, B. (2003). *Leonardo da Vinci: Renaissance genius.* Minneapolis: CarolRhoda. O'Connor has written an informative and interesting biography of this famous artist.

Ohno, A. A., with Richardson, N. A. (2002). *A journey: The autobiography of Apolo Anton Ohno.* New York: Simon & Schuster. Olympic speed skater and medalist Ohno recounts the best and the worst of his career on ice.

Opdyke, I. G. (1999). *In my hands: Memories of a Holocaust rescuer.* New York: Knopf. As a young Polish girl, Irene saved Jews during the Holocaust.

Partridge E. (1998). *Restless spirit: The life and works of Dorothea Lange.* New York: Viking. Lange took powerful photographs of migrant workers and Japanese American internees.

Partridge, E. (2002). *This land was made for you and me: The life and songs of Woody Guthrie.* New York: Putnam. Partridge examines the strong political views and personality that made Woody Guthrie an icon in American music.

Partridge, E. (2005). *John Lennon: All I want is the truth.* New York: Viking. Explores the fame and difficult times of Lennon's life.

Paulsen, G. (2000). *The beet fields: Memories of a sixteenth summer.* New York: Delacorte. After running away from home, Paulsen worked in the fields as a migrant laborer and with a carnival.

Paulsen, G. (2001). *Guts: The true stories behind "Hatchet" and the Brian books.* New York: Random House. Paulsen shares real-life experiences that influenced his writing.

Pollack, J. S. (1996). *Women on the hill.* New York: Watts. Pollack provides comprehensive profiles of women who have served in the U.S. Congress.

Porter, D. L. (2007). *Michael Jordan: A biography.* (Greenwood Biography series). Westport, CT: Greenwood. Explores Jordan's career on and off the court.

Robertson, J. I., Jr. (2001). *Standing like a stone wall.* New York: Atheneum. Primary resources enhance this biography of a Civil War general.

Rosen, M. (2001). *Shakespeare: His work and his world.* Cambridge, MA: Candlewick. Michael Rosen brings the bard and Elizabethan times to life.

Roy, J. (2006). *Yellow star*. Tarrytown, NY: Marshall Cavendish. Focuses on Syvia Perlmutter's childhood in the Lodz ghetto.

Santiago, E. (1993). *When I was Puerto Rican*. New York: Vintage. A sequel is Santiago's Alex Award–winning *Almost a Woman* (1999). In these classic coming-of-age biographies, Santiago recounts her life in Puerto Rico and in Brooklyn.

Schutz, S. (2006). *I don't want to be crazy*. New York: Scholastic. Written in verse. Schutz gives details about living with an anxiety disorder.

Severance, J. B. (1999). *Einstein: Visionary scientist*. New York: Clarion. This is a comprehensive biography of the famous scientist.

Sigerman, H. (2001). *Elizabeth Cady Stanton: The right is ours*. New York: Oxford University Press. Primary sources provide the basis for this biography of a woman and her fight for equal rights.

Sis, P. (2007). *The wall: Growing up behind the iron curtain*. New York: Farrar, Straus and Giroux. Sis describes his childhood in communist Czechoslovakia.

Sports Illustrated. (2008). *Brett Favre: The tribute*. New York: *Time*. Marketed to adults, this book includes text and photos that document the football star's career.

Stanley, D. (1996). *Leonardo da Vinci*. New York: Morrow. Stanley won the Orbis Pictus award for this biography of the great artist.

Stanley, D. (1998). *Joan of Arc*. New York: Morrow. Stanley examines the life of a familiar historical figure against the backdrop of a turbulent time in French history.

Stanley, D. (2000). *Michelangelo*. New York: HarperCollins. Filled with illustrations and artwork, this biography will appeal to middle schoolers and reluctant readers.

Stanley, D. (2002). *Saladin: Noble prince of Islam*. New York: HarperCollins. Stanley uses her art and writing to bring this historical figure to life for younger adolescents.

Stanley, G. (2004). *Harry S. Truman: Thirty-third president of the United States*. New York: Aladdin. This fictionalized biography looks at the early life of Truman.

Stravinsky, J. (1997). *Muhammad Ali*. New York: Random House. Photos, text, sidelights, and samples of Ali's poetry combine in this biography.

Streissguth, T. (1999). *Jesse Owens*. Minneapolis, MN: Lerner. Jesse Owens went from being a sharecropper's son to winning four gold medals at the 1936 Olympics in Berlin.

Stux, E. (2005). *Achievers: Great women in the biological sciences*. Greensboro, NC: Avisson. A collective biography of eight scientists, including Mary Leakey, Rosalind Franklin, and Rosalyn Yalow.

Tighe, M. A. (2006). *Sharon Creech: The words we choose to say*. Lanham, MD: Rowman & Littlefield. Part of the Scarecrow Studies in Young Adult Literature series.

Vizzini, N. (2000). *Teen angst naah . . . : A quasi-autobiography*. Minneapolis, MN: Free Spirit. A collection of essays about the author's teen years.

Walker, R. (2002). *Black, white, and Jewish: Autobiography of a shifting self*. New York: Riverhead Books. Born to a black mother and a white father who were civil rights activists, Rebecca Walker finds herself adrift when her parents divorce.

Weatherford, C. B. (2008). *Becoming Billie Holiday*. Honesdale, PA: Wordsong. Using poetry, Weatherford examines the life of a jazz singer.

Young, J. C. (2007). *Hugo Chavez: Leader of Venezuela*. Greensboro, NC: Morgan Reynolds. Chavez's childhood in Sabaneta, Venezuela, imprisonment, and rise to leadership.

Young, M. (Ed.). (2004). *Terrorist leaders*. Detroit: Greenhaven. A part of the Profiles in History series, this collective biography includes the biographies of people like Joseph Stalin, Adolf Hitler, and Timothy McVeigh.

Yount, L. (1994). *Contemporary women scientists*. New York: Facts on File. Yount looks at 10 women who have contributed significantly to the natural sciences.

Yount, L. (1996). *Twentieth-century women scientists*. New York: Facts on File. The author describes the struggles and discrimination that each of these scientists faced.

Yount, L. (2008). *Antoine Lavoisier: Founder of modern chemistry*. Berkeley Heights, NJ: Enslow. The life and contributions of the Frenchman said to have discovered oxygen.

Zach, K. K. (2002). *Hidden from history: The lives of eight American women scientists*. Greensboro, NC: Avisson. These biographies range from astronomer Annie Jump Cannon to bacteriologist Alice Evans and biologist Nettie Stevens, as well as well-known women such as Grace Hooper and Gertrude Elion.

Suggested Readings

Aronson, M. (2008). Selective memory. *School Library Journal*, *54*(3), 34.

Crew, H. S. (2008). Enhancing the curriculum using primary sources: Women engaged in war. *Teacher Librarian*, *35*(3), 28–32.

Fialkoff, F. (2008). Memoir or make-believe? *Library Journal*, *133*(6), 8.

Howard, S. C. (2006). Junior nonfiction: Biographies they will read! *Teacher Librarian*, *33*(3), 30.

Huckabee, H. (2006). Bio buddies. *English Journal*, *95*(6), 86–88.

Kirchhoff, A. (2008). Weaving the story of science. *The Science Teacher*, *75*(3), 33–37.

Lerner, B. (2005). Why teach biography? *Education Week*, *24*(27), 37.

References

All works of young adult literature referenced in this chapter are included in the Young Adult Books list and are not repeated in this list.

Akmal, T. T., and Ayre-Svingen, B. (2002). Integrated biographical inquiry: A student-centered approach to learning. *The Social Studies*, *93*(6), 272–276.

Bucher, K. T., and Manning, M. L. (1998). Telling our stories, sharing our lives: Collective biographies of women. *The ALAN Review*, *26*(1), 12–16.

Buehler, J. S. (2003). Dinner party. *Voices from the Middle*, *10*(4), 16–19.

Burns, M. M. (1995). Biography. In A. Silvey (Ed.), *Children's books and their creators*. Boston: Houghton Mifflin, 59–61.

Carter, B. (2003). Reviewing biography. *The Horn Book*, *79*(2), 165–174.

Daisey, P. (1996a). Promoting interest in plant biology with biographies of plant hunters. *The American Biology Teacher*, *58*(7), 396–407.

Daisey, P. (1996b). Promoting literacy in secondary content area classrooms with biography projects. *Journal of Adolescent and Adult Literacy*, *40*(4), 270–279.

Daisey, P. (1997). Promoting equity in secondary science and mathematics classes with biography projects. *School Science and Mathematics*, *97*(8), 413–418.

Daisey, P., and José-Kampfner, C. (2002). The power of story to expand possible selves for Latina middle school students. *Journal of Adolescent and Adult Literacy*, *45*(7), 578–587.

Didion, J. (2005). *The year of magical thinking*. New York, Knopf.

Habegger, A. (2001). *My wars are laid away in books: The life of Emily Dickinson*. New York: Random House.

Hillman, J. (2003). *Discovering children's literature*. Upper Saddle River, NJ: Merrill/Prentice Hall.

Hillebrand, L. (2001). *Seabiscuit: An American legend*. New York: Random House.

Hurst, C. O. (2001). Personalizing history. *Teaching PreK–8*, *32*(1), 106–109.

Lechner, J. V. (1997). Accuracy in biographies for children. *New Advocate*, *10*(3), 229–242.

Merriam-Webster's Encyclopedia of Literature. (1995). Springfield, MA: Merriam-Webster.

Mickenberg, J. (2002). Civil rights, history, and the left: Inventing the juvenile black biography. *MELUS*, *27*(2), 65–95.

Minchew, S. S. (2002). Teaching character through sports literature. *The Clearing House*, *75*(3), 137–141.

Moss, B., and Hendershot, J. (2002). Exploring sixth graders' selection of nonfiction trade books. *The Reading Teacher*, *56*(1), 6–17.

Rudelson, C. (2003). For teachers: Why use biographies? Accessed August 25, 2003, from: www.whitneystewart.com/ASSK/why_biography.htm.

Spence, J. (2003). *Becoming Jane Austen: A life*. London: Hambledon and London.

Taylor, D. (1996). *The healing power of stories: Creating yourself through the stories of your life*. New York: Doubleday.

Taylor, G. (2002/2003). Who's who? Engaging biography study. *The Reading Teacher*, *56*(4), 342–344.

Townsend, L. T., and Hanson, C. (2001). The self and the narrative: A conversation on educational biography. *Educational Studies*, *32*(1), 38–52.

Weinberg, S. (2003, November/December). American biographies: Vol 1. *Bookmarks*, *7*, 28–33.

York, S. (2001). What's new in Latino literature? *Book Report*, *19*(4), 19–24.

Chapter

10

Exploring Nonfiction/ Information Books

The nonfiction section of a large bookstore bursts with titles that promise to teach young adults to change the world (*It's Your World—If You Don't like It, Change It: Activism for Teenagers*, Halpin, 2004); sew (*Sew Teen: Make Your Own Cool Clothes*, Zent, 2006); get rid of losers (*30 Days to Getting over the Dork You Used to Call Your Boyfriend: A Heartbreak Handbook*, Hathaway, 2008); and party (*Jon and Jayne's Guide to Throwing, Going to, and "Surviving" Parties: Advice and More from Your Average but Xtraordinary Friends* (Rosenberg & Rosenberg, 2008). With such diverse titles available, it is easier than ever for teens to satisfy their curiosity about all kinds of topics.

Unfortunately, many adults do not think of nonfiction when they think about young adult literature. For example, Worthy, Moorman, and Turner (1999) noted instances of teachers who will not allow students to read nonfiction in sustained silent reading time, despite studies showing that some older children and adolescents prefer nonfiction. We do not want you to fall into that trap. Thus, although we have emphasized the pleasures of reading fiction, we also want to point out that reading well-written nonfiction is an enjoyable experience for many adolescents.

Doiron (1995) has found that nonfiction is no longer dry and boring, as authors employ "rich writing styles and a variety of forms not just to convey knowledge or list facts but also to infuse their subject with the same sense of wonder and awe that drew them to the topic in the first place" (p. 37). Similarly, Aronson (2006) has noted that nonfiction books can be innovative and original in both presentation and organization. A poll of adolescents ages 12–18 found that 35% read mainly to get information and facts and 26% prefer reading nonfiction books ("Reading remains popular among youth," 2001). "While still lagging somewhat behind fiction, young adult nonfiction is on the rise. . . . Teenagers enjoy biographies and creative non-fiction" (Furi-Perry, 2003). An instance of this popularity is Jack Canfield's best-selling inspirational and motivational series including *Chicken Soup for the Teenage Soul on Tough Stuff* (2001), and *Chicken Soup for the Teenage Soul: The Real Deal Friends* (2006).

Thus, all educators need to be knowledgeable about the many informational books written especially for young adults and the criteria to use to select them. In addition to examining information books and series for young adults, library media specialists and teachers have a professional responsibility to make these books an integral part of the curriculum as well as part of young adults' daily reading habits.

Young Adult Nonfiction

Do adolescents lose interest in reading as they reach middle school or do they just lose interest in reading what teachers expect them to read? Worthy, Moorman, and Turner (1999) have found that the gap between what students want to read and what schools provide them is widening. Adolescents do not find what they want to read in schools, and they see school reading as an imposition. In addition, some public libraries do not even include nonfiction in their young adult literature collections (Jones, 2001). Aronson (2001) has decried the adult mindset that assumes that young adults do not enjoy nonfiction and has cited the research of Betty Carter, which pointed out that nonfiction is popular with young adults but not with the school library media specialists who could purchase it or the teachers who could use it in the curriculum.

Why do young adults read nonfiction? To find part of the answer, go back to psychology and child development. As adolescents mature, they demonstrate a need to know about things and to explore concepts and subjects in more detail. According to Tracey Firestone of the Suffolk (New York) Cooperative Library System, adolescents turn to books to find information they do not feel comfortable asking someone else about (Jones, 2001). In addition, rather than focusing on the relationships or character development found in fiction, some boys prefer the action in "visual media—the Internet, nonfiction, newspapers, and magazines—that focus on sports, electronics, and games" (Guzzetti et al., 2002, p. 47). Jones (2001) has also reported that the research of Teri S. Lesesne has shown that non-fiction is especially important to "at-risk teens . . . [who are] less-than-enthusiastic readers" (p. 44). Lesesne further notes that even though adolescents may read non-fiction on a regular basis, "they do not see themselves as readers because nonfiction is not as valued in the English classroom" (p. 44). Lesesne's findings are echoed by Moss and Hendershot (2002), who have found that many reluctant middle school readers enjoy reading nonfiction trade books because they are interesting and use-ful for learning. Therefore, in this chapter, you will explore young adult nonfiction that while it has limitations and may be ambiguous, encourages discovery and lets the readers draw their own conclusions (Aronson, 2001). Connecting Adolescents and Their Literature 10–1 suggests one way to build on young adults' enthusiasm for nonfiction.

10-1 •••. CONNECTING ADOLESCENTS AND THEIR LITERATURE

To encourage adolescents to read nonfiction, educators can build on an idea discussed by Mary J. Lickteig (2003). While reading nonfiction, students are expected to locate interesting facts and to share this information with the class. At a given time, the teacher turns to one student and says, "Feed my brain." The student replies by sharing a specific, unusual, and/or interesting fact from the nonfiction book he or she is currently reading. In turn, that student asks another student in the class to "Feed my brain." Lickteig suggests limiting the sharing to three or four students at one time. An extension of this activity is to gather the shared information into a book of interesting facts or to have the class vote on the "best" facts to place on a bulletin board. This idea can be used in any subject across the curriculum.

Definition of Nonfiction

The simplest way to define nonfiction is to say it is literature that is not fiction and that focuses on facts and information; hence the often-used synonym *informational book*. However, the lines between fiction and nonfiction sometimes blur. Adult authors Truman Capote and John Hersey both wrote nonfiction "novels" in which they tell the story of actual people and events in the form of a novel without inserting their own comments (*Merriam-Webster's Encyclopedia of Literature*, 1995). Calling a writer of nonfiction a "writer of reality," author Penny Colman reports that some editors see a blurring of the boundaries between fiction and nonfiction, leading to a new category known as *edutainment*. While hard-core nonfiction writers do not make up anything, writers of edutainment do. Colman goes on to say that although she uses a style that she terms *creative nonfiction* or *literary journalism with fictional techniques*, she does not make anything up, including the dialogue, scenes, or characters ("Adventures in non-fiction: Talking with Penny Colman," 2002). The best nonfiction books present, interpret, organize, and document factual materials using an interesting presentation style. Table 10–1 shows the contrast between fiction and nonfiction.

TABLE 10-1   A Contrast of Fiction and Nonfiction

	Fiction	Nonfiction
Purpose	Pleasure	Information
Structure	Read from beginning to end	Read in parts or pieces
Language	Specific to the characters	Specific to the subject
Content	Created	Researched

EXPANDING YOUR KNOWLEDGE WITH THE INTERNET

You can use the Internet to find information about some selected authors of nonfiction for young adults, including the following.

Susan Campbell Bartoletti
www.scbartoletti.com/
www2.scholastic.com/browse/contributor.jsp?id=1907

Vicki Cobb
www.vickicobb.com/
www.peak.org/~bonwritr/AUTHORS_vcobb.htm

Penny Colman
www.pennycolman.com/

www2.scholastic.com/browse/contributor. jsp?id=1368

Jim Haskins
www.english.ufl.edu/faculty/jhaskins/

Milton Meltzer
www.wpi.edu/Academics/Library/Archives/ WAuthors/meltzer/bio.html

Jim Murphy
www.jimmurphybooks.com/content. scholastic.com/browse/contributor.jsp?id=1855

Types of Nonfiction

As with other genres, a number of ways exist to categorize nonfiction. One way is to distinguish between series and stand-alone works.

Individual Works. Like novels, nonfiction books may either be stand-alone works or part of a series. While an individual author may choose to write in a particular discipline or on a particular topic, he or she might write each stand-alone book in a different format with a different style and/or book design. Expanding Your Knowledge with the Internet has links to information about a few such nonfiction authors.

Series. In contrast to stand-alone books, nonfiction series consist of a number of books that may or may not be written by the same author. They are on the same general topic/subject and are linked by the publisher's book design for the series. These series should be evaluated not only on the books' content, but also on the books' design for the entire series (Zvirin, 1999). Poor design will detract from a good text, while a fancy design does not compensate for poor information. The publisher's challenge is to find a good design that will be appropriate for all of the books in the series. Some nonfiction series are written quickly to a specific formula and do not adhere to the same standards as nonseries nonfiction. While these books might meet the need to provide information for a specific report, they can be very pedestrian and rapidly become outdated (Lempke, 1999). However, a number of excellent series are available, and there is no doubt that young adults, including reluctant readers, find them appealing, especially those with photographs and other illustrations. Table 10–2 lists some currently popular nonfiction series.

TABLE 10-2   Several popular and well-written current nonfiction series

Series Title	Publisher
Drive. Ride. Fly	Motorbooks
Shapers of America	OTTN
Forensic Evidence	M. E. Sharpe
Science Concepts	Twenty-First Century
Groundwork Guides	Groundwood
Issues that Concern You	Gale/Greenhaven
Images and Issues of Women in the Twentieth Century	Lerner/Twenty-First Century
Political Profiles	Morgan Reynolds
Profiles in Science	Morgan Reynolds

One problem for educators is that many review editors, because of the number of series and the limited amount of review space in journals, focus on a series as a whole rather than on individual titles, unless a specific book deals with a highly controversial subject (Zvirin, 1999). This can cause problems when the books in a series are very uneven, especially if new books are added to the series over a period of several years. For example, an early review of a series may be very favorable, however, books published later may be of a lesser quality. Because the journal has published only one review of the whole series, you might not become aware of the decline in the later books' quality. Thus, it is important to review the individual books in a nonfiction series with the same care you use in evaluating stand-alone nonfiction.

Categories of Nonfiction

It is tempting to divide nonfiction into categories on the basis of the content of the school's curriculum. However, Dresang (1999) notes the changing boundaries in young adult nonfiction books, with the inclusion now of previously ignored or forbidden subjects, such as child slavery and child labor, contemporary political issues, sexuality, religion, violence, and environmental issues. Therefore, popular young adult nonfiction provides more than curriculum-related information. It is also full of information on growing up, popular culture, and the contemporary world. Seeing the wide range of nonfiction that is available and knowing that adolescents select nonfiction that goes beyond the subjects taught in school, we have chosen to divide these books into groups that roughly parallel some of the categories found in the Dewey Decimal System and have highlighted a few outstanding books. To help you select the categories your own students will enjoy, Connecting Adolescents and Their Literature 10–2 suggests using surveys as one way to identify their reading interests.

10-2 •••. CONNECTING ADOLESCENTS AND THEIR LITERATURE

Use surveys to find out your students' reading preferences. Be sure to include several categories of nonfiction, such as "how-to-do-it" books, true sports books, and books of interesting facts. Then, have books in the preferred categories available for your students and allow them to read them, especially in a sustained silent reading time. You can find sample inventories on the Internet at www.st.cr.k12.ia.us/reading/ readinginterestinventoriesChoicePage.htm.

General Works. Books of assorted and sometimes apocryphal "facts" are always popular with adolescents. In addition to the usual almanacs, two excellent choices are Jenifer Corr Morse's *Scholastic Book of World Records* (2006) and David Holt and Bill Mooney's *Exploding Toilet: Modern Urban Legends* (2004).

Religion and Mythology. While religion is not a popular topic with all young adults, some do begin to explore their personal religious beliefs. In Rahel Musleah's *Why on This Night? A Passover Haggadah for Family Celebration* (2000), Tahar Ben Jelloun's *Islam Explained* (2002), and Irshad Manji's *The Trouble with Islam: A Muslim's Call for Reform in Her Faith* (2004), the authors explore religions that are in the news. Two excellent historical accounts that provide a background on religion in America are Randall Balmer's *Religion in Twentieth Century America* (2001) and Grant Wacker's *Religion in Nineteenth Century America* (2000). Looking even farther to the past, *Gods, Goddesses, and Monsters: An Encyclopedia of World Mythology* (Keenan, 2000) and *Gods, Goddesses, and Mythology* (Littleton, 2005) explore mythology.

Social Sciences. A number of topics fall into the broad category of the social sciences. Several authors look at the changing face of America in books such as Pearl Fuyo Gaskins's *What Are You? Voices of Mixed-Race Young People* (1999), Milton Meltzer's *There Comes a Time: The Struggle for Civil Rights* (2001b), and Martha E. Kendall's *Failure Is Impossible: The History of American Women's Rights* (2001). Other books in the social sciences include:

- Michael L. Cooper, *Indian School: Teaching the White Man's Way* (1999)
- Penny Colman, *Corpses, Coffins, and Crypts: A History of Burial* (1997)
- Dennis Brindell Fradin and Judith Bloom Fradin, *5,000 Miles to Freedom: Ellen and William Craft's Flight from Slavery* (2006)

Science. Nonfiction can help adolescents explore the world of science. James M. Deem shows the mysteries hidden for centuries in *Bodies from the Bog* (1998). Likewise, Donna Jackson looks at scientists who hunt criminals in *The Wildlife Detectives: How Forensic Scientists Fight Crimes against Nature* (2000). Diane Swanson investigates science in *Nibbling on Einstein's Brain: The Good, the Bad, & the Bogus in Science* (2001). For pleasure and fun, Elizabeth Van Steenwyk takes readers to the ocean in *Let's Go to the Beach: A History of Sun and Fun by the Sea* (2001). Ken Croswell's *Ten Worlds:*

COLLABORATING WITH OTHER PROFESSIONALS

Some adolescents enjoy conducting experiments. Before they develop and implement their own (with sometimes disastrous results), teachers and library media specialists can work together to develop a display of science experiment books. A few to consider are:

- *Science Is . . . A Source Book of Fascinating Facts, Projects and Activities* (Bosak, 2000)
- *See for Yourself: More Than 100 Experiments for Science Fairs and Projects* (Cobb, 2001)
- *Mad Professor: Concoct Extremely Weird Science Projects* (Frauenfelder, 2002)

Everything That Orbits the Sun (2006) offers a fresh look at the planets, including Pluto. Adolescents can see how advanced weather forecasting has become by reading Jim Murphy's tale of the snowstorm of 1888 in *Blizzard!* (2000). There are a number of ways to introduce science nonfiction to adolescents; Collaborating with Other Professionals 10–1 offers one example.

Health. Given peer pressure and the need to assert their independence, many adolescents contemplate engaging in risky behaviors or begin to develop health problems. A number of nonfiction books address these issues in a nondidactic manner including, Magdalena Alagna's *Everything You Need to Know About the Dangers of Binge Drinking* (2001), Melanie Ann Apel's *Cocaine and Your Nose: The Incredibly Disgusting Story* (2000), and Margaret O. Hyde and Elizabeth H. Forsyth's *Depression: What You Need to Know* (2002). Other health-related nonfiction books include:

- Gael Jennings, *Bloody Moments: And Further Highlights from the Astonishing in History of Medicine* (2000)
- Ellen Schwartz, *I'm a Vegetarian: Amazing Facts and Ideas for Healthy Vegetarians* (2002)
- Kathlyn Gay, *Am I Fat? The Obesity Issue for Teens* (2006)
- Kim Etingoff, *Abusing Over-the-Counter Drugs: Illicit Uses for Everyday Drugs* (2007)

Growing Up as a Teenager. Young adults often turn to nonfiction to find answers to the questions they are reluctant to ask adults. For boys, there is Mavis Jukes's *The Guy Book: An Owner's Manual: Safety, Maintenance and Operating Instructions for Teens* (2002). Girls will similarly enjoy Anthea Paul's *Girlosophy: The Love Survival Kit* (2002). Several books provide all teens with a frank look at sexual information, including:

- Jane Pavanel, *The Sex Book: An Alphabet of Smarter Love* (2001)
- Linda and Area Madaras, *What's Happening to My Body?* (2000), with editions for both boys and girls

- Tania Heller, *Pregnant! What Can I Do? A Guide for Teenagers* (2002)
- Tina Radziszewicz, *Ready or Not: A Girl's Guide to Making Her Own Decisions About Dating, Love, and Sex* (2005)

Finally, teenager Aisha Muharrar relates the results of a Teen Labels Survey and frankly discusses the issues in *More Than a Label: Why What You Wear or Who You're with Doesn't Define Who You Are* (2002).

Applied Science and Technology. Many adolescents want to learn how things are made and how they work. For young adults who dream of actually building things, there are books such as David Burgess-Wise's *The Ultimate Race Car* (1999), Ed Sobey's *How to Build Your Own Prize-Winning Robot* (2002), and Chris Woodford and John Woodcock's *Cool Stuff 2.0: And How It Works* (2007). Other favorite nonfiction books on this subject include:

- Susan Goldman Rubin, *There Goes the Neighborhood: Ten Buildings People Loved to Hate* (2001)
- John B. Severance, *Skyscrapers: How America Grew Up* (2000)
- Elizabeth Mann, *Hoover Dam: The Story of Hard Times, Tough People, and the Taming of a Wild River* (2001)
- Angela Wilkes, *A Farm Through Time: The History of a Farm from Medieval Times to the Present Day* (2001)

The Arts. Art takes many forms, and most of them are represented in quality nonfiction for young adults. Caroline Desnoëttes presents famous paintings in *Look Closer: Art Masterpieces Through the Ages* (2006). Michael L. Cooper's *Slave Spirituals and the Jubilee Singers* (2001) looks at music. Kathlyn Gay and Christine Whittington's *Body Marks: Tattooing, Piercing, and Scarification* (2002) explores body art. Carol Sabbeth's *Monet and the Impressionists for Kids* (2002) examines an artistic movement. Jim Haskins and Kathleen Benson's *Conjure Times: Black Magicians in America* (2001) and Cherie Turner's *Stunt Performers: Life Before the Camera* (2001) look at two different types of entertainers. For budding cartoonists, there is Christopher Hart's *Manga Mania Villains: How to Draw the Dastardly Villains of Japanese Comics* (2003). Frank Augustyn and Shelley Tanaka's *Footnotes: Dancing the World's Best-Loved Ballets* (2001) and Olympid Dowd's *A Young Dancer's Apprenticeship: On Tour with the Moscow Ballet* (2002) examine the world of ballet.

Sports. Sports nonfiction is always popular. Steven Krasner presents information on sports with tips on how to be a better player in *Play Ball Like the Pros: Tips for Kids from 20 Big League Stars* (2002). Susan D. Bachrach combines sports and history in *The Nazi Olympics: Berlin 1936* (2000). Historical views of sports are found in Sandra and Susan Steen's *Take It to the Hoop: 100 Years of Women's Basketball* (2003), Marcos Bretón's *Home Is Everything: The Latino Baseball Story* (2002), *Baseball's Best Shots: The Greatest Baseball Photography of All Time* (2000), and Dave Caldwell's *New York Times Speed Show: How NASCAR Won the Heart of America*

(2006). In addition, there are a number of excellent sports biographies, as mentioned in Chapter 9.

Authors and Writing. Although some authors include information about their writing in their autobiographies, others write directly about the creative process of writing. In *Blood on the Forehead: What I Know about Writing* (1998), M. E. Kerr uses excerpts from her novels to explain the writing process. Leonard W. Marcus's *Author Talk* (2000) presents a series of interviews with 15 writers for young adults who talk about themselves and their craft. In *Writing Magic: Creating Stories That Fly* (2006), Gail Carson Levine encourages young aspiring writers. *What Is Poetry: Conversations with the American Avant-Garde* (2003), edited by Daniel Kane, explores poets who usually are not studied in school, and Ron Miller's *The History of Science Fiction* (2001) is an overview for younger adolescents.

Real Adventures. Nonfiction adventure books can be as exciting as fiction. Sir Earnest Shackleton's ill-fated Antarctic expedition has been chronicled in Jennifer Armstrong's *Shipwreck at the Bottom of the World: The Extraordinary True Story of Shackleton and the Endurance* (1998) and Caroline Alexander's *The Endurance: Shackleton's Legendary Antarctic Expedition* (1998). Collaborating with Other Professionals 10–2 shows how some high school teachers have used this adventure as a basis for an integrated unit. Other titles include:

- Kathy Pelta, *Rediscovering Easter Island* (2001)
- Joseph B. Treaster, *Hurricane Force: Tracking America's Killer Storms* (2007)

10-2   COLLABORATING WITH OTHER PROFESSIONALS

Katz, Boran, Braun, Massie, and Kuby (2003) used *Shipwreck at the Bottom of the World* (Armstrong, 1998) as the basis for an integrated thematic unit for high school students that allowed cooperation among several teachers, such as the reading teacher, social studies teacher, library media specialist, and language arts teacher. The strategies these teachers successfully used were similar to those used with fiction and included the following:

INTRODUCTORY ACTIVITIES

Linking the book to a video

Making predictions about the story/video

Using agree/disagree statements

Featuring quotations from the major character

DURING-READING ACTIVITIES

Continuation of some of the previous activities

Dramatization of scenes from the book

Vocabulary development activities

Verification of facts in the book

Study guide questions on the reading

AFTER-READING ACTIVITIES

Discussion of the book and/or links to fiction on the same topic

Inquiry, research, and electronic slide presentation of a topic from the book

- Andrew C. Revkin, *The North Pole Was Here: Puzzles and Perils at the Top of the World* (2006)
- Russell Freedman, *Who Was First? Discovering the Americas* (2007)

History. In nonfiction books, young adults can find a fresh look at historical events. Tom Feelings uses illustrations to document the Africa-to-America slave trade in *The Middle Passage: White Ships/Black Cargo* (1995). In Connecting Adolescents and Their Literature 10–3, Julia Johnson Connor (2003) describes how she used this wordless nonfiction book to provide a context for a discussion of African American literature in high school. Karen E. Lange provides new information about Jamestown, Virginia, in *1607: A New Look at Jamestown* (2007). Milton Meltzer looks at another type of immigration in *Bound for America: The Story of the European Immigrants* (2001a). Susan Campbell Bartoletti examines a great tragedy that led to massive emigration in *Black Potatoes: The Story of the Great Irish Famine, 1845–1850* (2001).

10-3 •••• CONNECTING ADOLESCENTS AND THEIR LITERATURE

When Julia Johnson Connor (2003) saw the pictures in Tom Feelings's wordless nonfiction book *The Middle Passage: White Ships/Black Cargo* (1995), she decided to use the book in her 11th- and 12th-grade English classes to provide a background for the discussion of slavery in African American literature. She suggests that, as adolescents examine the book, you can:

- Ask them to consider not only the information they have gained from the pictures but also the feelings the illustrations evoked.
- Ask students to think about why the author presented a visual representation of the Middle Passage rather than writing about it.
- Question students about their personal reactions to the book.

Connor found that the use of this book with an African American literature unit significantly increased the students' intellectual and emotional understandings of the Middle Passage and created a context for exploring other writings about the African American experience in literature.

Many adolescents want to read books about war. G. Clifton Wisler's *When Johnny Went Marching: Young Americans Fight the Civil War* (2001) provides a new view of this conflict. Karen Zeinert explores another hidden face of war in *Those Extraordinary Women of World War I* (2001). Amy Nathan and Eileen Collins have written *Yankee Doodle Gals: Women Pilots of World War II* (2001). Allan M. Winkler examines a modern conflict in *The Cold War: A History in Documents* (2001). Ted Gottfried records the aftermath of war in *Displaced Persons: The Liberation and Abuse of Holocaust Survivors* (2001).

from Page to Screen

NONFICTION AND INFORMATIONAL BOOKS

Like biographies, these books cover topics that are often also the subjects of films. Consider pairing a well-written informational text with one of the following films to deepen students' understanding of the subject matter, and as a means of comparing the authenticity of the tellers' fact-gathering.

INTO THE ARMS OF STRANGERS: THE STORY OF KINDERTRANSPORT
★★★ | 2000 | Unrated

This Academy Award–winner for Best Documentary follows the stories of many children who were secretly transported to Britain without their families to escape Nazi persecution. This film compares poignantly with Hana Volavkova's I Never Saw Another Butterfly, a collection of the writings of children who did not escape the Holocaust.

DOGTOWN AND Z-BOYS
★★★★ | 2001 | PG-13

This award winning documentary shares the story of some of the earliest professional skaters. Pair it

with Michael Brooke's nonfiction text The Concrete Wave: The History of Skateboarding for a detailed look into skating.

WHOSE CHILDREN ARE THESE?
★★★ | 2004 | Unrated

Theresa Thanjan's documentary focuses on the experiences of three Muslim teenagers after 9/11. The teens and their families faced prejudice, violence, and deportation.

IT'S NOT ABOUT SEX
★★★★ | 2007 | Unrated

High school students used research, including interviews with members of antirape organizations such as Men Can Stop Rape, to produce this documentary about sexual assault. The students were participants in a workshop sponsored by the Educational Video Center.

THE GRACE LEE PROJECT
★★★ | 2005 | Unrated

In this documentary, Grace Lee, a Korean-American filmmaker bothered by the image and preconceived notions her name suggests, searches around the world for women who share her name and defies the stereotypical (i.e., docile and innocent) image the name implies. Bruce Lee's mother is among the women she meets.

From Page to Screen lists a number of films that can be paired with young adult informational books in different categories.

Reasons for Using and Teaching Nonfiction

As we have indicated, young adult nonfiction is often ignored in schools. However, there are a number of reasons to make well-written nonfiction part of the curriculum and to encourage recreational nonfiction reading.

Reading nonfiction helps adolescents develop information literacy, a much-needed skill in modern society, in which students can no longer memorize everything in school that they will need to know as adults. Instead, they must develop the skills to locate, evaluate, and use information. In other words, they must become information literate. This form of literacy includes being able to:

- See the parts within the whole and their relationship
- Solve problems and think analytically
- Work in groups and communicate with others
- Work independently and assume responsibility (Benson, 2002)

To help adolescents become information literate, educators must use reading and writing strategies and critical thinking skills that focus on nonfiction. For example, in nonfiction, adolescents find tables, charts, graphic organizers, maps, drawings, diagrams, timelines, and other visual representations of information. To survive in contemporary society, adolescents need to develop the skills and abilities to decode this information. In addition, Hadaway, Vardell, and Young (2002) argue that although most educators use fiction in the classroom, high-stakes tests contain more nonfiction than fiction passages for students to read and analyze. Collaborating with Other Professionals 10–3 suggests how teachers and library media specialists can teach information literacy.

Several studies have found a link between the reading of nonfiction and the development of literacy skills. Generally, students who read magazines and nonfiction books have higher average reading proficiency than those who do not (Campbell, Kapinus, & Beatty, 1995). In addition, nonfiction that presents concepts and vocabulary in a concrete way can help teach literary skills and can provide a bridge to textbooks for nonnative as well as native English speakers (Hadaway, Vardell, & Young, 2002).

There are still other benefits of using nonfiction with young adults. Nonfiction:

- Helps adolescents learn and understand content-related vocabulary
- Provides current information in a more interesting way than textbooks
- May be more appealing visually than a textbook (Hadaway, Vardell, & Young, 2002)
- Is effective in moving adolescents from the Internet to the library (Jones, 2001)
- Generally has a clear focus in less than 200 pages
- Can provide a pleasurable reading experience

10-3   COLLABORATING WITH OTHER PROFESSIONALS

The National Science Education Standards provide broad, interdisciplinary goals for educators. Noting that both "emergent and sophisticated readers often choose science and nature as their favorite genre of reading material," Terrence E. Young (2003) has challenged teachers and school library media specialists to work together to identify quality nonfiction. Although his suggestions pertain only to science, the same principles can be adapted for other subjects in the curriculum.

- Content teachers and library media specialists should collaborate to help young adults understand curriculum concepts. They should identify quality nonfiction resources by:
  - Comparing the nonfiction books in a given subject in the school library's collection to a recognized standard
  - Identifying the most important topics to be developed in the collection
  - Purchasing nonfiction in these areas

Characteristics of Well-Written Nonfiction

You should evaluate nonfiction for young adults as carefully as you evaluate fiction. Just because a nonfiction book presents information does not mean that you should not examine its quality (Broderick, 1995; Jones, 1995) and its appeal to young adults, including the quality of the writing, the writing style, and the tone of the book. Fortunately, many nonfiction books have factual and unbiased material, clear photographs, and writing that reflects young adults' reading levels and interests. Unfortunately, not all do. Thus, teachers and library media specialists must read reviews and engage in firsthand evaluation.

What qualities should you look for in evaluating nonfiction? Considerations for Selecting Young Adult Literature: *Nonfiction* outlines a few questions that are

CONSIDERATIONS FOR
SELECTING YOUNG ADULT LITERATURE NONFICTION

When evaluating and selecting quality nonfiction for young adults, ask the following questions:

_____ Is the content accurate, current, and clear?

_____ Is there an unbiased presentation and perspective?

_____ Does the writing have a didactic or preachy tone?

_____ Is there a distinction between fact and conjecture or opinion?

_____ Is the content well-organized?

_____ Are the style and tone appropriate for the content and audience?

_____ What are the qualifications of the author?

_____ Does the book have a table of contents, index, glossary, timeline, or other organizers that help make the content accessible?

_____ Is there a useful index?

_____ Is the information up to date, with current research and documentation?

_____ Is there evidence of research—bibliographies, notes, suggestions for further reading, and mention of Internet sites or key words for searching?

_____ Are the illustrations appropriate, attractive, and accurate, with appropriate (and correct) captions?

_____ Is the book design appealing, with:

Attractive borders

Crisp, uncluttered pages

A readable and appropriate typeface

Features such as symbols and feature boxes

important to keep in mind. Obviously, accuracy and objectivity are of prime importance, as is an unbiased perspective (i.e., does the book present accurate representations of people with differing sexual orientations?). Nonfiction should not trivialize a subject. As Sullivan (2000) wonders, how can one book teach you everything you need to know about a topic (as some claim) in 100 pages or less? Also important is a style and organization that is appropriate to the content, appeals to young adults' interests, and is written at their reading levels. Because some authors write a number of books on different topics, it is necessary to look closely at their qualifications and the amount of research that they have done. Also examine the organizing features, such as the index and glossary. Check the usefulness of the index by trying to locate information in the book and determining whether key topics and concepts are included in the index. Whether the illustrations are in color or black and white, they should be sharp and appropriately positioned on the pages. They should also accurately portray or extend the text, and have correct descriptive captions. Credits for the illustrations should be included. An appealing and compatible book design is important to attract readers. Even the shape of a nonfiction book is important: short and thick books convey the impression of serious information; tall and skinny books appeal to reluctant readers.

As we have mentioned, one special consideration when evaluating nonfiction is the large number of published series. As Jones (1995) has noted, the editors of some journals and magazines that review young adult books believe that evaluating the large number of nonfiction series is an overwhelming task and thus choose not to review them. Other journals review a series only once, based only on the books available at that time. To add to the difficulty of reviewing, just as some series are better than others, individual books in a series may vary in quality. Unfortunately, publishers often try to get purchasers to buy an entire series by suggesting that a quotation about one book applies to all the books in the series (Jones, 1995). Lempke (1999) cautions against series books in which authors insert annoying comments and exclamation points in an attempt to be chatty or perky. In any work of nonfiction, the ideal is to provide a well-written, attractive, interesting book that makes even complex subjects simple enough for adolescents without trivializing the information.

Like single works of nonfiction, series must also be evaluated for accuracy and authenticity, content and perspective, style and organization, and the authors' qualifications. Considerations for Selecting Young Adult Literature: *Nonfiction Series* identifies some special items to look for when evaluating nonfiction series. Although it is tempting to look for well-known authors, it is just as important to determine the qualifications of all of the authors of books in the series. If the names of well-known authors are listed as editors or consultants for the series, you should determine exactly what their contributions are and whether they have actually written any of the books in the series. Make sure that the books in the series are not just out-of-print titles that have been given new covers and a new series title. Verify that the individual books are not padded with thick sections of incidental information that is repeated from title to title throughout the series (Boardman, 1997).

CONSIDERATIONS FOR
SELECTING YOUNG ADULT LITERATURE NONFICTION SERIES

When evaluating and selecting nonfiction series for young adults, ask the same questions you ask when evaluating nonseries nonfiction. Then ask the following:

_____ How do the contents of the books compare to the packaging of the series?

_____ Are the books in the series a consistent length?

_____ Is there evidence of consistent research throughout the series?

_____ Do the topics in each book in the series correlate with the curriculum or the interests of young adults?

_____ What are the qualifications of all of the authors of the books in the series?

_____ Is the book design consistent throughout the series?

_____ How much repetition is there in the books in the series?

Suggestions for Selecting and Using Nonfiction

Selecting appropriate nonfiction is just as important as selecting quality fiction. While the impulse may be to choose a book because it addresses a topic that is included in the curriculum or that reflects a current interest of young adults, it is important to evaluate nonfiction by applying the criteria listed previously in this chapter. Adolescents deserve accurate, appealing, well-written nonfiction books, and schools need to spend their resources wisely.

Awards and Best Books Lists.   As with fiction, the nonfiction books that win book awards and prizes are usually good ones to recommend to adolescents. Although there are no specific awards for young adult nonfiction, a number of nonfiction awards routinely include books that will appeal to young adult readers. These include the Orbis Pictus Award, given annually by NCTE to outstanding nonfiction for children, and the Robert F. Sibert Informational Book Award, given annually by the ALSC. The Boston Globe–Horn Book Award also has a category for nonfiction. The Society of School Librarians International gives a nonfiction K–12 award. The Children's Book Guild has a nonfiction award. The yearly best books lists prepared by the NCSS and NSTA consist of a large number of nonfiction books.

Nonfiction titles are often found among the winners and honor books in other awards and best books lists. Works of history are eligible for the Jefferson Cup, given by the Virginia Library Association. The Best Books for Young Adults, Quick Picks for Young Adults, and Popular Paperbacks for Young Adults, all annual lists from YALSA, often contain some recommended nonfiction titles. However, the best books lists are usually overwhelmingly composed of fiction books.

Print Reviews.   Several journals provide information on recommended nonfiction. Every year the August issue of *VOYA* presents a nonfiction honor list. Selected from books publishers nominate, this list consists of books recommended for middle school students and recently has included some additional comments by adolescents about the books.

EXPANDING YOUR KNOWLEDGE WITH THE INTERNET

The following Internet sites provide a sample of where you can find information about young adult nonfiction.

Orbis Pictus Award
www.ncte.org/elem/awards/orbispictus

Robert F. Sibert Information Book Award
www.ala.org/ala/alsc/awardsscholarships/
literaryawds/sibertmedal/sibert_medal.cfm

Boston Globe–Horn Book Nonfiction Award
www.hbook.com/bghb/default.asp

Washington Post–Children's Book Guild Nonfiction Award
www.childrensbookguild.org/2003award.htm

Outstanding Science Trade Books for Students K–12 (NSTA)
www.nsta.org/ostbc

Notable Social Studies Trade Books for Young People (NCSS)
www.socialstudies.org/resources/notable/

Jefferson Cup
www.co.fairfax.va.us/library/READING/YA/
JEFFCUP.HTM

Search It! Science
searchit.heinemann.com/

The journal *Science, Books & Films*, published by the American Association for the Advancement of Science (AAAS), has reviews of science books, including those for adolescents.

Some bibliographies highlight recommended nonfiction:

- *Reality Rules! A Guide to Teen Nonfiction Reading Interests* (Fraser, 2008)
- *Thematic Guide to Popular Nonfiction* (Adamson, 2006).
- *100 Most Popular Nonfiction Authors: Biographical Sketches and Bibliographies* (Drew, 2008)

Online Resources. On the Internet, Search It! Science is a subscription-based database of recommended science trade books that offers a free preview. Expanding Your Knowledge with the Internet provides additional information on specialized nonfiction awards and selection sources.

Teaching with Nonfiction in the Classroom

Educators can use a number of strategies to incorporate young adult nonfiction into the classroom. In many content areas, you can identify nonfiction books to supplement the curriculum. School health professionals and guidance counselors will find nonfiction books very useful in helping adolescents cope with developmental and health problems, as well as in career education. In addition, nonfiction can be used as a core book in literature-based instruction with a thematic approach, in interdisciplinary teaching, and for independent reading. Cheryl Thomas (2000), a sixth-grade language arts teacher, cites two professional books that have helped her integrate nonfiction into her classroom: *Nonfiction Matters* (Harvey, 1998) and *Strategies That Work* (Harvey & Goudvis, 2000). Thomas (2000) uses Walter Wick's *A Drop of Water* (1997) as a core book to teach reading, science, and math. Figure 10–1 illustrates her use of this book. Collaborating with Other Professionals 10–4 provides an idea for incorporating young adult nonfiction into the mathematics classroom.

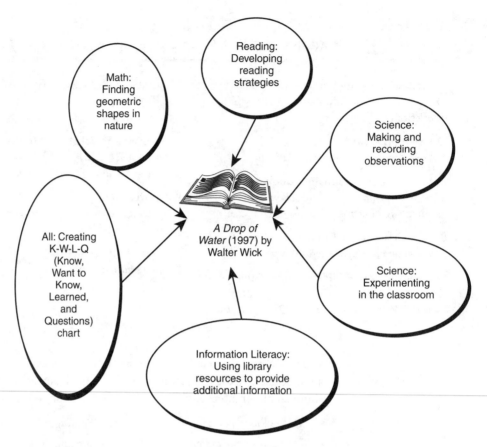

Figure 10-1   Nonfiction as a Core Book in the Curriculum

Here are some more ideas for using nonfiction in the classroom:

- Have students read two nonfiction books on the same subject and then compare their treatments. Do the authors use the same style? Are the books unbiased? What characteristics make one better than the other?

- Make nonfiction books the basis for reading activities along with fiction.

COLLABORATING WITH OTHER PROFESSIONALS

To use nonfiction in the mathematics classroom, work with science and/or social studies teachers to identify books that can also be used in their classes. Then you can:

- Divide the class into groups and have each group read a nonfiction book on a particular subject.

- Have each group take the information from the books members have read, combine it, organize it into a database, and develop graphic representations of the data, such as charts, graphs, and tables.

- In social studies, have students compare and contrast a fiction with a nonfiction book about the same subject.
- Have students use a chart to compare the information from nonfiction books, library reference sources, and Internet resources.
- When assigning readings, make nonfiction one of the choices.
- Use nonfiction books as the basis for discussion in student advisory sessions.
- Use concept maps to organize information from nonfiction books.
- Use text sets or theme baskets (see Figures 10–2, as well as 10–3 and 10–4).
- Make sure the school library has books that answer the questions adolescents are afraid to ask adults.

Text sets, or theme baskets, offer an opportunity to help students make connections across several texts, including multimedia and content areas. Teachers can work together to help students examine the difficult reality of sex-related assault and abuse using a text set like the one shown below.

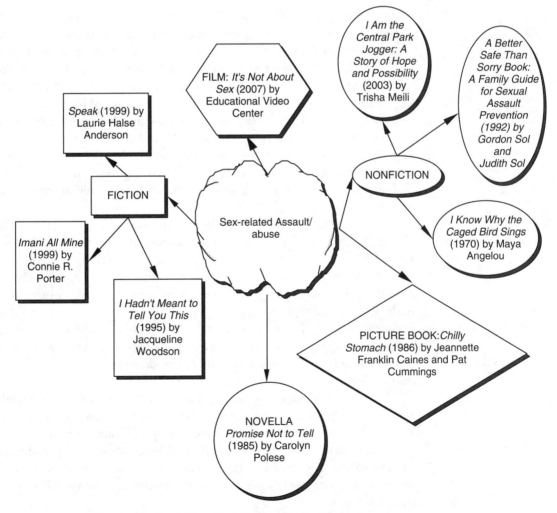

Figure 10-2 Using Text Sets or Theme Baskets

Content Area Reading. A natural use of nonfiction is to supplement or replace the textbook in the various subjects throughout the curriculum. Because nonfiction presents concepts and vocabulary in a concrete way, it can also be an excellent tool for teaching literacy development (Hadaway, Vardell, & Young, 2002). However, Benson (2002) maintains that teaching nonfiction in a content area means more than having students read a book. Even though students can decode words by the time they are in middle and high school, they still need help to understand the content of their reading (Donahue, 2003). Reading and information literacy skills involve going beyond merely accessing information to evaluating and using it. In other words, young adults must construct their own meaning from a text and must use different strategies for reading different texts. In doing so, they demonstrate comprehension by taking prior knowledge or topic knowledge and building on it to develop text knowledge or an understanding of the global structure of the text, the interrelationship of main concepts, and the organization of the text.

Literacy Skills. To teach these information literacy and content reading skills, teachers must employ a number of different strategies. Teachers cannot assume that young adults have these skills or that the literacy skills students employ when reading fiction will transfer to nonfiction. As Ogle points out (D'Arcangelo, 2002), students will apply different reading strategies to nonfiction material than to fiction. With fiction, they can anticipate the narrative structure of beginning, middle, and end; with nonfiction, they need help to understand the structure of the information. According to Richardson, Morgan, and Fleener (2009), expository text can be organized in at least 17 different ways, many of which may be new to younger adolescents. Six types of expository text that often appears in nonfiction are listing, analysis, cause and effect, comparison and contrast, definition, and analogy and example (Richardson et al., 2009).

You can teach a number of reading strategies with nonfiction, including predicting, thinking aloud, creating visual representations and graphic organizers, activating prior knowledge, previewing, taking notes, writing to learn, responding to study guides, preparing K-W-L (Know, Want to know, Learned) charts, establishing purposes for reading, developing questions on it, participating in directed reading-thinking activities, engaging in peer teaching, creating marginal notes, and participating in discussion webs (Barry, 2002). Text maps, based on the organizational features of a book, such as the chapter headings, subheadings, charts and tables, and boldfaced words, can also help readers become fluent in content area reading (Spencer, 2003).

To help students develop content reading skills, educators must model the appropriate strategies and expect students to focus on only one or two new strategies at a time, such as making a summary, comparing and contrasting an idea, creating a timeline, or determining cause and effect. When educators help students identify and use appropriate strategies for understanding text structure, students become better at not only reading but also understanding and recalling information (Rhoder, 2002).

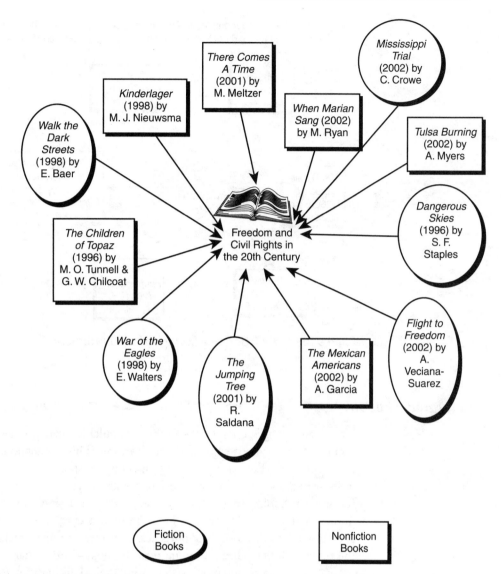

Figure 10-3   Fiction and Nonfiction on a Single Topic or Theme

When helping adolescents develop the appropriate reading and information literacy strategies to use with informational books, content teachers can use a work of young adult nonfiction as a core book, a supplement to the text, a part of interdisciplinary instruction, or for independent reading. Collaborating with the library media specialist, English/language arts teacher, and/or reading specialist, content teachers can identify nonfiction that can be taught in a number of classes throughout the curriculum. Educators can use just nonfiction or both fiction and nonfiction by relating the books to a central theme. Figure 10–3 shows a way to use both fiction and nonfiction books around a single topic or theme. Figure 10–4 illustrates the use of a fiction book as a springboard to the reading of several nonfiction books.

The following web on the theme of science, technology, and crime in the modern world features a fiction book as the core title leading to nonfiction books.

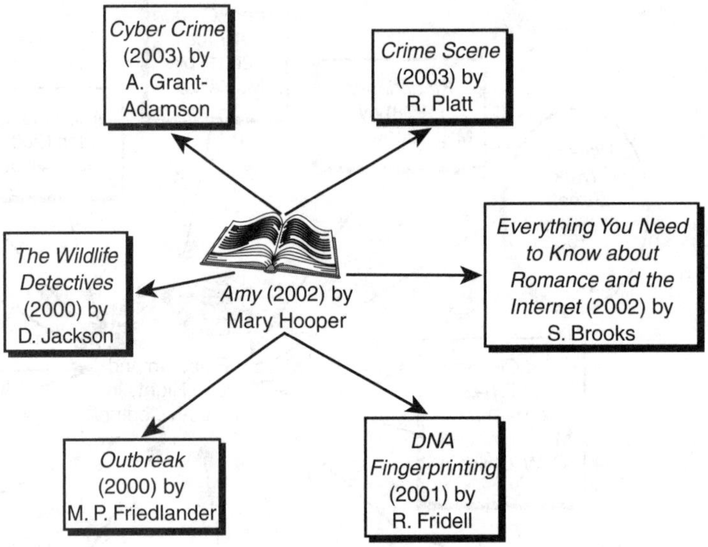

Figure 10-4   Fiction as a Springboard to Nonfiction

Concluding Thoughts

The wealth of nonfiction books and series available today provide young adults with opportunities for both enjoyment and learning. This tremendous selection can be a mixed blessing. Educators have a tremendous responsibility to select and suggest well-written and age-level-appropriate books for young adults. Although many informational books are attractive and appealing in design and format, teachers and library media specialists need to focus on their accuracy, perspectives, organization, and authors' qualifications and purposes. Considering today's technological advances, the future will likely bring even more such books—with enhanced photographs and more current topics, and more writers using their skills in this market.

Young Adult Books

This section includes young adult titles mentioned in this chapter.

Alagna, M. (2001). *Everything you need to know about the dangers of binge drinking.* New York: Rosen. Other books in this series include Sheldon Brooks, *Everything You Need to Know about Romance and the Internet* (2001); Cherie Turner, *Everything You Need to Know about the Riot Grrrl Movement* (2001); Katherine White, *Everything You Need to Know about Relationship Violence* (2001); and Sandra and Owen Giddens, *Everything You Need to Know about Crohn's Disease and Colitis* (2004).

Alexander, C. (1998). *The Endurance: Shackleton's legendary antarctic expedition.* New York: Knopf. This Alex Award–winner is full of adventure.

Apel, M. A. (2000). *Cocaine and your nose: The incredibly disgusting story.* New York: Rosen. After looking at the functions of the nose, Apel examines the effects of cocaine use, and options for treatment for addiction. Another book in this series is Allan B. Cobb's *Speed and Your Brain: The Incredibly Disgusting Story* (2000).

Armstrong, J. (1998). *Shipwreck at the bottom of the world: The extraordinary true story of Shackleton and the Endurance.* New York: Crown. In 1914, Sir Ernest Shackleton's ship was trapped in the Antarctic ice. Another book by this author is *Shattered: Stories of Children and War* (2002).

Augustyn, F., and Tanaka, S. (2001). *Footnotes: Dancing the world's best-loved ballets.* Brookfield, CT: Millbrook Press. The authors introduce seven ballets and the dancers who perform them.

Bachrach, S. D. (2000). *The Nazi Olympics: Berlin, 1936.* Boston: Little Brown. Readers go behind the sports events for the real story.

Balmer, R. (2001). *Religion in twentieth-century America.* New York: Oxford University Press. Religion and social issues combine in this history.

Bartoletti, S. C. (2001). *Black potatoes: The story of the Great Irish Famine, 1845–1850.* Boston: Houghton Mifflin. With period illustrations, Bartoletti presents the story of a great tragedy. Bartoletti has also written *Kids on Strike!* (1999) and *Growing Up in Coal Country* (1997).

Baseball's best shots: The greatest baseball photography of all time. (2000). New York: DK. A Quick Pick for Reluctant Young Adults Readers for 2001.

Ben Jelloun, T. (2002). *Islam explained.* New York: New Press. After a history of Islam, the author moves to a discussion of Muslim beliefs.

Bosak, S. V. (2000). *Science is . . . a source book of fascinating facts, projects and activities.* New York: Scholastic. Middle schoolers should enjoy the information and projects about weather, matter, energy, and biology.

Bretón, M. (2002). *Home is everything: The Latino baseball story.* El Paso, TX: Cinco Puntos Press. A bilingual book on the contributions of Latinos to baseball.

Burgess-Wise, D. (1999). *The ultimate race car.* New York: DK. A 2000 Quick Pick for Reluctant Young Adult Readers.

Caldwell, D. (2006). *New York Times speed show: How NASCAR won the heart of America.* New York: Kingfisher. Describes the history of stock-car racing.

Canfield, J., and Hansen, M. V. (2001). *Chicken soup for the teenage soul on tough stuff.* Deerfield Beach, FL: Health Communications. Another collection of inspirational stories and messages about life.

Canfield, J., Hansen, M. V., and Reber, D. (2006). *Chicken soup for the teenage soul: The real deal friends: Best, worst, old, new, lost, false, true, and more.* Deerfield Beach, FL: Health Communications. A collection of inspirational stories about friendship.

Cobb, V. (2001). *See for yourself: More than 100 experiments for science fairs and projects.* New York: Scholastic. Here are lots of ideas for science fair projects.

Colman, P. (1997). *Corpses, coffins, and crypts: A history of burial.* New York: Holt. Colman looks at the rituals and customs associated with burials. Other recommended books by Colman are *Rosie the Riveter: Women Working on the Home Front in World War II* (1995) and *Where the Action Was: Women War Correspondents in World War II* (2002).

Cooper, M. L. (1999). *Indian school: Teaching the white man's way.* New York: Clarion. Cooper uses various documents to explore the removal of Indian children to schools where they would learn the white man's culture.

Cooper, M. L. (2001). *Slave spirituals and the jubilee singers.* New York: Clarion. Cooper traces the spiritual from its roots to its presentation by the Jubilee Singers. Another book by this author is *Fighting for Honor: Japanese Americans and World War II* (2000).

Croswell, K. (2006). *Ten worlds: Everything that orbits the sun.* Honesdale, PA: Boyds Mills. Focuses on the planets, including Pluto and Eris.

Deem, J. M. (1998). *Bodies from the bog.* Boston: Houghton Mifflin. The bog of northern Europe has preserved bodies for thousands of years. Now the bodies have a tale to tell about our ancestors.

Desnoëttes, C. (2006). *Look closer: Art masterpieces through the ages.* New York: Walker. Encourages readers to carefully examine works by Leonardo da Vinci, Claude Monet, Vincent van Gogh, Marc Chagall, and others.

Dowd, O. (2002). *A young dancer's apprenticeship: On tour with the Moscow Ballet.* Brookfield, CT: Twenty-First Century Books. Follow this teenager as she joins the Moscow City Ballet.

Etingoff, K. (2007). *Abusing over-the-counter drugs: Illicit uses for everyday drugs.* Broomall, PA: Mason Crest. Describes the dangers of using over-the-counter drugs irresponsibly.

Feelings, T. (1995). *The middle passage: White ships/black cargo.* New York: Dial. This is a stark and moving visual portrayal of the African slave trade.

Fradin, D. B., and Fradin, J. B. (2006). *5,000 miles to freedom: Ellen and William Craft's flight from slavery.* Washington, DC: National Geographic Society. Shares a slave couple's struggle for freedom.

Frauenfelder, M. (2002). *Mad professor: Concoct extremely weird science projects.* San Francisco: Chronicle. The projects may be strange, but the science is sound.

Freedman, R. (2007). *Who was first? Discovering the Americas*. New York: Houghton Mifflin. Uncovers information about explorers who visited the Americas long before Christopher Columbus.

Gaskins, P. F. (1999). *What are you? Voices of mixed-race young people*. New York: Holt. Eight mixed-race young people describe their lives and the issues they face.

Gay, K. (2006). *Am I fat? The obesity issue for teens*. Berkeley Heights, NJ: Enslow. Provides information for readers concerned about being overweight.

Gay, K., and Whittington, C. (2002). *Body marks: Tattooing, piercing, and scarification*. Brookfield, CT: Twenty-First Century. This is a history of the art of body decorations and discusses the health risks involved.

Gottfried, T. (2001). *Displaced persons: The liberation and abuse of Holocaust survivors*. Brookfield, CT: Twenty-First Century Books. Unfortunately, anti-Semitism did not end with the fall of the Nazi regime. Another book by Gottfried is *Nazi Germany: The Face of Tyranny* (2000).

Halpin, M. (2004). *It's your world—if you don't like it, change it: Activism for teenagers*. Burnsville, MN: Tandem. Gives readers advice on how to speak out against injustices.

Hantman, C. (2008). *30 days to getting over the dork you used to call your boyfriend: A heartbreak handbook*. New York: Random House. Encourages readers to accept loss and move on with their lives.

Hart, C. (2003). *Manga mania villains: How to draw the dastardly villains of Japanese comics*. New York: Watson-Guptill, This book shows artists how to move from geometric shapes to characters such as the punk, the monster, and the mad scientist.

Haskins, J., and Benson, K. (2001). *Conjure times: Black magicians in America*. New York: Walker. The authors look at African American magicians. Other books by these authors are *Bound for America: The Forced Migration of Africans to the New World* (1999) and *African Beginnings* (1996).

Heller, T. (2002). *Pregnant! What can I do? A guide for teenagers*. Jefferson, NC: McFarland. This is a straightforward, nonbiased presentation of all aspects of this issue.

Holt, D., and Mooney, B. (2004). *Exploding toilet: Modern urban legends*. Little Rock, AR: August House. Includes legends from the Internet.

Hyde, M. O., and Forsyth, E. H. (2002). *Depression: What you need to know*. New York: Franklin Watts. Frankly discusses the causes, symptoms, and treatments of teenage depression.

Jackson, D. (2000). *The wildlife detectives: How forensic scientists fight crimes against nature*. Boston: Houghton Mifflin. Environmentalists use science to solve crimes.

Jennings, G. (2000). *Bloody moments: And further highlights from the astonishing in history of medicine*. Toronto: Annick Press. Lots of interesting and sometimes gory details from medicine.

Jukes, M. (2002). *The guy book: An owner's manual: Safety, maintenance and operating instructions for teens*. New York: Crown. The comparisons between boys and cars provides essential information.

Kane, D. (Ed.). (2003). *What is poetry? Conversations with the American avant-garde*. New York: Teachers and Writers Collaborative. Rather than presenting poems, Kane focuses on the writers who create them and their approach to writing.

Keenan, S. (2000). *Gods, goddesses, and monsters: An encyclopedia of world mythology*. New York: Scholastic. This book contains concise sketches from throughout the world.

Kendall, M. E. (2001). *Failure is impossible: The history of American women's rights*. Minneapolis, MN: Lerner. Kendall traces the movement from its beginning to modern times.

Kerr, M. E. (1998). *Blood on the forehead: What I know about writing*. New York: HarperCollins. Kerr talks about the sources of her ideas and how she turns ideas into stories.

Krasner, S. (2002). *Play ball like the pros: Tips for kids from 20 big league stars*. Atlanta, GA: Peachtree. Along with a little history of sports, there are plenty of tips, anecdotes, and guidance from professional players.

Lange, K. E. (2007). *1607: A new look at Jamestown*. Washington, DC: National Geographic. Using current research, the author provides new information about the Jamestown settlement.

Levine, E. (2000). *Darkness over Denmark: The Danish Resistance and the rescue of the Jews*. New York: Holiday House. This book includes stories of young people rescued from the Holocaust.

Levine, G. C. (2006). *Writing magic: Creating stories that fly*. New York: HarperCollins. Includes writing exercises for budding authors.

Littleton, C. S. (2005). *Gods, goddesses, and mythology*. New York: Marshall Cavendish. This encyclopedia looks at mythology from central Asia to the Incas and the Celts.

Madaras, L., with Madaras, A. (2000). *What's happening to my body? Book for boys: Growing up guide for parents and sons.* New York: Newmarket Press. The companion book is *What's Happening to My Body? Book for girls: Growing up guide for parents and daughters.*

Manji, I. (2004). *The trouble with Islam: A Muslim's call for reform in her faith.* New York: St. Martin's Press. The author offers controversial views about her religion.

Mann, E. (2001). *Hoover Dam: The story of hard times, tough people, and the taming of a wild river.* New York: Mikaya Press. It took an extraordinary feat of engineering to build this dam in the middle of the Great Depression. Another title by Mann is *Machu Picchu* (2000).

Marcus, L. S. (Ed.). (2000). *Author talk: Conversations with Judy Blume, Bruce Brooks, Karen Cushman, Russell Freedman, Lee Bennett Hopkins, James Howe, Johanna Hurwitz, E. L. Konisgburg, Lois Lowry, Ann M. Martin, Nicholasa Mohr, Gary Paulsen, Jon Scieszka, Seymour Simon, and Laurence Yep.* New York: Simon & Schuster. Fifteen young adult authors discuss their careers and their writing.

Meltzer, M. (2001a). *Bound for America: The story of the European immigrants.* New York: Benchmark Books. Meltzer focuses on the First Great Migration of Europeans from 1829 to 1920. Other books by Meltzer include *In the Days of the Pharaohs: A Look at Ancient Egypt* (2001) and *Piracy & Plunder: A Murderous Business* (2001).

Meltzer, M. (2001b). *There comes a time: The struggle for civil rights.* New York: Random House. Meltzer presents a concise history of the civil rights movement.

Miller, R. (2001). *The history of science fiction.* New York: Franklin Watts. An excellent introduction to the genre.

Morse, J. C. (2006). *Scholastic book of world records.* New York: Scholastic. Many adolescents are drawn to books like this that are full of interesting facts.

Muharrar, A. (2002). *More than a label: Why what you wear or who you're with doesn't define who you are.* Minneapolis, MN: Free Spirit. This survey of 1,000 teenagers uses personal stories to illustrate the problems of "labeling" people.

Murphy, J. (2000). *Blizzard!* New York: Scholastic. A single snowstorm paralyzes New York City. Other popular nonfiction books by Jim Murphy include *The Great Fire* (1995) and *An American Plague: The True and Terrifying Story of the Yellow Fever Epidemic of 1793* (2003).

Musleah, R. (2000). *Why on this night? A Passover Haggadah for family celebration.* New York: Simon & Schuster. This book presents the story of the ritual of the Seder.

Nathan, A., and Collins, E. (2001). *Yankee doodle gals: Women pilots of World War II.* Washington, DC: National Geographic. Meet the Women Airforce Service Pilots (WASPs).

Paul, A. (2002). *Girlosophy: The love survival kit.* St. Leonards, NSW, Australia: Allen & Unwin. The book contains commonsense advice about love and relationships. A companion volume is *Girlosophy: A Soul Survivor Kit* (2001).

Pavanel, J. (2001). *The sex book: An alphabet of smarter love.* Montreal: Lobster Press. Pavanel takes on the myths and provides frank information for teens of all sexual orientations.

Pelta, K. (2001). *Rediscovering Easter Island.* Minneapolis, MN: Lerner. Something about the monoliths of Easter Island have attracted explorers and scholars for ages.

Radziszewicz, T. (2005). *Ready or not? A girl's guide to making her own decisions about dating, love, and sex.* New York: Walker. Provides resources, contact information, and answers to thousands of questions about puberty, sexually transmitted diseases, homosexuality, and more.

Revkin, A. C. (2006). *The North Pole was here: Puzzles and perils at the top of the world.* New York: Kingfisher. The author traveled with scientists to explore the arctic.

Rosenberg, G., and Rosenberg, C. (2008). *Jon and Jayne's guide to throwing, going to, and "surviving" parties: Advice and more from your average but xtraordinary friends.* Deerfield Beach, FL: Health Communications. Helps readers learn to socialize at outings.

Rubin, S. G. (2001). *There goes the neighborhood: Ten buildings people loved to hate.* New York: Holiday House. Even famous structures like the Eiffel Tower were not always loved when they were first built.

Sabbeth, C. (2002). *Monet and the Impressionists for kids.* Chicago: Chicago Review Press. An introduction to Monet, Renoir, Degas, Cassatt, Cezanne, Gauguin, and Seurat.

Schwartz, E. (2002). *I'm a vegetarian: Amazing facts and ideas for healthy vegetarians.* Toronto: Tundra

Books. This is an excellent overview that looks at both factual issues and social ones.

Severance, J. B. (2000). *Skyscrapers: How America grew up*. New York: Holiday House. Look at the architects and the challenges they faced in building skyscrapers.

Sobey, E. (2002). *How to build your own prize-winning robot*. Berkeley Heights, NJ: Enslow. In addition to information on creating a robot, this book has lists of resources such as clubs and organizations.

Steen, S., and Steen, S. (2003). *Take it to the hoop: 100 years of women's basketball*. Brookfield, CT: Twenty-First Century. This short book provides information on a changing sport.

Swanson, D. (2001). *Nibbling on Einstein's brain: The good, the bad, & the bogus in science*. Toronto: Annick Press. Go beyond the surface of science to separate the good and the bad research.

Treaster, J. B. (2007). *Hurricane force: Tracking America's killer storms*. New York: Kingfisher. The author, a journalist, experienced Hurricane Katrina and reported on other hurricanes.

Turner, C. (2001). *Stunt performers: Life before the camera*. New York: Rosen. This is a book in the Extreme Careers series.

Van Steenwyk, E. (2001). *Let's go to the beach: A history of sun and fun by the sea*. New York: Holt. A short history of the appeal of the beach.

Wacker, G. (2000). *Religion in nineteenth-century America*. New York: Oxford University Press. Wacker looks at the individuals and movements that influenced the developing nation.

Wick, W. (1997). *A drop of water*. New York: Scholastic. Wick uses photographs to explore all of the states of water.

Wilkes, A. (2001). *A farm through time: The history of a farm from medieval times to the present day*. New York: Dorling Kindersley. Farmers change from using hand tools to driving modern machines.

Winkler, A. M. (2001). *The Cold War: A history in documents*. New York: Oxford University Press. Using documents and photographs, Winkler analyzes the Cold War.

Wisler, G. C. (2001). *When Johnny went marching: Young Americans fight the Civil War*. New York: HarperCollins. Wisler shows a less-than-glamorous view of the American Civil War.

Woodford, C., and Woodcock, J. (2007). *Cool stuff 2.0: And how it works*. New York: DK. Shows how products and inventions (e.g., recycling, game

consoles, helicopters, and so on) work. The authors also wrote *Cool Stuff: And How It Works* (2005).

Zeinert, K. (2001). *Those extraordinary women of World War I*. Brookfield, CT: Millbrook Press. The role of women during World War I is shown in vivid detail. Zeinert has also written *The Valiant Women of the Vietnam War* (2000).

Zent, S. (2006). *Sew teen: Make your own cool clothes*. New York: Sixth&Spring Books. Helps readers design clothes and accessories using 21 projects.

Suggested Readings

Aronson, M. (2007). Location is everything: The biggest challenge for writers of nonfiction for young people? Creating context. *School Library Journal, 53*(2), 31.

Aronson, M. (2007). A true and terrifying story: How to create a context that leaves readers begging for more. *School Library Journal, 53*(3), 36.

Brinda, W. (2008). "Can you name one good thing that comes out of war?" Adolescents' questions about war and conflict are answered in nonfiction. *The ALAN Review, 35*(2), 14–23.

Deahl, R. (2008). Call it Nonfiction . . . Sort of. *Publishers Weekly, 255* (12), 12–13.

Loertscher, D. (2007). Nonfiction texts and achievement. *Teacher Librarian 35* (1), 37.

Nicosia, L. (2006). Adolescent literature of witness. *Transformations, 17*(1), 85–97.

Young, T. A., Moss, B., and Corwell, L. (2007). The classroom library: A place for nonfiction, nonfiction in its place. *Reading Horizons, 48*(1), 1–18.

References

All works of young adult literature referenced in this chapter are included in the Young Adult Books list and are not repeated in this list.

Adamson, L. G. (2006). *Thematic guide to popular nonfiction*. Westport, CT: Greenwood Press.

Adventures in nonfiction: Talking with Penny Colman. (2002). *Journal of Children's Literature, 28*(2), 58–61.

Aronson, M. (2001). *Exploding the myths: The truth about teenagers and reading*. Lanham, MD: Scarecrow Press.

Aronson, M. (2006). Originality in nonfiction: A writer for young people makes a case for recognizing innovation. *School Library Journal, 52*(1), 42–43.

Barry, A. L. (2002). Reading strategies teachers say they use. *Journal of Adolescent & Adult Literacy, 46*(2), 132–141.

Benson, V. (2002). Shifting paradigms and pedagogy with nonfiction: A call to arms for survival in the twentyfirst century. *New England Reading Association Journal*, 38(2), 1–6.

Boardman, E. (1997). Series books: "Can we buy with confidence?" *The Book Report*, 16(3), 23–24.

Broderick, D. M. (1995). The history the young (and not so young) don't know. *Voice of Youth Advocates*, 17, 330–331.

Campbell, J. R., Kapinus, B., and Beatty, A. S. (1995). *Interviewing children about their literacy experiences.* Washington, DC: U.S. Department of Education.

Connor, J. J. (2003). "The textbooks never said anything about . . ." Adolescents respond to the Middle Passage; White Ships/Black Cargo. *Journal of Adolescent and Adult Literacy*, 47(3), 240–246.

D'Arcangelo, M. (2002). The challenge of content-area reading. *Educational Leadership*, 60(3), 12–15.

Doiron, R. (1995). An aesthetic view of children's nonfiction. *English Quarterly*, 28(1), 35–41.

Donahue, D. (2003). Reading across the great divide: English and math teachers apprentice one another as readers and disciplinary insiders. *Journal of Adolescent and Adult Literacy*, 47(1), 24–37.

Dresang, E. T. (1999). *Radical change: Books for youth in a digital age.* New York: H. W. Wilson.

Drew, B. A. (2008). *100 most popular nonfiction authors: Biographical sketches and bibliographies.* Westport, CT: Libraries Unlimited.

Fraser, E. (2008). *Reality rules! A guide to teen nonfiction reading interests.* Portsmouth, NH: Libraries Unlimited.

Furi-Perry, U. (2003, April/May). "Dude, that book was cool": The reading habits of young adults. *Reading Today* 20(5). Accessed January 5, 2004, from: www.findarticles.com/cf_dls/m0HQZ/5_20/100046846/print.jhtml.

Guzzetti, B., Young, J., Gritsavage, M., Fyfe, L., and Hardenbrook, M. (2002). *Reading, writing, and talking gender in literacy learning.* Newark, DE: International Reading Association.

Hadaway, N. L., Vardell, S. M., and Young, T. A. (2002). Highlighting nonfiction literature: Literacy development and English language learners. *The New England Reading Association Journal*, 38(2), 16–22.

Harvey, S. (1998). *Nonfiction matters.* York, ME: Stenhouse.

Harvey, S., and Goudvis, A. (2000). *Strategies that work.* York, ME: Stenhouse.

Jones, P. (1995). Homework helpers: The best in YA nonfiction series. *Voice of Youth Advocates*, 17(6), 324–329.

Jones, P. (2001). Nonfiction: The real stuff. *School Library Journal*, 47(4), 44–45.

Katz, C. A., Boran, K., Braun, T. J., Massie, M. J., and Kuby, S. A. (2003). The importance of being with Sir Ernest Shackleton at the bottom of the world. *Journal of Adolescent & Adult Literacy*, 47(1), 38–49.

Lempke, S. D. (1999). What makes a good nonfiction series? *Booklist*, 96(4), 431.

Lickteig, M. J. (2003). Feed my brain: Involving children with informational books. *School Library Media Activities Monthly*, 14(6), 29–30.

Merriam-Webster's Encyclopedia of Literature. (1995). Springfield, MA: Merriam-Webster.

Moss, B., and Hendershot, J. (2002). Exploring sixth graders' selection of nonfiction trade books. *The Reading Teacher*, 56(1), 6–17.

Reading remains popular among youth, according to poll (National Education Association survey). (2001, June). *Reading Today* 18(6). Accessed January 5, 2004, from: www.findarticles.com/cf_dls/m0HQZ/6_18/76332780/print.jhtml.

Richardson, J. S., Morgan, R. F., and Fleener, C. (2009). *Reading to learn in the content areas.* 7th ed. Belmont, CA: Thomson.

Rhoder, C. (2002). Mindful reading: Strategy training that facilitates transfer. *Journal of Adolescent & Adult Literacy*, 45(6), 498–512.

Spencer, B. H. (2003). Text maps: Helping students navigate information texts. *The Reading Teacher*, 56(8), 752–756.

Sullivan, E. (2000). More is not always better. *School Library Journal*, 46(4), 42–43.

Thomas, C. (2000). From engagement to celebration: A framework for passionate reading. *Voices from the Middle*, 8(2), 16–25.

Worthy, J., Moorman, M., and Turner, M. (1999). What Johnny likes to read is hard to find in school. *Reading Research Quarterly*, 34(1), 12–27.

Young, T. E. (2003). No pain, no gain . . . the science teacher and you working together. *Library Media Connection*, 21(4), 14–21.

Zvirin, S. (1999). Coping with series books. *Booklist*, 96(4), 432.

Chapter 11

Exploring Poetry, Drama, and Short Stories

Poetry, drama, and short stories are just as important as the other types of literature discussed in this book and deserve a place in any literature program for adolescents. Although these genres are often overlooked, books in these categories often appear on some of the recommended lists of young adult literature. For example, the short story collection *What They Found: Love on 145th Street* (Myers, 2007) was on YALSA's Best Books for Young Adults 2008 list. Marilyn Nelson's collection of sonnets *A Wreath for Emmett Till* (2005) was selected as a Michael L. Printz Honor Book in 2006. Paul Zindel's classic drama *The Effect of Gamma Rays on Man-in-the-Moon Marigolds* (1971) won the Pulitzer Prize. The 2008 Newbery Award went to Laura Amy Schlitz's collection of short plays *Good Masters! Sweet Ladies! Voices from a Medieval Village* (2007).

As with other forms of literature, to use this literature successfully with adolescents, educators must identify works that appeal to young adult readers and that they *want* to read. While selections may include classics in each genre, educators also need to share contemporary poetry, drama, and short stories with young adults and use appropriate titles that are written specifically for them.

Poetry, Drama, and Short Stories

Most educators readily recognize the need to provide adolescents with well-written poetry, drama, and short stories, often focusing on classics. Rather than reading only literary works that have claimed fame for years, young adults also want works that deal with their contemporary concerns and daily interests, such as beginning and maintaining a romance, coping with parental expectations, and struggling to grow into the adult world. These readers also want books that speak directly to them with words they can understand and situations they can relate to. Thankfully, there are excellent titles that satisfy all these criteria.

Poetry

Speaking of poetry in general rather than that written specifically for young adults, Charters (1997) has maintained that contemporary poetry pleases nearly everyone, from the most traditional to the most avant-garde. "Poetry in America is a diverse, highly contested field, crowded with a variety of practices and philosophies, none of which lends itself easily to generalization" (p. 38).

In the not-too-distant past, some people thought "poetry was best left in the hands of experts, those deemed knowledgeable enough to decipher and interpret the enigmatic language poets seem to so enjoy" (Steineke, 2002, p. 8). Fortunately, poetry has changed, and today students can personally connect to many contemporary poems. Thus, educators must provide adolescents with the tools to understand poetry and help them develop the confidence necessary to read, discuss, and enjoy it. When they have been taught effectively, using poetry they enjoy, young adults can meet even a challenging poem with enthusiasm and confidence (Steineke, 2002).

Called the language of emotions, poetry has an elusive character that defies exact definition. In general, the emphasis is not on how the reader feels about the poem but on how it makes the reader feel. Poetry is "writing that formulates a concentrated imaginative awareness of experience in language chosen and arranged to create a specific emotional response through its meaning, sound, and rhythm" (*Merriam-Webster's Encyclopedia of Literature*, 1995). When poem and reader connect, poetry has the power to elicit rich sensory images and deep emotional responses. These emotional responses are often age-related, so educators must ensure that the topics in the poetry they use relate to the experiences, emotions, concerns, and feelings of the readers (Aronson, 2008; Knowles & Smith, 1997).

Types of Poetry.   Part of what makes it difficult to select poetry for adolescents is that poetry affects readers in different ways (Heartwell, 2002). Some people like rhyming poetry; others enjoy free verse. Some think poetry should reflect the simple things in life; others believe it should explore the depths of a person's most complex emotions. The challenge for teachers and library media specialists is to pique the interest and curiosity of all students and help them learn to appreciate a variety of poetic styles.

Poetry for young adults comes in various forms. While some readers might like narrative poems, others might prefer lyrical poetry. Looking at studies of poetry preferences of young adults, Abrahamson (2002) found that, while adolescents enjoy narrative poetry, they also like humorous poems, including limericks, with older teens enjoying more subtle humor. Rhythm and rhyme are not as important to older teens as to younger teens, who also find that figurative language interferes with their ability to understand poems. Younger adolescents "prefer modern poetry over traditional or classic pieces" (Abrahamson, 2002, p. 22). Haiku comes in at the bottom of the list of preferred types of poems (Abrahamson, 2002). Thus, to decide what they like and enjoy, adolescents need to have the opportunity to explore various forms of poetry and to develop the skills to understand it. To help them, you must expose young adults to a wide variety of poems and teach them how to find individual poems and collections that appeal to their interests. Definitions of individual types of poetry and poetic devices are on the Internet at the Poetry Corner or Shadow Poetry. See Expanding Your Knowledge with the Internet on page 298.

Reasons for Using and Teaching Poetry. A number of reasons exist to use poetry with young adults. Poetry "has the power not only to delight but also has the potential to instruct" (Kazemek, 2003, p. 46) especially by providing "non-didactic moral education" (p. 44). In addition,

> poetry, like painting, reflects a special way of looking at the world. The poet, as the painter, looks at the world with an artist's vision, selecting images as vehicles for thoughts and feelings. The process is the same; only the mode of expression is different. The artist uses paint to convey a personal vision of the world: the poet uses words. (Marshall & Newman, 1997, p. 7)

Unfortunately, too much emphasis on poetic conventions can keep adolescents from enjoying the "words and music" (p. 23) of poetry (Thomas, 2000). For example, when Andrea Davis (1997) surveyed her eighth-grade students, their comments about poetry ranged from "I love it" to "It's boring, pointless, and mushy" (p. 17). However, she found that at the end of a carefully planned poetry anthology unit, the same students made the following comments:

> Before we did the anthology I hated poetry, I am glad my opinion changed. You're probably going to think I'm lying, but I thought the anthologies were the best thing we've done all year. . . . I even think I learned how to enjoy poetry a little better. (Davis, 1997, p. 20)

Lowery (2003) also found that poetry, with its short, concise thoughts, is an excellent way to help students who are at risk of failure learn to read. Poetry can help everyone (even preservice teachers) reflect on themselves and move "beyond those self-reflections to understanding the greater worldview" (p. 51).

Characteristics of Poetry for Young Adults. One essential key to identifying the best poetry to use with young adults is to remember their developmental period. While children are not developmentally "ready" for young adult poetry, adolescents do not usually enjoy children's poetry. While there are always some exceptions, such as the poems of Shel Silverstein and Jack Prelutsky (America's first children's poet laureate), in general, young adult poetry should be evaluated using the criteria listed in Considerations for Selecting Young Adult Literature: *Poetry*.

CONSIDERATIONS FOR
SELECTING YOUNG ADULT LITERATURE POETRY

When selecting poems for young adults, ask the following questions:

_____   Does the poem have meaning for the young adults—can they relate to the topic, setting, theme, and emotion being conveyed?

_____   Does the poem elicit rich sensory images or deep emotional responses that young adults will appreciate or understand?

_____   Does the poem allow adolescents to experience the power of words and to explore how words can elicit certain emotional responses?

_____   Does the poem have vivid imagery and vibrant language?

_____   Will the poem provide pleasure (i.e., can young adults relate to the poetry in some way either as an event or emotion they have experienced or would like to experience)?

Unfortunately, young adults might not like a poem that possesses all these characteristics because, like adults, adolescents have their own individual tastes, likes, and dislikes. Thomas (2001) goes so far as to contend that many contemporary poets who are writing for young adults disempower adolescent readers by writing in traditional ways and encourages adults to look for poems that push the boundaries of poetry by providing highly complex explorations of the feelings, emotions, and experiences of young adults. Thus, you must be sure to expose adolescents to a number of different poems in an attempt to interest as many readers as possible. Charles Simic, the 2007 U.S. poet laureate, explains, "What you do is you bring them [students] poems that are very difficult for any human being who has any imagination or thought processes to resist" (Aronson, 2008, p. 24).

When identifying poetry to use in a classroom or add to a library collection, educators must remember that females and males differ as readers, writers, and critics and bring their own perspectives to poetry, including their expectations for appropriate male and female behavior. To determine the gender messages, including the biases and stereotypes in adolescent poetry and the possible impact of poetry on gender identity, Johnson, McClanahan, and Mertz (1999) examined poetry anthologies for young adults. They identified five (Table 11–1) that "show both females and males as complex human

TABLE 11-1   Five Gender-Balanced Poetry Collections

Duffy, C. A. (Ed.). (1993). *I wouldn't thank you for a valentine: Poems for young feminists.* New York: Holt.

Glenn, M. (1982). *Class dismissed! High school poems by Mel Glenn.* New York: Clarion.

Hirschfelder, A. B., and Singer, B. R. (Eds.). (1992). *Rising voices: Writings of young Native Americans.* New York: Scribner.

Lyne, S. (Ed.). (1983). *Ten-second rainshowers: Poems by young people.* Scarsdale, NY: Bradbury.

Medearis, A. S. (1995). *Skin deep and other teenage reflections: Poems by Angela Shelf Medearis.* New York: Macmillan.

Source: Abstracted from Johnson, A. B., McClanahan, L. G., and Mertz, M. P. (1999). Gender representation in poetry for young adults. *The ALAN Review, 26*(3), 39–44.

beings rather than flat and one-dimensional subjects" and that could be used "in valuable ways to initiate classroom dialogue in an attempt to break various gender stereotypes before the stereotypes become permanent in the minds of adolescents" (p. 39).

Poetry Books for Young Adults. Books of poetry usually take one of three formats: edited anthologies consisting of the poems of a number of poets, collections of poems of one poet, or a single long poem or a group of poems meant to be read from beginning to end. An example of the latter category is Mel Glenn's *Split Image* (2000), the story of a young Asian American girl and the conflicts she faces at home and at school. In contrast, the poems within an anthology are often meant to be shared individually, though the collection as a whole may present a single theme. As poet Nikki Grimes (2000) says, a single poem can be "memorized or sung, or . . . carried in the back pocket of the mind" (p. 33). While you will want to share a number of classic poems with young adults, there are also a number of contemporary poems and collections of poetry that provide poems adolescents will want to carry with them.

Anthologies of poetry. There are a number of excellent collections of young adult poetry, some by adult poets and others by adolescents themselves. Patrice Vecchione has edited several anthologies that should appeal to adolescents, including *Faith and Doubt: An Anthology of Poems* (2007), *The Body Eclectic: An Anthology of Poems* (2002), and *Truth and Lies* (2000). Another anthology compiler is Paul Janeczko, who often combines information about poets with their poetry. His *Seeing the Blue Between: Advice and Inspiration for Young Poets* (2002) is a compilation of letters and poems from 32 poets that provides advice to adolescent writers. Other excellent poetry anthologies by Janeczko include:

- *Poetspeak: In Their Work, about Their Work* (1983)
- *The Music of What Happens: Poems That Tell Stories* (1985)
- *The Place My Words Are Looking For: What Poets Say About and Through Their Work* (1990)
- *Looking for Your Name: A Collection of Contemporary Poems* (1993)
- *Stone Bench in an Empty Park* (2000)
- *Blushing: Expressions of Love in Poems and Letters* (2004)

Adolescents often enjoy poems written by teenage authors. For example, the San Francisco Arts Commission's WritersCorps provides a workshop for young authors. Their yearly volume includes excellent poetry that is sometimes combined with prose or even photography. Some of their more recent volumes include *City of One: Young Writers Speak to the World* (DeDonato, 2004) and *Solid Ground* (Tannenbaum, 2006). *Movin': Teen Poets Take Voice* (2000), edited by Dave Johnson, consists of poems by participants in New York Public Library poetry workshops or teens who submitted their work via the Internet. Esther Pearl Watson and Mark Todd checked teen magazines and combed Internet sites to develop the anthology *The Pain Tree and Other Teenage Angst-Ridden Poetry* (2000). *You Hear Me? Poems and Writings by Teenage Boys* (2000), collected by Betsy Franco, contains expressions of the frank and sometimes raw emotions of adolescent boys. Franco's *Falling Hard: Teenagers on Love* (2008) explores love and romance from a teen's perspective. While boys and girls often appreciate the same type of poetry, there are times when their interests turn in other directions. In *I Wouldn't Thank You for a Valentine: Poems for Young Feminists* (1993), Carol Ann Duffy has collected poems that explore women's issues. In *I Feel a Little Jumpy Around You: Paired Poems by Men & Women* (1996), Naomi Shihab Nye and Paul B. Janeczko present pairs of poems on the same subjects.

Many young adult poetry anthologies incorporate multicultural poetry. Some of the classic collections are *I Am the Darker Brother*, compiled by Arnold Adoff in 1968 and expanded and updated in 1997, and *The Whispering Wind: Poetry by Young American Indians* (1972), edited by Terry Allen. *Pierced by a Ray of Sun: Poems About the Times We Feel Alone* (1995), featuring poems selected by Ruth Gordon, is an international collection that focuses on individual alienation and loneliness. Another favorite that focuses on young adult concerns (e.g., school and the future) is Lori M. Carlson's *Cool Salsa: Bilingual Poems on Growing Up Latino in the United States* (1994), in which she includes poets such as Sandra Cisneros and Gary Soto. Other collections about the Latino experience are *Wáchale! Poetry and Prose about Growing Up Latino in America* (2001), edited by Ilan Stavans, and *The Tree Is Older Than You Are: A Bilingual Gathering of Poems and Stories from Mexico with Paintings by Mexican Artists* (1995), edited by Naomi Shihab Nye. In *Shimmy Shimmy Shimmy Like My Sister Kate: Looking at the Harlem Renaissance Through Poems* (1996), Nikki Giovanni has collected poems that reflect the African American cultural experience in the early twentieth century.

There is no doubt that young adults enjoy a wide range of poetry. In *Light-Gathering Poems* (2000), Liz Rosenberg has produced a collection of classic and contemporary poems from throughout the world, including translations from poets such as Issa, Rilke, and Rumi. David Kherdian goes back to the 1960s and the Beat poets in San Francisco in his *Beat Voices: An Anthology of Beat Poetry* (1995). Other collections to consider are:

- June Cotner, *Teen Sunshine Reflections: Words for the Heart and Soul* (2002)
- Naomi Shihab Nye, *What Have You Lost?* (1999)
- Michael Stipe, *The Haiku Year* (1998)
- Zoe Anglesey, *Listen Up! Spoken Word Poetry* (1999)

Collections of a single poet. While Shel Silverstein, children's poet laureate Jack Prelutsky, and even Dr. Seuss remain favorites with some adolescents, there are a number of poets who write especially for young adults. In addition to his novels in various genres, Paul Fleischman has written several books of poetry that are meant to be read aloud, including *I Am Phoenix: Poems for Two Voices* (1989); *Joyful Noise: Poems for Two Voices* (1988); and *Big Talk: Poems for Four Voices* (2000). Naomi Shihab Nye has written *19 Varieties of Gazelle: Poems of the Middle East* (2002), a collection of her poems about the Middle East and Arab Americans, especially their feelings since September 11, 2001. Selecting works from her adult poems and adding new ones, Pat Mora has produced a collection of free verse poems in *My Own True Name* (2000). In *Remember the Bridge: Poems of a People* (2002), Carole Boston Weatherford combines poetry and history to chronicle African American history and culture. A perennial favorite is poet Arnold Adoff. In addition to compiling collections of the works of other poets, he has written a number of volumes of original work, including *Slow Dance: Heart Break Blues* (1995), *The Basket Counts* (2000), and *Sports Pages* (1986).

A story in poems. A number of authors have written poetic young adult novels by using a series of poems to tell a complete story. In *You Remind Me of You: A Poetry*

Memoir (2002), Eireann Corrigan, a high school student, reflects on her fight against an eating disorder. Although each poem can stand alone, the series presents a picture of the conflicting emotions and pressures teens feel. Another writer who looks at teenage problems through poetry is Sonya Sones. Her *Stop Pretending* (1999) tells the story of a teenager who is trying to cope with her sister's mental breakdown. Expanding Your Knowledge with the Internet provides Internet sites focusing on individual poets as well as young adult poetry in general.

A number of other authors have written stories in poems. In both the Newbery Medal–winning *Out of the Dust* (1997) and *Witness* (2001), Karen Hesse uses free verse to tell very complex tales. *True Believer* (2001) and *Make Lemonade* (1993), Virginia Euwer Wolff's stories of a girl named LaVaughn and her struggle to escape from the housing projects, are also written as free verse poems. Popular author Mel Glenn offers several stories in poetry, including *Class Dismissed! High School Poems* (1982) and his mysteries *Who Killed Mr. Chippendale? A Mystery in Poems* (1996) and *Foreign Exchange: A Mystery in Poems* (1999), as well as *Split Image: A Story in Poems* (2000). Other novels in verse include:

- Robert Cormier, *Frenchtown Summer* (1999)
- Jacqueline Woodson, *Locomotion* (2003)
- Helen Frost, *Keesha's House* (2003)
- Marilyn Nelson, *A Wreath for Emmett Till* (2005)

 EXPANDING YOUR KNOWLEDGE WITH THE INTERNET

You can use a number of Internet sites to expand your knowledge of poetry.

GENERAL INFORMATION

Favorite Poem Project
www.favoritepoem.org/

Poetry a Day for American High Schools
www.loc.gov/poetry/180/

The Poetry Corner—Poetry Definitions
www.english.uga.edu/cdesmet/class/engl4830/work/projects/brent/alphadef.htm

Shadow Poetry—Definitions
www.shadowpoetry.com/resources/wip/types.html

Clickable Poems
www.clickablepoems.com

INDIVIDUAL POETS

Academy of American Poets (includes information on poets)
www.poets.org/

Jack Prelutsky
www.jackprelutsky.com/

Mel Glenn
www.melglenn.com/

Naomi Shihab Nye
http://voices.cla.umn.edu/vg/Bios/entries/nye_naomi_shihab.html

Paul Fleischman
www.paulfleischman.net/

SITES THAT PUBLISH TEEN POETRY

Teen Ink
www.teenink.com/

Poetry by teens
links4teens.blogspot.com/

The Slam (hosted by *Cicada* magazine)
cricketmag.com/activity_display.asp?id=207

Suggestions for Selecting and Using Poetry. According to Georgia Heard (Smith & Zarnowski, 1999), "poetry is about recognizing and paying attention to our inner lives—our memories, hopes, doubts, questions, fears, [and] joys" (p. 66). Why, then, is poetry often a neglected genre? Unfortunately, many preservice teachers and library media specialists tell us that they do not like poetry because they had to analyze it to death in high school or memorize it in elementary school. Rather than focusing on the pleasure that can come from reading a well-crafted poem, these educators remember only the pain they felt when they were forced to dissect a poem. In an interview, Sonya Sones quoted a poem by poet laureate Billy Collins about people who want to "tie the poem to a chair with rope and torture a confession out of it" (Lesesne, 2002, p. 52). Fortunately, there are as many ways to use poetry as there are individual teachers and library media specialists. The key is to determine "what works" for an individual teacher and what young adults seem to enjoy. While some adolescents like to create anthologies, others enjoy writing poetry, performing poetry, or just discussing poems.

A number of excellent resources are available that educators can use to encourage young adults to read, write, and perform poetry. We have already mentioned several of the works of Paul B. Janeczko that incorporate poems with ideas for writing poetry. Another of his books is *How to Write Poetry* (1999). In addition, Kathi Appelt has written two books for budding poets: *Poems from Homeroom: A Writer's Place to Start* (2002) and *Just People & Paper/Pen/Poem: A Young Writer's Way to Begin* (1997). Alan Wolf's *Immersed in Verse: An Informative, Slightly Irreverent & Totally Tremendous Guide to Living the Poet's Life* (2006) is another resource for future poets. For teachers, excellent resources include:

- *Three Voices: An Invitation to Poetry Across the Curriculum* (Cullinan, Scala, and Schroder, 1995)
- *Teaching Poetry in High School* (Somers, 1999)
- *Today You Are My Favorite Poet: Writing Poems with Teenagers* (Hewitt, 1998)
- *Young Adult Poetry: A Survey and Theme Guide* (Schwedt and DeLong, 2002)
- *A Surge of Language: Teaching Poetry Day by Day* (Wormser and Cappella, 2004)
- *Writing in Rhythm: Spoken Word Poetry in Urban Classrooms* (Fisher, 2007)

Collaborating with Other Professionals 11–1 explains how to select poetry to complement a specific subject area.

The following are a few selected strategies to help you use poetry in instruction. We encourage you to consult the original sources for more detailed information.

- Share poems with young adults, but remember that the way you share them can be important. Much but not all poetry is meant to be read aloud. Abrahamson (2002) reported a study that found that adolescents who listened to poems that were read aloud "favored short poems with rhythm and rhyme. Students who read the poems and listened to them at the same time tended to give all poems the lowest ratings" (p. 21). In addition, poems that were serious, or without rhyme or obvious rhythm, scored highest when students read them silently (Abrahamson, 2002).

COLLABORATING WITH OTHER PROFESSIONALS

11-1

Teachers across the curriculum can work with school library media specialists to identify poetry that can be used in specific or even in several curricular areas. While the poems need not be long or difficult, they can set the mood for a unit or a lesson or just provide some humor. Teachers can read the poems aloud to the class or, following copyright guidelines, provide copies of a single poem from an anthology for everyone in the class. For example, social studies teachers might want to explore the poems in *Hour of Freedom: American History in Poetry* (2004), collected by Milton Meltzer, or J. Patrick Lewis's *The Brothers' War: Civil War Voices in Verse* (2007). Mathematics teachers can look at *Math Talk: Mathematical Ideas in Poems for Two Voices* (1991) by Theoni Pappas. *Poems for Teaching in the Content Areas: 75 Powerful Poems to Enhance Your History, Geography, Science, and Math Lessons* (Lewis and Robb, 2007) is another helpful resource.

- Use questions from various critical viewpoints to explore a novel in poetry form. Using Multiple Readings identifies questions from different critical viewpoints that can be used with *What My Girlfirend Doesn't Know* (2007) by Sonya Sones.

- Teach adolescents to read poetry out loud by reading slowly in a normal tone of voice and pausing at the punctuation, rather than at the end of the line. Poetry 180 is a website sponsored by the Library of Congress and presented by Billy Collins, former poet laureate of the United States. The site gives tips on how to read poetry aloud and offers 180 poems that can be shared daily. For more practical suggestions, visit *How to Read a Poem Out Loud* at www.loc.gov/poetry/180/p180-howtoread.html.

- Define poetry. Wendy King (1997) begins her poetry unit by encouraging students to develop a definition of poetry. Students are given excerpts of poetry and prose and asked to decide if the excerpt is poetry or prose. The students later develop a list of characteristics of poetry.

- Immerse students in poetry. Carol Jago (2001) uses the "Goldilocks assignment" to immerse her students in different types of poetry. After browsing a large number of poetry collections on different topics, students are asked to select three types of poems: one too easy, one too hard, and one just right. This activity allowed students to explore poetry and identify what type of poetry they easily comprehend.

- Link poems to a classic novel. Susan Jolley (2002) integrated poetry into the study of *To Kill a Mockingbird* by encouraging students to read poems that enhanced the theme of understanding others. Helping students examine the structure of the assigned poems, she asked them to create couplets or quatrains in their journals.

- Engage in authentic poetry discussions. Students find two poems they like and make four photocopies of each. Then, working in groups of four, the students:

USING MULTIPLE READINGS

The following questions reflect various critical viewpoints for the book *What My Girlfriend Doesn't Know* (2007), by Sonya Sones.

New Criticism
How many different forms (e.g., concrete poetry and comics) are used in the book? Why might the author have chosen to write the book in free verse rather than prose?

Archetypal Criticism
What archetypal images does this novel contain? Consider character types and the overall storyline.

Feminist Criticism
Does the narrator meet your expectations of a young man in love?

Deconstructionist Criticism
Is there anything in the novel that makes you think things are not as they appear? Is Robin a reliable narrator? Are his actions consistent with the type of character he seems to be?

Marxist Criticism
What power struggles are at work in the novel?

1. Discuss one of the poems
2. Take turns reading the poem in various interpretive ways
3. Share general impressions
4. Work individually and take notes on their impressions of the poem
5. Share ideas, making sure each reader has an opportunity to explain her or his personal views
6. Spend 10 to 15 minutes to reach a group consensus about the poem
7. Repeat the process with a different group member's poem (Steineke, 2002)

- Save words from a poem. Allen (2002) taught poetry by having students read a poem and then look for words they wanted to save for their own use. Using a writing workshop approach, students collected words on word walls or living charts. Some categories included (a) words/images that make me smile or laugh; (b) smells, sights, and sounds that bring tears to my eyes; (c) words/phrases that paint a picture; (d) words that make noise; (e) forbidden words; and (f) action words. By collecting words that capture their eyes and ears, adolescents can explore these words and make them part of their speaking and writing vocabularies.

- Write a line. Using familiar models such as William Carlos Williams's poems "This is Just to Say" and "The Red Wheelbarrow," students can write single-sentence poems.

- Create poems. While some students may enjoy writing poems that follow traditional forms such as haiku, sonnets, or cinquains, others might enjoy creating collage poems, found poems, group poems, character poems, riddle poems, raps, poems for two or more voices, or repeat poster poems. Some of these ideas are explained in detail in Bleeker and Bleeker (1996).

11-1 ●●●● **CONNECTING ADOLESCENTS AND THEIR LITERATURE**

Alan Lawrence Sitomer (2006) describes how students can make connections between rap music and classic poetry by selecting songs and poems that share themes. For example, Sitomer's students paired Tupac Shakur's "Me Against the World" with Dylan Thomas's "Do Not Go Gentle into That Good Night." This activity helped students learn elements of poetry while appealing to their interests.

- Create an Internet writer's workshop. Hommel (2003) encourages teachers to create an Internet writer's workshop where students can share their poetry and discuss poems other teens have written.
- Pair classic poetry with rap music. Connecting Adolescents and Their Literature 11–1 explains how to do this.
- Host a poetry jam/slam or spoken word event and display titles such as Nikki Grimes's *Bronx Masquerade* (2001). Connecting Adolescents and Their Literature 11–2 provides information on holding a poetry jam or poetry slam.

11-2 ●●●● **CONNECTING ADOLESCENTS AND THEIR LITERATURE**

Educators can build on the popularity of performance poetry by holding a poetry café or hosting a poetry jam/slam. In *Wham! It's a Poetry Jam: Discovering Performance Poetry* (2002), Sara Holbrook provides teenagers with ideas for poetry competitions, advice on presenting poetry, and suggestions for jamming. For a more formal poetry reading without the competition of a jam/slam, try a poetry celebration or poetry cafe. Cheryl Thomas (2000) reported that her students held one for parents, faculty, staff, and friends and found that the experience was "their finest day of the year" (p. 25). Other poetry slam resources are:

- *Slam* (von Ziegesar, 2000)
- *Slam Poetry Manual* (Bladwin, 2003)
- *The Spoken Word Revolution: Slam, Hip Hop and the Poetry of a New Generation* (Eleveld, 2004)
- *Hewitt's Guide to Slam Poetry and Poetry Slam* (Hewitt, 2005)
- *The Spoken Word Revolution Redux* (Eleveld, 2007)
- There is also information on the Internet at the following sites: www.ala.org/ala/yalsa/teenreading/trw/trw2003/wayscelebrate.htm www.e-poets.net/library/slam/

Drama

Jean Brown and Elaine Stephens (1995) called drama "probably the most neglected field for young adults" (p. 309). Now, a decade later, drama still has not assumed its rightful place in young adult literature. This is unfortunate, because carefully selected drama can provide adolescents with varied language situations, thought-provoking scenarios and dialogue, and considerable enjoyment.

Types of Dramatic Presentation. Educators can use a number of different styles of drama in the classroom, including:

- Oral interpretation (usually a one-person performance of a poem or brief prose passage)
- Story theater (a pantomime accompanied by a narrator who reads or tells the story while others act out the plot)
- Readers' theater (the reading of a script as opposed to acting it out)
- Creative dramatics (the dramatization of a story with an improvised dialogue)
- Role-playing (the actors invent both the dialogue and the action as they proceed) (Russell, 2009)

In addition, a number of short plays and monologues are written especially for young adults. When any of these dramatic forms are presented by enthusiastic teachers and library media specialists and are based on adolescent interests and developmental levels, middle and high school students usually enjoy dramatic activities.

Reasons for Using and Teaching Drama. Young adults are often eager to confront contemporary problems and relevant world issues. Authors and playwrights who are willing to write for adolescent audiences have an excellent opportunity to help young adults consider themes of diversity in race, religion, gender, and class in a way that profoundly affects them (Bontempo, 1995). Harding and Safer (1996) found that watching live theater can help young adults confront contemporary problems such as substance abuse by promoting reflection and stimulating discussion. Drama can transform people by making them think and sometimes by making them feel uncomfortable. However, educators often have to work to help adolescents deal with the feelings of discomfort that a play may cause and to transfer them to their own lives and the decisions they will personally have to make (Gonzalez, 2002). Therefore, when Abramovitz (2000) wanted to foster an appreciation and acceptance of diversity with her high school classes, she used a number of drama techniques such as interpretation sessions, role-playing, and Stanislavskian sensitivity exercises to help adolescents explore their feelings about ethnic conflicts. Abramovitz asked students to imagine they were trapped in a box so they could imagine how oppression feels. This Stanislavskian sensitivity exercise is based on the work of Konstantin Stanislavsky, who developed acting methods that enable cast members to experience the emotions of the characters they portray.

In addition to helping adolescents explore issues and the dilemmas of the human experience, educators can use drama to help secondary students develop their creativity. Another essential purpose of drama should be to help adolescents develop pleasure and skills in reading and interpreting drama, to acquaint students with dramatic traditions so they can evaluate dramatic performances, and to increase students' insights into themselves and others.

Characteristics of Drama for Young Adults. When selecting drama to use with young adults, remember that the key words are *young adults*. Drama that middle and

CONSIDERATIONS FOR
SELECTING YOUNG ADULT LITERATURE DRAMA

Ask the following questions when selecting drama for young adults:

_____   Can young adults relate to the topics or themes (e.g., relationships, struggling for or dealing with increased freedom from significant adults)?

_____   Will young adults be able to understand the language and communication, both verbal and nonverbal, and are these similar to their own?

_____   Will the drama provide real pleasure for young adults? Unlike the first item in this list, this item suggests that young adults can actually experience pleasure from either watching or participating in the drama.

_____   Is the drama cognitively appropriate in content and action, neither so low-level that young adults consider it "elementary" nor too advanced for young adults' thinking capacity?

secondary students enjoy and appreciate is usually different from drama for young children and older adults. While the playwright might not have had young adults specifically in mind, his or her drama still must appeal to young adults. Considerations for Selecting Young Adult Literature: *Drama* lists questions when selecting drama for young adults.

Drama for Young Adults.   Dramas for adolescents can take several forms. In addition to actual plays and monologues, there are also novels that are written or adapted as dramas or screenplays and poems that are meant to be performed.

There are several excellent anthologies of plays for young adults. In *Center Stage* (1990), Don Gallo has compiled short plays by young adult authors such as Walter Dean Myers and Susan Beth Pfeffer. Wendy Lamb has collected winning plays from the Young Playwrights Festival, which is sponsored by the Foundation of the Dramatist Guild, in several anthologies, including *Ten Out of Ten: Winning Plays from YPF 1* (1992) and *Ground Zero Club* (1987). Norma Bowles and Mark E. Rosenthal edited *Cootie Shots: Theatrical Inoculations Against Bigotry for Kids, Parents and Teachers* (2001), a collection of plays created by Fringe Benefits, a Los Angeles–based theatrical company. Other anthologies of dramas are:

- *Great Scenes for Young Actors* (Slaight and Sharrar, 1991)
- *Short Plays for Young Actors* (Slaight and Sharrar, 1996)
- *International Plays for Young Audiences: Contemporary Works from Leading Playwrights* (Ellis, 2000)
- *New Audition Scenes from Contemporary Playwrights: The Best New Cuttings from Around the World* (Ellis, 2005)
- *Thirty Short Comedy Plays for Teens: Plays for a Variety of Cast Sizes* (Allen, 2007)

Several authors have issued collections of their own plays for young adults. *Most Valuable Player and Four Other All-Star Plays for Middle and High School Audiences* (1999), by internationally known playwright Mary Hall Surface, contains scripts that

from Page to Screen

POETRY, DRAMA, AND SHORT STORIES

These film adaptations are particularly appropriate for adolescents. Consider comparing the film with the text of the original play and consider each medium's strengths and weaknesses in terms of the individual tale.

DRIVING MISS DAISY
★★★ | 1989 | PG

Alfred Uhry adapted his own Pulitzer Prize–winning stage play for the screen in this comedy–drama about aging, race relations, and friendship.

VANYA ON 42ND STREET
★★★★ | 1994 | PG

The film is an adaptation of David Mamet's play, which follows an actress (Julianne Moore) preparing to perform the Chekov play Uncle Vanya off Broadway. Exceptional writing and a luminous cast bring the film to life.

A RAISIN IN THE SUN
★★★ | 2008 | PG

This latest adaptation of A Raisin in the Sun (1957), written by Lorraine Hansberry, is directed by Kenny Leon.

ROMEO + JULIET
★★★★ | 1996 | PG-13

Retaining the original dialogue, director Baz Luhrman's dizzying, hip reimagining of Shakespeare's classic tale of star-crossed lovers is a surprisingly worthwhile adaptation.

focus on contemporary social issues. In *Nerdlandia* (1999), Gary Soto explores relationships in the Los Angeles barrio. In *Perspectives: Relevant Scenes for Teens* (1997), Mary Krell-Oishi provides short scenes that explore the range of teen emotions.

In other chapters, we have discussed realistic and historical fiction. Some of these books are written in the form of a play, including Paul Fleischman's *Seek* (2001) and *Mind's Eye* (1999), Walter Dean Myers's *Monster* (1999), and Julius Lester's *Day of Tears: A Novel in Dialogue* (2005). A popular young adult novel by Avi has been adapted into a play by Ronn Smith as *Nothing but the Truth: A Play* (1997).

Adolescents can also create drama through poetry. Some short poems with strong emotional themes are actually minidramas, often written in dialogue form, that are suitable for dramatization. While these poems may be found in a number of different anthologies, Paul Fleischman has created three volumes of poetry, *I Am Phoenix: Poems for Two Voices* (1989), *Joyful Noise; Poems for Two Voices* (1988), and *Big Talk: Poems for Four Voices* (2000), designed to be performed. Gasparro and Falletta (1994) have suggested that teachers of English as a second language could especially benefit from a multisensory approach because the dramatization of poetry is a powerful tool in stimulating learning. Many plays have been released as films. From Page to Screen lists a few of them.

Suggestions for Selecting and Using Drama. We have already mentioned a number of excellent anthologies and collections of plays as well as some complete plays. In addition, the Internet provides many resources that can help teachers and library media specialists select and use drama in schools. Expanding Your Knowledge with the Internet features a list of some of these sources.

EXPANDING YOUR KNOWLEDGE WITH THE INTERNET

A number of Internet sites have information about drama for young adults, including the following.

Theatre Education Database (from Brigham Young University)
tedb.byu.edu

Creative Dramatics
www.kmrscripts.com/cdguide.html

Philadelphia Young Playwrights
www.phillyyoungplaywrights.org

Drama Teacher's Resource Guide
www.msu.edu/~caplan/drama/resources.html

Scribbling Women—dramatization of stories by Amerian women writers
www.scribblingwomen.org

Outstanding Books for the College Bound: Drama
www.ala.org/ala/yalsa/booklistsawards/ outstandingbooks/dramaoutstanding.htm

Annual Nationwide Blank Theatre Company Young Playwrights Festival
www.youngplaywrights.com

Philadelphia Young Playwrights
www.phillyyoungplaywrights.org

Coterie's Young Playwrights Roundtable
www.thecoterie.com/YPL.htm

Delaware Young Playwrights Festival
www.delawaretheatre.com/education/ contentYPF2008.html

Earlier in this chapter we mentioned several reasons to use drama with young adults. Barbara T. Bontempo (1995) encourages teachers and young adults to explore prejudice through drama and role-playing. Other suggestions for using drama with young adults include the following:

- Integrate drama into subjects throughout the curriculum. Collaborating with Other Professionals 11–2 recommends the use of readers' theater to achieve this.

- After a dramatic performance, build on the play by asking students to:
    1. Write a short review of the play
    2. Discuss or write about the relationship of the theme of the play to contemporary life
    3. Write an alternative ending to the play
    4. Debate an issue presented in the play

11-2

COLLABORATING WITH OTHER PROFESSIONALS

You can identify short dramas that can be used throughout the curriculum to make subjects and concepts more meaningful and to encourage adolescents to develop their oral and physical communication skills. One excellent starting point is *Readers Theatre for American History* (2001) by Anthony D. Fredericks. Other helpful resources include *Born Storytellers:*

Readers Theatre Celebrates the Lives and Literature of Classic Authors (2005), by Ann N. Black, and *African Legends, Myths, and Folktales for Readers Theatre* (2008), by Anthony D. Fredericks. Working together, English and social studies teachers could use some of the scripts in this collection to help young adults explore historical events.

11-3 •••• CONNECTING ADOLESCENTS AND THEIR LITERATURE

Athletes are not the only ones who can perform in school activities. Many young adults welcome the opportunity to demonstrate their dramatic abilities. We have already suggested holding a poetry slam. This can be expanded to include the presentation of monologues and short dramatic scenes as well. A number of resources listed in the Young Adult Books section at the end of this chapter can serve as resources, including:

- *Acting Natural: Monologs, Dialogs, and Playlets for Teens* (Kehret, 1991)
- *Forensics Series, Duo Practice and Competition*, vol. 1 (Lhota and Milstein, 2003a)
- *Forensics Series, Duo Practice and Competition*, vol. 2 (Lhota and Milstein, 2003b)
- *Twenty 10-Minute Plays for Teens by Teens*, vol. 3 (Lamedman, 2006)
- *More Short Scenes and Monologues for Middle School Students Inspired by Literature, Social Studies, and Real Life* (Surface, 2007)

- Take a scene from a young adult novel and turn it into a dramatic presentation through Readers' theater, role-playing, or script writing.
- Encourage young adults to develop their creative talents by performing short plays. Connecting Adolescents and Their Literature 11–3 suggests one way to do this.
- Use monologues and dialogues in speech classes to develop oral presentation skills.
- Encourage students to participate in a national, state, or local young playwrights festival or organize a festival in your own school division.
- Work with other teachers to develop a drama workshop in your school to provide a place for adolescents who want to perform plays and who want to write them.
- Build on successful workshops such as the Bonderman (Newman, 2003), which was developed to support new playwrights.
- Build on the living newspaper format and use research, play design, scriptwriting, presentation, and puppets to present plays that articulate significant social studies issues (Chilcoat, 1996).

Short Stories

> A short story is, in some ways, like a photograph—a captured moment of time that is crystalline, though sometimes mysterious; arresting, though perhaps delicate. But while a photo may or may not suggest consequences, a short story always does. In the story's moment of time something important, something irrevocable has occurred. The change may be subtle or obvious, but it is definite and definitive. (Singer, 2000, p. 12)

Since the publication of Don Gallo's groundbreaking short story collection *Sixteen: Short Stories by Outstanding Writers for Young Adults* (1984), there has been a relative

EXPANDING YOUR KNOWLEDGE WITH THE INTERNET

These are a few of the many Internet sites that provide information about short stories for young adults.

Popular Paperbacks for Young Adults—Short Takes
www.ala.org/ala/yalsa/booklistsawards/
popularpaperback/2000popularpaperbacks.cfm

The Elements of the Short Story from the Yale–New Haven Teachers Institute
www.cis.yale.edu/ynhti/curriculum/units/1983/3/
83.03.09.x.html

A Chronology of the American Short Story
titan.iwu.edu/~jplath/sschron.html

Twenty Great American Short Stories (classics, not Young Adult)
www.americanliterature.com/SS/SSINDX.HTML

Literature: What Makes a Good Short Story?
learner.org/exhibits/literature/index.html

explosion in the number of quality short stories and short story collections written for young adults. Adolescents have welcomed this, shown their appreciation for short stories, and turned to reading short stories instead of or in addition to young adult novels. Because of their length, many short stories can be read in one sitting, often while waiting for class or for a friend. Through short stories, some young adults have been introduced to popular authors and have gone on to read complete novels by these writers. Expanding Your Knowledge with the Internet lists Internet sites that provide helpful information on short stories for young adults.

Types of Short Stories. Emerging as a distinct literary form in the nineteenth century, the short story's popularity was spurred by the tales of Edgar Allan Poe, especially his *Tales of the Grotesque and Arabesque*. In general, short stories are found in the same genres as novels: fantasy, science fiction, horror, historical and contemporary realism, adventure, mystery, and humor. A short story differs from a novel, in that the short story focuses on a single episode or scene with a limited number of characters. In a way, a short story is similar to the episodic plot found in chapter books for beginning readers where each chapter can almost stand on its own. In the short story, however, the entire plot must stand on its own, with the author using a concise setting, an economy of narration, and quickly developed characters.

Most frequently, short stories for young adults are collected into anthologies. The collection may contain works by a single author or by a number of individuals. Sometimes there is a connecting theme; in other cases, the connecting factor is that the stories are all written for young adults. According to editor Sharyn November,

> a short story collection is the literary equivalent of a Whitman's Sampler. The reader pokes around to see what's interesting—reads some stories the way you'd snap up the truffle or caramel, flips past others the way you'd put back the bad mint coconut swirl. (Singer, 2000, p. 13)

Reasons for Using and Teaching Short Stories. With the number of excellent short story collections currently available, a number of reasons exist to include short stories in the curriculum. Many teachers have found that using short stories for required reading helps students with a variety of reading and comprehension abilities. In addition, with their short length and quickly moving plot, short stories can also capture the attention of young adult readers. Finally, while young adults sometimes read short stories written for other age groups, especially short stories written for adults, many authors of short stories for adolescents deal with issues and concerns to which this age group can relate. Rather than just suggesting short stories on the basis of their long literary standing, educators and library media specialists who carefully select young adult short stories make a valuable contribution.

Characteristics of Short Stories for Young Adults.   What attributes or characteristics make a good short story for young adults? What kind of short story do young adults want? What separates the good from the mediocre? Like a novel, a short story must have a plot structure that provides the reader with an introduction, development, and conclusion and a character (or characters) who works through a conflict in less than 10,000 (sometimes less than 5,000) words. According to editor Sharyn November, a short story is

> bite-sized. Like good chocolate, it's intense. It's long enough to make you care about the characters—but it resolves in a way that's satisfying, rather than seeming unfinished or overdone. (Singer, 2000, p. 13)

Short stories should have "clarity and directness of vision, with no wasted words, no throwaway sentences" (Pearl, 2002, p. 31). While a novel is completeness, a short story is intensity. Considerations for Selecting Young Adult Literature: *Short Stories* provides several questions you can ask when selecting short stories young adults might enjoy.

When selecting short stories, educators also need to keep in mind the needs of both proficient and reluctant readers and try to find a balance between a reading level that challenges advanced readers and one that is appropriate for less accomplished

CONSIDERATIONS FOR SELECTING YOUNG ADULT LITERATURE SHORT STORIES

When selecting short stories for young adults, ask the following questions:

_____   Was the short story written specifically *for* young adult readers?

_____   Will the themes interest young adult readers? Will the young adult enjoy and want to continue reading the short story?

_____   Is the plot believable, interesting, and sufficiently fast-paced to hold readers' attention? Does it seem contrived or artificial in places?

_____   Is the characterization developed and free of racial, gender, social class, and other stereotypes?

_____   Is the length appropriate for young adults' attention spans?

_____   Is the setting appropriate and one with which young adults can relate?

_____   Will the short story contribute to integrated curricular approaches? Can the story be related to issues examined in a particular curricular area such as science or history?

readers. Connecting Adolescents and Their Literature 11–4 suggests the use of short story collections to appeal to a wide variety of readers, including those who have less than average reading skills or who simply do not enjoy reading.

11-4 • • • •   CONNECTING ADOLESCENTS AND THEIR LITERATURE

"Do we have to read the whole book?" While that question can come from an adolescent who feels pressured to find the time to read an entire novel, it can also come from a student who finds reading a book academically challenging. One advantage of short stories is that a complete story can often be read in a single sitting and may be more intellectually accessible for some students. Teachers and library media specialists can work collaboratively to compile a reading list of short stories (and the collection each can be found in) that includes:

- Stories for students who lack reading skills
- Stories for students who simply do not like to read
- Stories that vary in theme or subject

Provide a way for young adults to share what they read—this does not have to be the traditional book report, but some means of response that might motivate other readers.

Short Story Collections for Young Adults. There are several excellent collections for young adults. As with poetry, some of these are by a single author, while others feature stories by a number of the best young adult writers. Often the collections are centered around a single theme or contain stories in a specific literary genre.

Don Gallo is credited with creating and popularizing the young adult short story anthology that was more than a collection selected from adult short stories. His *Sixteen* (1984) is a collection of original short stories from popular young adult authors such as Richard Peck, Robert Cormier, and Bette Greene. Subsequent volumes have continued that emphasis, with authors such as Ellen Wittlinger, Bruce Brooks, and Chris Lynch. While some of his collections, such as *Visions* (1987) and *Connections* (1989) were eclectic, other anthologies, such as *Time Capsule* (1999), *Destination Unexpected* (2003), *On the Fringe* (2001), and *No Easy Answers* (1997), have focused on specific themes, such as tough choices for teens, adolescent outsiders, and transforming journeys.

With the popularity of fantasy, horror, and science fiction, it is not surprising that a number of recommended short story collections feature these genres. In *Firebirds: An Anthology of Original Fantasy and Science Fiction* (2003), Sharyn November collected stories by authors such as Megan Whalen Turner, Garth Nix, Nancy Farmer, and Lloyd Alexander. Other similar collections include *On the Edge: Stories at the Brink* (2000), *Trapped! Cages of Mind and Body* (1998), and *Night Terrors: Stories of Shadow and Substance* (1996), all edited by Lois Duncan; *Tomorrowland: Ten Stories about the Future* (1999), edited by Michael Cart; *Being Dead* (2001), edited by Vivian Vande Velde; and *The Restless Dead: Ten Original Stories of the Supernatural* (2007), edited by Deborah Noyes.

Some collections are centered around the theme of growing up in a multicultural world. Lori Carlson has collected tales of Asian Americans in *American Eyes: New Asian*

American Short Stories for Young Adults (1994) and of Native Americans in *Moccasin Thunder: American Indian Stories for Today* (2005). Paul Yee created 10 ghost stories related to the experiences of early Chinese immigrants in *Dead Man's Gold and Other Stories* (2002). Other anthologies include *Mixed: An Anthology of Short Fiction on the Multiracial Experience* (2006), edited by Chandra Prasad; *Half and Half: Writers on Growing Up Biracial and Bicultural* (1998), edited by Claudine Chiawei O'Hearn; and *America Street: A Multicultural Anthology of Stories* (1993), collected by Anne Mazer. Walter Dean Myers tells of the people who live in Harlem in *145th Street Stories* (2000) and *What They Found: Love on 145th Street* (2007). Gary Soto writes of life in the barrio in *Petty Crimes* (1998). Graham Salisbury takes readers to Hawaii in *Island Boyz* (2002). David Rice goes to the Rio Grande Valley in Texas in *Crazy Loco: Stories* (2001).

Girls are the target audience for some collections of short stories. In *No Missing Parts: And Other Stories About Real Princesses* (2003), Anne Carter has collected stories of girls who struggle to overcome adversity and to understand their place in life. Other collections for girls include *Stay True: Short Stories for Strong Girls* (1998), collected by Marilyn Singer; *Small Avalanches and Other Stories* (2004), by Joyce Carol Oates; and *Who am I Without Him? Short Stories about Girls and the Boys in Their Lives* (2005), by Sharon G. Flake.

Other collections focus on the problems both boys and girls face as they mature. Coretta Scott King Award–winning author Angela Johnson has written *Gone from Home* (1998), which contains 12 stories about the pressures and pains of growing up. James Howe has collected stories about the emotional life of adolescents in *Color of Absence: 12 Stories About Loss and Hope* (2001) and *13: Thirteen Stories That Capture the Agony and Ecstasy of Being Thirteen* (2006). *Sixteen: Stories About That Sweet and Bitter Birthday* (McCafferty, 2004) and *21 Proms* (Levithan & Ehrenhaft, 2007) are collections about important milestones for young adults.

A number of other subjects and themes appear in story collections. Sports stories range from the classic *Athletic Shorts* (1991), by Chris Crutcher, to *And Nobody Got Hurt 2!: The World's Weirdest, Wackiest Most Amazing True Sports Stories* (2007), a collection by Len Berman. Judy Blume collected short stories from authors who have felt the pressures of censorship, such as David Klass and Katherine Paterson, in *Places I Never Meant to Be* (1999). *Hear Us Out! Lesbian and Gay Stories of Struggle, Progress, and Hope, 1950 to the Present* (2007) is a collection of stories edited by Nancy Garden about what it has meant to be gay and lesbian in different eras. Finally, in *Shattered: Stories of Children and War* (2002), Jennifer Armstrong collected stories of young people living during times of war.

Suggestions for Selecting and Using Short Stories. Short stories should be selected with the same care and skills you use to select any quality literature for young adults. In fact, you can apply the criteria for each genre discussed in this book when selecting short stories in that genre. You can also apply some of the same ideas for using genre novels to using short stories. With teaching methods that reflect young adults' interests as well as their developmental, reading, and motivational levels, both teachers and library media specialists can enrich the curriculum with well-selected short stories. Short stories can be used to study the elements of fiction writing, including plot, characterization, setting, and themes; as the basis for literature discussions; and to practice reading skills, by using previewing, during-reading, and postreading activities.

COLLABORATING WITH OTHER PROFESSIONALS

11-3

To encourage students to read short stories for pleasure, a high school English teacher and a library media specialist worked together on a short story unit.

- Together they selected short story anthologies from the school library collection that had interesting covers, compelling titles, or topics or themes in which young adults are interested.
- The teacher developed a worksheet that focused on the elements of a short story the

students had been studying and encouraged students to select a story to read on their own.

- The class visited the library, selected stories of their choice, and used the Internet to find information about other books or story collections by the same author.
- Finally, the students completed a brief evaluation of the stories they selected. ("The short of it," 2000)

Suggestions for Collaborative Efforts 11–3 illustrates how a teacher and library media specialist can collaborate to encourage students to read short stories.

Concluding Thoughts

Carefully selected poetry, drama, and short stories can capture the interest of young adults, especially when educators and library media specialists collaboratively select works that young adults deem relevant. With the amount of quality literature available today, young adults are fortunate that they can enjoy collections and anthologies of poetry, drama, and short stories that include more literature written by women and authors of culturally diverse backgrounds, and literature that caters to their interests in romance, conflicts with parents and other adults, and contemporary issues. However, the challenge still remains for educators to introduce young adults to appropriate poetry, drama, and short stories that will interest them and, whenever possible, to integrate these three types of literature into the various curricular areas in a way that allows adolescents to see new and unique perspectives. When educators and library media specialists succeed in meeting these challenges, young adults will be the beneficiaries.

Young Adult Books

This section includes young adult titles mentioned in this chapter.

POETRY

Adoff, A. (1986). *Sports pages*. New York: Lippincott. Here are poems about the feelings and experiences adolescents find in sports.

Adoff, A. (1995). *Slow dance: Heart break blues*. New York: Lothrop Lee & Shephard. Here are poems for contemporary, urban teens.

Adoff, A. (1997). *I am the darker brother: An anthology of modern poems by African Americans*. New York: Aladdin. This is an updated collection of the 1968 edition with 21 new poems.

Adoff, A. (2000). *The basket counts.* New York: Simon & Schuster. Basketball takes center court in this collection.

Allen, T. (Ed.). (1972). *The whispering wind: Poetry by young American Indians.* Garden City, NY: Doubleday. A classic collection of poems by adolescents.

Anglesey, Z. (1999). *Listen up! Spoken word poetry.* New York: One World. A collection of poems that are designed to be used in performance.

Appelt, K. (1997). *Just people & paper/pen/poem: A young writer's way to begin.* Houston: Absey. A book of poems and ideas for young writers.

Appelt, K. (2002). *Poems from homeroom: A writer's place to start.* New York: Holt. Appelt matches the writing process to familiar school places such as study hall and homeroom.

Carlson, L. M. (1994). *Cool salsa: Bilingual poems on growing up Latino in the United States.* New York: Holt. Carlson's poems are for all adolescents.

Cormier, R. (1999). *Frenchtown summer.* New York: Delacorte. In free verse, Cormier tells of a 12-year-old boy in the summer of 1938.

Corrigan, E. (2002). *You remind me of you: A poetry memoir.* New York: Plush. These are autobiographical poems about a teen's battle with eating disorders.

Cotner, J. (Ed.). (2002). *Teen sunshine reflections: Words for the heart and soul.* New York: HarperCollins. This is an interfaith collection of poems and quotations.

DeDonato, C. (Ed.). (2004). *City of one: Young writers speak to the world.* San Francisco: Aunt Lute. Young adults express concerns about social issues.

Duffy, C. A. (Ed.). (1993). *I wouldn't thank you for a valentine: Poems for young feminists.* New York: Holt. Women from different cultures share their feelings and their fears.

Fleischman, P. (1988). *Joyful noise; Poems for two voices.* New York: HarperCollins. The 1989 Newbery Medal winner.

Fleischman, P. (1989). *I am Phoenix: Poems for two voices.* New York: HarperTrophy. Fleischman's poems celebrate birds.

Fleischman, P. (2000). *Big talk: Poems for four voices.* Cambridge, MA: Candlewick. These color-coded poems cover a range of topics and emotions.

Franco, B. (Ed.). (2000). *You hear me? Poems and writings by teenage boys.* Cambridge, MA: Candlewick. This is a no-holds-barred collection of poems.

Franco, B. (Ed.). (2008). *Falling hard: Teenagers on love.* Cambridge, MA: Candlewick. Poems about love written by young adults.

Frost, H. (2003). *Keesha's house.* New York: Frances Foster Books. Teen voices describe the problems that caused them to leave home.

Giovani, N. (Ed.). (1996). *Shimmy shimmy shimmy like my sister Kate: Looking at the Harlem Renaissance through poems.* New York: Holt. Giovanni includes poems by many of the writers of the Harlem Renaissance.

Glenn, M. (1982). *Class dismissed!: High school poems.* Poems about experiences in high school. New York: Houghton Mifflin.

Glenn, M. (1996). *Who killed Mr. Chippendale? A mystery in poems.* New York: Lodestar. Poems tell the story when a high school teacher is shot.

Glenn, M. (1999). *Foreign exchange: A mystery in poems.* New York: Morrow. It is easy to blame the visitors when a young girl is killed.

Glenn, M. (2000). *Split image: A story in poems.* New York: Morrow. Is Laura Li really as perfect as she seems?

Gordon, R. (1995). *Pierced by a ray of sun: Poems about the times we feel alone.* New York: HarperCollins. An international anthology of poems.

Grimes, N. (2001). *Bronx masquerade.* New York: Dial. The protagonist ignites his schoolmates' interest in poetry slams.

Hesse, K. (1997). *Out of the dust.* New York: Scholastic. Billie Jo uses poems to tell of her family's life in the Great Depression.

Hesse, K. (2001). *Witness.* New York: Scholastic. Poems tell the story of when the Ku Klux Klan comes to Vermont.

Hirschfelder, A. B., and Singer, B. R. (Eds.). (1992). *Rising voices: Writings of young native Americans.* New York: Scribner's.

Holbrook, S. (2002). *Wham! It's a poetry jam: Discovering performance poetry.* Honesdale, PA: Boyds Mills. Holbrook turns teens on to the world of performance poetry.

Janeczko, P. (1983). *Poetspeak: In their work, about their work.* New York: Macmillan. A collection of 148 poems by modern writers.

Janeczko, P. (1985). *The music of what happens: Poems that tell stories*. New York: Orchard. A collection of thought-provoking poems.

Janeczko, P. (1990). *The place my words are looking for: What poets say about and through their work*. New York: Macmillan. Thirty-nine American poets share their poems and memories.

Janeczko, P. (Ed.). (1993). *Looking for your name: A collection of contemporary poems*. New York: Orchard. Contemporary poets are featured in this collection.

Janeczko, P. (1999). *How to write poetry*. New York: Scholastic. This is an excellent guide to writing poetry.

Janeczko, P. (Ed.). (2000). *Stone bench in an empty park*. New York: Orchard. Haiku goes to the city in this modern collection in a traditional form.

Janeczko, P. (Ed.). (2002). *Seeing the blue between: Advice and inspiration for young poets*. Cambridge, MA: Candlewick. Thirty-two poets provide poems and letters explaining their craft and giving advice to aspiring writers.

Janeczko, P. (Ed.). (2004). *Blushing: Expressions of love in poems and letters*. New York: Orchard. Janeczko goes beyond the usual romantic poems in this collection.

Johnson, D. (2000). *Movin': Teen poets take voice*. New York: Orchard. This anthology contains the work of poets who participated in a New York Public Library workshop.

Kherdian, D. (1995). *Beat voices: An anthology of beat poetry*. New York: Holt. Both East and West Coast poets are represented in this collection.

Lewis, J. P. (2007). *The brothers' war: Civil War voices in verse*. Washington, DC: National Geographic. Explores the difficult reality of family members fighting on opposite sides of the war.

Lyne, S. (Ed.). (1983). *Ten-second rainshowers: Poems by young people*. Scarsdale, NY: Bradbury.

Medearis, A. S. (1995). *Skin deep and other teenage reflections: Poems by Angela Shelf Medearis*. New York: Macmillan. This is a collection of poems about the problems of being a teenager.

Meltzer, M. (Ed.). (2004). *Hour of freedom: American history in poetry*. Honesdale, PA: Boyds Mills. The major events in U.S. history reflected in 59 poems.

Mora, P. (2000). *My own true name*. Houston: Pinata Books. Although many of the poems reflect Mora's experience as a Latina in the Southwest, this collection will appeal to a wide range of adolescents.

Nelson, M. (2005). *A wreath for Emmett Till*. New York: Houghton Mifflin. Sonnets are used to tell the story of Till's brutal murder in 1955. Another book by Nelson is *The Freedom Business: Including a Narrative of the Life & Adventures of Venture, a Native of Africa* (2008).

Nye, N. S. (Ed.). (1995). *The tree is older than you are: A bilingual gathering of poems and stories from Mexico with paintings by Mexican artists*. New York: Simon & Schuster. Paintings by contemporary artists enrich this collection of translated poems.

Nye, N. S. (Ed.). (1999). *What have you lost?* New York: Greenwillow. From a lost memory to a lost friendship, these poems look at a range of experiences.

Nye, N. S. (2002). *19 varieties of gazelle: Poems of the Middle East*. New York: Greenwillow. Nye explores the emotions of Arab Americans. See also *Honeybee* (2008).

Nye, N. S., and Janeczko, P. B. (1996). *I feel a little jumpy around you: Paired poems by men & women*. New York: Simon Pulse. These poems share the views of both men and women on the same subject.

Pappas, T. (1991). *Math talk: Mathematical ideas in poems for two voices*. San Carlos, CA: Wide World Pub Tetra. From circles and fractions to Fibonacci numbers and tessellations, here are poems to share.

Rosenberg, L. (Ed.). (2000). *Light-gathering poems*. New York: Holt. Biographical sketches accompany the poems in this collection of contemporary and classic poetry.

Sones, S. (1999). *Stop pretending: What happened when my big sister went crazy*. New York: HarperCollins. How do you cope when your sister has a mental breakdown?

Sones, S. (2007). *What my girlfriend doesn't know*. New York: Simon & Schuster. Unpopular Robin Murphy begins dating beautiful Sophie.

Stavans, I. (Ed.). (2001). *Wáchale! Poetry and prose about growing up Latino in America*. Chicago: Cricket Books. From a Christmas poem to the verses of José Martí, this book explores the Latino culture.

Stipe, M. (1998). *The Haiku year*. New York: Soft Skull. A collection of haiku poems.

Tannenbaum, J. (Ed.). (2006). *Solid ground.* San Francisco: Aunt Lute. Poems commemorate the San Francisco earthquake of 1906.

Vecchione, P. (Ed.). (2000). *Truth and lies.* New York: Holt. This collection includes biographic notes and suggested readings along with a variety of poems.

Vecchione, P. (Ed.). (2002). *The body eclectic: An anthology of poems.* New York: Holt. Ruth Schwartz, Reginald Gibbons, and Li-Young Lee are some of the poets in this anthology that celebrates the body. Another collection by Vecchione is *Whisper and Shout* (2002).

Vecchione, P. (Ed.). (2007). *Faith and doubt: An anthology of poems.* New York: Holt. Poems explore notions of faith and doubt during different circumstances.

von Ziegesar, C. (Ed.). (2000). *Slam.* New York: Penguin Putnam. Ideas and poems pack this book of contemporary poetry.

Watson, E. P., and Todd, M. (Eds.). (2000). *The pain tree and other teenage angst-ridden poetry.* Boston: Houghton Mifflin. In 25 poems, young adults consider the problems of growing up.

Weatherford, C. B. (2002). *Remember the bridge: Poems of a people.* New York: Philomel. Poems complement a photo-essay on African American history. Another book by Weatherford is *Becoming Billie Holiday* (2008).

Wolf, A. (2006). *Immersed in verse: An informative, slightly irreverent & totally tremendous guide to living the poet's life.* New York: Sterling. Wolf gives advice to aspiring poets and includes poems from a variety of writers.

Wolff, V. E. (1993). *Make lemonade.* New York: Holt. LaVaughn sees the stress of being a teenage single parent when she babysits for Jolly.

Wolff, V. E. (2001). *True believer.* New York: Atheneum. LaVaughn has a crush on Jody, but Jody's feelings are for someone else.

Woodson, J. (2003). *Locomotion.* New York: Putnam. Lonnie discovers poetry as he reflects on the tragedies in his life.

DRAMA

Allen, L. (2007). *Thirty short comedy plays for teens: Plays for a variety of cast sizes.* Colorado Springs, CO: Meriwether. These plays, designed for four to six actors, are about realistic situations teenagers encounter. Also see *Sixty Comedy Duet Scenes for Teens: Real Life Situations for Laughter* (2008).

Bowles, N., and Rosenthal, M. E. (Eds.). (2001). *Cootie shots: Theatrical inoculations against bigotry for kids, parents and teachers.* New York: Theatre Communications Group. Each play, poem, or song in this collection focuses on tolerance and overcoming bigotry.

Ellis, R. (Ed.). (2000). *International plays for young audiences: Contemporary works from leading playwrights.* Colorado Springs, CO: Meriwether. These timely, sometimes edgy, dramas feature young characters. Another collection is *New International Plays for Young Audiences* (2002).

Ellis, R. (Ed.). (2005). *New audition scenes from contemporary playwrights: The best new cuttings from around the world.* Colorado Springs, CO: Meriwether. A collection of scenes and monologs from contemporary plays.

Fleischman, P. (1988). *Joyful noise: Poems for two voices.* New York: HarperCollins. Here are more poems that can be dramatized.

Fleischman, P. (1989). *I am Phoenix: Poems for two voices.* New York: HarperTrophy. Fleischman's poems are meant to be performed.

Fleischman, P. (1999). *Mind's eye.* New York: Holt. Courtney, 16 and a paraplegic, and Elva, 88 and losing her sight, are roommates in a nursing home.

Fleischman, P. (2000). *Big talk: Poems for four voices.* Cambridge, MA: Candlewick. Four people can perform these poems.

Fleischman, P. (2001). *Seek.* Chicago: Cricket Books. Radio sound bits and snippets of conversations create this interesting dramatic novel that includes instructions for performance.

Gallo, D. (Ed.). (1990). *Center stage.* New York: HarperCollins. A collection of 10 one-act plays.

Kehret, P. (1991). *Acting natural: Monologs, dialogs, and playlets for teens.* Colorado Springs, CO: Meriwether. These short scripts require no special props or costumes.

Krell-Oishi, M. (1997). *Perspectives: Relevant scenes for teens.* Colorado Springs, CO: Meriwether. From dating and teen pregnancy to family relationships and the problems of growing up, these short scenes explore adolescent life. Krell-Oishi has also written *Scenes That Happen* (1991).

Lamb, W. (Ed.). (1987). *Ground zero club.* New York: Laurel Leaf. These six plays were written by dramatists under the age of 19 for the Young Playwrights Festival.

Lamb, W. (Ed.). (1992). *Ten out of ten: Winning plays from YPF 1.* New York: Delacorte. More plays from the Young Playwrights Festival.

Lamedman, D. (Ed.). (2006). *Twenty 10-minute plays for teens by teens,* vol. 3. Lyme, NH: Smith & Kraus. A collection of plays by teen playwrights. Other volumes include *Twenty 10-Minute Plays For Teens,* vol. 1 (2004) and *Twenty 10-Minute Plays For Teens,* vol. 2 (2005).

Lester, J. (2005). *Day of tears: A novel in dialogue.* New York: Hyperion. A cast of characters describe how their lives were changed after over 400 slaves were sold from a Georgia plantation.

Lhota, B., and Milstein, J. B. (2003a). *Forensics series, Duo practice and competition: Thirty-five 8–10 minute original comedic plays,* vol. 1(young actors series). Hanover, NH: Smith & Kraus. This is a collection of short scripts for two actors.

Lhota, B., and Milstein, J. B. (2003b). *Forensics series duo practice and competition,* vol. 2. *Thirty-five 8–10 minute original dramatic scenes.* Hanover, NH: Smith & Kraus. This is a collection of short scripts for two actors.

Myers, W. D. (1999). *Monster.* New York: Harper-Collins. In this novel written as a screenplay, 16-year-old Steve Harmon is on trial for murder.

Schlitz, L. A. (2007). *Good masters! sweet ladies! voices from a medieval village.* Cambridge, MA: Candlewick. Set in England in 1255, short monologues introduce 22 characters in a village.

Slaight, C., and Sharrar, J. (Eds.). (1991). *Great scenes for young actors.* Newbury, VT: Smith & Kraus. These scenes from contemporary plays focus on the perspectives of young adults. Slaight has also edited *Multicultural Scenes for Young Actors* (1995).

Slaight, C., and Sharrar, J. (Eds.). (1996). *Short plays for young actors.* Newbury, VT: Smith & Kraus. This anthology includes both classic and modern plays.

Smith, R., and Avi. (1997). *Nothing but the truth: A play.* New York: Avon. When Philip is punished for humming the "Star-Spangled Banner," everything gets blown out of proportion.

Soto, G. (1999). *Nerdlandia.* New York: PaperStar. Martin, a nerd, likes Ceci, a chola girl. But while he is busy trying to become cool, Ceci is turning into a nerdish beauty.

Surface, M. H. (1999). *Most valuable player and four other all-star plays for middle and high school audiences.* Lyme, NH: Smith & Kraus. Surface explores a number of social themes in these plays.

Surface, M. H. (2007). *More short scenes and monologues for middle school students inspired by literature, social studies, and real life.* Lyme, NH: Smith & Kraus. These short works focus mainly on different types of relationships.

Zindel, P. (1971). *The effect of gamma rays on man-in-the-moon marigolds.* New York: Harper & Row. A widow and her daughters lead very interesting lives.

SHORT STORIES

Armstrong, J. (2002). *Shattered: Stories of children and war.* New York: Knopf. These short stories look at the effects of war on young people.

Berman, L. (2007). *And nobody got hurt 2! The world's weirdest, wackiest most amazing true sports stories.* New York: Little, Brown. Short and humorous stories about playing soccer, baseball, and other sports. The first volume is titled *And Nobody Got Hurt! The World's Weirdest, Wackiest True Sports Stories* (2005).

Blume, J. (Ed.). (1999). *Places I never meant to be.* New York: Simon & Schuster. These stories are accompanied by the author's observations on censorship.

Carlson, L. (Ed.). (1994). *American eyes: New Asian American short stories for young adults.* New York: Holt. These stories explore what it means to be an Asian American.

Carlson, L. (Ed.). (2005). *Moccasin thunder: American Indian stories for today.* New York: HarperCollins. These 10 stories focus on love, family, community, and friendship.

Cart, M. (1999). *Tomorrowland: Ten stories about the future.* New York: Scholastic. Stories about a new millennium in a number of different time periods.

Carter, A. (2003). *No missing parts: And other stories about real princesses.* Calgary: Red Deer College Press. The "princesses" in these stories confront contemporary issues.

Crutcher, C. (1991). *Athletic shorts.* New York: Greenwillow. Popular writer Chris Crutcher debunks the myth of the bonehead jock.

Duncan, L. (Ed.). (1996). *Night terrors: Stories of shadow and substance*. New York: Simon & Schuster. Annette Curtis Klause, Theodore Taylor, and Harry Mazer are some of the authors of these spooky tales.

Duncan, L. (Ed.). (1998). *Trapped! Cages of mind and body*. New York: Simon & Schuster. Teenagers are emotionally, physically, or mentally trapped in these stories.

Duncan, L. (Ed.). (2000). *On the edge: Stories at the brink*. New York: Simon & Schuster. Suspense is high in this collection.

Flake, S. G. (2005). *Who am I without him? Short stories about girls and the boys in their lives*. New York: Hyperion. A combination of interviews and short stories about teens in relationships.

Gallo, D. (Ed.). (1984). *Sixteen: Short stories by outstanding writers for young adults*. New York: Delacorte. The first in a series of original short story collections for adolescents.

Gallo, D. (Ed.). (1987). *Visions: Nineteen short stories about outstanding writers for young adults*. New York: Delacorte. A collection from outstanding authors.

Gallo, D. (Ed.). (1989). *Connections: Short stories by outstanding writers for young adults*. New York: Delacorte. Stories by 17 authors, including Gordon Korman, M. E. Kerr, and Sue Ellen Bridgers.

Gallo, D. (Ed.). (1997). *No easy answers: Short stories about teenagers making tough choices*. New York: Delacorte. The collection looks at the moral dilemmas adolescents face.

Gallo, D. (Ed.). (1999). *Time capsule: Short stories about teenagers throughout the twentieth century*. New York: Delacorte. Gallo looks at the trends, inventions, and values of the past in this collection.

Gallo, D. (Ed.). (2001). *On the fringe*. New York: Dial. These are stories of the geeks, the poor, the loners, the unathletic, and other outsiders.

Gallo, D. (Ed.). (2003). *Destination unexpected*. Cambridge, MA: Candlewick. In these stories, teenagers are transformed while on a variety of journeys. Published in 2004 is *First Crossing: Stories about Teen Immigrant*. See also *What are You Afraid of? Stories about Phobias* (2006).

Garden, N. (2007). *Hear us out! Lesbian and gay stories of struggle, progress, and hope, 1950 to the present*.

New York: Farrar, Straus and Giroux. This collection gives a historical view of gay and lesbian experiences.

Howe, J. (Ed.). (2001). *Color of absence: 12 stories about loss and hope*. New York: Atheneum. Stories about the different forms of loss in the lives of adolescents.

Howe, J. (Ed.). (2006). *13: Thirteen stories that capture the agony and ecstasy of being thirteen*. New York: Simon & Schuster. Well-known young adult writers such as Alex Sanchez and Ellen Wittlinger contribute to this collection about becoming a teenager.

Johnson, A. (1998). *Gone from home*. New York: DK. These are 12 stories of young people who face challenges when they leave home.

Levithan, D. and Ehrenhaft, D. (2007). *21 proms*. New York: Scholastic. Twenty-one stories about the prom from male and female perspectives.

Mazer, A. (Ed.). (1993). *America street: A multicultural anthology of stories*. New York: Persea. Fourteen authors present stories from diverse cultural and racial backgrounds. Another collection by this editor is *A Walk in My World: International Short Stories about Youth* (1998).

McCafferty, M. (2004). (Ed.). *Sixteen: Stories about that sweet and bitter birthday*. New York: Crown. Stories that explore the wonderment of being sixteen.

Myers, W. D. (2000). *145th Street stories*. New York: Delacorte. Myers writes about the people in Harlem.

Myers, W. D. (2007). *What they found: Love on 145th Street*. New York: Random House. A companion to *145th street: Short stories*, the fifteen stories explore the complexities of love and romance.

November, S. (Ed.). (2003). *Firebirds: An anthology of original fantasy and science fiction*. New York: Penguin. Here are 16 short stories from well-known authors.

Noyes, D. (Ed.). (2007). *The restless dead: Ten original stories of the supernatural*. Cambridge, MA: Candlewick. Vampires, ghosts, and devils are featured in these scary stories.

Oates, J. C. (2004). *Small avalanches and other stories*. New York: HarperTempest. Oates has collected some of her previously published stories in this volume.

O'Hearn, C. C. (1998). *Half and half: Writers on growing up biracial and bicultural*. New York:

Pantheon. Writers look at what it is like to grow up in a biracial or bicultural family.

Potok, C. (1998). *Zebra and other stories.* New York: Knopf. Six different young people experience a life-changing event.

Prasad, C. (Ed.). (2006). *Mixed: An anthology of short fiction on the multiracial experience.* New York: Norton. Eighteen stories feature biracial and multiracial characters.

Rice, D. (2001). *Crazy loco: Stories.* New York: Dial. These are stories of Mexican Americans in the Rio Grande Valley of Texas.

Salisbury, G. (2002). *Island boyz.* New York: Wendy Lamb. All of these stories are set in Hawaii.

Singer, M. (Ed.). (1998). *Stay true: Short stories for strong girls.* New York: Scholastic. Coming-of-age stories by several well-known writers.

Soto, G. (1998). *Petty crimes.* San Diego: Harcourt. These are the stories of life in the barrio.

Vande Velde, V. (2001). *Being dead.* San Diego: Harcourt. Ordinary teens wind up in creepy situations. Vande Velde takes one story and retells it five ways in *The Rumpelstiltskin Problem* (2000).

Yee, P. (2002). *Dead man's gold and other stories.* Toronto: Groundwood. Yee combines ghost stories with the experiences of early Chinese immigrants.

Suggested Readings

Collins, P. (2008). Using poetry throughout the curriculum. *Kappa Delta Pi Record, 44*(2), 81–84.

Danoff, S. (2008). Life ain't no crystal stair. *Educational Leadership, 65*(6), 76–79.

Eva-Wood, A. L. 2008). Does feeling come first? How poetry can help readers broaden their understanding of metacognition. *Journal of Adolescent & Adult Literacy, 51*(7), 564–576.

Rashid, L. (2008). When less is more: New short story collections to get teens reading. *School Library Journal, 5*(1), 16–19.

Wilkins, I. E., and Hines, R. A. (2008). "Shakespeare with Heart." An inclusive drama project. *The Exceptional Parent, 38*(3), 48–49.

Wissman, K. K. (2007/2008). "Making a way": Young women using literacy and language to resist the politics of silencing. *Journal of Adolescent & Ault Literacy, 51*(4), 340–349.

References

All works of young adult literature referenced in this chapter are included in the Young Adult Books list and are not repeated in this list.

Abrahamson, R. F. (2002). Poetry preference research: What young adults tell us they enjoy. *Voices from the Middle, 10*(2), 20–22.

Abramovitz, S. (2000). The power of performance in multicultural curricula. *Multicultural Education, 7*(3), 31–33.

Allen, J. (2002). Painting word pictures: The language of poetry. *Voices from the Middle, 10*(2), 52–53.

Aronson, D. (2008). Charles Simic: For the love of poetry. *Council Chronicle, 17*(3), 23–24.

Black, A. (2005). *Born storytellers: Readers theatre celebrates the lives and literature of classic authors.* Englewood, CO: Libraries Unlimited.

Bladwin, M. (2003). *Slam poetry manual.* Chicago: American Library Association.

Bleeker, G., and Bleeker, B. (1996). Responding to young adult fiction through writing poetry: Trying to understand a mole. *The ALAN Review, 23*(3), 38–40.

Bontempo, B. T. (1995). Exploring prejudice in young adult literature through drama and role play. *The ALAN Review, 22*(3), 31–33.

Brown, J. E., and Stephens, E. C. (1995). *Teaching young adult literature: Sharing the connection.* Belmont, CA: Brooks/Cole.

Charters, M. (1997). The different faces of poetry. *Publisher's Weekly, 244*(9), 38–41.

Chilcoat, G. W. (1996). Living newspaper puppet theater: An inquiry process for exploring—historical social issues in high-school social studies. *The Social Studies, 87*(6), 254–261.

Cullinan, B. E., Scala, M. C., and Schroder, V. (1995). *Three voices: An Invitation to poetry across the curriculum.* Portland, ME: Stenhouse.

Davis, A. (1997). Salamanca Hiddle is alive and well: Developing a palette for poetry. *Voices from the Middle, 4*(1), 16–21.

Eleveld, M. (Ed.). (2004). *The spoken word revolution: Slam, hip-hop, & the poetry of a new generation.* Naperville, IL: Sourcebooks.

Eleveld, M. (Ed.). (2007). *The spoken word revolution redux.* Naperville, IL: Sourcebooks.

Fisher, M. T. (2007). *Writing in rhythm: Spoken word poetry in urban classrooms*. New York: Teachers College.

Fredericks, A. D. (2001). *Readers theatre for American history*. Englewood, CO: Teacher Ideas Press.

Fredericks, A. D. (2008). *African legends, myths, and folktales for readers theatre*. Englewood, CO: Libraries Unlimited.

Gasparro, M., and Falletta, B. (1994). *Creating drama with poetry: Teaching English as a second language through dramatization and improvisation*. (ERIC Document Reproduction Service No. ED 368 214)

Gonzalez, J. B. (2002). From page to stage to teenager: Problematizing "transformation" in theatre for and with adolescents. *Stage of the Art, 14*(3), 17–21.

Grimes, N. (2000). The power of poetry. *Book Links, 9*(4), 32–35.

Harding, C. G., and Safer, L. A. (1996). Using live theatre combines with role playing and discussion to examine what at-risk adolescents think about substance abuse, its consequences, and prevention. *Adolescence, 31*(124), 783–796.

Heartwell, P. (2002). Masters as mentors: The role of reading poetry in writing poetry. *Voices from the Middle, 10*(2), 29–32.

Hewitt, G. (1998). *Today you are my favorite poet: Writing poems with teenagers*. Portsmouth, NH: Heinemann.

Hewitt, G. (2005). *Hewitt's guide to slam poetry and poetry slam*. Shoreham, VT: Discover Writing.

Hommel, M. (2003). Slamming on the net: A new writers workshop for teens. *Voice of Youth Advocates, 26*(1), 26–27.

Jago, C. (2001). *Beyond standards: Excellence in the high school English classroom*. Portsmouth, NH: Boynton/Cook.

Johnson, A. B., McClanahan, L. G., and Mertz, M. P. (1999). Gender representation in poetry for young adults. *The ALAN Review, 26*(3), 39–44.

Jolley, S. (2002). Integrating poetry and *To Kill a Mockingbird*. *English Journal, 92*(2), 34–40.

Kazemek, F. E. (2003). "And I wrote my happy songs, every child may joy to hear": The poetry of William Blake in the middle school classroom. *The ALAN Review, 30*(2), 44–47.

King, W. (1997). Stealing a piece of the world and hiding it in words. *Voices from the Middle, 4*(1), 22–29.

Knowles, E., and Smith, M. (1997). *The reading connection*. Englewood, CO: Libraries Unlimited.

Lesesne, T. (2002). Gaining power through poetry: An interview with Sonya Sones. *Teacher Librarian, 29*(3), 51–53.

Lewis, J. P., and Robb, L. (2007). *Poems for teaching in the content areas: 75 powerful poems to enhance your history, geography, science, and math lessons*. New York: Scholastic.

Lowery, R. M. (2003). Dreams of possibilities: Linking poetry to our lives. *The ALAN Review, 30*(2), 49–51.

Marshall, S., and Newman, D. (1997). A poet's vision. *Voices from the Middle, 4*(1), 7–15.

Merriam-Webster's Encyclopedia of Literature. (1995). Springfield, MA: Merriam-Webster.

Newman, J. D. (2003). The Bonderman and beyond: Developing new works for young audiences. *Stage of the Art, 15*(2), 9–12.

Pearl, N. (2002). The pleasures of short stories. *Alki, 18*(2), 31.

Russell, D. L. (2009). *Literature for children: A short introduction*, 6th ed. Boston: Pearson.

Schwedt, R. E., and DeLong, J. (2002). *Young adult poetry: A survey and theme guide*. Westport, CT: Greenwood.

Singer, M. (2000). What is a short story? *Journal of Youth Services in Libraries, 14*(1), 12–13.

Sitomer, A. L. (2006). Tupac Shakur in language arts class? *Instructor, 116*(2), 66–67.

Smith, K. P., and Zarnowski, M. (1999). Letting poetry in, sending poetry forth. *New Advocate, 12*(2), 209–213.

Somers, A. (1999). *Teaching poetry in high school*. Urbana, IL: National Council of Teachers of English.

Steineke, N. (2002). Talking about poetry: Teaching students how to lead the discussion. *Voices from the Middle, 10*(2), 8–14.

Thomas, C. (2000). From engagement to celebration: A framework for passionate reading. *Voices from the Middle, 8*(2), 16–25.

Thomas, J. (2001). Mel Glenn and Arnold Adoff: The poetics of power in the adolescent voice-lyric. *Style, 35*(3), 486–500.

Working with Teachers: The short of it. (2000). *The School Librarian's Workshop, 21*(2), 12.

Wormser, B., and Cappella, D. (2004). *A surge of language: Teaching poetry day by day*. Portsmouth, NH: Heinemann.

Chapter 12

Exploring Other Formats

Comics, Graphic (Comic-Format) Novels, Picture Books, and Magazines

"All those graphic novels are trash, and we don't have trash in our school library."

"Oh, I guess the boys would like the comics with those almost-naked, well-endowed heroines, but not in my classroom."

"These magazines are just not appropriate— where's the literary value in them?"

"Picture books in high school? They're for elementary children, not young adults."

These are just a few of the comments teachers and library media specialists may offer when talking about comics, graphic novels, picture books, and magazines—the most visual "literature" formats for young adults. However, before you dismiss these formats, we caution you to remember that contemporary adolescents are growing up in a visual and digital society where the use of pictures to present information is often the norm and where teenagers are comfortable with the visual styles found in these formats. According to Gorman (2008a), these visual formats are "perfect for promoting recreational or free voluntary reading—one of the most effective ways to increase literacy and create lifelong readers" (p. 43). If sales are any indication of popularity, the increase in sales of graphic novels from $75 million in 2001 (Raiteri, 2003b) to $207 million in 2004 (Reid, 2005) and $330 million for graphic novels and comics in 2006 (Gorman, 2008a) points out the growing interest in this visual genre. After adding graphic novels to the school library collection, one library media specialist found that graphic novels account for more than 25% of the circulation although they make up less than 1% of the total collection. Another library media specialist spent $1,000 on graphic novels and saw a 50% increase in circulation (Mcpherson, 2006).

Comics and graphic novels are beginning to gain acceptance. *Maus I*, Art Spiegelman's graphic novel, won the Pulitzer Prize and was later combined with *Maus II* to create *The Complete Maus* (1997). In 2002, the ALA annual conference featured a preconference workshop on graphic novels, and the ALA Teen Read Week theme was "Getting Graphic @ Your Library." By 2007, YALSA began to issue a best books list specifically for graphic novels, and in 2007, the graphic novel *American Born Chinese* (Yang, 2006) won the Printz Award and was a finalist for the National Book Award. The 2008 winner of the Randolph Caldecott Medal for the most distinguished American picture book was the graphic novel *The Invention of Hugo Cabret* (Selznick, 2007).

Comics, Graphic Novels, Picture Books, and Magazines

Many young adults enjoy these works, perhaps because they differ so dramatically from the genres that educators have traditionally encouraged adolescents to read—books that were, for the most part, all words and no pictures. In contrast to earlier generations, contemporary young adults have grown up with television and its "sound bites," as well as video games. Looking for print media that contain the same visual impact and a clipped, pared-down writing style, adolescents have turned to visual formats and to slick magazines that are designed to appeal to the teen market. There is no doubt that these media attract the attention and interest of adolescents and contribute to their enthusiasm for visual rather than written literacy. For many young adults, these formats represent a welcome move away from what they consider traditional "school" reading.

Researchers view literacy as more than reading and writing. "Students learn to be literate through multiple paths using multiple modalities" (McPherson, 2006, p. 67). Reluctant readers and second language learners find that the artwork in comics, graphic novels, picture books, or magazines helps their comprehension and serves as a bridge to more print-bound texts; and teachers find that using comics is a way to "build trust with a frustrated student" (Schneider, 2007, p. 57). Proficient readers of visual formats explore language and images in increasingly complex ways (Kress, 2003) and are "thinking differently from those adults who were brought up in a more print-dominated world" (Bearne, 2003, p. 98). Reading a visual format requires "active participation in the text . . . [as readers] make connections between the images and the text and create the links between the panels and the page as a whole" (Brenner, 2006, p. 125). This "reading between the panels" (p. 125) is an important literacy in a multimedia world.

As you explore each of the formats in this chapter, keep in mind the enthusiasm young adults have for these visual formats. Because we believe that one way to encourage young adults to read is to allow them to read things that interest them, we also believe that these formats belong in every school library and that they should, when appropriate, be incorporated into the school's curriculum. However, this also means that, as with any other formats or genres of literature, educators need to know about comics, graphic novels, picture books, and magazines; the materials that are available; and how to select high-quality, interesting works for young adults—items that teens will appreciate as well as items that will contribute to the formal and informal education of adolescents.

Comics

Contemporary comics have come a long way since a comic strip about the Yellow Kid appeared in an 1896 issue of *New York World* and a pamphlet featuring the comic characters Mutt and Jeff was offered as a premium for clipping newspaper coupons in 1911. By the late 1930s, readers could buy Action Comics and the *Superman Quarterly Magazine*. The industry continued to grow, and between 1940 and 1953, comics sales jumped from 17 million to 68 million copies a year (*Comic books and juvenile delinquency*, 1956). However, this growth was not always met with praise. In fact, many parents and educators questioned the deleterious effects comics might have on children. These fears led to a congressional investigation of the links between comics and juvenile delinquency, a call to raise the standards of decency and good taste in comics, and the establishment of the Comics Code Authority to monitor the content of comics. Another result was the growth of the underground comics publishing industry, which did not adhere to the code.

After many years of declining sales, comics have begun to regain their former popularity. Today, comics, along with graphic novels (which you will read about later in this chapter), are moving out of the traditional comic book stores and into the mainstream of American book publishing and sales. Comics are no longer cheap, with an average cost in 2004 of $2.85 (comicsworthreading.com). In 2007, Diamond Comic Distributors reported sales of $429.9 million, a 9% increase over the previous year, and estimated an overall U.S market of $600–700 million, not counting manga comic sales (Comic Buyers' Guide, 2008), which were estimated at $190–205 million in 2006 (Poitras, 2008). Each year, the North American comics industry hosts Free Comic Book Day on the first Saturday of May, when independent comic book stores give away comics to anyone who comes into their stores. Although some educators question whether this genre actually belongs in school library media centers and classrooms, other teachers and library media specialists have decided to explore the existing comics formats and identify strategies for making effective use of this genre.

Types of Comics. Essentially, comics and graphic novels are the same thing—*sequential art*, or a combination of text and images presented in a panel format. However, we will distinguish between the book-length graphic novel and the shorter comics. While most comics are issued in color, some publishers economize by producing black and white comics, often with a colored cover. Several ways exist to categorize comics. However, as with any listing of categories, there are some overlaps and some comics that do not fit into one of these categories.

Many comics belong in the publishing category known as serials: works, like magazines, that are issued in successive parts. Thus, one way to group comics is by publishing frequency. There are:

- Continuing or ongoing series that are published on a regular schedule, such as bimonthly or monthly, with no scheduled ending date.
- Miniseries, which usually have six or fewer issues.
- Maxiseries, which usually have more than six issues but with a definite ending point.

Miniseries and maxiseries are also referred to as limited series, to distinguish them from ongoing series. In addition to the comics series, there are:

- Annual comics, which are a yearly supplement to a series.
- One-shot comics, which are a single, stand-alone publications.

Sometimes comics are categorized by their format, including:

- *Standard format:* thirty-two 7"-by-10" pages stapled together. Variations on this are the 48-page *double-issues* and the 80-page *giants*.
- *Prestige format:* 8"-by-10" pages with a higher quality of paper and heavier covers.
- *Treasury editions:* specially published comics issued in a prestige or larger format.
- *Magazines:* comics series printed on magazine-size paper with stapled binding.
- *Trade paperbacks:* book-like volumes that usually collect and reprint a limited series. However, they may also include a number of different comics that are related to a single theme or are written by a single individual.
- *Graphic novels* (GN): complete, book-length stories or collections of original, related short stories that are bound with more durable cardstock or with hardcovers (http://ublib.buffalo.edu/libraries/units/lml/comics/pages/index.html; http://bookshelf.diamondcomics.com/public).

Scott McCloud has written a number of excellent books about comics that provide a background for this genre. These books include *Understanding Comics* (1993), *Reinventing Comics* (2000), and *Making Comics* (2006).

Reasons for Using and Teaching with Comics. With fast-paced action, powerful images, and dramatic plots that feature heroic adventures, contemporary comics address themes that are important to young adults, including issues of acceptance, nonconformity, prejudice, social injustice, coming of age, triumph over adversity, and personal growth. In comics, adolescents can explore current and historical events, legends and tall tales, mythology, and visual versions of classic novels and dramas. Some comics are even designed to raise social consciousness and interest in issues such as famine relief and environmental preservation, while others have antidrug or sex education themes. While some young adults may turn to comics to find familiar characters and cultural icons such as Superman, Batman, and Spider-Man, others are simply looking to enjoy a good story.

Many educators have discovered that they can interest reluctant readers by including comics in libraries and on reading lists. In addition, comics appeal to many poor readers and visual learners because in comics readers are expected to apply different "reading" skills. No longer following a single line of text, the reader must let the pictures direct the reading. Comics can also help adolescents develop their language arts skills and expand their vocabularies while conveying educational messages and serving as a bridge to other types of literature. According to Krashen (2004), "there is considerable evidence that comic books can and do lead to more 'serious' reading" (p. 97). The average comic has three times the vocabulary of a child and adult conversation and twice the vocabulary of an average children's book (Krashen, 1993).

Characteristics of Comics for Young Adults. Although the Comics Code Authority (CCA) began as a good way for a business group to police itself, today, with a few exceptions, most comics publishers do not participate in the CCA. Thus, educators need to examine comics carefully and identify those that are appropriate for various age levels of young adults and that will appeal to teenage readers. Considerations for Selecting Young Adult Literature: *Comics* contains suggestions for evaluating comics.

Archie Comics is one publisher that is committed to "wholesome, family-oriented products" (WFOP). Their website lists a number of situations in which a character in one of their comics will never participate, such as drinking alcoholic beverages, taking drugs, smoking, or knowingly engaging in illegal activities (www.archiecomics.com/note-to-parents.html).

Comics for Young Adults. Because of the serial format of many comics, one good way to explore comics is to look at the various series offered by major publishers. Table 12–1 identifies some of the series that are appropriate for young adults. Other comics series fall into the categories of crime comics, historical fiction, and literature-based (myths, legends, and visual representations of other classic literature). Although some publishers are offering nonfiction comics, these are often one-shots or graphic novels. However, we advise anyone who is interested in adding comics to a classroom or school library to visit a local comic book store or various Internet sites.

CONSIDERATIONS FOR SELECTING YOUNG ADULT LITERATURE COMICS

In general, ask the following questions when selecting comics for young adults:

_____   Does the comic present positive role models and/or positive themes without cultural or gender stereotypes?

_____   Is the comic tied to popular movies, video games, or television shows?

_____   Are there good visual qualities with an interesting layout, high-quality illustrations (color is not necessary, although new comic readers may be attracted to color comics), and good reproduction of the artwork?

_____   Is there good writing, with original characters, an intriguing plot, and a style that will keep the reader's interest?

_____   Does the comic avoid extreme violence, abusive behavior, or gratuitous profanity?

TABLE 12-1   Popular Comics Series for Young Adults and Their Publishers

	Series	Publisher
SUPERHEROES	Batman	DC Comics
	Generation X	Marvel Comics
	Justice Society of America	DC Comics
	Legion of Super-Heroes	DC Comics
	Spider-Girl	Marvel Comics
	Spider-Man	Marvel Comics
	Superman	DC Comics
	Wolverine	Marvel Comics
	X-Men	Marvel Comics
	Young Justice	DC Comics
HUMOR	Any series published by Archie	
	Geeksville	3 Finger Prints
	Groo	Dark Horse
	Sabrina the Teenage Witch	Archie
	The Simpsons	Bongo Entertainment
	Weirdsville	Blindwolf Comics
FANTASY/SCIENCE FICTION	Akiko	Sirius
	Bone	Cartoon Books
	Castle Waiting	Olio
	Elfquest	Warp Graphics
	Little White Mouse	Blue Line Pro Comics
	Star Wars	Dark Horse
	Usagi Yojimbo	Dark Horse
	Xeno's Arrow	Cup O'Tea Studios
MANGA	Princess Prince	CPM Manga
	Tenchi Muyo!	Viz

One type of comic that is very popular is manga (maw-nnn-gah), which, translated from Japanese, means whimsical pictures. Although *manga* is used in Japan to refer to all comics, in the United States, the term refers to Japanese or Asian-style comics. A spinoff of the Japanese anime or animation industry, manga is distinguished by intricate drawings and textures as well as sophisticated plot. It is common to use the term "anime" to refer to film animation and "manga" to refer to the print format. In the authentic format, manga has a right-to-left format instead of the traditional American left-to-right format. Although some publishers reverse the images for U.S. audiences, publishers such as Tokyopop issue manga in the original right-to-left format. Stuart Levy, the founder of Tokyopop, has called manga "chicklit for comics" (Reid, 2003, p. S6), as manga is more popular with females than with males (Reid, 2003). *Shojo* is a manga category that is aimed at younger girls and involves romance, while *shonen* appeals to boys with its action stories. Violent or sexually graphic manga are referred to as *hentai*. Connecting Adolescents and Their Literature 12–1 suggests using manga to introduce young adults to other literature and Japanese culture.

12–1 ●●●. **CONNECTING ADOLESCENTS AND THEIR LITERATURE**

For "otaku" (obsessed fans), many libraries host anime/manga clubs and programs that not only focus on these Japanese forms of comics and animated films but also help young adults learn about Japanese culture, language, fashions, and foods. The Evansville Vanderburgh Public Library in Indiana includes Japanese culture nights as well as programs on Japanese popular music and drawing lessons (Mori, 2007). Other libraries have included programs on sushi, origami, bonsai, martial arts, and the Japanese tea ceremony (King, 2006). Information on programming ideas and obtaining permission to show anime in schools and libraries is on the *VOYA* website: pdfs.voya.com/VO/YA2/VOYA200504AnimetedLibrary.pdf. Information on individual anime is online at www.abcb.com/parents.

Suggestions for Selecting and Using Comics. Selecting comics to use in schools can be difficult because, while educational publications are beginning to review graphic novels, few publish reviews of the more ephemeral comics. Some of the publishers such as Marvel do provide a rating system for their comics, including "all ages"; "A," ages 9 and up; "T+," ages 13 and up; and "parental advisory." To identify comics you might want to use with young adults, you can examine the winners of several comic awards, including:

- The Reuben Awards of the National Cartoonists Society, which has a category for comic books
- The Eisner Awards
- The Harvey Awards
- The Comics Buyer's Guide Fan Awards

On the Internet, Comics Worth Reading publishes reviews of comics, and Anime-News Network has information on manga along with very detailed reviews of some of the popular series. Diamond Comics, a distributor, has a special "bookshelf" website with information for librarians and teachers and a comic book shop locator, while Comic Books for Young Adults has detailed information on selecting and using comics. Although no longer being updated, Comic Book Conundrum provides information on many of the issues in the comics world. Finally, serving as a marketplace for comics collectors, *Comics Buyer's Guide* (magazine) provides news about comics, profiles of artists and writers, and information on new releases.

Because of the nature of comics, we suggest that educators preview all issues before making them available for adolescents. One of the best ways to remain current about comics is to work with a local comics retailer who can keep you informed about the new series and can identify comics that are popular with teens in your area. If that is not possible, visit the websites of some of the major publishers to see what they are producing.

Actually purchasing comics can also be a challenge, because many publishers do not offer subscriptions to their ongoing series. However, in addition to comic book stores, there are Internet sites that sell comics, although it is difficult to preview the comic on the Internet before ordering it. In contrast, trade paperbacks and graphic novels are now available in bookstores and on the Internet at places like Amazon.com. Published primarily for comics dealers and collectors, the standard reference guide to current and out-of-print comics is the *Official Overstreet's Comic Book Companion* (Overstreet, 2008). Expanding Your Knowledge with the Internet lists some of these sources.

EXPANDING YOUR KNOWLEDGE WITH THE INTERNET

The following websites provide further information about comics.

COMICS PUBLISHERS AND DISTRIBUTORS

Archie Comics
www.archiecomics.com/2.html

Dark Horse Comics
www.darkhorse.com/

DC Comics
www.dccomics.com/

Diamond Comics Bookshelf
bookshelf.diamondcomics.com/

Tokyopop
www.tokyopop.com/

COMIC AWARDS

Eisner Award
www.comic-con.org/cci/cci_eisners_main.shtml

Harvey Awards
www.harveyawards.org/

Comic Book Awards Almanac
users.rcn.com/aardy/comics/awards/index.html

COMIC BOOKS FOR YOUNG ADULTS

ublib.buffalo.edu/libraries/units/lml/comics/pages/index.html

Comic Books Conundrum
www.sideroad.com/comics/contents.html

Comics Worth Reading
www.comicsworthreading.com/

Free Comic Book Day
www.freecomicbookday.com

ONLINE COMIC BOOK NEWS

Newsarama
www.newsarama.com

Pulse (by Mile High Comics)
www.comicon.com/pulse

Tony'sOnlineTips (reviews by Tony Isabella)
www.worldfamouscomics.com/tony/

World Famous Comics
www.worldfamouscomics.com/

AnimeNews Network
www.animenewsnetwork.com/

Comic Book Internet Resources
ublib.buffalo.edu/libraries/asl/guides/comics.html

Cartoon America – Library of Congress exhibition
www.loc.gov/exhibits/cartoonamerica/

COLLABORATING WITH OTHER PROFESSIONALS

Vega and Schnackenberg (2006) established a multidisciplinary workshop to help middle school students. Using technology, writing and art, teachers helped the students develop and produce their own comics. They found that "cartooning and comics can be integrated into the curriculum to motivate and facilitate student learning" (p. 36).

- A science or social studies teacher can help students select a topic.

- An English teacher can help students write the dialogue and other verbal passages.
- An art teacher can help them illustrate the comic.
- A technology specialist can help the students visit appropriate websites and produce the comic.

The website, Writing for Comic Books, contains information on becoming a comics author (www.williamsullivanadvertising.com/joeedkin/writing.html).

Teachers and library media specialists can incorporate comics into the school in a number of ways. As Alvermann, Moon, and Hagood (1999) pointed out, when teachers use resources from popular culture, they appeal to the multiple literacies of students. Thus, educators can include comics in instructional units and use some of the same strategies used in teaching novels such as making predictions, identifying new vocabulary, preparing new illustrations, and comparing the comic to other literature. Spanish-language comics are excellent for encouraging reluctant readers and for encouraging Hispanic students to use library resources (Serantes, 2005). After visiting an Internet site (e.g., http://rec.arts.comics.reviews), young adults can review, compare, and contrast comics. Collaborating with Other Professionals 12–1 has an idea for creating comics. Finally, comics can serve as an introduction to reading for some reluctant readers or teens with limited reading abilities.

Graphic Novels

Graphic novels are one of the most popular and fastest-growing types of young adult literature. The format began in 1978 when cartoonist Will Eisner created *A Contract with God*, a collection of stories about a poor, crowded Jewish Bronx neighborhood, and coined the term *graphic novel* to describe a complex story told in comic book format in 64 to 179 pages. More than a collection of comic strips in book format (such as a collection of Garfield comics or Charles Schultz's tales of Charlie Brown), graphic novels are, according to Eisner, "the literary form of comics" (Kennedy, 2003, p. 110), which has finally received recognition and acceptance as a "valid, legitimate medium" (p. 110). Today, they are "legitimately considered as works of literary fiction" (O'English, Matthews, & Lindsay, 2006, p. 174). Obviously a visual medium, graphic novels are engaging, sometimes edgy, and often written for a mature audience. Comics publishers have embraced the medium and have issued graphic novels by outstanding artists such as Art Spiegelman, Neil Gaiman, Jeff Smith, and Coleen Doran. Even traditional publishers are now releasing "in-depth tales filled with rich themes, characters, and stories . . . works of both artistic and literary merit" (Gorman, 2008b, p. 38).

A graphic novel is a "dynamic format of image and word that delivers meaning and enjoyment" (Simmons, 2003, p. 12) and differs in subtle ways from both comics and picture books. Comprised of boxed pictures and text, a graphic novel may have several boxes per page. As in a picture book, the illustrations enrich and extend the text. However, in a graphic novel, readers must not only decode the words and the illustrations but must also identify what is happening between the visual sequences (Simmons, 2003). Diamond Comics, a major U.S. distributor, distinguishes a graphic novel from a comic by noting that the graphic novel is longer and that most graphic novels tell a complete stand-alone story, unlike comics, which are often issued in successive parts. Sometimes several issues of a comic are combined and reissued as a graphic novel. An excellent example of this is *Bone* (2004), by Jeff Smith. This winner of 10 Eisner and 11 Harvey awards was first published as a comic series and later reissued as a graphic novel (Bickers, 2007).

In addition, many graphic novels go beyond the superheroes found in traditional comics and address the issues and concerns reflected in more traditional types of literature. Thus, graphic novels have sometimes been called meatier comics (Gorman, 2002a) or "your favorite comics all grown up" (Lubbock, Texas, City-County Library). Graphic novels are usually issued in hardcover; the paperback format is called a trade paperback.

Types of Graphic Novels. Despite their popularity, graphic novels are often seen as nothing more than adventure stories. There are, however, a number of different types of graphic novels, including superhero tales; realistic stories; science fiction and fantasy novels; future, contemporary, and historical adventure stories; and manga tales, as well as humorous works, political satires, and adaptations of classics. Although fiction remains the most popular part of the genre (Weiner, 2001), the scope of graphic novels has widened to include more sophisticated subject matter, including nonfiction, biography, and autobiography. Whether fiction or nonfiction, the genre is still called the graphic novel.

Even the graphic novels that focus on the traditional superhero cannot be written off as mere fluff. Robert G. Weiner (2001) sees the superhero tale serving as an allegory to modern life while providing an escape for readers. Others believe that superheroes can be compared to the heroic figures in classical mythology.

Like manga comics, manga graphic novels and anime (Japanese animated cartoons on television or in movies or video games) are very popular with teenagers because of the "dynamic, eccentric, and very often sexy illustrations in combination with fast-paced science fiction, adventure, fantasy and martial arts stories" (Reid, 2003, p. 6), usually with teens as the main characters. There are four main genres of manga: *shojo* (girls' stories), *shonon* (boys' stories), *seinen* (adult) and *redilsu komikku* (ladies') (Schwartz & Rubinstein-Avila, 2006). Written to appeal to girls, *shonen-ai* manga is homoerotic, with "chaste and innocent boy love" (Cha, 2005b, p. 44), while *yaoi* has a more "graphically sexual" (p. 44) homoerotic emphasis. Recently, sports manga books with a focus on soccer, basketball, tennis, and football have appeared in the American market from Japan (Cha, 2005a). The growth of English-language manga graphic novels (either translations or original English language [OEL]) has been phenomenal (Reid, 2002), spurred in part by the release of related anime on television and in video/DVD format. Like manga comics, manga graphic novels, with their diverse subject matter, are more popular with females than males (Reid, 2003), with 60% to 70% of the manga sold in the United States being purchased by teen girls and women (Kan, 2006).

"Several scholars have claimed that manga require multimodal reading skills and a sharp critical inquiry stance" (Schwartz & Rubinstein-Avila, 2006, p. 42). The plots are often indirect and nonlinear, with subplots. The visuals consist of a "complex language of visual signals, from character design to sound effects to common symbols" (Brenner, 2006, 123). "Reading *manga* is like decoding a secret language because it requires puzzling through visual symbols, cultural references and histories to grasp the story line" (Brenner, 2007a, p. 60). Paul Gravett presents an excellent introduction to the history of manga in *Manga: Sixty Years of Japanese Comics* (2004).

Reasons for Using and Teaching with Graphic Novels. Too often, educators exclude graphic novels solely because of the format or the erroneous impression that all graphic novels are supernatural horror stories, or an expression of the male power fantasy. Instead, graphic novels are a fusion of text and art that builds on the impact of visuals to offer value, variety, and a new medium for literacy. Because graphic novels appeal to young people, educators can use them to offer alternatives to traditional texts and mass media and to introduce young adults to literature that they might otherwise never encounter. In fact, some educators use graphic novels to teach literary terms and techniques such as dialogue, serve as a bridge to other classics, and act as the basis for writing assignments. Although some educators might worry that reading graphic novels will discourage adolescents from reading other genres of literature, others believe that graphic novels may require young adults to use more complex cognitive skills than are required when reading text alone (Schwartz, 2002). Francisca Goldsmith notes that graphic novels provide information as well as telling stories and that they "require active, critical participation by the reader, who must not only be able to decode text, but also follow its flow and grasp essentials of narrative mood, character or plot through images" (Mooney, 2002, p. 18).

Characteristics of Graphic Novels for Young Adults. Tabitha Simmons (2003) maintains that

> graphic novel readers have learned to understand print, but can also decode facial and body expressions, the symbolic meanings of certain images and postures, metaphors and similes, and other social and literary nuances teenagers are mastering as they move from childhood to maturity. (p. 12)

It is, therefore, important to look for graphic novels that have visual impact while presenting a blending of text and art, because both the art and the text must be "read." Graphic novels are one genre where it is especially important to select books carefully, preview them when possible, and ensure that they are age-appropriate. Considerations for Selecting Young Adult Literature: *Graphic Novels* contains questions to ask during the selecting process. A number of popular graphic novels deal with controversial themes or have content that is more suited for adult readers, even though adolescents may read them. Thus, Gorman (2002a) advises educators to examine the genre, target audience, quality, and artistic merit as well as the reputation and style of the author

CONSIDERATIONS FOR
SELECTING YOUNG ADULT LITERATURE GRAPHIC NOVELS

When selecting graphic novels, ask the following questions:

_____ Does the graphic novel have visual impact that showcases the artistic ability of the creator?

_____ Does the graphic novel blend text and art?

_____ Does the use of color add to the graphic novel or is it unnecessary?

_____ Does the story have the best qualities of the literature genre (i.e., mystery, nonfiction, biography) it represents?

_____ Are the story and illustrations appropriate for adolescents?

and illustrator when evaluating graphic novels. Gorman has created a rating system for Tokyopop publishers that combines "familiar age categories . . . [with] a listing of 'content' indicators that strictly define the nature of the material" (Reid, 2007, p. 8).

Graphic Novels for Young Adults. Graphic novels reflect many of the genres of traditional literature, from fantasy and science fiction to adventure and nonfiction. In some books, including many by the award-winning Neil Gaiman, authors treat themes and depict situations that are most appropriate for mature young adults or for adult audiences. Therefore, we again mention the importance of previewing graphic novels before using them and recommending them to adolescents. Having noted that concern, we also believe that graphic novels can be used throughout the curriculum.

While Larry Gonick's *Cartoon History of the Universe* (1997) contains facts as well as enough trivia to keep readers interested, several authors of graphic novels have looked to specific historical events for their subjects. In *300* (1999), Frank Miller and Lynn Varley combine fact and fantasy to retell the story of the Spartans and the Battle of Thermopylae. In the Age of Bronze series, which begins with *A Thousand Ships* (2001), Eric Shanower writes of the Trojan War. Looking at more recent history, Art Spiegelman examines the Holocaust in *The Complete Maus* (1997).

Several graphic novels present interesting biographies. *Streetwise* (Cooke & Morrow, 2000) is a collection of autobiographies of people in the comics industry. *Dignifying Science* (Ottaviani, 2003) provides a look at famous women in science. *Two-Fisted Science* (Ottaviani, 2001b) presents stories of scientists like Newton, Einstein, and Galileo. *Bond Sharps, Cowboys, and Thunder Lizards* (Ottaviani, 2005) takes readers dinosaur-hunting in the American West. In *To Dance: A Ballerina's Graphic Novel* (Siegel, 2006), the author looks at her own life. Digital Manga Press has an "Edu-Manga" imprint featuring biographies of historical figures, including *Edu-Manga: Ludwig van Beethoven* (Kanda & Takase, 2006) and *Edu-Manga: Mother Theresa* (Kikai & Kishida, 2007).

Graphic novelists have also successfully adapted some classics, including David Wenzel's graphic novel version of Tolkein's *The Hobbit* (2001), a translation of Proust's *Remembrance of Things Past* (Heuet, 2001), Peter Kuper's rendition of Kafka's *The Metamorphosis* (2003), P. Craig Russell's adaptation of *The Ring of the Nibelung*

(2002) and *Beowulf* (2007) by Gareth Hinds. Will Eisner retold an African legend in *Sundiata: A Legend of Africa* (2002) and gave a new perspective to Charles Dickens's *Oliver Twist* in *Fagin the Jew* (2003). Kyle Baker takes text from *The Confessions of Nat Turner* (Styron, 1967) and adds the illustrations in the two-volume graphic novel *Nat Turner: Encore Edition* (2006). Several novels for middle school readers have been released in a graphic novel format, including:

- *Artemis Fowl: The Graphic Novel* (Colfer, Donkin, Rigano, and Lamanna, 2007)
- *Redwall: The Graphic Novel* (Jacques, Moore, and Blevins, 2007)
- *Stormbreaker: The Graphic Novel* (Horowitz, Johnston, Damerum, and Takasaki, 2006)

In other areas of the curriculum, science educators can use *Clan Apis* (Hosler, 2000) to study the life of the honeybee, *The Sandwalk Adventures* (Hosler, 2003) to look at Darwin's theory of natural selection, or *Fallout* (Ottaviani, 2001a) to examine the scientific and social aspects of the development of the atomic bomb. For social studies educators, Joe Kubert takes readers to the Balkans in *Fax from Sarajevo: A Story of Survival* (1998). Joe Sacco reports on his experiences in the Middle East in *Palestine* (2002). Ted Rall recounts his travels in *To Afghanistan and Back: A Graphic Travelogue* (2002). James Vining revisits the early space program in *First in Space* (2007). *Inside Out: Portrait of an Eating Disorder* (Shivack, 2007) is a good choice for health class.

Several graphic novels explore social issues, such as Judd Winnick's look at AIDS in *Pedro and Me* (2000) and Katherine Arnoldi's exploration of rape and pregnancy in *Amazing "True" Story of a Teenage Single Mom* (1998). For mature readers, Bryan Talbot's *The Tale of One Bad Rat* (1995) is a powerful story of sexual abuse. Pascal Blanchet looks at the growth and destruction of a town in *White Rapids* (2007). Other powerful graphic novels include collections of stories that look back at the attacks of 9/11, including *9–11 Artists Respond* (2002), *9–11: The World's Finest Comic Book Writers and Artists Tell Stories to Remember* (2002), and *In the Shadow of No Towers* (Spiegelman, 2004).

Within the genre of graphic novels are many fantasy and science fiction books, some of them based on comics that feature the same characters. For example, the X-Men move into graphic novels with *The Dark Phoenix Saga* (2003) from Chris Claremont and John Byrne's X-Men series or Peter Sanderson's *X-Men: The Ultimate Guide* (2003). In *Legion of Super-Heroes: The Beginning of Tomorrow* (1999), Tom McCraw tells the stories of teenage superheroes in the thirty-first century. In the three volumes of the *Daredevil: Visionaries* series (2000–2001), Frank Miller looks at another superhero. Similarly, Brian Bendis and Mark Bagley take a fresh look at another well-known character in *Ultimate Spider-Man: Power and Responsibility* (2002). Another well-developed fantasy graphic novel is *Castle Waiting* (Medley, 2006).

Appealing especially to girls are a number of graphic novels that reflect young adults' love of mystery and horror. *Buffy the Vampire Slayer: Origin* (Golden, 1999) and *Leave It to Chance: Shaman's Rain* (Robinson, 2000) are two books in series that feature female protagonists. Older teens will enjoy the mature subjects in Neil Gaiman's classics *The Sandman* (1993), *Death: The High Cost of Living* (1994), and *Black Orchid* (1996).

Other graphic novels bridge genres. In the realistic *Girl Stories* (2006), Weinstein follows a girl as she tries to shed her geek image. Myrick looks at a happy Midwestern childhood in *Missouri Boy* (2006). Fantasy and humor combine when the mummy of pharaoh

Imhotep IV meets a Victorian girl in *The Professor's Daughter* (Sfar & Guibert, 2007). *Polly and the Pirates* (Naifeh, 2006) is a fun adventure story for younger adolescents.

Like manga comics, manga graphic novels remain popular. *Rumiko Takahashi's Rumic Theater* (1996) and *Rumic Theater: One or Double* (1998) are excellent collections of the works of Rumiko Takahashi, the popular female artist of the Ranma ½ series. Other popular manga series with their authors and publishers are:

- *Boys over Flowers*, by Yoko Kamio (Viz Media)
- *Tarot Café*, by Sanag-Sun Park (Tokyopop)
- *After School Nightmare*, by Setona Mizushiro (Go! Media Entertainment)
- *Kare First Love*, by Kaho Miyasaka (Viz Media)
- *Steady Beat*, by Rivkah (Tokyopop)
- *Beauty Pop*, by Kiyoko Arai (Viz Media)
- *Buddha*, by Osamu Tezuka (Vertical, Inc.)
- *Honey Mustard*, by Ho-Kyung Yeo (Tokyopop)
- *Buso Renkin*, by Nobuhiro Watsuki (Viz Media)
- *YuYu Hakusho*, by Yoshihiro Togashi (Viz Media)
- *Chronicles of the Cursed Sword*, by Beop-Ryong Yeo (Tokyopop)
- *Densha Otoko: The Story of the Train Man Who Fell in Love with a Girl*, by Hitori Nakano and Wataru Wantanabe (DC Comics)
- *Gon*, by Masashi Tanaka (DC Comics) (a wordless graphic novel series)

Suggestions for Selecting and Using Graphic Novels. Like comics, graphic novels have just begun to achieve a level of acceptance by the publishing industry, and professional publications are now starting to include reviews of graphic novels. Some graphic novels even show up on the annual best books lists, as well as in the comics awards mentioned earlier. Several professional journals for librarians, such as *School Library Journal*, *VOYA*, and *Library Media Connection* have regular graphic novel columns. *Graphic Novels Core Collection*, a subscription database on WilsonWeb, provides descriptions and evaluations of over 2,000 titles; a trial subscription is available at www.hwwilson.com/trial. In 2007, YALSA began to issue a yearly list called Great Graphic Novels for Teens. Several writers, including Philip Crawford (2002, 2003b) and Michele Gorman (2002a, 2002b), have developed lists of recommended graphic novels. In addition to Roger Sabin's *Comics, Comix & Graphic Novels: A History of Comic Art* (2001), there are several publications on selecting graphic novels, including:

- *Developing and Promoting Graphic Novel Collections* (Miller, 2005)
- *Understanding Manga and Anime* (Brenner, 2007b)
- *The 101 Best Graphic Novels* (Weiner, 2006)
- *Graphic Novels: A Genre Guide to Comic Books, Manga, and More* (Pawuk, 2006)
- *Graphic Novels Now: Building, Managing, and Marketing a Dynamic Collection* (Goldsmith, 2005)
- *Graphic Novels: Everything You Need to Know* (Gravett, 2005)
- *Building Literacy Connections with Graphic Novels: Page by Page, Panel by Panel* (Carter, 2007)

EXPANDING YOUR KNOWLEDGE WITH THE INTERNET

A variety of Internet sites exist where you can find information about graphic novels. A few are listed below.

No Flying No Tights—Graphic Novels
www.noflyingnotights.com/index2.html

A Brief History of the Graphic Novel
www.graphicnovels.brodart.com/history.htm

Graphic Novels: suggestions for librarians
www.ala.org/ala/oif/ifissues/graphicnovels_1.pdf

Mercer County Library (New Jersey)—Comics and Graphic Novels Page
webserver.mcl.org/subj/grafnov.html

Columbia University's Graphic Novels Page
www.columbia.edu/cu/lweb/eguides/graphic_novels/

To learn more about graphic novels and keep informed about trends and new offerings, educators need to develop a relationship with a local comic book shop or a book store that carries graphic novels. Expanding Your Knowledge with the Internet provides more information on Internet sites about graphic novels.

Working with library media specialists, teachers should review all graphic novels for content, language, sexist and cultural stereotypes, and overall appropriateness for the particular class. Connecting Adolescents and Their Literature 12–2 provides ways to have young adults serve on youth advisory committees to assist in the selection.

Graphic novels can contribute to interdisciplinary thematic units or can serve as an introduction to a specific content area. For example, in the social studies, they can

CONNECTING ADOLESCENTS AND THEIR LITERATURE

As Gorman (2002a) has suggested, you can create a graphic novel youth advisory committee to help select graphic novels for a school library or classroom collection.

- Let members review new purchases and suggest ways to promote the graphic novel collection.

- Involve as many students as possible by having several small groups instead of one large group.

- Identify young adults who are familiar with graphic novels or who are interested in learning more about them.

- Provide guidelines and explain that the books should, at a minimum, be examined for content, reading level, language, sexist and cultural stereotypes, and overall appropriateness.

- Encourage the students to add other criteria.

- Remind students that their role is advisory and that while they can recommend novels for purchase, the school might not be able to purchase everything they recommend.

- Use the committee to review graphic novels that you are considering purchasing or that have been recommended by others.

help students develop an understanding of history and/or appreciation for differing cultures; in the sciences, they can help adolescents explore complex and sometimes confusing topics. We have mentioned several graphic novels that could support science and social studies units. In addition, graphic novels offer subject matter and viewpoints that students might not otherwise consider. For example, by providing an account of his parents' lives in England, Brigg's *Ethel & Ernest* (1998) shows how ordinary individuals reacted to major events like World War II (Schwartz, 2002). In *Graphic Novels in Your Media Center: a Definitive Guide* (Lyga & Lyga, 2004), the authors provide lesson plans for 12 graphic novels.

Educators can use graphic novels to give new voices to minorities and people with diverse viewpoints. In H. F. Kiyama's (1999) *The Four Immigrants Manga*, young adults can examine the lives of four Japanese immigrants in San Francisco from 1904 to 1924. In *Still I Rise* (Laird, Laird, & Bey, 1997), they can examine the history of African Americans (Schwartz, 2002). In addition, because of their comprehension supports including simple sentences and context and visual comprehension clues, graphic novels are excellent for English language learners.

Crawford (2003a) suggests that some graphic novels can be used with mature adolescents to address NCSS Standards that deal with individual development and identity and with power, authority, and governance. Christensen (2006) finds that graphic novels are excellent for teaching about global conflict. *A Jew in Communist Prague* (Giardino, 1997) chronicles a young Jew's coming of age in an era of communism and anti-Semitism. *Stuck Rubber Baby* (Cruse, 1995) examines racism and homophobia in the American South in the 1960s. To provide insight into global conflicts and power struggles, educators can use graphic novels such as *The Complete Maus* (Spiegelman, 1997), *Persepolis* (Satrapi, 2003), *Palestine* (Sacco, 2002), *Fax from Sarajevo* (Kubert, 1998), and *Echoes of the Lost Boys of Sudan* (Akol, Santino, Mabek, & Ngor, 2004). Collaborating with Other Professionals 12–2 suggests ways teachers and librarians can work together to add graphic novels to the school library and classrooms.

From Page to Screen identifies some film adaptations of comics and graphic novels and has suggestions for comparing the film and print versions.

COLLABORATING WITH OTHER PROFESSIONALS

Teachers and library media specialists should work together to add graphic novels to the school library's collection.

- Get the support of the school administration and the district library supervisor.
- Determine how the graphic novels will be:
  - Put in the library
  - Circulated
  - Displayed
  - Publicized
- Determine who (students? teachers?) will be involved in the selection process and who will be responsible for reviewing each novel before it is placed in circulation to teenagers (Mooney, 2002).

from Page to Screen

COMICS AND GRAPHIC NOVELS

Comics and graphic novels present unique critical opportunities when adapted to the screen. An excellent resource is *May Contain Graphic Material: Comic Books, Graphic Novels, and Film* (Booker, 2007). Because of their often hip and edgy realism, many of the best graphic novel adaptations receive an R-rating, making them unsuitable for sharing with adolescents.

Comics are often adapted for the screen in a much more general way than novels. Filmmakers pick up threads from several different issues and attempt to match the overall tone of the comic series. When viewing these big-screen comics heroes, you'll want to compare the film's faithfulness to the overall vision the comic series has of its hero, and discuss whether or not the film's take on the story and characters is as valuable as the original text.

HELLBOY
★★★ | 2004 | PG-13

Adapted from a series of popular graphic novels, this is a surprisingly high-quality film about a demon child raised by a kindly scientist. The film

touches on familiar adolescent issues of isolation and belonging.

THE DARK KNIGHT
★★★★ | 2008 | PG-13

An immediate classic, director Christopher Nolan's version of the darker side of Batman boasts one of the greatest villain performances in comic book history – Heath Ledger's Joker.

SPIDER-MAN 2
★★★ | 2003 | PG-13

Director Sam Raimi's video game–like visual style and Tobey Maguire's everyman good nature give this blockbuster a color, action, and human quality missing from some of the darker, more brooding superhero flicks. The sequel is even superior to the impressive original.

NAUSICAA OF THE VALLEY OF THE WIND
★★★★ | 1984 | PG

Japanese master animator Hayao Miyazaki creates a breathtaking vision of the Valley of the Wind and its heroine Nausicaa in just one of his many brilliant films.

The Simpsons Movie
★★★ | 2007 | PG-13

Animation's favorite family finally hit the big screen with a funny, irreverent film that fans of the comics and the TV show will appreciate.

Magazines

What is the role of the traditional magazine for young adults? Today, many librarians have problems deciding which, if any, popular magazines to purchase. Many teens are reading adult magazines rather than those targeted for them. In addition, with rising subscription costs, shrinking budgets, an emphasis on curriculum content, and the use of periodical databases for research, some school library media specialists have decreased the number of periodicals they purchase for entertainment and have instead looked for magazines that are both educational and entertaining. This has become more difficult as publishers of traditional quality periodicals resort to more glitz, glitter, and gloss (Fine & Kinney, 2000) in an effort to reach young adults who, increasingly, are turning to the Internet for information and entertainment. According to Rakestraw (2007), Webzines, blogs and social networking sites where young adults can "create their own content" (p. 397) seriously compete with magazines for young adult readership.

One result has been the growth of Webzines, or websites that focus on topics of interest to teenagers. Some magazines have switched entirely to an online format; others supplement print content with online content that includes interactive features (Rakestraw, 2007). Connecting Adolescents and Their Literature 12–3 looks at one way to build on the popularity of Webzines.

12-3 •••• CONNECTING ADOLESCENTS AND THEIR LITERATURE

Webzines (magazines on the Internet) use the power of the Internet to provide young adults with a wide range of choices in teen magazine literature. Many Webzines focus on topics that interest young adult girls (Norton, 2002). Review a few Webzines, and then follow the suggestions of Christie "CJ" Bott (2002) in *Zines—The Ultimate Creative Writing Project* and have students make their own Webzines as part of a creative writing project. A few Webzines are:

Girl Zone
www.girlzone.com/

gURL
www.gurl.com

Teen Voices
teenvoices.com/issue11_1/intro.html

Next Step
www.nextstepmagazine.com/NSMPages/home.aspx

React.com
www.react.com/index.asp

Ms. Quince Mag.
www.msquincemag.com

When young adults read magazines, they frequently turn to adult publications, such as the increasing number of specialty publications that are "written and designed for just about any interest or taste" (Waryncia, 2006, p. 40). Some traditional teen magazines are now being read by younger children, as adolescents turn to magazines that appeal to older readers, including the "celebrity weeklies *In Touch, US Weekly*, and the *Star*" (Tyre, 2004, p. 59). In response to an online survey, young adults included *People, Cosmopolitan, Newsweek, National Geographic, The New Yorker, Time*, the *New York Times Magazine*, and *Scientific American* as favorites, along with *Seventeen* and *CosmoGirl* (Rakestraw, 2007). An excellent picture of the young adult magazine market is contained in an online fact sheet, "Tweens, Teens and Magazines," produced by the Kaiser Family Foundation (2004).

Reasons for Using and Teaching with Magazines. Traditionally, magazine writers and publishers have produced magazines with appropriate reading levels, topics, and formats to interest young adults, especially reluctant readers and teens who feel challenged when asked to read a complete novel or even a long short story. Focusing on young adult concerns such as beauty, fitness, the opposite sex, cars, friendships and relationships, sports, and hobbies, these magazines have a variety of short and medium-length articles that are written in an exciting and enthusiastic style and can be read at one sitting.

CONSIDERATIONS FOR SELECTING YOUNG ADULT LITERATURE MAGAZINES

When examining magazines for adolescents, ask the following questions:

_____ Is the magazine visually appealing to adolescents?

_____ Does the content of the magazine appeal to the interests of adolescents?

_____ Is the content (both text and illustrations) of the magazine developmentally appropriate for adolescents?

_____ What is the reading level of the magazine?

_____ Does the magazine directly support the curriculum of the school?

_____ Is the magazine a good choice for recreational reading? Will it appeal to reluctant readers?

_____ Does the magazine avoid stereotyping or exploiting genders?

_____ Does the magazine duplicate information that can be found more easily in another resource (such as a database or on the Internet)?

Characteristics of Magazines for Young Adults. Just as with all young adult literature (i.e., series or informational books), magazines vary in quality, and educators need to evaluate and select them carefully. Considerations for Selecting Young Adult Literature: *Magazines* provides some questions you should ask when examining magazines.

Magazines for Young Adults. In magazines, young adults look for "browsability, informality, topic-focused approach, and glossy look" (Patron, 2006, p. 39). Special current events magazines for young adults include *New York Times Upfront* and *Teen Newsweek*. To support the curriculum, there are magazines like *Muse*, which focuses on science, history, and the arts, and *Cicada*, a literary magazine; Archaeology's *Dig*. *Teen Ink* features the writing of adolescents. In 2004, author Michael Cart began a semiannual journal, *Rush Hour*, for older adolescents. Looking more like a collection of short stories than a magazine, the literary journal includes short fiction, poems, nonfiction, and essays by recognized young adult authors.

Teachers and library media specialists should be careful to avoid stereotyping. However, it appears that while some magazines appeal to all young adults, others appeal primarily to either boys or girls. Magazines that appear to cater to female's interests include *Seventeen*, *CosmoGirl*, *Teen Vogue*, and *Shojo Beat*. Catering to males are periodicals such as *Shonen Jump*, *Beckett Baseball*, *Thrasher*, *TransWorld SKATE- boarding*, *Snowboarder*, and *BMX Plus*.

Suggestions for Selecting and Using Magazines. Suggestions for Selecting Young Adult Literature: *Magazines*, earlier in this chapter, listed questions to ask when evaluating magazines. One excellent list of magazines for young adults is a series of articles "Magazines for Teens on and off the Rack," parts 1 and 2, which appeared in *VOYA* (Rakestraw, 2007, 2008). Most of the magazines in the list are targeted to adults but enjoyed by younger readers as well.

With magazines, there is always a need to balance literary merit and popularity. Some educators want young adults to have magazines that will challenge readers to scale new heights and acquaint them with some of the classics of literature or with articles that expand their intellectual horizons. There are also educators who view magazines as one way to tempt the reluctant reader or to provide reading materials that academically challenged youth can enjoy. They believe that the immediate goal should be to encourage young adults to read and that once the love of reading is nurtured in young adults, these students will develop a desire to read more scholarly or educational materials. For example, in a survey sponsored by ALA, 64% of the boys indicated that they read sports magazines (Cox, 2003). We encourage you to examine a number of different magazines for young adults, talk to adolescents about their reading preferences, and then make up your own mind.

Magazines can be used in a number of ways throughout the curriculum. Obviously, some periodicals have subject tie-ins, such as *Muse* for the arts, *Dig* in science, and the many teen news magazines in social studies. Collaborating with Other Professionals 12–3 looks at ways teachers and library media specialists can help young adults get their writing published by focusing on literary magazines.

Picture Books for Young Adults

No longer designed solely for nonreaders, picture books, like comics, magazines, and graphic novels, are another visual format that has become popular with young adults. Defined as combining "the art of storytelling with that of illustration" (Russell, 2009, p. 134), picture books contain literature from a number of different genres, including realistic and historical fiction, science fiction and fantasy, poetry, biography, and nonfiction. Although they appear at first glance to be very simple, "good picture storybooks are very complex works dealing . . . with two distinct art forms" (p. 134). According to Albright (2002), teachers can use picture books to "engage adolescents, enrich content knowledge and stimulate higher order thinking" (p. 418). Across the

---

12–3

COLLABORATING WITH OTHER PROFESSIONALS

Some young adults would probably love to have their writing published. However, breaking into the publishing world can be difficult to do. Teachers and library media specialists can work together to help adolescents learn about magazines such *Teen Ink* that regularly publish student work. Librarians need to have this publication available for students to read, and teachers need to help students learn how to write for publication.

Some tips on writing for publication (Kellaher, 1999) include:

- Help adolescents get to *know* the publication where they will submit their work by examining current issues to determine:
  - The target audience (age group)
  - The types of articles published
  - The length of the articles

- The required submission format (paper or electronic)
- The submission process
- Encourage young adults to write about people, places, events, and issues they know about.
- Discuss plagiarism—what it is, the consequences, and how to avoid it.
- Remind young adults to consider Webzines that might be interested in receiving student work.
- Encourage young adults to be realistic in their expectations, not to take rejections personally, and to revise and resubmit.

An excellent article on writing for a student-produced magazine is "'When Can We Start Working on Magazines?' A Collaborative Language Arts-Computer Project" (Gillespie, 2005).

curriculum, a picture book can "act as a magnifying glass that enlarges and enhances the reader's personal interactions with a subject (Vacca & Vacca, 2005, p. 161).

Reasons for Using and Teaching with Picture Books. Picture books appeal to a wide range of readers (Neal & Moore,1991/1992), can bring humor into the class-room, can provide a basis for discussion, can serve as a model for creative writing, and can provide entertainment (Lesesne, Beers & Buckman, 1997). Not only are they excellent to use for a short period of instruction (Neal & Moore, 1991/1992), but they often take complex topics and provide a simple visual introduction, in some cases with several layers of meaning. In fact, many picture books require a more mature audience if they are to be completely understood. Albright (2002) found that "picture books can allow for both individual and collaborative meaning construction through aesthetic and efferent responses to literature and content" (p. 428). Ivey (2002) noted that picture books permit teachers to differentiate instruction when they allow students to select materials based on their interests and reading levels. "Reading picture books in secondary courses increases motivation, understanding of concepts, and aesthetic appreciation and provides easier material for less able readers" (Carr, Buchanan, Wentz, Weiss & Brant, 2001). Many secondary teachers also use picture books with English as a Second Language students (Hadaway & Mundy, 1999; Henry and Simpson, 2001) to help them increase their vocabulary and understanding.

Picture Books for Young Adults. There are too many excellent picture books to list in this chapter. Table 12-2 lists a few of our personal favorites and suggested subjects.

Characteristics of Picture Books for Young Adults. Because many picture books are written for younger readers, teachers and librarians must be careful when selecting picture books to use with young adults. Not only must the book meet the basic criteria for any picture book, but it must also appeal to young adults. Considerations for Selecting Young Adult Literature: *Picture Books* provides some questions you should ask when examining picture books.

CONSIDERATIONS FOR SELECTING YOUNG ADULT LITERATURE PICTURE BOOKS

When examining picture books for adolescents, ask the following questions:

_____ Are the illustrations visually appealing to adolescents and do they accurately represent and expand the text?

_____ Do the text and the illustrations complement each other?

_____ Will the content appeal to the interests of adolescents?

_____ Does the writing meet the standards for good literature?

_____ Does the picture book directly support the curriculum of the school?

_____ Does it include special materials for teachers or older readers?

_____ If the picture book is nonfiction or biography, does it meet the criteria for those genres?

_____ Does the picture book avoid stereotyping or exploiting genders and does it include diversity in both the pictures and the text?

TABLE 12-2   Selected Picture Books and Subject Suggestions

Title	Subject
Island of the Skog (Kellogg, 1973)	Social studies—government
Faithful Elephants (Tsuchiya, 1988)	World War II
Math Curse (Scieszka and Smith, 1995)	Mathematics
True Story of the 3 Little Pigs (Scieszka and Smith, 1989)	English—point of view
Mysteries of Harris Burdick (Van Allsburg, 1984)	English—creative writing
Rose Blanche (Innocenti and Gallaz, 1985)	Social Studies—World War II
The Wall: Growing Up Behind the Iron Curtain (Sis, 2007)	Cold War
Baseball Saved Us (Mochizuki, 1993)	Japanese internment in World War II
Pish, Posh, Said Hieronymus Bosch (Willard, 1991)	Art
Pink and Say (Polacco, 1994)	Civil War
Tough Cookie (Wisniewski, 1999)	Creative Writing—mysteries
No Star Nights (Smucker, 1989)	Environment, Social Studies
Snowflake Bentley (Martin, 1998)	Science

Suggestions for Selecting and Using Picture Books. A number of resources that teachers and librarians can use to identify picture books for young adults include:

- *Picture This: Picture Books for Young Adults: A Curriculum-Related Annotated Bibliography* (Matulka, 1997)
- *Using Picture Storybooks to Teach Literary Devices: Recommended Books for Children and Young Adults*, vol. 3 (Hall, 2002) and vol. 4 (Hall, 2007)
- *Worth A Thousand Words: An Annotated Guide to Picture Books for Older Readers* (Ammond & Sherman, 1996)
- *Teaching with Picture Books in the Middle School* (Tiedt, 2000)
- *Big Ideas in Small Packages: Using Picture Books with Older Readers* (Pearson, 2005)

A number of writers have reported on the use of picture books in secondary schools. For example, Albright (2002) reported on a study using picture books with middle school social studies students to study Latin America. Reading picture books aloud to students, she was able to engage them in high-level discussions and reinforce content knowledge. Giorgis (1999) reported similar findings when she read picture books aloud to students in a high school English class.

Costello and Kolodziej (2006) explained that a picture book biography such as *Leonardo da Vinci* (Stanley, 1996) can be used across the curriculum to supplement a social studies lesson on the Renaissance, an art history lesson, and a science lesson on inventors and inventions. Stone (2007) also believes that picture book biographies allow "writers to break free from the more standard structure of telling a person's life story from the beginning to the end" (p. 34). Some of her favorites are *Starry Messenger* (Sis, 1996) and the works of James Cross Giblin (e.g. 2000) and Diane Stanley (e.g. 1996).

At an Assembly on Literature for Adolescents workshop in 2006 (Smith, 2006), several authors participated in a session on using picture books to connect teens with young adult literature. For example, they suggested using *Show Way* (Woodson, 2005) as an introduction to the novel *Copper Sun* (Draper, 2006) and *William Shakespeare's Romeo and Juliet* (Coville, 1999) as an introduction to *Romiette and Julio* (Draper, 2001). The latter could also be used to introduce Shakespeare's original play, as could *William Shakespeare & the Globe* (Aliki, 1999). Using Multiple Readings suggests questions influenced by select literary theories for *Show Way* (2005) by Jacqueline Woodson.

USING MULTIPLE READINGS

The following are examples of questions critics might ask about *Show Way* (2005), by Jacqueline Woodson.

New Criticism
How does the relationship between text and pictures give meaning to the book?

Feminist Criticism
How are the women in *Show Way* depicted? What types of work do they do? How are men portrayed? What purpose do the men seem to serve?

Black Feminist Criticism
How does Soonie's family resist oppression during slavery and reconstruction?

Deconstructionist Criticism
What oppositional concepts (e.g., free/bound, justice/injustice, and biography/autobiography) are found in the book?

New Historical Criticism
What do the pictures suggest about slavery? The underground railroad? The civil rights movement? How does slavery impact contemporary society?

Concluding Thoughts

Comics, graphic novels, magazines, and picture books can motivate young adults to read. Unfortunately, some educators once thought, and perhaps some still do, these materials were not "real" literature and did not deserve recognition and use in schools. However, many young adults *do* read and enjoy them. Some teachers have been very successful in using comics, graphic novels, magazines and picture books for instructional purposes. Others use them to motivate students or supplement instructional resources. Comics have been read by many students since their earliest years; graphic novels appeal to students who grew up on video games and television; and magazines offer interesting possibilities for directing attention to young adults' concerns and interests. With their potential for getting young adults to read, comics, graphic novels, and magazines deserve serious consideration, rather than being relegated to second-class status or ignored altogether.

Young Adult Books

This section includes young adult titles mentioned in this chapter.

COMICS

Table 12–1 (p. 325) lists some recommended comic book series.

GRAPHIC NOVELS

9-11: Artists respond. (2002). Milwaukie, OR: Dark Horse Comics. Artists look back at the attacks of September 11, 2001.

9-11: The world's finest comic book writers and artists tell stories to remember. (2002). New York: DC Comics. Here are more stories of the September 11, 2001, attack.

Akol, G., Athian, S., Mabek, M., and Ngor, M. (2004). *Echoes of the lost boys of Sudan.* Dallas: Non-Fiction Reality Comics. Four young Sudanese boys tell their story of survival.

Arnoldi, K. (1998). *Amazing "true" story of a teenage single mom.* New York: Hyperion. After being raped, a young girl finds she is pregnant.

Baker, K. (2006). *Nat Turner: Encore edition.* vol. 1. New York: Kyle Baker. Follow Nat Turner, a slave, as he leads his famous slave rebellion in Virginia.

Bendis, B., and Bagley, M. (2002). *Ultimate Spider-Man: power and responsibility.* New York: Marvel Comics. This is the first volume in a series that takes a fresh look at a well-known character.

Blanchet, P. (2007). *White Rapids.* Montreal: Drawn & Quarterly. Follow a town from its birth, through its boom years, and into its decline.

Briggs, R. (1998). *Ethel & Ernest.* New York: Knopf. The story of the author's parents in England.

Claremont, C., and Byrne, J. (2003). *The Dark Phoenix saga.* New York: Marvel Enterprises. This is the second volume in the X-Men Legends series.

Colfer, E., Donkin, A., Rigano, G., and Lamanna, P. (2007). *Artemis Fowl: The graphic novel.* New York: Hyperion. The popular novel for middle schools is now out in graphic novel format.

Cooke, J. B., and Morrow, J. (Eds.). (2000). *Streetwise: Autobiographical stories by comic book professionals.* Raleigh, NC: TwoMorrows. This book contains biographies of individuals in the comic book industry.

Cruse, H. (1995). *Stuck rubber baby.* New York: Paradox. This frank coming-of-age story looks at the civil rights movement as well as a young man's emerging sexual identity.

Eisner, W. (1978). *A contract with God.* New York: DC Comics. This work began the graphic novel genre.

Eisner, W. (2002). *Sundiata: A legend of Africa.* New York: NMB. In this African legend, a crippled boy grows up and leads the fight against the evil Samanguru.

Eisner, W. (2003). *Fagin the Jew.* New York: Doubleday. This is *Oliver Twist* from a different perspective.

Gaiman, N. (1993). *The Sandman: A game of you.* New York: DC Comics. A young witch leads a group of women on a quest to destroy the evil Cuckoo. There are additional books in this multivolume, award-winning fantasy series with mature content.

Gaiman, N. (1994). *Death: The high cost of living.* New York: DC Comics. Every 100 years, Death comes back to Earth in this work for mature readers.

Gaiman, N. (1996). *Black orchid.* New York: DC Comics. Black Orchid tries to put together the pieces of her past and the biological tests that created her.

Giardino, V. (1997). *A Jew in communist Prague: Vol. 1. Loss of innocence.* New York: NBM. In this book for older adolescents, readers follow Jonas as he grows up in Prague in the 1950s.

Golden, C. (1999). *Buffy the vampire slayer: Origin.* Milwaukie, OR: Dark Horse Comics. Buffy becomes a vampire slayer.

Gonick, L. (1997). *Cartoon history of the universe.* New York: Broadway Books. Fun and fact are combined in this look at history. A similar book is *The Cartoon Guide to Statistics* (1993) by Gonick and Smith.

Heuet, S. (2001). *Remembrance of things past.* New York: NBM. Proust's work as a graphic novel.

Hinds, G. (2007). *Beowulf.* Cambridge, MA: Candlewick. Hinds adapts the epic tale to graphic format.

Horowitz, A., Johnston, A., Damerum, K., and Takasaki, Y. (2006). *Stormbreaker: The graphic novel.* New York: Philomel. Is Alex really the new boy-wonder superspy?

Hosler, J. (2000). *Clan apis.* Columbus, OH: Active Synapse. Follow the life cycle of a honeybee and explore the environment in which it lives.

Hosler, J. (2003). *The sandwalk adventures: An adventure in evolution told in five chapters.* Columbus, OH: Active Synapse. This easy-to-read graphic novel presents Darwin's theory of natural selection.

Jacques, B., Moore, S., and Blevins, B. (2007). *Redwall: The graphic novel.* New York: Philomel. Redwall Abbey is attacked by rats led by Cluny the Scourge.

Kanda, T., and Takase, N. (2006). *Edu-Manga: Ludwig van Beethoven.* Gardena, CA: Digital Manga. This is a manga biography of the famous composer.

Kikai, M., and Kishida, R. (2007). *Edu-Manga: Mother Theresa.* Gardena, CA: Digital Manga. This biography is in traditional manga format.

Kiyama, H. F. (1999). *The four immigrants manga.* Berkeley, CA: Stone Bridge Press. Young adults can examine the lives of four Japanese immigrants in San Francisco, from 1904 to 1924.

Kubert, J. (1998). *Fax from Sarajevo: A story of survival.* Milwaukie, OR: Dark Horse Comics. In this intense and sometimes explicit book, Kubert takes an up-front look at the horrors of war.

Kuper, P. (2003). *The metamorphosis.* New York: Crown. Kuper adapts Kafka's classic story.

Laird, R. O., Laird, T. N., and Bey, E. (1997). *Still I rise: A cartoon history of African Americans.* New York: Norton. This is a history of African Americans.

McCraw, T. (1999). *Legion of super-heroes: The beginning of tomorrow.* New York: DC Comics. Here are adventure and romance in the thirty-first century.

Medley, L. (2006). *Castle waiting.* Seattle: Fantagraphics. Twelve issues of the comic appear in this single volume that modernizes the tale of Sleeping Beauty.

Miller, F. (2000–2001). *Daredevil: Visionaries.* New York: Marvel Comics. There are three volumes in this series about the man who has no fear. Other superhero series by Miller are *Batman* and *X-Men.*

Miller, F., and Varley, L. (1999). *300.* Milwaukie, OR: Dark Horse Comics. The Spartans and Persians meet in the Battle of Thermopylae.

Mizushiro, S. (2006). *After school nightmare:* Vol. 1. Go! Comi. With both male and female traits, all Ichijou wants to be is normal.

Myrick, L. (2006). *Missouri boy.* New York: First Second. Myrick tells of life growing up in a small town.

Naifeh, T. (2006). *Polly and the pirates.* Portland, OR: Oni Press. Polly is too much a lady to be the daughter of a pirate queen—or isn't she?

Ottaviani, J. (2001a). *Fallout.* Ann Arbor: G. T. Labs. Examine the events that led to the creation of the atomic bomb.

Ottaviani, J. (2001b). *Two-fisted science: Stories about scientists.* Ann Arbor: G. T. Labs. These short stories feature real scientists such as Isaac Newton and Galileo.

Ottaviani, J. (2003). *Dignifying science.* Ann Arbor: G. T. Labs. This anthology presents biographies of famous women scientists.

Ottaviani, J. (2005). *Bone sharps, cowboys, and thunder lizards: A tale of Edward Drinker Cope, Othniel Charles Marsh, and the gilded age of paleontology.* Ann Arbor: G. T. Labs. American dinosaur hunting has real-life drama and adventure.

Rall, T. (2002). *To Afghanistan and back: A graphic travelogue.* New York: NBM. Rall recounts his trip to Afghanistan during the American bombing against the Taliban.

Robinson, J. (2000). *Leave it to Chance: Shaman's rain.* New York: DC Comics. Following in her father's footsteps, 14-year-old Chance Falconer wants to become a famous paranormal investigator.

Russell, P. C. (2002). *The Ring of Nibelung.* Milwaukie, OR: Dark Horse Comics. This series retells Richard Wagner's Ring cycle.

Sacco, J. (2002). *Palestine.* Seattle: Fantagraphics Books. Sacco describes his life among the Palestinians under Israeli occupation. Another of his books is *Safe Area Gorazade: The War in Eastern Bosnia 1992–1995.*

Sanderson, P. (2003). *X-Men: The ultimate guide.* New York: DK. The mutants with super abilities move from comic to graphic novel; Sanderson traces their history.

Satrapi, M. (2003). *Persepolis.* New York: Pantheon. A young girl's life is changed by the Islamic Revolution of 1979.

Selznik, B. (2007). *The invention of Hugo Cabret: A novel in words and pictures.* New York: Scholastic. Hugo, an orphan living in a Paris train station, meets a mysterious toy-seller.

Sfar, J., and Guibert, E. (2007). *The professor's daughter.* New York: First Second. Imhotep IV, a mummy, falls in love with the daughter of a professor of Egyptology.

Shanower, E. (2001). *A thousand ships.* Orange, CA: Image Comics. In this first book in the Age of Bronze series, Shanower begins his story of the Trojan War.

Shivack, N. (2007). *Inside out: Portrait of an eating disorder*. New York: Atheneum Books. This autobiographical graphic novels shows the author's struggle with bulimia.

Siegel, S. C. (2006). *To dance: A memoir*. New York: Atheneum Books for Young Readers. The dream of becoming a dancer takes the author from Puerto Rico to the New York City Ballet.

Smith, J. (2004). *Bone*. Columbus, OH: Cartoon Books. This combines the Bone comics into a single graphic novel.

Spiegelman, A. (1997). *The complete Maus*. New York: Pantheon. In this Pulitzer prize–winning graphic novel, Spiegelman looks at his family's struggle to survive as the racism of Nazi Germany spreads across Poland.

Spiegelman, A. (2004). *In the shadow of no towers*. New York: Pantheon. Spiegelman looks back at 9/11 and the aftermath of the tragedy.

Takahashi, R. (1996). *Rumiko Takahashi's Rumic Theater*. San Francisco: Viz Comics. A collection of stories from a great female manga author.

Takahashi, R. (1998). *Rumic Theater: One or double*. San Francisco: Viz Comics. This second collection from Takahashi contains more stories.

Talbot, B. (1995). *The tale of one bad rat*. Milwaukie, OR: Dark Horse Comics. A young girl tries to recover after sexual abuse.

Tanaka, M. (2000). *Gon*. New York: DC Comics. This is a wordless manga graphic novel.

Tezuka, O. (2005). *Buddha*. Vol. 1. New York: Vertical. First of the eight-volume biography of Siddhartha Buddha.

Vining, J. (2007). *First in space*. Portland, OR: Oni Press. Vining looks at the chimpanzees in the early NASA space program.

Watsuki, N. (2006). *Buso Renkin*. Vol. 1. San Francisco: Viz Media. Kazuhiko is a reluctant monster-slaying warrior.

Weinstein, R. L. (2006). *Girl stories*. New York: Holt. A young girl faces the trials of growing up.

Wenzel, D. (2001). *The Hobbit: An illustrated edition of the fantasy classic*. New York: Ballantine Books. Wenzel brings Middle-Earth to life in this adaptation.

Winnick, J. (2000). *Pedro and me: Friendship, loss, and what I learned*. New York: Holt. Winnick looks at AIDS in his examination of his friendship with the late Pedro Zamora, an HIV-positive AIDS activist.

Yang, G. L. (2006). *American-born Chinese*. New York: First Second. Yang tells three stories of young Chinese Americans.

PICTURE BOOKS

Aliki. (1999). *William Shakespeare & the globe*. New York: HarperCollins. Picture help tell the story of the playwright and the Globe Theatre.

Coville, B. (1999). *William Shakespeare's "Romeo and Juliet."* New York: Dial Books. Coville simplifies the classic story.

Giblin, J. C. (2000). *The amazing life of Benjamin Franklin*. New York: Scholastic. Franklin was a printer, inventor and statesman.

Innocenti, R., and Gallaz, C. (1985). *Rose Blanche*. Mankato, MN: Creative Education. A young German girl discovers a concentration camp in World War II.

Kellogg, S. (1973). *The island of the Skog*. New York: Dial Press. Jenny and her friends escape to an island inhabited by the fearsome Skog.

Martin, J. B. (1998). *Snowflake Bentley*. Boston: Houghton Mifflin. This is the story of the scientist who investigated the formations found in snowflakes.

Mochizuki, K. (1993). *Baseball saved us*. New York: Lee & Low. A young Japanese American boy learns to play baseball in a World War II Internment camp.

Polacco, P. (1994). *Pink and Say*. New York: Philomel. Two young boys meet during the American Civil War.

Scieszka, J., and Smith, L. (1989). *The true story of the 3 little pigs*. New York: Viking. A. Wolf tells his side of the story.

Scieszka, J., and Smith, L. (1995). *Math curse*. New York: Viking. Can everything in the day really be a math problem?

Sis, P. (1996). *Starry messenger: A book depicting the life of a famous scientist, mathematician, astronomer, philosopher, physicist, Galileo Galilei*. New York: Farrar, Straus and Giroux. Pictures show the life of the man who changed the way we see our galaxy.

Sis, P. (2007). *The Wall: Growing up behind the Iron Curtain*. New York: Farrar, Straus and Giroux.

Sis recounts his childhood in communist Europe.

Smucker, A. E. (1989). *No star nights.* New York: Knopf. A steel mill changes life for children.

Stanley, D. (1996). *Leonardo da Vinci.* New York: Morrow Junior Books. The life of a famous artist and inventor shows his amazing mind.

Tsuchiya, Y. (1988). *Faithful elephants: A true story of animals, people, and war.* Boston: Houghton Mifflin. World War II comes to the Tokyo zoo.

Van Allsburg, C. (1984). *The mysteries of Harris Burdick.* Boston: Houghton Mifflin. Each picture is accompanied only by a brief caption.

Willard, N. (1991). *Pish, posh, said Hieronymus Bosch.* San Diego: Harcourt Brace. What strange creatures inhabit the painter's home?

Wisniewski, D. (1999). *Tough Cookie.* New York: Lothrop, Lee & Shepard Books. Tough Cookie sets out to find out what happened to his friend Chips.

Woodson, J. (2005). *Show way.* New York: Putnam. The tradition of making map quilts passed from mother to daughter.

Suggested Readings

Fingerson, J., and Killeen, E. B. (2006). Picture books for young adults. *Teacher Librarian, 33*(4), 32–34.

Greyson, D. (2007). GLBTQ content in comics/graphic novels for teens. *Collection Building, 26*(4), 130–134.

Ho, J. D. (2007). Gender alchemy: The transformative power of manga. *The Horn Book, 83*(5), 505–512.

Jacobs, D. (2007). More than words: Comics as a means of teaching multiple literacies. *English Journal, 96*(3), 19–25.

Schwarz, G. (2006). Expanding literacies through graphic novels. *English Journal, 95*(6), 58–64.

Seyfried, J. (2008). Reinventing the book club: Graphic novels as educational heavyweights. *Knowledge Quest, 36*(3), 44–48.

Snowball, C. (2007). Researching graphic novels and their teenage readers. *Library and Information Science Research Electronic Journal, 17*(1). Accessed November 18, 2008 from http://libres.curtin.edu.au/libres17n1/.

Wright, G., and Sherman, R. B. (2006). Comics redux. *Reading Improvement, 43*(4), 165–172.

References

All works of young adult literature referenced in this chapter are included in the Young Adult Books list and are not repeated in this list.

Albright, L. K. (2002). Bringing the Ice Maiden to life: Engaging adolescents in learning through picture book read-alouds in content areas. *Journal of Adolescent & Adult Literacy, 45*(5), 418–428.

Alvermann, D. E., Moon, J. S., and Hagood, M. C. (1999). *Popular culture in the classroom: Teaching and researching critical media literacy.* Newark: International Reading Association.

Ammon, B. E., and Sherman, E. W. (1996). *Worth a thousand words: An annotated guide to picture books for older readers.* Englewood, CO: Libraries Unlimited.

Bearne, E. (2003). Rethinking literacy: Communication, representation and text. *Reading Literacy and Language, 37*(3), 98–103.

Bickers, J. (2007). The young and the graphic novel. *Publishers Weekly, 254*(8), 62–63.

Booker, M. K. (2007). *May contain graphic material: Comic books, graphic novels, and film.* Westport, CT: Praeger.

Bott, C. (2002). Zines: The ultimate creative writing project. *English Journal, 92*(2), 27–38.

Brenner, R. (2006). Graphic novels 101 FAQ. *The Horn Book, 82*(2), 124–125.

Brenner, R. (2007a). Core collection: Japanese manga for teens. *Booklist, 103*(14), 60.

Brenner, R. (2007b). *Understanding manga and anime.* Westport, CT: Libraries Unlimited.

Carr, K. S., Buchanan, D. L., Wentz, J. B., Weiss, M. L., and Brant, K. J. (2001). Not just for the primary grades: A bibliography of picture books for secondary content teachers. *Journal of Adolescent & Adult Literacy, 45*(2), 146–153.

Carter, J. B. (2007). *Building literacy connections with graphic novels: Page by page, panel by panel.* Urbana, IL: National Council of Teachers of English.

Cha, Kai-Ming. (2005a). Sports manga gets in the game. *Publishers Weekly, 252*(16), 25–26.

Cha, Kai-Ming. (2005b). Yaiu manga: What girls like? *Publishers Weekly, 252*(10), 44–46.

Christensen, L. L. (2006). Graphic global conflict: Graphic novels in the high school social studies classroom. *The Social Studies, 97*(6), 227–230.

Comic books and juvenile delinquency. (1956). Accessed March 1, 2004, from: www.geocities.com/Athens/8580/kefauver.html.

Comic buyers guide. (2008). Final North American Comics Market Estimates for 2007. Accessed April 5, 2008, from: www.cbgxtra.com.

Comics worth reading March 2004 previews. Accessed March 2, 2004, from: www.comicsworthreading.com/previews/0403.html.

Costello, B., and Klodziej, N. J. (2006). A middle school teacher's guide for selecting picture books. *Middle School Journal, 38*(1), 27–33.

Cox, R. (2003). From "Boys' Life" to "Thrasher:" Boys and magazines. *Teacher Librarian, 30*(3), 25–26.

Crawford, P. (2002). Graphic novels: Selecting materials that will appeal to girls. *Knowledge Quest, 31*(2), 43–45.

Crawford, P. (2003a). Beyond *Maus:* Using graphic novels to support social studies standards. *Knowledge Quest, 31*(4), 41–42.

Crawford, P. (2003b). Graphic novels of 2002: Superheroes and more. *Knowledge Quest, 31*(5), 46–47.

Draper, S. M. (1999). *Romiette and Julio.* New York: Atheneum Books for Young Readers.

Draper, S. M. (2006). *Copper sun.* New York: Atheneum Books for Young Readers.

Fine, J., and Kinney, M. (2000). Magazine mania. *School Library Journal, 46*(8), 40–43.

Gillespie, J. D. (2005). "When can we start working on magazines?" A collaborative language arts–computer project. *English Journal, 94*(5), 117–121.

Giorgis, C. (1999). The power of reading picture books aloud to secondary students. *The Clearing House, 73*(1), 51–53.

Goldsmith, F. (2005) *Graphic novels now: Building, managing, and marketing a dynamic collection.* Chicago: American Library Association.

Gorman, M. (2002a). What teens want: Thirty graphic novels you can't live without. *School Library Journal, 48*(8), 42–44.

Gorman, M. (2002b). More of what teens want. Accessed December 30, 2002, from http://slj.reviewsnews.com/index.asp?layout=articlePrint&articleID=CA261476.

Gorman, M. (2008a). Graphic novels rule! *School Library Journal, 51*(3), 42–47.

Gorman, M. (2008b). A new generation of graphic novels: Expect the unexpected. *Library Media Connection, 26*(6), 38.

Gravett, P. (2004). *Manga: Sixty years of Japanese comics.* New York: Collins Design.

Gravett, P. (2005). *Graphic novels: Everything you need to know.* New York: Collins Design.

Hadaway, N. L., and Mundy, J. (1999). Children's informational picture books visit a secondary ESL classroom. *Journal of Adolescent & Adult Literacy: 42*(6), 464–476.

Hall, S. (2002). *Using picture storybooks to teach literary devices: Recommended books for children and young adults:* Vol. 3. Westport, CT: Oryx.

Hall, S. (2007). *Using picture storybooks to teach literary devices: Recommended books for children and young adults.* Vol. 4. Westport, CT: Libraries Unlimited

Henry, R., and Simpson, C. (2001). Picture books & older readers: A match made in heaven. *Teacher Librarian, 28*(3), 23–28.

Ivey, J. (2002). Getting started: Manageable literacy practices. *Educational Leadership, 60*(3), 20–23.

Kaiser Family Foundation. (2004). *Tweens, teens and magazines: Fact sheet.* Accessed April 28, 2008, from: www.kff.org/entmedia/upload/Tweens-Teens-and-Magazines-Fact-sheet.pdf.

Kan, K. (2006). The comics industry takes a look at itself. *Voice of Youth Advocates, 29*(20), 136–137.

Kellaher, K. (1999). Get kids' work published! Top tips on how to do it from children's magazine editors. *Instructor, 108*(6), 14.

Kennedy, M. H. (2003). Wisdom from the Old Master: Will Eisner discusses the graphic novel. *Library of Congress Information Bulletin, 62*(5), 110–111.

King, K. A. R. (2006). Godzilla vs. the librarian. *Voice of Youth Advocates, 29*(3), 224–225.

Krashen, S. D. (1993). *The power of reading: Insights from the research.* Englewood, CO: Libraries Unlimited.

Krashen, S. D. (2004). *The power of reading: Insights from the research*. 2nd ed. Westport, CT: Libraries Unlimited.

Kress, G. (2003). *Literacy in the new media age*. London: Routledge.

Lesesne, T. S., Beers, G. K., and Buckman L. (1997). Not just for kids: Picture books for older readers. *Journal of Adolescent & Adult Literacy, 40*(7), 584–589.

Lubbock (Texas) City-County Library. Accessed December 11, 2003 from: library.ci.lubbock.tx.us/opac/.

Lyga, A. A. W., and Lyga, B. (2004). *Graphic novels in your media center: A definitive guide*. Westport, CT: Libraries Unlimited.

Matulka, D. (1997). *Picture this: Picture books for young adults: A curriculum-related annotated bibliography*. Westport, CT: Greenwood Press.

McCloud, S. (1993). *Understanding comics*. Northampton, MA: Kitchen Sink Press.

McCloud, S. (2000). *Reinventing comics: How imagination and technology are revolutionizing an art form*. New York: HarperCollins.

McCloud, S. (2006). *Making comics: Storytelling secrets of comics, manga and graphic novels*. New York: HarperCollins.

Mcpherson, K. (2006). Graphic literacy. *Teacher Librarian, 33*(4), 67–69.

Miller, S. (2005). *Developing and promoting graphic novel collections*. New York: Neal-Schuman.

Mooney, M. (2002). Graphic novels: How they can work in libraries. *Book Report, 21*(3), 18–19.

Mori, M. (2007). Graphic novels: Leading the way to teen literacy and leadership. *Indiana Libraries, 26*(3) 29–32.

Neal, J. C., and Moore, K. (1991/1992). *The Very Hungry Caterpillar* meets *Beowulf* in secondary classrooms. *Journal of Reading, 35*(4), 290–296.

Norton, B. (2002). When is a teen magazine not a teen magazine? *Journal of Adolescent & Adult Literacy, 45*(5), 296–299.

O'English, L., Matthews, J. G., and Lindsay, E. B. (2006). Graphic novels in academic libraries: From *Maus* to manga and beyond. *Journal of Academic Librarianship, 32*(2), 173–182.

Overstreet, R. M. (2008). *Official Overstreet comic book companion*. New York: Random House.

Patron, W. (2006). Children's magazines and collection development. *Children and Libraries 4*(3), 39–44.

Pawuk, M. (2006). *Graphic novels: A genre guide to comic books, manga, and more*. Westport, CT: Libraries Unlimited.

Pearson, M. B. (2005). *Big ideas in small packages: Using picture books with older readers*. Worthington, OH: Linworth.

Poitras, G. (2008). What is manga? *Knowledge Quest, 36*(3), 49.

Raiteri, S. (2003a). Graphic novels. *Library Journal, 128*(8), 94.

Raiteri, S. (2003b). Graphic novels. *Library Journal, 128*(14), 138.

Rakestraw, M. (2007). Magazines for teens on and off the rack: Part 1. *Voice of Youth Advocates, 30*(5), 397–402.

Rakestraw, M. (2008). Magazines for teens: On and off the rack: Part 2. *Voice of Youth Advocates, 30*(6), 492–497.

Reid, C. (2002). Asian comics delight U.S. readers. *Publishers Weekly, 249*(51), 26.

Reid, C. (2003). Manga is here to stay: Tokyopop's format leads manga into the bookstore market. *Publishers Weekly, 250*(42), S6.

Reid, C. (2005). U. S. graphic novel market hits $200M. *Publishers Weekly, 252*(16), 15.

Reid, C. (2007). Tokyopop bows new ratings. *Publishers Weekly, 254*(8), 8.

Russell, D. L. (2009). *Literature for children: A short introduction*. 6th ed. Boston: Pearson.

Sabin, R. (2001). *Comics, comix & graphic novels: A history of comic art*. London: Phaidon.

Schneider, N. (2007). Holy reading, Batman! *Teaching PreK–8, 37*(4), 56–57.

Schwartz, G. E. (2002). Graphic novels for multiple literacies. *Journal of Adolescent and Adult Literacy, 46*(3), 262–265.

Schwartz, A., and Rubinstein-Avila, E. (2006). Understanding the manga hype: Uncovering the multimodality of comic-book literacies. *Journal of Adolescent & Adult Literacy, 50*(1), 40–49.

Serantes, L. C. (2005). ¿Es un pájaro? ¿Es un Avión? . . . ¡Es Superman! Spanish comics for American libraries. *Young Adult Library Services, 3*(4), 46–48.

Simmons, T. (2003). Comic books in my library? *PNLA Quarterly, 67*(2), 12, 20.

Smith, C. L. (2006). *Picture this: Picture books for young adults: Notes from ALAN 2006.* Accessed May 2, 2008, from: cynthialeitichsmith.blogspot.com/2006/11/picture-this-picture-books-for-young.html.

Stone, T. L. (2007). From spark to story. *School Library Journal, 53*(11), 34–35.

Styron, W. (1967). *The confessions of Nat Turner.* New York: Random House.

Tiedt, I. M. (2000). *Teaching with picture books in the middle school.* Newark, DE: International Reading Association.

Tyre, P. (2004, April 19). No longer most likely to succeed. *Newsweek.* Accessed April 8, 2005, from

Lexis-Nexis database: http://web.lexis-nexis.com/universe/.

Vacca, R. T., and Vacca, J. L. (2005). *Content area reading: Literacy and learning across the curriculum.* Boston: Pearson.

Vega, E. S., and Schnackenberg, H. L. (2006). Integrating technology, art, and writing to create comic books. *Middle School Journal, 37*(4), 30–36.

Waryncia, L. (2006). Why I love children's magazines. *Children and Libraries, 4*(3), 40–42.

Weiner, R. (2001). Graphic novels in libraries. *Texas Library Journal, 77*(4), 130–135.

Weiner, S. (2006). *The 101 best graphic novels.* 2nd ed. New York: NBM.

Index